List of Exhibits

Valuing Small Businesses and Professional Practices

Second Edition

Shannon P. Pratt, DBA, CFA, FASA
Managing Director
Willamette Management Associates

with

Robert F. Reilly, CFA, ASA, CPA
Managing Director
Willamette Management Associates

and

Robert P. Schweihs, ASA
Managing Director
Willamette Management Associates

IRWIN
Professional Publishing®
Chicago • London • Singapore

Project editor: Rita McMullen
Production manager: Ann Cassady
Designer: Jeanne M. Rivera
Art coordinator: Mark Malloy
Compositor: Precision Typographers
Typeface: 11/13 Century Schoolbook
Printer: The Maple Press

Library of Congress Cataloging-in-Publication Data

Pratt, Shannon P.
    Valuing small businesses and professional practices / Shannon P.
Pratt—2nd ed.
        p.   om.
    Includes bibliographical references and index.
    ISBN 1-55623-551-8
    1, Small business—Valuation.   2. Professions—Valuation.
I. Title.
HG4028.V3P73   1993
    338.6'42—dc20   92-26337

Printed in the United States of America

    3 4 5 6 7 8 9 0 MP 9 8 7 6 5

To Pam
who has cheerfully lent a helping hand to scores of our
fellow professionals around the country at one time or another

and whose dedication, good spirit, and professionalism
have been a benefit to all of us and an inspiration to those of us
that know her.

Preface

In the seven years since the publication of the first edition of this book, the business valuation community has made great strides in raising its level of professionalism through research, writing, education, and the development of widely accepted business valuation standards. This edition reflects that progress and the current "state of the art" of the business valuation profession.

What Is a "Small" Business?

While "small" is difficult to define, this book deals with the range from "mom and pop" businesses up through those worth around $5 million, plus professional practices of all sizes. One of the hallmarks of "small" in most cases in this context is personal involvement of the owner or owners in the operation of the business or practice.

Objective and Audience

This book provides the guidance necessary for both those who are performing small business and professional practice appraisals and those who are evaluating or using appraisals performed by others. The intended audience includes:

- Business and professional practice appraisers.
- Attorneys and judges.
- CPAs.
- Business and professional practice owners.
- Bankers.
- Academics in the fields of finance, economics, and valuation.
- Financial and estate planners.
- Other business consultants.

Changes since the First Edition

All material is updated if appropriate, the subject matter coverage is substantially broadened, and all relevant recent developments are reflected.

Entirely new chapters have been added which cover the following topics:

- Business valuation standards.
- S corporations.
- ESOPs.
- Transaction data bases.

Significantly expanded coverage includes the following:

- **Source materials**. Hundreds of new and updated source materials and bibliographical references (many of which are placed at the ends of relevant chapters).
- **Professional practices**. A full 100-page, six-chapter section, with added illustrative case studies.
- **Litigation support and dispute resolution**. A full four-chapter section, including a chapter on valuations prepared for divorces and a chapter on valuations prepared for damage claims.

Other changes and expansions include the following:

- A brand new sample case and suggested solution.
- Understanding Discount and Capitalization Rates (Chapter 12) is updated and expanded.
- Asset Based Methods (Chapter 17) is much more fully developed.
- Valuing Intangible Assets (Chapter 34) is greatly expanded.
- Business Valuation Standards adopted by the American Society of Appraisers in 1992 are included as Appendix A.

As noted in the Acknowledgments following this Preface, this book has benefited greatly from extensive peer review. We have attempted to present the current professional consensus on the issues addressed and definitions used, many of which had little or no discernable consensus at the time of the first edition of this book.

While great progress has been made, the profession is still evolving. We solicit your critiques, corrections, and suggestions for future printings and editions. Please address your comments or suggestions to us at Willamette Management Associates, 111 S.W. Fifth Avenue, Suite 2150, Portland, Oregon 97204, or call us at 503-222-0577.

Shannon Pratt
Portland, Oregon
March 1993

Acknowledgments

Readers will note that I wrote this edition of the book along with two of my colleagues, Robert Reilly and Bob Schweihs. Robert was responsible for the greatly expanded chapter on Asset-Based Methods and the extended Intangible Asset chapter. These are chapters to which his background contributes significant experience and expertise. Robert and Bob also drafted much of the other material, and both reviewed and edited the entire volume.

Other chapters were drafted or updated for this edition by various other colleagues, who are individually recognized as the principal authors of those respective chapters.

This book has had the benefit of extremely extensive peer review from which literally hundreds of corrections and suggestions have been incorporated. The following individuals reviewed the entire manuscript:

Jay E. Fishman, ASA
Financial Research, Inc.

Jim Rigby, ASA
The Financial Valuation Group

James M. (Mike) Hill, ASA
J. Michael Hill & Associates

Erich Sylvester, ASA
The Financial Valuation Group

Jeffrey D. Jones, ASA
Certified Business Appraisers, Inc.

Tom West
Business Brokerage Press

Portions of the manuscript were also reviewed by individuals with particularly relevant expertise. These individuals included:

Michael J. Bolotsky, ASA

Robert L. Dunn
Bancroft & McAlister

William A. Cerillo
Kornblum & Ferry

Roger K. Hill, ASA
Business & Professional Associates

Robert Coulson
American Arbitration Association

Michael J. Wagner
Putnam, Hayes & Bartlett

I particularly want to thank those individuals who contributed material for the chapter on Transaction Data Bases, including:

Robert G. Berry
*Geneva Business Research
  Corporation*

Ray Miles
Institute of Business Appraisers

John Cahill
Carroll/Cahill Associates

Jack R. Sanders
Asset Business Appraisal

Mike Carroll   David J. Scribner
Carroll/Cahill Associates   *UBI Business Brokers*

Three members of the Willamette Management Associates professional staff deserve special recognition for contributions that greatly helped to "fine tune" this book: Scott Beauchene for his assistance in a variety of technical applications; Jim Rabe for his concise "summary of steps" exhibits in several of the chapters; and Jeff Tarbell for verifying the accuracy of each of the mathematical formulas and calculations.

For permission to use material, I wish to thank:

American Society of Appraisers   Practitioners Publishing Co.
Bank of America   Prentice Hall Law & Business
Financial Research Associates   Robert Morris Associates
Ibbotson Associates   Simon & Schuster

The bibliography (much of which has been conveniently placed at the ends of the relevant chapters) was prepared by Pam Mastroleo, the Willamette Management Associates manager of library and information services. The hundreds of source materials and references she has documented add immeasurably to the value and usefulness of the book. Pam was also the project manager for the book and coordinated the entire effort, a challenging task which she carried out masterfully.

The bulk of the manuscript (in some cases several drafts) was typed by my executive secretary, Charlene Cottingham, in between managing me and my kaleidoscopic schedule. Charlene was also responsible for the design and production of most of the exhibits throughout the entire book.

The unstinting efforts of all these people have made a meaningful contribution to the quality of this book and to the entire profession, and I express my great gratitude. Final responsibility for all judgments and content rests, as always, with the authors.

Shannon Pratt

About the Author

Shannon P. Pratt is a managing director of Willamette Management Associates, a national valuation consulting, economic analysis, and financial advisory firm. Willamette Management Associates serves clients on a national basis from Portland, Oregon; Chicago, Illinois; and Washington, DC. Over the past 24 years, Dr. Pratt and the Willamette staff of valuation analysts have become widely recognized and respected as leading contributors to the conceptual development of the business appraisal profession. Having completed thousands of appraisal assignments, Dr. Pratt and his professional associates are frequently called upon to testify in international, federal, state, and local courts as expert witnesses in matters related to the valuation of assets, properties, and business interests.

Sometimes characterized as the "quintessential researcher" for his endeavor to keep abreast of the issues in the business appraisal profession, Dr. Pratt has been instrumental in developing within Willamette Management Associates one of the most extensive business valuation research libraries in existence, with a constantly updated collection of hundreds of books, articles, transaction data sources, and court cases involving business valuation issues. This book draws heavily on that resource.

Dr. Pratt holds a Doctorate in Finance from Indiana University. He is a Fellow of the American Society of Appraisers in Business Valuation (the highest designation awarded by the Society for outstanding contribution to this field). He also holds the professional designations of Chartered Financial Analyst, Certified Review Appraiser, Certified Business Counselor, and Certified Financial Planner.

Dr. Pratt has been a member of the American Society of Appraisers Business Valuation Committee since its inception in 1980. He was recently honored by being named the first and only Life Member Emeritus of that committee. He has also been named a Life Member of The ESOP Association Valuation Advisory Committee, after serving on that committee for over a decade, including five years as its chairman. He currently serves as the Chairman of the Business Valuation Task Force of The Appraisal Foundation.

Author of numerous articles on business valuation topics, published in a variety of national professional and trade journals, Dr. Pratt is a frequent speaker at professional appraisal meetings, as well as at bar and CPA meetings, industry associations, and financial and estate planning groups. He is also the author of the first edition of this book, *Valuing Small Businesses and Professional Practices* (1986), and the first and second editions of *Valuing a Business* (see outside back cover), both published by Business One Irwin. He is also coauthor with Jay Fishman, Cliff Griffith, and Keith Wilson, of *Guide to Business Valuations*, published by Practitioners Publishing Company.

Contents

Plans.   Estate, Gift, Inheritance, and Income Taxes.   Ad Valorem Taxes (Property Taxes).   Charitable Contributions.   Buy-Sell Agreements.   Property Settlements in Divorces.   Damage Cases.   Mergers.   Determining Life Insurance Needs.   Squeeze-Out Mergers and Dissenting Stockholder Actions.   Minority Stockholder Oppressing Actions.   Valuations for Multiple Purposes.   Considering Alternatives: Estate Planning and Other Types of Choices.   Summary.

Equity. *Defining the Earnings Base. Capitalization Rate by the "Build-Up" (Summation) Method. Capitalization Rate by Direct Market Comparison Method. Applying the Rate to Determine the Value.* Capitalizing Earnings Available to Overall Investment ("Invested Capital"). *Defining the Earnings Base. Capitalization Rate by the Weighted Average Method. Applying the Rate to Determine the Value.* How Expected Growth Affects Capitalization Rates. Adjusting for Excess Assets or Capital Deficiency. Examples of Valuations by the Capitalized Earning Approach. *Sole Proprietorship Example. Corporation Example.*

*bilities.   Discrete (Separate) Revaluation of Assets and Liabilities.
Partial Revaluation of Individual Assets and Liabilities.*   Steps
in Application of the Asset Accumulation Method.   *Obtain or Develop GAAP Basis Balance Sheet.   Identify Assets and Liabilities
to Be Revalued.   Identify Off-Balance Sheet Assets that Should
Be Recognized.   Identify Off-Balance Sheet and Contingent Liabilities that Should Be Recognized.   Value the Items Identified
Above.   Construct a Valuation Basis Balance Sheet.*   Premises
of Value for Individual Assets.   *Value in Continued Use, as Part
of a Going Concern.   Value in Place, as Part of a Mass Assemblage of Assets.   Value in Exchange, in an Orderly Disposition.
Value in Exchange, in a Forced Liquidation.*   Selecting a
Premise of Value.   Individual Asset Valuation Approaches and
Methods.   *Financial Assets.   Tangible Real Property.   Tangi-
ble Personal Property.   Intangible Real Property.   Intangible
Personal Property.*   Illustrative Example.   Avantages of the
Asset Accumulation Method.   Disadvantages of the Asset Accu-
mulation Method.   Summary.   Selected Bibliography.

Multiplier.   Price/Book Value Method.   Valuation Summary.
Valuation Conclusion.

Part I

Introduction: Understanding the Valuation Process

Chapter 1

Business Valuation Standards

Introduction

The most important development in the business appraisal profession since the 1986 edition of this book is the evolution of business valuation standards. That is why Business Valuation Standards is not only one of the new chapters in this edition, but also the first chapter in the book.

There has been an increasing awareness of the existence and efficacy of business appraisal standards in recent years. This trend of increased awareness is not only continuing but accelerating. An important aspect of this awareness is recognition of business valuation standards by the courts.

It is absolutely imperative that those responsible for preparing, reviewing, and using business appraisals be aware of both the existing standards and also the development of future standards as they evolve. The need for this awareness extends to all business owners and directors, fiduciaries, business advisors, consultants, and intermediaries, including attorneys, CPAs, business brokers, and lenders.

Since the 1986 edition, business valuation standards have been promulgated by both The Appraisal Foundation and the Business Valuation Committee of the American Society of Appraisers. These organizations and their current work are described briefly in this chapter, and the American Society of Appraisers' business valuation standards are included as Appendix A at the end of the book. This appendix presents the existing standards as they stood at the last moment before press time. The descriptions of The Appraisal Foundation and the American Society of Appraisers (ASA) include sources that will enable the reader to keep up with future developments.

The chapter also briefly describes the work of certain other professional and regulatory bodies that address business appraisals in various ways.

The Appraisal Foundation

Background

In 1987, nine of the leading U.S. professional appraisal organizations adopted a landmark document titled "Uniform Standards of Professional Appraisal Practice." Eight of the nine groups are composed entirely of real estate appraisers. One, the American Society of Appraisers, is multidisciplinary; that is, it awards certification in real estate, machinery and equipment, personal property, business valuation, and technical valuation.

Content of Uniform Standards of Professional Appraisal Practice (USPAP)

1. Prefatory material contains, among other things, an Ethics Provision, a Competency Provision, and a Departure Provision, which apply to all appraisers.

2. Standards 1 through 6 deal with real estate appraisal. Standard 3 deals with reviewing an appraisal. It is oriented to real estate, but is applicable to business appraisal with only minor modification.
3. Standards 7 and 8 deal with personal property appraisal.
4. Standards 9 and 10 deal with business appraisal.

Developments and Status

Government Recognition. At this writing, five federal government agencies[1] have adopted the uniform standards as requirements for real estate appraisals over which they have jurisdiction, and it is generally expected that other agencies will adopt these standards as mandatory for real estate appraisals. Several states now are studying USPAP with a view toward incorporating all or part of it into state law or regulation.

Business Valuation Task Force. The Appraisal Foundation appointed a five-person task force to review and recommend changes to Standards 9 and 10 and the other standards to the extent that they may apply to business appraisal. As we go to press, the task force has completed this review and The Appraisal Foundation Standards Board has approved the revised version of Standards 9 and 10, which are included in the January 1993 edition of USPAP. One important modification is that Standards 9 and 10 have been broadened to include all forms of intangible property.

The address of The Appraisal Foundation is 1029 Vermont Avenue, N.W., Suite 900, Washington, D.C. 20005, (202) 347-7722.

The Appraisal Foundation makes its developments known through a service called Appraisal Foundation Subscription Service. At press time the annual rate for this service was $150.

The Appraisal Standards Board of The Appraisal Foundation maintains a mailing list for distribution and comment on any new standards or revisions to standards. There is no charge to be included on this list. The address to request inclusion on this list is the same as The Appraisal Foundation above.

American Society of Appraisers

Background

The need for a broad program of education and professional accreditation in the discipline of business valuation was finally met with the formation in 1981 of the Business Valuation Committee of the American Society of Appraisers (ASA). The ASA is a long-standing, multidisciplinary orga-

---

[1]The five agencies are National Credit Union Administration; Department of the Treasury, Office of Thrift Supervision; Department of the Treasury, Office of the Comptroller of the Currency; Federal Deposit Insurance Corporation; and Federal Reserve System.

nization that offers education and professional accreditation in many appraisal disciplines, including real property, machinery and equipment, personal property, and a number of technical valuation specialties.

The ASA had for many years offered accreditation in Intangible Property, which included stocks or other interests in businesses as well as patents, copyrights, and other intangible property. However, there were few candidates for accreditation under that designation. In 1980, the name of the accreditation category was changed from Intangible Property to Business Valuation, and the content of the examinations was revised to include a heavy emphasis on current techniques for appraising businesses of all sizes, professional practices, and partial interests in them.

Shortly following adoption of the business valuation designation, the Business Valuation Committee of the ASA was formed. The Business Valuation Committee now has the support of almost all the leading U.S. business appraisal firms, as well as accounting firms offering business appraisal services, and from 1984 through 1992 the business valuation discipline was the fastest-growing category of accreditation in the American Society of Appraisers.

The professional designation ASA stands for *Accredited Senior Appraiser*. In order to acquire this designation, one needs to do the following: acquire five years of experience in the discipline in which the designation is granted; pass the relevant examinations; and submit two appraisal reports that meet the examining committee's standards. The American Society of Appraisers also awards the professional designation AM, Accredited Member, which has all the same requirements as ASA except only a two-year experience requirement.

The American Society of Appraisers offers a series of four three-day basic courses in business valuation, each presented several times per year at various locations around the United States. In addition, the ASA holds an annual meeting for members from all appraisal disciplines. In recent years, this event has included two days of educational meetings on business appraisal topics. Also, the Business Valuation Committee sponsors a two-day Advanced Business Valuation Seminar each fall. Local chapters or regional groups of chapters of the ASA occasionally sponsor educational programs.

The Business Valuation Committee also publishes a quarterly journal, *Business Valuation Review*, and the ASA publishes a multidisciplinary appraisal journal, *Valuation*.

The society's code of ethics requires an appraiser using the professional designation of ASA or AM as a credential in connection with a valuation report to set forth the discipline in which certification was achieved in the statement of qualifications and/or limiting conditions presented to, or received by, clients (e.g., Peter Plausible, ASA, Business Valuation). It would be a breach of ethics for someone accredited in machinery and equipment appraisal, for example, to write a business valuation report and be identified only as "Sandy Shoveler, ASA," which might mislead the reader to think that the author is accredited in business valuation when in fact the accreditation is in a different appraisal discipline.

Information on the American Society of Appraisers, its courses, and a list of members accredited in Business Valuation may be obtained from the ASA National Headquarters, P.O. Box 17265, Washington, D.C. 20041, (703) 478-2228.

Business Valuation Standards

The American Society of Appraisers, through its Business Valuation Committee, in 1992 completed the process of issuing a series of Standards for Business Valuation. As of this writing, all standards have been adopted by the Business Valuation Committee and approved by the Board of Governors.

1. Business Valuation Standard I: Terminology
2. Business Valuation Standard II: Full Written Business Valuation Report
3. Business Valuation Standard III: General Performance Requirements for Business Valuation
4. Business Valuation Standard IV: Asset Based Approach to Business Valuation
5. Business Valuation Standard V: The Guideline Company Valuation Method
6. Business Valuation Standard VI: Market Approach to Business Valuation
7. Business Valuation Standard VII: Income Approach to Business Valuation
8. Business Valuation Standard VIII: Reaching a Conclusion of Value
9. Business Valuation Standard IX: Financial Statement Adjustments

Business Valuation Standards I through IX, as approved by the Board of Governors are included as Appendix A. It is contemplated that they will be reorganized slightly in the final version but with no change to content. The final version of the Business Valuation Standards will be published in the *Business Valuation Review*, P.O. Box 24222, Denver, Colorado 80224, (303) 758–6148.

Both USPAP and the ASA Business Valuation Standards are mandatory for all members of ASA. From this point forward, the Business Valuation Committee will develop a set of "Procedural Guidelines." These guidelines will note acceptable but not mandatory methods and procedures for use in business appraisal.

Other Professional and Regulatory Bodies

Canadian Institute of Chartered Business Valuators (CICBV)

The Canadian Institute of Chartered Business Valuators (CICBV), originally called the Canadian Association of Business Valuators, was founded on January 6, 1971. Since then it has held biennial meetings, with the proceedings published as *The Journal of Business Valuation*. The CICBV holds educational meetings for its members at varying intervals.

The CICBV has developed a rigorous examination for testing a candidate's professional skills in business valuation. It awards the professional designation of CBV (Chartered Business Valuator) to those who demonstrate three years of full-time experience in business appraisal, five years of part-time experience, or two years and a required course of study, pass the exam, and meet certain other requirements.

The CICBV publishes a code of ethics, which includes general content of a valuation report and requirements for the disclosure of information sources.

Information on the CICBV may be obtained from the Canadian Institute of Chartered Business Valuators, 150 Bloor Street West, Second Floor, Toronto, Ontario M5S 2Y2, (416) 960-1254.

Institute of Business Appraisers

The Institute of Business Appraisers (IBA) offers one-day and two-day seminars on business appraisal topics. It publishes a code of ethics and at this writing has an exposure draft of a suggested set of standards. The address of the IBA is P.O. Box 1447, Boynton Beach, Florida 33435, (407) 732-3202. The IBA awards the professional designation CBA, Certified Business Appraiser. This involves an examination and the submission of reports, but no experience requirement.

The ESOP Association

The ESOP Association Valuation Advisory Committee meets twice a year, primarily to discuss issues concerning the valuation of Employee Stock Ownership Plan (ESOP) shares in privately held companies. The committee has worked toward developing valuation guidelines and in 1989 issued a revised edition of its 75-page booklet titled *Valuing ESOP Shares*.[2] Committee members also conduct educational sessions for ESOP Association members and companies considering ESOPs.

While The ESOP Association is contributing a worthwhile effort to the refinement and sophistication of ESOP stock valuation, it should be understood that it neither certifies nor endorses business appraisers or any other specialists, nor does it issue standards as such. At the present time it has a number of subcommittees studying specific valuation issues relating to ESOP stock. For example, one is a subcommittee on the relationship between control and minority interest issues, and another is on discounts for lack of marketability. Anyone valuing ESOP shares should be aware of the work of The ESOP Association Valuation Advisory Committee.

Information on The ESOP Association may be obtained from The ESOP Association, 1100 17th Street, N.W., Suite 1207, Washington, D.C. 20036, (202) 293-2971.

---

[2]*Valuing ESOP Shares* (Washington, D.C.: The ESOP Association, 1989).

Internal Revenue Service (IRS)

The IRS issues Revenue Rulings. These do not have the force of law, but present the position of the Service on various tax matters, including valuations of businesses and business interests.

Over time many of the positions espoused by the IRS through their Revenue Rulings come up in court case disputes. The resolution of these issues by the courts establishes case law precedent. Most, but not all, of such case law have been supportive of positions taken in the Revenue Rulings. The most important of those that relate to business valuation are:

59-60   Valuing Closely Held Stock
68-609   Formula Method (this revenue ruling also extends 59-60 to apply to business interests of any type)
83-120   Valuation of Preferred Stock

Revenue Ruling 59-60 is reprinted in Appendix B at the end of this book. Revenue Ruling 68-609 is reproduced in Exhibit 15–1 in Chapter 15. Revenue Ruling 83-120 is Exhibit 26–2 in Chapter 26. In particular, Revenue Ruling 59-60 has been issued for over 30 years, and certain parts of it are widely quoted by professionals and courts, even in some valuation matters not involving taxation issues.

Department of Labor

Like the IRS Revenue Rulings, regulations issued by the Department of Labor do not have the force of law. They represent the Department's position with respect to interpretation of the law as it applies to certain issues.

In May of 1988, the DOL issued a proposed draft of a Regulation Relating to the Definition of Adequate Consideration (for ESOP stock). Hearings have been held and written comment received. At this writing there is no indication as to when they expect to issue a final regulation.

Summary

Unlike the situation when the first edition of this book was published, business valuation standards now exist. Importantly, they are recognized not only by professionals, but also by courts. Consequently, it is important that all parties dealing with business valuations be aware of them.

The standards are quite general. They make good sense. They have been developed by people who represent all segments of the professional business appraisal community. Consequently, they contain important guidance applicable to all business appraisals, no matter whether the person or persons performing the appraisal belong to any of the professional appraisal organizations.

The standards will evolve further and be refined over the next few years. Knowledge of and adherence to these evolving standards will be an important part of the foundation for sound business appraisal practice.

Bibliography

American Society of Appraisers Business Valuation Standards. (Standards I through IX, as approved by the committee in 1992, are included as Appendix A. Copies of the final version will be available at no charge from the Publisher of *Business Valuation Review*, P.O. Box 24222, Denver, Colo. 80224, (303) 758-6148.)

Pratt, Shannon P. *Reviewing a Business Appraisal Report.* National Association of Review Appraisers & Mortgage Underwriters (1989), 8383 East Evans Road, Scottsdale, Ariz. 85260-3614, (602) 998-3000. (Single copies are available at no charge from Willamette Management Associates, 400 S.W. Sixth Avenue, Suite 1115, Portland, Ore. 97204, (503) 222-0577, while supplies last.)

Principles of Appraisal Practice and Code of Ethics. American Society of Appraisers (1992), P.O. Box 17265, Washington, D.C. 20041, (703) 478-2228. (This publication is available free of charge from the ASA.)

Regulation Relating to the Definition of Adequate Consideration; Notice of Proposed Rulemaking. Department of Labor, 29 CFR Part 2510, as published in the *Federal Register* 53, no. 95 (May 17, 1988), pp. 17632-17638.

Uniform Standards of Professional Appraisal Practice. The Appraisal Foundation (1992), 1029 Vermont Avenue, N.W., Suite 900, Washington, D.C. 20005, (202) 347-7722. Henceforth from 1992, The Appraisal Foundation will publish an annually updated version of USPAP.

Valuing ESOP Shares. The ESOP Association (1989), 1100 17th Street, N.W., Suite 1207, Washington, D.C. 20036, (202) 293-2971.

Chapter 2

Defining the Valuation Assignment

First Things First

In order to have the valuation job on track from the very beginning, the first step is to define clearly and completely the valuation problem.

Defining the valuation assignment is the logical beginning of the valuation process, providing the focus for all the valuation considerations and efforts to be undertaken. The appraiser should assist the client (and the attorney, if one is involved) in specifying the exact appraisal assignment. In my experience, anyone who does not engage in business appraisals on a regular basis is unlikely to consider all the key elements in an appraisal assignment. Furthermore, such persons often would not have the technical knowledge to adequately specify such complex elements of the appraisal assignment as the standard and premises of value. Inadequacies in specification of the appraisal assignment often result in misdirected efforts and invalid conclusions.

I highly recommend that the definition of the valuation assignment be written. Writing valuation objectives and requirements forces those responsible for the valuation to think carefully through all of its essential elements. It also helps them avoid misdirecting the valuation process and helps the various parties involved, such as the principals, brokers, attorneys, and professional appraisers, avoid misunderstandings that otherwise may arise. The knowledge and experience of the professional appraiser can be invaluable in helping to assure that the appraisal assignment is specified completely and correctly.

Basic Elements of the Valuation Assignment

In simple terms, the first step in valuation is to make the following decisions and incorporate them into a valuation assignment:

1. Exactly what asset, property, or business interest is to be valued.
2. The applicable standard of value.
3. The appraisal date (the date as of which the appraiser's opinion of value applies).
4. The applicable premise of value.
5. The legal interest that is subject to appraisal.
6. The use or uses to which the valuation exercise is expected to be put.
7. Instructions to be given to a professional appraiser, if one is to be retained.

Exhibit 2–1 is a suggested checklist for use in defining the valuation assignment.

Exhibit 2–2 gives examples of written definitions of an appraisal assignment covering points one through seven above.

Exhibit 2–1

VALUATION ASSIGNMENT CHECKLIST

Name of entity _____

Form of ownership

      ☐ Regular corporation   ☐ Limited partnership

      ☐ Subchapter S corporation   ☐ Sole proprietorship

      ☐ General partnership   ☐ Other (please specify)

State in which incorporated or registered

Valuation being done on   ☐ stock basis, or   ☐ asset basis
      (If asset basis, list assets to be included and liabilities to be assumed, if any)

Are there other classes of equity interests outstanding?   ☐ Yes   ☐ No
      (If yes, please specify)

Proportion of total entity being valued

Any restrictions on transfer?

Purpose or purposes of the valuation

Applicable standard of value (If pursuant to a federal or state statute, corporate bylaw or other governing law or document, so indicate)

Appraisal date

Is covenant not to compete involved?   ☐ Yes   ☐ No

Is employment agreement(s) involved?   ☐ Yes   ☐ No

If independent appraiser is retained:
    Name of appraiser

    Name of client

    Form and extent of appraisal report

    Expected completion date (specify due date of various phases)

    Fee arrangement

SOURCE: Willamette Management Associates

Exhibit 2–2

SAMPLE WRITTEN DEFINITIONS
OF THE APPRAISAL ASSIGNMENT

Value for a divorce

    To determine the fair market value of a 20 percent interest in Gotham Insurance Agency (Gotham), a New York general partnership, as of the present time, for the purpose of a property settlement in the marital dissolution of Mr. and Mrs. Randolph.

Value for ESOP transactions

    To determine the fair market value of minority shares of common stock of Gotham Insurance Agency, Inc., a Delaware corpora-

tion, owned by Gotham's Employee Stock Ownership Plan as of April 30, 1991, for the purpose of ESOP stock transactions.

Value for a dissenting stockholder action

    To determine the fair value of 500 shares of common stock (out of 2,500 outstanding) of Gotham Insurance Agency, Inc. (Gotham), a Delaware corporation, as of April 30, 1991, pursuant to Del. Code Ann. tit. Section 8 262()-262(d), for the purpose of a dissenting stockholder action.

SOURCE: Willamette Management Associates

Property to Be Valued

Much of the confusion and apparent disagreement among appraisers and appraisal writings arises simply because it is not clear exactly what asset, property, or business interest is to be valued. To determine the applicable approach and steps to be taken, *exactly* what is to be valued must be made clear. An important determination is whether the stock or the assets of the business are to be valued. More small businesses and professional practices are sold on the basis of an asset sale rather than on the basis of a stock sale, in which case it is essential to specify the assets that are included in the appraisal.

Stock represents an indirect ownership interest in whatever bundle of assets and liabilities (actual or contingent) exists in a corporation. Stock ownership is quite different from direct ownership of assets and direct obligation for liabilities.

If stock is to be valued, it must be identified in the appraisal assignment. If assets are to be valued, those assets (and any liabilities to be assumed) must be specified.

If a partial interest in an entity is to be valued, the proportionate relationship of the partial interest to the whole is obviously important.

Valuation of the Stock of a Business

Identification of the Corporation. The name of the corporation and the state of incorporation should be specified when valuing stock; this avoids the ambiguity frequently caused by the existence of many corporations with the same name, incorporated in different states. Also, most legal factors that have a bearing on valuation are matters of state laws, which, on some issues, vary considerably. So, for some valuation purposes, the state of incorporation has an important effect on certain valuation criteria.

State law and state case law precedents are especially variable in regard to valuations of businesses and professional practices for property settlements in divorces, as discussed in Chapter 39.

If the corporation has any special corporate registration, such as federal income tax chapter S tax status or a nonprofit corporation, that should be specified as part of the corporate identification, because it may have a bearing on the valuation process and conclusion.

Specification of the Stock Interest to be Valued. To preclude any uncertainty, specify if 100 percent of the stock is to be valued. If not, then specify the proportionate interest to be valued.

If there is only one class of common stock, it is generally sufficient to state the number of shares being valued out of the total number of shares outstanding. If there is more than one class of common stock, the appraisal assignment should specify the number of shares in each class being valued out of the total number of shares in that class. Where one or more classes of stock are outstanding but not subject to valuation, the assignment should nevertheless mention them.

If the number of shares that may be involved in a contemplated transaction is unknown, the assignment may contain general wording, such as ''minority shares of common stock'' or ''controlling shares of common stock.'' A more exact specification should be determined as soon as possible and noted in the work paper file.

The valuation of stock in a small business or professional practice is usually done on an equity basis, that is, net of all liabilities. However, the appraiser is sometimes asked to provide an opinion on the total value of all the invested capital (usually defined to mean the stock plus the long-term debt). If so, that assignment should be clearly specified.

Restrictions on Transfer. If there are any restrictions on transferring the shares of stock to be valued, it is a good idea to note them in the appraisal assignment, because restrictions on transfer usually affect the value of the shares to be appraised.

Valuation of the Assets of a Business

Even if a small business or professional practice is incorporated, it is quite common to transfer it on the basis of a sale of assets rather than a sale of stock. In such a case, the assets to be transferred (and liabilities, if any) must be specified.

The following assets are commonly included in the sale of a small business or professional practice:

1. Inventory.
2. Fixed assets—leasehold improvements, furniture, fixtures, equipment, and so forth.
3. Intangible assets—leasehold, trade name, patents, copyrights, customer lists, goodwill, advantageous financing arrangements, and so forth.

The seller frequently keeps the cash, collects the accounts receivable, and pays off all the existing liabilities. If the inventory is substantial and is financed by a manufacturer, the buyer may assume the liability for the inventory, subject, of course, to the manufacturer's approval.

Real estate may or may not be included in the sale. If it is and is subject to a mortgage, the buyer may or may not assume the mortgage. (As discussed in later chapters, it is generally preferable, if possible, to separate, or unbundle, the real estate value from the value of the business, especially if the real estate is multipurpose rather than an integral part of the business.)

Sometimes a buyer may purchase most or all of the receivables and assume most or all of the liabilities. If so, it must be determined whether these transfers are unconditional or if contingencies or recourses exist.

Treatment of Covenants Not to Compete and Employment Agreements

Two types of intangible assets are frequently created specifically for the purpose of facilitating the sale of a business or professional practice. These two types of intangible assets include covenants not to compete and employment agreements. It is important to specify if either or both of these assets are to be included. Many small businesses and professional practices would have little or no value without such agreements.

If such contracts are included, the matter of how they are treated in the purchase agreement has income tax consequences for both the buyers and the sellers. This matter is discussed in Chapter 26.

The Purpose or Purposes of the Valuation

This book focuses both on valuation for the purpose of buying or selling a business or practice, and also on special aspects of valuations for many other needs: property settlements, taxes, damage cases, minority stockholder appraisal rights, and so on. Valuations for each of these different purposes are often affected by a mass of complex federal and state statutes and legal precedents. The result is that different standards of value, and different valuation criteria, must be applied in different cases, depending both on the purpose of the valuation and on the jurisdiction in which it is taking place. Consequently, the purpose of the valuation is an integral part of the valuation assignment, and the valuation process must meet the applicable standard of value and valuation criteria.

The next two chapters are devoted to an overview of the different standards of value and how they may apply for different valuation purposes.

Parts IV, VI, and VII contain chapters devoted to some of the most important purposes for business and professional practice valuation, and the peculiarities of valuations for these different purposes.

It is desirable for both the engagement letter and the ultimate written report to state that the valuation is valid only for the purpose or purposes stated and only as of the stated appraisal date (as discussed in the next section).

Appraisal Date

The date, or dates, at which the business or practice is being valued is critically important, because circumstances can cause values to vary materially from one date to another, and the valuation date directly influences data available for valuation.

Choosing an Applicable Appraisal Date

It is usually easier to arrive at the most reliable valuation at the end of an entity's fiscal year, because most companies take physical inventories then and also analyze and adjust other accounts in the normal course of business. If a transaction is to take place at the end of a fiscal year, it often involves arriving at a value before the end of the fiscal year. This valuation is then subject to certain adjustments for physical inventory, accounts receivable, and/or certain other accounts, depending on exactly what is being transferred as part of the sale.

Valuations shortly after the end of a fiscal year can often rely on year-end data, in most cases with some minor adjustments. If the effective date of the closing is some other time, it may be necessary to go through a complete year-end closing of the books to arrive at the final price. More often, especially in smaller businesses and practices, a value can be arrived at without such a complete accounting exercise, but subject to adjustment for a physical inventory count if inventory is a significant item.

Valuations for Employee Stock Ownership Plans (ESOPs) are usually pegged to a fiscal year-end, and valuations for some other purposes, such as gifts, charitable contributions, and incentive stock options, can be pegged to a specific date.

Appraisal Dates Determined by Law

For many purposes, the effective date for valuation is out of the parties' hands. In most states, the valuation date for inheritance taxes is the date of death. For federal estate taxes, the taxpayer can elect the date of death or six months after, so the parties should determine which is more advantageous. For divorces, the most common valuation date is the effective date of the divorce, which could be the date of trial or the date the decree was entered. However, this varies from state to state and from situation to situation (see Chapter 39, which addresses divorce litigation). For dissenting stockholder actions, the valuation date is almost always the date that the stockholders approved the action creating the dissenters' appraisal rights. Relevant valuation dates for damage cases must be determined case-by-case, and may themselves be a matter of dispute among the parties.

If possible, the valuation date or alternate possible valuation dates should be specified in both the engagement letter and the valuation opinion report.

There are times when the valuation date is not known at the time the appraisal assignment is initially made. This is often a problem in valuations for divorces, where courts in many jurisdictions have discretion to set the valuation date at the date of separation, date of filing, date of trial, or some other date.

If the valuation date is ambiguous, it is generally desirable to try to get it resolved by the court as early as possible in order to save the cost of valuations as of dates the court ultimately deems to be irrelevant. Sometimes, however, resolution of this issue before trial is not possible, and it is necessary to go to court prepared to present valuations as of two or more different dates.

If the valuation date or dates are changed or clarified after the initial valuation assignment, it is desirable to document this in writing with a copy to the client.

Applicable Standard of Value

As discussed in the following chapters, different standards of value govern valuations for different purposes. Some of these standards have fairly clear-cut definitions and interpretations that appraisers and courts widely accept; others do not.

Although fair market value is the most widely used standard of value, it does not apply to all valuation situations. Specify the standard of value applicable to the particular situation, if known.

Where possible, this book attempts to identify the applicable standard of value for each common kind of valuation situation. If in doubt, consult a professional appraiser.

Instructions to the Independent Professional Appraiser

If an outside appraiser is to be retained, discuss and agree to certain factors, such as extent and type of report expected, the time schedule, and the expected cost.

Form and Extent of the Appraisal Report

The appraiser's report to the client can be oral, written, or a combination. An oral report can be anything from a quick phone call to lengthy meetings with the principals, attorneys, brokers, and/or other parties involved. The form and extent of a written report can range from a single-page letter report to a detailed, hundred-page-plus volume. Obviously, at least general expectations should be discussed and referenced in the assignment.

Schedule

Most first-time, or infrequent, business appraisal clients tend to underestimate the amount of appraiser lead time needed for a thorough and professional job. The "comfort zone" is usually 60 days for a completely documented, written appraisal for a medium-sized company (as discussed more fully in Chapter 37). Often, however, it is necessary for the appraiser to act immediately and give a client at least minimal guidance about an imminent deal.

Perhaps the most serious lead-time problem that appraisers encounter is a sudden attorney request for expert witness testimony, in court, on a disputed valuation issue. An attorney may jeopardize his client's position when he fails to allow enough lead time for an expert witness to prepare thoroughly for court testimony.

The best plan is to give the appraiser all the lead time possible, and agree at the beginning about the expected schedule.

Fee Arrangements

An appraiser may work on a fixed fee, a range of estimated fees, hourly, or daily. The more clearly defined the appraisal assignment, the more likely it is that the appraiser will be able to quote a fixed fee or a very close estimate. For most types of appraisal assignments, an independent professional appraiser is legally and ethically prohibited from entering into an arrangement making the appraiser's fee contingent on completed settlement negotiations or the outcome of a court decision. More on all these points is discussed in Chapter 37.

The fee arrangements should include the terms of payment as well as the basis for establishing the fee.

Summary

In summary, the valuation assignment should address all of the following elements:

1. Precise and complete description of the property to be valued, including description of liabilities to be assumed, if any.

2. The purpose or purposes of the valuation (e.g., the use or uses to which the valuation work product will be put).
3. The effective date or dates of the valuation.
4. The applicable standard of value (including reference to any legal or documentary source that governs the applicable standard).
5. The form and extent of the expected valuation work product (appraisal report).
6. The schedule.
7. The fee arrangements.

Exhibit 2–3 is a sample engagement letter that covers the elements discussed in this chapter, as well as a few other important points such as indemnification of the appraiser.

Exhibit 2–3

PROFESSIONAL SERVICES AGREEMENT

John Doe Associates, an Oregon corporation, hereafter called "Doe," and ___Estate of Alan B. Client___, hereafter called "Client," agree as follows:

1.   **Description of services.** Doe agrees to perform certain professional services for Client, described briefly as follows as to purpose and assignment, with the understanding that any modification to the assignment as stated below will be by a letter agreement signed by both parties.

Appraisal of the fair market value of a 100% interest in ABC, Inc., an Illinois corporation, held by the estate of Alan B. Client, as of August 30, 1991, for estate tax purposes.

2.   **Use of Appraisal.** Client warrants that this appraisal will be relied on only for the use indicated above and only as of the date indicated above. Client understands that this appraisal is not valid for any other use or for any other appraisal date.

3.   **Date(s) services due.** Doe will begin performance upon receipt of all information requested of Client, and will complete assignment(s), unless delayed or prevented by matters beyond Doe's control, according to the following schedule:

Full, formal report within 90 days of receipt of all requested documents.

4.   **Fees.** Doe's fees for such professional services will be calculated on standard hourly rates in effect at the time services are rendered for staff members assigned to Client's project, plus out-of-pocket expenses. The fee is estimated at a range of $_____ to $_____, exclusive of expenses such as travel, long distance telephone, purchases of data, copying and printing costs. The fee will not exceed such estimate by more than 25% without prior notification to Client.

5.   **Retainer.** $_____ is due as a retainer upon execution of this Agreement. Retainer paid by Client will be applied to the **final** billings.

6.   **Payment terms.** Client will receive regular twice-monthly invoices, including fees and expenses incurred, for which payments will be due at Doe offices within 15 days of dates of invoices. Balances which remain unpaid 30 days from dates of invoices will be assessed a finance charge of 1.5% monthly (18% annual percentage rate).

If Doe is to provide expert witness testimony as part of its assignment, Client agrees that payment of all fees and expenses invoiced and/or incurred to date will be received at Doe offices before Doe provides expert witness testimony, or if travel for testimony is necessary, payment will be received before travel is incurred.

Client agrees that the fees and expenses invoiced by Doe must be paid current per the terms of this Agreement before Doe provides any report or analysis conclusions.

7.   Client understands that Doe will need prompt access to documents, materials, facilities, and/or Client's personnel in order to perform its services in a timely and professional manner, and Client agrees to fulfill all such requests in a timely manner and to cooperate fully with Doe. Client further understands and agrees that delays in providing data or information may result in a delay of the completion date of the project.

8.   Doe agrees to perform its services in a professional and objective manner. Client understands that Doe does not guarantee the results of any analysis which it may undertake, but only agrees that any report or analysis shall represent Doe's professional opinion based on the data given to or compiled by it. Doe attempts to obtain and compile its data from reliable sources, but it cannot guarantee its accuracy or completeness.

Exhibit 2–3 (*concluded*)

9.   Client warrants that the information and data it supplies to Doe will be complete and accurate in every respect to the best of Client's knowledge; that any reports, analysis, or other documents prepared by Doe will be used only in compliance with all applicable laws and regulations; and that Client will hold Doe harmless for any breach of this warranty.

10.   Client agrees to indemnify and hold Doe harmless against any and all liability, claim, loss, cost, and expense, whatever kind or nature, which Doe may incur, or be subject to, as a party, expert witness, witness or participant in connection with any dispute or litigation involving Client. This indemnity includes all out-of-pocket expenses (including travel costs and attorney fees) and payment for all Doe staff members' time at standard hourly rates in effect at the time rendered to the extent Doe attends, prepares for, or participates in meetings, hearings, depositions, trials, and all other proceedings, including travel time. If Doe must bring legal action to enforce this indemnity, Client agrees to pay all costs of such action, including any sum as the Court may fix as reasonable attorney fees.

11.   If this Agreement, or any monies due under the terms hereof, is placed in the hands of an attorney for collection of the account, Client promises and agrees to pay Doe's attorney fees and collection costs, plus interest at the then legal rate, whether or not any legal action is filed. If any suit or action is brought to enforce, interpret, or collect damages for the breach of this agreement, Client agrees to pay Doe's reasonable attorney fees and costs of such suit or action, including any appeal as fixed by the applicable Court or Courts.

Dated this 30th day of September 1991, at Portland, Oregon.

Estate of Alan B. Client   **John Doe Associates**

By:_____   By: _____
Name: Martha Client, Executor   Name: John Doe, President

Address: 100 North 4th Street, Decatur, Illinois 64156
Telephone: (708) 555-4455
FAX: (708) 555-4457

SOURCE: Willamette Management Associates

Chapter 3

Defining Value

> *Many terms are used to define value. . . . Only a few of these terms have some definition. Others have the definition which the parties choose to place upon them.*[1]

Since the task of this book is to assist readers in reaching, understanding, or evaluating conclusions about value, its logical beginning is to identify and define different standards and premises of value that may apply in different situations. Many terms are used to describe various notions of value; but, unfortunately, such terms mean different things to different people.

I cannot emphasize enough how critical it is to clearly delineate the definition of the value being sought in the particular engagement. Clients rarely give it much thought. Most attorneys do not have enough technical background in valuation of businesses to think the matter of defining the value all the way through and raise the right questions. One of the professional valuer's most important tasks is to work carefully and thoroughly with the client and/or attorney to arrive at a definition of value that is appropriate to the specific valuation engagement.

This chapter presents the concepts of value (both standards and premises) that are most widely encountered and most useful in business valuation.

Standards of Value

A standard of value as used in this book is a definition of the type of value being sought. For some valuation situations, the standard of value is legally mandated, either by law or by binding legal documents or contracts. In other cases, it is a function of the wishes of the parties involved. I could tell horror stories by the dozens about disputes, often resulting in litigation, that arose because the parties had differing understandings as to the standard of value applicable to the situation. Basic standards of value are often further clarified by various premises relating to the value as discussed in the next major section.

Fair Market Value

In the United States, the most widely recognized and accepted standard of value is *fair market value*. It is the standard that applies to all federal and state tax matters, such as estate taxes, gift taxes, inheritance taxes, income taxes, and ad valorem taxes. It is also the legal standard of value in many other—though not all—valuation situations.

The ASA definition of fair market value is the amount at which property would change hands between a willing seller and a willing buyer when neither is acting under compulsion and when both have reasonable knowledge of the relevant facts.

---

[1]John E. Moye, *Buying and Selling Businesses* (Minneapolis, Minn.: National Practice Institute, 1983), p. 25.

There is general agreement that the definition implies that the parties have the ability as well as the willingness to buy or to sell. The market in this definition can be thought of as all the potential buyers and sellers of like businesses or practices.

In legal interpretations of fair market value, the willing buyer and willing seller are hypothetical persons dealing at arm's length, rather than any particular buyer or seller. In other words, a price would not be considered representative of fair market value if influenced by special motivations not characteristic of a typical buyer or seller.

The concept of fair market value also assumes prevalent economic and market conditions at the date of the particular valuation. You have probably heard someone say many times, "I couldn't get anywhere near the value of my house if I put it on the market today," or, "The value of XYZ Company stock is really much more (or less) than the price it's selling for on the New York Stock Exchange today." The standard of value that those people have in mind is some standard *other than* fair market value, since the concept of fair market value means the price at which a transaction could be expected to take place under *conditions existing at the valuation date*.

The terms *market value* and *cash value* are frequently used interchangeably with the term *fair market value*.[2] Real estate appraisers generally use the term *market value* rather than *fair market value*.

The Appraisal Foundation defines *market value* as follows:

MARKET VALUE: Market value is the major focus of most real property appraisal assignments. Both economic and legal definitions of market value have been developed and refined. A current economic definition agreed upon by agencies that regulate federal financial institutions in the United States of America is: The most probable price which a property should bring in a competitive and open market under all conditions requisite to a fair sale, the buyer and seller each acting prudently and knowledgeably, and assuming the price is not affected by undue stimulus. Implicit in this definition is the consummation of a sale as of a specified date and the passing of title from seller to buyer under conditions whereby:
1. buyer and seller are typically motivated;
2. both parties are well informed or well advised, and acting in what they consider their best interests;
3. a reasonable time is allowed for exposure in the open market;
4. payment is made in terms of cash in United States dollars or in terms of financial arrangements comparable thereto; and
5. the price represents the normal consideration for the property sold unaffected by special or creative financing or sales concessions granted by anyone associated with the sale.

Substitution of another currency for *United States dollars* in the fourth condition is appropriate in other countries or in reports addressed to clients from other countries.

Persons performing appraisal services that may be subject to litigation are cautioned to seek the exact legal definition of market value in the jurisdiction in which the services are being performed.

---

[2]A leading authority on real estate appraisal terminology in the United States says that the definition of market value is synonymous with fair market value. Byrl N. Boyce, ed., *Real Estate Appraisal Terminology* (Cambridge, Mass.: Ballinger Publishing Company, 1982), p. 98.

It is generally understood that fair market value means a value in cash or cash equivalents (as indicated in The Appraisal Foundation definition of *market value*) unless otherwise stated. However, very few small businesses and professional practices actually sell for cash. Consequently, it is common for business brokers to think of the value of a business or practice on the basis of the face value of a transaction on the terms at which the particular type of business or practice typically sells in the marketplace. Some term other than fair market value (such as *transaction value*) might avoid confusion. However, it is not uncommon for brokers to use the term *fair market value* in this context.

Investment Value

In the first edition of this book, I used the terms *investment value, intrinsic value,* and *fundamental value* interchangeably, as many people do.[3] I noted, however, that "some writers make certain distinctions among these standards of value." After studying several score more books, articles, and court cases that use these terms, I decided that the distinctions in their typical usage should be brought to readers' attention. Therefore, I am treating *intrinsic* or *fundamental value* separately from *investment value.*

In real estate terminology, investment value is defined as "value to a particular investor based on individual investment requirements, as distinguished from the concept of market value, which is impersonal and detached."[4] In real estate appraisal, calculations of investment value conventionally involve discounting an anticipated income stream.

One of the leading real estate appraisal texts makes the following comments regarding the distinction between market value and investment value:

> Market value can be called "the value of the marketplace"; *investment value is the specific value of goods or services to a particular investor (or class of investors) for individual investment reasons.* Market value and investment value are different concepts, although the values estimated for each may or may not be numerically equal depending on the circumstances. In addition, market value estimates are commonly made without reference to investment value, but investment value estimates are frequently accompanied by a market value estimate to facilitate decision making.
>
> Market value estimates assume no specific buyer or seller. Rather, the appraiser considers a hypothetical transaction in which both the buyer and the seller have the understanding, perceptions, and motivations that are typical of the market for the property or interests being valued. Appraisers must distinguish between their own knowledge, perceptions, and attitudes and those of the market or markets for the property in question. The special considerations of a given client are irrelevant to a market value estimate.[5]

---

[3]For example, in Chapter 11 of his classic *Valuation of Property*, James Bonbright describes the concept of *intrinsic value* as including both *value to the owner* (which other authors refer to as *investment value*) and *justified price* (the general notion that other authors ascribe to *intrinsic value*).

[4]Boyce, *Real Estate Appraisal Terminology*, p. 140.

[5]*The Appraisal of Real Estate*, 10th ed. (Chicago: The Appraisal Institute, 1992), p. 29–30.

In their well-received text *The Stock Market: Theories and Evidence*, Lorie and Hamilton discuss investment value by reference to the classic work of John Burr Williams:[6]

> He considers the appropriate rate of discounting, the effects of stock rights and assessments, risk premiums, the effect of the capital structure of the firm, and the marketability of the security. His treatment of these various subjects leads to the grand conclusion that the investment value of a stock is determined by discounting the "expected" [authors' term] stream of dividends at the discount rate appropriate for the individual investor. . . .[7]

There can be many valid reasons for the investment value to one particular owner or prospective owner to differ from the fair market value. Among these reasons are the following:

1. Differences in estimates of future earning power.
2. Differences in perception of the degree of risk.
3. Differences in tax status.
4. Synergies with other operations owned or controlled.

The discounted future returns valuation method (see Chapter 13) is essentially oriented toward developing an investment value. Whether or not the value thus developed also represents fair market value depends on whether the assumptions used would be accepted by a consensus of market participants.

If sound analysis leads to a valid conclusion that the investment value to a particular owner exceeded market value at a given time, the rational economic decision for that owner would be not to sell at that time unless a particular buyer could be found to whom investment value would be higher than the consensus of value among a broader group of typical buyers.

Of course, the concept of investment value as described above is not completely divorced from the concept of fair market value, since it is the actions of many specific investors, acting in the manner just described, that eventually lead to a balancing of supply and demand through the establishment of an equilibrium market price that represents the consensus value of the collective investors.

Finally, the term *investment value* has a slightly different meaning when used in the context of dissenting stockholder suits. In this context, it means a value based on earning power, as described above, except that the appropriate discount or capitalization rate is usually considered to be a consensus rate rather than a rate peculiarly appropriate for any specific investor.

Intrinsic or Fundamental Value

Intrinsic value (sometimes called *fundamental value*) differs from *investment value* in that it represents an analytical judgment of value based

---

[6] John Burr Williams, *The Theory of Investment Value* (Cambridge, Mass.: Harvard University Press, 1938). Reprinted in Amsterdam by North Holland Publishing Company, 1956.

[7] James H. Lorie and Mary T. Hamilton, *The Stock Market: Theories and Evidence* (Homewood, Ill.: Richard D. Irwin, 1973), pp. 116–17.

on the perceived characteristics inherent in the investment, not tempered by characteristics peculiar to any one investor, but rather tempered by how these perceived characteristics are interpreted by one analyst versus another.

Financial Decision Making defines *intrinsic value* as follows:

> *Value, intrinsic of common stock.* The price that is justified for a share when the primary factors of value are considered. In other words, it is the real worth of the stock, as distinguished from the current market price of the stock. It is a subjective value in the sense that the analyst must apply his own individual background and skills to determine it, and estimates of intrinsic value will vary from one analyst to the next.

The financial manager estimates intrinsic value by carefully appraising the following fundamental factors that affect common stock values:

1. *Value of the firm's assets.* The physical assets held by the firm have some market value. In liquidation approaches to valuation, assets can be quite important. In techniques of going-concern valuation, assets are usually omitted.
2. *Likely future earnings.* The expected future earnings of the firm are the most important single factor affecting the common stock's intrinsic value.
3. *Likely future dividends.* The firm may pay out its earnings as dividends or may retain them to finance growth and expansion. The firm's policies with respect to dividends will affect the intrinsic value of its stock.
4. *Likely future growth rate.* A firm's prospects for future growth are carefully evaluated by investors and are a factor influencing intrinsic value.[8]

Further concurrence on the meanings of intrinsic value and fundamental value is found in the following definitions from an authoritative reference in the accounting field:

> *Intrinsic value.* The amount that an investor considers, on the basis of an evaluation of available facts, to be the "true" or "real" worth of an item, usually an *equity security.* The value that will become the market value when other investors reach the same conclusions. The various approaches to determining intrinsic value of the *finance* literature are based on expectations and discounted cash flows. See *expected value; fundamental analysis; discounted cash flow method.*[9]
>
> *Fundamental analysis.* An approach in security analysis which assumes that a security has an "intrinsic value" that can be determined through a rigorous evaluation of relevant variables. Expected earnings is usually the most important variable in this analysis, but many other variables, such as dividends, capital structure, management quality, and so on, may also be studied. An analyst estimates the "intrinsic value" of a security on the basis of those fundamental variables and compares this value with the current market price of this security to arrive at an investment decision.[10]

In the analysis of stocks, intrinsic value is generally considered the appropriate price for a stock according to a security analyst who has completed a fundamental analysis of the company's assets, earning

[8]John J. Hampton, *Financial Decision Making: Concepts, Problems and Cases,* 3rd ed. (Englewood Cliffs, N.J.: Prentice Hall, 1983), pp. 429–30.

[9]W. W. Cooper and Yuri Ijiri, eds., *Kohler's Dictionary for Accountants,* 6th ed. (Englewood Cliffs, N.J.: Prentice Hall, 1983), p. 285.

[10]Ibid., p. 228.

power, and other factors. Lorie and Hamilton comment on the notion of intrinsic value as follows:

> The purpose of security analysis is to detect differences between the value of a security as determined by the market and a security's "intrinsic value"—that is, the value that the security *ought* to have and will have when other investors have the same insight and knowledge as the analyst.[11]

If the market value is below what the analyst concludes is the intrinsic value, the analyst considers the stock a "buy." If the market value is above the assumed intrinsic value, the analyst suggests selling the stock.

It is important to note that the concept of intrinsic value cannot be entirely divorced from the concept of fair market value, since the actions of buyers and sellers based on their *specific* perceptions of intrinsic value eventually lead to the *general* consensus market value and the constant and dynamic changes in market value over time.

Case law often refers to the term *intrinsic value*. However, almost universally such references do not define the term other than by reference to the language in the context in which it appears. Such references to *intrinsic value* can be found both in cases where there is no statutory standard of value and in cases where the statutory standard of value is specified as *fair value* or even *fair market value*. When references to *intrinsic value* appear in the relevant case law, the analyst should heed the notions ascribed to that term as discussed in this section.

Fair Value

The expression *fair value* is an excellent example of ambiguous terminology used in the field of commercial appraisal. In order to understand what the expression means, you have to know the context of its use. The accepted definition of fair value in real estate appraisal terminology is totally different from the interpretation the courts have given to fair value as a statutory standard of value applicable to a business appraisal.

A leading authority on real estate terminology states that fair value is synonymous with market value or fair market value.[12] However, in most states, fair value is the statutory standard of value applicable in cases of dissenting stockholders' appraisal rights. In these states, if a corporation merges, sells out, or takes certain other major actions, and the owner of a minority interest believes that he is being forced to receive less than adequate consideration for his stock, he has the right to have his shares appraised and to receive fair value in cash.

There is no clearly recognized consensus about the definition of fair value in this context but precedents established in the courts of the various states certainly have not equated it to fair market value. I have served as an advisor or expert witness for one side or the other in many dissenting stockholder suits, and I can say that when a situation arises

---

[11]Lorie and Hamilton, *The Stock Market*, p. 114.
[12]Boyce, *Real Estate Appraisal Terminology*, p. 98.

of actual or potential stockholder dissent, it is necessary to research carefully the legal precedents applicable to each case.

The term *fair value* is also found in the dissolution statutes of those few states in which minority stockholders can trigger a corporate dissolution under certain circumstances (e.g., California Corporations Code Section 2000). Even within the same state, however, a study of case law precedents does not necessarily lead one to the same definition of fair value under a dissolution statute as under that state's dissenting stockholder statute.

Premises of Value

The premise of value is an assumption as to the set of circumstances under which the sale transaction will take place. The premise of value will define or specify how, or under what conditions, a buyer and a seller will exchange the subject assets, properties, or business interests. The premise of value answers the question: "value under what set of hypothetical transaction circumstances?"

The standard of value is an assumption as to who will be the buyer and who will be the seller in the hypothetical or actual sales transaction regarding the subject assets, properties, or business interests. The standard of value will define or specify what parties will be involved in the exchange transaction. The standard of value generally answers the question: "value to whom?",[13] although the standard of value sometimes is a product of the legal system, e.g., defined by statute or case law.

As such, premises of value are often in the nature of modifiers (adjectives) to the standard of value, such as "fair market value on a minority, marketable basis."

Sometimes premises of value are imposed artificially in a particular legal context. To give an example, under California Corporations Code Section 2000 (the California corporate dissolution statute), the case law is generally interpreted to mean that a minority interest is valued *as if* it were a proportional share of a control value.[14]

Going-Concern Value

The concept of *going-concern value* is not a standard of value, but an assumption about the status of the business. It merely means that the business or practice is being valued as a viable operating entity: It has its assets and inventory in place, its work force in place, and its doors open for business, with no imminent intent to liquidate or threat of discontinuance as a going concern.

As noted earlier, fair market value, fair value, investment value, and

---

[13]For a further discussion of premises of value, see, for example, Robert F. Reilly, "Tackling a Common Appraisal Problem," *Journal of Accountancy,* October 1992; and Robert F. Reilly, "Real Estate Valuation Issues in Bankruptcy," *Real Estate Accounting and Taxation,* Fall 1991.

[14]See, for example, *Roland* v. *4-C's Electronic Packaging,* 168 Cal.App.3d 290 (1985) and *Brown* v. *Allied Corrugated Box Co.,* 91 Cal.App.3d 477 (1979).

intrinsic or fundamental value are examples of standards of value. Thus, in many instances, it would be correct to characterize the value being estimated as "fair market value on a going-concern basis," "fair value on a going-concern basis," or "investment value on a going-concern basis." Unless otherwise noted, we will assume in this book that we are dealing with values of businesses or practices on a going-concern basis.

In most cases, the phrase *going-concern value* is used to mean the total value of the entity as a going concern. Sometimes, however, if the total value of the firm on a going-concern basis exceeds the net value of its tangible assets, the phrase *going-concern value* is used to refer to the difference between the two, that is, to the intangible value that exists over and above the net tangible asset value.[15]

Liquidation Value

Liquidation value is, in essence, the antithesis of *going-concern value*. *Liquidation value* means the net amount that can be realized if the business is terminated and the assets sold off piecemeal. The term *orderly liquidation* means that the assets are sold over a reasonable period of time, in an attempt to get the best available price for each asset. The term *forced liquidation* means that the assets are sold as quickly as possible, frequently all at one time at an auction sale.

When computing liquidation value, it is essential to recognize all costs associated with the liquidation of the enterprise. These costs normally include commissions, the administrative cost of keeping the company alive until the liquidation is completed, taxes of the entity, and legal and accounting costs. Also, in computing the present value of a business on a liquidation basis, it is necessary to discount the estimated net proceeds, at a rate reflecting the risk involved, from the time the net proceeds are expected to be received back to the effective valuation date. For these reasons, the liquidation value of the business as a whole is normally less than the sum of the liquidation proceeds of the underlying assets.

Control versus Minority

The degree of control versus minority represented by the interest being valued often is not necessarily a black and white issue. The degree of control or lack of it may fall anywhere across a broad spectrum, depending on the percentage ownership, the distribution of other ownership interests, and state laws governing rights of various percentage ownership interests in circumstances pertinent to the valuation situation at hand.

The premise with respect to the degree of control or lack of it may be a very important factor in the determination of value. In most valuation situations, the premise as to the degree of control can be stated clearly and unequivocally at the outset. In some cases, however, the degree of

---

[15]For a more complete discussion of the phrase *going-concern value* in this latter context, see Benjamin N. Henszey, "Going Concern Value after *Concord Control, Inc.,*" *Taxes,* November 1983, p. 699.

control represented in the interest being valued is a matter of controversy.

Degree of Marketability

All other things being equal, investors prefer to own something that they
can liquidate immediately without any depressing effect on value rather
than something that is difficult, time-consuming, and/or costly to liquidate. The benchmark usually used to represent full marketability is an
actively traded stock of a public company, which the owner can sell at
or very near the last reported transaction price merely by a phone call
to a broker, receiving cash within five business days. The premise as
to the extent to which the entity or business being valued is or is not
marketable is usually considered in relation to this benchmark.

The Business Interest Being Valued

Equity versus Invested Capital

Stated conclusions as to the value of a business or practice are often
ambiguous in the sense that it is not clear what part of the right-hand
side of the balance sheet is intended to be included.

Equity means the ownership interest. In a corporation, equity is represented by stock. If there is more than one class of stock, the term equity
by itself usually means the combined value of all classes of stock. If it is
intended that the value represents only one class of stock in a multiclass
capital structure, there should be a statement as to which class of equity
the value purports to represent.

In a partnership, equity is represented by partners' capital. If it is
a multiclass partnership (such as a limited partnership), there should be
a statement as to which class or classes of partnership interests the value
purports to represent.

In a sole proprietorship, equity is the owner's interest.

Invested capital is not always as clearly defined. Therefore, if the
term is used, it should be supplemented by a definition of exactly what
it means in the given valuation context.

The most commonly used definition of invested capital is all equity
and long-term debt. Sometimes it is used to mean all equity and all
interest-bearing debt, whether short-term or long-term. (This latter definition often applies in small businesses and professional practices because debt shown on the books as short-term often is actually being used
as long-term debt and in some cases, in reality, even represents equity—
that is, loans from owners that are never really expected to be repaid.)
Another balance sheet category that is occasionally included under the
umbrella of invested capital is deferred liabilities. Taken to the extreme,
the term *invested capital* has been used occasionally to represent *all*
equity and debt.

I hope that this little section has made it abundantly clear that *the value of the business* is a highly ambiguous term until it is clear exactly what elements of equity and debt are or are not intended to be included in that value.

What Assets Are Included

As with the right-hand side of the balance sheet, it is equally important to understand what elements of the left-hand side of the balance sheet are included in an appraised value.

In the absence of information to the contrary, the value of the business or the value of the practice would very likely be interpreted to mean that the value figure encompassed *all* the assets. However, small businesses and professional practices are usually sold without cash or cash equivalents, and are often sold without the receivables, leaving the former owner to collect them. Similarly, it is fairly common practice to deal with the value of the business or practice separately from the inventory, handling the transfer of the inventory either as a totally separate transaction or as an add-on to what is called the value of the business or practice. In the extreme, the value being sought of the business or practice may represent only the intangible value, with *all* the tangible assets somehow being handled separately.

These distinctions are encountered most often when valuing sole proprietorships. However, even if the subject of the valuation is organized as a corporation or partnership, it may not be stock or partnership interests that are actually transferred in the transaction. In many cases, the transaction is structured as an asset sale, which may include all or any part of the assets.

It is important to understand what the assumption is as to what assets are or are not included within the definition of the value being sought.

Book Value

Book value is something of a misnomer because it *does not represent any standard or premise of value at all. It is an accounting term, not an appraisal term.* Book value means the sum of the asset accounts, net of depreciation and amortization, less the liability accounts, as shown on a balance sheet.

Assets are usually accounted for at historical cost, less depreciation computed by one of various methods. Some assets may be completely written off the books. Liabilities are usually shown at face value. Intangible assets normally do not appear on the balance sheet unless they were purchased or the actual cost of development was recorded. Neither contingent assets nor contingent liabilities are recorded on the books.

The longer the time after an individual asset or liability item is placed on the books, the less likely the book value of that item will bear any identifiable relationship to any standard of value for the individual item, much less for the entity as a whole.

Sources of Guidance as to Applicable Standards and Premises of Value

The expertise and craft of the professional valuer include the skill to seek out and interpret guidance as to the standard and premises of value that are relevant to the assignment at hand. Some of the most important sources of guidance as to the applicable standard and premises of value for the given situation are the following:

- Statutory law (state and federal).
- Case law (cases decided under the controlling statutory or common law).
- Administrative regulations (e.g., IRS Revenue Rulings).[16]
- Company documents (e.g., articles of incorporation or partnership, bylaws, meeting minutes, agreements).
- Contracts between the parties (e.g., buy-sell agreements, arbitration agreements).
- Precedent established by prior transactions.
- Directives issued by the court (in some litigated cases where the standards or premises are not clear, the valuer may take the initiative to seek direction from the court regarding the relevant definition of value).
- Discussions with an attorney involved in the valuation matter or experienced in similar matters.
- Legal case documents (e.g., complaint, response, and so forth).
- The valuer's experience and judgment.

Effect of Terms on Value

As noted earlier in the chapter, most small businesses and professional practices do not sell for cash or cash equivalents. The majority of small businesses and professional practice sales include a cash down payment, typically 20 to 40 percent of what we will call the *transaction price*, with the balance on a contract to be paid over some period of time, usually a few years.

The contracts for the balance of the transaction price are usually interest-bearing contracts, but the rate of interest is almost always below a market rate. In other words, third-party lenders would generally charge higher rates on loans that have comparable collateral and the same terms as those in the contract for the balance of a transaction price. Consequently, the fair market values of such contracts in terms of cash or cash equivalents accepted as part of the consideration in a sale are usually less than their face values. The procedure for converting the face value of such a contract to cash value is the subject of Chapter 19.

---

[16]Note that administrative rulings do not have the force of law, but represent the position of the agency administering the law as to their interpretation of the law and rules for applying it.

Some contracts may include a contingency clause, which makes the full expected amount that the seller will realize depend on certain future events; such an event could be the level of future earnings or retention for some time period of the clients who were doing business with the seller at the time of the transaction.

As discussed more fully in Chapter 19, I know of no other class of transactions whose prices diverge as far from a cash equivalent fair market value as the values of contracts arising from sales of small businesses and professional practices. It is not at all uncommon for the terms of the contract to be such that the cash equivalent value is 20 percent or more below the face value of the transaction.

Summary

This chapter has explained why the notion that there can only be one value is a myth. For reasons either mandated by law or driven by investor objectives and perspectives, different standards of value may be applicable in different circumstances. Various premises, or assumptions, relating to the business or business interest being valued also have an important impact on the valuation methodology and conclusion.

Differing opinions as to the appropriate standard and/or premise of value may have greater impact on the ultimate conclusion of value than differences in methodology or estimates of figures affecting the value that follow once the standard and premises have been established.

Failure to accord adequate attention to establishing the appropriate standard and premises of value historically has been a major contributor to flawed conclusions of value. This chapter has provided a road map as to the alternatives to consider. It has also provided guidance as to sources that will help in selecting the appropriate standard and premises for the particular valuation situation.

Chapter 4

How Valuations Differ for Different Purposes

Before you can value a company, you must know the purpose for which you need the valuation. Different purposes will provide differing values and different valuation methods.[1]

When I give speeches on valuing businesses and professional practices, I frequently tell the listeners that the purpose of the valuation has an important bearing on the valuation process that should be undertaken, and, in some cases, on the conclusion that will be reached. This revelation usually shocks at least some of the members of the audience, who had never realized that different valuation considerations and conclusions can be appropriate for the same interest in a business or professional practice, depending on the purpose of the valuation.

While some people's first reaction is to think that there can be only one value for any given property at any one time, it simply isn't so. Different state and federal statutes, regulations, and legal precedents found in court cases impose different standards of value and different sets of criteria for valuations for different purposes. Also, apart from the valuation process and conclusion, the extent and form in which the valuation should be presented, oral and/or written, are influenced to a considerable extent by the purpose of the valuation.

Buying or Selling a Business or Practice

A valuation for a purchase or sale is subject to all the forces that affect supply and demand, including all relevant economic factors prevalent at the time and all the vagaries of the market for the business or practice in question. As noted in the previous chapter, the *market* can be thought of as all the potential buyers and sellers of like businesses or practices.

It is logical for a potential seller to think of value in two ways. The first way is to identify what is acceptable to him, by whatever value criteria and parameters he chooses. This idea can be expressed as intrinsic value, fundamental value, or investment value, as discussed in the previous chapter. The other way is to identify what potential buyers are willing to pay or what the market will bear, called market value or fair market value.

There can be many reasons why the value of a business or practice to the present owner may be more than anyone else is willing to pay at any given time. In that case, the logical decision is to keep the business or practice. If the market value appears to be at, or above, the value acceptable to the prospective seller, the objective then becomes to find the buyer who is willing to pay the most.

It is logical for a potential buyer to think of value in the same two ways. He may first decide on his own valuation criteria and parameters, given his particular set of circumstances. He would use these criteria and parameters to determine his intrinsic, fundamental, or investment value for any given business or practice in which he might consider

---

[1] Paul B. Baron, *When You Buy or Sell a Company*, rev. ed. (Meriden, Conn.: The Center for Business Information, Inc., 1983), pp. 8–9.

investing. He might also survey the prices at which businesses or practices that interest him would be available, and he could think of these prices as the market available to him.

If nothing is available at a price the prospective buyer would be willing to pay at the time, the logical decision is not to make an investment until a later time when market prices may be more appealing. If several investments do appear to be available at acceptable prices, then the objective is to find the one that represents the best value according to that buyer's criteria and parameters.

Market conditions for various types of businesses and practices vary considerably from time to time and from one locality to another. When many buyers are willing to pay prices at or above a typical seller's notion of fundamental value for a given type of business or practice, the condition is called a *seller's market*. When many sellers are willing to sell for an amount at or below a typical buyer's notion of fundamental value, the condition is called a *buyer's market*.

Partly because of these ever-changing market conditions, as well as because of the unique nature of each business and practice and other circumstances that may be unique to certain potential buyers, no formula can ever be devised that will produce a reliable conclusion about the market value of any particular business or practice at any given time. Chapter 36 discusses the various valuation factors that should be considered by prospective buyers or sellers. These factors may differ in relative importance from factors relevant for other valuation purposes.

Buying or Selling a Partial Interest

A partial interest in a business or practice may or may not be worth a proportionate value of the total entity. Put another way, depending on the circumstances, the sum of the values of the various parts taken individually may or may not add up to the value of the business or practice if it were valued as one total entity.

Minority interests are typically worth something less than their proportion of the total entity value. This matter is discussed in some detail in the chapters on valuations for specific purposes, and especially Chapter 35, "Valuing Minority Interests."

Obtaining or Providing Financing

The typical bank lending officer has no conception of the total value of the entity to which he is lending. He usually has some conception of the value of assets pledged as collateral, but neither has nor avails himself of expertise in the field of business appraisal. Many businesses and practices have far greater value than is indicated by their financial statements alone. If this value can be demonstrated convincingly, it may be helpful in obtaining desired financing.

There are many sources of *venture capital* today, including venture capital funds, insurance companies, and special venture capital departments or affiliates of some banks. Such sources almost always seek an equity participation, such as convertible debt or warrants. Owners who approach such sources should go in with a soundly based notion of the market value of their business, and, of course, the question of value will be of prime importance to the providers of the financing.

Going Public

While the public market is composed mainly of the stocks of large companies, hundreds of successful public stock offerings were made in the $500,000 to $5,000,000 range in the 1980s. That market for small initial public offerings (IPOs) continues to be available in the early 1990s, as this edition goes to press. Most companies that succeeded in such offerings had innovative products or services offering the prospect of rapid growth and thus a high potential rate of return to the investor in the form of appreciation in the stock price. Most such offerings are sold to the public through small, regional investment banking firms.

When appraising a company for the purpose of a public stock offering, the appraiser must pay special attention to other public offerings that may be considered comparable in some respect, and also to the receptiveness of the public market to the type of offering being considered. These factors are subject to constant change, sometimes changing dramatically in very short periods.

Leveraged Buyouts

Leveraged buyouts became increasingly popular in the 1980s, but are subject to more stringent credit criteria in the early 1990s. For businesses that have considerable unused borrowing capacity, prospective buyers may arrange to borrow a significant portion of the total purchase price by using the assets, and possibly also the stock, of the business as collateral, thus "cashing out" the seller. Both banks and insurance companies have become quite involved in leveraged buyouts in recent years.[2] Also, a group of specialized financial institutions has sprung up to participate in this market. They frequently want some equity participation. A well-documented appraisal of the fair market value of the business can be important to the implementation of a leveraged buyout.

Employee Stock Ownership Plans

The Tax Reform Act of 1984 substantially enhanced the financial advantages of selling stock to employees through an Employee Stock Owner-

---

[2]At this writing, banks are the primary source of funds for leveraged buyouts for small businesses, while most insurance companies are interested only in multimillion dollar deals.

ship Plan (ESOP), and the 1986 Tax Reform Act further enhanced the attractiveness of ESOPs. The stock to be sold through an ESOP can range from small minority interests to 100 percent of the company. The tax advantages of an ESOP make the vehicle attractive to use in conjunction with a leveraged buyout. The tax advantages of ESOPs are discussed in the chapter on estate planning considerations.

Valuations for ESOPs follow the guidelines of Revenue Ruling 59-60, used for gift and estate tax purposes, with certain special modifications necessary to accommodate the unique nature of ESOPs.

In recent years, many smaller companies have implemented ESOPs as ownership success with employee involvement has become more widespread. Consequently, in this edition we have devoted an entire chapter to Employee Stock Ownership Plans (Chapter 25) in small businesses and professional practices.

Estate, Gift, Inheritance, and Income Taxes

The universal standard of value for estate, gift, and inheritance taxes is fair market value, which is defined and interpreted in the previous chapter. Guidelines for federal estate and gift taxes are found in Revenue Ruling 59-60. Revenue Ruling 68-609, which basically is the "excess earnings" ruling, contains important language broadening the application of Revenue Ruling 59-60:

> The general approach, methods, and factors, outlined in Revenue Ruling 59-60. . . are equally applicable to valuations of corporate stocks for income and other tax purposes as well as for estate and gift tax purposes. They apply also to problems involving the determination of the fair market value of business interests of any type, including partnerships and proprietorships, and of intangible assets for all tax purposes.[3]

Valuation guidelines for state inheritance taxes are generally consistent with federal estate and gift tax guidelines.

Although the standard of value for estate, gift, and inheritance taxes is fair market value, there can be many differences between a valuation for tax purposes and a valuation for the sale of a business or for other purposes. For example, estate and gift tax valuations are based on the value of a business to a hypothetical buyer who would have no special synergy with, or relationship to, the seller. In a normal tax valuation, the fact that the seller might be able to command a higher price because of some feature that might be uniquely valuable to a particular buyer would not be considered. According to legal precedents, assets with intangible value are taxable only if the owner has the legal right to transfer them. However, a seller without the unequivocal legal right to transfer ownership to any buyer of his choice, as would be normal with an automobile dealership, would seek the necessary manufacturer's approval for a specific prospective buyer; with that approval obtained, the seller would expect to receive a price that would include whatever intangible value the operation may possess.

---

[3]Revenue Ruling 68-609 (1968-2 C.B. 327).

Another distinction between estate and gift tax valuations and valuations for the sale of a business is how much each relies on the historical record, as opposed to projections. Some buyers may be willing to pay for the opportunity for future profits that they envision; but such projections may not exist or may be considered too speculative to be relied on as a basis of value in a legal context, such as an estate or gift tax valuation.

Revenue Ruling 59-60 specifically recognizes that "valuation of securities is, in essence, a prophecy as to the future. . . ."[4] Nevertheless, as a practical matter, valuations for tax purposes rely relatively more heavily on a company's historical record than do valuations for sales, which are more prone to rely on projections. This difference is a matter of emphasis rather than of concept.

Ad Valorem Taxes (Property Taxes)

Ad valorem is a Latin expression that has found its way into English dictionaries. It means "according to value," and is the basis for assessing property taxes in virtually all state and local taxing jurisdictions.

Municipal taxing authorities have been hard-pressed to raise adequate funds; sometimes assessing officers are pressured to be aggressive in their opinions of the values of taxable properties. Many sudden and huge increases in property taxes have been levied on such businesses as manufacturers, shopping centers, and motels. In many cases, the economics of the respective businesses have not justified the increases. Businesses have often been assessed for real estate values that exceeded the entire going-concern value of the total business, *including* the real estate.

I believe that taxpayers can save millions of dollars by properly valuing businesses in which the business and the physical property are integrally interrelated. Fair market value is the legal standard of value in many ad valorem cases.[5] The real-world market values such properties on their ability to produce income, which is this book's primary valuation focus. Proper application of business valuation principles should be able to counteract some methods used in many assessing jurisdictions. These methods sometimes produce values well in excess of the applicable legal standard of fair market value.[6]

Charitable Contributions

Revenue Ruling 59-60 is also the basic guideline for charitable contributions.

---

[4]Revenue Ruling 59-60 (1959-1 C.B. 237), Section 3.

[5]For a further discussion of ad valorem valuation issues, see Robert F. Reilly, "Property Tax Valuation Services," *Tax Management Advisor,* Spring 1989.

[6]For further discussion of this concept, see Shannon P. Pratt, "Rates of Return as an Influence on Value" (*Third Annual Proceedings,* New York University, *Institute on State and Local Taxation,* 1985).

If the claimed value of securities donated is more than $10,000, the Tax Reform Act of 1984 makes it mandatory that the value be supported by a qualified appraisal attached to the return. The appraisal must be made by a qualified appraiser and must be received by the donor before the due date (including extensions) of the return on which the deduction is claimed.

Buy-Sell Agreements

Valuations for buy-sell agreements can be based on whatever criteria the parties mutually agree to and may or may not bear any relationship to any recognized standard of value. Valuations for this purpose are discussed more fully in the chapter on estate planning (Chapter 26).

Property Settlements in Divorces

State laws govern disputed property settlements that involve marital dissolutions. However, state statutes fail to specify what standard of value applies to businesses and professional practices in divorces. The law governing various aspects of the valuation of businesses and professional practices in divorces is often established by case precedent in each state, and the cumulative result of such precedents varies greatly from state to state, and can vary from case to case within a state.

On some valuation issues, some state courts have established precedents that are diametrically opposed to those of courts of other states on the same issues.

For some valuation issues, many state courts have established no precedents at all. It is no wonder that the parties and their appraisers frequently find themselves far apart on the matter of valuation of a business or professional practice in a divorce! Added to the confusing and contradictory legal guidance is the acrimony and distrust that frequently accompany matrimonial dissolutions. Although we do far more appraisals of businesses and professional practices for purposes other than for divorces, my staff and I wind up presenting expert testimony in court more often for divorces than for any other single purpose.

Valuations for divorces have become so important to certain valuation practitioners that this edition devotes an entire new chapter to valuations of businesses and professional practices for divorces (Chapter 39).

Damage Cases

The most common damage situations that may require a business valuation to establish the amount of damages are the following:

- Breach of contract.
- Condemnation.
- Lost business opportunity.
- Lost profits.
- Antitrust.
- Personal injury.
- Insurance casualty claims.
- Wrongful termination of a franchise.

Each must be approached with as thorough an understanding as possible of the legal precedents that affect the valuation in the specific case, since the precedents vary considerably, not only from one type of damage situation to another but also from one jurisdiction to another. Chapter 40 presents more detail on valuations for damage actions.

Mergers

A merger involves the combination of two entities so that stock or partnership interests in one are exchanged for stock or assets of another. Some amount of cash may be offered in addition to stock or a partnership interest.

The situation usually requires the valuation of each entity in order to establish an exchange ratio. Sometimes, however, an exchange ratio may be established by some criterion without actually valuing the entities.

Determining Life Insurance Needs

Life insurance can serve three important uses in a business or professional practice:

1. To fund the redemption of stock or a partnership interest from the estate of the deceased.
2. To pay estate and inheritance taxes.
3. To provide for the continuity of the business or practice for a period of time in the absence of a key person.

Valuation factors to determine the amount of life insurance needed to meet these objectives are discussed in Chapter 26.

Squeeze-Out Mergers and Dissenting Stockholder Actions

In virtually all states, controlling stockholders have the right to effect certain actions that give rise to minority stockholders' appraisal rights. In general, these actions include a merger or sale of the company or the disposition of a major portion of its business or assets.

If controlling stockholders wish to eliminate minority stockholders, they can form a new corporation, sell the stock of the old corporation to the new corporation, and pay off the minority stockholders. This action gives rise to the term *squeeze-out merger*, since the result is to force out the minority stockholders.

If any minority stockholder believes that the consideration offered in the transaction is inadequate, he has the right to have his shares appraised and to be paid off, in cash, the amount finally determined. Almost all state statutes specify that the standard of value for such actions is fair value, as discussed briefly in the previous chapter. A stockholder who exercises his dissenting stockholder rights may end up receiving more than, less than, or the same amount as was originally offered.

A study of the relevant legal precedents is extremely important in a valuation under dissenting stockholder rights. Such valuations are discussed in Chapter 38.

Minority Stockholder Oppressing Actions

In several states (including California, Rhode Island, and Delaware),[7] there are procedures whereby certain minority stockholders who are unable to achieve satisfaction regarding operations can sue for dissolution of the company. In these states, the other stockholders can avoid dissolution of the company by having the stock appraised and paying off the disgruntled stockholder at the appraised value.

The standard of value for these minority stockholder dissolution actions is *fair value*. Note that this is the same phrase that is used in the dissenting stockholder statutes discussed in the previous section. Do not, however, be misled into thinking that they mean the same thing in the two different legal contexts. Within the given state, you will find that case law interprets fair value differently in actions under dissolution statutes than in actions under dissenter statutes. This is a good example of the importance of the valuation practitioner's study and understanding of relevant case law.

Valuations for Multiple Purposes

The situation can become tricky when the same valuation is intended to be used for two or more different purposes. For example, a valuation for the purpose of selling the company or attracting outside investment capital may contain speculative elements based on future potential that may be acceptable to a risk-oriented investor, but not acceptable to a court charged with determining value under some set of statutory standards and legal precedents.

As noted earlier, valuations pursuant to buy-sell agreements can be

---

[7]Cal. Corp. Code §§1300, 2000; Del. Code Ann. §262; R.I. Gen. Laws §7-1.1-74.

just as arbitrary as the parties mutually agree to make them, but such valuations will not necessarily (or even usually) be appropriate for determining property settlements in divorces or estate and inheritance taxes.

Setting a value for a tender offer to buy out minority shareholders is quite a different matter from setting a price at which to effect a squeeze-out merger, in which all the stockholders are required to sell, whether they like it or not. A valuation for a tender offer may be at a lower price than a valuation for a squeeze-out merger. If so, and that valuation is subsequently used for a squeeze-out merger, a dissenting stockholder suit is likely to follow.

The material in this book should provide the reader with considerable guidance on when a certain valuation procedure will be suitable for two or more specific contemplated uses and when it will not. When in doubt, seek professional help.

Considering Alternatives: Estate Planning and Other Types of Choices

An owner may need to find out a range of possible values for the business or practice in order to decide what to do. For example, the owner may be considering making charitable contributions, giving gifts within the family, selling stock to employees, and/or initiating an Employee Stock Ownership Plan. The decision to implement any of these choices is likely to depend to some extent on the values of the shares or interests to be transferred in each case. In such cases, the valuation process should proceed so that it addresses all of the possible alternatives contemplated. Differences in valuation procedures and/or conclusions that may be applicable, depending on which of the possible alternatives are finally implemented, should be noted and brought to the client's attention.

Summary

I hope that readers of this chapter are convinced that the purpose of the valuation has a bearing on how (and even whether) certain elements of value will be reflected in the applicable standard of value, valuation procedures, and ultimate conclusion of value. It is always important to determine whether or not the appraisal is governed by a legally mandated standard of value. If it is, then it is also important to gain an understanding of the case law interpretation of that standard of value.

Later chapters go into more detail about the specific nuances of valuations for the most commonly encountered valuation purposes: buying or selling a company or a partial interest; buy-sell agreements; divorces, damage cases, and other litigated valuation contexts; gift and estate taxes; and Employee Stock Ownership Plans.

Chapter 5

Differences between the Valuation of Large and Small Businesses

Although the basic theory underlying the valuation is the same for any size business, many practical differences dictate different valuation techniques. As noted in the preface, there is no clear-cut line of demarcation between small and large. Some businesses have some characteristics commonly associated with small businesses and other characteristics more commonly found in larger businesses. In general, even very large professional practices have characteristics that, for the purpose of determining applicable valuation techniques, fall more in line with the characteristics of small businesses than with large businesses.

The most important general categories of differences between small and large businesses, which determine the appropriate valuation techniques to be employed, are the following:

Status of financial statements. Larger companies are more likely to have statements that are audited, or at least reviewed, by outside CPAs, while smaller businesses are more likely to have statements that are merely compiled.

Cash versus accrual accounting. Most large companies use accrual accounting, while many small businesses and most professional practices use cash accounting.

Length of "track record." On the average, larger businesses have longer histories available for analysis by the appraiser.

Form of business ownership. Large operations are more likely to be regular corporations, while smaller operations are more likely to be sole proprietorships, partnerships, or S corporations.

Stock versus asset transaction. The larger the company, the more likely it is that stock is to be transferred in case of a sale, while a smaller entity is more likely to involve a transfer of selected assets.

Considerations offered by purchaser. The smaller the business, the more likely it is to be sold for a cash down payment and a term contract for the balance; the larger the business, the more likely it is to be sold for cash and/or stock in a public company.

Comparative transaction data available. The smaller the company, the fewer the comparative transaction data that are publicly available; while for valuations of larger companies, it is much more likely that useful, comparative, publicly traded stock data will be available.

Role of owner/manager. The smaller the company, the less the depth of management and the more important the role of one or a few owner(s)/manager(s). In small companies, it is quite common to find that the only stockholders are persons active in the business.

Compensation policies. Larger companies are more likely to remunerate owners at something near a market rate of compensation, while small companies tend to pay owners what they can afford, which may be above or below a market rate.

Accounting policies for financial reporting. Smaller firms usually have a single set of financial statements, normally following whatever accounting policies will minimize their tax liabilities. Larger companies are more likely to have a set of financial statements designed to present

---

Reliance on Audit Opinions
by Erich Sylvester, ASA

You will often hear an unqualified audit opinion called a "clean" opinion or a "clean bill of health." In my opinion, this metaphorical language reflects a widely held misconception that the principal meaning of an unqualified opinion is that the CPA firm has performed a financial "health check-up" and that a clean audit opinion is a guarantee that the client firm is "healthy," not in danger of insolvency or bankruptcy, and even a safe investment. This belief results in lawsuits against CPA firms when their audit clients become insolvent or bankrupt by creditors and investors who claim that they relied on the auditors' clean opinion in extending credit or investing.

There is a type of audit qualification that states that, in the auditors' opinion, certain factors "raise substantial doubt about the company's ability to continue as a going concern." However, it is too simplistic to view an audit as a "thumbs up" or "thumbs down" verdict on the financial health or investment prospects of a firm.

Remember that the principal conclusion of an audit opinion is that the financial statement is presented "in conformity with generally accepted accounting principles." Conformity with GAAP may assist lenders and investors in evaluating the financial position and past performance of a company, but the lack of a going-concern (or any other) qualification should not be read as a guarantee of financial health.

Another reason to preach against this misconception is that it promotes the parallel misconception that a business appraisal is a guarantee of value. Do you want lenders and investors to believe that appraisers should be sued whenever lenders and investors rely on an appraisal to their detriment?

---

a truer picture for financial reporting than their tax statements would convey. Some larger companies may even lean toward maximization of reported earnings to enhance stock value.

Status of Financial Statements

Audited Statements

If a company's financial statements are audited, it means that a CPA firm has done a complete audit and that the statements are presented in accordance with generally accepted accounting principles (GAAP), unless otherwise noted. Audited statements contain footnotes that explain accounting policies and provide some details beyond just the line items on the balance sheet and income statement. Audited statements are the most complete and reliable type of statements with which an appraiser works. An example of an auditor's unqualified audit opinion and of an auditor's qualified opinion are shown as Exhibits 5–1 and 5–2.

Reviewed Statements

From an appraiser's viewpoint, the next most preferred level of statement presentation after audited statements is reviewed statements. They are also "reviewed" by independent outside CPAs and often contain

Exhibit 5–1

EXAMPLE OF UNQUALIFIED AUDITOR'S OPINION

Concise Precise Advice Company
Certified Public Accountants

REPORT OF INDEPENDENT AUDITORS

To the Board of Directors
Albatross Aviation, Inc.

We have audited the accompanying consolidated balance sheet of Albatross Aviation, Inc. and Subsidiaries as of March 31, 1992 and 1991, the related consolidated statements of income, and changes in stockholders' equity and cash flows for the years then ended. These consolidated financial statements are the responsibility of the company's management. Our responsibility is to express an opinion on these consolidated financial statements based on our audit.

We conducted our audit in accordance with generally accepted auditing standards. Those standards require that we plan and perform the audit to obtain reasonable assurance about whether the consolidated financial statements are free of material misstatements. An audit includes examining, on a test basis, evidence supporting the amounts and disclosures in the consolidated financial statements. An audit also includes assessing the accounting principles used and significant estimates made by management, as well as evaluating the overall consolidated financial statements presentation. We believe that our audit provides a reasonable basis for our opinion.

In our opinion, the consolidated financial statements referred to above present fairly in all material respects, the consolidated financial position of Albatross Aviation, Inc. and Subsidiaries as of March 31, 1992 and 1991, and the results of its consolidated operations and its cash flows for the years then ended, in conformity with generally accepted accounting principles.

CONCISE PRECISE ADVICE COMPANY

Portland, Oregon
August 21, 1992

the same detail of footnote disclosures as audited statements. Although all the audit verification procedures are not done, the statements are often prepared in accordance with generally accepted accounting principles. An example of a CPA firm's opinion regarding reviewed statements is shown as Exhibit 5–3.

Compiled Statements

A compilation involves merely putting together and presenting information supplied by management. Compiled statements may be prepared

Exhibit 5-2

EXAMPLE OF "QUALIFIED" AUDITOR'S OPINION

Lima, Pinto & Bush
Certified Public Accountants

REPORT OF INDEPENDENT PUBLIC ACCOUNTANTS

To the Stockholders and Board of Directors of
Colossal Conifer Corporation

We have examined the consolidated balance sheets of Colossal Conifer Corporation (a Washington corporation) and subsidiaries as of December 31, 1991, and 1990, and the related consolidated statements of income, stockholders' equity and changes in financial position for each of the three years in the period ended December 31, 1991. Our examinations were made in accordance with generally accepted auditing standards and, accordingly, included such tests of the accounting records and such other auditing procedures as we considered necessary in the circumstances.

As discussed further in the notes to the accompanying financial statements, an action by Colossal Conifer Corporation to recover the value of property taken by the U.S. Government in March 1987 for expansion of Staggerbush State Park is pending. The Company has recorded $550 million which management considers a conservative measure of the value of the land and timber taken. While management believes that its calculation is a conservative measure for financial reporting purposes, it is not possible for us to form an opinion as to the amount which will be eventually recovered through this action.

In our opinion, subject to the effect of any adjustments that might have been required had the final outcome of the Company's action against the U.S. Government mentioned in the preceding paragraph been known, the financial statements referred to above present fairly the financial position of Colossal Conifer Corporation and subsidiaries as of December 31, 1991, and 1990, and the results of their operations and the changes in their financial position for each of the three years in the period ended December 31, 1991, in conformity with generally accepted accounting principles which, except for the change made as of January 1, 1989 (with which we concur) in the method of computing depreciation on certain assets as described in the notes to the accompanying financial statements, were applied on a consistent basis.

Lima, Pinto, and Bush

Seattle, Washington
February 15, 1992

either by an outside CPA firm or by the company itself. They may include footnote disclosures similar to those found in audited or reviewed statements, but usually they do not. An example of a CPA firm's typical opinion regarding compiled statements is shown as Exhibit 5-4.

Tax Returns Only

Some small entities prepare no financial statements other than their tax returns. In such cases, the appraiser will usually want to recast the data

Exhibit 5–3

COVER LETTER TO REVIEWED STATEMENTS

The Shareholders and Board of Directors
Mary's Machinery & Equipment, Inc.

We have reviewed the accompanying balance sheet of Mary's Machinery & Equipment, Inc., as of December 31, 1991, and the related statements of income, retained earnings, and changes in financial position for the year then ended, in accordance with standards established by the American Institute of Certified Public Accountants. All information included in these financial statements is the representation of the management of Mary's Machinery & Equipment, Inc.

A review consists primarily of inquiries of company personnel and analytical procedures applied to financial data. It is substantially less in scope than an examination in accordance with generally accepted auditing standards, the objective of which is the expression of an opinion regarding the financial statements taken as a whole. Accordingly, we do not express such an opinion.

Based on our review, we are not aware of any material modifications that should be made to the accompanying financial statements in order for them to be in conformity with generally accepted accounting principles.

Green, Eye, Shade & Co.

Exhibit 5–4

COVER LETTER TO COMPILED STATEMENTS

Annie's Apparel Store

We have compiled the accompanying balance sheet of Annie's Apparel Store as of December 31, 1991, and the related statements of income, retained earnings, and changes in financial position for the year then ended, in accordance with standards established by the American Institute of Certified Public Accountants.

A compilation is limited to presenting in the form of financial statements information that is the representation of management. We have not audited or reviewed the accompanying financial statements and, accordingly, do not express an opinion cr any other form of assurance on them.

Audit, Review & Co.

from the tax returns into financial statement form. If the business is a sole proprietorship, the appraiser should be able to rely on Schedule C to Form 1040 of the federal income tax return, which is supposed to separate business from personal items.

Responsibility for Forensic Accounting

It is not necessarily the responsibility of the appraiser to perform forensic accounting procedures. If there are questions as to the accuracy of statements, they may be referred to a CPA, or the client may hire a forensic accountant.

Records in a Shoe Box

Sometimes, there are no statements or tax returns, only journals and/ or ledgers, or maybe even just invoices, vouchers, check stubs, and so on, in a shoe box. This form of record-keeping will usually entail a fair amount of work even to create a semblance of a statement, which may or may not be reliable once it is done.

Cash versus Accrual Accounting

In accrual accounting, revenues are recognized when they are earned, and expenses are recognized when they are incurred. For example, if a dentist does work and bills it to his patient in January, it shows as revenue on the income statement for January, and the account receivable shows as an asset on the balance sheet at the end of January.

In cash accounting, revenues and expenses are recognized when the money is received or paid. In the dentist example, the work done and the bill would be reflected on cash-basis statements only when the money was received from the patient.

Valuations are usually based on accrual accounting information. Therefore, if an entity is on cash-basis accounting, conversion to an accrual basis usually needs to be made for valuation purposes.

Length of Track Record Available

For most valuation purposes, it is useful to look at five years or so of comparative income and expense data, if it is available. However, this is not the case for many small businesses. The business may not be that old; the business may have changed hands, and the prior owner's records are not available; or the business may have changed accounting procedures so that some of the data may not be comparable. The more cyclical or variable the business, the more important it is to look at data over a period of years. The appraiser simply has to do the best he can with what he has to work with. Many valuations are based only on the latest year's data and/or a projection.

On the one hand, we want data for as long a period as possible providing that it is relevant to the current valuation. On the other hand, it would be folly (sometimes encountered) to base a valuation on an average of five years' historical earnings or cash flow that bears no relationship to current earnings or expectations.

Form of Business Ownership

In a corporation, all stockholders of a given class of stock share pro rata in earnings, at least on the books, because earnings are related to a retained earnings account that is part of stockholders' equity. In other words, each stockholder of a given stock class shares equally in the earnings and capital accounts, and each stockholder of the class shares equally in all distributions, whether in the form of dividends or the sale of stock. If there is more than one class of stock, the appraiser must assess the relative rights of each class being appraised.

In a partnership, partners may share on different bases in earnings and in the capital accounts. Therefore, if appraising the interests of one or more partners, it is necessary to read the partnership agreement carefully and to analyze the distributions to each partner and the capital account balances.

Stock versus Asset Transaction

Before one can determine a value, it is necessary to define precisely what business interest is being valued, as noted in Chapter 2.

In a stock valuation, the appraiser needs to determine whether there will be any major changes from the statements on which the valuation is based, such as any major cash withdrawal or any significant off-balance sheet liabilities or assets.

In an asset transaction, it is necessary to define just what assets are being transferred and what, if any, liabilities are being assumed by the buyer. Typically, in an asset transaction, the seller keeps the cash and receivables and pays off all liabilities. What is being transferred usually is the inventory, plant, and equipment, and whatever intangible values may exist, if any. What is typical in this respect varies from one industry to another and from deal to deal in any industry. This variability is one of the many problems with rule of thumb valuation approaches or valuations done on some "formula" basis. Such rules of thumb or formulas usually fail to specify exactly what is being transferred.

Since asset transfers often do not include cash or accounts receivable, the buyer may have to provide some working capital in addition to the purchase price of the business. If the buyer has to invest additional cash for working capital, that should be regarded as an add-on to the purchase price of the total business on a going-concern basis. If the buyer is planning to borrow to meet working capital requirements, the cost of such borrowing should be considered in his projected earnings and cash flow. The seller, of course, may net out a considerable amount that is more or less than the transaction price, by collecting receivables and liquidating payables.

Consideration Offered by Purchaser

In addition to determining just what is being sold, it is also necessary to think about the nature of the consideration being received. Most businesses are sold for some combination of cash, a contract balance, and/or stock of the acquiring company. In some cases, some portion of the contract balance may be contingent on certain future events.

It is simplest, of course, if the price is all in cash. However, as noted elsewhere, most small businesses and professional practices do not sell for 100 percent cash.

If a contract is involved, the strength of the commitment and all the terms must be evaluated. If the stock of the acquiror is part or all of the consideration, the stock of the acquiror must be valued. Chapter 19 discusses the conversion of a price on terms to a fair market value on a cash equivalent basis.

Comparative Transaction Data Available

Valuing a business or property by the market approach basically means finding actual transaction prices for similar businesses or practices and using value ratios developed from those prices to guide in valuing the subject business or practice. (We discuss this in more detail in Chapter 6, comparing real estate appraisal and business appraisal approaches.)

Large businesses, even ones closely held, can usually be valued by reference to transactions in stocks of publicly traded companies in the same or a similar industry. However, many small businesses and practices are in industries or professions in which there are no publicly traded companies. Even if publicly traded companies exist, there may be so many differences between the small business and its much larger, publicly traded counterpart that it would be very difficult to derive meaningful valuation parameters from the publicly traded big brother.

In spite of a variety of efforts, at this writing there still are no truly reliable publicly available data bases on prices of transactions in small businesses and professional practices. In conjunction with the first edition of this book, my company, Willamette Management Associates, spent significant time and effort attempting to start such a data base. We found it very difficult to collect consistently reliable data, and ultimately decided that the cost/benefit ratio did not justify the effort to keep it current.

The Institute of Business Appraisers, through its members, attempts to maintain a data base. However, for many industries, the data are sparse and/or out of date, and there is no way to verify the reliability of the data. Business brokers may be useful sources of transaction data. References to certain proprietary business brokers' data bases are found elsewhere in the book. Many business brokers specialize in specific types of businesses on a regional or national basis. Lists of brokers by geographical location and specialty are available from the International Business Brokers Association, P.O. Box 704, Concord, Massachusetts 01742, (508) 369-2490. For some types of professional practices, some data are available (see Part V on "Valuing Professional Practices").

If comparative transaction data are available, they should be very helpful. Otherwise, the appraiser can use the generalized approaches described in subsequent chapters, tempered by factors pointed out in later parts of the book that are applicable to certain industries and professions. See Chapter 33, Transaction Data Bases, for a current review of what is available.

Role of the Owner/Manager

The smaller the business or practice, the more important looms the role of the owner/manager. How much of the success of the operation is due to the talents and efforts of the owner/manager(s)? How much of that success can be transferred to new ownership? Is the seller including a noncompete agreement in the deal? Is the seller providing assistance in the transition? These types of questions need to be addressed as part of the valuation process. Usually, in a small business or practice, growth will not be automatic but will depend on continuing entrepreneurial skill and effort. In general, smaller businesses require much more personal involvement on the parts of their owners and are much less suitable for absentee ownership than medium-sized and larger businesses. In other words, the labor and ownership are much more difficult to separate.

In fact, not only is growth on its own less likely to occur in a smaller enterprise than in a medium-sized or larger one that has momentum, but considerable personal effort is usually required just to *maintain* the earnings stream. There is no point in paying a sizable sum for a business or practice from which the customers will disappear as soon as the new owner takes over, or which is dependent on a seller's talents that will not be available to the new owner. In other words, the buyer or appraiser must judge whether profit-contributing factors will persist or whether they are strictly attributable personally to the former owner.

Sometimes, profit factors attributable to the seller can stay with the business for a time, if the seller is willing to enter into an employment agreement under which he will work for the new owner for some specified period.

Motivation of the Buyer

Related to the role of the owner/manager is the matter of the motivation of the buyer. Clearly, some small businesses are sold because the buyer is looking to acquire a job. In such cases, we could say that the applicable standard of value is investment value (the value to a particular buyer, as discussed in Chapter 3). However, when there are enough buyers and sellers of certain types of businesses with demonstrably common valuation parameters, application of these parameters tends to produce evidence that also represents fair market value regardless of the motivations that resulted in the value parameters.

Businesses and practices that sell based on the motivation to "buy a job" do have value, even if they would be expected to produce no income after deduction of reasonable owner/manager's compensation. The greater the start-up costs or other barriers to entry, the more the value such businesses and practices have.

Compensation to Owners

Whenever a closely held business is appraised partly or entirely on the basis of profits, compensation to owners must be examined. The smaller the business or practice, the more important this factor becomes. Few small businesses or professional practices compensate their owners on the basis of what their services are worth. Large companies are more likely to remunerate officers at something near a market rate of compensation, while smaller entities tend to pay owners on the basis of what the business or practice has available in earnings and/or cash flow, which can be above or below a market rate of compensation.

In computing profits, it is necessary to figure out what a competent person who is not the owner would have been paid to do the same job or jobs, and substitute that amount for the actual compensation paid to the owners. It is necessary to consider all the compensation, including benefits and perks of all kinds. Some guidance on sources of reasonable compensation data is included in Chapter 8 and in Appendix D.

Accounting Policies for Financial Reporting

The valuation analyst must determine the extent to which accounting policies conform either to economic reality or to the policies of other entities with which the subject is being compared, and make adjustments as necessary. Such adjustments are discussed in Part II, "Analyzing the Company."

Earnings Analysis on Pretax or After-Tax Basis

When valuing a large corporation, one usually states earnings and cash flow figures on an after-tax basis. When valuing small businesses and professional practices, the opposite is usually true; that is, one usually states earnings and cash flow figures on a pretax basis.

In the final analysis, of course, what should be of greatest interest to an investor is what he can keep in his pocket after taxes. However, many small businesses are partnerships or sole proprietorships, and personal tax brackets differ from individual to individual. Also, accounting and compensation policies tend to greatly affect small corporations, often resulting in little or no taxable income to the business. Consequently, comparisons on a pretax basis tend to be more expedient for small businesses and professional practices.

Make sure that you compare any earnings or cash flow figures being used on an "apples-to-apples" basis. One valuation error I often encounter is a price/earnings multiple being taken from a group of public companies in an industry on an after-tax basis and then applied to a private company's pretax earnings to conclude a value. P/E multiples quoted for publicly traded stocks are always on an after-tax basis. If such a multiple is going to be used for valuation guidance for a private company, the subject company's earnings must also be on an after-tax basis.

One way to make these bases comparable is simply to deduct taxes at statutory state and federal corporate rates from the subject company's pretax earnings, whether the subject company is actually a corporation or not, and regardless of the taxes it actually pays. Alternatively, the public company's financial statements may be obtained and a ratio of the company's price to pretax earnings can be computed.

Complexity of Capital Structure

Capital structure is generally defined as the equity (ownership interest) plus the long-term debt. Smaller entities tend to have simple capital structures; larger ones are likely to be more complex. The person doing the valuation should determine whether there are any complexities in the capital structure. Examine closely any debts owed to owners; their characterization as short-term or long-term (or even as debt at all) may be arbitrary.

Classes of Corporate Stock

Most corporations have only one class of common stock. Some corporations, however, have one or more classes of common and, in some cases, one or more classes of preferred. Classes of stock authorized in the articles of incorporation but never issued are of no concern in the valuation; it is the stock actually outstanding that matters.

Treasury Stock

Treasury stock is stock that has been issued and subsequently reacquired by the corporation. Regarding the valuation of stock of a company, treat treasury stock as if it had never been issued. If the balance sheet shows that there is treasury stock, subtract the number of shares of treasury stock from the number of shares of stock shown issued to get the number of shares outstanding; this is the relevant number of shares to use to determine a value per share. The book value of the common stock should be net of any amounts shown on the balance sheet for the purchase of treasury stock.

Limited Partnerships

A *limited partnership* has two or more classes of partners, each class usually with significantly different rights and obligations regarding partnership earnings, assets, and liabilities. It is called a limited partnership because the limited partners have only limited personal obligation for debts of the partnership (as is also true of a corporate stockholder); by contrast, general partners are personally liable for debts of the partnership. These differences obviously have a significant impact on the relative values of the respective partners' interests.

General Partnerships

Even in general partnerships, however, every partner is not necessarily on the same footing. The most common differences among partners is that all partners may not have the same percentage interest in the partnership earnings as they do in the partnership capital account. Therefore, when valuing the interest of any particular partner, you must carefully study the articles of partnership (or the partnership agreement) and the statement of partners' capital accounts in order to determine exactly what the interest involves. In some cases (as with some corporations), voting control may be lodged in what on the surface would appear to be simple minority interests.

Summary

While the same in theory and broad approaches, the differences in methods and procedures typically employed in the valuation of small businessess and professional practices are different enough from those typically employed in valuation of larger businesses to warrant the effort of this book in addition to *Valuing a Business.*[1]

The primary categories of differences are as follows:

---

[1]Shannon P. Pratt, *Valuing a Business: The Analysis and Appraisal of Closely Held Companies,* 2nd ed. (Homewood, Ill.: Business One Irwin, 1989).

1. Small business and professional practice statements typically have a lower level of professional accounting treatments, e.g., usually not audited or reviewed.
2. Cash-basis accounting is common rather than accrual-basis accounting.
3. The historical record of operations typically is shorter (and often more erratic) than for larger businesses.
4. Sole proprietorships, partnerships, and S corporations are much more common than for larger businesses.
5. Sales of small businesses usually are on terms other than cash.
6. Very little reliable comparative transaction data are available compared to the wealth of publicly traded company and merger and acquisition data for larger companies.
7. The role of the owner/manager, and how that role will evolve in an ownership transition, takes on great importance in a small business or professional practice.
8. Small businesses and professional practices frequently are bought and sold pursuant to other than strictly financial investment motivations.
9. Accounting policies vary, with small businesses often motivated to minimize taxable income while public companies may wish to make a good income showing for stockholders.
10. Owner's compensation is a far more important variable in the small business or professional practice, varying from strictly a market rate of compensation for services performed more often than not.
11. Analysis of earning power frequently is performed on a pretax basis for small businesses and professional practices versus the typical after-tax basis for larger businesses.
12. One of the few factors tending to make small business easier is that they usually have fairly simple capital structures.

All of these factors cause different types of differences in data collection and analysis. Financial statement analysis often requires more judgment and results in more adjustments than for larger businesses. Comparative transaction data, if available at all, must be evaluated very carefully for reliability and comparability and often must be adjusted to cash equivalent value.

Weaknesses in comparative data often tend to lead to less reliance on a guideline company (market) approach than for larger businesses. On the other hand, nonfinancial motivations of buyers and sellers may cause a market approach to be more relevant than an income approach in some instances.

Owner's compensation is almost always an important aspect of the analysis in a small business, and frequently requires adjustment for valuation purposes.

One caveat, however: as noted at the beginning of this summary, in spite of all the practical differences in small and large business valuation, the underlying theory and applicable broad aproaches are the same as for larger businesses. It is important to be sure that results of practices employed in small business and professional practices can be reconciled with sound general business valuation theory.

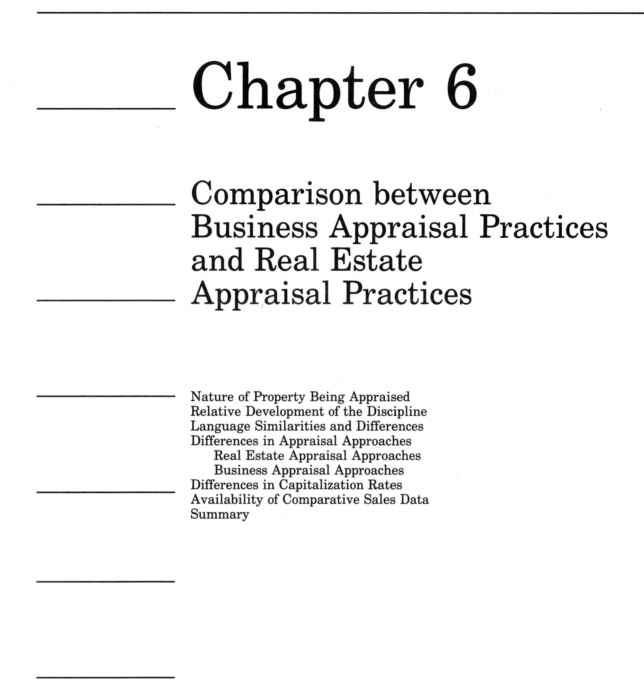

Chapter 6

Comparison between Business Appraisal Practices and Real Estate Appraisal Practices

While both real estate appraisal and business valuation are sophisticated professional disciplines with conceptual commonality, the procedures, language, knowledge, and experience required are very different. This flows from the fact that what is being appraised is quite different.

Business valuation has to do with the value of the rights inherent in ownership of a commercial, industrial, or service organization pursuing an economic activity. Real estate appraisal involves the valuation of land, improvements, and associated rights.[1]

The appraisal of small businesses and professional practices differs in significant ways from the appraisal of real estate. Certainly, both are sophisticated, professional disciplines with many common concepts. The most important difference, of course, is the nature of the property being appraised. A business is a complex and dynamic entity, involving the interaction of many resources. Real estate, by definition, is physical property, which may be one part of a total business. The valuation of a business integrates the total entity: all of the assets (current assets, real estate, personal property, intangible assets), the liabilities (current liabilities, long-term debt), and various classes of equity.

Other differences have arisen from the historical development of the two appraisal disciplines and the backgrounds of the people involved. Some terminology overlaps and some terminology contradictions have caused and continue to cause confusion.

There are also many similarities between business appraisal and real estate appraisal. The purpose of this chapter is to provide the reader with some perspective by highlighting some of the differences and similarities between business and real estate appraisal.

Nature of Property Being Appraised

Real estate, by definition, is static property. The leading authority in the field of real estate defines real estate as "physical land and appurtenances affixed to the land, e.g., structures."[2]

A business, by contrast, is a complex and dynamic organization of interrelated resources, including people, capital, and a wide variety of tangible and intangible assets, one of which may be real estate. In other words, real estate may be one component of a business.

The major categories of rights that need to be appraised in conjunction with real property are interests in the fee estate (ownership of the property itself) and the leasehold estate (rights of a lessee). Other rights may include items such as underground rights, air rights, and easements.

By contrast, the appraisal of a business involves an almost limitless

---

[1] John D. Emory, "Why Business Valuation and Real Estate Appraisal Are Different," *Business Valuation Review*, March 1990, pp. 3–7.

[2] *The Appraisal of Real Estate*, 10th ed. (Chicago: The Appraisal Institute, 1992), p. 6.

amalgam of rights and opportunities, some contractual and others not, including any or all of the bundle of rights that may be associated with a parcel of real estate or, in some cases, many different parcels of real estate.

Furthermore, the valuation of partial interests in a corporation or a partnership that is dominated by real estate will usually involve the valuation of the entity's equity on a minority basis. The minority equity holder has no direct claim on the entity's assets. A minority's value may have little relationship to its pro rata share of the entity as a whole.

In most cases, especially with respect to properties utilized by small businesses and professional practices, the real estate is separable from the business. In such cases, as is discussed in various chapters throughout this book, the real estate and the business should be appraised separately, with the income stream to the business charged with an appropriate rent expense.

When the business and the real estate it occupies are virtually inseparable, as in the case of a single-use property, for example, I suggest that the intertwined business/real estate entity will have more of the economic characteristics of a business entity than the economic characteristics normally associated with real estate. When that is true, approaches normally associated with business appraisal are likely to lead to a more reliable appraisal result than approaches normally associated with real estate appraisal.

Relative Development of the Discipline

An organization that provides leadership in the discipline of business appraisal is the American Society of Appraisers, a multidisciplinary appraisal society conferring professional certification in several fields. Its members certified in business appraisal number in the hundreds, while its members certified in one or more aspects of real estate appraisal number in the thousands. In addition, in the field of real estate appraisal, The Appraisal Institute (formed through a merger in 1991 of the American Institute of Real Estate Appraisers and the Society of Real Estate Appraisers) offers an extensive array of publications, course offerings, and the MAI (Member of the Appraisal Institute) professional designation.

Unlike real estate appraisal theory, which has been published and taught widely for decades, most of the organized development of business appraisal theory and practice has taken place since 1980, and has been spearheaded by the Business Valuation Committee of the American Society of Appraisers.

The development of the business appraisal discipline has drawn heavily on the theory and practice of corporate finance and security analysis. The use of the theory and knowledge of corporate finance and security analysis is eminently reasonable, since the umbrella labeled *corporate finance* really covers the financing of all kinds of business entities, regardless of whether they happen to be corporations, partnerships, or sole proprietorships. The basic thrust of security analysis is the appraisal of an interest in an operating entity; the discipline of security analysis, therefore, is really a specialized variation of business appraisal.

The business appraisal discipline combines the relevant elements of these fields of expertise, along with the requisite understanding of economics, business management, and accounting; it formulates an appraisal process that incorporates and focuses the considerations necessary to estimate the value of an operating entity within the economic and industry environment prevalent at any given time.

Language Similarities and Differences

A term may have a certain well-accepted definition in the language of finance and security analysis and a different and equally well-accepted definition in the language of real estate. Similarly, practitioners in business finance and security analysis may label a concept with one name, and practitioners in real estate appraisal may identify the same concept by some other name. The language of business appraisal logically follows the language of finance and security analysis, since the common subject matter is operating businesses.

Under generally accepted accounting principles (GAAP), the term *net operating income* is typically defined to be income after the deduction of depreciation and amortization, and the literature of finance follows the accounting definition.[3] By contrast, real estate terminology does not include noncash items such as depreciation or amortization within its definition of operating expenses, and therefore the definition of net operating income as used in real estate terminology is before deduction of depreciation or amortization expense.[4]

In business finance and security analysis terminology, the term *cash flow* (or *cash throwoff*) is most commonly (although not universally) used to mean net income after all cash expenses, which means after interest costs but before noncash items such as depreciation and amortization.[5] However, in real estate terminology, cash flow is defined to mean "income remaining from net operating income after debt service is paid,"[6] which means after principal payments as well as interest payments.

It is beyond the scope of this book to provide a comparative lexicon of terminology used in the fields of real estate and business appraisal. Hopefully, the foregoing examples will alert the reader to the problem, so that he will be aware of which definition is intended when he encoun-

---

[3]For example, a typical finance text defines net operating income as "income before interest and income taxes but after depreciation produced by operating assets." Charles O. Kroncke, et al., *Managerial Finance: Essentials* (St. Paul: West Publishing Company, 1976), p. 479. Business appraisers regard a property the company utilizes in its operations as an operating asset.

[4]*The Appraisal of Real Estate*, p. 450.

[5]For example, the *Dictionary of Banking and Finance* defines cash flow as "the reported net income of a corporation, plus amounts charged off for depreciation, depletion, amortization, and extraordinary charges to reserves which are bookkeeping deductions and not actually paid out in cash." (New York: John Wiley & Sons, 1982), p. 92.

[6]*The Dictionary of Real Estate Appraisal*, 2nd ed. (Chicago: American Institute of Real Estate Appraisers, 1989), p. 234.

ters one of the many terms that have ambiguous usage. The ambiguities prevalent in current usage are responsible for miscommunications and many erroneous appraisal results.

Most real estate appraisals provide market value (in exchange): that is, an estimate of the price of the property as if separated from the existing business. The value of real estate as part of a going-concern business is its market value (in use). It is not unusual for the market value in exchange of a piece of real estate to be quite different from its market value in use. An example would be an old-fashioned factory still in use by the original firm—to which it has considerable value in use—which would require substantial renovation to be productive for another use.

Differences in Appraisal Approaches

As a generalization, I would say that approaches to business appraisals are less rigidly structured than approaches to real estate appraisal. That is not to say that any approach used in business appraisal can or should be any less rigorously carried out; however, the variations and complexities of business appraisal require more flexibility in the choice and design of appraisal methodology.

Real Estate Appraisal Approaches

In the field of real estate appraisal, there are three generally accepted valuation approaches:

1. *Income approach (income capitalization approach)*: "A set of procedures in which an appraiser derives a value indication for income-producing property by converting anticipated benefits into property value. This conversion is accomplished either by (1) capitalizing a single year's income expectancy or an annual average of several years' income expectancies at a market-derived capitalization rate or a capitalization rate that reflects a specified income pattern, return on investment, and change in the value of the investment; or (2) discounting the annual cash flows for the holding period and the reversion at a specified yield rate."[7]

2. *Cost approach*: "A set of procedures in which an appraiser derives a value-indication by estimating the current cost to reproduce or replace the existing structure, deducting for all accrued depreciation in the property, and adding the estimated land value."[8]

3. *Market approach (sales comparison approach)*: "A set of procedures in which an appraiser derives a value indication by comparing the property being appraised to similar properties that have been sold recently, applying appropriate units of comparison, and making adjustments, based on the elements of comparison, to the sales prices of the comparables."[9]

---

[7]*The Appraisal of Real Estate*, p. 81.
[8]Ibid., p. 80.
[9]Ibid.

Business Appraisal Approaches

In business appraisal, there is no universal acceptance of any specific number of approaches. Individual writers sometimes make such categorical statements as "There are five approaches for valuing a business," or "Seven approaches are acceptable," but there is no consensus that the discipline of business appraisal should be practiced according to some specific number of structured approaches.

Within the income capitalization approach, the real estate appraisal profession recognizes certain variations closely parallel to variations of earning power capitalization approaches used in business appraisal. For example, what real estate appraisers call "direct capitalization"[10] is essentially the same procedure as I have described as capitalizing normalized earnings in Chapter 14. Within the category of direct capitalization, the real estate profession includes gross income multipliers, recognizing, as we do in Chapter 16, that the assumption underlying their validity is that a given level of gross income generated by a certain type of property or business should be able to generate a certain level of net income. What real estate appraisers call "yield capitalization"[11] is essentially the same procedure I have described as "The Discounted Future Returns Method" in Chapter 13.

Income capitalization approaches are conceptually similar in business appraisal and real estate appraisal. However, in most cases, estimating an income stream for an operating business is much more difficult than estimating an income stream for an apartment or office building or some similar income-producing real estate property. Furthermore, the risks of an operating business are typically more complex to assess and quantify than are the risks of operating real estate, and therefore the selection of appropriate capitalization rates is more difficult in the context of business appraisal. To cope with these challenges adequately, the business appraiser needs a broad understanding of relevant economic and industry factors, capital market conditions, business management, and accounting.

As a generality, the business appraiser's asset approaches have some similarities to the real estate appraiser's cost approach. Referred to as the Asset Accumulation Approach or the Adjusted Net Worth Approach to business valuation, the Asset Approach really provides an indication of the value of the business enterprise by developing a fair market value balance sheet. All of the business's assets are identified and brought to fair market value in use, and all of the business's liabilities are brought to current value as of the valuation date. The difference between fair market value of the assets and the current value of the liabilities is an indication of the business enterprise equity value under this approach.

As for the market or sales comparison approach, the real estate appraiser will seek data on sales of comparable properties, and the business appraiser will seek data on transactions in comparable businesses. The business appraiser will interpret the comparable transaction data for

---

[10]Ibid., p. 419.
[11]Ibid., p. 420.

guidance in determining applicable valuation parameters—such as capitalization rates for earnings or cash flow, and gross revenue multipliers—and ratios of the entity's market value to asset value measures, such as book value or adjusted net tangible asset value. Sometimes the business appraiser will set out a separate valuation approach, using the market value indicators based on some specific transaction data with each approach drawing to the fullest possible extent on available comparative sales data.

Differences in Capitalization Rates

There is a tendency for the market for businesses to change more rapidly than the market for real estate. The reason is that a business is typically a collection of tangible and intangible assets each with its own price volatility and risks of ownership.

Pretax income streams from direct investment in real estate tend to be capitalized at lower rates of return than comparably defined pretax income streams from investments in non-real estate oriented businesses. The primary reason for this is the tax advantages of real estate, which usually result in a comparably defined pretax income stream translating into a higher after-tax income stream. Another reason may be a lower perceived level of risk in direct real estate investment compared with the typical investment in a small business.

On a value-in-exchange basis, real estate investors may accept a lower rate of return from their cash flow stream than they would accept from other assets because they expect extra return in the form of capital appreciation on the property. This is in sharp contrast to a business investment that includes both machinery and equipment that will eventually become worthless through wear and tear and/or obsolescence and intangible assets that will become obsolete over time.

Availability of Comparative Sales Data

Useful comparative sales data are much harder to obtain for sales of businesses than for sales of real estate. The problem of obtaining comparative transaction data is greater for small businesses and professional practices than for large businesses.

Real estate transaction data are readily available in county courthouses, and sales of public companies are reported in great detail. However, there is no requirement for public reporting of data on sales of closely held companies. As a consequence, unless the business appraiser has access to a private data source, there may be no comparative transaction data available for guidance.

Another problem with the use of comparative sales data for business appraisers is the uniqueness of every business. Each parcel of real estate is also unique, of course; but the large number of variables, many of which are impossible to measure numerically, usually make the matter of comparability a greater problem when using comparative business sales transaction data than when using comparative real estate transaction data.

Summary

When performed correctly, real estate appraisal practices and business appraisal practices are totally compatible with each other. In fact, logically, valuation of income-producing real estate may be viewed as a special case of business valuation, in the sense that income-producing real estate is logically equivalent to a business that has very limited assets. When each is done properly, the significant differences in approaches and emphases emerge logically from the basic differences in the nature and scope of the property being appraised. It is unfortunate, however, that the terminology used by the two disciplines is not interchangeable. The differences in usage of certain important terms are so ingrained that there may be no realistic prospect for developing a set of mutually compatible terms.

Part II

Analyzing the Company

Chapter 7

Adjusting the Balance Sheet

The process of determining the price begins with "normalizing" the company's financial records. Neither the balance sheets nor the income statements of smaller, privately held companies necessarily bear any relationship to reality.[1]

The value of most businesses and practices generally depends on the assets being transferred and/or how much the business or practice can earn. The starting place, then, is to adjust the financial statements so that they reflect *a best estimate of economic reality.* Making these adjustments is often referred to as normalizing the financial statements.

This chapter deals with adjusting the balance sheet to get a realistic picture of the assets being transferred; the next chapter deals with adjusting the income statement to get a realistic picture of the entity's earnings power. Many of the factors involved in these adjustments are interrelated; many of them have a bearing on both the balance sheet and the income statement.

Accounts Receivable

When a small business or professional practice is sold, the seller typically collects the accounts receivable, and they are not part of the transaction. In other cases, a buyer may agree to collect the accounts on a contingent basis, paying the seller 85 percent or so of collections.

If accounts receivable are to be transferred on other than a contingent basis, it should be questioned whether they may be worth more or less than the net amount at which they are carried on the books. For companies using accrual accounting, accounts receivable are usually shown on the balance sheet in the following format:

Accounts Receivable	$100,000
Less: Allowance for doubtful accounts	5,000
	$95,000

The collectibility of receivables is evaluated based upon many factors. Among the most common are:

- Historical experience.
- State of the economy and its effect on the company's customers.
- The aging of the receivables.
- The financial stability of the customers.
- The company's credit-granting policies.

Some companies are extremely conservative and accrue a greater amount for doubtful accounts than will ultimately be necessary to offset uncollectible accounts. At the other extreme, some companies do not accrue any allowance for doubtful accounts. They just write off an ac-

---

[1]Thomas P. Murphy, "What Price Independence?" *Forbes,* September 27, 1982, pp. 208–9.

Exhibit 7–1

MARY'S MACHINERY & EQUIPMENT, INC.
AGED ACCOUNTS RECEIVABLE
AS OF DECEMBER 31, 1991

Account Name	Total	Current	30–60 Days	60–90 Days	90–120 Days	Over 120 Days
	$	$	$	$	$	$
Ace Widget Co.	1,000	1,000				
A-1 Equipment	20,000					20,000
Best Rentals	5,000				5,000	
Cascade Construction	500			500		
Davidson Machine	6,000			6,000		
E & F Transportation	70,000	35,000	35,000			
Frank Industries	2,000	2,000				
General Equipment	3,000					3,000
Holt Industries	1,500				1,500	
I.K. Industries	12,000					12,000
Jay Manufacturing	500			500		
K Construction	25,000	25,000				
Long's Machinery	6,500				6,500	
Mountain Resources	30,000	15,000	15,000			
Nelson Excavating	2,000					2,000
Power Enterprises	8,000					8,000
Rolling Transportation	25,000	20,000	5,000			
Sam's Equipment	40,000	12,000	20,000	8,000		
T.X. Resources	2,000				2,000	
Vic's Manufacturing	10,000	10,000				
Western Industries	30,000					30,000
TOTAL	300,000	120,000	75,000	15,000	15,000	75,000
	100.0%	40.0%	25.0%	5.0%	5.0%	25.0%

count directly against accounts receivable when they determine it to be uncollectible.

An aged accounts receivable schedule (Exhibit 7–1) is the starting place to try to examine whether the net amount shown on the books is really a good estimate of the amount that will actually be collected.

The lower the percentage of receivables in older categories the better. The percentages can be compared with prior years' results or industry data to better understand collectibility.

Some buyers of businesses value accounts receivable by some arbitrary rule of thumb. For example, they may accept current accounts at face value, discount those over 30 days by 10 percent, those over 60 days by 20 percent, those over 90 days by 30 percent, and allow little or nothing for accounts over 120 days. It is generally possible, however, to get a much more accurate estimate of net collectibility by analyzing each account, looking at the past payment history of any accounts that are sizable or that are more than 30 or 60 days old, taking into consideration the typical collection period for businesses in the particular industry. (Sources for average collection periods for different types of businesses are discussed in Chapter 9.)

A buyer may be willing to accept most of the accounts receivable, either at face value or at some discount, but will leave some for the seller to try to collect. In other cases, a buyer may accept accounts receivable on a contingent basis, reserving some portion to be paid to the seller when, and if, the accounts are collected.

Inventory

Inventory is accounted for in three categories: raw material, work in process, and finished goods.

For accounting purposes, raw material is generally valued by multiplying the quantity of each usable item on hand by the lower of either the actual cost of the item or its market value, depending on prevailing accounting policy. Work in process value is determined by adding the costs incurred to bring the item from raw material to its current condition. For accounting purposes, finished goods are valued at the total cost of material, labor, and overhead required to prepare the item for sale.

Ideally, the inventory account would be adjusted by taking a physical inventory count and extending it at current costs. If the inventory account must be adjusted by the appraiser on the basis of the books and records, the two main questions to answer involve the basic accounting policy (generally either FIFO or LIFO) and the write-off and/or write-down policy.

FIFO versus LIFO

FIFO, or *first-in, first-out,* means that the first unit of an inventory item purchased is the first unit considered sold for accounting purposes. LIFO, or *last-in, first-out,* means that the unit of an inventory item purchased last is the first unit considered sold for accounting purposes. The difference between FIFO and LIFO accounting appears in the ending inventory on the balance sheet; this affects the cost of goods sold and thus the earnings on the income statements.

To the extent that prices go up, LIFO results in lower figures for ending inventory, a higher cost of goods sold, and therefore lower earnings than result with FIFO. Since LIFO accounting is acceptable for federal income tax purposes and results in less taxable income in a rising price scenario, there has been a widespread tendency for companies to adopt LIFO rather than FIFO inventory accounting in response to inflation.

Take a simple example of a company that started its accounting period with 30 widgets, purchased for $10 each, then purchased 60 more widgets for $15 each during the accounting period, and ended the period with an inventory of 40 widgets. Using FIFO versus LIFO accounting, compute the comparative inventory and cost of goods sold as follows:

	FIFO			LIFO		
Beginning inventory	30 units @ $10	=	$300	30 units @ $10	=	$300
Purchases	60 units @ $15	=	900	60 units @ $15	=	900
Goods available for sale			$1,200			$1,200
Ending inventory	40 units @ $15	=	$600	30 units @ $10	=	$300
				10 units @ $15	=	150
			$600			$450
Cost of goods sold			$600			$750

In other words, under LIFO, the accounting perpetuates the fiction that the original units in the inventory are the ones still there. In the case above, under LIFO accounting, the ending inventory would be shown on the balance sheet at $450; under FIFO accounting, the same ending inventory would be shown on the balance sheet at $600.

Since the FIFO method results in showing more current values on the balance sheet, that method comes closer to portraying the inventory at an economically realistic current value. Therefore, if the subject company uses LIFO, you can adjust the balance sheet to a FIFO basis. If the company reporting on LIFO has audited statements, the footnotes usually provide the information necessary to adjust the inventory values from LIFO to FIFO. All that needs to be done is to add the amount shown as LIFO Reserve to the amount of the inventory account shown on the balance sheet. If the statements of a company reporting on LIFO are not audited, then the company's accountant should be able to provide the analyst with the necessary information to adjust to a FIFO basis. Inventory writeups should normally be offset by recognition of the tax effect, as discussed in a subsequent section.

Some companies account for inventory on some type of an average-cost basis, but that practice is so uncommon that it does not warrant a discussion in this book.

Write-Down and Write-Off Policies

Regardless of whether the FIFO, LIFO, or average-cost inventory method is used, most companies adhere to the "lower-of-cost-or-market" principle, which holds that the carrying value should be reduced if the market value is less than the cost. Market value for this purpose is defined as "current replacement cost except that market shall not be higher than net realizable value, nor should it be lower than net realizable value reduced by the normal profit margin."[2]

Implementation of the lower-of-cost-or-market principle varies tremendously—one company may have a stockroom full of obsolete inventory, while another company may have an aggressive program of automatic write-downs and write-offs of inventory on the basis of the number of months it has been in stock. Appropriate adjustments to inventory values

---

[2]Leopold A. Bernstein, *Financial Statement Analysis: Theory, Application, and Interpretation*, 3rd ed. (Homewood, Ill.: Richard D. Irwin, 1983), p. 149.

may be necessary when a company goes to one extreme or the other in making, or not making, adjustments to inventory values in its implementation of the lower-of-cost-or-market principle. The more extreme the inventory accounting policies, the less the accounting records can be relied on to assist in obtaining an economically realistic inventory value.

Tax Effect

If we are valuing a corporation as a going concern for a transaction involving 100 percent of the equity, we must recognize that the cost basis of the inventory, not our adjusted value, will still be its book value for federal income tax purposes. Therefore, any adjustment made should net out the income tax effect.

For example, if we revalue inventory upward from a book value of $100,000 to an adjusted value of $150,000, the effect is that the $50,000 gain will be taxed to the corporation at the corporation's ordinary income tax rate when the inventory is sold. If the corporation is in the 30 percent tax bracket, the markup of $50,000 in the inventory account should be net of, or offset by, $15,000 in income taxes that will eventually come out of the $50,000 markup. Therefore, the net markup for the purpose of valuing the stock should be only $35,000.

Prepaid Expenses

The components of the prepaid expense account shown on the balance sheet should be examined. The most common components are rent, insurance, and office supplies. If these items will be necessary for the going concern, no adjustment may be necessary. However, if they are not necessary, the prepaid expense account should be adjusted accordingly. An example of such an item would be $10,000 worth of stationery and promotional materials that will not be used by a new buyer because he plans to change the name of the company. There could also be some valuable prepaid expenses that do not show up on the balance sheet because they were charged directly to expenses when paid, and it may be appropriate to make an adjustment for these items.

Other Current Assets

If other current assets are involved in the valuation, such as marketable securities or short-term notes or contracts receivable, they should be adjusted to market values. As with the inventory account adjustment, if equity in a corporation is being valued, any adjustment to current asset account values should net out the related income tax effect: that is, the income tax that will be incurred when the asset is sold. This may be shown by bringing a deferred tax account onto the balance sheet.

Real Estate

In valuing most small businesses and professional practices, my preference is to deal with real estate separately from the value of the business or practice. For one thing, many sellers who own the premises being occupied by the business are willing to sell the business or practice with or without the real estate. This means the business has to be valued separately. Since many small businesses and professional practices do not own the real estate they occupy, balance sheet and income statement data can usually best be compared from one entity to another and to industry averages without real estate on the balance sheet. Also, appraisal approaches appropriate for the real estate may be different from those appropriate for the operating entity. Finally, environmental concerns and regulations have affected the transferability of real estate, which can complicate the sale of the business.

Sometimes, appraising the real estate and appraising the business entity separately may lead to more meaningful conclusions than appraising only one or the other.

If the real estate is to be removed from the balance sheet, items related to real estate must also be removed from the income statement and a reasonable rent included in the expenses. Examples of such items that may be included on the income statement are interest, taxes, and insurance related to the property ownership. In some cases some rental income may require an adjustment.

If real estate is to be left on the balance sheet, it may be adjusted to appraised fair market value if a current appraisal is available. If the appraisal available is outdated, or if the real estate changed hands a few years ago, the real estate value should be updated.

The Real Estate Appraisal Process

Just as there are several approaches available to value businesses, real estate is appraised by considering the three traditional approaches to asset appraisal: the market approach, the income approach, and the cost approach.

Market Approach. The market approach provides a systematic framework for estimating the value of the subject property based on an analysis and correlation of actual transaction prices reflecting the purchase and sale of properties comparable to the subject property. This approach requires the comparison and correlation of the subject property to comparable properties that have been listed for sale or actually sold in the appropriate primary or secondary market. Considerations such as the location of the comparable properties, the time of the sale, physical characteristics, and special financing or other terms and conditions of the sale are discretely analyzed for each comparable property, and these data are appropriately adjusted in the correlation of data used to indicate the current value of the subject property.

Income Approach. The income approach provides a systematic framework for estimating the value of the subject property based on the capitalization or present value determination of the prospective economic income to be derived from property ownership. In the income approach, economic income can be defined several ways, including:

- Net income.
- Net operating income.
- Gross or net rental income.
- Gross cash flow.
- Net cash flow.

The income capitalization procedure can also be accomplished in several ways, including:

- Capitalizing current year's income.
- Capitalizing a normalized period's income.
- Projecting future income over a discrete time period.
- Determining a present value.

The quantification of the appropriate capitalization or discount rate is an essential element of the income approach to asset appraisal. The appropriate capitalization or discount rate should reflect a fair return on stakeholders' invested capital and should consider the opportunity cost of capital, the time value of money, the term of the investment, and the risk of the investment.

Cost Approach. The cost approach provides a systematic framework for estimating the value of the subject property based on the principle of substitution. A prudent investor would pay no more for a property than the amount necessary to replace the asset with a comparable substitute. Replacement cost new (cost of a new asset with equal utility) establishes the maximum amount that a prudent buyer would pay for a property.

To the extent that the subject property has less utility than an ideal replacement, the value of the subject property must be adjusted for this measurable decrease in utility. The property's replacement cost new is then adjusted for losses in value due to physical deterioration, functional obsolescence, technological obsolescence (a specific form of functional obsolescence), and economic obsolescence (often called external obsolescence).

Due to budget constraints and to other factors, business appraisers typically rely on the cost approach to determine the fair market value of the operating assets.

Under the cost approach, the typical formula for quantifying an asset's fair market value is as follows: *Reproduction cost new less incurable functional and technological obsolescence equals replacement cost new. Replacement cost new, less physical deterioration, less economic obsolescence, and less curable functional and technological obsolescence equals fair market value.*

The proper sequencing of the appropriate decrease in asset value due to deterioration, depreciation, and obsolescence is important to the correct application of the cost approach. The previously indicated sequence of cost and obsolescence analyses is typically most appropriate for determining the fair market value of assets for ad valorem taxation purposes. Each of the previously indicated terms will be defined briefly in the following paragraphs.

Reproduction Cost. Reproduction cost is the cost to construct, at current prices, an exact duplicate or replica of the subject asset. This duplicate would be created using the same materials, construction standards, design, layout, and quality of workmanship that was used to create the original asset. Therefore, an asset's reproduction cost will encompass all of the deficiencies, enhancements, and obsolescence that exist in the subject asset. Many of these inadequacies, enhancements, and so forth, inherent in the subject asset are incurable.

An asset's deficiencies are considered curable when the prospective economic benefit of enhancing or modifying the asset exceeds the current cost—in terms of material, labor, and time—to change the asset. An asset's deficiencies are considered incurable when the current costs of enhancing or modifying the asset—in terms of material, labor, and time—exceed the expected future economic benefits.

Replacement Cost. The replacement cost of a subject asset is the cost to create, at current prices, an asset having equal utility to the asset being appraised. The replacement asset, however, would be created with modern materials, current construction standards, state-of-the-art design and layout, and the highest available quality of workmanship.

The difference between an asset's reproduction cost and its replacement cost is, typically, the quantification of incurable functional and technological obsolescence. That is, in an ideal replacement asset, all elements of incurable functional and technological obsolescence have been removed or "reengineered" from the subject asset.

An asset's replacement cost is sometimes quantified using a "green field" approach. That is, the replacement cost of a subject asset or property is the cost to build a redesigned and reengineered ideal replacement from scratch—on an undeveloped "green field."

Physical Deterioration. Physical deterioration is the reduction in the value of an asset due to physical wear and tear and the impact of continued use and the elements of nature on the subject asset. Physical deterioration affects the value of an asset in two ways. First, an asset experiencing physical deterioration looks old and used. This appearance will impact the value of that asset in its secondary market. Second, continued use or the effect of natural elements on an asset will ultimately reduce its remaining useful life and its anticipated remaining utility. In effect, the asset will be partially used up. Quite obviously, this also affects the value of the asset in its secondary market.

Functional Obsolescence. Functional obsolescence is the reduction in the value of an asset due to its inability to perform the function (or yield the periodic utility) for which it was originally designed. Due to structural deficiencies (in the case of tangible real property) or due to mechanical deficiencies (in the case of tangible personal property), the subject asset can no longer do the job for which it was designed (i.e., perform at design specifications) at the same cost as available replacement assets. Unlike elements in physical deterioration, elements of functional obsolescence may not be visually evident.

An asset manifesting functional obsolescence may not be physically damaged in any way. In fact, the asset may be brand new. However, due to faulty construction or to changes in its use or mechanism, the asset can no longer perform (in terms of a standardized measure of utility produced) as designed. Like physical deterioration, however, elements of functional obsolescence are physically inherent in the subject asset.

Technological Obsolescence. Technological obsolescence is often considered a special category of functional obsolescence. Technical obsolescence is a decrease in the value of the subject asset due to improvements in technology that make the subject asset less than the ideal replacement for itself. Technological obsolescence occurs when, due to improvements in design or engineering technology, a new replacement asset will produce a greater standardized measure of utility production than the subject asset.

For example, due to technological improvements in construction engineering, a replacement building can perform the same function as the subject building, but with 20 percent less square footage. Or due to enhancement in design technology, a replacement machine can produce its output better, cheaper, or faster than the subject machine.

With respect to technological obsolescence and unlike physical deterioration, the subject asset need not be physically damaged at all. Unlike functional obsolescence, the subject asset can be performing exactly to design specification. As a result of technological improvements, however, the design specifications of a replacement asset have materially improved compared with those of the subject asset. Accordingly, the subject asset will have a lower value in its secondary market compared with that of a replacement asset that meets the technologically enhanced specifications.

Economic Obsolescence. Economic obsolescence is a reduction in the value of real property or tangible personal property due to the impact of events, or conditions that are external to, and not controlled by, the physical nature or the structural or mechanical operation of the asset. The impact of economic obsolescence is typically beyond the control of the asset's owner. For that reason, economic obsolescence is typically considered to be incurable.

Approximations of Real Estate Values

Rather than adopt this rigorous, three-approach process, sometimes a friendly local real estate broker can help. Or an earlier, slightly outdated real estate appraisal may be adjusted to an estimate of current value by using an index of real estate values for the subject property type and locale.

If no better approximation of current value is available, a tax-assessed value might be helpful. However, even in jurisdictions where tax-assessed values purportedly represent market value, they frequently do not. If there is a way of knowing the typical relationship between tax-assessed values and market values in a particular jurisdiction, the tax-assessed values can be adjusted accordingly. Incidentally, since Proposition 13, tax-assessed values are virtually worthless as indicators of market value in California; tax-assessed values there are limited by a formula ceiling, unless the property changes hands.

Tax Effect

If equity is being valued, the question arises, should any tax effects of adjusting real estate values be taken into consideration on the balance sheet. If the real estate is likely to be sold, tax effects may be netted out of the real estate value adjustment. (Alternatively, the tax effects could be recognized by a deferred taxes payable account in the liability section of the balance sheet.)

If a buyer would not be expected to sell the real estate (a premise often used in appraisals for divorce purposes in some jurisdictions, for example), it is debatable whether implied taxes on the markup should be recognized on the adjusted balance sheet. When recognizing the tax effect, one method is to account for the capital gains taxes implied in the markup with a deferred tax account. Alternatively, they could be footnoted as a contingent liability.

Tangible Personal Property

Generally speaking, to adjust a balance sheet on a going-concern basis, the furniture, fixtures, and equipment should be adjusted to their market values. Different people, however, have different ideas of what that means for this category of assets. The replacement cost for most used equipment is twice, or several times, as much as could be realized in a liquidation sale if the operation were closed.

Used Replacement Cost

The consensus is that *used replacement cost* best applies when adjusting the furniture, fixtures, and equipment account on the balance sheet on a going-concern basis. This term is generally interpreted to mean the price at which used equipment in comparable condition could be purchased on the open market, plus the cost of transporting and installing it so it works. Estimates of such costs can be obtained from equipment appraisers or dealers. This is the concept of value usually meant when people use the term *market value* in reference to the furniture, fixtures, and equipment account on an adjusted balance sheet. This is a reasonable way to look at the value of these assets on a going-concern basis, because in essence it represents an *opportunity cost,* an alternative that the buyers have available to them if they don't buy the entity being valued.

Depreciated Replacement Cost

One of the common approaches to valuing the furniture, fixtures, and equipment for an adjusted balance sheet on a going-concern basis is *depreciated replacement cost.* In simple terms, depreciated replacement cost means the current cost to replace the item new, less an allowance for the length of time it has been in service. For example, if a new comparably productive machine would cost $1,000 new and could be expected to have a useful economic life of 10 years (with no salvage value), and the present machine had been in use for 4 years and could be expected to last 6 more years, the appraiser could estimate the depreciated replacement cost at $600 ($6/10 \times \$1,000 = \$600$).

This calculation assumes that the subject machine has been maintained in reasonably good operating order. If the condition of the equipment is exceptionally good or bad, an upward or downward adjustment would be in order. If the subject equipment suffers from functional obsolescence, a downward adjustment must be made to arrive at a proper value based on the depreciated replacement cost approach. For example, if the subject machine can do the same job as the new replacement machine, but only at a higher operating cost (perhaps because of a difference in energy efficiency, for example) a downward adjustment in value must be made to recognize this factor.

The depreciated replacement cost approach is commonly used by industrial appraisers analyzing asset values for manufacturing companies for ad valorem (property tax) appraisals.

Liquidation Value

Orderly liquidation value is the net amount that could be expected to be received if the assets were sold off in an orderly manner. Estimates of orderly liquidation value can be obtained from equipment appraisers or wholesale dealers. Although a creditor might focus heavily on the balance sheet adjusted to liquidation value, that is not normally the primary focus for an adjusted balance sheet on a going-concern basis.

Forced liquidation value is the net amount that could be expected to be received if the assets were sold off piecemeal immediately. Some creditors rely on this value for tangible personal property as a basis for collateral. Estimates of forced liquidation value can be obtained from equipment appraisers or auctioneers.

It should be kept in mind, however, that leasehold improvements are usually worthless in a liquidation sale, and most furniture, fixtures, and equipment bring prices in a liquidation sale that are heavily discounted even from used replacement cost.

Intangible Assets

At this stage of the valuation process, balance sheet adjustments are usually limited to those necessary to arrive at an adjusted net tangible asset value. If the value of the business based on earning capacity is greater than the net tangible asset value, some intangible value is indicated. Frequently, this intangible value is simply called goodwill. However, that may be an improper characterization of the intangible value; and for other reasons, it may be worthwhile to quantify the amount of value attributable to specific intangible assets such as patents, copyrights, customer lists, and many other possibilities. This concept is discussed more fully in Chapter 34.

Liabilities

If equity is being valued, or if liabilities are to be assumed in conjunction with an asset sale, then the liability side of the balance sheet should also be examined for possible adjustments. Most liabilities, of course, would be left on an adjusted balance sheet at their face value. An adjustment can be made on an interest-bearing obligation with an interest rate significantly different from current market rates, or on a deferred taxes account, for example.

Interest-Bearing Debt

It is common to read or hear the phrase "assume favorable financing" as a selling point, to make a business more attractive to a potential buyer. Most people, however, fail to resolve this important question: in valuing the business in question, how many dollars' worth of difference does the favorable financing that is available really make?

For example, suppose that the buyer assumes a mortgage or bond or note with a remaining principal balance of $500,000, payable in 84 equal monthly installments (seven years), including interest at 8 percent, when the current market rate for comparable debt financing is 14 percent. The payments on the obligation would be $7,793.21 per month. The present value of the mortgage can be computed as follows:

$$\text{PV} = \sum_{i=1}^{84} \frac{\$7,793.21}{(1.011667)^i} = \$415,834$$

In other words, the $500,000 face value of the obligation should be adjusted to a present value of $415,834 for the adjusted balance sheet under current economic conditions.

The procedures for computing the amounts of the payments and present values for such contracts are covered in Chapter 19.

Suppose an adjusted gross asset value is $700,000. Without adjusting the liability, the face amount of $500,000 would be deducted, resulting in an adjusted net asset value of $200,000. Applying the appropriate adjustment to the liability results in a deduction of only about $416,000, leaving an adjusted net asset value of $284,000. In other words, in this example, the ability to use favorable financing to control $700,000 worth of assets makes the business worth $84,000 more than it would if such financing were not available as part of the package.

Deferred Taxes

An item called *deferred taxes* sometimes appears on the balance sheet, because income taxes have been incurred but are not yet due to be paid. The analyst should inquire about the likely timing of such payments, or even whether they will have to be paid at all. Frequently it is appropriate to reduce the deferred taxes item, or possibly eliminate it entirely, in constructing the adjusted balance sheet from an appraisal viewpoint. (As noted earlier, it is sometimes also appropriate to bring a deferred tax item onto the balance sheet to partly offset certain writeups.)

Contingent or Off-Balance Sheet Assets and Liabilities

Many items that do not actually appear on the balance sheet should be considered in the course of the balance sheet analysis. These are items for which it has not been established for certain whether or not a payment (complete or partial) actually will be made or received. The factors giving rise to such off-balance sheet items may already be in place: a lawsuit filed, accrued vacation, or pension liabilities; or the item may be dependent on some future event—such as a change in taxation or some aspect of the regulatory environment. Whether or not such items warrant specific attention depends on their potential magnitude and the probability of their actually resulting in future payments or receipts.

Sometimes, when constructing the adjusted balance sheet, one or more of these contingencies should be added to the line items in the statements at their probable value (e.g., estimated amount after adjusting for taxes times probability of payment times time value factor). More often, because of their uncertain nature, it would be appropriate to call attention to these items in a footnote. The following are a few fairly common examples of off-balance sheet liabilities and assets.

Product Liability

If a company manufactures or sells widgets, it may have an obligation for repairs, replacements, or other restitution for defective widgets, through express warranty or otherwise. Many small manufacturing companies just charge the expense of such claims against earnings as they occur. If a company is exposed, but has no reserve or liability account on its balance sheet to cover it, a good procedure is to estimate the probable cost of such future claims, perhaps from the history of such claims, and establish a liability account on the balance sheet to recognize these obligations.

In general, one of the reasons that many buyers prefer an asset purchase rather than a stock purchase is to avoid the obligation for any possible contingent liabilities of the selling corporation. However, under various states' bulk sales laws, this type of contingent liability is likely to be transferred to a new owner even through an asset transaction rather than a stock transaction. If that is a prospect, a buyer should seek his attorney's advice as to what his position will be on this matter.

Lawsuits

Actual or potential lawsuits of all kinds are an area far too broad to treat in any detail. If such possibilities exist, they should be investigated as thoroughly as possible. It is also possible, of course, that the company could have a suit pending against someone else, which could be resolved with a great benefit to the company (i.e., a contingent asset).

Regulatory Compliance

In these days of extensive bureaucratic regulation, often administered with utter disregard for economic consequences to the individual business, community, or nation, the specter of the potential cost of complying with government mandates cannot be ignored.

Some of the most common sources of such mandatory expenditures are asbestos and real estate environmental clean up, which may not be indemnified away, pollution control requirements, and Occupational Safety & Health Administration (OSHA) requirements. A potential buyer should inquire into possible costs of compliance and should recognize a liability for incurring such costs.

A potential cost could be uncertain, perhaps pending the outcome of an administrative or legal proceeding that may require considerable time to resolve; therefore, a buyer might establish a reserve for the potential cost, with the seller entitled to any residual in the reserve not actually required to meet the final compliance mandate.

Past Service Liability

There may be obligations to employees for past services, perhaps in the form of unfunded pension liabilities, accrued vacations, or arrangements with individual employees. These obligations should be quantified, if possible, and shown as a liability on the balance sheet.

Employment Agreements

Some companies may have employment agreements or consulting agreements, under which regular payments are made to former owners or employees. When that is the case, from an appraisal viewpoint, the obligations under such agreements should be viewed as liabilities.

Exhibit 7–2

ANNIE'S APPAREL STORE
ADJUSTED BALANCE SHEET
AS OF DECEMBER 31, 1991

	Balance Sheet as Reported		Adjustments	Balance Sheet as Adjusted	
	$	%	$	$	%
ASSETS					
Current Assets:					
Cash	5,000	2.2	(5,000) a	0	0.0
Accounts Receivable	30,000	13.2	(3,000) b	27,000	9.6
Inventory	180,000	78.9	40,000 c	220,000	78.6
Prepaid Expense	3,000	1.3		3,000	1.1
Total Current Assets	218,000	95.6		250,000	89.3
Fixed Assets:					
Fixtures & Equipment	50,000	21.9			
Less: Depreciation	40,000	17.5			
	10,000	4.4	20,000 d	30,000	10.7
TOTAL ASSETS	228,000	100.0		280,000	100.0
LIABILITIES & OWNER'S EQUITY					
Current Liabilities:					
Accounts Payable	110,000	48.2	(110,000) e	0	0.0
Notes Payable	1,000	0.4	(1,000) e	0	0.0
Accrued Payroll	2,000	0.9	(2,000) e	0	0.0
Total Current Liabilities	113,000	49.5		0	0.0
Long-term Debt					
Contract Payable	100,000	43.9	(10,984) f	89,016	31.8
Total Liabilities	213,000	93.4		89,016	31.8
Owner's Equity	15,000	6.6	175,984 g	190,984	68.2
TOTAL LIABILITIES & EQUITY	228,000	100.0		280,000	100.0

a   Cash to be retained by seller.

b   It is easier for an ongoing operator to collect accounts receivable--accounts receivable discounted 10% for doubtful accounts and time to collect.

c   Aggressive policy in inventory markdowns has been followed. This adjustment results from taking a physical inventory, extending at probable selling prices, and allowing a 45% gross margin, the store's average historical gross margin.

d   Adjustment to furniture and fixtures based on talks with dealers--approximate used replacement cost.

e   Will pay out of proceeds of sale.

f   Buyer will assume remaining balance of 7% note from Annie's purchase of store--60 payments of $1,980.12, discounted at 12% (See Chapter 19).

g   The net amount of adjustments a through f.

Unrecorded Obligations

The appraiser should investigate whether there may be any outstanding obligations, not recorded on the books, for goods or services. In one case, for example, a balance sheet on which a sale of a company was based showed accounts receivable for sales that had been made, but did not show the liability for the salesmen's commissions that would have to be paid out of the accounts receivable when collected.

Liens

If the company has any of its assets pledged, either to secure its own indebtedness or because it is contingently liable for someone else's indebtedness, such facts should be noted.

Examples of Adjusted Balance Sheets

The following are hypothetical examples of the procedures discussed in this chapter. These examples assume that the respective companies have done their accounting on an accrual basis. An example of how to handle balance sheet adjustments for companies accounting on a cash basis is included in Chapter 23.

Sole Proprietorship Example

Annie was a good merchandiser and a shrewd businesswoman. When she decided to retire, the apparel shop she had bought a few years before was well maintained and operating profitably. Exhibit 7–2 is the adjusted balance sheet her appraiser prepared in connection with selling her business.

Corporation Example

Mary's Machinery & Equipment, Inc., distributes and services industrial machinery and equipment. Mary's is well known for its top-notch mechanics and rebuilding expertise. Mary wants to sell the business and move to Hawaii for rest and relaxation. The company felt the brunt of the recession for a couple of years, but returned to profitability in 1991. Exhibit 7–3 is the adjusted balance sheet prepared by the company's appraiser in connection with the sale of the business.

Summary

This chapter discussed the most common asset and liability account adjustments that business appraisers frequently make to bring the balance sheet account balances to current value. This helps to provide a better perspective on the values of assets employed in the business.

Exhibit 7–4 summarizes the steps in adjusting the balance sheet.

Many of the balance sheet adjustments imply related income statement adjustments. The next chapter discusses adjustments to the income statement.

Exhibit 7–3

MARY'S MACHINERY & EQUIPMENT, INC.
ADJUSTED BALANCE SHEET
AS OF DECEMBER 31, 1991

	Balance Sheet as Reported		Adjustments	Balance Sheet as Adjusted	
	$	%	$	$	%
ASSETS					
Current Assets:					
Cash & Equivalents	65,000	7.2		65,000	6.0
Accounts Receivable	300,000	33.3	(70,000) a	230,000	21.3
Inventory	320,000	35.6	105,000 b	425,000	39.5
Prepaid Expense	15,000	1.7		15,000	1.4
Marketable Securities	10,000	1.1	7,800 c	17,800	1.7
Other	5,000	0.6		5,000	0.5
Total Current Assets	715,000	79.5	42,800	757,800	70.4
Furniture, Fixtures & Equipment:					
Equipment	110,000	12.2			
Furnishings	40,000	4.4			
Vehicles	200,000	22.2			
	350,000	38.8			
Less: Accumulated Depreciation	225,000	25.0			
Net Furn., Fix. & Equip.	125,000	13.8	125,000 d	250,000	23.2
Leasehold Interest	0	0.0	8,200 e	8,200	0.8
Other Assets	60,000	6.7		60,000	5.6
TOTAL ASSETS	900,000	100.0	176,000	1,076,000	100.0
LIABILITIES & STOCKHOLDER'S EQUITY					
Current Liabilities:					
Notes Payable	50,000	5.7		50,000	4.6
Current Maturity LTM	40,000	4.4		40,000	3.7
Accts. & Notes Payable--Trade	120,000	13.3		120,000	11.2
Accrued Expenses	40,000	4.4		40,000	3.7
Other	30,000	3.3		30,000	2.8
Total Current Liabilities	280,000	31.1		280,000	26.0
Long-term Debt	100,000	11.1	(4,855) f	95,145	8.8
Other Liabilities	20,000	2.2		20,000	1.9
Contingent Liabilities	0	0.0	50,000 g	50,000	4.6
Total Liabilities	400,000	44.4	45,145	445,145	41.4
Stockholder's Equity:					
Common Stock	25,000	2.8			
Paid-In Capital	25,000	2.8			
Retained Earnings	525,000	58.3			
	575,000	63.9			
Less: Treasury Stock	(75,000)	(8.3)			
Total Stockholder's Equity	500,000	55.6	130,855 h	630,855	58.6
TOTAL LIABILITIES &					
STOCKHOLDER'S EQUITY	900,000	100.0	176,000	1,076,000	100.0

Note: Percentages may not total due to rounding.

Exhibit 7–3 (concluded)

a   The following accounts are believed to be uncollectible (see Exhibit 7-1).

A-1 Equipment	$20,000
I.K. Industries	12,000
Power Enterprises	8,000
Western Industries	30,000
	$70,000

b   Inventory needs to be adjusted to a FIFO basis as follows:

LIFO Reserve	$110,000

In addition, the inventory needs to be reduced by $5,000 for obsolete inventory.

c   200 shares of IBM common stock

200 shares of IBM common stock	200
(closing price 12/31/91)	$89
	$17,800

d   Adjustment to Furniture, Fixtures, and Equipment based on talks with dealers--approximate cost to replace used, including delivery.

e   Rent paid by Mary's is approximately $200 per month below fair market rent. Discount this amount at Mary's weighted cost of capital, computed as follows:

Balance sheet composition:	2/3 debt @ 7.5% after tax cost	=	5%
	1/3 equity @ 27% cost	=	9%
	Cost of Capital		16%

The lease has a five-year term. The present value of $200 discounted for 60 months at 16% annually is $8,200.

f $50,000 of the long-term debt is at current market interest rates. However, $50,000 is payable in 36 equal monthly installments (3 years), including interest at 6%, resulting in monthly payments of $1,521.10 per month. The current market rate for comparable debt financing is 13%. The present value of favorable financing is $45,144.51, or approximately $45,145.

g   Mary's is currently involved in a lawsuit for which the probable judgment against the company will amount to $50,000.

h   The net amount of adjustments a through g.

Exhibit 7–4

SUMMARY OF STEPS IN
ADJUSTING THE BALANCE SHEET

Step 1   Obtain a copy of the subject company's balance sheet as of or just before the valuation date.

Step 2   Adjust each of the company's assets from their stated book value to reflect appraised fair market values. Although not considered to be comprehensive, a list of potential adjustments to the company's assets as stated on the balance sheet includes the following:

- Adjust the cash and cash equivalents of the company to that required for normalized operations of the firm, eliminating any non-operating cash and cash equivalents or including an adjustment for any operating cash deficiency.
- Adjust the accounts receivable as shown on the balance sheet to eliminate any accounts considered uncollectible.
- Review the inventory as stated on the company's balance sheet. Ideally, adjust the inventory through a physical count and extend the inventory at current costs while eliminating any obsolete inventory. Otherwise, review the company's inventory accounting policy and write-off or write-down policy.
- Adjust components of the prepaid expense account if these items will not be necessary for the on-going operations of the company.
- Adjust other assets as listed on the balance sheet to reflect fair market values.
- Adjust real estate to appraised fair market value using a current appraisal.
- Adjust the furniture, fixtures, and equipment to their market values.
- Adjust any identifiable intangible assets to their appraised values.
- If appropriate, make any adjustments necessary to income taxes to reflect the adjustments made to the assets as stated on the balance sheet.

Step 3   Adjust each of the company's liabilities from their stated book value to reflect appraised fair market values. Although not considered to be comprehensive, a list of potential adjustments to the company's liabilities includes the following:

- Adjust any interest-bearing debt with favorable financing to reflect fair market value at current interest rates.
- Adjust the deferred taxes account to accurately reflect the likelihood and timing of income tax payments.

Step 4   Adjust the balance sheet to include any assets and liabilities of the company that are not stated on the balance sheet, such as contingent or off-balance sheet assets and liabilities.

Step 5   Compute the adjusted value of the equity by subtracting the liabilities stated at fair market value from the assets as stated at fair market value. If the company has preferred stock, the common equity should be reduced by the value of those securities.

Chapter 8

Adjusting the Income Statement

The objective of adjusting the income statement to a normalized basis is to make the best possible estimate of the true economic earning power of the entity in question. The first set of income statement adjustments is generally done on the assumption that the entity will continue to remain independent essentially in its present mode of operation. Adjustments under that assumption are the subject of this chapter.

> Normalization adjustments are unique to business valuation engagements. The purpose of normalization adjustments is to give the consultant insight into:
> a. What prior operations might have looked like under normal conditions (and on a consistent basis with comparable companies), or
> b. What a prospective buyer might reasonably be expected to obtain from the company in the future, using history as a guide.
> Normalization adjustments may be affected by the size of the ownership interest, type of entity, definition of value, and purpose of the valuation.[1]

If a particular buyer contemplates changes that will affect revenues and/or expenses, it is a good idea for him to prepare an income statement as he would expect it to look with the change implemented. We will call this a *pro forma* income statement, or a *buyer's* income statement, to distinguish it from an *adjusted* income statement. The *pro forma* or *buyer's* income statement is discussed in Chapter 11.

In this chapter we will assume that the adjustments are being made in order to assist in valuing a controlling interest. Differences in procedures that might be appropriate for valuing minority interests are discussed in Chapter 35.

Compensation to Owners

The item that most often begs adjustment on the income statements of a privately held entity is the compensation to the owners. Actual compensation tends to be based on what the entity can afford or how the owners desire to be compensated, and may bear little or no relationship to the economic value of the services actually performed by the owners.

The general idea of the compensation adjustment is to substitute for the compensation actually paid the cost of hiring a nonowner outsider to perform the same function. Another way to look at it is to substitute for actual compensation paid some average amount that other people are normally compensated for performing similar services. For example, if we are valuing a small restaurant whose owner is being paid $50,000 per year, and a competent, full-charge manager could be hired for $30,000 to perform the same services, the owner's compensation would be adjusted downward by $20,000 on the adjusted income statement, resulting in a $20,000 addition to pretax profit.

---

[1] Jay E. Fishman, Shannon P. Pratt, et al., *Guide to Business Valuations*, 2nd ed. (Fort Worth, Tex.: Practitioners Publishing Co., 1992), pp. 4–21.

Analyzing the Components of Compensation

The adjustment should reflect all components of compensation, many of which may be buried in various expense accounts. Expenses considered discretionary on the owner's part should normally be adjusted. Many types of expenses are perfectly legitimate from an income tax viewpoint that would not be considered essential by an owner whose objective was to maximize bottom-line profits.

All salary, bonuses, and direct payments to owners are part of the compensation. Payments into pension, profit sharing, or other retirement accounts for the benefit of the owners should also be included. In some cases, there are substantial life insurance premiums that should be included. However, when comparing to industry averages (as discussed in the next chapter), it may be necessary to exclude certain compensation components. For example, neither *Annual Statement Studies* nor the *Almanac of Business and Industrial Financial Ratios* includes either pension or life insurance payments in compensation.

Some of the most common expense items that may be considered discretionary are automobile expenses, travel and entertainment, and costs of maintaining boats, airplanes, various condominiums, and other residences. When analyzing compensation to owners, don't overlook the various kinfolk, in-laws, and outlaws who may be on the payroll or otherwise receiving benefit from the business.

Sources of Comparative Compensation Data

Employment agencies and executive recruiters are good sources of informal estimates of how much it would cost to fill a particular job. The large compensation consulting firms also maintain data on compensation levels for various positions in various locales. Many trade associations compile and publish data on compensation in their respective industries.

Three commonly used sources that provide average levels of compensation to owners in various business and professional classifications are the Robert Morris Associates' *Annual Statement Studies*, the *Almanac of Business and Industrial Financial Ratios*, and *Financial Studies of the Small Business*. These sources are discussed more fully, with sample pages of each, in Chapter 9. Additional sources of compensation data include *Source Book Statistics of Income* (Internal Revenue Service, Washington, D.C.), *Officer Compensation Report* (Panel Publishers, New York), and *Executive Compensation Survey Results* (National Institute of Business Management, New York).

Depreciation

Depreciation accounting policies differ greatly from one company to another. As noted in Chapter 5, large companies often account for depreciation in one way for tax purposes and in another way for financial reporting purposes; smaller businesses and professional practices tend to account for depreciation one way only: in whatever acceptable manner minimizes their income tax burdens. Exhibit 8–1 is a condensed primer on acceptable alternative depreciation methods currently in use.

Depreciation is a noncash charge against earnings; that is, the business makes no cash outlay at the time it charges the depreciation against earnings. (The cash outlay was made at the time the equipment was purchased.)

If the analyst wishes to normalize *net free cash flow*, the preferred approach is to add back all the depreciation to earnings, and then deduct a separate charge that is an estimate of the annual average cost to replace the equipment necessary to sustain the level of revenues that the income statement assumes.

Alternatively, if the object is to normalize net income, depreciation may be adjusted to an economically realistic life or to a basis typically used by comparable companies. (The latter procedure typically is appropriate if comparative company analysis is being used as a valuation approach.)

Cost of Goods Sold

For a merchandising or manufacturing business, the cost of goods is obviously a critical item. Like depreciation, it is an area where accounting practices differ significantly from one company to another. Moreover, cost of goods is an area where it is not uncommon to find accounting practices varying significantly from one year to another within the same company. It is desirable, if possible, to analyze statements for several years and to be able to explain any significant differences in the cost of goods sold as a percentage of sales from year to year, as well as any significant departures from the industry average.

Adjustment for Companies Using LIFO Accounting

For companies using LIFO for their inventories, both the beginning and ending inventories shown on the income statement should be converted to a FIFO basis to get a good approximation of the true economic cost of goods sold. This adjustment can be done by adding back the LIFO reserve provided in the footnotes to the financial statements, as follows:

		Add LIFO Reserve	FIFO Basis
Beginning Inventory	$100,000	$40,000	$140,000
Add: Purchases	300,000		300,000
Goods Available for Sale	$400,000		$440,000
Less: Ending Inventory	120,000	50,000	170,000
Cost of Goods Sold	$280,000		$270,000

Exhibit 8–1

ALTERNATIVE DEPRECIATION METHODS

Data used for the following examples:
Piece of equipment, purchased at beginning of Year 1
Cost of equipment $50,000
Estimated useful life   5 years

Year	Computation			Year's Depreciation Charge	Balance Accumulated Depreciation	Book Value Year-End

STRAIGHT-LINE METHOD

Year	Computation			Year's Depreciation Charge	Balance Accumulated Depreciation	Book Value Year-End
1	1/5 (20%)	x	$50,000	$10,000	$10,000	$40,000
2	20%	x	50,000	10,000	20,000	30,000
3	20%	x	50,000	10,000	30,000	20,000
4	20%	x	50,000	10,000	40,000	10,000
5	20%	x	50,000	10,000	50,000	0

200% DECLINING BALANCE METHOD

Year	Computation			Year's Depreciation Charge	Balance Accumulated Depreciation	Book Value Year-End
1	40%	x	$50,000 a	$20,000	$20,000	$30,000
2	40%	x	30,000	12,000	32,000	18,000
3	40%	x	18,000	7,200	39,200	10,800
4	40%	x	10,800	4,320	43,520	6,480
5	40%	x	6,480	2,592	46,112	3,888

a Based on double the straight-line rate of 20%, multiplied by the undepreciated book value.

SUM OF THE YEAR'S DIGITS METHOD

Year	Computation			Year's Depreciation Charge	Balance Accumulated Depreciation	Book Value Year-End
1	5/15	x	$50,000 b	$16,667	$16,667	$33,333
2	4/15	x	50,000	13,333	30,000	20,000
3	3/15	x	50,000	10,000	40,000	10,000
4	2/15	x	50,000	6,667	46,667	3,333
5	1/15	x	50,000	3,333	50,000	0

b Numerator is the remaining estimated useful life. Denominator is the sum of the years (5 + 4 + 3 + 2 + 1 = 15).

MODIFIED ACCELERATED COST RECOVERY SYSTEM

Year	Computation			Year's Depreciation Charge	Balance Accumulated Depreciation	Book Value Year-End
1	20.00%	x	$50,000 c	$10,000	$10,000	$40,000
2	32.00%	x	50,000	16,000	26,000	24,000
3	19.20%	x	50,000	9,600	35,600	14,400
4	11.52%	x	50,000	5,760	41,360	8,640
5	11.52%	x	50,000	5,760	47,120	2,880
6	5.76%	x	50,000	2,880	50,000	0

c Statutory percentages for MACRS five-year property used for tax purposes.

Note: The above are examples of the more popular depreciation methods now in use. Salvage value has not been considered in the examples. An introductory accounting text can be consulted for a thorough presentation of potential depreciation methods. The Modified Accelerated Cost Recovery System (MACRS) was enacted as part of the Economic Recovery Tax Act of 1986 and is used for federal tax purposes. One of the periodic tax guides can be consulted for a thorough presentation of the provisions of the MACRS.

On a LIFO basis, the cost of goods sold was $10,000 more than it was on a FIFO basis, so the LIFO basis would have resulted in $10,000 less pretax earnings than the FIFO basis. (See also the example of the widgets in Chapter 7, where LIFO accounting produced a cost of goods sold of $750, versus $600 by the FIFO method. In that example, if the sales were $1,000, the gross margin would be $400 under FIFO accounting and $250 under LIFO accounting.)

Unconventional but Not Uncommon Practices

When counting and pricing the inventory at the end of a particularly prosperous year, the owner(s) of a company may decide to take write-offs or markdowns on slow or questionable inventory, in order to avoid paying a higher amount of income tax. If the company counts and prices the inventory in a more optimistic manner in the following year, there will be a pickup in inventory on a comparative basis and a commensurate reduction in cost of goods sold, resulting in a dislocation of gross margin and pretax earnings. One way to recognize and adjust for such erratic practices is to analyze income statements for several years, discounting an abnormally high gross margin in some years, unless there is evidence that such a higher-than-average margin is sustainable in future years.

The notion that unconventional inventory accounting practices exist is reinforced by the following quote:

> Understating year-end inventory is a simple and relatively safe—though improper—means of reducing a profitable concern's taxes. When goods are sold, their cost is deducted from sales revenue to determine taxable profit. Falsely reducing inventory has the effect of falsely increasing that deduction because the hidden goods are presumed to have been sold. . . . Cheating is the little guy's LIFO. . . . The New York garment maker who hides $500,000 of inventory at tax time uses a different fiscal period for financial statements to his bank. After writing down the inventory as of December 31, he writes it up six months later when the financial statement year ends. In this way, he underpays the IRS and impresses his banker. Some describe that kind of inventory accounting as WIFL—Whatever I Feel Like.[2]

Occupancy Costs

Occupancy costs are the costs of occupying the premises, primarily rent and utilities. If the premises are owned, the occupancy costs shown on the statements would usually include depreciation, insurance, property taxes, building repairs, and interest on any mortgage balance outstanding, as well as utilities.

Rented or Leased Premises

If the premises are rented or leased, it should be determined whether rent or lease payments are on an arm's-length basis. If the premises are

---

[2]*The Wall Street Journal*, August 4, 1981, quoted in Philip L. Cooley, *How to Value an Oil Jobbership for Purchase or Sale* (Bethesda, Md.: Petroleum Marketing Education Foundation, 1982), pp. 3–16.

rented from the owner or his affiliates, kinfolk, or friends at something above or below a market rate of rent, an adjustment to a market rate should be made, unless the existing rate can be expected to prevail for a long period of time under a new, unrelated owner.

If a lease is about to expire, or if an existing month-to-month arrangement is tenuous, occupancy costs should be adjusted to the probable cost under a new lease or a new month-to-month arrangement. If the lessee is responsible for such variable items as taxes, common area maintenance, and/or insurance, the status and possible changes in those items should be investigated and adjusted as appropriate.

Owner-Occupied Premises

As noted elsewhere, and except for certain kinds of special-use or single-use properties, my preference is to treat valuation of the business occupying the premises separately from the valuation of the premises themselves. To separate the real estate value from the business value, described in Chapter 7, it is necessary to remove from the income statement (and in another manner from the balance sheet) all expenses associated with the property ownership and to substitute a market rate of rent for the premises occupied.

Nonrecurring Items

Since the objective of the adjustment is to get a normalized income estimate, it is necessary to adjust historical income statements for any items that would not be expected to recur in the future. Such items include a much broader spectrum than just those that would meet the narrow definition of extraordinary items under generally accepted accounting principles (GAAP). The following are a few examples of frequently encountered items that would call for an adjustment.

Business Interruptions

Business interruptions may occur for any of a wide variety of reasons, such as strikes, storm or fire damage to premises, lack of access to premises due to street repair, extended closure for remodeling, interruption in availability of critical supplies, illness of a key person or owner, withdrawal of bank financing, loss of lease, or many other occurrences of a temporary but significant nature.

When such items are identified, their effect should be removed from the historical income stream being used as a basis for estimating a normalized income stream. If the amount of the effect can be reliably estimated, the income figures for that period of time can be adjusted accordingly. If not, then the period during which the business interruption occurred can be omitted from the historical income statement data being used to derive a normalized statement.

Insurance Proceeds

A business may receive proceeds from life insurance on a key person, or from some type of property and casualty claim. The amount of such proceeds can be based on any of a number of factors, and the amount is not likely to be an exact offset to the amount of current earnings lost during the accounting period in which the proceeds are received. Consequently, such proceeds are usually removed from the normalized earnings stream calculations.

Lawsuit Settlements

Sometimes, companies have substantial payments or receipts as a result of lawsuits, which can arise from a wide variety of circumstances, such as property and casualty losses, breach of contract, patent or copyright infringement, product liability, antitrust actions, income or property tax disputes, and many other situations. Usually, the amount of the settlements paid or received are taken out for a normalized earnings calculation.

Gains or Losses on Disposal of Assets

Gains or losses on the sale of assets should be adjusted out of the normalized income stream to the extent that they are nonrecurring in nature. If a company sells its only building or airplane, the gain or loss should be removed from computation of normalized earnings. On the other hand, if a construction company, for example, has $20,000 to $50,000 in gains from disposal of equipment almost every year, that would be recurring in nature. Be careful, however, not to "double count" earnings by adding back depreciation in excess of the actual economic decrement in value, but at the same time leaving in the earnings stream the gain on the depreciated asset that was sold.

Discontinued Operations

If a company had earnings or losses in the past from operations that were discontinued, and consequently are not relevant to the company's expected future earning power, such earnings or losses should be adjusted out when computing a normalized earnings stream.

Payments on Employment Contracts and Covenants Not to Compete

It is common to find included in expenses on the income statement payments to a former owner arising from an employment contract and/or a covenant not to compete. An analysis should be made of the extent to which such payments were actually for services rendered to the company during the accounting periods in which they were paid. If not for services rendered, and if a new buyer is to assume such payments, the value of such future payments should be deducted from the value of the business as otherwise determined.

Abnormal Market Conditions

From time to time, businesses experience abnormally high or low profits (or losses) due to abnormal market conditions. For example, some service stations made unprecedented profits because of the very high gross margins they were able to achieve during periods of gasoline shortages. Some stations were sold at prices that were very high by historical standards, apparently to buyers who thought the high margins and lack of price competition at the retail level were here to stay. Buyers who paid high prices on the basis of that assumption never realized a good return on their investments, and many went broke because they couldn't service the debt they had incurred in the purchases.

During the early 1980s, when interest rates were high and automobile production and sales were low, many automobile dealerships sold at very low prices compared to prices for dealerships before and after that period. Those who bought dealerships during that period made handsome returns on their investments in the years not far ahead.

Some industries, such as sawmills, for example, are cyclical by nature and seem to have abnormally good or bad years from time to time; but for some companies, such so-called abnormalities keep recurring over the years. In cyclical industries, statements for several years should be examined to try to normalize the especially good and bad years.

The problem, of course, if we are trying to estimate normalized earnings, is to identify what part of the historical record is abnormal. People tend to extrapolate future expectations on the basis of the most recent past, a practice that can be very misleading. Some informed and dispassionate judgment about the economy and the industry and its prospects should be brought to bear on the question of what adjustments, if any, should be made to the historical income statements for abnormal market conditions.

Unrecognized Costs

Sometimes actual or potential expenses have not been recognized on the income statement. If any such items exist, the statements should be adjusted to reflect them. The following are a few examples of such items that are frequently encountered.

Accrued Expenses

Sometimes companies do not recognize incurred costs as expenses. In the previous chapter, for example, I mentioned an occasion when salesmen's commissions, payable when the accounts were collected, were not recorded as expenses, even though the revenues were recorded when the sale was made. This oversight resulted in an overstatement of income, since the unrecorded commissions were really a cost of generating the revenue.

Sometimes invoices for purchases may not come in, or may not be recorded, until after the end of the accounting period, even though the merchandise was received and counted in the ending inventory. This lack of cost recognition would result in an understatement of cost of goods and an overstatement of profit.

The objective of accrual accounting is to match expenses with the associated revenues. Whenever revenues are recognized on the income statement, it is also important to recognize the expense associated with those revenues, and vice versa.

Bad Debts

Most companies and professionals who sell goods or services on credit have some accounts that don't get collected. Recommended accrual accounting practices call for recognizing some bad debt expense on the income statement at the time the revenues are recorded (and an allowance for doubtful accounts as a deduction from accounts receivable on the balance sheet) or sales (on the income statement) when the specific accounts are determined to be uncollectible.

Generally speaking, the appropriate amount of bad debt expense to be charged against revenues at the time the revenues are recognized can be determined by examining the company's historical amount of uncollectible accounts as a percentage of revenues. To the extent that the bad debt expense actually recorded for a period differs significantly from the company's historical bad debt experience, an adjustment to that expense item is indicated.

Insurable Liabilities

Most companies exposed to product liabilities take out insurance to protect themselves against product liability claims. Sometimes, insurance for officers and directors is appropriate. Similarly, most professional practitioners have some type of errors and omissions and/or malpractice liability insurance. If a company or professional with such exposure lacks appropriate liability insurance, an additional expense in the amount of the premiums for the insurance that the company or practice "should" have is an appropriate adjustment.

Imminent Changes

When normalizing the income statement, adjustment should be made to revenues and expenses for changes that are close at hand and predictable from the information available. For example, if the company has lost, or is about to lose, a major customer, with no replacement in sight, an adjustment to revenues would seem appropriate.

Nonoperating Income and Expenses

When the business or practice has nonoperating items of income and/or expense, they should usually be removed when creating a normalized income statement. For example, if a company owns some property from which it is deriving income unrelated to the basic business or practice, such nonoperating income and any expenses (including the tax effects) associated with it should not be included in the normalized income statement. Then the entity can be valued on an operating basis, and the assets not part of the basic operations can be dealt with separately if they are to be a part of the total package being valued. Another common income-producing nonoperating asset would be a portfolio of marketable securities. Nonoperating assets that often have associated nonoperating costs include boats, airplanes, and recreational properties.

Adjusting for Taxes, if Necessary

If it is desired to obtain an after-tax rather than a pretax earnings figure, each adjustment to pretax earnings must also be accompanied by an adjustment for the applicable income taxes. If the entity is incorporated, the appropriate rate to use is the corporation's marginal tax rate, that is, the tax rate applicable to its last dollar of taxable income. State and local income taxes should be included, when applicable, as well as federal income taxes.

If the entity is a sole proprietorship, a partnership, or an S corporation, the normalized income statement usually stops at pretax income, because each different owner may be subject to a different tax rate. If an estimated after-tax figure is desired, then one way to do it is to find out, or make an assumption about, the owner's tax bracket and use the owner's marginal tax rate. Another method is to use what the corporate tax rate would be if it were a corporation, since incorporation is almost always an available option.

Examples of Adjusted Income Statements

The accompanying examples illustrate the procedures discussed in this chapter. The two examples carry on with the same two hypothetical companies used in the previous chapter.

Sole Proprietorship Example

Exhibit 8–2 is an adjusted income statement for Annie's Apparel Store, a sole proprietorship, which her appraiser prepared when she was ready to sell her business.

Exhibit 8–2

ANNIE'S APPAREL STORE
ADJUSTED INCOME STATEMENT
FOR THE YEAR ENDED DECEMBER 31, 1991

	Income Statement as Reported		Adjustments	Adjusted Income Statement	
	$	%	$	$	%
Sales	1,000,000	100.0		1,000,000	100.0
Cost of Goods Sold:					
Beginning Inventory	170,000		15,000 a	185,000	
Plus: Purchases	570,000			570,000	
	740,000			755,000	
Less: Ending Inventory	180,000		40,000 b	220,000	
Cost of Goods Sold	560,000	56.0		535,000	53.5
Gross Margin	440,000	44.0		465,000	46.5
Expenses:					
Owner's Salary	70,000	7.0	(20,000) c	50,000	5.0
Other Salaries	150,000	15.0		150,000	15.0
Payroll Taxes	30,000	3.0		30,000	3.0
Employee Benefits	23,000	2.3		23,000	2.3
Rent	65,000	6.5		65,000	6.5
Utilities	3,000	0.3		3,000	0.3
Telephone	3,000	0.3		3,000	0.3
Insurance	0	0.0	2,000 d	2,000	0.2
Supplies	5,000	0.5		5,000	0.5
Advertising	25,000	2.5		25,000	2.5
Travel & Entertainment	25,000	2.5	(20,000) e	5,000	0.5
Automobile Expense	5,000	0.5		5,000	0.5
Outside Accountants	5,000	0.5		5,000	0.5
Legal	3,000	0.3		3,000	0.3
License, Registrations, etc.	2,000	0.2		2,000	0.2
Dues & Subscriptions	1,000	0.1		1,000	0.1
Allow. for Doubtful Accts.	0	0.0	2,400 f	2,400	0.2
Depreciation	13,000	1.3		13,000	1.3
Interest	7,000	0.7		7,000	0.7
Total Expenses	435,000	43.5	(35,600) g	399,400	39.9
Pretax Income	5,000	0.5		65,600	6.6

a In order to arrive at a realistic cost of goods sold, we have adjusted the beginning inventory to Annie's best estimate of what it would have been at the then–current market price.

b From inventory adjustment made in Exhibit 7-2.

c According to Robert Morris Associates' *Annual Statement Studies,* 1991 edition, the median officer's compensation/sales ratio for companies with assets of less than $2 million was 4.0%, or approximately $40,000 for a store the size of Annie's. Since Annie is such an excellent operator, we felt $50,000 compensation is reasonable.

d Annie's should carry fire, casualty, and liability insurance at a cost of approximately $2,000 per year.

e Annie has had an above–average amount of travel and entertainment expenses through her business in an amount of approximately $20,000. In fact, a retail store the size of Annie's might not incur even $5,000 in travel and entertainment expense.

f About 24%, or $240,000, of Annie's sales are made on credit. Historically about 1%, or $2,400, has been uncollectible.

g Summary of adjustments a through f.

Corporation Example

Exhibit 8–3 shows the income statements as reported for Mary's Machinery & Equipment, Inc., for the years ended December 31, 1987 through 1991. Exhibit 8–4 shows the adjusted income statements for Mary's over the same time period. Both the reported and adjusted statements were prepared by Mary's appraisers; the adjusted statements were prepared in connection with the sale of the business.

Summary

This chapter discussed the most common income and expense account adjustments that business appraisers frequently make to bring the income statement accounts close to a presentation of economic reality on a going-concern basis. These are the most commonly needed adjustments, but many others are called for in certain instances.

Exhibit 8–5 summarizes the steps in adjusting the income statement. In some cases, income statement adjustments beget related balance sheet adjustments. However, many do not. The adjusted balance sheet must show what is there, not what might have been there but for extravagant expenditures.

Finally, we caution the analyst to carefully explain and justify each adjustment and to be cautious not to overreach in making income statement adjustments.

Exhibit 8–3

MARY'S MACHINERY & EQUIPMENT, INC.
INCOME STATEMENTS

(000s, except Per–Share Data)

	1991		1990		1989		1988		1987	
	$	%	$	%	$	%	$	%	$	%
Sales	2,400	100.0	2000	100.0	2,200	100.0	2,400	100.0	2,200	100.0
Cost of Goods Sold:										
Beginning Inventory	300		320		340		320		320	
Plus: Purchases	1,620		1,380		1,480		1,610		1,450	
	1,920		1,700		1,820		1,930		1,770	
Less: Ending Inventory	320		300		320		340		320	
Cost of Goods Sold	1,600	66.7	1,400	70.0	1,500	68.2	1,590	66.2	1,450	65.9
Gross Margin	800	33.3	600	30.0	700	31.8	810	33.8	750	34.1
Operating Expenses:										
Officers' Compensation	120	5.0	100	5.0	110	5.0	120	5.0	110	5.0
Salaries & Wages	230	9.6	210	10.5	220	10.0	230	9.6	220	10.0
Employee Benefits	50	2.1	45	2.3	45	2.0	50	2.1	45	2.0
Payroll Taxes	50	2.1	40	2.0	45	2.0	50	2.1	45	2.0
Rent	24	1.0	24	1.2	24	1.1	24	1.0	24	1.1
Depreciation	33	1.4	35	1.8	37	1.7	39	1.6	41	1.9
Insurance	20	0.8	20	1.0	20	0.9	20	0.8	20	0.9
Travel & Entertainment	30	1.3	25	1.3	25	1.1	30	1.3	25	1.1
Policy Adjustments	26	1.1	32	1.6	30	1.4	24	1.0	35	1.6
Transportation Vehicles	24	1.0	28	1.4	30	1.4	26	1.1	25	1.1
Prov. for Bad Debt	13	0.5	21	1.1	15	0.7	13	0.5	10	0.5
Other	90	3.8	100	5.0	95	4.3	92	3.8	100	4.5
Total Oper. Expenses	710	29.7	680	34.2	696	31.6	718	29.9	700	31.7
Operating Income	90	3.6	(80)	(4.2)	4	0.2	92	3.9	50	2.4
Other Income (Expense):										
Interest Expense	(15)	(0.6)	(18)	(0.9)	(20)	(0.9)	(18)	(0.8)	(18)	(0.8)
Dividend Income	1	Nil	1	Nil	1	Nil	1	Nil	1	Nil
Gain (Loss) on Sale of Assets	–	–	10	0.5	–	–	–	–	–	–
Fire Damage	–	–	–	–	(15)	(0.7)	–	–	–	–
Discont. Operations	–	–	–	–	–	–	(10)	(0.4)	20	0.9
Total Other Income (Exp.)	(14)	(0.6)	(7)	(0.4)	(34)	(1.6)	(27)	(1.2)	3	0.1
Income Before Taxes	76	3.0	(87)	(4.6)	(30)	(1.4)	65	2.7	53	2.5
Income Taxes	16	0.7	–	–	–	–	14	0.6	10	0.5
Net Income	60	2.3	(87)	(4.6)	(30)	(1.4)	51	2.1	43	2.0
Average No. Shares Outstanding	200		200		250		250		250	
Earnings Per Share	$300		($435)		($120)		$204		$172	
Dividends Per Share	$50		–		–		$50		$50	
Effective Tax Rate	21.2%		–		–		21.2%		19.1%	

NOTE: Figures may not total due to rounding.

Nil = Inconsequential amount, greater (or less) than zero.

SOURCE: Company financial statements.

Exhibit 8–4

MARY'S MACHINERY & EQUIPMENT, INC.
ADJUSTED INCOME STATEMENTS
(000s, except per–share data)

	1991		1990		1989		1988		1987	
	$	%	$	%	$	%	$	%	$	%
Sales	2,400	100.0	2000	100.0	2,200	100.0	2,400	100.0	2,200	100.0
Cost of Goods Sold:										
Beginning Inventory	400 a		430 a		460 a		425 a		420 a	
Plus: Purchases	1,620		1,380		1,480		1,610		1,450	
	2,020		1,810		1,940		2,035		1,870	
Less: Ending Inventory	430 a		400 a		430 a		460 a		425 a	
Cost of Goods Sold	1,590	66.2	1,410	70.5	1,510	68.6	1,575	65.6	1,445	65.7
Gross Margin	810	33.8	590	29.5	690	31.4	825	34.4	755	34.3
Operating Expenses:										
Officers' Compensation	120	5.0	100	5.0	110	5.0	120	5.0	110	5.0
Salaries & Wages	230	9.6	210	10.5	220	10.0	230	9.6	220	10.0
Employee Benefits	50	2.1	45	2.3	45	2.0	50	2.1	45	2.0
Payroll Taxes	50	2.1	40	2.0	45	2.0	50	2.1	45	2.0
Rent	24	1.0	24	1.2	24	1.1	24	1.0	24	1.1
Depreciation	33	1.4	35	1.8	37	1.7	39	1.6	41	1.9
Insurance	20	0.8	20	1.0	20	0.9	20	0.8	20	0.9
Travel & Entertainment	30	1.3	25	1.3	25	1.1	30	1.3	25	1.1
Policy Adjustments	26	1.1	32	1.6	30	1.4	24	1.0	35	1.6
Transportation Vehicles	24	1.0	28	1.4	30	1.4	26	1.1	25	1.1
Prov. for Bad Debt	13	0.5	21	1.1	15	0.7	13	0.5	10	0.5
Other	90	3.8	100	5.0	95	4.3	92	3.8	100	4.5
Total Oper. Expenses	710	29.7	680	34.2	696	31.6	718	29.9	700	31.7
Operating Income	100	4.1	(90)	(4.7)	(6)	(0.2)	107	4.5	55	2.6
Other Income (Expense):										
Interest Expense	(15)	(0.6)	(18)	(0.9)	(20)	(0.9)	(18)	(0.8)	(18)	(0.8)
Dividend Income	1	Nil	1	Nil	1	Nil	1	Nil	1	Nil
Gain (Loss) on Sale										
of Assets	0	0.0	0	0.0 b	0	0.0	0	0.0	0	0.0
Fire Damage	0	0.0	0	0.0	0 c	0.0	0	0.0	0	0.0
Discont. Operations	0	0.0	0	0.0	0	0.0	0 d	0.0	0 d	0.0
Total Other Income (Exp.)	(14)	(0.6)	(17)	(0.9)	(19)	(0.9)	(17)	(0.8)	(17)	(0.8)
Income Before Taxes	86	3.5	(107)	(5.6)	(25)	(1.1)	90	3.7	38	1.8
Income Taxes	20	0.8	0	0.0	0	0	23	1.0	7	0.3
Net Income	66	2.7	(107)	(5.6)	(25)	(1.1)	67	2.7	31	1.5
Average No. Shares										
Outstanding	200		200		250		250		250	
Earnings Per Share	$330		($535)		($100)		$268		$124	
Dividends Per Share	$50		$0		$0		$50		$50	
Effective Tax Rate	23.3%		0.0%		0.0%		25.6%		18.4%	

NOTE: Figures may not total due to rounding.

Nil = Inconsequential amount, greater (or less) than zero.

a

	As of December 31:					
	1991	1990	1989	1988	1987	1986
	(in 000s)					
Inventory as Stated	$320	$300	$320	$340	$320	$320
Add: LIFO Reserve	110	100	110	120	105	100
Adjusted Inventory	430	400	430	460	425	420

b   The $10,000 gain was from the sale of the company's condominium. Since that was a nonrecurrring item, the gain was eliminated in the adjusted income statement.

c   The $45,000 loss was from a fire in the warehouse in 1989. That represented the amount of the loss not recovered from insurance proceeds. Since it was a nonrecurring item, it needed to be eliminated from the adjusted income statement.

d   Mary's discontinued a retail parts store in 1988. Since we are interested only in Mary's current earning power, those gains were eliminated from the adjusted income statement.

Exhibit 8–5

SUMMARY OF STEPS IN
ADJUSTING THE INCOME STATEMENT

Step 1   Obtain copies of the subject company's income statements for the five-year period preceding the valuation date, or for whatever period is considered relevant to the valuation assignment.

Step 2   Adjust the company's historical income statements to a normalized basis to determine the true economic earning power of the company. Although not intended to be comprehensive, a list of potential adjustments to expenses on the company's income statements include the following:

- Adjust total owner compensation (including salary, bonuses, and profit sharing payments) to reflect the cost of hiring a nonowner employee to perform the same function.
- Adjust depreciation to reflect an economically realistic life or to a basis typically used by comparable companies.
- For companies using LIFO inventory accounting, both the beginning and ending inventories shown on the income statement should be converted to a FIFO basis to get a good approximation of the true economic cost of goods sold.
- Adjust rent expense to reflect the rent expense resulting from an arm's length lease. If the lease is about to expire, adjust occupancy costs to the probable cost under a new lease.

Step 3   Adjust the income statement to exclude any items that are not expected to recur in the future. These nonrecurring items could include the following:

- Eliminate the effect of any business interruptions that are unexpected in the future, such as strikes, fire damage, illness of a key person, etc.
- Adjust the income statement to exclude any insurance proceeds, such as proceeds from life insurance on a key person or a property and casualty claim.
- Eliminate the amount of any lawsuit settlement payments paid or received from the company's income statements.
- To the extent that they are nonrecurring, adjust any gains or losses from the sale of assets out of the historical income stream of the company.
- Eliminate earnings or losses from discontinued operations of the company from the historical income statements.
- Adjust the historical income stream to eliminate abnormally high or low profits or losses due to abnormal market conditions that are considered nonrecurring.

Step 4   Adjust the income statements to include any actual or potential expenses that have not been recognized on the income statements. These expenses may include the following:

- Include any accrued expenses that have not been reflected in the latest income statement.
- Adjust the bad debt expense to reflect the bad debt that was actually recorded if it significantly differs from the company's historical bad debt experience.

Step 5   Adjust the latest income statement prior to the valuation date to reflect any imminent changes in business, such as the expected loss of a major customer.

Step 6   Adjust the historical income statement to eliminate any nonoperating income and expenses.

Step 7   Adjust the income statements for applicable income taxes.

Chapter 9

Comparisons with Industry Averages

One of the benefits of having normalized the balance sheet and income statement is that it makes it possible to make valid comparisons between the entity being valued and others in the same business or profession. While comparison with peers is not an essential step in the valuation process, it can be helpful in several ways, especially for businesses and professional practices for which a good body of comparative data is available. However, care must be exercised in this process to be sure that comparison of income statement and balance sheet items is conducted under like accounting treatment and ratio definitions.

Advantages of Comparative Analysis

Comparative analysis provides some insight into how the entity in which we are interested compares with its peers. This information is especially useful, of course, for those who do not have a great deal of financial experience with the business or profession in question, even though they may have considerable experience with it from other viewpoints. Even the veteran buyer, however, will sharpen his perspective on the entity at hand by going through a comparative analysis exercise.

Identifying Errors

Comparative analysis makes it eminently apparent when the subject entity in some respect differs markedly from industry averages. This disparity could cause the appraiser to recheck balance sheet and/or income statement data for possible errors. In some cases, the appraiser may seek the company accountant's explanation when wide divergences from industry averages appear.

Identifying Strengths and Weaknesses

Comparative analysis points up the relative strengths and weaknesses of the subject entity compared to its peers, from both a balance sheet and an income statement point of view. It shows where the company shines compared with its peers, and what financial items need to be improved and by how much in order to bring it into line with industry averages.

Identifying Opportunities

Comparative analysis can point out opportunities that become apparent from studying balance sheets, income statements, and ratios that use the two statements together.

For example, if a company has little or no debt compared with others in its line of business, its assets might be used as collateral for borrowing to help finance the purchase. That is the basic concept of the *leveraged buyout*, or using debt financing, supported by the company's assets, to pay a significant portion of the purchase price. If the bottom-line profits fall below industry averages after appropriate income statement adjustments, this suggests room for improvement. The income statement comparisons may reveal specific categories of costs that might be reduced to improve profitability. If a retailer's gross margin is below the industry average, profits might be improved considerably by bringing the margin up to, or better than, standard. If the salary costs for a service business are out of line, it suggests that there should be room to generate the same revenue with less labor cost or to generate more revenue with the existing amount of labor.

Ratios that utilize both the balance sheet and the income statement include, for example, accounts receivable turnover (average collection period) and inventory turnover (average length of time merchandise is held in inventory). Improvements in these ratios would mean a reduction in working capital requirements, thus reducing interest costs if the company is borrowing money to finance receivables and inventory.

Sources of Comparative Industry Data

Sources of comparative industry data can be classified into two broad groups: (1) general sources that provide data for a wide variety of businesses and professional practices; (2) specialized sources that provide data on some specific category of businesses or professional practices.

General Sources

Three of the most widely used general sources for comparative financial data for small businesses are RMA *Annual Statement Studies*, the *Almanac of Business and Industrial Financial Ratios*, and *Financial Studies of the Small Business*. Each is published annually. The degree of usefulness of the data varies considerably from one type of business to another, depending largely on how many reasonably homogeneous businesses the publications are able to collect data for in each category.

RMA *Annual Statement Studies.* Probably the most popular source is the RMA *Annual Statement Studies*, which is a product of a national association of bank loan and credit officers. The 1991 edition was based on financial statements of over 95,000 businesses and professional practices submitted by member banks. One reason for the broad appeal of the *Annual Statement Studies* is the over 350 different industries it covers. *Annual Statement Studies* is also available in computerized form from several sources.

Exhibit 9–1 is a typical page from RMA *Annual Statement Studies*, in this case retailers of women's ready-to-wear. Note that each industry group is broken down into six size categories, based on total assets. (No figures are shown for the two largest size categories in this particular industry group because RMA considers that fewer than 10 financial statements in a particular size category is too small a sample to be considered representative and could be misleading.) Also, data are shown in the aggregate for five years, so that year-to-year comparisons can be made.

Exhibit 9–1

RETAILERS - WOMEN'S READY-TO-WEAR SIC# 5621

Current Data Sorted By Assets						Type of Statement	Comparative Historical Data	
2	3	13	4	2	3	Unqualified	63	39
2		1	2			Qualified	4	1
21	23	10	2	1		Reviewed	94	91
83	26	6				Compiled	141	142
5						Tax Returns		
18	21	5	2	2	1	Other	63	41
	102(4/1-9/30/90)		156(10/1/90-3/31/91)				6/30/86-3/31/87	6/30/87-3/31/88
0-500M	500M-2MM	2-10MM	10-50MM	50-100MM	100-250MM		ALL	ALL
131	73	35	10	5	4	NUMBER OF STATEMENTS	365	314
%	%	%	%	%	%	**ASSETS**	%	%
8.8	9.8	10.0	12.7			Cash & Equivalents	10.9	10.2
10.7	13.9	13.5	9.4			Trade Receivables - (net)	12.9	13.3
55.8	50.2	43.5	36.6			Inventory	50.4	49.9
1.6	.7	2.5	3.1			All Other Current	1.3	1.1
76.8	74.7	69.5	61.8			Total Current	75.5	74.5
16.2	19.4	23.7	29.6			Fixed Assets (net)	17.7	18.4
1.5	1.6	1.7	3.3			Intangibles (net)	.8	1.2
5.5	4.3	5.1	5.3			All Other Non-Current	5.9	5.8
100.0	100.0	100.0	100.0			Total	100.0	100.0
						LIABILITIES		
16.5	9.4	11.5	20.7			Notes Payable-Short Term	10.9	12.4
4.3	3.4	3.2	1.7			Cur. Mat.-L/T/D	3.3	3.4
11.4	16.9	20.0	18.1			Trade Payables	18.2	17.2
.6	.4	.2	.2			Income Taxes Payable	1.0	1.0
10.4	7.7	8.8	14.6			All Other Current	8.2	7.7
43.2	37.8	43.7	55.3			Total Current	41.6	41.7
13.2	12.5	13.9	10.1			Long Term Debt	11.6	13.4
.2	.2	.2	.5			Deferred Taxes	.5	.4
2.2	3.9	3.1	3.2			All Other Non-Current	3.1	1.6
41.1	45.5	39.1	30.8			Net Worth	43.2	42.8
100.0	100.0	100.0	100.0			Total Liabilities & Net Worth	100.0	100.0
						INCOME DATA		
100.0	100.0	100.0	100.0			Net Sales	100.0	100.0
40.4	43.0	40.8	29.9			Gross Profit	40.7	39.5
37.5	41.8	39.6	29.6			Operating Expenses	37.8	37.3
2.9	1.2	1.2	.4			Operating Profit	2.9	2.2
1.3	.8	1.1	1.7			All Other Expenses (net)	.4	.4
1.6	.4	.1	−1.4			Profit Before Taxes	2.5	1.8
						RATIOS		
3.2	2.8	2.4	2.2				2.8	2.7
2.1	2.0	1.6	1.3			Current	2.0	1.9
1.4	1.5	1.1	.7				1.3	1.3
1.0	1.2	.8	1.2				1.1	1.0
(130) .4	.6	.5	.3			Quick	(364) .5	(311) .5
.2	.2	.3	.1				.2	.3
1 390.0	1 276.4	1 363.9	0 905.5				1 285.3	2 234.2
6 59.5	12 29.6	5 69.1	1 262.2			Sales/Receivables	9 41.0	11 33.8
22 16.6	38 9.5	26 14.1	6 60.4				31 11.7	34 10.7
78 4.7	74 4.9	64 6.8	38 9.6				74 4.9	73 5.0
114 3.2	122 3.0	74 4.9	86 4.3			Cost of Sales/Inventory	104 3.5	107 3.4
169 2.3	174 2.1	135 2.7	114 3.2				146 2.5	152 2.4
6 72.2	21 17.5	28 12.9	13 28.3				22 16.7	19 19.5
20 18.7	37 9.8	41 9.0	37 10.0			Cost of Sales/Payables	37 9.9	34 10.6
38 9.5	54 6.8	64 6.8	62 5.9				56 6.6	51 7.1
4.6	4.8	8.2	7.4				4.9	4.9
9.2	7.2	14.7	15.5			Sales/Working Capital	8.0	8.4
18.3	15.0	34.9	−21.3				17.3	18.6
5.9	3.6	4.0					7.7	5.8
(116) 2.4	(68) 2.0	(32) 1.3				EBIT/Interest	(298) 2.7	(261) 2.4
−.5	.0	−.3					1.1	.7
2.7	2.4	2.0				Net Profit + Depr., Dep.,	6.4	4.0
(34) .6	(35) .5	(18) 1.1				Amort./Cur. Mat. L/T/D	(157) 2.1	(132) 1.6
−1.4	−.6	.3					.8	.7
.1	.2	.3	.4				.2	.1
.3	.4	.6	.6			Fixed/Worth	.4	.4
1.1	.6	1.7	−9.4				.7	.9
.6	.6	.9	1.3				.6	.7
1.5	1.4	1.6	2.0			Debt/Worth	1.2	1.3
4.1	2.6	3.9	−16.0				2.6	2.7
38.5	16.4	18.6				% Profit Before Taxes/Tangible	34.5	29.0
(115) 12.2	(71) 7.4	(33) 6.1				Net Worth	(343) 15.4	(297) 11.3
−3.8	−8.5	−10.6					2.2	.7
12.9	7.4	7.8	10.6			% Profit Before Taxes/Total	14.5	11.4
4.4	3.7	1.7	−1.7			Assets	5.9	4.4
−7.1	−4.5	−3.7	−24.2				.7	−.0
85.4	29.5	25.9	32.4				47.5	47.3
28.1	18.6	16.3	13.4			Sales/Net Fixed Assets	19.6	20.5
13.1	10.2	8.9	3.8				10.8	9.5
4.0	3.5	4.5	3.3				3.7	3.5
3.0	2.6	3.4	2.4			Sales/Total Assets	2.8	2.7
2.2	1.9	2.0	1.7				2.2	2.1
.6	.7	.8					.9	.9
(105) 1.0	(67) 1.3	(32) 1.5				% Depr., Dep., Amort./Sales	(306) 1.5	(261) 1.5
1.8	1.7	2.6					2.2	2.1
3.8	2.4	1.1				% Officers', Directors',	2.8	2.5
(61) 6.7	(33) 4.0	(14) 2.6				Owners' Comp/Sales	(149) 4.4	(129) 4.2
9.6	8.7	4.7					7.1	7.3
62434M	214265M	554249M	367230M	1026332M	1014809M	Net Sales ($)	3517516M	2871584M
27442M	71169M	164314M	152896M	381073M	510069M	Total Assets ($)	1415222M	1072340M

©Robert Morris Associates 1991

M = $thousand   MM = $million
See Pages 1 through 15 for Explanation of Ratios and Data

SOURCE: *RMA Annual Statement Studies*, 1991, p. 482. Reprinted with permission from Robert Morris Associates. RMA cautions that the studies be regarded only as a general guideline and not as an absolute industry norm. This is due to limited samples within categories, the categorization of companies by their primary Standard Industrial Classification (SIC) number only, and different methods of operations by companies within the same industry. For these reasons, RMA recommends that the figures be used only as general guidelines in addition to other methods of financial analysis.

Each of the ratios presented is defined in a section several pages long at the beginning of each RMA annual volume. Note that "all ratios computed by RMA are based on year-end statement data only." For example, the cost of sales/inventory (inventory turnover ratio) is computed by dividing the cost of goods sold for the year by the ending inventory. A truer picture of inventory would be derived by dividing cost of goods sold by average inventory, but the data on which the RMA ratios are based are not sufficient to make that computation.

Almanac of Business and Industrial Financial Ratios. The source of all data used in the *Almanac* is the data compiled from corporate tax returns by the U.S. Treasury, Internal Revenue Service. It is broken down into 181 fields of business and industry, about half the number offered by RMA.

Exhibit 9–2 is a typical data presentation from the *Almanac*, in this case apparel and accessory stores. Each industry group is presented in two tables. One table includes corporations that reported a profit as well as those that did not; the second table includes only those that reported a profit.

Each group for which there are sufficient data is broken down into 12 asset size categories, compared with six in the RMA data. The *Almanac* gives more income statement line items than does RMA, while RMA gives more balance sheet line items and more ratios.

The various ratios used are defined in the front part of the *Almanac*. Computations of some of the ratios differ from computations used by RMA.

The biggest drawback to the *Almanac* is the degree to which the information is outdated. The 1992 edition covers tax returns for fiscal years ended July 1988 through June 1989, the most recent year for which authoritative figures derived from tax return data of the Internal Revenue Service are available. Nevertheless, operating figures for most industries have at least some degree of stability over time, and the *Almanac* offers some income statement items not found elsewhere.

Financial Studies of the Small Business. The *Financial Studies of the Small Business*, published by Financial Research Associates (FRA), is a compilation from over 30,000 financial statements submitted by over 1,500 independent certified public accountant firms, from all across the country. Slightly less than 70 small business and professional services categories are included.

Exhibit 9–3 is a typical data presentation from *Financial Studies*, in this case, retail apparel stores with total assets of $100,000 to $250,000. *Financial Studies* differs particularly from *Annual Statement Studies* and the *Almanac* in that it focuses on especially small firms. Within each business or professional services group for which sufficient data are available, four size breakdowns are presented by total assets: $10,000 to $100,000; $100,000 to $250,000; $250,000 to $500,000; and $500,000 to $1,000,000. In addition, an overall presentation from $10,000 to $1,000,000 follows the individual breakdown. If any one breakdown did not contain 10 or more firms, the data were omitted.

Exhibit 9–2

TABLE I: CORPORATIONS WITH AND WITHOUT NET INCOME, 1992 EDITION

5600 RETAIL TRADE:

APPAREL AND ACCESSORY STORES

Item Description For Accounting Period 7/88 Through 6/89	A Total	B Zero Assets	SIZE OF ASSETS IN THOUSANDS OF DOLLARS (000 OMITTED)										
			C Under 100	D 100 to 250	E 251 to 500	F 501 to 1,000	G 1,001 to 5,000	H 5,001 to 10,000	I 10,001 to 25,000	J 25,001 to 50,000	K 50,001 to 100,000	L 100,001 to 250,000	M 250,001 and over
1. Number of Enterprises	48723	3658	21200	14278	4089	3077	1927	265	121	39	27	24	18
2. Total receipts (in millions of dollars)	77812	1593	3685	5887	2809	5693	8723	4808	3871	2951	3990	5416	28387
Selected Operating Factors in Percent of Net Sales													
3. Cost of operations	59.5	56.2	57.4	61.1	60.8	62.4	62.1	57.8	57.5	58.7	57.5	59.1	59.1
4. Compensation of officers	2.1	3.6	5.6	3.8	5.7	3.9	3.3	2.6	2.5	1.0	0.8	1.1	0.4
5. Repairs	0.4	0.3	0.3	0.3	0.4	0.3	0.4	0.4	0.6	0.4	0.5	0.5	0.4
6. Bad debts	0.3	0.4	-	0.2	0.2	0.2	0.3	0.2	0.2	0.3	0.2	0.6	0.4
7. Rent on business property	6.4	8.2	9.1	9.0	6.6	5.0	5.6	5.0	5.7	5.5	8.3	5.8	6.0
8. Taxes (excl Federal tax)	2.3	2.4	2.5	2.4	2.4	2.0	2.4	2.1	2.3	2.3	2.4	2.5	2.3
9. Interest	1.5	0.5	0.7	0.8	1.4	0.9	1.1	1.0	1.3	1.9	1.7	3.0	1.7
10. Deprec/Deplet/Amortiz	2.2	1.3	1.4	1.3	1.5	1.2	1.4	1.3	1.8	1.7	2.6	2.6	3.2
11. Advertising	2.6	2.2	2.2	2.3	2.2	2.8	3.0	4.8	3.6	5.1	2.4	2.8	2.0
12. Pensions & other benef plans	0.9	0.8	0.5	0.2	0.2	0.7	0.6	0.8	0.7	0.8	0.7	0.9	1.3
13. Other expenses	22.1	30.3	21.1	20.8	20.0	20.7	21.4	24.1	23.3	22.1	23.9	23.8	21.8
14. Net profit before tax	A	A	A	A	A	A	A	A	0.5	0.5	A	A	1.5
Selected Financial Ratios (number of times ratio is to one)													
15. Current ratio	1.9	·	2.0	2.4	1.9	1.9	1.9	1.6	1.8	2.0	2.0	2.2	1.7
16. Quick ratio	0.6	·	0.4	0.6	0.5	0.6	0.6	0.5	0.7	0.7	0.7	0.8	0.7
17. Net sls to net wkg capital	7.1	·	9.2	5.6	5.7	6.7	6.2	9.1	6.3	5.9	6.9	4.6	8.5
18. Coverage ratio	2.9	·	0.9	0.6	0.9	2.0	2.1	3.0	3.4	2.9	1.9	1.3	4.4
19. Asset turnover	2.0	·	3.7	2.4	2.1	2.6	2.3	2.5	2.1	2.0	2.1	1.4	1.6
20. Total liab to net worth	1.5	·	4.0	2.5	2.2	1.8	1.4	1.6	1.6	1.7	1.8	2.5	1.1
Selected Financial Factors in Percentages													
21. Debt ratio	59.5	·	80.1	71.7	69.2	64.6	57.6	62.2	62.1	62.9	63.8	71.1	51.7
22. Return on assets	8.4	·	2.1	1.2	2.6	4.9	5.5	7.6	9.0	11.0	6.7	5.3	11.9
23. Return on equity	8.2	·	-	-	-	5.4	4.7	9.7	11.8	14.9	4.3	-	12.3
24. Return on net worth	20.6	·	10.6	4.3	8.3	13.7	12.9	20.1	23.8	29.7	18.6	18.3	24.7

Exhibit 9–2 (concluded)

TABLE II: CORPORATIONS WITH NET INCOME, 1992 EDITION

5600 RETAIL TRADE:
APPAREL AND ACCESSORY STORES

Item Description For Accounting Period 7/88 Through 6/89	A Total	B Zero Assets	C Under 100	D 100 250	E 251 500	F 501 1,000	G 1,001 5,000	H 5,001 10,000	I 10,001 25,000	J 25,001 50,000	K 50,001 100,000	L 100,001 250,000	M 250,001 and over
SIZE OF ASSETS IN THOUSANDS OF DOLLARS (000 OMITTED)													
1. Number of Enterprises	25736	954	10886	7415	2478	2309	1307	214	95	35	18	11	13
2. Total receipts (in millions of dollars)	60386	1108	2189	3573	1916	4685	6180	3945	3319	2810	2770	3135	24756
Selected Operating Factors in Percent of Net Sales													
3. Cost of operations	59.3	54.6	59.4	59.0	60.2	62.2	61.9	56.9	57.0	58.7	57.8	58.8	59.3
4. Compensation of officers	1.9	1.9	3.7	2.9	6.9	4.0	3.5	2.8	2.7	1.0	0.8	0.8	0.4
5. Repairs	0.4	0.3	0.2	0.2	0.4	0.3	0.3	0.4	0.6	0.4	0.5	0.3	0.4
6. Bad debts	0.3	0.5	-	0.2	0.2	0.1	0.4	0.2	0.2	0.3	0.1	0.5	0.4
7. Rent on business property	5.9	4.2	9.5	8.9	5.3	4.6	5.3	5.0	5.5	5.3	7.6	5.2	5.9
8. Taxes (excl Federal tax)	2.3	1.5	2.0	2.6	2.5	1.9	2.4	1.7	2.2	2.2	2.5	2.8	2.3
9. Interest	1.1	0.5	0.5	0.5	1.0	0.8	0.7	1.0	1.1	1.6	1.4	1.6	1.3
10. Deprec/Deplet/Amortiz	2.1	1.2	0.9	0.9	1.1	1.0	1.2	1.2	1.7	1.6	2.4	2.1	3.1
11. Advertising	2.5	2.4	1.9	2.2	1.7	2.7	2.7	5.0	3.3	5.2	1.9	2.2	1.8
12. Pensions & other benef plans	0.9	0.7	-	0.2	0.2	0.8	0.6	0.9	0.7	0.8	0.7	0.9	1.3
13. Other expenses	21.0	31.0	17.7	19.6	16.8	19.9	19.6	23.3	22.7	20.7	23.0	21.3	21.2
14. Net profit before tax	2.4	1.3	4.2	2.8	3.7	1.8	1.3	1.7	2.3	2.2	1.4	3.5	2.7
Selected Financial Ratios (number of times ratio is to one)													
15. Current ratio	1.9	-	2.5	3.0	3.5	2.1	2.2	1.7	1.9	2.1	1.9	2.1	1.7
16. Quick ratio	0.7	-	0.6	0.8	1.1	0.8	0.8	0.5	0.8	0.7	0.6	0.8	0.6
17. Net sls to net wkg capital	7.1	-	7.8	5.1	3.9	6.4	5.5	8.2	6.1	6.0	7.7	5.6	8.9
18. Coverage ratio	6.1	12.7	12.0	12.6	6.0	4.7	7.1	5.1	5.5	4.2	4.1	4.5	6.5
19. Asset turnover	2.1	-	3.7	2.8	2.2	2.9	2.4	2.5	2.3	2.2	2.2	1.8	1.7
20. Total liab to net worth	1.0	-	1.5	0.9	0.7	1.4	0.9	1.6	1.3	1.3	1.5	1.6	0.8
Selected Financial Factors in Percentages													
21. Debt ratio	50.3	-	59.6	46.7	42.8	58.4	47.8	61.3	56.4	56.8	59.9	60.8	45.7
22. Return on assets	14.0	-	20.3	16.8	13.1	10.3	12.5	12.7	13.9	14.5	12.3	13.2	14.1
23. Return on equity	17.7	-	-	24.8	17.9	18.0	18.1	22.0	20.4	21.4	16.7	18.7	14.7
24. Return on net worth	28.1	-	50.2	31.5	22.8	24.9	24.0	32.9	31.8	33.6	30.6	33.8	25.9

SOURCE: *Almanac of Business and Industrial Financial Ratios*, 1992 edition, pp. 256–57. Reprinted with permission of publisher.

Exhibit 9-3

RETAIL APPAREL — TOTAL ASSETS $100000-$250000

ASSETS

CURRENT ASSETS	AS A PCT OF CURRENT ASSETS
CASH	12.08
ACCOUNTS RECEIVABLES	4.14
INVENTORIES	73.26
OTHER CURRENT ASSETS	0.00

FIXED ASSETS	AS A PCT OF FIXED ASSETS
LAND, BUILDINGS, LEASE-HOLD IMPROVEMENTS	0.00
EQUIPMENT	100.00
OTHER FIXED ASSETS	0.00

LIABILITIES & CAPITAL

CURRENT LIABILITIES	AS A PCT OF CURRENT LIABILITIES	AS A PCT OF TOTAL LIABILITIES
ACCOUNTS PAYABLE/TRADE	53.19	35.90
SHORT TERM BANK LOANS	0.00	0.00
OTHER CURRENT DEBT	24.23	15.06

LONG TERM DEBT	AS A PCT OF LONG TERM DEBT	AS A PCT OF TOTAL LIABILITIES
NOTES PAYABLE	0.00	0.00
MORTGAGES PAYABLE	0.00	0.00
LONG TERM BANK LOANS	0.00	0.00
STOCKHOLDER LOANS (DUE TO OWNERS)	0.00	0.00
OTHER LONG TERM DEBT	0.00	0.00

RETAIL APPAREL — TOTAL ASSETS $100000-$250000

INCOME DATA

	AS A PCT OF NET SALES
NET SALES (GROSS INCOME)	100.00
COST OF SALES	60.96
GROSS PROFIT	39.04
GENERAL/ADMINISTRATIVE EXP	34.27
OPERATING PROFIT	4.77
INTEREST EXPENSE	0.67
DEPRECIATION	0.85
PROFIT BEFORE TAXES	3.25

ADDITIONAL OPERATING ITEMS

LABOR	11.22
ADVERTISING EXPENSE	1.98
TRAVEL EXPENSE	0.56
RENT	4.67
INSURANCE	0.92
OFFICER/EXECUTIVE SALARIES	8.85

RATIOS

	MEDIAN	UPPER QUARTILE	LOWER QUARTILE	UNITS
CURRENT	2.5	6.9	1.6	TIMES
QUICK	0.7	2.0	0.3	TIMES
CURRENT ASSETS/TOTAL ASSETS	86.0	95.3	76.7	PCT
SHORT TERM DEBT/TOTAL DEBT	86.2	100.0	58.7	PCT
SHORT TERM DEBT/NET WORTH	57.1	234.2	11.3	PCT
TOTAL DEBT/NET WORTH	60.7	346.9	17.1	PCT
SHORT TERM DEBT/TOTAL ASSETS	30.1	51.2	11.8	PCT
LONG TERM DEBT/TOTAL ASSETS	2.7	31.3	0.0	PCT
TOTAL DEBT/TOTAL ASSETS	52.1	81.4	17.2	PCT
SALES/RECEIVABLES	16.7	62.5	5.3	TIMES
AVERAGE COLLECTION PERIOD	6.	24.	0.	DAYS
SALES/INVENTORY	4.0	7.0	2.6	TIMES
SALES/TOTAL ASSETS	2.7	3.5	1.8	TIMES
SALES/NET WORTH	5.4	13.2	2.8	TIMES
PROFIT (PRETAX)/TOTAL ASSETS	7.9	22.5	-5.0	PCT
PROFIT (PRETAX)/NET WORTH	14.2	57.1	-5.9	PCT

SOURCE: *Financial Studies of the Small Business*, 14th edition, 1991, pp. 23-24. Reprinted with permission of publisher.

Median figures are used for financial statement line items, and it is necessary to read the explanation in order to interpret those figures correctly. Definitions of ratios are included in the front of the loose-leaf book, and most are similar, if not identical, to those used by RMA. As is the case with the RMA ratios, upper and lower quartile figures, as well as medians, are presented.

I found it quite interesting to note that the 1991 edition (as well as earlier editions) offered the following statement:

> Again data has revealed noticeable differences when compared to studies including large firms in their sampling. FRA compared data on retail establishments to other studies containing a substantial number of firms with larger asset sizes. This comparison revealed the typical FRA firm to be more liquid, employing less debt, and earning a higher return on investment. These differences are significant and we would hope that one in an evaluating position would now be better able to make valid comparisons for the particularly small firm.[1]

Specialized Sources

Many trade and professional associations compile and make available composite financial data on businesses or professions that are members. Also, some trade and professional publications offer financial data. Each issue of the RMA *Annual Statement Studies* now contains a bibliography listing 115 separate sources of composite financial data for specific lines of business. One advantage of franchise operations is that most franchisers provide comparative financial data. Also, many manufacturers that sell through networks of retail outlets provide comparative financial data to their retailers. Certain CPA firms, and management consultants that specialize in particular lines of business, provide clients with comparative financial data.

Interpretation of Financial Statement Ratios

Comparisons between financial statement ratios for the subject company and industry averages can indicate both specific opportunities for possible improvement and situations that could cause problems. Financial statement ratios fall into four broad categories:

1. Short-term liquidity measures.
2. Balance sheet leverage ratios.
3. Activity ratios.
4. Profitability ratios.

In addition to the traditional categories of ratios, each line item on the income statement can be compared with industry averages.

---

[1] *Financial Studies of the Small Business*, 14th ed. (Orlando, Fla.: Financial Research Associates, 1991), p. i.

Short-Term Liquidity Measures

The two primary short-term liquidity ratios are the *current ratio* and the *acid test ratio* (also called the *quick ratio*); both are discussed in some detail in Chapter 11 in the section on analyzing working capital requirements. Their most important use is to indicate the extent to which a company may have either inadequate or excessive working capital.

Balance Sheet Leverage Ratios

The primary balance sheet leverage ratios are the *equity ratio* (owner's equity as a percent of total assets) and the *long-term debt-to-equity ratio*. These ratios are one indicator of the degree of risk; the less the equity, relative to the total assets and to the long-term debt, the greater the degree of risk. For some companies, these ratios might also indicate borrowing power; leverage ratios well below industry averages may indicate unused borrowing power.

Activity Ratios

The general idea of activity ratios is to measure how efficiently the assets are being employed. The primary activity ratios are *accounts receivable turnover, inventory turnover* (both discussed in Chapter 11 under working capital analysis), and *asset turnover* (sales divided by total assets).

Profitability Ratios

Profitability ratios fall into two broad categories: income statement profitability ratios and rates of return on some measure of investment. Income statement profitability ratios are usually expressed as a percentage of sales. Rate-of-return ratios are usually expressed either as a percentage of equity or as a percentage of investment, with investment usually defined to mean either equity plus long-term debt, or equity plus all interest-bearing debt. The following measures of profitability are often expressed as a percentage of one or more of the four variables above:

1. EBDIT: Earnings before depreciation, interest, and taxes.
2. EBIT: Earnings before interest and taxes.
3. EBT (pretax profit): Net income before taxes.
4. EBDT: Earnings before depreciation and taxes.
5. Net Income: Earnings after interest, depreciation, and taxes.

When comparing any ratios with industry averages, it is important to be sure that the comparison is on an apples-to-apples basis; that is, the industry average measures of comparison and the subject company ratios are being computed in exactly the same way. The following section offers some examples that compare company financial statement ratios with industry averages.

Exhibit 9–4

ANNIE'S APPAREL STORE AND
ALMANAC OF BUSINESS & INDUSTRIAL FINANCIAL RATIOS
RETAIL TRADE: APPAREL AND ACCESSORY STORES
COMPARATIVE ANALYSIS

Asset Size	The Almanac $251,000 – $500,000	Annie's Apparel a $280,000
Revenues	$797,632 b	$1,000,000
Cost of Operations	61.5 %	53.5 %
Compensation of Officers	4.7	5.0
Bad Debts	0.2	0.2
Rent on Business Property	5.5	6.5
Interest	0.9	0.7
Depreciation	1.3	1.3
Advertising	1.9	2.5
Pension and Other Benefit Plans	0.5	2.3
Other Expenses	17.8 c	21.4
Net Profit before Taxes	2.9	6.6
RATIOS		
Coverage Ratio	5.0	10.4
Asset Turnover	2.4	3.5
Total Liabilities/Net Worth	1.1	0.5
Return on Assets	11.1	25.9
Return on Equity	16.0	34.4

a   Figures used are from the adjusted income statement and balance sheet (see Exhibits 7-2 and 8-2).

b   Average revenues for the 4,686 companies in this asset size.

c   Includes repairs and taxes (excluding federal income tax).

SOURCE: *Almanac of Business and Industrial Financial Ratios,* 1991 edition.

Examples of Comparative Industry Analysis

The following hypothetical examples illustrate how the average industry data discussed in this chapter can be compared with data from the entity in which we are interested. The two examples continue to refer to the same two hypothetical companies used in the two previous chapters.

Sole Proprietorship Example

Exhibit 9–4 shows how Annie's Apparel Store compares with other apparel and accessory stores. The *Almanac of Business and Industrial Fi-*

nancial Ratios is used as the basis of comparison in this example, in order to compare as many expense items on the income statement as possible.

It is apparent that Annie's gross margin is far above the industry average, as is her return on equity. Her inventory does not turn over as fast as the industry average, but the slower-moving inventory may be necessary to have a merchandise mix with an above average gross margin. (Because the adjusted balance sheet eliminates the current liabilities for Annie's, several ratios that would normally be computed are omitted in this example.)

Corporation Example

Exhibit 9–5 shows how Mary's Machinery & Equipment, Inc., compares with other wholesale machinery and equipment distributors. Robert Morris Associates' *Annual Statement Studies* is used as the basis of comparison in this example.

Many more comparisons are available by comparing Mary's with the industry averages, as shown in RMA data.

Mary's is well above the industry average short-term liquidity measures for both the current ratio and the quick ratio. She has much less balance sheet leverage, with a debt/equity ratio of only 0.8. This leverage position definitely suggests a very strong financial position and probable borrowing power, if she wanted to use it.

The activity ratios show that she is above the industry median for accounts receivable turnover, but her inventory turnover is between the industry median and the lower quartile. She is at the industry lower quartile for sales to total assets. These statistics suggest that she might be able to use her assets a little more intensively to get a little more sales out of the assets in use.

Most importantly, however, Mary's is ahead of industry averages in all categories of profitability ratios. Her gross profit, operating profit, and pretax profit as a percent of sales are all above industry averages. Her pretax return on equity is between the industry median and the upper quartile.

Each of the various industry comparison services does not necessarily compute all the ratios of interest, but they offer enough to make very useful generalizations in many respects about how the subject company compares with its peers.

Summary

Comparing the subject company with industry averages is a useful and often revealing exercise as a part of the valuation process. It may help the analyst spot errors and/or areas for further inquiry. It helps to reveal the company's strengths, weaknesses, and opportunities.

Several generalized sources of comparative data have been presented. In addition to these, many trade and professional associations and trade and professional publishers generate comparative financial

Exhibit 9–5

MARY'S MACHINERY & EQUIPMENT, INC. AND
RMA FINANCIAL STATEMENT STUDIES
COMPARATIVE ANALYSIS

	RMA	MARY'S
Asset Size:	$500m – $2mm	
Statement Date:	4/1/90 to 3/31/91	1991

COMPOSITION OF THE BALANCE SHEET AND THE INCOME STATEMENT

	%	%
ASSETS:		
Cash & Equivalents	6.5	6.3
Accounts & Notes Receivable	35.1	22.3
Inventory	36.4	36.7
All Other Current	1.6	2.5
Total Current	79.6	67.7
Fixed Assets (Net)	14.1	24.2
Intangibles	0.6	0.8
All Other Noncurrent	5.7	7.3
Total Assets	100.0	100.0
LIABILITIES AND NET WORTH		
Notes Payable--Short Term	15.0	4.8
Current Maturity Long-Term Debt	3.8	3.9
Accounts & Notes Payable--Trade	23.8	11.6
All Other Current	7.7	2.9
Total Current	50.8	27.1
Long-Term Debt	10.5	9.2
All Other Noncurrent	2.3	6.8
Net Worth	36.3	56.9
Total Liabilities & Net Worth	100.0	100.0
INCOME STATEMENT DATA		
Net Sales	100.0	100.0
Gross Profit	29.1	33.8
Operating Expenses	26.9	29.6
Operating Profit	2.2	4.2
All Other Expenses (Net)	0.6	0.6
Profit Before Taxes	1.7	3.6

RATIOS

	Upper Quartile	Median	Lower Quartile	Mary's
Current Ratio	2.2	1.6	1.2	2.5
Quick Ratio	1.2	0.8	0.6	1.1
Sales/Receivables	11.4	8.8	6.9	10.4
Cost of Sales/Inventory	9.6	6.2	3.9	4.2
Cost of Sales/Payables	17.4	9.7	6.4	13.3
Sales/Working Capital	6.5	11.2	22.7	5.7
EBIT/Interest	4.9	2.3	1.2	6.7
Fixed Assets/Net Worth	0.1	0.3	0.8	0.4 a
Debt/Net Worth	0.9	1.9	3.7	0.8
% Pretax Income/Tangible Net Worth	27.5	12.6	4.1	14.9
% Pretax Income/Total Assets	8.7	4.2	1	8.3
Sales/Net Fixed Assets	69.6	33.8	14.9	9.6 a
Sales/Total Assets	3.7	3.0	2.3	2.3
% Deprec., Amort./Sales	0.5	1.0	1.6	1.4
% Officers' Comp./Sales	2.9	4.3	7.3	5.0

a Mary's assets have been adjusted upward to reflect replacement cost, while RMA companies' fixed assets are unadjusted; therefore, Mary's ratio would be higher in the case of fixed assets/net worth and lower in the case of sales/fixed assets if they were computed as the RMA ratios were.

LTD = Long-term debt

SOURCE: *Annual Statement Studies,* 1991 edition.

data for their industry or profession. Exhibit 9–6 summarizes the steps in comparing industry averages.

When using comparative industry data, the analyst must be careful to check definitions of both financial statement line items and ratios. Different sources use different definitions. The analyst may have to adjust the subject company data to conform to the comparative source's definitions to get an apples-to-apples comparison.

In the course of the analysis, the appraiser should think about how any deviations from industry norms impact value. These points should be noted in the ultimate valuation analysis.

Exhibit 9–6

SUMMARY OF STEPS IN
COMPARING INDUSTRY AVERAGES

Step 1   Normalize the balance sheet and income statement of the subject company as described in Chapters 7 and 8.

Step 2   Collect comparative financial data for the average company of similar size in the industry in which the subject company operates through sources such as RMA *Annual Statement Studies*, the *Almanac of Business and Industrial Financial Ratios*, the *Financial Studies of the Small Business*, or other specialized sources.

Step 3   Calculate the financial ratios that are available in the industry sources for the subject company.

Step 4   Calculate the balance sheet line items as a percent of total assets for the subject company.

Step 5   Calculate the income statement line items as a percent of total revenues for the subject company.

Step 6   Compare the common-size balance sheet (from Step 4) for the subject company to the industry norms.

Step 7   Compare the common-size income statements (from Step 5) for the subject company to the industry norms.

Step 8   Compare the financial ratios (including liquidity ratios, activity ratios, leverage ratios, and profitability ratios) for the subject company to the industry norms.

Step 9   List the subject company's strengths and weaknesses compared to the average company of similar size in the industry.

Chapter 10

Analyzing Qualitative Factors

Relevant Economic Data
    National Economic Data
    Regional and Local Economic Data
Industry Factors
    Markets
    Channels of Distribution
    Technology
    Sources of Industry Information
Competition
    Existing Competition
    Potential Competition
Regulation
    Present Regulations
    Potential Changes in Regulatory Environment
Product or Service Lines
    Existing Lines
    Opportunities for Related Lines
    Patents, Copyrights, Trademarks
    Relative Profitability of Lines
    Service or Warranty Obligations
Supplier Relationships
    Continuity
    Degree of Exclusivity
    Contractual Relationships
Market Position
    Reputation
    Geographic Scope
    Method of Marketing and Distribution
    Pricing Policies
    Customer Base
    Customer Relationships
    Market Continuity, Growth Opportunities, and Weaknesses
Management and Employees
    Size and Composition of Work Force
    Key Employees
    Other Employees
    Compensation
    Personnel Policies, Satisfaction, Conflict, and Turnover

Adequacy of Physical Facility
>   Condition
>   Heat, Light, Plumbing, and Other Systems
>   Size
>   Continuity of Occupancy
Operating Efficiencies and Inefficiencies
>   Physical Plant
>   Accounting and Other Controls
Reason for Sale
Summary

Qualitative factors are the characteristics of the business, industry, and the economy as a whole that affect the future of the company and whether its performance will be consistent with past results. Many of these factors are difficult or impossible to quantify, such as the effects of competition or unanticipated upturns or downturns in the economy; others are more easily quantifiable, such as the expected cost of improvement to facilities and future compensation. A thorough analysis of these factors will assist the appraiser in assessing the company's ongoing earning power. It will also help the appraiser to estimate the degree of risk involved in the enterprise, which in turn will have an important bearing on the applicable capitalization rates. And it may bring to light additional capital investment that may be required in order to produce some expected level of income.

One good way of acquiring information on some of the factors discussed in this chapter is to visit the entity's operating facilities and talk with current owners, managers, and others, as well as outside sources. In some cases, the potential buyer may be wise to work in the operation for a day, a week, or even longer, to get a good look at the operation from the inside.

The relevance of the various factors will differ from one industry to another, and sometimes from one business to another within an industry. The following sections discuss the major categories of qualitative factors that should be considered in valuing a typical business or professional practice. (There is further discussion of certain qualitative factors specific to professional practices in Part V.) For some companies, some of the factors discussed in this chapter obviously will not apply. For other companies, these factors and others will be relevant.

Relevant Economic Data

The importance of economic data varies greatly from one kind of business or practice to another. As a broad generality, businesses providing goods or services for which demand is highly elastic are more affected by changes in economic conditions than are businesses providing goods or services that people regard as daily necessities. The discretion available to buyers to avoid or postpone purchase of certain goods and services can determine how much broad economic influences affect the enterprise. The appraiser must use his judgment and experience when considering which economic factors will have a bearing on the fortunes of the business or practice being valued.

National Economic Data

Relevant national economic data will provide clues to people's propensity to spend money for the goods or services offered by the business or practice being valued, along with anything else that might affect profit margins. Depending on the line of business, the following economic variables could have a bearing on the company's outlook:

1. *Gross Domestic Product (GDP)*[1]: The value of all goods and services produced in a country. GDP covers the goods and services produced by labor and property located in the United States.
2. *Gross National Product (GNP)*: The value of all goods and services produced in a country plus income earned in foreign countries less income payable to foreign sources. GNP covers the goods and services produced by labor and property supplied by U.S. residents. As long as the labor and property are supplied by U.S. residents, they may be located either in the United States or abroad.
3. *Disposable Personal Income*: The total income received by individuals, available for consumption and savings; this is total personal income less personal taxes.
4. *Business Capital Spending*: The total amount of business expenditures on durable assets, such as plant and equipment, during a specific time period.
5. *Consumer Durable Goods Expenditures*: The total amount of consumer expenditures on such items as appliances and automobiles during a specific time period.
6. *Housing Starts*: Total number of housing units started during a specific time period.
7. *Consumer Price Index (CPI)*: The most common means of measuring the price changes of goods and services purchased by the typical household. The CPI indexes the cost of the typical market basket purchased by an urban family against its cost in a base year. The market basket includes such items as food, clothing, shelter, fuels, transportation fares, charges for doctors' and dentists' services, drugs, and other goods and services purchased for daily living.
8. *Producer Price Index* (formerly called the *Wholesale Price Index*): Designed to measure average changes in prices of all commodities at all stages of processing, produced or imported for sale in primary markets in the United States. It is based on more than 3,000 commodities. All prices used in constructing the index are collected from sellers and generally apply to the first significant large-volume trans-

---

[1]Beginning with the late 1991 comprehensive revision of the National Income and Product Accounts (NIPAs), the Bureau of Economic Analysis (BEA) will feature gross domestic product (GDP), rather than gross national product (GNP), as the primary measure of U.S. production. This change in emphasis recognizes that GDP is more appropriate for many purposes for which an aggregate measure of the nation's production is used.

action for each commodity, for example, the manufacturer's or other producer's selling price.

Unfortunately, economists historically have not been able to predict relevant demand and other economic variables with enough accuracy to be very useful for this purpose. Nevertheless, the analyst must do the best he can with what is available. There are literally thousands of sources of such data. A few readily available ones include the following:

1. Government Publications

The *Federal Reserve Bulletin* (The Board of Governors of the Federal Reserve System in Washington, D.C.): Published monthly, the *Federal Reserve Bulletin* includes such data as employment, industrial production, housing and construction, consumer and producer prices, GDP, personal income and savings, and key interest rates. Three years of annual historical data are usually presented for each set of statistics, and data for the current year are provided in monthly or quarterly units. It is usually available at public and university libraries. This is the best single service for finding current U.S. banking and monetary statistics. The Board also publishes a quarterly *Federal Reserve Chart Book* with an annual *Historical Chart Book*, providing graphic trends for many of the statistics in the *Bulletin*.

Survey of Current Business (U.S. Department of Commerce): This monthly publication has two sections. The first deals with basic business trends, and starts with an article, "The Business Situation," which reviews business developments, pointing out relative strengths and weaknesses. The second section contains an extensive compilation of basic statistics on all phases of the economy. This is the most important single source for current U.S. business statistics. It can be found in most major libraries.

Statistical Abstract of the United States (U.S. Department of Commerce): This annual publication contains statistics on all phases of U.S. life—economic, social, political, industrial—and some comparative international statistics. It is well-indexed and easy to use, and is available at most public libraries.

2. Banks

Economic Trends (Federal Reserve Bank of Cleveland): This monthly publication is an excellent source of economic variables, ranging from GDP and its components to money supply aggregates. The figures for such indicators as consumer income, business fixed investment, housing starts, producer and consumer prices, and so on, are usually given quarterly and monthly. Most major libraries have *Economic Trends* on hand, along with publications of all the other 11 Federal Reserve Bank Districts, which also contain economic information. *U.S. Financial Data*, published weekly by the Federal Reserve Bank of St. Louis, is an especially good compilation of statistics on the money supply, commercial paper and business loans, interest rates, and securities yields.

Economic and Business Outlook (Bank of America): Issues are published six times a year and feature a particular aspect of the economy such as the U.S. economy and long-term outlook; short-term outlook; the California economy; and the global economy. This publication was previously known as *Economic Report,* published by Security Pacific National Bank prior to its merger with the Bank of America.

3. Popular Materials

Barron's: This weekly newspaper includes a wealth of statistical information. It includes articles covering a wide range of business and financial topics.

Business Week: As its name implies, this weekly publication covers all aspects of the business world. One of the strengths of this publication is that it offers intelligent business articles in an easy-to-read magazine format. The first issue of each year gives forecasts on a wide array of industries.

Fortune: Perhaps one of the most comprehensive sources for economic forecasts. In addition to monthly comments in each issue, the magazine makes quarterly and yearly forecasts for nearly all major economic indicators.

The Wall Street Journal: This is the daily newspaper of the business world. The paper is divided into three sections: the first covering the world news; the second containing special reports on a particular aspect of business; the third covering money and investing. The highlight of the *Journal* is the daily statistical tables for stock, mutual funds, bonds, and so on. Statistics released by the Fed on Friday appear in the next Monday's *Journal*.

Regional and Local Economic Data

Obviously, the more a business or practice depends on the economy of some locality, the more relevant is the analysis of economic data about that area. An automobile dealership located in a town dependent on an economically troubled industry is not worth nearly as much as one with comparable sales and profits the prior year but located in a rapidly growing metropolis. Population, employment, and income forecasts are generally the most relevant types of local economic data. If a business depends on a certain industry, such as travel or construction, then estimates of such variables as the level of tourism or the number and dollar amounts of construction starts are relevant.

The primary sources for regional and local economic data are bank economics departments, public utilities, chambers of commerce, and various state agencies, such as departments of economic development and bureaus of labor statistics. Most major local banks publish statistical tabulations of economic indicators, although their availability is limited. Although major libraries usually subscribe to one or more bank economic publications, the selections at libraries are usually limited to those published nearest to the particular library. The best way to obtain regional bank publications is to write or call the particular bank's economic department.

Some universities publish regional and local economic data, sometimes focused on one or a few industries important to the region. Most

states and multistate regions now have regular monthly business magazines that give economic statistics, and most metropolitan areas now
have weekly newspapers that focus on business developments. I have
found that the business sections of some metropolitan daily newspapers
are offering more economic analysis and statistics, sometimes regularly
in Sunday editions and sometimes irregularly in special features that
focus on some specific part of the local economic scene.

Additional Data Sources for Regional and Local Economies.

Regional Economies and Markets: Published quarterly by the Economic
and Business Environment Program of The Conference Board, this analysis looks at groups of states in terms of manufacturing production,
employment, and income.

The Complete Economic and Demographic Data Source: Published by
Wilson & Poole Economics, this is an excellent source for statistical
profiles of metropolitan areas, counties, and states. Historical as well as
projected data are included in this source. Other publications from Wilson & Poole include *State Profiles* and *MSA Profiles*, which currently
include statistical economic data and forecasts through the year 2010.

Metro Insights: For larger metropolitan areas, this publication of Data
Resources Inc./McGraw Hill provides 10 to 15 pages of narrative economic discussion well supported with statistics. This source contains
information on the 100 largest metropolitan areas in the United States.
Each area profile includes an economic profile, forecasts for growth,
infrastructure evaluation, and construction and demographic data.

Survey of Buying Power: Published annually in two monthly editions of
Sales & Marketing Management magazine, this publication breaks down
demographic and income data by state, metropolitan area, and county.
Retail sales data are presented for store groups and merchandise lines.
Also included are population and retail sales forecasts for local areas.

Industry Factors

Knowing something about the prospects and problems of the industry
can provide a useful perspective for the valuation process. Quantitative
comparisons between the subject company and industry-average operating figures were covered in the previous chapter. This section suggests some qualitative aspects to be considered, as well as some available
information sources. The following sections on "Competition" and "Regulation" also address some topics that may be industrywide matters,
and some of the sources of information listed below will address those
subjects.

Markets

The industry factor most important to the value of most businesses and
practices is the market outlook for the products or services being offered.

For a given dollar amount of physical asset value, historical sales, or historical profits, a business or practice with a growing market for its products or services would be expected to be worth more than one facing a stagnant or declining market demand, all other things being equal.

Channels of Distribution

For many industries, channels of distribution evolve over time. The most obvious and widespread trend is that of consolidation, which has at least three important aspects: (1) cutting out the middle man, (2) a trend toward larger business units, and (3) a trend toward more corporate chain and/or franchised units and fewer independent business units.

Independent wholesalers have been getting closer to extinction for many years in such fields as groceries, jewelry, and many, if not most, other consumer goods, as more and more manufacturers sell directly to retailers. Manufacturers' representative firms and brokerage firms, such as food brokers, have found the suppliers they represent to be a fickle lot, as accounts they have successfully built are taken away in favor of direct distribution by the manufacturer. Industrial distributors of all kinds are constantly in jeopardy of losing one or more of their leading lines because of the supplier's shift to a direct distribution policy.

Economic efficiencies of scale have been operating for years to increase the average size of such diverse entities as farms and ranches, motels and hotels, and grocery and discount merchandising stores. The effect, of course, has been a dramatic increase in the amount of investment required for such entities. In some cases, however, this trend toward bigness has opened up opportunities for businesses at the small end of the spectrum. As consolidation provides strategic advantages to the larger entities in a particular industry group, the smaller participants in the industry carefully identify, protect, and promote their position.

While the impact of consolidation increases the competitive pressure on independent operators, there can also be some advantages. One of the obvious ones is that national and regional acquirors provide an important group of prospective buyers for the owners of businesses and professional practices in lines in which such acquisitions are taking place. Another is that hundreds of chains are expanding through franchising. Some business owners may be able to benefit by becoming local franchise operators. In any case, some understanding of how the channels of distribution of an industry or professional practice area are evolving should add perspective to the valuation of most businesses and professional practices.

Technology

In today's dynamic environment, as economic philosopher Robert Heilbroner so aptly put it, "the curve of technology is rising exponentially beneath our feet." Some products or services will be completely or nearly obsolete within a few years, while others will skyrocket in usage as technological advances make them more attractive because of such factors as lower costs, miniaturization, improved performance, and greater compatibility with other related products.

There is hardly a business or profession for which the dynamics of technological change do not have implications for the value of the entity. For some, technology will determine the very viability of the enterprise. For others, such as retail establishments, technological changes will merely mandate capital expenditures for new equipment, such as the latest electronic bar code readers and reading and transmission equipment for the new generation of bank debit cards. The effects of technological change should be considered in terms of their impact on earnings potential, capital expenditure requirements, and risk for the entity being valued.

Sources of Industry Information

Generally, the best sources of industry information are trade and professional associations and publications. The owners of the entity being appraised can usually direct the appraiser to the relevant associations and publications, although we have found that many small business owners are unaware of many of the sources of information relating to their own businesses. Several directories for such sources exist. The most comprehensive directory of trade and professional associations is *The Encyclopedia of Associations*, published annually by Gale Research, Inc. Also useful is *National Trade & Professional Associations of the United States*, published annually by Columbia Books. One of the most comprehensive directories of trade and professional publications is *Business Publication Rates and Data*, published annually by Standard Rate & Data Service. Another is *Ulrich's Periodical Directory*, published every other year by R. R. Bowker.

Other sources of industry information are government publications, such as the *U.S. Industrial Outlook,* published annually by the U.S. Department of Commerce, and investment publications such as Standard & Poor's *Industry Surveys* and *ValueLine Investment Survey*. Several of the most useful of these sources are located in the bibliography included in the book as Appendix D. There also exist a number of indexing services that can be used to find industry information.

Competition

It would seem to go without saying that a buyer trying to place a value on a prospective acquisition would want to check out the existing and potential competition, but this important qualitative factor is often neglected.

Existing Competition

Analysis of the competition takes different forms in different lines of business or professional practice, so I can offer only broad suggestions. In general, it is desirable to know the number of competitors, their names, their locations, the sizes of their respective operations, and how long they have been in business. One or more significant *new* competitors could be an important factor, since the full effects of their competition would probably not be reflected in the historical financial statements of the entity being valued. It is also desirable to know in what ways the competition is similar or differentiated along product or service lines, pricing policy, marketing methods, and other factors.

The statement "We have no competition" is simply not adequate. Everyone has competition. The world has finite buying power and infinite demands. There are very few products or services for which there is absolutely no substitute. The appraiser should probe the question of competition until a satisfactory picture is developed.

Of course, a certain amount of competition can be healthy. A cluster of related retailers, though competitors, are often successful because they collectively draw a good flow of traffic interested in their line of wares. Wineries have found it profitable to be located among groups that collectively promote tours and local wines. And we have all heard the old saw that an attorney in town with no competition will starve to death, but when a second attorney comes to town they will both prosper.

Potential Competition

From the point of view of the person trying to value an operation, the most dangerous competition is the competition that isn't there yet, because its effect on the subject entity's earning power is a matter of guesswork. A unit of a large retail chain opening near a small or medium-sized independent store can sometimes put the independent out of business completely. Introduction of a technically superior or lower-cost competitive product may damage or even destroy some manufacturers and their distributors. A manufacturer may authorize an additional distributor in the same territory, or even open a company store in competition with its distributor. The easier the entry into the line of business, the more likely that new competition may be lurking just around the corner. It is never possible to know all the competitive problems that the future will bring, but an effort should be made to avoid being blindsided by new competition that might have been foreseen.

Regulation

Various industries and professional practices are subject to greater or lesser degrees of regulation, mostly from government agencies, but sometimes from their own professional associations. From a valuation viewpoint, the regulation can have either positive or negative implications. In any case, it is desirable to understand the regulatory situation.

Present Regulations

The gamut of existing regulations that affect the values of businesses and professional practices defies comprehensive categorization, but a few general groupings deserve special note.

Compliance Requirements. Two major government bodies administering regulations that cost the private sector hundreds of millions of dollars are the Occupational Safety and Health Administration (OSHA) and the Environmental Protection Agency (EPA). The appraiser should inquire whether there are any OSHA, EPA, or other compliance requirements that may cost some money to satisfy.

Restrictions on Entry. Some protection from excessive competition may be provided by restrictions on others entering the field. These restrictions range from the monopoly status of most utilities (gas, electric, water, local telephone, cable TV, and so on) to merely the requirements of passing certain competency tests in order to obtain licenses.

Licenses for many activities, such as paging systems, taxicabs, and (in most states) liquor outlets, are available only in limited numbers. Wherever there are regulatory restrictions to entry, there is likely to be some intangible value to the existing entities.

Potential Changes in Regulatory Environment

The political and social moods of the country and its leaders have been changing rapidly in recent years, causing dramatic changes in regulations affecting businesses and professions, which in turn have had dramatic impacts on the values of businesses and practices in many lines. Generally, the widespread move toward deregulation allows new competition and reduces the premium values that entrenched entities may have formerly commanded.

Costs of regulatory compliance are driving the values of many businesses to zero, as they shut down because the costs of compliance are too great. Others sell far below book value because the economic return possible under current conditions is not enough to justify the amount of investment made at an earlier time.

On the other hand, changes in regulatory requirements can create bonanzas for entities in a position to provide products or services to assist companies in meeting newly mandated requirements.

Another area of government regulation that undergoes constant review and change is the amount of federal and state subsidies and reimbursements available for various activities, as well as import restrictions and tariffs. As attitudes vacillate between subsidies and restrictions, businesses dependent on them face considerable risk, and their values are likely to be discounted considerably. Import/export firms may enjoy substantial windfall increments in their values when import restrictions are relaxed for selected goods. The values of nursing homes and other health care facilities, for another example, are very sensitive to changes in the programs of cost reimbursements available for their patients.

The foregoing comments and examples just scratch the surface of the major problem of anticipating and assessing the effect of a myriad of potential regulatory changes on the values of existing businesses and professional practices.

Product or Service Lines

The product or service lines being offered are another qualitative factor that will have different degrees of impact on value in different situations.

Existing Lines

The appraiser can get an understanding of the product or service lines being offered through sales literature, a visit to the premises, and/or interviews with an owner or manager. The appraiser should inquire about the relative size of each major product line and how long the company has offered it. He should also ask about any prior lines that may have been discontinued. This information should help him judge the extent to which historical operating information for the company represents a reasonable basis for extrapolating the future.

The more the market demand that already exists for the particular product or service, as opposed to others that are merely comparable, the more valuable is the entity that sells or distributes it. Good examples of this principle are found in the pricing of soft drink bottlers and beer distributorships, where almost all of the goodwill value is associated with the volume of the leading brands that are sold.

Opportunities for Related Lines

From the buyer's point of view, there could be value in the opportunity to add related lines. For example, there may be a perfect opportunity for a professional practice to enhance its position by bringing in someone with a related specialty not adequately represented in the market. A small food packer may have established a strong local brand recognition and a route distribution system for a specialty line, which may provide an opportunity to sell related specialty items under the same brand name through the existing distribution system.

Related lines may be either developed internally or brought in from outside. Even though a buyer may recognize opportunities, however, he will be reluctant to pay for opportunities that have not been seized and developed.

Patents, Copyrights, Trademarks

Like any intangible asset, the value of patents, copyrights, and trademarks lies in their ability to contribute to profits. Specific methods for placing values on each of these items are discussed in Chapter 34. In many small business and professional practice valuation assignments, however, no attempt is made to value each item individually; rather, the items are considered general qualitative factors in the valuation of the overall entity.

The importance of patents, copyrights, and trademarks lies in their ability to contribute to continuity of revenues, hopefully at higher margins of profit than would be possible if such legal protections did not exist. Only to the extent that they fulfill this function do they genuinely contribute to the value of the enterprise, and their contributions should be reflected in the income approaches to value. To the extent that patents, copyrights, and trademarks are well protected or have been tested in court, and are long-lived, the appraiser can have more confidence in the continuity of the income stream associated with them.

If the value of the total entity is determined to be greater than its net tangible asset value, it may be desirable for income tax purposes to allocate the value above the tangible asset value to specific intangible assets. As noted earlier, that is the subject of Chapter 34.

Relative Profitability of Lines

Sometimes it is revealing to inquire into the relative profitability of different lines. It is not unusual for a business to have one or more lines that generate impressive gross volume, but on examination are found to be marginal or even negative in contributing to profitability. That may explain why an operation produces profit margins below industry averages. If the business is being valued on an income capitalization basis, the low level of profitability will be reflected in the income stream being capitalized. However, if the business is being valued by some other method, the negative impact of low-margin lines needs somehow to be reflected within that valuation method. For example, if some version of a multiple of gross revenues method is being used in the valuation, the revenues from the substandard lines may not be included in the revenues to be capitalized, or they could be capitalized at a lower multiplier than other lines.

Service or Warranty Obligations

Obligations to service products sold can be either a positive or a negative influence on value, depending on the situation. If the company is a manufacturer with off-balance sheet warranty liability, this factor should be recognized, either as a lump-sum deduction from the enterprise value or as an expense deduction from the income stream being capitalized. On the other hand, if a company is a distributor that performs warranty service work, and adequate reimbursements come from the manufacturer for such work, the customer traffic generated by warranty service can be a very positive factor in assuring continuity of revenues and profits.

Supplier Relationships

If supplier relationships are important to the entity, then this subject should be investigated carefully.

Continuity

The continuity of a supplier relationship is of considerable importance to many businesses. The ultimate disaster would be the single-product distributor facing the loss of his supplier. Often, there are strong personal relationships between an owner and one or more key suppliers; the new owner will need to ascertain whether he can maintain a business relationship with this supplier now that the personal relationship is gone, or, if that is not possible, find another supplier. It is important to determine the extent to which continuity of supplier relationships can be assured or are at risk under new ownership.

The issue of prices may be important, as well as merely keeping the supplier relationship. The existing owner may have favorable pricing because of existing relationships, either contractual or noncontractual, which may be amended in a relationship with a new buyer. If the buyer faces this possibility, the effect on profit margins obviously must be assessed.

Degree of Exclusivity

An exclusive relationship for a market is generally more valuable than a nonexclusive relationship, because it is more conducive to continuity of revenues and maintenance of profit margins. An example of this would be a fast food franchise agreement. If the degree of exclusivity is threatened, that may be regarded as a negative factor in the valuation picture. Of course, if the transfer of an exclusive distributorship is contemplated, the willingness of the supplier to maintain the arrangement under new ownership must be ascertained.

Contractual Relationships

As a general rule, the strongest type of contractual relationship with a supplier is a franchise, which is often—but not always—transferable. Most distributorship agreements are not actually franchises and are not transferable without the supplier's consent. That may pose a perplexing valuation problem, since considerable value may depend on whether or not a new owner could take over the distributorship agreement, a decision which may be entirely up to the supplier.

For income tax purposes, case history shows some reluctance to accept any value dependent on a relationship that the owner does not have the legal right to transfer. When selling a business, however, intangible value relating to the relationship is usually included in the price; but the deal is subject to the supplier's approval of the new owners. The arguments that go on over this issue in divorces, damage cases, dissenting stockholder suits, and other valuation disputes are voluminous enough to fill a book by themselves.

Market Position

Whether the entity is a professional practice, a service business, a retailer, a manufacturer, or any other kind of business, its market position has an important bearing on the amount and certainty of its ability to generate earnings, and thus on its value.

Reputation

Reputation is critically important to a professional practice, while it would be less important to a retailer of standard merchandise selling primarily on a price basis. As with many factors, the degree of importance should help to determine how much investigation is warranted. Sources of information can include customers, suppliers, competitors, current and/or former employees, outside consultants of various kinds who may be familiar with the business or practice, and creditors.

Geographic Scope

An understanding of the entity should include the geographic scope of the markets its serves. The company's geographic scope can either be a positive or negative factor, depending on costs involved in doing business in the area, competitive factors, opportunities to increase market penetration, and other characteristics of the market.

Method of Marketing and Distribution

The appraiser should understand the company's methods of marketing and distribution. If revenues are generated primarily because of referrals or location, the appraiser should assess the potential continuity of the referral sources and the continued availability of the location. If revenues depend on continuous advertising, the business may not be able to continue without the advertising. If marketing is based heavily on personal sales efforts, will existing sales people or adequate replacements be available?

Another factor is whether the distribution system will continue to be available at a reasonable cost. If distribution is by mail, contract delivery service, or freight, will there be significant changes in costs?

In summary, it is important to understand how the revenues are generated, what brings the buyers to the entity, and how the goods and services are delivered, in order to assess the potential continuity of revenues and profit margins.

Pricing Policies

Commodity versus Specialized Products. In general, on the bottom of the value scale is a company that prices its products or services on a commodity basis, that sells on a price basis alone, without differentiating between its products or services and those offered by several direct competitors in the market. Such companies' pricing policies are totally subject to the external forces of the marketplace; they have no control over their own destiny in that respect. Their profit depends on their ability to operate more efficiently than their competitors. These companies include those that distribute branded merchandise but compete primarily on a price basis.

At the other end of the spectrum is the company whose product or service is so unique or so superior that it is insulated from direct competition; such a company has a high degree of discretion over its own pricing policies. Such companies are usually able to maintain consistently high profit margins and returns on investment and usually sell at a premium price over their net tangible asset value, in some cases very handsome premiums.

Most companies and practitioners are, of course, somewhere between these extremes, and the appraiser must use his judgment to assess how the entity's pricing situation bears on the level and reliability of its earning power.

Bid versus Negotiated Contract Prices. For companies that do a large portion of their business on fixed-price contracts (or fixed prices, subject to certain variables), it is desirable to ascertain how much is done on a bid basis instead of on a negotiated basis. As a generality, companies that have a large portion of their contracts strictly on a bid basis are considered to be in the category of commodity firms in terms of pricing, while those with more contracts on a negotiated basis are considered to be in the category of specialty firms. However, in some lines of business, buyers exercise considerable discretion in accepting bids, with quality and service considered as well as price. In those cases, bidder firms are considered a step removed from commodity firms in pricing.

Customer Base

Several aspects of the customer base are important, including diversification, persistence, and quality.

Diversification. For some companies, diversification or concentration of the customer base is a major factor. The low-value end of the spectrum would be represented by a company performing a single government contract that will be completed soon with no follow-up business presently in sight. (One might even question whether that situation should be classified as a going concern.) At the high-value end of the spectrum is a customer base so broad that losing a few customers would have no perceptible impact on the entity's revenues or profits.

Small businesses, and certain types of professional practices, commonly have one or a few large customers whose loss would deal a serious blow to the entity's earning capacity, or even to its viability. In these cases, the continuity of the key customers' business must be analyzed carefully and the risk assessed accordingly. Companies with very concentrated customer bases usually sell at discounts compared with other companies of comparable revenues and earnings but having more diversified customer bases, all other things being equal.

Persistence. Another aspect of the customer base is *persistence*, the extent to which the same customers tend to repeat. This characteristic has the dimensions of both longevity and frequency. In businesses such as insurance agencies and periodical publications, for example, first-year customers are not considered as valuable as longer-term customers because statistics have shown a positive correlation between longevity and propensity to renew. A service business that provides its services regularly to the same clientele, such as annual audits provided by a CPA firm, is generally worth more per dollar of historical revenues and earnings than the kind of service business in which each service performed is a new piece of business, even though some of the customers may have patronized the firm previously.

Quality. Appraising the quality of the customer base is certainly a very subjective judgment, but nevertheless important. Some of the measures of quality are the customers' ability and willingness to pay their bills on time, their ability to pay the kind of prices the operation would like to charge, their ability to increase their purchases over time, and their ability and propensity to refer other customers of comparable quality.

Customer Relationships

Closely akin to the analysis of the customer base is the analysis of customer relationships. If one or several major customers are family members, or have close personal or other business ties with the owner or a key person, then the appraiser should candidly assess the ability to retain those customers under new ownership.

Another aspect of customer relationships is customer satisfaction. Talks with some customers and former customers can help shed some light on this factor.

Market Continuity, Growth Opportunities, and Weaknesses

The point of this whole analysis of market position is to assess both the level and the degree of certainty of future revenues, along with the level and degree of certainty of the margins that those revenues will be able to generate in light of the pricing forces to which the company is subject. The greater the degree of continuity promised by the market position, the lower the risk. Growth opportunities are more valuable to the extent that they seem likely to evolve naturally from forces already in place than from large doses of entrepreneurial effort and expenditures. Weaknesses should be listed, evaluated, and reflected in the earnings stream and/or capitalization rates used in the valuation.

Management and Employees

The people factor is certainly a key qualitative element in most businesses and professional practices; this is especially true in small businesses, where typically there is substantial owner involvement in management, or the business focuses around one or a few key people.

Size and Composition of Work Force

A basic factor that influences the health of a business is the size and composition of the work force: the number of employees, their functions, their general backgrounds, qualifications, and levels of competence, and their basis and level of compensation. Whether the company is adequately staffed, understaffed, or overstaffed will have a bearing on the extent to which the company's long-term earning capacity will conform to its recent history.

Key Employees

The importance of the owner or other key employees to the success of the business is a matter that must be given the utmost attention in valuing small businesses and professional practices. Information should be acquired as to age, length of service, education, and prior experience of each key employee; whether he works full-time or part-time; whether he has outside work or financial interests that may dilute his efforts or cause any conflict of interest; his level of compensation, including all fringe benefits and discretionary expenses; and how long he intends to stay with the entity.

If key employees' expertise and customer relationships would take some time to transfer to a new owner, then the value of the transaction to the buyer would depend on their willingness to enter into an employment contract for the ownership-transition period. Furthermore, if customers would follow the seller if he or she left and opened a new shop or joined a competitor, then the value of the transaction probably also depends on a noncompete agreement. Employment agreements and noncompete agreements, if applicable, are usually calculated in the total value arrived at for the business or practice. However, in negotiating the actual deal, they are often separated and the total transaction value allocated among the purchase price for the business, employment agreements, and the covenants not to compete. This matter is discussed further in Chapter 36.

Other Employees

It is helpful to have an idea of the nature of the work force, the extent to which it is unionized, or may be unionized, the history of any strikes or work stoppages, and its general adequacy for the tasks at hand. This analysis may give some indication of necessary or possible changes that may affect profitability.

Compensation

Nonowner Employees. The main consideration with respect to nonowner employees is whether the compensation is adequate, inadequate, or too high. If inadequate, some additional costs should be allowed when estimating earning power. If compensation is too high, there should be room for savings, but perhaps not immediately.

Owner Employees. If an owner is going to stay on as an employee, his value in his employment role should be estimated. If he wants to take out more than the value of his employment in direct compensation and benefits, the purchase price can be adjusted downward accordingly.

Personnel Policies, Satisfaction, Conflict, and Turnover

A prospective owner should know the main features of past personnel policies. Only a small percentage of small businesses and professional practices have personnel policies in writing, and those that do may or may not follow them closely. Consequently, such information usually needs to be gleaned through interviews. This study may also uncover some additional cost requirements or some possible savings.

Informal discussions with employees should give clues as to whether they are satisfied or dissatisfied and costs that might be necessary for the new owner to incur to correct existing problems. If there are internal conflicts, it may be possible to bring them to light during the valuation process. People do like to talk, especially about things that are bothering them. Interviews can bring many problems to light, enabling their impact on the value of the entity to be assessed. Sometimes the problems are frustrations over being unable to pursue opportunities an employee envisions—they may be true opportunities for the enterprise, as well.

A personnel turnover rate below the average for the kind of business is usually regarded as a plus, and a high turnover rate is usually considered a negative. Some businesses, however, intentionally have a high turnover rate in order to avoid the higher direct compensation and benefits that tend to accrue with seniority.

Adequacy of Physical Facility

The physical facility may allow for considerable expansion; it may be just about adequate for current operations; it may require capital expenditures; or it may be so inadequate that a move is imminent. If the physical facility is important, its adequacy or lack of it obviously has a bearing on value.

Condition

As discussed in Chapter 7, an important concern in the valuation of facilities is deferred maintenance, which can include such items as needed painting, repair of leaks, repair of broken or cracked windows, doors, and walls, equipment maintenance, and anything necessary to put the facility in good operating condition. For retail outlets or service establishments with considerable foot traffic, maintenance can also include modernizing, even though existing equipment and decor are not necessarily in bad condition, in order to keep up with current trends and upscale consumer expectations.

Heat, Light, Plumbing, and Other Systems

Special attention should be paid to the adequacy of all operating systems, including all utility hookups, heating and air conditioning, all electrical systems, burglar alarms, sprinkler system, and plumbing, including the adequacy of rest rooms. There may be deferred maintenance, but more importantly, certain systems may be antiquated in their abilities to serve current needs, especially electrical systems, because commercial electrical appliances have come to be used far more extensively since most electrical systems were installed. These factors need to be assessed and any cost implications reflected in the valuation.

Size

The size of the facility should be considered not only in relation to current needs, but also in relation to needs in the foreseeable future. If a move appears to be in prospect, its cost and the likely changes in occupancy cost should be taken into consideration.

Continuity of Occupancy

If it seems preferable to continue occupying the present location, it is important to determine the length of time that the premises will be assured to be available, and at what cost. Any increased costs should be reflected in the valuation.

Operating Efficiencies and Inefficiencies

Any special efficiencies or inefficiencies that may be identified should be helpful in assessing ongoing earning power and future costs. By *efficiency* in this context, I mean getting the job done at the lowest possible cost, and by *inefficiency*, I mean any circumstance that would cause higher-than-necessary costs.

Physical Plant

Plant-related efficiency, or lack of it, generally arises from location, size, and layout, and the extent to which the equipment is or is not state-of-the-art. Some causes of plant inefficiency are easily correctable, some may be difficult or costly to correct, and some may be impossible to change. The valuation must consider the impact on earnings power of any inefficiencies not correctable, such as extra transportation costs because of remote location, functional obsolescence of equipment, or extra labor costs because of inefficient layout, as well as the costs of correcting any existing inefficiencies that will be worthwhile to correct. It is also possible that correction of inefficiencies will result in some profitability gains that should be reflected.

Accounting and Other Controls

Accounting systems can be adapted to be very useful tools of management control, but few small businesses and professional practices even approach getting maximum management benefit out of their accounting systems. The extent of controls implemented should be investigated. To the extent that good controls are in place and being utilized effectively, the risk of an unexpected earnings decline is reduced, although most of the upside profit potential from efficiency may have already been achieved. To the extent that controls are poor, of course, the risk of an unanticipated drop in earnings is increased.

Reason for Sale

It is always desirable to know why the business is being offered for sale. If the sale is under pressure, the price is likely to be less than if there is no pressure to sell. If the business is in an estate, in most cases it is worth less than if the former owner/manager were still living; usually some value is lost due to the lack of an orderly transition period. This factor varies considerably, depending on the role of the former owner/manager in the operations of the business and his relationships with its public. The value implications of all the many reasons to sell vary greatly, but it is another qualitative item to take into consideration.

Summary

This chapter covered a wide variety of qualitative factors that most frequently have a bearing on the value of a business or professional practice; it has not covered all the vast number of possible factors that might be encountered in any specific case. Exhibit 10-1 summarizes the steps in analyzing qualitative factors.

It should be clear that it is impossible to create any cookbook or formula valuation models or methods that can fully reflect and evaluate all the subjective factors that have a bearing on value. In most individual cases, one or a few subjective or qualitative factors really have a significant influence on value; a dozen or more others may have a minor influence.

While the chapter has suggested factors to look for, the appraiser will require considerable experience and judgment to put them in perspective and to determine how they will influence his ultimate opinion of value, or the price that a buyer would be willing to pay, or that a seller should be willing to accept.

Exhibit 10–1

SUMMARY OF STEPS IN
ANALYZING QUALITATIVE FACTORS

Step 1   Collect and analyze national economic data that could have a bearing on the subject company's outlook.

Step 2   Collect and review relevant regional and local economic data that could impact the subject company's future profitability.

Step 3   Collect and analyze sources of information on the industry in which the subject company operates.

Step 4   Analyze the existing competitors of the subject company and consider the potential for new entrants into the company's markets.

Step 5   Review government regulations that affect the business, especially with a view toward potential changes.

Step 6   Review the product lines offered by the subject company as of the valuation date and review the following:

- Opportunities for the subject company to add related business lines.
- The extent of the continuity of the income stream associated with any patents, copyrights, or trademarks of the company.
- The relative profitability of each of the company's product lines.

Step 7   Examine the continuity, degree of exclusivity, and contractual relationships of any supplier relationships of the subject company.

Step 8   Evaluate the market position of the company being appraised, including, but not limited to, the following:

- The reputation of the company.
- The geographic scope of the company's operations.
- The company's methods of marketing and distribution.
- The pricing policies of the company.
- The diversification, quality, and persistence of the company's customer base.
- The strengths and weaknesses of the company's overall market position.

Step 9   Review the employees of the subject company, including the following:

- Review the size and composition of the work force.
- Summarize each of the key employees of the company, including background information such as age, length of service, education, and prior experience.
- Evaluate the level of owner compensation.
- Review the historical turnover rates of the company's work force.

Step 10   Analyze the physical facility of the company to determine its condition, adequacy of operating systems, and capacity.

Step 11   Summarize the operating efficiencies and inefficiencies related to the subject company.

Chapter 11

The Buyer's Perspective—
Pro Forma Statements

Up until this point, we have been looking at the financial statements of the business in question under its current operations and as it stands. However, from the viewpoint of a prospective buyer, some changes may be necessary or desirable. The thrust of this chapter is to step into the buyer's shoes, to consider the financial statements and possible changes from the viewpoint of a knowledgeable buyer. Before coming to grips with the question of how much to offer, there are a number of factors a buyer should take into consideration.

The buyer must look at his total investment in the business, not just what he pays the seller. Apart from how much the buyer pays the seller for the business or practice, how much additional financing will be necessary, what will be its source, and what will it cost? Or will the business itself be a source of financing for the purchase?

Analysis of Working Capital Requirements

If it will be necessary to provide additional working capital, the buyer's pro forma balance sheet should reflect the amount needed and the source. If the buyer will be providing extra dollars for working capital, that amount should be reflected in the pro forma balance sheet and recognized as part of the buyer's total investment in the business when deciding how much to offer the seller. If the buyer plans to borrow from a bank to finance working capital needs, the pro forma balance sheet should reflect the average amount of borrowing expected, and the interest should be reflected on the buyer's pro forma income statement. For definitions and examples of working capital and its components, see Exhibit 11–1.

Steps in Analyzing Working Capital

If the prospective buyer doesn't know how much working capital it will take to operate the business, he can get some guidance from the industry-average data discussed in Chapter 9. For example, Exhibit 9–1 shows that the average ratio of sales to working capital for women's ready-to-wear stores of all sizes is 7.2:1. Therefore, among those in the RMA sample the average women's ready-to-wear store expecting to do $1 million in sales would have about $139,000 in working capital.

Note, however, that in Exhibit 11–1 the sales to working capital range is quite wide. The upper quartile figure is 4.8 ($208,000 working capital to support $1 million sales), and the lower quartile is 15.0 ($67,000 working capital to support $1 million). One of the biggest variables, of course, would be whether or not the store has a policy of selling on credit. The other major variables on the asset side are how often the inventory turns over (average length of time the merchandise stays in inventory) and, if the company sells on credit, the average length of time it takes to collect accounts receivable. On the liability side, the two main variables are the trade terms available from suppliers and the terms under which other financing (usually bank borrowing) can be arranged.

Exhibit 11–1

ANALYSIS OF WORKING CAPITAL
AND ITS MAJOR COMPONENTS

Definitions

Working Capital = Current Assets - Current Liabilities

Current Assets. Cash and items expected to be converted to cash or used up in the business within one year. Major items are cash, marketable securities, accounts receivable, notes receivable within a year, prepaid expenses, and inventory.

Current Liabilities. Items expected to be paid within one year. Major items are accounts payable, notes payable within a year (including any portion of longer-term debt that is due within a year), and accrued expenses.

Current Ratio $= \dfrac{\text{Current Assets}}{\text{Current Liabilities}}$

Quick Ratio $= \dfrac{\text{Cash \& Equivalents + Receivables}}{\text{Current Liabilities}}$

Working Capital Turnover $= \dfrac{\text{Sales}}{\text{Working Capital}}$

Preferably, this ratio is computed using *average* working capital as the denominator. However, as a matter of expedience, it is often computed using working capital at the end of the period as the denominator.

Accounts Receivable Turnover $= \dfrac{\text{Sales}}{\text{Accounts Receivable}}$

Preferably computed using *average* accounts receivable; for expedience, often computed using ending accounts receivable.

Average Collection Period (Days) $= \dfrac{365}{\text{Accounts Receivable Turnover}}$

Inventory Turnover $= \dfrac{\text{Cost of Goods Sold}}{\text{Inventory}}$

Preferably computed using *average* inventory; for expedience, often computed using ending inventory. Many companies have unusually low inventories at the end of their fiscal periods because they let the inventories run down to make it easier to take the physical inventory count and/or because they set the end of the fiscal year to coincide with a seasonally slow time, when inventories would normally be low. In such cases, doing the computation on the basis of ending inventory will overstate the true inventory turnover.

Average Day's Inventory $= \dfrac{365}{\text{Inventory Turnover}}$

Exhibit 11–1 (concluded)

Example of Working Capital Analysis

Sales	$100,000	Cost of Goods Sold	$ 60,000

Current Assets:		Current Liabilities:	
Cash	$ 1,000	Accounts Payable	$ 8,000
Accounts Receivable	10,000	Bank Note Payable	12,000
Inventory	15,000		
Prepaid Expenses	2,000		
Total Current Assets	$ 28,000	Total Current Liabilities	$ 20,000

Working Capital $= \$28,000 - \$20,000 = \$8,000$

Current Ratio $= \dfrac{\$28,000}{\$20,000} = 1.4$

Quick Ratio $= \dfrac{\$11,000}{\$20,000} = .55$

Working Capital Turnover $= \dfrac{\$100,000}{\$8,000} = 12.5$

Accounts Receivable Turnover $= \dfrac{\$100,000}{\$10,000} = 10$

Average Collection Period $= \dfrac{365}{10} = 36.5$ Days

Inventory Turnover $= \dfrac{\$60,000}{\$15,000} = 4.0$ times per year

Average Days' Inventory $= \dfrac{365}{4.0} = 91$ days

To summarize, the buyer's analysis of his working capital needs consists of the following steps:

1. Estimate sales volume.
2. Decide on credit policy, and estimate the average amount of accounts receivable on the basis of the average estimated collection period.
3. Estimate the amount of inventory needed on the basis of estimated average inventory turnover.
4. Estimate the amount of prepaid expenses needed.
5. Estimate the average amount of accounts payable on the basis of trade terms available from suppliers.
6. Estimate the average amount of bank financing on the basis of the terms of the bank financing available.
7. Allow for some extra cash, because the steps above are estimates and averages; there may not be enough cash at peak periods. (If the

business is highly seasonal, this analysis should be done on the basis of the high seasonal requirements rather than on the averages.)

8. From the steps above, compute the amount of working capital that will be necessary.

9. As a check, compute the current ratio, quick ratio, and working capital turnover based on the results of steps 1 through 8, and compare them with industry averages.

An Example of Working Capital Analysis

1. Annie's Apparel has been doing $1 million volume. Industry sources expect retail selling prices to go up by about 5 percent this year. The shopping center's consultant has predicted a 4 percent increase in foot traffic. Considering these factors, and assuming no major changes in the operation, an estimated sales volume of approximately $1.1 million seems reasonable.

2. Annie's accounts receivable turnover has been 33 times per year, because she has extended only very limited credit. If the new buyer follows the same policy, on $1.1 million sales, we would estimate average accounts receivable at about $35,000.

3. Using the adjusted balance sheet (Exhibit 7–2, page 88), we see that the inventory value at current prices is $220,000. Using the adjusted income statement (Exhibit 8–2, page 102), we see that the cost of goods sold was $535,000. If the buyer can maintain the same gross margin, the cost of goods sold will be about $589,000 (0.535 × $1,100,000 = $589,000). Inventory turnover last year was 2.6 times. If we maintain the same inventory turnover, we will need about $227,000 average inventory.

4. Annie's $3,000 of prepaid expenses includes a rental deposit only. The new buyer will need to pay a rent advance of $5,000 immediately. Also, as noted in Exhibit 8–2, Annie's has not been carrying any fire, theft, or liability insurance. The buyer will need to take out a policy with a $2,000 annual premium, bringing total prepaid expenses to $10,000.

5. Trade credit is on a 30-day basis. With estimated purchases of $589,000 (from step 3 above), average estimated trade accounts payable would be about $49,000.

6. We find that we can get a bank line of credit of $200,000 based on 60 percent of inventory and accounts receivable under 90 days old. If we assume $227,000 average inventory and an average of $30,000 eligible account receivable (under 90 days old), average bank financing would be about $155,000 (0.6 × $257,000 = $155,000).

7. There is not a great deal of seasonality to the business, and some flexibility is available in suppliers' trade terms at peak periods, so we will assume that $10,000 extra cash will cover fluctuations and contingencies.

8. On the basis of steps 1 through 7, working capital requirement can be estimated as follows:

Current assets: Current liabilities:
Cash $10,000   Accounts payable $49,000
Accounts receivable   35,000   Bank note payable   155,000
Inventory   227,000
Prepaid expenses   10,000
Total current assets $282,000   Total current liabilities $204,000

Working capital: $282,000 − $204,000 = $78,000

$$\text{Current ratio} = \frac{\$282,000}{\$204,000} = 1.4$$

$$\text{Quick ratio} = \frac{\$10,000 + \$35,000}{\$204,000} = .22$$

$$\text{Working capital turnover} = \frac{\$1,100,000}{\$78,000} = 14.1$$

9. Exhibit 9–1 shows that the average current ratio for women's ready-to-wear stores with total assets of $500,000 to $2,000,000 is 2.0, but the lower quartile is 1.5, approximately equal to our estimate. The average quick ratio is 0.6, with a lower quartile of 0.2, also fairly close to our estimate. The median sales/working capital (working capital turnover) ratio is 7.2, with a lower quartile of 15.0, again just a little above our estimate. The result is that Annie's new owners would be in the bottom 25 percent of similar companies in short-term liquidity. This is within a reasonable operating range and isn't necessarily alarming. The new owners will have to exercise cash flow controls.

In summary, the above analysis suggests a balance sheet that will include $282,000 of current assets, of which $49,000 will be financed by trade payables, $155,000 by short-term bank borrowings, and $78,000 by long-term debt and/or owner's equity.

This analysis of Annie's assumes business to be pretty much as usual, based on recent history. It should be noted that the inventory turnover of 2.6 times per year is near the bottom quartile of the industry average (from Exhibit 9–1), considerably below the median of 3.0. It would appear that there might be room for improvement in inventory turnover. On the other hand, Annie's gross margin of 44 percent is slightly above the industry average of 43.0 percent, which may be partly due to a merchandise mix that turns more slowly than the industry's average merchandise mix.

Analysis of Fixed Assets

The buyer should analyze the fixed assets to determine whether an additional investment in fixed assets will be necessary, or whether any existing assets are above the needs of the business and could be sold without affecting the entity's earning power.

Deferred Maintenance and Replacement Requirements

It is not at all uncommon to find that physical premises and equipment have not been kept up to the standard necessary to continue to perform their functions effectively. Owners may have deferred normal maintenance and equipment for a wide variety of reasons, anything from inadequate capital to just plain apathy.

When such conditions are present, the buyer should estimate the cost of the deferred maintenance and replacements and consider that cost as part of the investment in the business. As a generality, if a buyer would pay $100,000 for a business with equipment in average condition, but it will cost $20,000 in repairs and replacements to bring the equipment in the subject business to average condition, he might be willing to pay $80,000 for the business "as is."

Compliance Requirements

As noted in Chapter 7, there may be some off-balance-sheet liabilities, such as costs of equipment to comply with environmental clean-up regulations, OSHA, pollution control, zoning standards, building codes, or other governmental requirements. A buyer should make provision for any such costs as part of his investment.

Other Asset Inadequacies

Sometimes a company has simply outgrown its physical capacity to do its job because of inadequate space and/or equipment. Costs of moving, or any capital additions necessary to maintain the level of revenues on which the valuation analysis is based, should be provided for as part of the buyer's investment.

Excess Assets

In some cases, businesses have assets that are not really needed in the operations, usually excess equipment and/or real estate. Any net proceeds a buyer could expect to receive from disposals of such assets could be used to reduce the amount of permanent investment he might otherwise require. If disposal of excess assets is contemplated, any revenues and/or expenses associated with such assets should be removed when compiling the buyer's pro forma income statement.

Contingent Liabilities

It is important that the buyer analyze any contingent liabilities that may carry forward into new ownership and determine what provision needs to be made for them. As noted in Chapter 7, they may be recognized on the balance sheet either by a line item in the liability section or by a footnote.

Structure of Long-Term Liabilities

At the time he is preparing to offer to buy a business or practice, the buyer should take into consideration the likely structure of his long-term liabilities. The structure of the buyer's financing has a bearing on the cost of capital, which in turn may influence the price offered for a business. This interrelationship is discussed in Chapter 12. The structure of the long-term liabilities also affects the buyer's ability to service the debt, as discussed in Chapter 20.

A buyer may elect to pay off some existing long-term liabilities because he considers the financing cost high, and either doesn't need it or can get it cheaper elsewhere. The buyer may be forced to pay off certain long-term liabilities because they are not assumable, a matter that must be checked in each case if a buyer is considering assuming any existing liabilities.

A buyer who has the desire and ability to obtain long-term financing for the purchase should investigate the probable amount and terms and reflect them in his pro forma balance sheet and income statement.

One option, which is very popular in sales of small businesses and professional practices, is to have the seller carry a long-term contract for a significant portion of the transaction price. Whether this contract will be technically the obligation of the business under the new owner, or a personal obligation of the new owner, putting the obligation on pro forma financial statements of the business makes clear the amounts that will have to be paid, one way or another, relative to the other financial variables of the business. As a practical matter, if it is technically a personal obligation of the buyer, the resources of the business will probably be pledged to secure its payment anyway.

The Buyer's Income Statement

A sophisticated buyer will make a pro forma income statement for an entity he is considering purchasing, based on how he thinks he will operate the business.

Broadly speaking, a buyer's income statement might differ from the adjusted (normalized) income statements, as developed in Chapter 8, for three reasons:

1. Changes in the prospects for the business that the buyer anticipates while still viewing the operation as a stand-alone, independent entity, with no basic changes in its business.
2. Changes the buyer contemplates as a result of effecting some change

in the nature or in the operations of the business, but still viewing it as an independent entity.
3. Synergies and efficiencies that arise as a result of combining the entity income in some way with other entities controlled by the buyer.

This categorization of possible changes is somewhat arbitrary, and the categories are not mutually exclusive. In most cases, the changes would sooner or later make the business worth more to the buyer than it would be worth if the business were assumed to continue to operate as it has in the past. Obviously, such considerations have a bearing on how much any "particular" buyer might be willing and able to pay. Since these items are predicated on the buyer's perception of his ability to change things to his advantage, he wants as little as possible of the potential benefit of such changes reflected in the transaction price. Consequently, in most cases, the seller and his representative never see the buyer's pro forma income statement.

Changes in Existing Operations

Revenues. The buyer may believe that revenues can be increased, perhaps significantly, without major changes in the basic nature of the business. These improvements could result from a number of things, such as changes in the promotional theme, changes in the merchandise mix, or improved service to increase repeat business. Obviously, the buyer's pro forma statement must reflect any increased costs associated with the hypothetical increases in revenues.

Operating Expenses. The buyer should analyze all the operating expenses to determine whether he or she would anticipate their being higher or lower than in the past. The analysis may be based on personal experience or on industry averages, as developed in Chapter 9. Some of the items most likely to be adjusted might be wage costs and promotional expense items.

At this point in the analysis, the new owner/manager should set his own salary at something approximating a market rate for his services, regardless of what he actually thinks he may or may not take out of the business in salary and perks.

Interest Expense. Since the buyer would probably finance the operation somewhat differently from how it was financed in the past, there may be a difference in interest cost. The buyer's pro forma income statement should reflect interest based on how the buyer contemplates financing the business.

Sensitivity Analysis. Often, the buyer will consider several "states of the world" in order to understand the sensitivity of various factors. For example, the buyer might analyze the required changes in the operations of the business (and the resulting change in purchase price) due to a decrease in revenues of 20 percent or an increase in revenues of 20 percent.

New Business Directions

The potential for this category of change is so vast that it almost defies any comprehensive discussion of the many possibilities. The buyer may plan to turn a conventional retailer into a discounter. He may add entire new product lines. He may eliminate or implement a credit policy. He may discontinue a losing or marginal aspect of the operation. In any case, the buyer's income statement should reflect the anticipated consequences of the contemplated changes.

Synergies and Efficiencies

A particular buyer may be in a unique position to effect changes because of other related operations under his control. He may benefit from eliminating a competitor, controlling a source of supply, controlling a distribution outlet, or reducing costs by combining activities. No two potential buyers' pro forma statements will be alike, but the category of synergies is where they are likely to differ the most. From the strategic buyer's perspective, the most important aspects of the potential acquisition might be the synergies, without which he might have little or no interest in the seller's operation. The buyer will want to see what the income statement would look like when the benefits of the available synergies appear.

Samples of Buyer's Pro Forma Statements

The following are hypothetical examples of buyers' pro forma income statements that illustrate the considerations from the buyer's perspective discussed in this chapter. The two examples continue the same two hypothetical companies used in the last three chapters.

Purchase of a Sole Proprietorship

Exhibit 11–2 is a buyer's pro forma income statement for Annie's Apparel Store from the perspective of one hypothetical buyer. The prospective buyer of Annie's Apparel Store is Rags, Inc. Rags operates a chain of 10 women's ready-to-wear stores. Rags plans to continue to operate the new store as Annie's Apparel Store, although the merchandising mix will change somewhat, and thus the gross margins will probably be more in line with the 40 percent experienced by most of the Rags Stores. However, Rags does expect operating expenses to be less, due to efficiencies effected through combining the stores. Such expense as legal, accounting, insurance, automobile, travel and entertainment, and supplies should be lower. Rags projects that Annie's sales will increase 10 percent

Exhibit 11–2

ANNIE'S APPAREL STORE
BUYER'S PRO FORMA INCOME STATEMENT

	Income Statement as Reported 1991		Adjusted Income Statement 1991		Pro Forma Income Statement	
	$	%	$	%	$	%
Sales	1,000,000	100.0	1,000,000	100.0	1,100,000	100.0
Cost of Goods Sold:						
Beginning Inventory	170,000		185,000		185,000	
Plus: Purchases	570,000		570,000		695,000	
	740,000		755,000		880,000	
Less: Ending Inventory	180,000		220,000		220,000	
Cost of Goods Sold	560,000	56.0	535,000	53.5	660,000	60.0
Gross Margin	440,000	44.0	465,000	46.5	440,000	40.0
Expenses:						
Owner's Salary	70,000	7.0	50,000	5.0	50,000	4.5
Other Salaries	150,000	15.0	150,000	15.0	150,000	13.6
Payroll Taxes	30,000	3.0	30,000	3.0	30,000	2.7
Employee Benefits	23,000	2.3	23,000	2.3	20,000	1.8
Rent	65,000	6.5	65,000	6.5	65,000	5.9
Utilities	3,000	0.3	3,000	0.3	3,000	0.3
Telephone	3,000	0.3	3,000	0.3	3,000	0.3
Insurance	0	0.0	2,000	0.2	1,000	0.1
Supplies	5,000	0.5	5,000	0.5	4,000	0.4
Advertising	25,000	2.5	25,000	2.5	20,000	1.8
Travel & Entertainment	25,000	2.5	5,000	0.5	3,000	0.3
Automobile Expense	5,000	0.5	5,000	0.5	3,000	0.3
Outside Accountants	5,000	0.5	5,000	0.5	3,000	0.3
Legal	3,000	0.3	3,000	0.3	1,500	0.1
License, Registrations, etc.	2,000	0.2	2,000	0.2	2,000	0.2
Dues & Subscriptions	1,000	0.1	1,000	0.1	1,000	0.1
Allow. for Doubtful Accts.	0	0.0	2,400	0.2	3,500	0.3
Depreciation	13,000	1.3	13,000	1.3	13,000	1.2
Interest	7,000	0.7	7,000	0.7	7,000	0.6
Total Expenses	435,000	43.5	399,400	39.9	383,000	34.8
Pretax Income	5,000	0.5	65,600	6.6	57,000	5.2

NOTE: Figures may not total due to rounding.

due to a more effective advertising campaign, which will be less expensive than what Annie's used. Rags' employee benefit program is not as generous as Annie's and will be less expensive.

Purchase of Corporate Stock

Exhibit 11–3 is a buyer's pro forma income statement for Mary's Machinery & Equipment, Inc., from the perspective of Barney Backhoe, who has been working as general manager for Mary's. Mr. Backhoe and two associates want to purchase Mary's.

Mr. Backhoe plans to keep the name of the business as it is because Mary's has a reputation for good quality and service. He expects to be able to maintain sales at their current level. Mr. Backhoe does want to emphasize the service end of the business more, because Mary's has

Exhibit 11–3

MARY'S MACHINERY & EQUIPMENT, INC.
BUYER'S PRO FORMA INCOME STATEMENT

	Income Statement as Reported 1991		Adjusted Income Statement 1991		Pro Forma Income Statement	
	$	%	$	%	$	%
Sales	2,400,000	100.0	2,400,000	100.0	2,400,000	100.0
Cost of Goods Sold:						
Beginning Inventory	300,000		400,000		400,000	
Plus: Purchases	1,620,000		1,620,000		1,590,000	
	1,920,000		2,020,000		1,990,000	
Less: Ending Inventory	320,000		430,000		430,000	
Cost of Goods Sold	1,600,000	66.7	1,590,000	66.2	1,560,000	65.0
Gross Margin	800,000	33.3	810,000	33.8	840,000	35.0
Expenses:						
Officers' Compensation	120,000	5.0	120,000	5.0	110,000	4.6
Salaries & Wages	230,000	9.6	230,000	9.6	230,000	9.6
Employee Benefits	50,000	2.1	50,000	2.1	50,000	2.1
Payroll Taxes	50,000	2.1	50,000	2.1	50,000	2.1
Rent	24,000	1.0	24,000	1.0	24,000	1.0
Depreciation	33,000	1.4	33,000	1.4	33,000	1.4
Insurance	20,000	0.8	20,000	0.8	20,000	0.8
Travel & Entertainment	30,000	1.3	30,000	1.3	25,000	1.0
Maintenace & Repair	0	0.0	0	0.0	20,000	0.8
Policy Adjustments	26,000	1.1	26,000	1.1	26,000	1.1
Transportation Vehicles	24,000	1.0	24,000	1.0	29,000	1.2
Prov. for Bad Debt	13,000	0.5	13,000	0.5	13,000	0.5
Other	90,000	3.8	90,000	3.8	90,000	3.8
Total Expenses	710,000	29.7	710,000	29.7	720,000	30.0
Operating Income	90,000	3.6	100,000	4.1	120,000	5.0
Other Income (Expense):						
Interest Expense	(15,000)	(0.6)	(15,000)	(0.6)	(20,000)	(0.8)
Dividend Income	1,000	Nil	1,000	Nil	0	0
Total Other Inc. (Exp.)	(14,000)	(0.6)	(14,000)	(0.6)	(20,000)	(0.8)
Income Before Taxes	76,000	3.0	86,000	3.5	100,000	4.2
Income Taxes	16,000	0.7	20,000	0.8	25,750	1.1
Net Income	60,000	2.3	66,000	2.7	74,250	3.1

NOTE: Figures may not total due to rounding.

Nil = Inconsequential amount, greater (or less) than zero.

an excellent team of mechanics and service people. That should cause margins to improve slightly.

Summary

It is typical for a knowledgeable buyer to make up a pro forma balance sheet and income statement for the business or practice under consideration reflecting the buyer's plans and expectations. In this chapter we have addressed the pro forma statements on a single-year basis, but many buyers will go out three to five years with pro forma statements. This analysis helps the buyer to quantify and assess expectations for the business.

Almost all buyers expect businesses to do *better* under the new ownership than they have historically. Generally, this is due to the buyer's plans to improve the operation. Thus, the buyer's pro forma results, if translated into a value, would result in what we have called *investment value* (value to that particular buyer) in Chapter 3. This may set an absolute upper limit on what the buyer is willing to pay. The buyer, of course, wants little, if any, of the value resulting from future changes to be reflected in the purchase price. However, buyers are sometimes willing to pay *something* over the value indicated by historical results in order to purchase the opportunity.

Exhibit 11–4

SUMMARY OF STEPS IN
PREPARING PRO FORMA STATEMENTS

Step 1   Analyze the working capital requirements of the business based on industry sources.

Step 2   Analyze the fixed assets of the company to determine whether an additional investment in fixed assets is necessary, or whether any existing assets are above the needs of the business and could be sold without affecting the entity's earning power.

Step 3   Review any contingent liabilities and determine what provision needs to be made for them.

Step 4   Determine the desired structure of long-term liabilities.

Step 5   Summarize a pro forma income statement for the subject company.

Part III

Reaching the Value Conclusion

Chapter 12

Understanding Discount and Capitalization Rates

Discount Rate: A rate of return used to convert a monetary sum [or series of monetary sums], payable or receivable in the future, into present value.[1]
Capitalization Rate: Any divisor [usually expressed as a percentage] that is used to convert income into value.[2]

Introduction

Converting expected income to value—this is the core of valuation of businesses and professional practices. Obviously, this chapter is one of the most critical chapters in the book.

The most important approach to valuing most going-concern businesses or practices is to discount or capitalize some measure of earning power. Whether we classify the many discounting and capitalization methods of doing this under the "income approach," "the cost approach," or the "market approach" is irrelevant. In all discounting and capitalizing methods, we convert one or more measures of actual or estimated earning power to an indication of value, using discount or capitalization rates derived from market data.

An understanding of the nature of discount rates and capitalization rates and the selection of the applicable rate for a given situation is probably the most difficult problem in the entire process of business valuation.

Perfectly valid methods of valuation will produce perfectly meaningless results unless one uses valid numbers. The ability to select applicable discount and capitalization rates in a wide variety of situations is an indispensable skill of the expert business appraiser. It is also one of the most difficult skills to understand and implement thoroughly. Mistakes and poor judgment in the selection of discount and capitalization rates are probably the most common sources of error in business valuation.

"Discounting" versus "Capitalizing"

In the introduction, the terms *discounting and capitalizing methods* and *discount and capitalization rates* were used several times. Before proceeding, we need to understand the difference between a discounting method and a capitalizing method. From this understanding we can then proceed to understand the difference between discount rates and capitalization rates.

As we shall see in the next sections, discounting is a procedure applied to one or a series of returns expected in the future, while capitalizing is a procedure that can be applied to historical, current, or expected future level of returns.

Note that up to this point, we have talked about discounting or capitalizing *income, earnings power,* or *returns*—all generic terms with no specific meaning. Later, we will deal with the critical matter of exact

---

[1]American Society of Appraisers, Business Valuation Standard I—BV I Terminology (American Society of Appraisers, June 1992) (parenthetical note supplied).
[2]Ibid.

definitions of the many measurements of economic income that may be discounted or capitalized.

Discounting

Discounting is the exact opposite of compounding. In compounding, we ask the question, "If I invest a dollar today at x percent interest for a period of x years, how much will it be worth at the end of x years?" In discounting, we ask the opposite question: "In order to receive a dollar x years in the future, based on x percent assumed compound rate of return, how much do I have to invest today?" Exhibit 12–1 shows the basic arithmetic of discounting.

Discounting is a procedure that converts an expected future return, or a series of expected future returns, to a present value using a discount rate. The discount rate is the assumed periodic compound total rate of return on the investment over the life of that investment. The total return is comprised of one or both of two components:

1. *Income.* Amounts received while holding the investment (usually in the form of interest on debt, dividends on stock, or withdrawals from a partnership or sole proprietorship).
2. *Appreciation (or depreciation).* The incremental (or decremental) amount received at the time of liquidating the investment, over and above (or below) the amount paid for the investment.

Perhaps the purest form of discounting a lump-sum future payment to a present value is found in zero-coupon U.S. Treasury bonds. You buy a bond that pays a lump sum of $1,000 at some specified date in the future. The term *zero coupon* means that they pay you no interest along the way. Instead, the bonds are sold at a discounted price to give the investor the annually compounded rate of return that the market requires to attract investment in those bonds at the time that the bonds are issued. For example, if current market conditions require a rate of return of 8 percent on a 10-year "zero," the present market value would be computed as follows (using the arithmetic shown in Exhibit 12–1):

$$\text{PV} = \frac{\$1,000}{(1+.08)^{10}}$$
$$= \$463.19$$

A reader can look in *Barron's* or other financial publications and see the current price and rate of return assuming the bond is held to maturity for all maturities of zero coupon U.S. Treasury bonds.

Exhibit 12–1 shows an example using a bond that pays regular interest plus face value at maturity.

There are many different measures of expected future returns that can be discounted when valuing a business or practice. Some of the most commonly used examples include:

1. Net free cash flow available to all invested capital.
2. Net free cash flow available to common equity.

Exhibit 12–1

ARITHMETIC OF DISCOUNTING VS. COMPOUNDING

COMPOUNDING

The formula to determine the future value of an amount invested at annually compounded interest for a certain number of years is as follows:

$$FV = PV(1 + r)^i$$

where:

FV	=	Future Value
PV	=	Present Value
r	=	rate
i	=	ith year (the number of years into the future that the principal plus the compound rate of return will be received)

Example

Assume that we invest $1,000 for 3 years at 10% interest. Substituting in the above formula gives us the following:

$$
\begin{aligned}
FV &= \$1,000(1 + .10)^3 \\
&= \$1,000(1.10 \times 1.10 \times 1.10) \\
&= \$1,000(1.331) \\
&= \$1,331
\end{aligned}
$$

DISCOUNTING

Start with the formula for compounding:

$$FV = PV(1 + r)^i$$

As we learned in basic algebra, we can divide both sides of an equation by the same factor:

$$\frac{FV}{(1 + r)^i} = \frac{PV(1 + r)^i}{(1 + r)^i}$$

Also, if the same factor appears in both the numerator and the denominator of an expression, we can cancel them out:

$$\frac{FV}{(1 + r)^i} = \frac{PV\cancel{(1 + r)^i}}{\cancel{(1 + r)^i}}$$

And lo and behold, we have the formula for discounting from a future value to a present value! Since it is customary to put the dependent variable (the value we are solving for) on the left hand side, the basic formula for discounting is written as follows:

$$PV = \frac{FV}{(1 + r)^i}$$

Exhibit 12–1 (concluded)

Example

If we can get 10% annually compounded interest, how much do we have to invest today to get a lump-sum payment of $1,331 exactly 3 years from now? Substituting in the above formula gives us the following:

$$PV = \frac{\$1,331}{(1 + .10)^3}$$

$$= \frac{\$1,331}{1.331}$$

$$= \$1,000$$

DISCOUNTING A SERIES OF FUTURE RETURNS

Discounting a series of future returns simply involves discounting each individual future return, and adding up the present values of each return to get a total present value for the series of returns. The formula for discounting a series of future returns may be written as follows:

$$PV = \Sigma \frac{FV_i}{(1 + r)^i}$$

The capital Greek letter Sigma (Σ) stands for "sum of." It means to add up each of the components that follow, in this case the present values of each of the expected future amounts.

Example

Assume that a bond pays $100 interest at the end of each year for 3 years, and pays $1,000 principal at the bond's maturity date at the end of 3 years. If the market requires a 10% total rate of return on bonds of this quality and maturity at this time, what is the present value of the bond? Substituting in the above formula gives us the following:

$$PV = \frac{\$100}{(1 + .10)} + \frac{\$100}{(1 + .10)^2} + \frac{\$100}{(1 + .10)^3} + \frac{\$1,000}{(1 + .10)^3}$$

$$= \frac{\$100}{1.10} + \frac{\$100}{(1.10 \times 1.10)} + \frac{\$100}{(1.10 \times 1.10 \times 1.10)} + \frac{\$1,000}{(1.10 \times 1.10 \times 1.10)}$$

$$= \frac{\$100}{1.10} + \frac{\$100}{1.21} + \frac{\$100}{1.331} + \frac{\$1,000}{1.331}$$

$$= \$90.90 + \$82.64 + \$75.13 + \$751.31$$

$$= \$1,000$$

It can readily be seen from the above that if the discount rate (the rate of return required to attract capital to the investment) goes up, the present value goes down, and vice versa.

---

[a] In all the examples in this book, for simplicity, it is assumed that compounding is on an annual basis and that all returns are received at the end of each year. With minor adjustments in the arithmetic, assumptions of semiannual, quarterly, monthly, daily, or even continuous compounding can be accommodated. It can also be assumed that proceeds are received at some time other than the end of the year. For example, proceeds received at the middle of the year are accommodated by the "mid-year discounting convention."

3. Net income.
4. Dividends or other withdrawals.

Obviously, it is essential that the discount rate selected be appropriate for the future measure of return that is to be discounted. More will appear on this in future sections.

Capitalizing

Capitalizing is a procedure that converts a single flow of returns to an indication of value. The arithmetic of capitalization is very simple: the return flow to be capitalized is divided by the capitalization rate. The formula to determine indicated value by capitalization is as follows:

$$PV = \frac{A}{C}$$

where:
    PV = Present value
     A = Amount of return flow to be capitalized (usually expressed as dollars per annum)
     C = Capitalization rate (expressed as a percentage)

Suppose that a stock paid $.48 per share annual dividend, and that we believe that 4 percent is an appropriate capitalization rate for that stock's dividend. The indicated value of that stock based on capitalizing its dividend would be:

$$PV = \frac{\$.48}{.04}$$
$$= \$12$$

Note that the capitalization rate is the reciprocal of the valuation multiple or ratio. In other words, to convert a valuation multiple or ratio into a capitalization rate, you divide 1 by the multiple or ratio.

Suppose that the aforementioned stock had earned $1.00 in the last 12 months and it was determined that an appropriate P/E (price/earnings) multiple is 12. The stock should be worth 12 × $1.00 = $12.00. Another way to say the same thing is to say we will capitalize the latest 12 months' earnings. Since the capitalization rate is the reciprocal of the multiple,

$$\text{Cap rate (for latest 12 months' earnings)} = \frac{1}{12}$$
$$= .0833$$

Using the capitalization of earnings procedure, the indicated value of the stock based on capitalizing its latest 12 months' earnings would be:

$$PV = \frac{\$1.00}{.0833}$$
$$= \$12$$

Note that virtually any measure of returns can be capitalized. Examples include:

1. Revenues (gross or net).
2. Earnings (any of many definitions).
3. Cash flow (any of many definitions).
4. Dividends (or interest, or partnership withdrawals).

Note also that any of the above economic income variables can be measured over any of an almost infinite variety of time periods in determining the level of return to be capitalized. The time periods for measurement could include, for example:

1. Latest fiscal year.
2. Latest available 12 months.
3. Simple or weighted average of last three years, five years, or any other historical period.
4. Forecast for current or following fiscal year.
5. Forecast for next 12 months.
6. A "normalized" estimate of the return variable to be capitalized.

Quite obviously, it is essential that the capitalization rate selected be appropriate for the return variable to be capitalized, both in terms of the definition of the return variable and the time period for which it is measured or estimated.

After understanding the basic methodologies of discounting and capitalizing, one should realize that a discount rate and a capitalization rate clearly are not the same thing. They are two different concepts that should not be confused. The relationship between discount rates and capitalization rates is discussed in subsequent sections.

Components of a Discount Rate

The discount rate is the expected total rate of return required to attract capital to the particular investment. The *total return* includes all the financial benefit the investor expects to receive from the investment. The total return includes both income and capital appreciation, if any is expected. As noted earlier, this includes payouts (interest, dividends, withdrawals) plus or minus any change from the purchase price of the investment to the proceeds expected to be realized on its sale.

The *discount rate* is the total return expressed as a periodic compounded percentage of the amount to be invested to produce that return over the life of the investment. Put another way, the discount rate (required total rate of return) is the cost of capital for a particular category of investment. It is the expected total rate of return that the market requires in order to attract money to any category of investment, considering the risks and other characteristics of the investment. In other words, the discount rate (i.e., the required total rate of return) is the rate of return available in the market on other investments comparable in risk, liquidity, and other characteristics of importance to investors. In economic terms, it can be thought of as an *opportunity cost* (the cost of giving up the opportunity to do something else with the same money).

A simple example of the total rate of return available in the market on one category of investment would be a bond that is only one year away from maturity, at which time the issuer would pay back the face value (usually $1,000 per bond) to the holder, along with any interest due. If the bond carried an interest rate of 10 percent, the interest would be $100 per year, because interest is computed on the face value of the bond ($1,000 × .10 = $100). If an investor bought the bond for $950, he would also expect to earn $50 in capital appreciation ($1,000 − $950 = $50), which would also be part of this total expected return. These two components of expected return would be expressed as a total expected rate of return by dividing the total expected return by the amount invested, as follows:

$$\frac{\$100 \text{ (interest)} + \$50 \text{ (capital appreciation)}}{\$950 \text{ (amount paid for bond)}}$$

In the example above, the total expected rate of return is 15.8 percent. (In bond terminology, the total expected rate of return is called the *yield to maturity*.)

The discount rate (i.e., the required total rate of return) for an investment in the ownership of a closely held business or professional practice can be thought of as being comprised of the following four components:

1. The rate of return available in the market on investments that are essentially free of risk, highly liquid, and virtually free of any administrative costs associated with ownership.
2. The premium required to compensate the investor for risk.
3. The premium required to compensate the investor for illiquidity.
4. The premium required to compensate the investor for administrative costs.

These four components of the required rate of return are discussed in the following four subsections.

Risk-Free Rate of Return

The concept of the risk-free investment is that the investor can be sure to get back the exact amount of money promised, exactly when it is promised. The investor can count on receiving the principal at a certain time, along with a stated amount of interest. To make it even sweeter, if he decides he wants his money before the principal is due, there is a ready liquid market in which he can instantly sell the investment to someone else, paying only a nominal commission cost.

The *risk-free rate* is the rate of return available to an investor at any given time on such an investment, such as U.S. Treasury bills or the highest-quality money market funds. The rates of return available on such investments usually cover the expected rate of inflation plus a "real" rate of return, that is, something for renting out the money for a period of time. For example, if U.S. Treasury bills yielded 6 percent, and economists' expectations were that inflation was running at an annual rate of about 4 percent, the investor in T-bills would get enough interest to keep up with inflation, plus a real rate of return of about 2 percent for loaning the money on a risk-free basis.

For reasons discussed in a later section, the total rate of return available on long-term U.S. Government bonds is frequently used as a proxy for the risk-free rate when developing a required total rate of return for an equity investment.

Premium for Risk

Risk is the uncertainty as to exactly when or how much return an investor will receive on a given investment. In order to induce an investor to put his money into something with risk, he must have a reasonable expectation that he will earn a higher rate of return than that available on a risk-free basis.

There are two categories of risks inherent in investing in a small business or professional practice: (1) risk factors peculiar to the specific business or practice, including those peculiar to the particular industry or profession within which it operates; (2) risk factors arising from general economic conditions, such as interest rates, availability of credit, and expansionary or recessionary conditions.

Premium for Illiquidity

In contrast to the ready marketability noted as a hallmark of the risk-free investment, small businesses and professional practices are relatively illiquid. A sale usually requires a few months to accomplish, during which time the seller usually expends considerable time and effort on the sale. The seller will either pay a brokerage commission or incur other direct selling costs. It is hard to predict how long it will take to sell, or what the price will be relative either to what the owner paid for it or what his notion of its intrinsic value may be. When he does sell the business, more often than not, he will receive only part of the price in cash and the balance on a contract over some extended period of time.

In the practice of valuing businesses and business interests, there are two procedures in common usage for dealing with the adverse characteristic of illiquidity. Either procedure can be acceptable, if properly applied; but the procedures typically used for large businesses differ from those typically used for small businesses. In valuing interests in large businesses for which a liquid public trading market is not readily available, the typical procedure is to reach a value as if a public trading market existed and then take a percentage discount for the lack of ready marketability. This procedure is attractive in valuing illiquid interests in large companies because there is considerable market evidence available to help one quantify the discount for illiquidity (lack of immediate marketability).[3]

In valuing small businesses and professional practices, however, it is a common procedure to build the adverse characteristic of illiquidity into the

---

[3]For a discussion of this procedure and related market data, see Pratt, "Data on Discounts for Lack of Marketability," *Valuing a Business*, 2nd ed., pp. 239–62.

discount rate. The relative impact of this factor is somewhat subjective, since little empirical evidence has been developed up to this point to quantify this factor as it applies to small businesses and professional practices.

In any case, it obviously requires a fairly high expected rate of return to induce investors to accept the risks and illiquidity of small businesses compared with available risk-free investments.

Premium for Administrative Costs

Some analysts also recognize that the total required rate of return contains a component for the cost of administering the investment, which is separate from any compensation for services in managing the business. This component would be analogous to a bank's custodial fee for collecting, depositing, and accounting for receipts and expenditures from a client's investments. Such administrative costs tend to be higher for direct proprietary investments in small businesses or practices, even if the investment is made as a silent partner, than for passive holdings in such things as publicly traded securities. Usually, time is spent communicating with people active in the business, and the tax aspects are usually more complicated than they are for a securities investment.

Relationship between Discount Rates and Capitalization Rates

A *discount rate* converts *all* of the expected future return on investment (however defined) to an indicated present value. It is generally accepted that the discounted future returns method is theoretically the most correct way to value income-producing investments, including businesses and professional practices.

In contrast to the more comprehensive method of discounting *all* of the expected returns, a *capitalization rate* converts *only a single return flow number* to an indicated present value.

This leads us to the logical answer to the difference between the discount rate and the cap rate:

> For an investment with perpetual life, the difference between the discount rate and the cap rate is the annually compounded percentage rate of growth or decline in perpetuity in the economic income variable being discounted or capitalized.

The above relationship can be expressed as a formula very simply:[4]

$$c = r - g$$

---

[4]For further discussions of this concept and step-by-step mathematical proofs showing that the cap rate equals the discount rate less growth as defined above, see Greg Gilbert, "Discount Rates and Capitalization Rates—Where Are We?" *Business Valuation Review*, December 1990, pp. 108–13, and Philip L. Cooley, *How to Value an Oil Jobbership for Purchase or Sale* (Bethesda, Md.: Petroleum Marketing Education Foundation, 1982), pp. 7-34–7-37.

where:

> c = capitalization rate (a rate to be used as a divisor to convert a return flow variable, such as net free cash flow, to an indication of value)

> r = discount rate

> g = annually compounded rate of growth in the economic income variable being capitalized over the life of the investment (if there is an expected rate of decline, the g is negative, so the effect is that the rate of decline is *added* to the discount rate to get the capitalization rate)

Reflecting Growth or Decline in Expected Returns

If the economic income stream to be capitalized does not include all of the total return expected on the investment, then the rate of return expected from some source other than the amount of the current income stream being capitalized must be subtracted from the required total rate of return (discount rate) in order to get an applicable rate at which to capitalize the current income stream. For example, suppose that the required total rate of return on an equity investment has been estimated to be 30 percent, that the investment is expected to produce an income stream of $10,000 in the coming year, and that the income stream is expected to increase at a rate of 3 percent per year. In that case, the 3 percent incremental expected return can be subtracted from the 30 percent total required rate of return in determining the applicable rate at which to capitalize the $10,000 expected next year's income. In this case, the capitalized value would be computed as follows:

$$\frac{\$10,000}{(.30-.03)} = \frac{\$10,000}{.27} = \$37,037$$

Regardless of whether the appraiser plans to use the required total rate of return (discount rate) directly to develop a capitalization rate in one of the valuation methods, it is important that he have a pretty good idea of what the required total rate of return should be for the specific type of investment. Knowledge of the required total rate of return enables one to judge reasonably whether the capitalization rates used for certain streams of income, plus other elements of the total expected rate of return not reflected in the income stream, will actually sum up to the required total rate of return for the type of investment.

Some guidance as to developing required total rates of return (discount rates) and capitalization rates is presented in a later section.

The above discussion shows that there is one unique situation where the discount rate and the capitalization rate are equal to each other: where the return stream to be discounted or capitalized is constant in perpetuity. The best example of this is a U.S. preferred stock with a constant dividend in perpetuity and no sinking fund or redemption provision. If the stock pays a $5 annual dividend and the market requires a

10 percent total rate of return, the stock can be valued by dividing the annual dividend by the market required rate of return, which in this unique situation can correctly be characterized as *both* the discount rate and the capitalization rate:

$$\frac{\$5.00}{.10} = \$50.00$$

In summary, the consensus of current professional appraisal thinking is that the capitalization rate impounds all the components of the discount rate (assuming that the two rates are to be applied to the return variable defined in exactly the same way except for the time period of measurement or estimation). For any given valuation date, values of the components of the discount rate (risk-free rate, risk premiums, etc.) are the same for the capitalization rate as for the discount rate. The difference is that the capitalization rate impounds one additional component: the annually compounded rate of change in the return variable being capitalized over the life of the investment, plus any increment or decrement to the value of the investment not reflected in the return variable being capitalized. (The following paragraphs illustrate the development of a cap rate where the value of the investment goes to zero over the life of the investment.)

Return *on* Investment versus Return *on and of* Investment

In business appraisal, capitalization rates are usually stated in the form of some variation of return on investment. For example, if an investor were willing to invest $100,000 to receive an annual return of $25,000, we would say that the *return on investment* is 25 percent ($25,000 ÷ $100,000 = .25). In reverse, we would say that the $25,000 income stream was capitalized at a rate of 25 percent, meaning that the income stream was valued at $100,000 ($25,000 ÷ .25 = $100,000).

In some cases, however (more often in real estate appraisal, but occasionally in business appraisal), a capitalization rate is stated in a form that represents a return *on and of* investment. We found an example of this method in a business appraisal in which a broker was valuing a restaurant by a variation of the excess earnings method (described in Chapter 15). He capitalized earnings before depreciation. However, he assumed that the used restaurant equipment would have an average remaining life of five years. He accounted for this finite life by using a capitalization rate that gave him an 18 percent return on his investment in the equipment plus enough additional to amortize his investment completely in five years. In other words, he used a rate that got him an 18 percent return on his investment plus the return of his investment in five years.[5]

In the example above, the capitalization rate worked out to be 30.5 percent, or 12.5 percent over that investor's required return on capital. The additional amount was built into the capitalization rate instead of recognizing either depreciation or a reserve for replacements as an ex-

---

[5]Dick Fraser, "How Much Is Your Business Worth?" *Restaurant Business*, August 1, 1981, pp. 85–88.

pense. This form of capitalization rate, in lieu of depreciation expense, is used quite commonly in the appraisal of buildings and of certain limited life intangible assets, but it is not found frequently in business appraisals.

Distinguishing between *Return on Equity* (ROE) and *Return on Invested Capital* (ROI)

Much confusion arises among different people involved in valuing businesses because of failure to distinguish between return on equity and return on total investment (or invested capital). *Equity* is the ownership interest. If the business is financed entirely by equity, then equity and invested capital are one and the same. However, *investment* (also frequently called *invested capital*) is a broader term, including debt as well as equity. Therefore, if the business is financed by debt as well as equity, then equity is a subset, or only a portion, of the total investment.

Return on Equity

Return on equity (ROE) is defined as follows:

$$\frac{\text{Earnings}}{\text{Equity}}$$

For example, if a company had earnings of \$10,000 and equity of \$50,000, the return on equity would be computed as:

$$\frac{\$10,000}{\$50,000} = .20$$

Return on Invested Capital

Return on investment (ROI) is a term used more ambiguously than *return on equity*. In some contexts, *investment* (or *invested capital*) is defined to be synonymous with *capital*, that is, all equity plus long-term debt.[6] In other contexts, *investment* is defined to include all equity and interest-bearing debt, including short-term debt.

None of these ways of defining return on equity or return on investment is necessarily right or wrong. The point of all this discussion is that it is necessary to be explicit about the exact meaning of these expressions in any given context.

One of many formulas for return on investment is:

$$\frac{\text{Earnings before interest and taxes (EBIT)}}{\text{Investment}}$$

For example, if a company had \$75,000 worth of interest-bearing debt and \$50,000 equity, and it paid \$7,500 in interest on the debt and had

---

[6]If the balance sheet also has deferred items in the long-term liability section, such as deferred taxes or unearned subscription revenues, such items sometimes are included in "capital" and sometimes not.

$10,000 worth of pretax earnings, the return on investment would be computed as:

$$\frac{\$7,500 + \$10,000}{\$75,000 + \$50,000} = \frac{\$17,500}{\$125,000} = .14$$

Another commonly used formula is:

$$\frac{\text{Debt-Free Net Income (DFNI)}}{\text{Investment}}$$

The above formulation is called debt-free because it assumes there is no debt and therefore no interest, and all the assumed pretax earnings in this formulation are charged with the applicable equity tax rate.

Implication for Discount and Capitalization Rates

If the economic income stream being discounted or capitalized is that available to common equity (after any payments of interest or preferred dividends), then the discount or capitalization rate is strictly an equity rate. The discount rate should represent the best available approximation of the cost of equity capital for the subject enterprise as of the valuation date.

If, on the other hand, the economic income stream being capitalized represents income available to *both* debtholders and equityholders, then the discount rate should reflect a blending of the cost of debt capital and the cost of equity capital. This blending is based on the assumed proportions of debt and equity capital. The blended rate is called the *weighted average cost of capital* (WACC). The development of a weighted average cost of capital is discussed in a subsequent section of this chapter, and its application in discounted or capitalized return valuation methods is discussed in the following two chapters.

Relating Discount or Capitalization Rate to Income Stream

Economic income streams can be defined in many ways. It is essential to understand the nature of the economic income stream being capitalized and to select a capitalization rate that is applicable to that particular economic income stream.

To appreciate this problem, consider the simple example of Sally's Salons, a small chain of hairdressing shops, well established in upscale apartment and hotel locations. As illustrated in Exhibit 12–2, several common ways of defining earnings are the following:

1. *Owner's discretionary cash.* Earnings before owner's compensation (as discussed in Chapter 8), depreciation, interest, and taxes.
2. *EBDIT.* Earnings before depreciation, interest, and taxes (but after owner's compensation).

Exhibit 12–2

SALLY'S SALONS, INC.
INCOME STATEMENT

Sales	$1,000,000
Operating Expenses (Excluding Owner's Compensation)	730,000
Owner's Discretionary Cash	270,000
Owner's Compensation	150,000
Earnings before Depreciation, Interest & Taxes	120,000
Depreciation	40,000
Earnings before Interest & Taxes	80,000
Interest	50,000
Earnings before Taxes	30,000
Income Taxes	5,000
Net Income	$25,000

3. *EBIT.* Earnings before interest and taxes (but after owner's compensation and depreciation).
4. *EBT.* Earnings before taxes (but after owner's compensation, depreciation, and interest).
5. *Net income.* The bottom line, earnings after all expenses, including income taxes if incorporated.

When Sally asks a business broker what she can get for her business, he replies: "Businesses like yours in this metropolis usually sell for net assets at market value plus one year's earnings." What does he mean by *earnings*? He may be referring to any of the five definitions above, or any of many possible variations. For example, as discussed in Chapter 8, depreciation may be included in expenses, but at an adjusted amount; or earnings may be stated before depreciation, but after an allowance for replacements. Similarly, the owner's compensation may be deducted from sales as an expense, but at an adjusted amount.

Another variation sometimes encountered is the treatment of principal repayments on borrowed funds as an expense in determining the earnings variable to capitalize. That is done in order to get a capitalization rate in the form of a return on a cash-on-cash basis. A *cash-on-cash* return is the amount of cash per year expected to be available to the investor, divided by the amount of cash invested. In real estate appraisal, this concept is called the *equity dividend rate*.

In summary, there are many ways to define the economic income

Exhibit 12–3

LEVELS OF RETURNS THAT MAY BE DISCOUNTED OR CAPITALIZED

Level of Return	Returns to Equity	Returns to Total Invested Capital
Gross or net revenues	X	X
Owner's discretionary cash		X
EBDIT		X
EBIT		X
EBT	X	
Net income	X	
DFNI		X
Net free cash flow to invested capital		X
Net free cash flow to equity	X	

Note: With the exception of gross or net revenues, the levels of returns falling in the "Returns to Invested Capital" column by definition include returns available to debt holders as well as to equity holders.

stream, none of which is right or wrong. No matter how the economic income stream is defined, it is essential that the discount or capitalization rate selected be the rate that is appropriate to the particular definition of the income stream being discounted or capitalized.

Several definitions of economic income streams that may be discounted or capitalized are shown in Exhibit 12–3, along with the distinctions as to which income streams represent return to equity and which economic income streams represent return to all invested capital.

Developing a Discount Rate

Methods directly employing capitalization rates are used more frequently than methods directly employing discount rates in valuing small businesses and professional practices. We present the development of discount rates first, however, because in theory, as noted in an earlier section, the capitalization rate should reflect all the elements of the discount rate plus one or two others. The appraiser should be able to mentally reconcile the reasonableness of the capitalization rates used with reasonableness of the levels of discount rates theoretically impounded in them.

Discount Rates for Debt

Discount rates for debt instruments are widely observable in the market-place. If a company borrows, its actual cost of borrowing provides significant evidence as to its cost of debt. If it does not, but is in a position to do so if desired, the cost of borrowing for other companies of comparable risk can be utilized to develop a cost of debt for the subject company.[7]

Discount Rate for Net Free Cash Flow to Equity

Unlike discount rates for debt, discount rates for equity are *not* directly observable in the marketplace. Therefore, the cost of equity capital generally has to be pieced together or "built up" by adding the components of the discount rate as discussed in an earlier section of this chapter.

   The return variable for which an equity discount rate is most frequently built up is *net free cash flow*. There are two reasons for this. One is conceptual, the other a matter of empirical expediency (ready availability of data). The conceptual reason is that net free cash flow represents the return on the investment that the investor has completely available to take out of the business or to do with as he wishes with absolutely no impairment of the ongoing ability of the business to continue to produce the expected level of cash flows in the future. The empirical reason to prefer discounting net free cash flow over other measures of economic income is the availability and acceptance of market data by which to help quantify the discount rate applicable to net free cash flow.

Definition of Net Free Cash Flow.   For the purpose of developing and applying an equity capitalization rate, net free cash flow is defined as follows:

   Net income (after taxes)
+ Noncash charges
− Capital expenditures (the net changes in fixed and other noncurrent assets)*
− Changes in working capital*
+ Net changes in long-term debt*
= Net free cash flow

* Assumes amounts are those necessary to support projected operations.

If there are preferred dividends, they would have to be subtracted, of course, if the objective is to determine cash flow available to the common equity.

---

[7]For step-by-step direction on costs of debt capital, see Chapter 16, "Valuing Debt Securities," in Pratt, *Valuing a Business*, 2nd ed., pp. 406–20.

Risk-Free Rate of Return. The truly risk-free benchmark rate of return is the short-term Treasury bill rate. Longer maturities have some risk inherent in them because the market prices of the bonds fluctuate with changes in interest rates.

It is intuitively appealing, however, to use long-term government bond rates as the base from which to build an equity discount rate for two related reasons:

1. The long-term bonds come closer to matching the expected life of most equity investments.
2. Long-term interest rates fluctuate less over time. This lesser fluctuation seems more consistent with the fluctuations of required rates of return on equity investments.

Fortunately, data have now been developed allowing the 20-year government bond rate to be used as the risk-free base in developing an equity discount rate for net free cash flow. These data are described in the following section.

Premium for Risk. The annual yearbook, *Stocks, Bonds, Bills, and Inflation,*[8] publishes several series which quantify data on rates of return on equity over and above rates of return on government securities. The two series of greatest usefulness in this context are the long-horizon expected equity risk premium and the expected small stock premium. Exhibit 12–4 shows these series for the 1992 yearbook.

The median market value of the common equity for the stocks comprising the "small stock" group at year-end 1991 was $19.4 million. Small stocks as we have defined them in this book are smaller than these. Whether that warrants any additional risk premium for size is unknown as a generality. Studies of equity risk premiums for stocks smaller than the Ibbotson "small stock" group have not been conducted up to this point. It is a matter of the appraiser's analysis of risk factors of the subject company to determine whether or not any additional adjustment for specific risk for the subject company is warranted.

Premium for Illiquidity. The data referred to above are from publicly traded minority interests. Investors as a whole cherish liquidity and loathe illiquidity. Certainly, if one is valuing a minority interest in a closely held company, some further discount for the illiquidity of the subject securities is warranted. When valuing a business or practice overall, there is still an illiquidity factor associated with the closely held nature of the business. When valuing a closely held company, the illiquidity factor is usually reflected in a separate step at the end of the process. However, some appraisers of smaller companies like to reflect the illiquidity factor in the discount rate. (It is also common for venture capitalists to impound the illiquidity factor into their discount rate.)

When one is dealing with capitalization rates, impounding the discount for illiquidity into the cap rate is a matter of very simple arithme-

---

[8]*Stocks, Bonds, Bills, and Inflation: 1992 Yearbook* (Chicago: Ibbotson Associates, annual).

Exhibit 12–4

Differences of Means   **(1926 – 1991)**
of Annual Returns

Series Difference	Difference of Means
STOCKS MINUS BONDS AND BILLS	
Long-horizon expected equity risk premium: Common stock total returns minus long-term government bond income returns	7.4 %
Common stock total returns minus long-term government bond total returns	7.3
Intermediate-horizon expected equity risk premium: Common stock total returns minus intermediate-term government bond income returns	7.7
Common stock total returns minus intermediate-term government bond total returns	7.1
Short-horizon expected equity risk premium: Common stock total returns minus U.S. Treasury bill total returns	8.6
SMALL STOCKS	
Expected small stock premium: Small stock total returns minus common stock total returns	5.1
BONDS AND BILLS	
Expected default premium: Long-term corporate bond total returns minus long-term government bond total returns	0.6
Expected horizon premium: Long-term government bond total returns minus U.S. Treasury bill total returns	1.3
Long-term government bond total returns minus intermediate-term government bond total returns	-0.2
Long-term government bond income returns minus intermediate-term government bond income returns	0.3
Intermediate-term government bond total returns minus U.S. Treasury bill total returns	1.5
Intermediate-term government bond income returns minus U.S. Treasury bill total returns	0.9

tic. The cap rate before the discount for illiquidity is multiplied by one divided by one minus the discount for illiquidity. For example, assume that the cap rate is 20 percent before the discount for illiquidity, and the discount for illiquidity is determined to be 30 percent. The arithmetic would be as follows:

$$.20\left(\frac{1}{1-.30}\right)$$
$$= .20\left(\frac{1}{.70}\right)$$
$$= .20(1.43)$$
$$= .286 \text{ Cap rate adjusted for illiquidity}$$

Note that this adjustment is only applicable when the cap rate itself is derived from publicly traded company data. If the cap rate is derived from closely held company data, this adjustment is not applicable. When dealing with discount rates instead of cap rates, there is no simple arithmetic for impounding the discount for illiquidity into the discount rate. For this reason, I still prefer to take a separate discount for illiquidity as a separate step when valuing minority interests in small businesses and professional practices. Discounts for lack of marketability for minority interest in closely held businesses can cover a very wide range, but most fall in the area of about 25 percent to 45 percent.[9]

Controlling interests are generally much easier to sell than minority interests and may not require any discount for lack of marketability. If the facts and circumstances of the case suggest that there should be any discount for lack of marketability for a controlling interest, it would usually not be more than 15 percent.[10]

Premium for Administrative Costs. We rarely see any premium for administrative costs specifically reflected in a discount rate. More commonly, such costs are taken into consideration in the economic income stream being discounted or capitalized.

Weighted Average Cost of Capital (WACC)

When developing a discount rate to apply to an economic income stream available to all invested capital (equity plus interest-bearing debt), the discount rate is a weighted average of the costs of debt and equity based on the assumed relative proportions of each in the capital structure.

When valuing a minority interest, the assumed weighting of debt and equity should normally be as it exists, because the minority stockholder would generally not have the ability to change it. When valuing a controlling interest, an industry average capital structure is often used on the theory that a control owner would have the ability to put an optimal capital structure in place.

---

[9]For more explanation and a summary of empirical market data, see Chapter 10, "Data on Discounts for Lack of Marketability," in Pratt, *Valuing a Business*, 2nd ed., pp. 238–62.

[10]Ibid., especially pp. 256–57.

When computing the cost of debt, its cost normally is caculated on an after-tax basis, that is, reduced by the tax savings, since interest is a deductible expense for income tax purposes. The formula for this is:

$$r_d = K_d (1 - t)$$

where:

r_d = after tax cost of debt

K_d = before tax cost of debt

t = effective income tax rate

As an example, assume that a company has 40 percent debt at a 10 percent borrowing rate, 60 percent equity at a 20 percent cost of equity, and an effective tax rate of 30 percent. The weighted average cost of capital would be computed as follows:

	Cost		Proportion in Capital Structure		
Debt (.10 × .7) =	.07	×	.40	=	.028
Equity	.20	×	.60	=	.12
Weighted average cost of capital					.148

Data on industry-average leverage (proportions of debt and equity) for more than 350 industry groups are contained in Robert Morris Associates' *Annual Statement Studies.*

Discount Rate for Other Return Variables

Defensible discount rates for economic income measures other than net free cash flow are difficult (but not impossible) to develop. The measure of economic income most commonly discounted other than net free cash flow is net income. There are two basic methods for developing a discount rate for an economic income measure other than net free cash flow:

1. Convert a discount rate developed for net free cash flow to a discount rate applicable to some other economic income measure.
2. Attempt to develop a discount rate for the desired economic income measure from directly observed market data for that variable.

Converting a Net Free Cash Flow Discount Rate. The key to converting a net cash flow discount rate to a discount rate for some other economic income measure is to estimate the typical percentage difference between the two measures and adjust the net cash flow discount rate accordingly. One way is to compute the historical percentage difference between net cash flow and the desired economic income measure (such as net income) for the subject company. Another way is to research public companies in the industry to estimate the percentage difference.

Net free cash flow is almost always lower than net income or any other economic income measures that the appraiser is likely to discount or capitalize. Therefore, the discount rate applicable to other measures is almost inevitably higher than the discount rate applicable to net free cash flow.

Developing a Discount Rate Directly from Market Data. Sometimes a discount rate can be estimated from market data by converting observed market capitalization rates to discount rates. The most likely economic income measure to lend itself to this exercise is net income.

Recall that we said that the primary difference between the discount rate and the capitalization rate is growth. For some companies, earnings growth estimates can be obtained for as much as five years ahead.[11] Adding the growth rate to the capitalization rate (the reciprocal of the P/E ratio in the case of net income) gives a rough estimate of the implied discount rate. There are at least two problems with this method. First, to be valid, the growth rate used in the conversion should be an expected growth rate in perpetuity. The five-year growth rate could differ considerably from the longer-term growth rate. Secondly, the five-year forecasted growth rates found in such publications leave much to be desired in terms of accuracy. Nevertheless, in some cases the method provides at least a useful "rough cut" at getting a ballpark estimation.

Developing a Capitalization Rate

Unlike discount rates, capitalization rates for almost any level of return to either equity or overall invested capital are directly observable in the market. If enough reliable guideline company transaction data are available, the direct market comparison method (often called the "Guideline Company Method"—see Business Valuation Standard V in Appendix A) may be the easiest and most reliable way to develop capitalization rates to apply to various income variables for the subject company. Alternatively, for some income variables, it is possible to convert a discount rate to a capitalization rate.

Direct Market Comparison Method

The direct market comparison method of developing a capitalization rate consists of finding transactions in the market involving the sale of entities with comparative economic income streams and computing the capitalization rates implied in the prices at which the transactions took place. The example most familiar to people is price/earnings multiples in the public stock market.

For example, if a small restaurant chain wants to value shares of its stock for the purpose of selling shares to the public (going public), the appraiser will look at the prices at which similar small restaurant chain stocks are selling in the public market in relation to various measures of earning power, one of which will be the latest 12 months' earnings per share. The price/earnings multiple reported in daily newspapers is the

---

[11]*Value Line Investment Survey* is one source of such estimates.

current market price of a stock, divided by the latest reported 12 months' earnings per share. In the public market, price/earnings multiples are quoted on the basis of after-tax earnings. If the appraiser finds that most similar stocks are selling between six and nine times their latest 12 months' earnings, that provides a ballpark within which to capitalize the subject company's latest 12 months' earnings to determine a public offering price. The appraiser will then very carefully examine all the guideline companies' characteristics relative to the subject company and make an estimate of just where within that ballpark the subject company belongs.

Then, using the guideline companies' financial statements, the appraiser will do the same exercise to develop market-indicated capitalization rates for several other measures of earning power. Such measures could include, for example, the last three and five years' straight and/or weighted average earnings, projected next year's earnings, and perhaps one or several measures of cash flow. In other words, for each of several measures of earning power, the market will provide a range of capitalization rates for various guideline companies, and the appraiser will have to exercise his judgment to determine where in each range the subject company best fits.

The most important thing about the above example is that the appraiser derives a different applicable capitalization rate from the public market for each different measure of earning power considered for the subject company. Capitalization rates derived directly from transaction data should be based on the same measure of earning power as the measure of the subject company's earning power to which that capitalization rate will be applied. Otherwise, adjustments must be made; and such adjustments may be difficult to support.

It is obvious from the above example that the appraiser could conceivably develop quite a wide array of capitalization rates. These capitalization rates could include those based on each of several different definitions of earnings, each involving several different historical and/or projected time periods. The appraiser must judge which measure or measures of earning power, along with the respective indicated capitalization rate(s), most realistically indicate value in each case. Any capitalization rate found in a market transaction reflects expectations of the level and risk of future earnings. In order for capitalization rates found in the market to be realistic guides for valuing the subject company, there must be a reasonable basis for expecting the subject company's earnings stream to be at least approximately parallel to what was expected from the earnings streams from which the capitalization rates were derived.

In the small restaurant chain example, if the average stock was selling at 12 times last year's earnings, the market is capitalizing *last year's earnings* at 8.33 percent ($1 \div 12 = .0833$). The market is certainly not buying those stocks because it expects their future earnings to be only 8.33 percent of the current stock price; the market obviously expects earnings growth, since earnings of 8.33 percent are available on much safer investments. To realistically capitalize the subject company's latest year's earnings at the market-derived capitalization rate of 8.33 percent, one must reasonably expect the growth and risk characteristics of the subject company's future earnings to be somewhat similar to the industry, or, more specifically, to that subset of the industry from which the capitalization rate was derived.

The point of the example above is to stress the need for comparability between the subject company and the companies from which the capitalization rate is derived; the comparability should be reflected in the definition of the earnings base being capitalized and also in the assumptions regarding it.

Also, note that the purpose of the valuation clearly influences the appraiser's choice of data. Since the purpose is a public offering, public market data are used for comparison. That is not to say that public market data cannot be used at all for other purposes for which small business valuations may be undertaken but, as discussed in Chapter 5 and elsewhere in this book, it is much more difficult to make useful comparisons between public companies and small private companies than between public companies and medium-sized to larger private companies.

The same kind of exercise can be used to derive capitalization rates from closely held company market transaction data. The problem is that the data themselves are much harder to obtain, because there is no requirement for public reporting of most private transaction data. Sources of such data that do exist are discussed in Appendix D of this book.

The direct market comparison method is generally considered the best method if a sufficient number of directly comparable transactions are available for comparison; but that is a big "if." As noted above, comparative data are not always readily available. Moreover, because of the unique nature of each business, the appraiser must exercise a great deal of analytical judgment to ascertain the degree of comparability between the subject company and the comparative transactions found in the market.

Converting a Discount Rate to a Capitalization Rate

As discussed in the earlier section in this chapter on the "Relationship between Discount Rates and Capitalization Rates," one way to develop a cap rate is to convert from a discount rate as a starting place. In this method, the appraiser subtracts from the discount rate a number that represents the expected annually compounded growth in perpetuity of the variable to be capitalized.

Warning! Historical Industry Returns Not Reliable for Discount and Cap Rates

We have said consistently that discount and capitalization rates are determined by the market, and that some type of market transaction data is the proper type of source for developing such rates. A common error is to use some source of industry historical data (such as RMA *Annual Statement Studies*) as a basis for such rates. If the sawmill industry returned 5 percent on equity over the last five years, would you buy equity in a sawmill for an expected 5 percent long-term total expected return? Of course not! Only expected future returns count. Recent historical returns for an industry are often not representative of expected future returns, and therefore are generally not a valid source of discount and capitalization rates.

Relationship between Payback Period and Capitalization Rate

Some purchasers of businesses use the *payback period* as a criterion to determine the maximum amount they will be willing to pay. The payback period is based on cash flow and can be defined as follows:

> The time required (usually in years) for estimated future net cash receipts to equal the initial cash outlay for a project. If the estimated receipts are the same amount each year, the payback period is equal to the investment outlay divided by this annual amount.[12]

Since the payback period is a cash flow concept, income before depreciation expense but after allowance for replacements should be used to compute the payback period. If the expected cash flow thus defined was $30,000 each year, and the asking price for the business was $120,000, the payback period could be computed as follows:

$$\frac{\$120,000}{\$30,000} = 4 \text{ years}$$

If a buyer sets a maximum payback period as a limit to the amount he would consider paying, and the expected cash flow is an even amount each year, the maximum price becomes the payback period times the expected annual cash flow. In the example with the $30,000 expected cash flow each year, if the buyer sets a maximum payback period of three years, the maximum price he would pay would be computed as follows:

$$\$30,000 \times 3 \text{ years} = \$90,000$$

When the expected cash flow is an even amount each year, the reciprocal of the payback period could be regarded as the capitalization rate applicable to cash flow. In other words, a three-year payback period would be equivalent to a 33.33 percent capitalization rate applicable to cash flow (1 ÷ 3 = .3333), in the same manner that the reciprocal of the price/earnings multiple is a capitalization rate for the earnings stream on which the price/earnings multiple is based.

The payback period becomes most relevant when returns beyond a relatively short time horizon are highly uncertain. For example, during the housing boom of the 1970s, we encountered a company buying small sawmills on the basis of a maximum payback period of three years,

---

[12]W. W. Cooper and Yuji Ijiri, eds., *Kohler's Dictionary for Accountants*, 6th ed. (Englewood Cliffs, N.J.: Prentice Hall, 1983), p. 375.

recognizing that the industry was highly cyclical and its future very uncertain.

The primary disadvantage of the payback period is that it gives no recognition whatsoever to expected returns beyond the payback period. Another, less important, criticism of the payback period is that it gives no recognition to the timing of the cash flows within the payback period. The payback period can be a useful supplemental tool, but it should not be used alone.

Different Rates for Different Buyers

The cost of capital, either debt or equity, is different from one potential buyer to another. For an individual buying a sole proprietorship from another individual, the cost of capital would probably be about the same for the buyer as for the seller. On the other hand, the cost of capital to a sizable public company is probably somewhat less than the cost of capital to the typical small entrepreneur.

The buyer will usually use a capitalization rate based on that buyer's own cost of capital. The seller should consider the cost of capital to the likely classes of buyers and estimate the capitalization rates that they are likely to use.

A pair of small business consultants offer this explanation:

> The appropriate discount rate is defined as the required rate of return of the investor. Thus, when valuing a business, the buyer and seller will almost always have different required rates of return, as each individual will have different investment opportunities available, each of which has a different return and a different risk. Risk and return are directly related—if one opportunity poses a riskier situation than another it must consequently promise a higher return to compensate the investor for taking the additional risk. Therefore, if one investor perceives an investment opportunity as being riskier than does a second investor considering the same opportunity, the former will require a higher rate of return on that investment than the latter.[13]

As discussed earlier, when fair market value is the applicable standard of value, capitalization rates used should be representative of a market consensus. However, when determining investment value of a business to a particular party, the applicable discount or capitalization rates are those based on that party's cost of capital, risk perceptions, and other relevant factors.

Summary

Discount and capitalization rates are two different concepts, but there is a clearly identifiable relationship between the two. The capitalization

---

[13]James W. Carland, Jr., and Larry R. White, "Valuing the Small Business," *Journal of Small Business Management*, October 1980, p. 44.

rate is, in effect, a variable rooted in the discount rate, but also reflecting other factors. The discount rate is applied to *all* the returns expected by the investor. The capitalization rate is applied to a single amount of return at some point in time. Therefore, the capitalization rate must differ from the discount rate by the amount necessary to reflect in the indicated value any expected return not impounded directly in the economic income stream being capitalized. The most common such element is expected growth in the economic income stream being capitalized. Another element, in the case of a limited life investment, is any increase or decrease in the value of the investment from purchase to sale or liquidation.

Discount or capitalization rates are meaningless until we define the investment base to which they apply. The most common investment bases are either the equity of the company or all the invested capital of the company, generally including equity plus interest-bearing debt.

There are a wide variety of definitions of economic income streams that may be discounted or capitalized. A discount or capitalization rate is meaningless until there is a clear definition of the economic income stream to which it is applicable. *It is absolutely critical to properly match the discount or capitalization rate to the economic income stream being discounted or capitalized.*

Finally, discount and capitalization rates are determined by the market. They reflect economic and industry conditions as well as internal company conditions at the time of the valuation. These conditions particularly include interest rates, inflation expectations, the industry and company outlook, and investor perceptions of the risk of the prospective investment as of the valuation date. All these factors are subject to constant change and must be analyzed by the appraiser as of the valuation date as part of the process of determining the appropriate discount and/or capitalization rates.

Selected Bibliography

Arneson, George S. "Capitalization Rates for Valuing Closely Held Companies." *TAXES*, May 1981, pp. 310–17.

Boykin, James H. "Seeking the Elusive Discount Rate." *Appraisal Journal,* July 1990, pp. 328–33.

Brock, Thomas. "More on Capitalization Rates." *ASA Valuation*, June 1986, pp. 68–71.

Dietrich, William C. "Capitalization Rates—Seeing Is Believing." *Business Valuation News*, December 1985, pp. 3–4.

Gilbert, Gregory A. "Discount Rates and Capitalization Rates—Where Are We?" *Business Valuation Review*, December 1990, pp. 108–13.

Honnold, Keith L. "The Link between Discount Rates and Capitalization Rate: Revisited." *Appraisal Journal*, April 1990, pp. 190–95.

Kenny, Thomas J. "Closely Held Corporation Valuation: Determining a Proper Discount Rate." *Business Valuation Review*, March 1992, pp. 22–30.

Leung, Tony T. S. "Myths about Capitalization Rate and Risk Premium." *Business Valuation News*, March 1986, pp. 6–10.

Ling, David C. "Implementing Discounted Cash Flow Valuation Models: What Is the Correct Discount Rate?" *Appraisal Journal*, April 1992, pp. 267–74.

McMullin, Scott G. "Discount Rate Selection." *Business Valuation News*, September 1986, pp. 16–19.

Nevers, Thomas J. "Capitalization Rates." *Business Valuation News*, June 1985, pp. 3–6.

Pratt, Shannon P. "Understanding Capitalization Rates." *ASA Valuation*, June 1986, pp. 12–29.

_____. "Valuing a Practice: Choosing the Right Capitalization Rates." *CA Magazine*, April 1987, pp. 49–52.

Schilt, James H. "Selection of Capitalization Rates—Revisited." *Business Valuation Review*, June 1991, pp. 51–52.

Slay, Kelley D. "The Capitalization Rate, the Discount Rate, and Projected Growth in Value." *Appraisal Journal*, July 1990, pp. 324–27.

Chapter 13

The Discounted Future Returns (DFR) Method

The valuation of an ongoing business is the present worth of the future stream of net income.[1]

The real value of any going business is its future earnings power. Accordingly, the discounted cash flow approach, more than any other, determines the true value of your business.[2]

This chapter is short because the two major variants of the discounted future returns (DFR) method, the discounted cash flow (DCF) method and the discounted future earnings (DFE) method, are not often used in the valuation of small businesses and professional practices. They are used more often in the valuation of medium-sized and large businesses. Nevertheless, in spite of their practical difficulties, they are conceptually valid methods and at least deserve to be discussed here.[3] In fact, in 1991 the Delaware Chancery Court accepted the DCF method in valuing a radiology practice.[4]

Pros and Cons of the Discounted Future Returns Method

The discounted future returns method of valuation is based on the widely accepted theory that the value of the business depends on the future benefits it will produce (denominated in terms of cash flow or earnings), discounted back to a present value at an appropriate discount rate.

The method is not often used in the valuation of small businesses and professional practices, partly because it requires projections of cash flow or earnings for several years into the future. Many owners or prospective buyers of small businesses and professional practices would consider such projections too speculative to be useful.

Another reason why the method is not used more in small businesses and professional practices is that what will happen in the future often is more a function of the personal efforts of the owner/operator than of forces that will carry forward with the business itself, independent of the owner's personal contributions. Consequently, buyers are naturally reluctant to include in the present value any future benefits that really depend on their own efforts rather than automatically resulting from forces already in place.

A buyer may wish, however, to do a discounted future cash flow and/or earnings exercise for his or her own analysis. Certainly there are some small business and professional practice valuations to which the discounted future returns method of valuation would apply; those would be businesses and practices whose returns could be predicted with enough reliability to make the exercise useful and whose earnings result largely from forces already in place.

---

[1] Walter Jurek, *How to Determine the Value of a Business* (Stow, Oh.: Quality Services, Inc., 1977) p. 28.

[2] Thomas J. Martin and Mark R. Gustafson, *Valuing Your Business* (New York: Holt, Rinehart & Winston, 1980), p.14.

[3] For a more complete exposition of the discounted future returns method, see Chapter 3 in Pratt, *Valuing a Business*, 2nd ed.

[4] *In re Radiology Associates, Inc.*, C.A. No. 9001 (November 1991).

The Discounted Future Returns Formula

The basic formula for valuing an entity by the DFR method is as follows:

$$PV = \Sigma \ \frac{E_i}{(1+r)^i}$$

Where:
   PV = Present Value
   Σ = Sum of
   E_i = Expected economic return in the ith period in the future
   r = Discount rate
   i = The period (usually stated as a number of years) in the future
         in which the economic return to be discounted is expected to
         be received

Quantifying the Variables

Only two principal variables need to be quantified:

1. The expected cash flow or earnings for each future year.
2. The applicable rate by which to discount those projected future economic returns back to a present value.

Forecasting the Future Returns

Forecasting the future returns is really a matter of carrying out for several years the adjusted income statement exercises discussed in Chapter 8 and Chapter 11. The forecast can be done either on the basis of cash flow or earnings available to equity or on the basis of cash flow or earnings available to overall investment (including borrowed funds as well as equity).

Length of Forecast.   There is no *right* answer to the question of how far into the future one should try to carry the forecasts. Theoretically, the further the better. As a practical matter, for most small operations, it is not possible to forecast earnings very far before the forecasts become so unreliable that they are useless. The best guidance that can be offered is that the appraiser should forecast as many years into the future as he has a realistic basis for predicting. At the end of that period, it might be reasonable to assume either some constant growth rate or a given level of sustainable earnings, either for a limited period or into infinity.

Constant or Nominal Dollars.   One question that frequently arises is whether the forecasts should be done on the basis of constant dollars (1993 dollars, for example, if the forecast is being done in 1993), or whether an estimate of the effects of inflation should be included in the forecasted cash flow or earnings figures. The answer is that the forecast can be based on either assumption, but the choice of constant or inflation-adjusted dollars affects the choice of discount rate, as discussed in the next section.

Who Prepares the Forecasts? Another question that frequently arises is: "Who should prepare the forecasts, the appraiser or the company?" A related question is: "If the company prepares the forecasts, what is the appraiser's role in judging the credibility of the forecasts?" In some cases, the appraiser will prepare forecasts with the assistance of management input. More often, the company (or the buyer) will make the forecasts. When the appraiser does not make the forecasts, there is often an opportunity to review the underlying assumptions with management. In this case, the appraiser may make some adjustments based on an evaluation of the reliability of the assumptions. In any case, the source of the forecasts should be disclosed in any written or oral report that uses them. The appraiser's evaluation of the forecasts' credibility will be a factor in the judgment as to the weight to be accorded to the DFR method in determining the final opinion of value of the entity being appraised.

Selecting the Discount Rate

The appropriate present value discount rate to use in the denominator is the rate of return that the market requires for comparable investments, as discussed in Chapter 12. If the future returns projection is the returns available to equity, then the appraiser should use the discount rate that applies to an equity investment. If the projection is for the returns available to a total investment that includes borrowed funds, then the appraiser should use a discount rate applicable to the overall investment (weighted average cost of capital).

Recall that Chapter 12 pointed out that one component of the discount rate is inflation, which is intended to compensate the investor for the decreased buying power of future dollars when he receives them. If the returns projections are in dollars that include the effects of inflation, a discount rate that includes the inflation component (as developed in Chapter 12) should be used as the discount rate. That is, if the earnings or cash flow projections are in constant dollars, then the inflation component should be subtracted out of the total required rate of return to arrive at the appropriate discount rate. Economic forecasts available from banks, government agencies, or other publications can be used to obtain a consensus forecast of the long-term inflation rate.

Please refer back to Chapter 12 for more detail on developing the present value discount rate.

An Example

The Ace Widget Company has developed an outstanding patented widget, and its market acceptance has grown steadily over the last few years. The market potential for continued growth in sales and earnings seems assured, but Mr. Ace himself has decided to sell out and seek new challenges.

We carefully prepared a set of pro forma adjusted income statements for the next five years (prepared in accordance with Chapters 8 and 11), which indicate the following forecasted net free cash flow:

Year 1	Year 2	Year 3	Year 4	Year 5
$20,000	$30,000	$40,000	$50,000	$60,000

For years 6 and beyond, it appears that the market will have reached saturation and that net free cash flow will level off at around $65,000 per year.

We have great confidence in the future of Ace's widgets. We have decided that it would be worthwhile for us to buy the business from Ace at a price that would provide us a rate of return on our investment of 20 percent or more (our estimate of our weighted average cost of capital developed in accordance with Chapter 12).

Using the discounted future returns formula presented earlier, the present value of the cash flows for the first five years can be computed as follows:

$$\frac{\$20,000}{(1+.20)} + \frac{\$30,000}{(1+.20)^2} + \frac{\$40,000}{(1+.20)^3} + \frac{\$50,000}{(1+.20)^4} + \frac{\$60,000}{(1+.20)^5}$$

At the end of five years, we forecast a business with net free cash flows of $65,000 per year. If we capitalize $65,000 per year at 20 percent, the value of that forecasted cash flow stream starting at the end of the fifth year can be computed as follows:[5]

$$\frac{\$65,000}{.20} = \$325,000$$

However, that value is five years away and has to be discounted back to a present value. The present value of the cash flow stream starting five years from now can be computed as follows:

$$\frac{\$325,000}{(1+.20)^5}$$

Putting the whole thing together, we can compute the value of Ace Widget Company as follows:

$$\frac{\$20,000}{(1+.20)} + \frac{\$30,000}{(1+.20)^2} + \frac{\$40,000}{(1+.20)^3} + \frac{\$50,000}{(1+.20)^4} + \frac{\$60,000}{(1+.20)^5} + \frac{(\$65,000 \div .20)}{(1+.20)^5}$$

$$= \$16,667 + \$20,833 + \$23,148 + \$24,113 + \$24,113 + \$130,610$$

$$= \$239,484 \text{ (or } \$240,000, \text{ rounded)}$$

On the basis of this analysis, we would decide to purchase Ace Widget if we can negotiate a deal with Mr. Ace at less than $240,000, cash or cash equivalent. (As we will see in Chapter 19, we can afford to pay Mr. Ace a price of $300,000 or more, if he is willing to take a substantial portion of it in a long-term contract at a low interest rate; but that is another story.)

The calculations above can be done using present value tables, or they may be done easily on an inexpensive pocket calculator such as the

---

[5]Note that we *capitalize* the expected cash flow for year 6 and beyond because of the assumption that it is a constant expected amount in perpetuity.

Texas Instruments Business Analyst III (BA III). For example, computing the present value of $325,000 five years from now, discounted at 20 percent compounded annually, simply requires putting the Texas Instruments calculator in the *finance* mode and entering the following:

Input	Key
325,000	FV
5	N
20	%i
	CPT
	PV

The answer should show as $130,610.

In the above example, we simplified the calculations by assuming that there would be no more growth in net free cash flows beyond the sixth year. A more common assumption is that there will be some level of growth continuing, perhaps just at the rate of expected inflation. If that is the expectation, then the capitalization rate for the sixth year's forecasted cash flow would be the discount rate *minus* the expected growth rate. In the above example, if th expected continued growth were 4 percent, the capitalization rate for the sixth year's forecasted cash flow would be: .16 (.20−.04 = .16). In that case, the computation would be as follows:

$$\frac{\$20,000}{(1+.20)} + \frac{\$30,000}{(1+.20)^2} + \frac{\$40,000}{(1+.20)^3} + \frac{\$50,000}{(1+.20)^4} + \frac{\$60,000}{(1+.20)^5} + \frac{(\$65,000/(.20-.04))}{(1+.20)^5}$$

$$= \$16,667 + \$20,833 + \$23,148 + \$24,113 + \$24,113 + \$163,263$$
$$= \$272,137$$

In this case, the assumption of a continued 4 percent compounded growth in perpetuity adds a little over $30,000 to the indicated value.

Values calculated by the DFR method can cover a wide range, depending on the cash flow or earnings forecasts used and the present value discount rate selected. Exhibit 13–1 shows how the indicated value can vary using pessimistic, most likely, and optimistic earnings forecasts, and varying the discount rate from 16 to 24 percent. By varying the cash flow forecasts up or down by 20 percent, and the discount rates up or down by 4 percent, we get a range of values from a high of $380,000 to a low of $150,000, a differential of well over 2 to 1 on the indicated value of the business.

No wonder different people can have wide disagreements about the value of any particular business!

Summary

There are two principal variables in the discounted future returns method:

1. The forecasted future returns (the numerator).
2. The discount rate (the denominator).

Exhibit 13–1

PRESENT VALUE OF ACE WIDGET COMPANY
By the Discounted Future Returns Method

Optimistic Forecast

Year	Projected Cash Flow	Present Value Discounted At				
		16%	18%	20%	22%	24%
1	$24,000	$20,690	$20,339	$20,000	$19,672	$19,355
2	36,000	26,754	25,855	25,000	24,187	23,413
3	48,000	30,752	29,214	27,778	26,434	25,175
4	60,000	33,137	30,947	28,935	27,084	25,378
5	72,000	34,280	31,472	28,935	26,640	24,560
6 on	78,000	232,105	189,414	156,732	131,182	110,860
Total Value		$377,718	$327,241	$287,380	$255,199	$228,741

Most Likely Forecast

Year	Projected Cash Flow	Present Value Discounted At				
		16%	18%	20%	22%	24%
1	$20,000	$17,241	$16,949	$16,667	$16,393	$16,129
2	30,000	22,295	21,546	20,833	20,156	19,511
3	40,000	25,626	24,345	23,148	22,028	20,979
4	50,000	27,615	25,789	24,113	22,570	21,149
5	60,000	28,567	26,227	24,113	22,200	20,466
6 on	65,000	193,421	157,845	130,610	109,318	92,383
Total Value		$314,765	$272,701	$239,484	$212,665	$190,617

Pessimistic Forecast

Year	Projected Cash Flow	Present Value Discounted At				
		16%	18%	20%	22%	24%
1	$16,000	$13,793	$13,559	$13,333	$13,115	$12,903
2	24,000	17,836	17,236	16,667	16,125	15,609
3	32,000	20,501	19,476	18,519	17,623	16,784
4	40,000	22,092	20,632	19,290	18,056	16,919
5	48,000	22,853	20,981	19,290	17,760	16,373
6 on	52,000	154,737	126,276	104,488	87,454	73,907
Total Value		$251,812	$218,160	$191,587	$170,133	$152,495

The forecasted returns can be either those available to equity or those available to overall invested capital (usually defined to include equity plus interest-bearing debt, although other definitions sometimes are used).

The returns that are forecasted usually are either net free cash flow or earnings, although other definitions of economic returns sometimes are used.

The returns may be forecasted either in the actual expected dollars in the year received (including inflation), or in "constant" or "real" dollars (today's dollars, *not* including inflation).

The discount rate includes a riskless rate of return (usually based on yields on U.S. Government Treasury bonds or bills yield to maturity as of the valuation date) plus a premium for the risk incurred in the investment. Sometimes a premium is added to the rate to reflect illiquidity (lack of marketability), but in other cases, the matter of illiquidity, if significant, is handled as a separate discount at the end of the valuation process.

If the forecasted returns are those available to equity holders, then the present value discount rate applicable to equity is used. If the forecast returns include what is available to cover interest on debt, then a weighted-average cost of capital is an appropriate present value discount rate.

If the forecasted returns are net free cash flow, a discount rate applicable to net free cash flow is appropriate. If the forecasted returns are earnings, a discount rate applicable to earnings is appropriate. (The discount rate applicable to earnings can be developed by starting with a net free cash flow discount rate and adjusting it, as discussed in Chapter 12.)

The "riskless rate" (government bond yield) includes investors' expectations of inflation over the life of the bond. If the forecasts are in constant dollars ("real" dollars—today's dollars without inflation), then the expected inflation must be subtracted from the present value discount rate.

In any written or oral presentation, the definition of the forecasted returns must be clearly spelled out. The derivation of the present value discount rate must also be explained so that it can be understood.

The critical thing is that the present value discount rate used be an appropriate rate that is matched to the definition of the forecasted economic returns. The most common error in application of the discounted future returns method is using a present value discount rate that is not appropriate for the particular level of economic returns used in the forecast.

Selected Bibliography

Bielinski, Daniel W. "How to Capture Equity Value in Pricing a Target." *Mergers & Acquisitions*, November/December 1991, pp. 26–31.

————. "The Debt-Free DCF Model: A Fix on Intrinsic Values." *Mergers & Acquisitions*, September/October 1989, pp. 43–47.

Black, Fischer. "A Simple Discounting Rule." *Financial Management*, Summer 1988, pp. 7–11.

Colborn, Asli F. "Estimating a Firm's Continuing Value." *Business Valuation Review,* December 1991, pp. 157–62.

Cooper, Glen. "How Much is Your Business Worth?" *In Business*, September/ October 1984, pp. 50–54.

Hartl, Robert J. "DCF Analysis: The Special Case of Risky Cash Outflows." *Real Estate Appraiser & Analyst*, Summer 1990, pp. 67–72.

Hempstead, John E. "Delaware Court Embraces Cash Flow Valuation Method with Both Arms." *Business Valuation Review*, December 1991, pp. 182–83.

Kane, Walter M. "Discounted Cash Flow Analysis and Newton's Apple." *Appraisal Journal*, July 1991, pp. 328–37.

Pratt, Shannon P., and Ralph Arnold. "Misuse of the Discounted Future Returns Valuation Method." *FAIR$HARE: The Matrimonial Law Monthly*, March 1990, pp. 3–5.

Pratt, Shannon P., and Craig S. Hugo. "Pricing a Company by the Discounted Future Earnings Method." *Mergers & Acquisitions*, Spring 1972, pp. 18–32.

Reilly, Robert F. "Pricing an Acquistion: A 15-Step Methodology." *Mergers & Acquistions,* Summer 1979, pp. 14–31.

Wincott, D. Richard. "Terminal Capitalization Rates and Reasonableness." *Appraisal Journal*, April 1991, pp. 253–260.

Chapter 14

Basic Capitalized Earnings Methods

A basic capitalization of earnings method means the application of one divisor or multiplier to one economic earnings figure; the result is an indication of value derived from that single division or multiplication. In real estate terminology, this process is called *direct capitalization*, defined as follows:

> The capitalization method used to convert an estimate of a single year's income expectancy or annual average of several years' income expectancies into an indication of value in one step, either by dividing the income estimate by an appropriate rate or by multiplying the income estimate by an appropriate factor.[1]

The economic income stream to be capitalized can be the latest year's, a straight or weighted average of past years, a normalized income stream, a forecast of the coming year's, or some other variation. The economic income stream can be either before or after any or all of several items, such as interest, depreciation, allowance for replacements, and/or other capital expenditures, owner's compensation, taxes, principal payments on debt, and many more.

As a practical matter, there are many more variations of earnings in common usage in basic capitalized earnings methods than in the discounted future returns method. This is because capitalization rates for a wide variety of return variables can be observed directly in the market from comparative company data.

The key is that the economic income stream being capitalized must be clearly defined, and the capitalization rate chosen must be a rate that is appropriate for the particular economic income stream, as defined. In order to avoid being encyclopedic, this chapter discusses only the most common few among the many possible variations.

Deciding on the Earnings Base to Be Capitalized

There are many possible earnings bases to capitalize to derive indications of the value of a business or practice. The appropriate choices depend on many factors; perhaps the most important of these are (1) the purpose of the appraisal, (2) the availability of reliable and valid data, and (3) the ability to develop a realistic capitalization rate that is applicable to the earnings base chosen.

How the Purpose Affects the Selection of the Earnings Base

An owner who wants to sell his business or practice obviously wishes to present as optimistic an earnings base as possible. If the latest year is the best year, he is likely to want to rely on that. If the latest year was not the best year, he will probably point to the average of whatever

---

[1] *The Dictionary of Real Estate Appraisal* (Chicago: American Institute of Real Estate Appraisers, 1984), p. 93.

number of years it takes to show the best results. Alternatively, he may adjust his historical results to his concept of a normalized earnings base, or he may forecast earnings for the year ahead. If he has a large amount of depreciation, he may choose to focus on gross or net cash flow rather than earnings. If interest was high, he may want to focus on operating income (earnings before interest). Certainly there is nothing wrong with a seller putting his best foot forward, as long as the information is accurate and complete enough not to mislead. As long as the information is clearly labeled as to exactly what it represents, a buyer can judge for himself how he will use it in deciding what he is willing to pay.

On the other hand, the same owner who will be paying gift, estate, inheritance, or ad valorem taxes on the basis of the valuation will be inclined to be conservative when selecting an earnings base to be capitalized.[2] He will not want to pay taxes on the basis of projected future earnings increases that may or may not materialize. When it comes to paying taxes based on the value of the business, he is not likely to believe that the highest level of earnings he has ever achieved is the best basis for the valuation of the business.

As a generalization, valuations for taxes and many other legal purposes should be based as far as possible on the actual historical record, whereas valuations for transactions, damage cases, and other purposes that tend to look to future results may rely more on estimates. Business executives are accustomed to making decisions on the basis of estimates. Except in certain types of damage cases and certain other instances, courts generally prefer to rely on an actual historical record, if that record is meaningful.

Valuations for divorce purposes also tend to lean more toward historical than estimated future results, at least to the extent that historical results are reasonably representative of ongoing expectations. One reason for this is that a family law court does not usually want to reflect in the valuation any future earnings improvement that would be a result of the postdivorce efforts of the operating spouse. Therefore, any estimated earnings used in a divorce case should reflect only expected results of forces already in place.

Exhibit 14–1 shows a variety of levels of earnings that may be capitalized.

Availability of Reliable and Valid Earnings Data

By *reliable* earnings data, we mean dependable and accurate data. For many small businesses, obtaining reliable earnings data on which to base a valuation is a major problem. In many cases, the problem arises from inadequate recordkeeping. In other cases, discretionary expenses that some people might regard as part of owner's compensation are so

---

[2]*Ad valorem* is Latin for "according to value." This is the expression commonly used for property taxes, because they are assessed according to value. Tax assessors tend to favor a cost approach to estimating value for property taxes. Because many businesses do not earn enough return to support the value of their property as indicated by a cost approach, they are paying too much in property taxes by not appealing the assessment based on income methods of valuation.

Exhibit 14–1

SEVEN EXAMPLES OF VARIOUS
LEVELS OF EARNINGS THAT MAY BE CAPITALIZED[a]

(1)	**Pretax earnings**[b]	
	Plus:	Interest expense
(2)	Equals:	**Earnings before interest and taxes (EBIT)**
	Plus:	Depreciation, amortization, and all other noncash charges
(3)	Equals:	**Earnings before depreciation, interest and taxes (EBDIT)**
	Pretax earnings	
	Less:	Income taxes
(4)	Equals:	**Net income**
	Plus:	Tax affected interest expense (computed as interest expense x (1 - tax rate))
(5)	Equals:	**Debt-free net income (DFNI)**
	Plus:	Depreciation, amortization and all other noncash charges
(6)	Equals:	**Debt-free cash flow (DFCF)**
	Net income	
	Plus:	Depreciation, amortization and all other noncash charges
	Less:	Capital expenditures
	Less:	Increase (or plus decrease) in working capital
	Plus:	Increase (or less decrease) in debt balance
(7)	Equals:	**Net cash flow**

---

[a] Note that it is important to adjust the capitalization rate to match the various earnings streams to be capitalized.

[b] The earnings base can be the last 12 months, average, weighted average or projected earnings for the subject company normalized to exclude any unusual or non-recurring events.

intertwined with essential expenses that it is virtually impossible to separate them. In some cases, it is necessary to work with only a single year's earnings or even an estimate, simply for lack of any other reliable data.

By *valid* earnings data, we mean data that are relevant to the current circumstances and expectations as of the valuation date. When a fire closes down a business for months, or when a major product line is discontinued, there may be perfectly reliable records of earnings for last year, but the difference in circumstances may render such historical data inapplicable to the situation at hand.

In summary, the earnings base or bases chosen to be capitalized should be both reliable and relevant to future expectations.

Ability to Develop an Applicable Capitalization Rate

It is easier to develop an applicable capitalization rate for certain earnings bases than for others, especially if the rate is to be developed by the direct market comparison method. There simply may be no market capitalization rate data available for many definitions of an earnings base, which otherwise are acceptable for valuation. Consequently, the appraiser may believe that one definition of earnings is best for conceptual reasons but may have to rely on an earnings base defined some other way just because of the availability of comparative market data from which to develop a capitalization rate.

Capitalizing Earnings Available to Equity

In direct capitalization of earnings, there are only two principal variables: (1) the definition of the income stream to be capitalized and (2) the capitalization rate. The capitalization rate may be expressed either as a divisor or as a multiplier. As discussed earlier, the key is to select a capitalization rate applicable to the particular earnings base.

Defining the Earnings Base

In the typical small business or professional practice, appraisers often use the normalized earnings base, if sufficient data are available. By *normalized,* we mean adjusted as necessary to represent a sustainable level of ongoing earning power.

Income taxes are a genuine economic cost. However, for reasons already discussed (lack of availability of data and different tax rates among various parties), most capitalizations of small business and professional practice earnings are done on a pretax basis.

If the cap rate is developed by the direct market comparison method, it is rarely possible to get the necessary data to compute net free cash flow for the comparative companies. Therefore, the earnings base to be used with the direct market comparison method of developing a capitalization rate will necessarily be dictated by availability of data. If market data are available for more than one earnings base, it usually is helpful to look at the value indications from several different levels of earnings.

Capitalization Rate by the "Build-Up" (Summation) Method

Having developed a normalized level of economic earnings available to equity, next develop the capitalization rate applicable to the economic earnings stream. If the standard of value is fair market value, the correct capitalization rate is the rate available on the most comparable investments for which data are available, adjusted for differences in risk and other characteristics between the subject investment and the nearest comparable investments for which data are available. As discussed in the previous chapter, the two primary methods for developing a capitalization rate applicable to earnings available to equity are (1) the summation method and (2) the direct market comparison method.

In the summation method, the first step is to develop a required total rate of return to equity; the second step is to adjust that rate for any portion of the expected return that may not be reflected in the economic earnings stream being capitalized. One good starting place for the summation method is the rate of return available on 20-year U.S. government bonds,[3] a rate readily available in *The Wall Street Journal* and many metropolitan daily newspapers. To that rate can be added the long-term historical average difference in rate of return on small stocks over long-term U.S. government bonds; through 1991, this was 7.4 percent, as discussed in the last chapter.[4] That total can be adjusted upward or downward for differences in perceived risk between the average small NYSE stock (comprising 20 percent of the smallest companies on the NYSE as measured by market value of common stock) and the subject company.

Adjustment can also be made for the fact that the small NYSE stocks are readily marketable, while a closely held business is less liquid. It is not uncommon to adjust the required rate of return upward, up to 10 percentage points, to reflect these factors, or sometimes even more, but there is little empirical evidence available for guidance in quantifying this adjustment. On the other hand, the investments in publicly traded stocks are minority interests, but we are discussing a controlling interest in the closely held business. Some investors would be willing to trade off the advantage of liquidity of investment, as found in a public company stock, for control of a small business, thus partially or even fully offsetting the upward adjustment to the capitalization rate for risk and lack of liquidity.

As discussed in the previous chapter, the total required rate of return includes, as a component, the expected rate of inflation. If we can assume that the economic earnings stream will grow in perpetuity at the rate of inflation, we can subtract the expected inflation rate from the total required rate of return in order to get a capitalization rate to apply to the current level of normalized earnings.

An example of the development of a capitalization rate, as described above, is as follows:

Long-term U.S. government bond rates	12%
Plus: Long-horizon expected equity risk premium	7.4
Expected small stock premium	5.1
Average premium return on small stocks over U.S. government bonds	12.5
Expected total rate of return on small public stocks	24.5
Plus: Premium for greater risk and illiquidity	4
Total required expected rate of return for subject company, including inflation component	28.5
Less: Consensus long-term inflation expectation	5
Capitalization rate to apply to current earnings	23.5%

[3]The reason for using 20-year U.S. government bonds, rather than 30-year or some other long maturity, is that the equity risk premium data are available only for 30-day, 5-year, and 20-year maturities.

[4]Ibbotson Associates, *1992 Yearbook*, p. 117.

Capitalization Rate by Direct Market Comparison Method

If pertinent data are available, it is also desirable to develop a capitalization rate, or range of capitalization rates, by the direct market comparison method. The best opportunity for using this method is when the appraiser has data available on the sales of other comparable closely held companies. For example, if data indicated that several comparable companies had sold for prices ranging from 3.2 to 5 times earnings, with earnings defined the same way as for the subject company, that data would imply a range of capitalization rates from .313 to .200 (1 ÷ 3.2 = .313; 1 ÷ 5 = .200). This range would suggest some upper and lower boundaries for the capitalization rate suggested by the summation method. The values should take into consideration the qualitative factors discussed in Chapter 10 in deciding where within the indicated range the capitalization rate applicable to the subject company should fall.

Keep in mind that published price/earnings multiples on publicly traded stocks are based on after-tax earnings. For reasons discussed elsewhere, the smaller the business, the less likely that public stock information will be useful for the purpose of valuing the business. However, if the appraiser decides that the subject company's stock is such that capitalization rates for earnings of public companies are relevant, he can compute price/pretax earnings multiples for the public companies by using current stock prices and earnings data from the companies' annual and interim reports.

Applying the Rate to Determine the Value

If a 25 percent capitalization rate were selected and applied to expected annual earnings available to equity of $10,000, the value of the equity in the business would be computed as follows:

$$\frac{\$10,000}{.25} = \$40,000$$

In other words, if a buyer requires a 25 percent return on equity for an investment to be attractive to him, he or she would capitalize the $10,000 expected earnings at 25 percent. That is, he or she would be willing to pay $40,000 for the $10,000 expected economic earnings stream because the *earnings yield* would be 25 percent ($10,000 ÷ $40,000 = .25).

Capitalizing Earnings Available to Overall Investment ("Invested Capital")

The difference between overall investment (or "invested capital") and equity in this context is that overall investment includes interest-bearing debt as well as equity. This method is appropriate when a portion of total investment may be financed with borrowed funds. This method is also sometimes called the *debt-free method*.

In some versions, the method includes all interest-bearing debt; in other versions, it includes only long-term debt. As noted elsewhere, many small businesses use short-term debt as if it were long-term debt. Neither version is necessarily right or wrong, but much confusion arises when the appraiser fails to specify whether or not short-term borrowing is included in his definition of overall investment.

Defining the Earnings Base

The economic earnings base should be the amount available to whatever has been defined as the overall investment. Except for interest, the most common convention is to define earnings as in the previous section. If overall investment means equity and long-term debt only, the earnings should be after any interest on short-term debt and before interest on long-term debt.

If overall investment includes all interest-bearing debt, the economic earnings base should be earnings before any interest. The economic earnings base thus defined is sometimes referred to as EBIT (earnings before interest and taxes), and also as *net operating income*.[5]

Capitalization Rate by the Weighted Average Method

When capitalizing earnings available to overall investment, it is appropriate to use a weighted average capitalization rate, consisting of one capitalization rate for the portion of the investment to be financed by equity, and one or more other rate(s) for the portion(s) of the investment to be financed by debt, as discussed in the previous chapter. (There may be more than one rate for debt because there may be different portions of the debt at different rates.)

Capitalization Rate for Equity Portion. The procedure for developing the capitalization rate applicable to the equity portion of the investment is the same as outlined in the previous section. When deciding what rate to use, within a reasonable range, one should consider that the higher the leverage (the amount of debt capital compared to the amount of equity capital), the higher the capitalization rate applicable to the equity capital portion. This is because increasing the amount of leverage increases the risk of the equity ownership.

Capitalization Rate for Debt Portion. The capitalization rate for the debt portion is basically the cost of the borrowed funds. Since interest is a tax-deductible expense, the cost of borrowing is the borrowing rate times one minus the effective tax.

Weighted Average Capitalization Rate. Once the capitalization rate has been determined for each of the components of the total investment,

---

[5]Net operating income is the income remaining after all expenses except interest, income taxes, and items not directly related to the company's operations. In accounting terminology, it is after depreciation. In real estate terminology, it is before depreciation, but in some usages it is after allowance for replacement expenditures.

the next step is to weight them on the basis of the proportion each is of the total investment.

For example, let's say it has been determined that the borrowing rate for the portion to be financed by debt should be 15 percent and the required return for the portion to be financed by equity should be 25 percent. Let's also say that the debt portion will carry 40 percent of the total investment, leaving 60 percent to be financed by equity. Then the weighted average capitalization rate can be computed as follows:

	Cost	**Proportion**		
Debt	.15	.4	=	.06
Equity	.25	.6	=	.15
Weighted average capitalization rate				.21

The above capitalization rate is also referred to as an *overall capitalization rate* or a *blended capitalization rate*.

Applying the Rate to Determine the Value

If an overall capitalization rate of 20 percent were applied to earnings of $20,000 before interest charges, the value of the total investment would be computed as follows:

$$\frac{\$20,000}{.20} = \$100,000$$

In other words, if $50,000 debt were available at a cost of 15 percent, the interest cost would be $7,500 per year (.15 × $50,000 = $7,500). Subtracting the $7,500 in interest from the $20,000 of earnings would leave $12,500 available for earnings on the equity portion, or 25 percent ($12,500 ÷ $50,000 = .25).

The above example implies no taxes at the entity level, either because it is a nontaxable entity or because the return to equity is modest enough that it could be paid out in salary or bonus without being treated as a dividend for tax purposes. If the entity were tax-paying, then the cost of debt would be tax-affected and the tax expense would be considered on computing the return to equity.

Of course, if there were excess assets or capital deficiencies, appropriate adjustments should be made in reaching the final value conclusion.

How Expected Growth Affects Capitalization Rates

When a stock is selling at 12 times earnings, its earnings yield is 8.3 percent. (The earnings yield is the reciprocal of the P/E multiple; thus, $1 \div 12 = .083$.) This is, in effect, the rate at which the market is capitalizing earnings. The fact that a stock is selling at 12 times earnings should not be interpreted to mean that investors are satisfied with a total return of 8.3 percent on their investment. What it means is that the investors will accept a current earnings yield of 8.3 percent because they expect the economic earnings stream to grow in the future. The consensus of investors' expectations about the future rate of earnings growth is incorporated into the rate at which they are willing to capitalize current earnings.

If an appraiser can project into the future a specific amount of expected earnings for each of several years, then the discounted future returns method (Chapter 13) is an appropriate method to use. More commonly, however, specific projections would be little more than mere guesses; but it is, nonetheless, intuitively reasonable to expect at least some growth in earnings. That expectation definitely has a bearing on value, so it needs somehow to be reflected in the valuation procedure.

The simplest way to look at expectations regarding future earnings growth is to assume some constant rate of growth in perpetuity. For the practical purpose of this analysis, 15 to 20 years is almost as good as perpetuity, since earnings expected to be generated after that length of time would have only a very minor effect on the value of the business today.

Consider, for example, a business operating in an environment with a 20-year forecast of 5 percent annually compounded inflation and 2 percent annually compounded population growth. Couple these assumptions with the expectations that the profit margins will keep up with inflation and that the business will maintain its share of the market; now there is a basis for a reasonable expectation of a 7 percent annually compounded rate of earnings growth as a result of the forces in place. How does the appraiser reflect these assumptions in determining the proper rate at which to capitalize current earnings?

Under the assumption of a constant annually compounded rate of growth in the economic earnings or cash flow stream in perpetuity, the correct rate at which to capitalize the current level of earnings or cash flow is the required total rate of return less the assumed growth rate. If the analysis leads to the conclusion that the required total rate of return should be 32 percent and the expected growth rate is 7 percent, then the current economic earnings stream should be capitalized at 25 percent (.32 − .07 = .25).

Obviously, a seller would like to convince a buyer to expect a high growth rate. From the buyer's viewpoint, however, only growth that is virtually assured as a result of forces already in place should be reflected in deciding on a rate at which to capitalize current earnings or cash flow. The buyer would not expect to pay for potential future growth that may result from his own successful entrepreneurial efforts.

Adjusting for Excess Assets or Capital Deficiency

The $40,000 value developed in the previous section represents the total value of the investment on a going-concern basis. If assets not needed in the operation of the business are to be included in the transaction, the buyer could add to the $40,000 his estimate of the net proceeds that would be available from selling those excess assets.

On the other hand, if additional investment would be necessary to sustain the $10,000 economic earnings stream (for working capital, deferred maintenance, or anything else), then such additional investment should be subtracted from the amount to be paid.

Examples of Valuations by the Capitalized Earnings Method

The following are hypothetical examples to illustrate the procedures discussed in this chapter. The two examples continue to use the same two hypothetical companies used in Part II on analyzing the company.

Sole Proprietorship Example

Annual pretax income available to the owner of Annie's Apparel, according to the adjusted income statement (Exhibit 8–2, page 102), is $65,600. This figure allows for a normal salary for the owner/manager and for interest on a long-term contract payable to be assumed by the buyer.

In the previous chapter, we discussed required total rates of return for equity investments in small businesses and practices ranging from 20 to 40 percent, with most falling in the 25 to 35 percent range. If we assume that about 5 percent of the total required rate of return will come more or less automatically as a result of the profits of the business keeping up with inflation, capitalization rates for current earnings will range from about 20 percent to 30 percent.

When one is deciding where in the range the appropriate capitalization rate falls for Annie's earnings available to the owner (after a reasonable salary), one should recognize at least two risk factors. First, leverage is present because of the $100,000 contract being assumed. Second, the $65,600 earnings represents 6.6 percent return on sales, considerably above the industry average, as shown in Exhibits 9–1, 9–2, and 9–3, pages 110, 112–13, and 114; this would lead one to question whether that level of earnings can be sustained for the long run.

If we decide that the upper end of the range, 30 percent, is the appropriate rate, a valuation calculation can be made as follows:

$$\frac{\$65,600}{.30} = \$218,667$$

From the buyer's perspective, if Annie's were to capitalize the pro forma earnings of $57,000 at 25 percent, reflecting a lower degree of risk inherent in the lower pro forma earnings estimate, a calculation can be made as follows:

$$\frac{\$57,000}{.25} = \$228,000$$

Corporation Example

Since Mary was leaving the business, one of her key employees, Barney Backhoe, and two of his associates decided that they would like to try to buy Mary's Machinery and Equipment, Inc., through a leveraged buyout. That is, they would use borrowed funds with the collateral being the company's assets. Based on the financial statements and adjusted balance sheets and income statements, the bank indicated interest in making a term loan of approximately 60 percent of the purchase price at 12 percent interest. The term loan will have monthly interest payments and annual principal reductions, with the note personally guaranteed by each of the three parties involved in the purchase. There are no significant extra costs associated with the loan.

Because the business has been well established for several years, the buyers feel that a 25 percent total pretax rate of return on equity would be satisfactory in order to make the deal attractive. They also believe that the combination of inflation and population growth in their area will bring a 5 percent annual growth in earnings, so they are willing to accept a 20 percent return on the first year $(.25 - .05 = .20)$. On this basis, they would capitalize the first year's expected earnings as follows:

	Capitalization Rate		Proportion		
Debt	.12	×	.60	=	.072
Equity	.20	×	.40	=	.080
Weighted average capitalization rate					.152
EBIT*			$101,000	=	$664,474
Capitalization rate			.152		

*When using the weighted average cost of capital, it is appropriate to use an earnings base before interest expense. $101,000 is derived from the sum of the interest expense and the income before taxes (see Exhibit 8–4). See p. 204 for definition and discussion of EBIT.

It is easy to capitalize the economic income stream using any proportion of leverage the buyer considers reasonable. For example, if a buyer believed that only 40 percent of the purchase price could be financed with debt, with the same costs of the debt and equity components of the capital structure, he could calculate the capitalized value of the income stream as follows:

	Capitalization Rate		Proportion		
Debt	.12	×	.40	=	.048
Equity	.20	×	.60	=	.120
Weighted average capitalization rate					.168
EBIT			$101,000	=	$601,190
Capitalization rate			.168		

As can be seen in the example above, an increase of 1.6 percent in the assumed weighted average capitalization rate makes a difference of over $60,000 in the amount that the buyer would be willing to pay. The lesson should be clear. As the cost of capital goes up, the values of existing businesses come down, and vice versa. To the extent that low-cost debt financing is available to a buyer to finance a purchase, the weighted average cost of capital for that buyer is lower than it would be if such financing were less available or not available at all. As economic conditions change, the cost and availability of financing change. These changes have an important impact on the values of businesses.

Summary

There are two variables in the basic capitalized earnings method:

1. The measure of economic income to be capitalized (the numerator).
2. The capitalization rate (the denominator).

The measure of economic income to be capitalized may be defined in a variety of ways. The purpose of the valuation, the availability of reliable and valid data for a particularly defined measure of income, and the ability to develop a capitalization rate applicable to the particular definition of income all may influence the choice of the measure of income to capitalize.

The measure of income to be capitalized may be income available to equity, in which case an equity capitalization rate would be used. If the economic income stream capitalized includes returns available to cover interest on debt, then a capitalization rate applicable to overall invested capital should be used.

Capitalization rates may be built up by developing a discount rate and adjusting for differences, usually growth, between the expected total returns and the specific measure of income being capitalized. Alternatively, a capitalization rate may be developed by directly observable market capitalization rates on comparative economic income streams.

In either case, it is absolutely critical that the capitalization rate used be an appropriate rate that is matched to the definition and procedures for measurement of the economic income stream being capitalized. The most common error in the application of the capitalization of earnings method is using a capitalization rate that is not appropriate for the particular definition and/or measurement of the economic income stream being capitalized.

Chapter 15

The Excess Earnings Method

In applying the "formula" approach, the average earnings period and the capitalization rates are dependent on the facts pertinent thereto in each case.

The past earnings to which the formula is applied should fairly reflect the probable future earnings.[1]

The above quotations from Revenue Ruling 68–609 are all too frequently overlooked, resulting in some of the more egregious misapplications of the excess earnings method.

The *excess earnings method* of valuation can be considered a hybrid method of valuation. If the balance sheet used represents (or is adjusted to represent) reasonably current values, the method may be regarded as either an asset approach or an income approach. We devote a separate chapter to it because it is the most widely used and, arguably, the most misused of all methods for valuing small businesses and professional practices.

It is widely written about, and more than half of the business and professional practice brokers that we have encountered use some version of it. It is widely used by courts in divorce proceedings for determining the value of goodwill in professional practices. Yet the Internal Revenue Service, which spawned the method back in 1920, now often denounces it.

History of the Excess Earnings Method

The excess earnings method is sometimes called the *Treasury method* because the method originally appeared in a 1920 publication by the U.S. Treasury Department, ARM 34, which stands for Appeals and Review Memorandum Number 34. It was adopted to compute the value of goodwill that breweries and distilleries lost because of prohibition.

Since then, both taxpayers and IRS agents have widely used (and misused) it in connection with valuations of businesses for gift and estate taxes. Also, perhaps partly because of its wide publicity and partly because its apparently simplistic nature is appealing, it has been widely adopted in one form or another for pricing small businesses and professional practices.

In 1968, the Internal Revenue Service updated and restated the ARM 34 method with the publication of Revenue Ruling 68–609, which is reproduced on the following page as Exhibit 15–1. Revenue Ruling 68–609 is still in effect.

How It Works

A Step-by-Step Explanation

While there are several variations to this methodology, the typical steps in the excess earnings method can be summarized as follows:

---

[1]Revenue Ruling 68–609, 1968–2, C.B. 327.

Exhibit 15–1

REVENUE ruling 68–609 (formula method)

The "formula" approach may be used in determining the fair market value of intangible assets of a business only if there is no better basis available for making the determination; A.R.M. 34, A.R.M. 68, O.D. 937, and Revenue Ruling 65-192 superseded. (1968-2, C.B., 327).

REVENUE RULING 68-609

The purpose of this Revenue Ruling is to update and restate, under the current statute and regulations, the currently outstanding portions of A.R.M. 34, C.B. 2, 31 (1920), A.R.M. 68, C.B. 3, 43 (1920), and O.D. 937, C.B. 4, 43 (1921).

The question presented is whether the "formula" approach, the capitalization of earnings in excess of a fair rate of return on net tangible assets, may be used to determine the fair market value of the intangible assets of a business.

The "formula" approach may be stated as follows:

A percentage return on the average annual value of the tangible assets used in a business is determined, using a period of years (preferably not less than five) immediately prior to the valuation date. The amount of the percentage return on tangible assets, thus determined, is deducted from the average earnings of the business for such period and the remainder, if any, is considered to be the amount of the average annual earnings from the intangible assets of the business for the period. This amount (considered as the average annual earnings from intangibles), capitalized at a percentage of, say 15 to 20 percent, is the value of the intangible assets of the business determined under the "formula" approach.

The percentage of return on the average annual value of the tangible assets used should be the percentage prevailing in the industry involved at the date of valuation, or (when the industry percentage is not available) a percentage of 8 to 10 percent may be used.

The 8 percent rate of return and the 15 percent rate of capitalization are applied to tangibles and intangibles, respectively, of businesses with a small risk factor and stable and regular earnings; the 10 percent rate of return and 20 percent rate of capitalization are applied to businesses in which the hazards of business are relatively high.

The above rates are used as examples and are not appropriate in all cases. In applying the "formula" approach, the average earnings period and the capitalization rates are dependent upon the facts pertinent thereto in each case.

The past earnings to which the formula is applied should fairly reflect the probable future earnings. Ordinarily, the period should not be less than five years, and abnormal years, whether above or below the average, should be eliminated. If the business is a sole proprietorship or partnership, there should be deducted from the earnings of the business a reasonable amount for services performed by the owner or partners engaged in the business. See Lloyd B. Sanderson Estate v. Commissioner, 42 F 2d 160 (1930). Further, only the tangible assets entering into net worth, including accounts and bills receivable in excess of accounts and bills payable, are used for determining earnings on the tangible assets. Factors that influence the capitalization rate include (1) the nature of the business, (2) the risk involved, and (3) the stability or irregularity of earnings.

The "formula" approach should not be used if there is better evidence available from which the value of intangibles can be determined. If the assets of a going business are sold upon the basis of a rate of capitalization that can be substantiated as being realistic, though it is not within the range of figures indicated here as the ones ordinarily to be adopted, the same rate of capitalization should be used in determining the value of the intangibles.

Accordingly, the "formula" approach may be used for determining the fair market value of intangible assets of a business only if there is no better basis therefor available.

See also Revenue Ruling 59-60, C.B. 1959-1, 237, as modified by Revenue Ruling 65-193, C.B. 1965-2, 370, which sets forth the proper approach to use in the valuation of closely-held corporate stocks for estate and gift tax purposes. The general approach, methods, and factors, outlined in Revenue Ruling 59-60, as modified, are equally applicable to valuations of corporate stocks for income and other tax purposes as well as for estate and gift tax purposes. They apply also to problems involving the determination of the fair market value of business interests of any type, including partnerships and proprietorships, and of intangible assets for all tax purposes.

A.R.M. 34, A.R.M. 68, and O.D. 937 are superseded, since the positions set forth therein are restated to the extent applicable under current law in this Revenue Ruling. Revenue Ruling 65-192, C.B. 1965-2, 259, which contained restatements of A.R.M. 34 and A.R.M. 68, is also superseded.

1. Determine a net tangible asset value, as in Chapter 7. (Note that this value is typically for net tangible assets only and would not normally include intangible items such as leaseholds, patents, copyrights, and so on.)

2. Determine a normalized level of earnings, as in Chapter 8.

3. Determine an appropriate percentage rate of return, or, in the parlance of this book, a capitalization rate on the net tangible asset value. Multiply the net tangible asset value from Step 1 by that rate to determine the amount of earnings attributable to the tangible assets. Subtract that amount from the normalized earnings developed in Step 2. The result of this step is called the *excess earnings*, that is, the amount of earnings above a fair return on the net tangible asset value.

4. Determine an appropriate capitalization rate to apply to the excess earnings, which are presumably the earnings attributable to goodwill or other intangible assets, as opposed to tangible assets. Capitalize the excess earnings at that rate.

5. Add the values from Steps 1 and 4.[2]

Ah . . . Sweet Simplicity!

Don't you believe it!

In a subsequent section, we will examine the many decisions and pitfalls encountered in each of the above steps. But first, let's look at a simple example, a popularly accepted summary presentation, and a few choice words from the IRS.

An Example

Let's suppose that Flora's Flower Shop has a net tangible asset value of $20,000. Let's also suppose that after allowance for a reasonable salary for Flora, the shop earns about $8,000 per year. For the purpose of this example, we will use a rate of return of 15 percent on the tangible assets, and will capitalize the excess earnings at $33\frac{1}{3}$ percent. (The matter of determining applicable rates is discussed later in the chapter.) In this scenario, the value of Flora's Flower Shop would be computed as follows:

Net tangible asset value		$20,000
Normalized earnings	$8,000	
Earnings attributable to tangible assets ($20,000 × .15) =	3,000	
"Excess" earnings	$5,000	
Value of excess earnings ($5,000 ÷ .333) =		15,000
Total value		$35,000

---

[2]As an alternative to using the present net tangible asset value and normalized earnings, some appraisers base the computations of the value of excess earnings on average net tangible assets and average earnings for some period of time, usually five years. This procedure is satisfactory if the period used is representative of reasonable future expectations. If this procedure is used, the value of excess earnings is still added to the present net tangible asset value to arrive at the value for the total entity. Also, if there is interest-bearing debt, some analysts use returns available to overall capital (debt and equity), and then subtract the value of the interest-bearing debt as a final step to arrive at an equity value.

A Popular Version

Exhibit 15–2 is typical of the summaries of the excess earnings method in popular usage. The text accompanying the formula offers the following comments:

> The buyer looks at the business for its ability to earn a fair return on investment, after deducting his or her salary. The present and future earning power of the business is of prime importance. If the business is not at least equal in earning power to an outside investment in a comparable business or in securities, the buyer usually will not be willing to pay more than the price of tangibles. In fact, the buyer may not want to buy the tangible assets—even at bargain prices—if the business is not profitable. . . .
>
> Goodwill can be thought of as the difference between an established successful business and one that has yet to establish itself and achieve success. The price the buyer should be willing to pay for goodwill depends on the earning power and potential of the business.
>
> The price the seller should be content with is the amount considered as compensation for the transfer of intangible values and for the surrender of the expected earning power of the business. The seller should base the value of goodwill on the actual condition and earning power of the business. If past efforts and capital were used effectively, the current earning power of the business should be above average. If earnings are low, the buyer probably will resist paying any amount for intangibles. . . .
>
> Because each business and sales transaction is different, the formula should be used only to indicate some of the major considerations in pricing a business.[3]

Denunciation by the IRS

The IRS Appellate Conferee Valuation Training Program uses colorful language to denounce the use of ARM 34 or the excess earnings method of valuation. Following are some pertinent excerpts:

> One of the most frequently encountered errors in appraisal is the use of a formula to determine a question of fact, which on a reasonable basis must be resolved in view of all pertinent circumstances. . . . ARM 34 has been applied indiscriminately by tax practitioners and by members of the Internal Revenue Service since it was published. On occasion the Tax Court has recognized ARM 34 as a means of arriving at a fair market value. The latest and most controlling decisions on valuation, however, relegate the use of a formula to a position of being a last resort. ARM 34 was published in 1920, but since that time it has continually appeared in the annals of tax valuation and resulted in many improper appraisals.
>
> By such a formula the same value would be found in 1960 as in 1933, although values per dollar of earnings were very different in those two years. The basic defect is apparent; the rates of return which are applied to

[3]*How to Buy or Sell a Business*, Small Business Reporter series (San Francisco: Bank of America, 1982), p. 8.

Exhibit 15–2

A Popular Version of the Excess Earnings Method

The Pricing Formula	**Example:**	**Business A**	**Business B**
Step 1. Determine the adjusted tangible net worth of the business. (The total market value of all current and long-term assets less liabilities.)	**1.** Adjusted value of tangible net worth (assets less liabilities).	$100,000	$100,000
Step 2. Estimate how much the buyer could earn annually with an amount equal to the value of the tangible net worth invested elsewhere.	**2.** Earning power at 10%* of an amount equal to the adjusted tangible net worth, if invested in a comparable risk business.	10,000	10,000
Step 3. Add to this a salary normal for an owner-operator of the business. This combined figure provides a reasonable estimate of the income the buyer can earn elsewhere with the investment and effort involved in working in the business.	**3.** Reasonable salary for owner-operator in the business.	18,000	18,000
Step 4. Determine the average annual net earnings of the business (net profit before subtracting owner's salary) over the past few years. This is before income taxes, to make it comparable with earnings from other sources or by individuals in different tax brackets. (The tax implications of alternate investments should be carefully considered.) The trend of earnings is a key factor. Have they been rising steadily, falling steadily, remaining constant, or fluctuating widely? The earnings figure should be adjusted to reflect these trends.	**4.** Net earnings of the business over recent years (net profit before subtracting owner's salary).	30,000	23,350
Step 5. Subtract the total of earning power (2) and reasonable net salary (3) from this average net earnings figure (4). This gives the extra earning power of the business.	**5.** Extra earning power of the business (line 4 minus lines 2 and 3).	2,000	(4,650)
Step 6. Use this extra, or excess, earning figure to estimate the value of the intangibles. This is done by multiplying the extra earnings by what is termed the "years-of-profit" figure. This "years-of-profit" multiplier pivots on these points. How unique are the intangibles offered by the firm? How long would it take to set up a similar business and bring it to this stage of development? What expenses and risks would be involved? What is the price of goodwill in similar firms? Will the seller be signing an agreement with a covenant not to compete? If the business is well established, a factor of five or more might be used, especially if the firm has a valuable name, patent, or location. A multiplier of three might be reasonable for a moderately seasoned firm. A younger, but profitable, firm might merely have a one-year profit figure.	**6.** Value of intangibles —using three-year profit figure for moderately well-established firm (3 times line 5).	6,000	None
Step 7. Final Price equals Adjusted Tangible Net Worth plus Value of Intangibles. (Extra Earnings times "Years of Profit.")	**7.** Final price (lines 1 and 6).	$106,000	$100,000 (or less)

In **example A**, the seller receives a value for goodwill because the business is moderately well established and earning more than the buyer could earn elsewhere with similar risks and effort. Within three years, the buyer should have recovered the amount paid for goodwill in this example.

In **example B**, the seller receives no value for goodwill because the business, even though it may have existed for a considerable time, is not earning as much as the buyer could through outside investment and effort. In fact, the buyer may feel that even an investment of $100,000— the current appraised value of net assets—is too much because it cannot earn sufficient return.

This is an arbitrary figure, used for illustration. A reasonable figure depends on the stability and relative risks of the business and the investment picture generally. The rate of return should be similar to that which could be earned elsewhere with the same approximate risk.

SOURCE: *How to Buy or Sell a Business*, Small Business Reporter Series (San Francisco: Bank of America, 1982), p. 8.

tangibles and to intangibles are completely arbitrary and have no foundation in fact. . . .

The 8 percent rule, or any other arbitrary rate of earnings as a normal return on tangible assets, cannot be demonstrated to have a reasonable basis. Similarly, the 15 percent rate or any specific rate on intangible assets is not in itself a supportable figure. If there were a somewhat comparable business which had earned $50,000 per year as an average for five years and which had been sold for $400,000 cash, it could be said that there was a 12½ percent indicated rate of return on total investment but no one could ascertain what have been the rates of return on the tangible and intangible assets. All that can be said for ARM 34, or a similar formula method of capitalization using two rates of interest, is that you hope to get a good answer based upon two bad guesses. It is difficult enough to get one reasonably accurate rate of capitalization using normal appraisal methods. . . . To get two fairly accurate rates, one for tangibles and the other for intangibles, other than by the use of pure guesswork, is impossible. . . .

Any capitalization of earnings must take into consideration the economic conditions prevailing at the specific date of appraisal, including those conditions controlling in the industry in this particular company's area, and even in the national economy.

If we assume that a fair rate of return for this type of business is 8 percent, the better procedure is to capitalize a representative earnings figure (in this instance 1953 income) at that rate. To attempt to segregate value based on earnings as between normal income and that induced by whatever goodwill or other intangible assets the business may possess is to aspire to a higher degree of clairvoyance than has yet been demonstrated as obtainable by mere man.[4]

Analysis of the Method

A method that has been so thoroughly denounced by its own promulgators, and yet is one of the most widely used methods in existence today, certainly deserves some analysis.

First of all, the Treasury Department did not initiate the method to value the total entity by the method, but specifically to value the goodwill or other intangible value, if any, above the tangible asset values. However, since it seems logical that any intangible value identified by the method must be added to tangible value to get a total value, the method has attained popularity for valuing the total entity.

Revenue Ruling 68–609 contains many ambiguities, and leaves many unanswered questions. Various practitioners have adopted a wide variety of interpretations to the ambiguities, and a wide variety of answers to the unanswered questions. We will discuss these ambiguities and open questions in the same order as the "Step-by-Step Explanation" in an earlier section.

Determining Net Tangible Asset Value

Step 1 in the excess earnings method is to determine a net tangible asset value. Revenue Ruling 68–609 does not define tangible asset value, nor is it very specific with respect to the important question "net of what?"

Defining Tangible Asset Value. Revenue Ruling 68–609 offers absolutely no guidance as to either the appropriate standard or premise of value that is intended in conjunction with the phrase "tangible asset

---

[4]U.S. Internal Revenue Service, *IRS Appellate Conferee Valuation Training Program* (Chicago: Commerce Clearing House, 1978), pp. 82–86. The section was repeated with no substantive changes in the 1980 revision.

value." Does it mean replacement value? Liquidation value? Book value? Or what?

There is some consensus among careful valuation practitioners that the best conceptual interpretation of the phrase "tangible asset value" in this context is fair market value on a going-concern basis. Typically, this would be measured by replacement cost new less an allowance for physical deterioration and depreciation or for any functional or economic obsolescence.[5] An alternative would be to use replacement cost used.

Furthermore, IRS Private Letter Ruling 79–05013 (also promulgated as an IRS National Office Technical Advice Memorandum) takes a firm position that the standard of value for the tangible assets should be fair market value:

> Rev. Rul. 68–609 addresses the determination of fair market value of intangible assets by the formula approach, and for this reason it is proper that all terms used in the formula be consistent. The formula uses value in terms of fair market value, so the term " . . . value of the tangible assets used in a business," in the formula, should be in terms of fair market values, as defined in Rev. Rul. 59–60.

As a practical matter, only rarely will the practitioner engage in such a careful valuation of the tangible assets. Typically, the practitioner will attempt to make some rough approximation of the fair market value of the tangible assets on a going-concern basis. Often the practitioner is stuck with book value simply because there are no readily available data to aid in reaching a better approximation.

Should Asset Value Adjustments be Tax-Affected? Because the purpose of the analysis is to determine the value of tangible assets on a going-concern basis on which a reasonable rate of return should be earned, the appraiser normally does not make any adjustment to recognize the tax effect of unrealized gains or losses. However, there could be cases (e.g., a large inventory write-up where a tax payment on the sale of the inventory is imminent) where a tax adjustment may be appropriate.

Are Any Intangibles Ever Included? Typically, as the phrase "tangible asset value" implies, all intangibles would be removed from the balance sheet in performing the excess earnings exercise. However, some practitioners would leave in (or even add to the balance sheet) certain identifiable intangible assets with readily ascertainable market values, especially if such intangible assets could be sold independent of the business.[6]

Treatment of Nonoperating Assets. There is general consensus that it is preferable to remove nonoperating and/or excess assets from the balance sheet (and related revenue from the income statement) and treat such items separately in the excess earnings method.

---

[5]"Replacement cost" means the cost of acquiring and putting in place an asset that will accomplish the same task as the existing asset, e.g., extrude 1,000 plastic widget handles per hour.

[6]See, for example, Thomas L. West and Jeffrey D. Jones, eds., *Handbook of Business Valuation* (New York: John Wiley & Sons, 1992), Chapter 15.

Treatment of Real Estate Owned. Many practitioners also prefer to remove real estate from the balance sheet and impute fair market rental expense on the income statement.

What Is "Netted Out" in Determining Tangible Asset Value? Depreciation? All liabilities? All current liabilities? All noninterest-bearing liabilities?

I have not encountered any exception to the notion that tangible asset value should be net of all depreciation, amortization, and obsolescence. However, it often is not practical to measure all these items in terms of current economic values.

In the simplest straight equity application of the excess earnings method, all liabilities would be deducted to arrive at a net tangible asset value.

However, the only reference to netting out liabilities in Revenue Ruling 68–609 is taking out noninterest-bearing current liabilities.[7] Furthermore, experienced valuation practitioners recognize that differences in leverage from one company or practice to another can lead to distortions in valuation results derived from the excess earnings method. Furthermore, most sales of small businesses and professional practices are consummated on a debt-free basis. That is, the old owner pays off liabilities rather than the new owner assuming them, and the new owner establishes a new set of financing arrangements.

Therefore, in many cases, a more reliable result will be achieved by using a "debt-free" version of the excess earnings method. This involves removing all interest-bearing debt from the balance sheet and all interest (adjusted for taxes) from the income statement. The excess earnings exercise is then carried out to produce an indicated value for all invested capital (defined here to include all equity and interest-bearing debt). Finally, the value of interest-bearing debt would be subtracted to determine the value of the equity.

Do You Value Debt at Face Value or at Fair Market Value? The conceptual answer to this question is that it depends on when the debt is likely to be paid. If payment at face value is imminent (e.g., payment triggered by the very transaction for which the valuation is being performed), then it is appropriate to value the debt at face value. If it is contemplated that the debt will remain outstanding, then most practitioners would prefer to value the debt at fair market value.

Determining a Normalized Level of Earnings

Step 2 in the excess earnings method is to determine a normalized level of earnings. Revenue Ruling 68–609 does not make any attempt to define *earnings*. It does, however, make the key statement that the earnings "*should fairly reflect the probable future earnings* (emphasis supplied)." In suggesting the use of past years' earnings as a basis, it notes that

---

[7]The actual phrase used in Revenue Ruling 68–609 is "accounts and bills receivable in excess of accounts and bills payable."

abnormal years should be eliminated. Practitioners also agree that non-recurring items should be eliminated from any year used for earnings base calculations.

Treatment of Nonoperating Income.   Consistent with removing non-operating assets from the tangible asset base, related nonoperating income should be removed from the earnings base.

Treatment of Owners' Compensation.   Revenue Ruling 68–609 states that "if the business is a sole proprietorship or partnership, there should be deducted from the earnings of the business a reasonable amount for services performed by the owner or partners engaged in the business." Valuation practitioners also concur that abnormal compensation should be adjusted to a normal level. The "normal level" is generally considered to be the cost of employing someone else to perform like services.

Treatment of Income Taxes.   Earnings to be capitalized should normally be net of federal and state income taxes paid by the entity being valued. Most small businesses and professional practices are organized as sole proprietorships, partnerships, or S corporations; the entities normally pay no federal or state income taxes, so the matter may be moot. Even small businesses and professional practices organized as C corporations often manage their affairs to eliminate or nearly eliminate corporate income taxes.

However, there are instances where a case can be made for tax-affecting the income even where the entity does not pay income taxes. For example, if the entity were to be sold to a corporation that would have to pay taxes on the entity's income, in determining that buyer's investment value, the buyer would almost surely tax-affect the income in doing a valuation calculation. If that buyer were the typical buyer, the tax-affected earnings probably would also lead to the fair market value. Also, a significant (and not uncommon) problem arises when tax liability is flowed through to an owner but the earnings giving rise to the tax liability are not paid out. Tax-affecting the entity's earnings is one of several possible ways to treat this problem for purposes of valuation.

Definition of "Earnings."   Revenue Ruling 68–609 is totally silent with respect to any definition of *earnings*. Is it net income? Net cash flow? Or what?

There is some consensus among valuation practitioners that the variable best suited to represent earnings in the context of the excess earnings method is net cash flow (as defined in Chapter 13). For most small businesses and professional practices, the difference between net income and net cash flow is so minimal that it doesn't matter. If there is any significant difference between net income and net cash flow, it is important to use an equity rate of return applicable to the variable being capitalized, as discussed in Chapter 12 on "Understanding Discount and Capitalization Rates."

Appropriate Rate of Return on Tangible Assets

No one has totally and convincingly refuted the position stated by the IRS that any arbitrary rate of earnings as a normal return on tangible assets cannot be demonstrated to have a reasonable basis. Nevertheless, there are some ways to look at the problem of determining a fair rate of return on tangible assets that could be helpful.

There is a strong consensus among valuation practitioners today that the appropriate percentage rate of return on tangible assets in the excess earnings method depends on the asset mix in each case.[8] Assets that are highly liquid, low in risk, and/or readily acceptable as loan collateral require lower rates of return than assets that are less liquid, more risky, and/or less acceptable as loan collateral.

Loan officers look at the liquidity and riskiness of assets available as collateral in determining how much they will lend. Therefore, the asset values that can be used as collateral have a bearing on the company's cost of capital because they influence how much capital will be available at bank loan rates. Since banks will usually not make loans to 100 percent of the assets used as collateral, and since there are some costs to bank borrowing that are in addition to the basic interest rate, it is reasonable to suggest that businesses need to earn a rate of return on their investment in tangible assets that is at least a few points above the rate at which bank loan money is available to them.

Appropriate Capitalization Rate for Excess Earnings

Tangible assets provide at least a modicum of safety in that, if earnings fail to materialize as expected, the assets can usually be liquidated for something. Goodwill, on the other hand (as well as many other intangible assets), has no liquidation value in the absence of earnings, since its very value depends on its ability to generate earnings. Therefore, the risk attached to the intangible portion of the assets would seem to be greater and demand a higher rate of return.

Furthermore, a good case can be made that the tangible assets have a much more persistent and predictable life than goodwill or other intangible assets in many, if not most, cases. Despite the IRS fiction that purchased goodwill cannot be amortized because its value does not diminish, in most cases goodwill values do diminish over time. And the rate of diminution in value is often much greater than the rate of economic depreciation of tangible assets.[9] One might say that goodwill, if not nourished, will perish.

In general, investors are not willing to pay cash up front for more than one to five years' worth of earnings from commercial goodwill,

---

[8]See, for example, Jay E. Fishman, Shannon P. Pratt, et al., *Guide to Business Valuations,* 2nd ed. (Fort Worth, Tex.: Practitioners Publishing Co., 1992), Chapter 7; and Thomas L. West and Jeffrey D. Jones, eds., *Handbook of Business Valuation* (New York: John Wiley & Sons, 1992), Chapter 15.

[9]For an interesting discussion of the diminution of the value of goodwill, see Jerald H. Udinsky, "Goodwill Depreciation: A New Method for Valuing Professional Practices in a Marital Dissolution," *Community Property Journal,* Fall 1982, pp. 307–22.

sometimes even less. The length of expected future earnings from good-will for which investors are willing to pay depends primarily on the perceived persistence of those earnings in the future, independent of further investment of time and effort to perpetuate them.

One way to develop a capitalization rate to apply to excess earnings is to think in terms of converting the number of years' worth of expected future excess earnings the investor would be willing to pay for in terms of cash up front into a capitalization rate. The capitalization rate in this scenario is simply the reciprocal of the number of years' expected excess earnings for which the investor would be willing to pay cash up front. For example, if the typical investor would pay cash equivalent to four years' excess earnings, the calculation would be:

$$1 \div 4 = .25$$

The following table shows capitalization rates for excess earnings based on assumed investors' tolerances for a range of payback periods (the length of time the investor is willing to accept to recover the initial outlay):

Payback Period	Capitalization Rate
3 months	400%
6 months	200
1 year	100
2 years	50
3 years	33⅓
4 years	25
5 years	20

Summary: Conceptual Basis for the Two Capitalization Rates

In light of the foregoing discussion, it is reasonable, conceptually, to determine appropriate capitalization rates to apply to earnings generated both from a base of tangible assets and from intangible factors over and above an acceptable return on the investment in tangible assets. The conceptual basis is that the difference in the cost of capital depends on the presence or lack of tangible assets. Generally, the greater the value of the tangible assets the buyer receives for his investment, the less risky the buyer perceives the investment to be, thus the lower his required rate of return. Furthermore, the assets support borrowing, thus reducing the weighted average cost of capital.

We suggest, therefore, that the rate to be applied as a return on tangibles be a weighted average of the cost of borrowing and the cost of equity. The weighting would logically depend on what percentage of the assets could be financed by borrowing.

We also suggest that the capitalization rate for the excess earnings be at or above the high end of a range of reasonable required rates of return on equity, because the risk would be perceived to be greater with no tangible asset backing. The determination of the rate in each case should depend on the expected duration and the perceived risk of the excess earnings.

The capitalization rates applied to current earnings might be adjusted to reflect how much the economic earnings stream is expected to grow as a result of the forces in place, as discussed in Chapter 11. However, recognizing that such adjustments assume growth in perpetuity, a questionable assumption for most small businesses and professional practices, the validity of any such adjustment must be examined carefully.

An example of the application of the excess earnings method is shown as Exhibit 15–3.

Negative Goodwill

The excess earnings method deals with how to value the earnings, if any, over and above a reasonable rate of return on the tangible assets. What if the earning power is less than a reasonable rate of return on the tangible assets? Such a circumstance could indicate negative goodwill; it could be an indication that the value of the total entity would be less than the value of its tangible assets (on a replacement value basis, as discussed in Chapter 7).

In such a situation, earnings are insufficient to justify buying the business on the basis of the replacement value of its assets, and the lower value indicated by the capitalized earnings should predominate over the adjusted tangible asset value, as developed in Chapter 5. Should the value indicated by the earning power fall below the liquidation value of the assets, one could conclude that the business would be worth more dead than alive, and liquidation of the subject business would be a rational economic choice.

Common Errors in Applying the Excess Earnings Method

The excess earnings method is widely misused in valuing small businesses and professional practices. Some of the errors most commonly encountered are discussed in the following sections.

Failure to Allow for Owner's Salary

As noted in Revenue Ruling 68–609 (Exhibit 15–1), "If the business is a sole proprietorship or partnership, there should be deducted from the earnings of the business a reasonable amount for services performed by the owner or partners engaged in the business." This point is also covered in Chapter 8.

Unfortunately, valuations are often done by the excess earnings method that do not include a reasonable allowance for compensation to the owner or owners for services performed. This error results in an

Exhibit 15–3

SAMPLE VALUATION BY EXCESS EARNINGS METHOD

Assumptions:

Net current assets	$400,000	
Fixed assets, net	100,000	
(Above assets at fair market value)		
Borrowing base	80%	of net current assets
Borrowing rate	10%	
Cost of equity capital	25%	
Capitalization rate for excess earnings	$33^{1}/_{3}\%$	
Pretax net free cash flow	80,000	
(After reasonable compensation to owner/ manager, as defined in Chapter 12)		

Scenario A: Company pays no income taxes

Borrowing base:

Net current assets	$400,000	
	x .80	
Tangible assets financed by debt	$320,000	64%
Tangible assets financed by equity	180,000	36%
Total net tangible assets	$500,000	100%
(Before interest bearing debt)		

	Proportion in the Capital Structure	Cost	Weighted Cost
Debt	.64	.10	.064
Equity	.36	.25	.09
Required return on net tangible assets			.154

Pretax net free cash flow		$100,000
Net tangible assets	$500,000	
Required return on net tangible assets	.154	
		77,000
"Excess" earnings		$ 23,000
Capitalized at		$33^{1}/_{3}\%$
Value of excess earnings		$ 69,000
Add: Value of net tangible assets		500,000
Total value		$569,000

In the above scenario, the buyer could pay $569,000 for the fixed assets, net current assets, and intangible value. If the buyer used the full borrowing power, the purchase price could be financed with $320,000 debt and $249,000 equity.

Exhibit 15–3 (concluded)

Scenario B: Company pays 20% income taxes

Borrowing base is same as in Scenario A, but cost of debt reduced 20% of debt cost because of deductibility of taxes.

	Proportion in the Capital Structure	Cost	Weighted Cost
Debt	.64	(.10x.80) = .08	.0512
Equity	.36	.25	.09
Required return on net tangible assets (rounded)			.141

Pretax net free cash flow		$100,000
Less: Income taxes at 20%		20,000
After tax net free cash flow		$ 80,000
Net tangible assets	$500,000	
Required return on net tangible assets	.141	
		70,500
"Excess" earnings		$ 9,500
Capitalized at		33-1/3%
Value of excess earnings		28,500
Add: Value of net tangible assets		500,000
Total value		$528,500

In the above scenario, the buyer could pay $528,500 for the fixed assets, net current assets, and intangible value. If the buyer used the full borrowing power, the purchase price could be financed with $320,000 debt and $208,000 equity.

---

overstatement of the true economic earnings, which in turn leads to an overstatement of the value of the business.

Failure to Use Realistic Normalized Earnings

To the extent that the method is valid, it depends on a reasonable estimate of normalized earnings, developed as discussed in Chapter 8. As noted in Revenue Ruling 68–609, "The past earnings to which the formula is applied should fairly reflect the probable future earnings."

We have frequently seen the method applied blindly to the latest year's earnings, or to some simple or weighted average of recent years' earnings, without regard to whether or not the earnings base used reflects fairly the probable future earnings. Such completely uninformed use of some historical earnings base usually results in an undervaluation or overvaluation.

Using Book Values of Assets without Adjustment

As noted in Chapter 3, book value is something of a misnomer, since it is not a value at all, but rather an accounting term meaning the dollar amount at which the item is carried on the company's financial records. The book value of assets usually represents the acquisition cost of assets less any depreciation recorded for financial accounting and/or income tax purposes. The longer the company has held the assets, the less likely it is that the book value will be a reasonable approximation of any kind of economic value, such as replacement or liquidation value.

Net tangible asset value used in the excess earnings approach should reflect an informed judgment about the value of the tangible assets, as discussed in Chapter 7. Understatement of the value of the net tangible assets results in a high capitalization rate being applied to too large a portion of the total earnings, which leads to an undervaluation of the total entity, or vice versa if the net tangible asset value is overstated.

Errors in Choosing Appropriate Rates

The choice of the two capitalization rates is critical to the validity of the result of the excess earnings method. A conceptual approach to the determination of the rates to use was suggested in an earlier section. However, one clearly erroneous practice that recurs in the selection of the rates is using the rates suggested in the ruling itself.

The ruling, written in 1968, suggests rates of 8 to 10 percent on tangible assets, with 15 to 20 percent applied to the excess earnings. However, the ruling states that "the percentage of return . . . should be the percentage prevailing in the industry involved at the date of the valuation. . . . The above rates are used as examples and are not appropriate in all cases. . . . The capitalization rates are dependent upon the facts pertinent thereto in each case."[10]

Both the wording of the ruling and common sense indicate that the specific rates mentioned in the ruling are examples, and the actual rates to use depend on the facts at the time. In spite of that, even in the 1990s, we find people using the rates for the excess earnings method used in the ARM 34 example back in 1920, and again in Revenue Ruling 68–609 in 1968, when prevailing rates were much lower. The average yield on long-term government bonds in 1968 was about 5 percent. They have not been that low in recent history. Using capitalization rates that are too low inevitably results in overstating the value of the entity.

Summary

The "excess earnings method" (also called the "formula method") dates back to the period of Prohibition. It was the U.S. Treasury Department method of determining the amount to compensate distilleries for their loss of goodwill. The IRS's current position on the method is embodied in Revenue Ruling 68–609, the IRS Appellate Conferee Valuation Training Program, and Private Letter Ruling 79–05013, all referenced in this chapter. The IRS says that the method "may be used in determining the

---

[10]Revenue Ruling 68–609, 1968–2 C.B. 327.

value of intangible assets of a business only if there is not a better basis for making the determination."

In spite of this lack of enthusiasm on the part of the IRS, the excess earnings method is one of the most widely used and misused methods of valuation for small businesses and professional practices. Moreover, the guidance in the proper implementation of the method contained in the above three references is widely ignored, resulting in a plethora of misapplications.

This chapter has developed the proper use of the excess earnings method. It has quoted the relevant guidance provided in each of the IRS references cited above. Of most critical importance, the chapter has provided guidance on how to develop the four key variables in the excess earnings method:

1. Net tangible asset value.
2. Earnings base to be capitalized.
3. Reasonable rate of return on tangible assets.
4. Capitalization rate to be applied to "excess earnings."

Finally, the chapter concluded with a discussion of each of the most commonly encountered errors found in attempted implementations of the excess earnings method. By following the guidance in this chapter, the reader should be able to implement the excess earnings method properly and identify any of the most common errors in other implementations of the excess earnings method.

Selected Bibliography

Fox, Jeffery D. "Closely Held Business Valuations: The Uninformed Use of the Excess Earnings/Formula Method." *TAXES*, November 1982, pp. 832–36.

Gallinger, George W., and Glenn A. Wilt, Jr. "The Excess Earnings Model's Necessary Assumptions." *ASA Valuation*, February 1988, pp. 74–78.

Gomes, Glenn M. "Excess Earnings, Competitive Advantage, and Goodwill Value." *Journal of Small Business Management*, July 1988, pp. 22–31.

Schilt, James H. "An Objection to the Excess Earnings Method of Business Appraisal." *TAXES*, February 1980, pp. 123–26.

———. "Goodwill and Excess Earnings." *Business Law News*, Winter 1982, pp. 18–20.

———. "Challenging Standard Business Appraisal Methods." *ASA Valuation*, June 1985, pp. 2–10.

Shayne, Mark. "A Reexamination of Revenue Ruling 68-609." *FAIR$HARE: The Matrimonial Law Monthly*, July 1992, pp. 5–8.

Vinso, Joseph D. "Excess Earnings Estimation of Intangibles (A Note)." *Business Valuation News*, December 1984, pp. 15–17.

Chapter 16

_____ Gross Revenue Multipliers

One of the most widely used and abused methods used in the valuation of small businesses and professional practices is gross revenue multipliers. They can be useful, but their usefulness has severe limitations. When gross revenue multipliers are used for valuation without the user completely understanding the limitations that apply to each case, the result can be an extremely misleading estimate of value.

The Basic Concept

Another, and perhaps more descriptive, name for the gross revenue multiplier is the *price-to-sales ratio*. In other words, the basic concept is that the value is some multiple of the amount of revenue that the entity generates.

For example, if data on sales of a certain type of business or practice indicated that they almost always sell in a range of .40 to .75 times revenue, and we are interested in a business or practice that generates $200,000 in annual revenues, the range of multiples of sales would indicate that the entity should be worth $80,000 to $150,000 (.40 × $200,000 = $80,000 and .75 × $200,000 = $150,000). Where our subject entity should fall within that range would depend on its profitability, if that information is available, and on a variety of other factors. Some of the other relevant general factors are discussed in Chapter 10.

The concept of the gross revenue multiplier as a method in the valuation of a business or practice might be categorized either as a method within the broader category of an income approach, or as a method within the broader category of a market approach, depending on how the multiplier is developed. If a buyer develops a multiple of gross revenue that he is willing to pay strictly on the basis of his own expectations of return on sales, it can logically be regarded as a form of an income approach. If the gross revenue multiplier is developed from observed data on sales of comparative companies, it can be thought of as a form of the market approach. In either case, the method implicitly assumes that there is some relatively consistent relationship between revenues and profits for the particular type of business or practice. The usefulness of the method obviously varies from one type of business or practice to another, to the extent that that assumption holds true.

When Gross Revenue Multipliers May Be Useful

As a broad generalization, gross revenue multipliers may be useful for the following objectives:

1. To get a very rough range of possible values with a minimum of time and effort.
2. To get an estimate of value when other data are unavailable or inadequate.

3. As one indicator of a value or a range of values used in conjunction with other valuation approaches.

The following sections discuss some of the situations in which gross revenue multipliers may be useful.

When Gross Sales Are the Only Reliable Income Data Available

For many entities, especially small sole proprietorships, a record of profitability may be impossible, or nearly impossible, to construct. This is either because there have never been complete records or because personal and business receipts and expenditures are difficult to clearly separate from each other.

For Companies with Losses or Erratic Earnings

For many reasons, a company may not have demonstrable earnings to capitalize, even though it has considerable potential; this may be because of adverse economic conditions that are expected to improve, because the company is in a start-up or research and development stage, or because of significant nonrecurring factors. In cases such as these, most buyers would construct a pro forma income statement for one or several years into the future. However, ratios of price to revenues at which sales of comparative companies took place can offer one indication of value.

Earnings of some companies may be highly erratic, either because of economic factors affecting the industry or because of special factors affecting the particular company. Attempts to normalize the earnings may require a great deal of subjective judgment about what level of past earnings best suggests future earnings expectations. Gross revenue multipliers derived from recent sales of comparable companies or practices may give some indication of how others assess the future of the industry or profession.

Finally, recent earnings may have experienced a "spike," an unprecedented upward thrust, which may or may not be sustainable. In this case, analysis of the gross revenue multipliers of other recent sales of comparable companies may prevent a buyer from paying too much, based on an unsustainable earnings level.

For Highly Homogeneous Industries and Professions

The more similar many businesses or practices within an identifiable industry are, the more valid the indication of value provided by the gross revenue multiplier approach. If an industry or profession tends to have a fairly standard cost structure, then a given level of revenue should be expected to produce a somewhat predictable amount of profit. In the limited number of industry or professional segments for which this homogeneity is characteristic, entities may sell within a fairly tight range of each other in terms of multipliers of revenue.

Even for relatively homogeneous industry or professional practice segments, gross revenue multipliers can usually be expected to vary quite a bit at any given time from one geographical region to another.

Estimating Value of Intangible and/or Other Assets

A method used by some appraisers of professional practices is to appraise tangible assets on some form of a market value basis, and then estimate intangible asset value based on some multiple of practice revenue. As with other gross revenue multipliers, the multiple to be used might be developed on the basis of some expected level of returns per dollar of revenue, or it may be developed on the basis of reported multiples of revenue paid for goodwill and/or other intangibles in comparative practice transactions.

Some wholesalers that help to finance franchised retailer customers (or to facilitate sales of franchises) use a gross revenue multiplier method to set value on fixtures and intangible assets. Typically, they take the view that a store should be worth the value of its inventory plus x weeks' sales for its fixtures and intangibles. Where the particular store falls within the range of the high and low boundaries of the number of weeks' sales should be based at least in part on profitability. In the limited instances where the appraiser can obtain data on comparative transactions priced this way, it can be a very useful method.

Where There Is a High Industry Correlation between Price and Return on Sales

In some industries there is a high degree of correlation between the sale price of a company and its percentage return on sales. In others there is not. If there is such a correlation evident (not necessarily to an extremely high degree of statistical significance), the industry transaction data can be helpful in developing an appropriate gross revenue multiplier for the subject company.

Consider the data tabulated and graphed in Exhibit 16–1 for industries A and B. In industry A, there is a nice smooth progression (high degree of correlation) between return on sales and gross revenue multipliers. If we know or can make a good estimate of return on sales for our subject company, it is pretty easy to see approximately what gross revenue multiplier it is likely to command. This can be developed either visually on the graph or statistically. For industry B, return on sales provides virtually no guidance as to selection of an appropriate gross revenue multiplier.

Gross Revenue Multipliers Generally Indicate Debt-Free Value

Gross revenue multipliers generally lend themselves better to developing an indication of the total value of invested capital (total of debt and equity or debt-free value) than a straight equity value. If all the companies in the industry are essentially unleveraged (financed all or mostly by equity), or if all the firms have essentially similar capital structures, it doesn't much matter whether the gross revenue multiplier is used to indicate the value of invested capital or the value of equity. But if capital structures vary, it is generally best to do the analysis on a debt-free basis and then subtract the debt if the value of equity is the ultimate objective.

Consider Company A and Company B, with equal revenues and equal EBITs, but Company A with debt and Company B with no debt. If you suggested that the equity of each was worth the same multiple of gross revenue, you would conclude that the equity of the one burdened with debt was worth as much as the one with no debt. Analysis on a debt-free basis would probably produce a more plausible result.

Problems in Using Gross Revenue Multipliers

Those using gross revenue multipliers as indicators of value should do so with their eyes wide open. Everything possible should be done to assess the impact on value of whatever differences there may be between the subject entity and the population from which the range of gross revenue multipliers was drawn. Even after being as thorough as possible, the appraiser should realize that there still may be considerable latitude in the resultant range of reasonable values. Following are some of the problems with using gross revenue multipliers as indicators of value.

Ambiguity as to Exactly What Was Sold

As noted in Chapter 2, value is meaningless until it is clear what is being valued. Some people tend to bandy about figures purported to be representative gross revenue multipliers, without making it clear just what they supposedly represent. Does the multiplier value only the intangibles? Intangibles and fixed assets? Inventory? Other assets? Liabilities? When a gross revenue multiplier is quoted, one should take care to understand what the multiplier is supposed to represent before judging its meaningfulness.

Ambiguity as to Terms of Sale

Is the gross revenue multiplier at issue supposed to represent a cash value, or does it relate to a price on some noncash terms that may be typical for sales of entities in the particular business or profession? A price on long, easy terms may be half again as much as a value in cash, as discussed in Chapter 19.

When gross revenue multipliers are discussed, they more often than not relate to terms of sale typical in the business or profession rather than to cash values for the business or practice.

Exhibit 16–1

CORRELATION BETWEEN PRICE AND RETURN ON SALES

Company	Industry A		Industry B	
	Return on Sales %	Price per $ of Sales	Return on Sales %	Price per $ of Sales
1	1.190	0.235	1.169	0.475
2	2.010	0.355	2.019	0.245
3	2.830	0.385	2.790	0.630
4	3.650	0.510	3.830	0.325
5	4.780	0.485	4.579	0.445
6	5.750	0.615	5.779	0.419
7	6.800	0.665	6.779	0.555

Industry A

Regression Output		Regression Line	
		ROS	P/R
Constant	0.186357445	1.190	0.272
Standard Error of Y Estimate	0.040195190	2.010	0.331
R Squared	0.940741036	2.830	0.390
Number of Observations	7	3.650	0.449
		4.780	0.531
		5.750	0.601
X Coefficient(s)	0.072028799	6.800	0.676
Standard Error of Coefficient	0.008084696		

Price/Revenues Multiple = 0.1864 + 0.0720 x Return on Sales

Correlation = 96.99%

Industry B

Regression Output		Regression Line	
		ROS	P/R
Constant	0.384834717	1.169	0.402
Standard Error of Y Estimate	0.139181500	2.019	0.415
R Squared	0.052756267	2.790	0.426
Number of Observations	7	3.830	0.442
		4.579	0.453
		5.779	0.471
X Coefficient(s)	0.148397460	6.779	0.485
Standard Error of Coefficient	0.028121296		

Price/Revenues Multiple = 0.3848 + 0.0148 x Return on Sales

Correlation = 22.97%

Exhibit 16–2 (concluded)

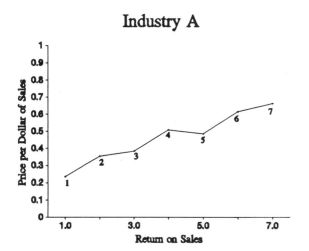

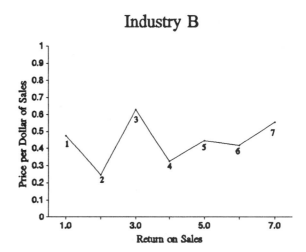

A Profit Factor Usually Comes into Play

As noted earlier, for most kinds of businesses or industries for which gross revenue multipliers are commonly used, the assumption of some level of profitability is inherent in the range of multipliers generally quoted. To apply the gross revenue multiplier approach intelligently, the appraiser should have some idea what level of profitability is implicit in the multiplier and what the chances are that the subject entity will achieve the implied level of profitability.

Differences in Persistence of Revenues

Another factor implied in any industry average gross revenue multiplier is some industry average persistence of the revenues to which it is applied. In other words, if a buyer thinks of the value of an entity in terms of a multiple of its revenues, he is thinking in terms of "buying a book of business" (as insurance people put it). He must have some idea about how much of that business is likely to stay with the entity after he buys it, and for how long.

In order to use gross revenue multipliers intelligently, the appraiser must have some idea of the degree of expected persistence on which the industry average multiplier is based and the likelihood that the persistence for the subject entity will be better or worse than the industry standard expectation.

Uniqueness of Each Entity

As noted earlier, the validity of gross revenue multipliers as indicators of value depends on some degree of homogeneity among a class, which, typically, is not characteristic among diverse entrepreneurs and professional practitioners. The historical developments of different entities, as well as the unique personalities and preferences of the personally managed operations, may create a uniqueness not characteristic of real estate or other commercial investments. The appraiser may have great difficulty adjusting data for any group of entities for which a range of multipliers supposedly is representative so that it can be usefully applied to any particular entity.

Multipliers Change Considerably over Time

A business broker once told us that the multipliers of revenue at which sales of businesses through his office were being consummated were running 30 percent lower than a year earlier. In other words, at the time of our conversation, he would have expected to sell at 70 percent of a year's revenues a business that would have sold for 100 percent of a year's revenues a year earlier.

Even when gross revenue multipliers may be useful, it must be recognized that they are volatile and change over time for several reasons.

Ease of Entry.   The degree to which it is easy, or even feasible, to start one's own operation may vary over time, either because of supply and demand in the business or practice category or because of changes in the regulatory environment, such as the amount or method of allocating licenses for a certain activity. These factors obviously influence what people will pay to get into an established business or practice.

Consider an extreme but very real example. Assume that a city for a long time limited licenses to do taxicab business on its streets to a certain number of cabs, then suddenly changed the rules to allow licensing of an unlimited number. The value of a taxi company per dollar of historical revenue would be expected to drop dramatically. As another example, municipalities differ greatly from one another in the way they allocate garbage collection routes, and municipalities occasionally make changes in their allocation procedure. These changes would usually impact gross revenue multiples for such companies.

Fashions, Fads, and Fantasies.   Certain types of businesses and practices may be in or out of fashion in the market at any given time, just as certain groups of stocks can be the darlings of the market one year and the dogs the next. Innovative ideas and scarce opportunities are the kinds of things that drive multipliers up; fading glitter and a glut of participants can move multipliers down.

Economic and Industry Conditions.   Economic and industry conditions can considerably influence the outlook for persistence of revenues for both the near-term and long-term future. They can also affect the profit margins that those revenues can generate. Obviously, these factors will have an impact on what a buyer will be willing to pay per dollar of revenues currently being attained.

Even Gross Revenue Data May Not Be Reliable

For some businesses, it is not even possible to get reliable data on the amount of gross revenues being generated. That is especially true of cash businesses, including many types of retail and service establishments. This fact poses a dilemma. Will the buyer rely on somebody's oral estimate of revenues, or will he consider only data that can be verified? There is no right answer to that question. Different buyers have different criteria by which they judge the reliability of the data they may be willing to accept.

Multiples of Some Measure of Physical Volume

In a few industries, some buyers look at some measure of physical volume in determining how much they are willing to pay. For example, the cable TV industry looks at the number of subscribers. Funeral homes are priced partly on the basis of the average number of services per year, although that pricing approach is less dominant today than it used to be. Buyers of soft drink bottlers and beer distributors look at the number of cases sold, with most of the value related to the premium brands. Taverns sometimes are priced on the basis of the monthly volume of draft beer purchased from the distributor.

But even gross physical volume measures are not always reliable. A business broker told us of an owner who bought and sold taverns frequently and usually owned two or more at any one time. When he planned to sell a tavern, the purchase invoices showed that the tavern bought a lot of kegs of beer from the distributor during the months prior to his offering the tavern for sale. What the prospective buyer inspecting the records didn't know was that some of the kegs went out the back door and were actually sold through one of the owner's other taverns.

In one appraisal we planned to use the quantity of liquor purchased to help estimate the true sales volume of a cocktail lounge. However, the owner told us that he was pretty sure that a recently terminated employee had been bringing in significant amounts of liquor on his own so that his skimming would go undetected.

Using Industry Earnings Data to Check Gross Revenue Multipliers

Logically, the multiplier of revenue at which a company should sell would be the company's profits, expressed as a percentage of sales, divided by the applicable rate at which its earnings should be capitalized. For example, suppose that a manufacturing company earned an average of 5 percent on its sales, and buyers of companies in that industry demanded a 20 percent return on their investment. The buyers would be willing to pay:

$$\frac{.05}{.20} = .25, \text{ or } 25 \text{ percent of sales}$$

If someone proposes to price a company or group of companies in an industry on the basis of a gross revenue multiplier, the average return on sales for the industry can be looked up in any of the sources discussed in Chapter 9 or from trade association statistics, if they are available. If the average profit on sales, divided by a satisfactory capitalization rate, comes out somewhere near the proffered gross revenue multiplier, then the multiplier would appear to be fairly accurate.

Some data on gross revenue multipliers for specific types of businesses and practices are presented in Chapter 33.

Summary

The gross revenue multiplier method of valuation is used much more with small businesses and professional practices than with larger businesses. This is primarily because reliable data on income at other levels for both the subject and comparative companies tends to be less readily available than is typically the case for larger companies.

The implication of a gross multiplier for valuation is that the subject business or practice is about equally profitable with about the same level of risk as the population or sample of comparative companies from which the revenue multiplier is drawn, or, if not, that the appraiser has adjusted the multiplier appropriately to reflect differences. Another implication is that the assets being valued are similar in nature relative to the revenue level as the population or sample from which the multiplier is drawn.

The multiple of gross revenue or physical volume is less than an ideal valuation method. However, it often is useful when other reliable data are not available, or as a check on other methods.

Chapter 17

Asset-Based Methods

Although the concept of current value is becoming more popular in the accounting literature, business financial statements prepared in accordance with generally accepted accounting principles (GAAP) are still prepared based on the historical cost principle. That is, all assets and liabilities recognized on a business's balance sheet are recorded at their historical acquisition price (i.e., historical cost). This GAAP-based historical cost asset valuation approach allows for conservatism, consistency, and cost-efficiency in the preparation of periodic financial statements.

As the most fundamental business *accounting* principle: the book value of assets minus the book value of liabilities equals the book value of equity.

One fundamental approach to business *valuation* is to assume that the current value of assets minus the current value of liabilities equals the value of equity.

From a business valuation perspective, the most appropriate standard (or definition) of value is the one that is appropriate given the purpose and objective of the appraisal. Chapter 3 presented several alternative standards of value, including fair market value, fair value, intrinsic or fundamental value, and investment value. These and other similar standards of value are the appropriate value definitions to use in a small business or professional practice valuation performed by using an asset-based valuation method.

Accordingly, based upon the purpose and objective of the appraisal, the appraiser will first select the appropriate standard of value to apply to the equity interest subject to appraisal. If an asset-based method is used as one of the basic valuation approaches, the appraiser will apply an appropriate standard of value to all of the assets and liabilities of the firm. (The standard of value for the assets and liabilities may be fair market value, even if the standard for the equity interest ultimately is something else.)

In other words, the appraiser will restate all of the assets and liabilities of the firm from their historical cost values to, for example, fair market value. After the restatement of all asset and liability accounts from their historical cost to fair market value, the appraiser can then apply the axiomatic "assets minus liabilities" formula to conclude the fair market value of the firm's equity interests.

At this point, the business appraiser has typically concluded the value of 100 percent of the equity of the firm, on a marketable, controlling interest basis. If the appraisal subject is other than 100 percent of the equity of the firm (e.g., the value of a nonmarketable, minority interest), clearly several security analysis discounts and/or premiums will need to be considered. (In some cases a discount for lack of marketability and/or other premiums or discounts will be appropriate even when valuing 100 percent of the equity. Such premiums or discounts often are affected by the standard of value applicable to the subject equity interest.)

Fundamentals of Asset-Based Methods

If properly applied, asset-based methods are, arguably, the most complex and challenging small business and professional practice valuation techniques from an appraisal perspective. The costs and benefits of asset-based business valuation methods will be described below. Before we consider these costs and benefits, or the various asset-based valuation methods, several important fundamentals should be reiterated.

First, in properly applying asset-based methods, historical cost-based financial statements are a starting point only. They are not an ending point.

Appraisers use the firm's balance sheet prepared in accordance with generally accepted accounting principles only as a point of departure from which to begin their appraisal analyses. While the final format of the valuation basis balance sheet is usually similar to the historical cost basis balance sheet (e.g., the assets may be on the left and the liabilities may be on the right), it usually differs in content.

The valuation basis balance sheet is materially different from the historical cost balance sheet in at least two ways: (1) the balances in the asset and liability accounts have been revalued, as of the valuation date, and (2) several new asset and liability accounts are likely to be added.

Second, in properly applying asset-based methods, all assets and liabilities should be restated to an appropriate standard of value consistent with the standard of value selected for the business valuation. As will be described below, if the assets and liabilities are immaterial, or if the revaluation change is immaterial, the appraiser may elect to leave those account balances at their historical cost value. Otherwise, the appraiser will separately consider and analyze each asset and liability, either item by item or grouped by categories.

The appraiser will then conclude the defined value (e.g., fair market value) of each asset and liability, in the process of ultimately concluding the defined value (e.g., fair market value) of the firm's equity structure. As will be explained below, it is generally inappropriate to conclude the value of the firm's assets and liabilities—and of the firm's equity value—at its "net book value."

Third, in properly applying asset-based methods, *all* of the firm's assets and *all* of the firm's liabilities should be considered for revaluation to the selected appropriate standard of value. In many cases, the appraiser will need to rely on experts in real estate, machinery and equipment, or other appraisal disciplines.

Many of a firm's most valuable assets are not recorded on the firm's historical cost basis balance sheet. This includes the whole category of the firm's intangible assets and intellectual properties. These assets are typically not included on a historical cost basis balance sheet prepared in accordance with GAAP (unless the intangible assets were acquired as part of a business acquisition, accounted for as an asset purchase transaction).

Also, many of the firm's most significant liabilities are not recorded on the firm's historical cost basis balance sheet. This includes the whole category of the firm's contingent liabilities. Accordingly, as part of the asset-based valuation, new asset and, possibly, new liability accounts will be recorded on the firm's revaluation balance sheet.

Asset-Based Methods versus Book Value

It is important to distinguish between asset-based business valuation methods and the naive reliance upon "book value" as a valuation conclusion. The true defined value of a business enterprise, under any standard of value, may equal the firm's book value only by chance and happenstance; more likely it will be either higher or lower than book value.

There is no theoretical underpinning, conceptual justification, empirical data, or practical reasoning to suggest that the value of a business enterprise (under any standard of value) would equal the firm's historical cost-basis book value.

The terms *book value* or *net book value* are unfortunate colloquialisms from an appraisal perspective because book value is not related to economic value or to the valuation process at all. Book value is an accounting convention.

From an accounting perspective, the book value of a firm is the historical cost of all of the firm's assets less total accumulated reserves for depreciation. Net book value is the firm's book value less the recorded liabilities. Net book value (often called book value, in the vernacular) is synonymous with the firm's owners' equity. Therefore, net book value can also be calculated as the sum of the owners' equity investments in the firm plus the cumulative amount of the firm's retained earnings.

In any event, book value is not a rigorous business valuation method. And book value is not a conceptually sound asset-based valuation method. It is naive and generally inappropriate to conclude a business valuation based upon book value. Not only are the values shown on the balance sheet often not representative of an appropriate value for business valuation purposes, but also there may be one or several important assets and/or liabilities not shown on the accounting balance sheet at all.

Various Asset-Based Methods

In the appraisal literature, there are several names for very similar asset-based methods. These methods are often referred to as the net asset value method, adjusted net worth method, adjusted book value method, asset build-up method, or asset accumulation method. In fact, these are all very similar methods within the same broad approach.

Accordingly, as a convention, these methods will be referred to collectively as the asset accumulation method for the remainder of this chapter.

The asset accumulation method is a balance sheet oriented valuation method. Essentially, the firm's balance sheet is restated to current value (as defined). This typically involves the identification and valuation of otherwise unrecorded tangible and intangible assets, as well as the revaluation of assets and liabilities already on the balance sheet.

The Asset Accumulation Method

There are two extreme alternatives in the application of the asset accumulation method:

1. The collective revaluation of all of the firm's assets.
2. The discrete (separate) revaluation of all of the firm's assets.

Each of these two alternative applications will be described briefly below. In many cases, practicality will dictate procedures somewhere between the two extremes.

Collective Revaluation of Assets and Liabilities

In the collective revaluation application, all of the revaluation of the firm's assets and liabilities (and, hence, owners' equity) is made in one analysis and calculation. Typically, this collective revaluation is concluded in the identification and quantification of the firm's incremental value over and above the book value of its recorded assets.

Using this application, goodwill is often defined globally as all of the appreciation (or depreciation) in the value of the firm, as compared to the book value of the firm.

Under the capitalized excess earnings method, the value of the firm's equity is the value of the firm's net tangible assets plus the value of the firm's intangible assets, much or all of which may be in the nature of goodwill. This intangible value is quantified using the capitalized excess earnings method.

So, when viewed from the perspective of asset-based business valuation methods, the capitalized excess earnings method may be considered one application of the asset accumulation method (where all asset revaluation is concluded on a collective basis).

It should be noted, however, that in the strictest application of the excess earnings method, as discussed in Chapter 15 and Revenue Ruling 68–609, all tangible assets are revalued to fair market value, and the excess earnings method is used only to quantify the intangible value.

Discrete (Separate) Revaluation of Assets and Liabilities

In the discrete revaluation application, all of the firm's assets and liabilities are analyzed and appraised individually.

This involves a separate identification and revaluation of the firm's:

1. Financial assets (e.g., cash, receivables, etc.).
2. Tangible personal property (e.g., inventories, machinery and equipment, furniture and fixtures, etc.).
3. Tangible real property (e.g., land, land improvements, buildings, etc.).
4. Intangible real property (e.g., leasehold interests, easements, mineral rights, air and water rights, etc.).

5. Intangible personal property (e.g., patents, trademarks, computer software, customer relationships, going-concern value, goodwill, etc.).
6. Current liabilities (e.g., accounts payable, taxes payable, salaries payable, etc.).
7. Long-term liabilities (e.g., bonds, notes, mortgages, and debentures payable, etc.).
8. Contingent liabilities (e.g., pending tax disputes, pending litigation, etc.).
9. Special obligations (e.g., unfunded pensions, earned vacations, ESOP repurchase liabilities, etc.).

Under this application, the value of the discretely appraised assets (both tangible and intangible) less the value of the discretely appraised liabilities (both recorded and contingent) represents the business value of the firm.

Theoretically and practically, the business value concluded under the collective revaluation application should equal the business value concluded under the discrete revaluation application.

The determination of which application to use in a given appraisal should be a function of:

1. The experience and judgment of the professional appraiser.
2. The quantity and quality of available data.
3. The purpose and objective of the appraisal.
4. The scope and timing of the appraisal assignment.

As will be discussed below, both costs and benefits are associated with the discrete application of the asset accumulation method.

Partial Revaluation of Individual Assets and Liabilities

Very often, it is practical to revalue some but not all of the firm's specific assets and liabilities before using the capitalized excess earnings method to quantify the balance of the remaining increment or decrement to the firm's total equity value. When choosing a capitalization rate to apply to "excess earnings," the appraiser should consider the extent to which the excess earnings arise totally from intangibles (auguring toward a higher rate) and the extent to which the "excess earnings" partially reflect unrecognized tangible asset values.

Since the collective revaluation application of the asset accumulation method was discussed in detail in Chapter 15 (with regard to the capitalized excess earnings method), the remainder of this chapter will focus on the discrete revaluation application of the asset accumulation method.

Steps in Application of the Asset Accumulation Method

This section lists and briefly discusses the asset accumulation method as divided into the following six steps:

1. Obtain or develop a GAAP basis balance sheet.
2. Determine which assets and liabilities on the GAAP basis balance sheet require adjustment.
3. Identify off-balance sheet assets that should be recognized and valued.
4. Identify off-balance sheet or contingent liabilities that should be recognized and valued.
5. Value the items identified in steps 2 through 4.
6. Construct a valuation basis balance sheet based on the results of steps 1 through 5.

Obtain or Develop GAAP Basis Balance Sheet

As mentioned above, first, the appraiser starts with a GAAP, historical cost basis balance sheet for the subject small business or professional practice, prepared as of the valuation date. If a historical cost basis balance sheet is not available because the valuation is being conducted as of an interim date, the appraiser has three options:

1. The client (or an accountant retained by the client) may prepare a historical cost basis balance sheet as of the valuation date and give it to the appraiser as a basic tool to start the appraisal.
2. The appraiser may prepare a historical cost basis balance sheet as of the valuation date, assuming the appraiser has the requisite basic accounting expertise to prepare such a financial statement.
3. The appraiser may rely upon the most recent historical cost basis balance sheet prepared at a fiscal period end just prior to the valuation date. A recent fiscal period end balance sheet will require more revaluation adjustments than a valuation date balance sheet, but it is usually better than not having a starting point at all.

Identify Assets and Liabilities to Be Revalued

Second, the appraiser will carefully analyze and understand each material recorded asset and liability of the firm. The objective of this analysis is to determine which material recorded assets and liabilities will need to be revalued according to the selected standard of value appropriate for the subject business valuation.

As a convention throughout the remainder of this discussion, let's assume that fair market value is the appropriate standard of value for the subject business valuation. Accordingly, in this step, the appraiser will analyze which material recorded assets and liabilities of the firm should be revalued in order to conclude fair market value.

Identify Off-Balance Sheet Assets that Should Be Recognized

Third, the appraiser will identify which unrecorded (sometimes called "off-balance sheet") assets need to be recognized on the valuation balance sheet of the firm. For example, while, tangible and intangible assets are not normally recorded on the firm's financial statements under GAAP, they often represent the largest component of economic value for small businesses and professional practices.

The firm's tangible and intangible assets represent the allocation of the elements of the overall business value into specific assets. They represent the identification of the specific factors (i.e., the specific assets or asset groups) responsible for the firm's earning capacity, cash flow generation capacity, and dividend paying capacity. In the case of intangible assets, they normally would not appear on the balance sheet if developed internally, only if they were acquired in a purchase. Some tangible assets may have been expensed rather than capitalized when acquired, and others may be fully depreciated even though they still have remaining economic life.

Identify Off-Balance Sheet and Contingent Liabilities that Should Be Recognized

Fourth, the appraiser will identify what unrecorded material contingent liabilities, if any, need to be recognized on the valuation balance sheet of the firm. If there are potential environmental liabilities, specialized expert opinion may be needed.

Under GAAP accounting, contingent liabilities are not recorded on a historical cost basis balance sheet. However, in audited and reviewed financial statements, material contingent liabilities are subject to footnote disclosure.

The identification and valuation of contingent liabilities is a relatively rare step in an asset accumulation method business valuation, only because most small businesses and professional practices do not have material contingent liabilities. However, the appraiser should consider this procedure in every asset accumulation method business valuation. Certainly, for those firms that have material pending litigation against them, tax claims against them, environmental claims against them, and so forth, these contingent liabilities have a significant (and often quantifiable) effect on the risk of the business. Therefore, these material contingent liabilities have a significant effect on the business enterprise value of the subject firm.

Value the Items Identified Above

Fifth, after the analysis of recorded assets and liabilities and the identification of unrecorded assets and liabilities, the appraiser will begin the quantitative process of revaluing each of the subject firm's assets and, if necessary, each of the subject firm's liabilities.

Typically, the appraiser will perform these valuation analyses by category of assets. The standard categorization of assets, for purposes of applying the asset accumulation method, was described above. These standard categories of assets are (1) financial assets, (2) tangible personal property, (3) tangible real property, (4) intangible real property, and (5) intangible personal property. For some of these categories, the business appraiser may need to rely on specialized experts.

The general valuation approaches, methods, and premises for appraising these asset categories (and the component tangible and intangible assets) will be summarized in the next section of this chapter.

Construct a Valuation Basis Balance Sheet

Sixth, after concluding the value for all of the firm's tangible and intangible assets—and for all of the firm's recorded and contingent liabilities, the appraiser will construct a valuation basis balance sheet for the firm, as of the valuation date.

From this valuation basis (as opposed to historical cost basis) balance sheet, it is mathematically simple for the appraiser to subtract the value of the firm's liabilities (recorded and contingent) from the value of the firm's assets (tangible and intangible). The remainder of this subtraction is the value of a 100 percent interest in the firm's equity structure (on a marketable, controlling business enterprise basis).

At this point, the asset accumulation method has produced the value of the total owners' equity of the firm. Of course, if the firm has several classes of equity securities outstanding, then additional valuation and allocation procedures are required.

In addition, if the appraisal assignment relates to something less than the overall business equity value (e.g., to a nonmarketable minority interest in the class B nonvoting common stock of the firm), then additional business valuation discount and/or premium analyses and procedures are required. Also, if foreseeable sales of appreciated assets are contemplated, the tax liability on the potential gain usually should be recognized.

Premises of Value for Individual Assets

Before considering the various valuation methods with respect to the individual assets of the firm, the appraiser should first consider both the appropriate standard (or definition) of value and the appropriate premise of value for each asset category. Usually (but not always), the appropriate standard of value selected for each asset category should be the same standard of value as selected for the overall business valuation.

With regard to individual asset appraisal, appraisers may elect from among four alternative premises of value. Each of these four alternative premises of value may apply under each of the alternative standards of value.

While the standard (or definition) of value answers the general question "value to whom?", the premise of value answers the general question "value under what type of hypothetical market transaction?" For example, under the fair market value standard of value, the same asset category may be appraised under four different premises of value.

So, while fair market value answers the question of "value to whom?" (i.e., a hypothetical willing buyer and a hypothetical willing seller), the selected premise of value answers the question "in what type of market transaction will these parties interact?"

The four alternative premises of value for individual asset appraisal are (1) value in continued use, as part of a going concern; (2) value in place, as part of a mass assemblage of assets; (3) value in exchange, in an orderly disposition; and (4) value in exchange in a forced liquidation.

Value in Continued Use, as Part of a Going Concern

Under this premise, it is assumed that the subject assets are sold as a mass assemblage and as part of an income-producing business enterprise.

This premise of value contemplates the mutually synergistic relationships of the firm's tangible assets to the intangible assets and of the intangible assets to the tangible assets.

Value in Place, as Part of a Mass Assemblage of Assets

Under this premise, it is assumed that the subject assets are sold as a mass assemblage, but that the mass assemblage is capable of, but not currently operating as, an income-producing business enterprise.

This premise of value contemplates some of the mutual contributory value of the tangible assets vis-à-vis the intangible assets and of the intangible assets vis-à-vis the tangible assets. However, while there is a value in place component to the subject assets, this premise would specifically exclude the contributory value of such common intangible assets as a trained and assembled work force, going-concern value, and goodwill.

Value in Exchange, in an Orderly Disposition

Under this premise, it is assumed that the subject assets are sold piecemeal and not as part of a mass assemblage. It is assumed that the assets are given an adequate exposure to their normal secondary market.

However, due to the orderly disposition market transaction assumption, this premise does not contemplate any contributory value effect of the tangible assets on the intangible assets, or of the intangible assets on the tangible assets.

Value in Exchange, in a Forced Liquidation

Under this premise, it is assumed that the subject assets are sold piecemeal and not as part of a mass assemblage. It is also assumed that the assets are not allowed a normal exposure to their normal secondary market. Rather, the assets are permitted an abbreviated exposure to a market of the highest bidders present (who may or may not represent the collective demand-side marketplace for that asset).

Due to the forced liquidation market transaction assumption, this premise assumes no contributory value (or other interrelationships) from tangible assets to intangible assets, or vice versa.

Selecting a Premise of Value

Any of the four above described premises of value may be applied to the same asset (or category of assets) being appraised under the same standard of value. For example, an appraiser may select the fair market value standard and assume that a willing buyer and a willing seller transact to exchange an asset.

The selected premise of value describes the assumed market conditions under which this willing buyer and willing seller meet (i.e., during the sale of an up-and-running business, during the sale of a temporarily closed business, during the brokered sale of individual assets, or during the auction sale of individual assets).

The appraiser will select the appropriate premise or premises of value based upon the purpose and objective of the appraisal and based upon the most likely form of the ultimate sale of the subject business (and, accordingly, of the assets of the subject business). Needless to say, the selection of the appropriate premise or premises of value is a critical decision in the application of the asset accumulation method to business valuation.

Even under the same standard of value, the subject business can have materially different business enterprise valuation conclusions—given the premise or premises of value selected for valuing various assets.

Individual Asset Valuation Approaches and Methods

After the appropriate premise of value is selected, the next step in the asset accumulation method is to apply one or more widely recognized appraisal approaches to each individual asset category.

The conceptual cornerstone of the asset accumulation method is the identification and valuation of all of the firm's assets. This includes the financial assets, the tangible assets (real and personal), and the intangible assets (real and personal).

In Chapter 7, the procedures related to "adjusting the balance sheet" were discussed. Those adjustment procedures should be considered when analyzing the firm's balance sheet in preparation for the application of *any* business valuation approach or method. The procedures discussed below are common asset appraisal procedures, as compared to common balance sheet adjustment procedures. These asset appraisal procedures should be considered when using the asset accumulation method of business valuation.

Since this is not a text devoted to individual asset appraisal, this discussion will be introductory in nature. In the bibliography to this chapter, appropriate references to specialized textbooks will be presented with regard to the appraisal of individual tangible assets for those business appraisers who wish to study these subjects in detail. References to specialized texts and articles on appraising intangible assets are included in the bibliography at the end of Chapter 34.

Financial Assets

The most common assets included in this category include cash, accounts and notes receivable, and prepaid expenses.

With regard to cash, no revaluation procedures need to be performed, of course.

In the sale of a small business, it is common for the seller to retain some or all of the cash balances on hand. This is true in a transaction involving the sale of stock as well as in a transaction involving the sale of assets. Accordingly, the appraiser should verify the amount of cash, if any, that will actually be transferred with the business enterprise.

With regard to accounts and notes receivable, the appraiser will estimate the net realizable value of these receivables. The net realizable value is, essentially, the present value of the expected realization of (i.e., collection of) the receivables.

For businesses with audited or reviewed financial statements (or more sophisticated acccounting systems), a reserve for uncollectible accounts is typically established as a contra-asset valuation account. Particularly if the valuation date is other than a fiscal period end, the appraiser should assess the adequacy of this reserve for uncollectible accounts.

For smaller businesses that have not established reserves for uncollectible accounts, the appraiser should assess the ultimate collectibility of the gross receivables.

Based upon this assessment of historical collection patterns, the appraiser will, typically, discount the gross accounts receivable in order to conclude an estimate of net cash collections.

Lastly, if the expected realization of the receivables is anticipated to occur over an extended period of time (i.e., longer than the normal collection cycle), then the appraiser may also apply a present value analysis to the longer-term receivables.

The net balance of the accounts and notes receivable, after the analysis for uncollectible accounts and the present value of extended period receivables (if applicable), represents the net realizable value of this asset category.

With regard to prepaid expenses, the appraiser will estimate the net realizable value of this asset category. Prepaid expenses typically include deposits and prepaid rent, insurance, utilities expenses, and so forth.

Normally, the business expects to realize the economic benefit of these assets within the normal course of one business cycle. Therefore, normally, no revaluation adjustment is required with respect to recorded prepaid expenses.

However, if the appraiser determines that the company will not enjoy an economic benefit from a prepaid expense during a normal business cycle, then a revaluation adjustment is appropriate. For example, if the company has recorded prepaid rent expense on a facility that it is no longer using, then that asset will likely have little economic value.

The expected realization of the prepaid expenses represents the net realizable value of this asset category.

Tangible Real Property

Tangible real property includes such assets as owned land, land improvements, buildings, and building improvements.

Technically, in the appraisal literature, tangible real property is called real estate. Real estate is distinguished from intangible real property, which represents a limited legal interest (i.e., less than a fee simple interest) in real estate.

There is a prodigious body of literature with respect to the appraisal of real estate, and both the appraisal regulatory agencies and the various professional appraisal membership organizations have promulgated professional standards with respect to the valuation of tangible real property.

Nonetheless, all real estate is valued by reference to these three generally accepted valuation approaches: (1) the cost approach, (2) the income approach, and (3) the sales comparison approach. However, each of these three approaches represents a general category of several discrete appraisal methods.

Each of these three general real estate valuation approaches will be described briefly below.

Cost Approach. The cost approach is based upon the economic principle of substitution. That is, no one would pay more for an asset than the price required to obtain (by purchase or construction) a substitute asset of comparable utility. This assumes, of course, that the subject asset is fungible.

In other words, the cost approach assumes that substitute properties of comparable utility may be obtained.

If, in fact, the subject asset is unique in one or more respects, then the cost approach may not be a viable valuation approach.

Using the cost approach, the value of land is appraised separately from the value of all appurtenances to land.

The subject land is valued as if vacant and unimproved. The value of vacant land is determined by reference to the sale of comparable land parcels in the reasonably proximate marketplace.

The appraiser collects and analyzes data with respect to recent sales of vacant land parcels. If necessary, quantitative adjustments are made for size, access, services, frontage, topography, distance, time of sale, and special terms of sale.

Based upon an analysis of these adjusted comparable property sales data, the appraiser concludes the value of the subject land.

The subject buidings and improvements are valued by reference to the current cost to recreate their functional utility. There are several commonly used cost approach methods. One of the most common methods is the depreciated reproduction cost method.

This method is algebraically described as follows:

	reproduction cost new of buildings and improvements
less:	allowances for incurable functional and technological obsolescence
equals:	replacement cost
less:	allowance for physical deterioration
equals:	depreciated replacement cost
less:	allowance for economic or external obsolescence
less:	allowances for curable functional and technological obsolescence
equals:	fair market value of buildings and improvements

To complete the cost approach, the value of the land is added to the value of the buildings and improvements. The sum of these two values represents the value of the subject tangible real property, per the cost approach.

Income Approach. The income approach is based upon the economic principle of risk and return investment analysis. Using this approach, the value of the real estate is the present value of the expected economic income that could be earned through the ownership of the subject asset.

There are two categories of valuation methods under the income approach: (1) the direct capitalization method and (2) the yield capitalization method.

From an investment analysis perspective, both of these methods are conceptually identical, and, therefore, from a theoretical perspective, both methods should conclude identical values for the same parcel of real estate.

Using the direct capitalization method, the appraiser first estimates the normalized economic income that would be earned from the rental (whether hypothetical or actual) of the subject real estate. Economic income may be defined many ways (i.e., before tax, after tax, before interest expense, after interest expense, etc.).

The most common definition of economic income used in the direct capitalization method is before-tax net operating income. This estimate of economic income is normalized to represent an average or typical period's rental income (including normal rental rates and occupancy levels) and operating expenses (including normal repairs, maintenance, etc.).

The normalized economic income is capitalized typically, as an annuity in perpetuity, by a capitalization rate commensurate with the risk of investment and consistent with the measurement of economic income. For example, if projected economic income is measured on an after-tax basis, then the capitalization rate should be derived on an after-tax basis. If economic income is measured before tax, then the capitalization rate should be derived before tax, and so forth.

Consistent with the definition of economic income as before-tax net operating income, the most common derivation of the direct capitalization rate is a blended rate or weighted average cost of capital.

The equity component of this blended rate represents the typical real estate investor's current income yield expectation for similar rental properties; it excludes the investor's derived long-term capital appreciation expectation for the subject property. The debt component of this blended rate represents the typical mortgage debt rate for similar rental properties; it includes a yield component for the amortization of mortgage principal as well as the payment of mortgage interest.

The debt component and the equity component are blended, or weighted together, based upon the typical loan-to-value ratio for new mortgages offered on comparable rental properties. The result of this analysis is the direct capitalization rate.

Using the direct capitalization method, the value of the subject real estate is presented algebraically, as follows:

$$\text{Value} = \frac{\text{Normalized economic income}}{\text{Direct capitalization rate}}$$

Using the yield capitalization method, the value of the subject real estate is the present value of the projected economic income to be derived from the property over a discrete period of time.

While there is no theoretically correct project period, discrete projection periods of from 5 to 10 years are common.

The appraiser projects the economic income to be derived from the rental of the subject property for each individual year in the discrete projection period. Again, before-tax net operating income is the most common measurement of economic income.

The appraiser next derives a present value discount rate to calculate the present value of the discrete projection of economic income. This present value discount rate is often called the *going-in capitalization rate.*

A blended cost of debt and cost of equity is the most common derivation of the going-in capitalization rate.

The appraiser then estimates the normalized economic income to be generated by the property after the conclusion of the discrete projection period. This is sometimes called an estimate of the residual value (or reversionary period) income. This is the average or typical level of income to be generated by the property after the end of the projection period.

The appraiser next derives a capitalization rate consistent with this estimate of residual value (or reversionary period) income. This rate is often called the *residual (or reversionary) capitalization rate*; it is sometimes called the *coming-out capitalization rate.*

The coming-out capitalization rate is often different from the going-in capitalization rate due to the changing relative remaining life of the property and the different risk positions of the two investment periods.

The estimate of residual normalized economic income is capitalized by the residual capitalization rate. The result is the estimated value of the property at the end of the discrete projection period.

This residual value is brought back to its present value, using the discrete projection period present value discount rate.

Finally, under the income approach, the value of the subject real estate is the sum of discrete projection period present value plus the residual value present value.

Sales Comparison Approach (Market Approach). The sales comparison approach is based upon the economic principle of efficient markets. That is, when there is a relatively efficient and unrestricted secondary market for comparable properties, and that market accurately represents the activities of a representative number of willing buyers and willing sellers, then the market is most determinative of the value of the subject property.

Using the sales comparison approach, the appraiser first collects data with regard to relatively recent sales of comparable real estate properties. Next, the appraiser analyzes each of these sale transactions to determine if any quantitative adjustments are necessary due to the lack of comparability of the subject property when compared to the comparable properties.

The appraiser would consider these factors, among others, when determining if quantitative adjustments to the sales comparison data are necessary:

1. Age of each transaction (i.e., elapsed time from the valuation date).
2. Land to building ratio of each property.
3. Absolute location and relative location of each property compared to population centers, highways, and so forth.
4. Age of each property.
5. Physical condition of each property.
6. Municipal and other services available to each property.
7. Frontage and access of each property.
8. Topography of land and soil type of each comparable property.
9. Environmental aspects of each property.
10. Special financing or other terms regarding each sales transaction.

Accordingly, if necessary, the appraiser adjusts the sales comparison data to make each transaction as comparable to the subject property as possible. Based upon these adjusted sales comparison data, the appraiser will conclude a market-derived valuation multiple.

This multiple is typically expressed in terms of value per square foot of improved building space.

Next, the appraiser applies the market-derived valuation multiple to the size characteristics of the subject property. The resulting product is the estimate of value of the subject real estate, per the sales comparison approach.

To reach a final valuation synthesis and conclusion regarding the subject real estate, the appraiser will carefully consider the quantitative results of each of the valuation approaches used. In reaching the valuation conclusion, the appraiser will consider the quantity and quality of available data used in each valuation approach.

The appraiser will also assess the appropriate degree of confidence in the applicability and validity of each approach with respect to unique characteristics of the subject real property. Based upon these factors, the appraiser will synthesize the results of each approach and conclude an overall value for the subject real estate.

Tangible Personal Property

The tangible personal property category of assets include such assets as inventory, office furniture and fixtures, computer and office automation equipment, store racks and fixtures, manufacturing machinery and equipment, processing equipment, tools and dies, trucks and automobiles, and material handling and transportation equipment.

There is a considerable body of literature with regard to the appraisal of industrial and commercial tangible personal property. There is also authoritative literature regarding the appraisal of special purpose and technical tangible personal property, such as scientific and laboratory equipment, medical and health care equipment, mining and extraction equipment, and so forth. Many of these references are presented in the bibliography related to this chapter.

Nonetheless, all of the various tangible personal property appraisal methods and procedures can be grouped into the three traditional asset appraisal approaches: (1) the cost approach, (2) the income approach, and (3) the market approach.

Inventory. With regard to inventory, the appraiser should distinguish between the work in process inventory of a professional service firm (e.g., accounting firms, law firms, etc.) and the merchandise inventory of a manufacturer or wholesale/retail firm.

The work in process inventory of a professional service firm is, essentially, the unbilled receivables of the firm. Therefore, with regard to this asset category, the same net realizable value rules discussed with respect to accounts and notes receivable would apply to this asset as well.

With regard to tangible merchandise inventory, there are at least three common valuation methods. These alternative valuation methods apply equally to raw material, work in process, and finished goods inventory.

These three common merchandise inventory valuation methods are (1) the cost of reproduction method, (2) the comparative sales method, and (3) the income method.

While these three inventory valuation methods are discussed elsewhere in the appraisal literature, they are concisely summarized in Internal Revenue Service Revenue Procedure 77-12, 1977-1 C.B. 569.

Revenue Procedure 77-12 (Exhibit 17–1) was originally issued with respect to the valuation of merchandise inventory for purchase price allocation purposes. Nonetheless, these valuation methods provide reasonable guidelines for the appraisal of merchandise inventory for business valuation purposes, as well.

The cost of reproduction valuation method generally provides a good indication of fair market value if the inventory is readily replaceable in the volume and in the mix equal to the subject quantity on hand. In valuing an inventory under this method, however, other factors may be relevant. For example, a well-balanced inventory available to fill customers' orders in the ordinary course of business may have a fair

Exhibit 17–1

Rev. Proc. 77-12

SECTION 1. PURPOSE.

The purpose of this Revenue Procedure is to set forth guidelines for use by taxpayers and Service personnel in making fair market value determinations in situations where a corporation purchases the assets of a business containing inventory items for a lump sum or where a corporation acquires assets including inventory items by the liquidation of a subsidiary pursuant to the provisions of section 332 of the Internal Revenue Code of 1954 and the basis of the inventory received in liquidation is determined under section 334(b)(2). These guidelines are designed to assist taxpayers and Service personnel in assigning a fair market value to such assets.

SEC. 2. BACKGROUND.

If the assets of a business are purchased for a lump sum, or if the stock of a corporation is purchased and that corporation is liquidated under section 332 of the Code and the basis is determined under section 334(b)(2), the purchase price must be allocated among the assets acquired to determine the basis of each of such assets. In making such determinations, it is necessary to determine the fair market value of any inventory items involved. This Revenue Procedure describes methods that may be used to determine the fair market value of inventory items.

In determining the fair market value of inventory under the situations set forth in this Revenue Procedure, the amount of inventory generally would be different from the amounts usually purchased. In addition, the goods in process and finished goods on hand must be considered in light of what a willing purchaser would pay and a willing seller would accept for the inventory at the various stages of completion, when the former is not under any compulsion to buy and the latter is not under any compulsion to sell, both parties having reasonable knowledge of relevant facts.

SEC. 3. PROCEDURES FOR DETERMINATION OF FAIR MARKET VALUE.

Three basic methods an appraiser may use to determine the fair market value of inventory are the cost of reproduction method, the comparative sales method, and the income method. All methods of valuation are based on one or a combination of these three methods.

.01 The cost of reproduction method generally provides a good indication of fair market value if inventory is readily replaceable in a wholesale or retail business, but generally should not be used in establishing the fair market value of the finished goods of a manufacturing concern. In valuing a particular inventory under this method, however, other factors may be relevant. For example, a well balanced inventory available to fill customers' orders in the ordinary course of business may have a fair market value in excess of its cost of reproduction because it provides a continuity of business, whereas an inventory containing obsolete merchandise unsuitable for customers might have a fair market value of less than the cost of reproduction.

.02 The comparative sales method utilizes the actual or expected selling prices of finished goods to customers as a basis of determining fair market values of those finished goods. When the expected selling price is used as a basis for valuing finished goods inventory, consideration should be given to the time that would be required to dispose of this inventory, the expenses that would be expected to be incurred in such disposition, for example, all costs of disposition, applicable discounts (including those for quantity), sales commissions, and freight and shipping charges, and a profit commensurate with the amount of investment and degree of risk. It should also be recognized that the inventory to be valued may represent a larger quantity than the normal trading volume and the expected selling price can be a valid starting point only if customers' orders are filled in the ordinary course of business.

.03 The income method, when applied to fair market value determinations for finished goods, recognizes that finished goods must generally be valued in a profit motivated business. Since the amount of inventory may be large in relation to normal trading volume the highest and best use of the inventory will be to provide for a continuity of the marketing operation of the going business. Additionally, the finished goods inventory will usually provide the only source of revenue of an acquired business during the period it is being used to fill customers' orders. The historical financial data of an acquired company can be used to determine the amount that could be attributed to finished goods in order to pay all costs of disposition and provide a return on the investment during the period of disposition.

.04 The fair market value of work in process should be based on the same factors used to determine the fair market value of finished goods reduced by the expected costs of completion, including a reasonable profit allowance for the completion and selling effort of the acquiring corporation. In determining the fair market value of raw materials, the current costs of replacing the inventory in the quantities to be valued generally provides the most reliable standard.

SEC. 4. CONCLUSION.

Because valuing inventory is an inherently factual determination, no rigid formulas can be applied. Consequently, the methods outlined above can only serve as guidelines for determining the fair market value of inventories.

market value in excess of its cost of reproduction because it provides a continuity of business. However, an inventory containing obsolete merchandise unsuitable for customers might have a fair market value of less than the cost of reproduction.

The comparative sales valuation method utilizes the actual or expected selling prices of finished goods to customers as a basis of determining the fair market value of that inventory. When the expected selling price is used as a basis for valuing inventory, consideration should be given to the time that would be required to dispose of this inventory, the expenses that would be expected to be incurred in such disposition, applicable discounts (including those for quantity), sales commissions, and freight and shipping charges, and a profit commensurate with the amount of investment and degree of risk.

It should also be recognized that the inventory to be valued may represent a larger quantity than the normal trading volume and that the expected selling price can be a valid starting point only if customers' orders are filled in the ordinary course of business.

The income valuation method when applied to the fair market value determination of inventory recognizes that the subject inventory must generally be valued in a profit-motivated business. Since the amount of inventory may be large in relation to the normal trading volume, the highest and best use of the inventory will be to provide for a continuity of the marketing operation of the going business.

Additionally, the subject inventory will usually provide the only source of revenue of the subject business during the period it is being used to fill customers' orders. The historical financial data of the subject company can be used to determine the amount that could be attributed to inventory in order to pay all costs of disposition and provide a return on the investment during the period of disposition.

The appraiser will apply one or more of these inventory valuation methods based upon the quantity and quality of available data and based upon the most likely ultimate disposition of the subject inventory.

The appraiser will estimate the value of the subject inventory based upon the results concluded from one or more of these inventory valuation methods.

Other Tangible Personal Property   The conceptual underpinnings of the cost approach for tangible personal property are essentially identical to that for tangible real property. Again, the cost approach is based upon the economic principle of substitution.

Particularly with respect to tangible personal property, a willing buyer will pay no more to a willing seller than the cost associated with replacing the subject asset with an asset of comparable functional utility.

As with real estate, there are several common cost approach methods that appraisers use as a starting point related to tangible personal property. These methods include depreciated reproduction cost method, depreciated replacement cost method, creation cost method, recreation cost method, and others.

For special purpose tangible personal property (which may experience considerable incurable forms of obsolescence), the depreciated reproduction cost method is a common valuation method. However, for most general purpose tangible personal property, the depreciated replacement cost method is the most common valuation method.

The depreciated replacement cost method for tangible personal property is presented algebraically below:

	replacement cost new of the subject asset
less:	allowance for physical deterioration
equals:	depreciated replacement cost
less:	allowance for economic or external obsolescence
less:	allowance for curable functional and technological obsolescence
equals:	fair market value of the subject asset

If the subject asset is no longer produced, the replacement cost of the most comparable available substitute asset is used as the starting point in the cost approach (and, specifically, in the depreciated replacement cost method).

Using the income approach, the value of the tangible personal property is often quantified as the present value of the rental income from the hypothetical rental of the subject property over its remaining useful life.

First, the appraiser estimates the remaining useful life of the subject asset. This is typically the shortest of the asset's remaining physical, functional, technological, or economic lives.

Second, the appraiser estimates a fair rental rate for the subject asset. This gross rental income is reduced by insurance, maintenance, and other expenses that are the responsibility of the lessor.

The result is a projection of the net rental income (real or hypothetical) to be derived from the subject asset over the asset's expected remaining life.

Next, the appraiser derives an appropriate present value discount rate. This discount rate is intended to provide for a fair, risk-adjusted rate of return to the property lessor over the term of the lease.

The present value of the projected rental income over the expected remaining life of the property represents the value of the subject asset, per the income approach. (Since tangible personal property has a finite life, appraisers typically do not have to consider a residual value to tangible personal property—as would be appropriate with tangible real property.)

Using the market approach, the value of the subject asset is the price that it would command in its appropriate secondary market. This valuation approach is based upon the principle of efficient markets.

The use of this approach assumes that an efficient secondary market exists with regard to the exchange of the subject asset. The use of this approach also assumes that reliable information is available regarding this tangible personal property exchange market.

Using this approach, appraisers first obtain data regarding secondary transactions with respect to comparable assets. Next, appraisers analyze these data with regard to a set of reasonable comparability criteria. The market transactional data are adjusted, if necessary, to enhance their comparability and applicability to the subject asset.

Based upon the adjusted transactional data base, the appraiser selects comparable sales most indicative of a hypothetical transaction involving the subject asset. These adjusted sales data are used to conclude the value of the subject asset, per the market approach.

Lastly, the appraiser concludes an overall value of the subject asset based upon a synthesis of the results of the various valuation approaches used.

Based upon the appraiser's perceived reliability of, and confidence in, the various approaches, the appraiser will reach an overall valuation conclusion for the subject tangible personal property.

Intangible Real Property

Intangible real property assets represent intangible legal claims on tangible real estate. The type of assets encompassed by this category of assets includes leasehold interests (and various other leasehold estates), possessory interests (associated with franchise ordinances or other permits), exploration rights, air rights, water rights, land rights, mineral rights, use rights, development rights, easements (including scenic easements), and associated intangible rights and privileges related to the use or exploitation of real estate.

As intangible claims on tangible real estate, the value of these assets is generally a subset of, or derivative of, the value of the associated tangible real estate.

As with tangible real estate, there are many individual methods and techniques to appraise intangible real property. However, as with real estate, all of these methods can be conveniently grouped into the three traditional appraisal approaches: (1) the cost approach, (2) the income approach, and (3) the sales comparison approach.

Each of these three approaches (and some associated methods) were discussed above, with respect to the value of tangible real estate. Accordingly, we will not reiterate those general discussions here.

It is noteworthy, however, that the cost approach is rarely used to value intangible real property. Intangible real property typically represents a legal claim on the use of, exploitation of, development of, or forbearance of real estate.

Accordingly, the cost of the underlying real estate is generally irrelevant to the intangible property right holder. Rather, the income approach is typically the most widely used approach with respect to the valuation of intangible real estate interests.

The sales comparison approach is also used to value certain intangible real estate interests. For example, there is a reasonable sales transaction secondary market for certain intangible real estate interests—such as the unexpired portion of assignable below-market industrial and commercial leases (i.e., leasehold interests).

As with the appraisal of real estate, the appraisal of intangible real property interests is based upon a synthesis of all available valuation data and upon the conclusions of whatever valuation approaches were used. The appraiser considers and synthesizes the results of the various valuation approaches and concludes the value for the subject intangible real property interests.

Intangible Personal Property

Intangible personal property assets include most of the assets generally called intangible assets and intellectual properties. There are, arguably, over 100 different types of intangible assets and intellectual properties. However, many of these individual intangible assets are industry-specific.

Generally, all intangible assets can be conveniently grouped into the following eight categories of intangible assets:

1. Customer-related (e.g., customer lists).
2. Contract-related (e.g., favorable supplier contracts).
3. Location-related (e.g., certificates of need).
4. Market-related (e.g., trademarks and trade names).
5. Data processing-related (e.g., computer software).
6. Technology-related (e.g., engineering drawings and technical documentation).
7. Employee-related (e.g., employment agreements).
8. Goodwill-related (e.g., going-concern value).

In addition, all intellectual properties can be conveniently grouped into the following two categories of intellectual properties:

1. Creative (e.g., copyrights).
2. Innovative (e.g., patents).

Chapter 34 will discuss in detail the identification, valuation, and remaining useful life analysis of intangible assets and intellectual properties. Therefore, we will not expand upon these issues here.

As with all other assets, intangible personal property assets are valued by application of one or more of the three basic asset valuation approaches: (1) the cost approach, (2) the income approach, and (3) the market approach.

The appraiser will apply one or more of these approaches to the valuation of each intangible personal property asset. Then, the appraiser will derive a conclusion of value based upon a synthesis of the results of the various intangible personal property valuation approaches used.

Although the discussion of intangible asset valuation is deferred to Chapter 34, the identification, valuation, and remaining useful life analysis of intangible personal property assets is the conceptual cornerstone of the asset accumulation method.

It is quite possible that, in any particular business valuation, a rigorous and thorough analysis of intangible personal property assets may indicate a nominal or even a zero economic value for the subject intangible assets.

It is also quite possible that, in any particular business valuation, a rigorous and thorough analysis of intangible personal property assets may even indicate a negative economic value for the subject intangible assets. In such a case, the overall business valuation of the firm can not generate adequate economic support for the values assigned to the discrete tangible real and personal property assets.

When that situation occurs, the valuation phenomenon of economic obsolescence exists. Economic obsolescence is defined as the amount, if any, of negative intangible asset value calculated in an asset accumulation method business valuation (given the indicated values for the tangible real and personal property assets).

When economic obsolescence exists in a business valuation using the asset accumulation method, the indicated values of the tangible real and personal property assets are overstated—from an economic perspective—and must be reduced. In fact, the indicated values of the tangible real and personal property assets must be reduced (i.e., allocated down, typically in direct proportion to their indicated values) until the final concluded values for these assets indicates no economic obsolescence.

At that valuation conclusion, there may be no positive intangible personal property value indicated by the intangible asset valuation. But there will also be no negative intangible personal property value indicated by the intangible asset valuation.

In other words, after any calculated economic obsolescence is allocated to the subject firm's tangible real and personal property assets, then the remaining amount of intangible asset value in the subject firm will be zero.

Of course, based upon the standards and premises of value applied, based upon the industry in which the firm operates, and based upon the microeconomic dynamics of the firm, the analysis and appraisal of the subject assets of any subject firm may indicate little or no (or even negative) intangible asset value. Nonetheless, such an analysis and appraisal should be performed as an integral part of any asset-based method business valuation.

As mentioned above, when using the asset accumulation method of business valuation, the firm's intangible assets may be valued collectively (e.g., using the capitalized excess earnings method) or the firm's intangible assets may be valued individually and discretely. But the firm's intangible assets must be appraised as part of the valuation process.

As will be discussed in Chapter 34, several important concepts with regard to the valuation of intangible assets are part of an asset accumulation method business valuation. Several of these concepts will be introduced briefly below.

First, there is an important sequencing to the identification and valuation of these intangible assets; it is important to understand and follow the flow (or funnel) of income from customers/clients/patients into the firm and appraise the intangible assets in the order of how they are affected by this flow.

Second, there is an important prioritization to the identification and valuation of intangible assets. Typically, intangible assets to be appraised using a market approach will be valued first; intangible assets to be appraised using a cost approach will be valued second; and intangible assets to be appraised using an income approach will be valued last.

Third, it is important to carefully avoid double counting (or over counting) of economic business value when appraising intangible assets. For example, the appraiser must procedurally avoid identifying one component of economic business value and then, inadvertently through various valuation techniques, assign some or all of the same economic value to the firm's trademarks and trade names, patents, customer relationships, goodwill, and so forth.

Fourth, like tangible assets, intangible assets may be valued using either a cost approach, an income approach, or a market approach. If several different intangible assets are identified as part of an asset accumulation method business valuation, it is quite likely that some intangible assets will be valued using a cost approach, while some others will be valued using an income approach, and some others may still be valued using a market approach. Clearly, given the function and purpose of each individual intangible asset, the appraiser should use the valuation approach (or approaches) that is (are) most determinative of the true economic value of the subject intangible asset.

Nonetheless, as a general rule, at least one intangible asset should be valued using an income approach as part of each asset accumulation method business valuation. In this way, the appraisal will verify and validate the income-earnings economic capacity of the subject assets. The intangible assets valued using the income approach confirm the economic support for the tangible real and personal property assets (and other intangible assets) of the firm. And the intangible assets valued using the income approach confirm that there is no (or that there is) economic obsolescence associated with the tangible real and personal property assets of the firm.

Illustrative Example

To illustrate the general application of the asset accumulation method, let's create a hypothetical small business. Let's call this small business Client Company, Inc.

Client Company, Inc. is a successful family-owned widget manufacturing company. To make this example relatively simple, let's assume that the owners of Client Company, Inc. are contemplating the sale of this going-concern business enterprise.

Therefore, the objective of this appraisal is to determine the fair market value of the overall business enterprise. In other words, we can eliminate from consideration the identification and quantification of various business valuation discounts and premiums.

The purpose of this appraisal is to provide an independent valuation opinion to the current owners to allow them to assess the most likely transaction price regarding the sale of the company.

In order to more finitely identify the components of the Client Company, Inc. business value by the selling family members and to potential buyers, we have elected to use the asset accumulation method. Specifically, we will apply this business valuation method on a discrete asset valuation basis (as opposed to a collective asset valuation basis).

Given the purpose and objective of the appraisal, we will conclude the fair market value (as the standard of value) of all of the tangible and intangible assets of Client Company, Inc., as of the valuation date.

Given the successful historical operations of the firm and management's plans to sell the business as an ongoing business, we have selected the individual asset valuation premise of value in continued use, as a going-concern business enterprise.

Exhibit 17–2 presents the statement of financial position (i.e., balance sheet) of Client Company, Inc. as of the June 30, 1992, valuation date. Let's assume that this statement of financial position is prepared in accordance with generally accepted accounting principles. In other words, the Exhibit 17–2 statement of financial position is prepared on a historical cost basis.

Exhibit 17–2, then, is the basis working document that is the point of departure to start our asset accumulation method business valuation.

Exhibit 17–3 presents the final summary of the asset accumulation method business valuation for Client Company, Inc.

Exhibit 17–3 presents both the historical cost values for all recorded assets and liabilities of Client Company, Inc. (just slightly rearranged from the GAAP basis balance sheet). And Exhibit 17–3 presents the fair market values for all assets and liabilities—both tangible and intangible—of Client Company, Inc.

Let's review each of the asset and liability fair market value conclusions in Exhibit 17–3. The following paragraphs describe an illustrative valuation conclusion for each asset and liability and a typical valuation approach that may be used in a business valuation such as Client Company, Inc.

The cash balance remains at its historical cost value. The appraiser would confirm whether or not the cash balances would be transferred to the new owner when the business was sold.

The accounts and notes receivable assets remain at their historical cost value. This conclusion was reached after an assessment of the timing and collectibility of the receivables.

Prepaid expenses remain at their historical cost value. This conclusion was reached after an assessment of the value of the prepaid expenses to the going-concern business.

Inventory is revalued upward. This revaluation is based upon the sales comparison method described in IRS Revenue Procedure 77-12.

Long-term notes receivable are valued at their historical cost. This conclusion is based upon an analysis of the stated interest rate versus current interest rates for similar risk notes and based upon the historical and likely prospective payment pattern regarding the notes.

The note receivable from supplier is revalued downward. Some years ago, this business extended a loan to one of its key suppliers. This decremental revaluation was based upon an analysis of the below-market interest rate on the note and of the erratic historical payment history from the supplier on the note.

Exhibit 17–2

CLIENT COMPANY, INC.
STATEMENT OF FINANCIAL POSITION
AS OF JUNE 30, 1992

ASSETS

Current Assets:

Cash	$200,000
Accounts and notes receivable	500,000
Prepaid expenses	200,000
Inventory	600,000
Total Current Assets	1,500,000

Non–current Assets:

Plant, property, and equipment, at cost:

Land	200,000
Buildings and improvements	1,200,000
Office furniture and fixtures	300,000
Machinery and equipment	500,000
Tools and dies	300,000
Total plant, property, and equipment	2,500,000
Less: Accumulated depreciation	1,000,000
Net plant, property and equipment	1,500,000

Other non–current assets:

Long–term notes receivable	250,000
Note receivable from supplier	250,000
Total other non–current assets	500,000

TOTAL ASSETS	**$3,500,000**

LIABILITIES AND OWNERS' EQUITY

Current Liabilities:

Accounts payable	$400,000
Wages payable	200,000
Taxes payable	100,000
Accrued liabilties	300,000
Total Current Liabilities	1,000,000

Non–current Liabilities:

Bonds payable	200,000
Notes payable	200,000
Mortgages payable	700,000
Debentures payable	200,000
Total Non–current Liabilities	1,300,000

Owners' Equity:

Capital stock	200,000
Additional paid–in capital	500,000
Retained earnings	500,000
Total Owners' Equity	1,200,000

TOTAL LIABILITIES AND OWNERS' EQUITY	**$3,500,000**

Exhibit 17–3

CLIENT COMPANY, INC.
BUSINESS ENTERPRISE VALUATION
ASSET ACCUMULATION APPROACH
AS OF JUNE 30, 1992

	At Historical Cost	At Fair Market Value
ASSETS		
Financial Assets:		
Cash	$200,000	$200,000
Accounts and notes receivable	500,000	500,000
Prepaid expenses	200,000	200,000
Inventory	600,000	700,000
Long-term notes receivable	250,000	250,000
Note receivable from supplier	250,000	150,000
Total Financial Assets	2,000,000	2,000,000
Tangible Real Property:		
Land	200,000	300,000
Buildings and improvements	1,200,000	1,000,000
Less: Accumulated depreciation	400,000	
Net Tangible Real Property	1,000,000	1,300,000
Tangible Personal Property:		
Office furniture and fixtures	300,000	200,000
Machinery and equipment	500,000	300,000
Tools and dies	300,000	200,000
Less: Accumulated depreciation	600,000	
Net Tangible Personal Property	500,000	700,000
Intangible Real Property:		
Leasehold interests	0	100,000
Net Intangible Real Property	0	100,000
Intangible Personal Property:		
Trademarks and trade names	0	200,000
Computer software	0	150,000
Patents	0	150,000
Favorable supplier contracts	0	100,000
Goodwill	0	100,000
Net Intangible Personal Property	0	700,000
TOTAL ASSETS	$3,500,000	$4,800,000
LIABILITIES AND OWNERS' EQUITY		
Current Liabilities:		
Accounts payable	$400,000	$400,000
Wages payable	200,000	200,000
Taxes payable	100,000	100,000
Accrued liabilties	300,000	300,000
Total Current Liabilities	1,000,000	1,000,000
Non-current Liabilities:		
Bonds payable	200,000	200,000
Notes payable	200,000	200,000
Mortgages payable	700,000	650,000
Debentures payable	200,000	200,000
Total Non-current Liabilities	1,300,000	1,250,000
Contingent Liabilities:		
Contingent claims	0	150,000
Total Contingent Liabilities	0	150,000
TOTAL LIABILITIES	2,300,000	2,400,000
TOTAL LIABILITIES AND OWNERS' EQUITY	$3,500,000	$4,800,000
TOTAL OWNERS' EQUITY	$1,200,000	$2,400,000

Land is revalued upward. This incremental revaluation is based upon a market value appraisal of the land, as if vacant and unimproved, using the sales comparison approach.

Buildings and improvements are revalued incrementally, as fair market value exceeds the (depreciated) historical cost of these properties. This appraisal is based upon depreciated reproduction cost analysis of the subject properties.

Office furniture and fixtures, machinery and equipment, and tools and dies are revalued incrementally—that is, the fair market value conclusions for each asset category exceed their (depreciated) historical cost. The depreciated replacement cost method would be a typical valuation method for the appraisal of these assets.

A leasehold interest is identified and capitalized on the valuation balance sheet. In this illustrative example, Client Company, Inc. enjoys a favorable rental advantage (i.e., below-market rental rates) on some warehouse space that it leases. The appraiser used the income approach to project and capitalize this favorable (below-market) lease rate advantage and to conclude the fair market value of the leasehold interest. This leasehold interest intangible asset was not previously recorded on the historical cost basis balance sheet.

The entire category of intangible personal property would not be recorded on a GAAP historical cost basis balance sheet. However, these intangible assets are identified and appraised for business valuation purposes.

Trademarks and trade names are an important intangible asset for Client Company, Inc. Company management spends a great deal of time and money promoting the company's name: they advertise, send promotional announcements, sponsor booths at trade shows, and so forth.

The appraiser used the recreation cost method to quantify the value of this intangible asset. The appraiser estimated the current cost required for the firm to recreate its current level of customer awareness, brand recognition, and consumer loyalty. This estimated cost to recreate this level of name awareness is capitalized as the value of this intangible asset.

Computer software is an important intangible asset for Client Company, Inc. This computer software was internally developed, instead of externally purchased. Accordingly, the value of this computer software typically will not be recorded on a GAAP basis balance sheet.

The systems analyst at Client Company, Inc. has developed and implemented an automated materials requirement planning (MRP) system. This system is extremely useful to the company with regard to material purchasing, labor scheduling, and production planning.

The appraiser used the market approach to estimate the value of this intangible asset, as there is a relatively similar (in terms of functionality) MRP system available on the market from a commercial software vendor. After consideration of the market value of a comparable commercial system, and after including the costs of customization, installation, testing, and training, the appraiser concluded the fair market value of the Client Company, Inc. computer software.

The patent that Client Company, Inc. holds is a valuable intangible asset to them. The widgets that Client Company, Inc. manufactures have certain unique and proprietary technological feature advancements compared to the widgets manufactured by competitors. And other manufacturers can not reverse-engineer and copy the Client Company, Inc. advanced features, because the subject product is protected by a U.S. product patent.

Because of the advanced features (protected by the patent), Client Company, Inc. estimates that it sells more widgets than it would otherwise, and its average selling price per widget is higher than its competitors' prices. Accordingly, the appraiser used the income approach to value the intangible value of the Client Company, Inc. patent.

Client Company, Inc. has a favorable supply contract with a key supplier. The buyer for Client Company, Inc. is a skilled negotiator. Using these superior negotiating skills, the buyer convinced the key supplier to agree to supply an essential raw material to Client Company, Inc. at 20 percent below the prices that the supplier charges to its other, similar sized customers. This agreement is documented in a three-year-term supply contract.

The appraiser used the income approach to estimate the economic value of the Client Company, Inc. favorable supply contract.

Goodwill is typically considered the accumulation of all the other economic value of the firm not specifically identified with (or allocated to) individual tangible and intangible assets. The analysis and quantification of goodwill (or the lack of goodwill) is an important component in the asset accumulation method business valuation of a firm like Client Company, Inc.

With respect to the subject firm, the appraiser used a capitalized excess earnings method to identify and value goodwill. First, the appraiser identified and valued all of the other individual assets of Client Company, Inc.—both tangible and intangible. Second, the appraiser assigned a fair rate of return against each asset of the firm—both tangible and intangible. Third, the appraiser compared the total calculated fair return on the total tangible and intangible assets to the total economic income actually earned by the firm. Fourth, any excess economic income (above a fair return on all identified tangible and intangible assets) was capitalized as an annuity in perpetuity.

This capitalization conclusion, then, is the fair market value of the Client Company, Inc. goodwill.

The current liabilities of Client Company, Inc. were analyzed by the appraiser. Given the short-term nature of these monetary liabilities, the appraiser estimated their fair market value at their historical cost carrying amounts.

The noncurrent liabilities were also analyzed by the appraiser. Given the term of these liabilities and their stated (or implied) interest rates, the appraiser estimated the fair market value of the bonds, notes, and debentures at their historical cost carrying amounts.

The mortgage payable, however, has a substantial remaining term and has an interest rate that is considerably below current market rates.

The appraiser confirmed with the bank that they would allow Client Company, Inc. to pay off the mortgage at a discount compared to the principal balance. The appraiser estimated this discount and concluded the fair market value of the mortgage payable.

There is an outstanding lawsuit against Client Company, Inc. The plaintiff, a former employee, alleges that Client Company, Inc. violated the employee's exclusive marketing territory agreement. Although there were extenuating circumstances, Client Company, Inc. management realized that it did violate the agreement and that it owes damages to the former employee.

While the trial is not yet scheduled, and no one can predict the court's final decision regarding either liability or damages, Client Company, Inc. management believes that an offer of $150,000 will be adequate to settle the case and satisfy all future liability to the plaintiff.

The appraiser analyzed this estimate and then used it to capitalize a contingent liability on the Client Company, Inc. valuation balance sheet.

Finally, the appraiser summed the estimated fair market values for all of the tangible and intangible assets of Client Company, Inc. Next, the appraiser summed the estimated fair market values for all of the recorded and contingent liabilities of Client Company, Inc. Last, the appraiser subtracted the total liability value from the total asset value. The remainder is the fair market value of the total owners' equity of Client Company, Inc., per the asset accumulation method.

Advantages of the Asset Accumulation Method

As should be apparent from the above discussion of the theoretical concepts and the practical applications of this method, there are a number of advantages of the asset accumulation method of business valuation.

First, the results of the asset accumulation method are presented in a traditional balance sheet format. This format should be comfortable and familiar to anyone who has worked with basic financial statements.

Second, this method componentizes all of the business value of the firm. In the illustrative example above, the valuation conclusion was exactly two times book value for Client Company, Inc. Other valuation methods would, presumably, reach the same valuation conclusion. But those methods would not explain why the company is worth two times book value.

This method identifies exactly which assets (tangible and intangible) are contributing value to the firm and how much value each asset is contributing.

Third, this method is useful when structuring the sale of a business. This method can immediately quantify the effects on business value of many common seller structural considerations, such as:

1. What if the seller retains the company's cash on hand?
2. What if the seller retains (or leases back to the company) the operating real estate facilities?
3. What if the seller personally retains title and the patent or some other valuable assets of the company?
4. What if the seller personally retains any or all of the debt instruments of the company?

Fourth, this method is useful to the seller when negotiating the sale of the company. If the buyer offers a lower price than the asset accumulation method concludes, the seller can ask: "Since you're not willing to pay for all of the assets of the business, which of these assets don't you want me to sell to you as part of the transaction?

Fifth, this method is useful to the buyer when negotiating the purchase of the company. If the seller wants a higher price than the conclusions of the asset accumulation method, the buyer can ask: "What other assets are you willing to sell to me—in addition to what has already been appraised on this balance sheet—to justify the price that you are asking?"

Sixth, after the sale transaction is consummated, this business valuation method allows for a fast and reasonable allocation of the lump-sum purchase price among the assets acquired. This purchase price allocation is often required for both financial accounting purposes and tax accounting purposes. Many of the identified intangible assets may be subject to amortization cost recovery for federal income tax purposes.

Seventh, this method is useful with regard to financing the subject transaction. Typically, all categories of lenders (secured, unsecured, mezzanine, etc.) will want to know the value of the company's assets—both tangible and intangible—before they will commit to financing the deal. This business valuation method generally provides lenders with the information they need.

Eighth, this method is particularly useful in litigation support and dispute resolution matters. Since it identifies the individual value components of the individual assets of the firm, it allows for the easy measurement of the impact of certain alleged actions (or lack of actions) on the firm.

Also, this method can be used to allocate assets (as well as—or instead of—stock) in a stockholder/partner dissolution dispute or in a marital dissolution dispute.

Ninth, this method can be used with virtually any standard of value or premise of value. In other words, using the same comparative balance sheet format, appraisers can value the same business under several alternative standards (i.e., definitions) of value. Likewise, using the same comparative balance sheet format, appraisers can value the same business under several alternative premises of value.

Therefore, the impact of changing standards of value or premises of value can be immediately identified and quickly quantified.

Tenth, this method requires the most rigorous analysis and thorough understanding of company operations on the part of the appraiser. Such required rigorous analyses can only help to enhance the quality of the valuation. Also, this method generally requires much more active participation of company management in the valuation process. This active interest and participation can only help to enhance the quality of the valuation.

Disadvantages of the Asset Accumulation Method

The primary disadvantage of the asset accumulation method is that, if taken to its ultimate extreme, it could be quite expensive and time consuming. It also may necessitate involvement of appraisal specialists in several fields, which may be more suitable for larger businesses than for small businesses and professional practices.

Also, as described in this chapter, capturing all the assets means the intangibles as well as the tangibles. Most intangible asset values depend especially heavily on income approaches. Therefore, taken to its extreme, the asset accumulation method may ultimately depend as much or more on income variables as on values of tangible assets, especially for small businesses and professional practices. In this sense, the appellation *asset accumulation method* may seem to some like a misnomer. However, this latter is a semantic problem, not a conceptual problem.

Summary

The asset accumulation method is a common asset-based business valuation method. The theoretical underpinning of this method is simple: the value of the business is the value of the business assets (tangible and intangible) less the value of the business liabilities (recorded and contingent).

Basically, this method recognizes that all of the economic value of a business has to come from—and be identified back with—the productive assets of the business.

The asset accumulation method can be applied on a collective basis, where all of the economic value of the firm greater than the tangible value is aggregated and called goodwill. A common implementation of this method is the capitalized excess earnings method.

Also, the asset accumulation method can be applied on a discrete basis, where all of the firm's tangible and intangible assets are individually identified and appraised. The discrete application of the asset accumulation method was illustrated in this chapter.

It is naive and conceptually incorrect to automatically conclude that the value of a business is based upon the value of the tangible assets of the business only. Likewise, it is naive and conceptually incorrect to conclude that the value of a business is equal to its accounting book value—without substantial valuation procedures and rigorous fundamental analysis to support that conclusion.

The intangible assets of the firm may contribute substantial economic value. They may contribute little or no economic value. Or they may contribute negative economic value, which is recognized as economic obsolescence—or a decrease in the value of the tangible assets of the firm. Again, the ultimate application of an asset-based valuation method requires a structured, rigorous, and comprehensive valuation analysis of all of the assets of the firm.

There are numerous advantages to the asset accumulation method of business valuation—particularly to small business and professional practices. These advantages include application to transaction pricing and structuring, deal negotiation, acquisition financing, purchase accounting, and dispute resolution.

However, there are "costs" associated with the asset accumulation method of business valuation. This method requires more time and effort on the part of the appraiser than many other business valuation methods. This method requires more access to company facilities and management than many other business valuation methods. And this method requires more access to company data, particularly operational data, than many other business valuation methods. This method also requires more time and effort on the part of company management and more involvement of company management in the valuation process.

Lastly, the asset accumulation method requires that the appraiser have experience and expertise with regard to the identification and valuation of both the tangible and intangible assets of the firm. Certainly, this method is only recommended for appraisers who have adequate experience and expertise in the appraisal of the individual component assets of a business enterprise. The use of supporting appraisers with the requisite experience and qualifications may fill the void for a particular asset type for which the business appraiser lacks the technical expertise.

Selected Bibliography

Articles

Andresky, Jill. "The Big Easy (Asset Valuation)." *Forbes,* November 2, 1987, p. 142.

Churchill, Michael. "Asset Valuation." *Australian Accountant,* April 1992, pp. 35–39.

DeThomas, Arthur R., and Don Seat. "Asset Valuation: A Practical Approach for Decision Making." *CPA Journal,* September 1991, pp. 82–83.

Lynn, Daniel M., and Robert R. Neyland. "Asset Valuation: Softening the Bankruptcy Blow." *Bank Management,* April 1992, pp. 48–49.

Northrup, C. Van, and Patti J. Geolat. "What's It Worth?" *Best's Review (Property/Casualty Insurance Edition),* March 1986, p. 62.

Reilly, Robert F. "The Valuation of Computer Software." *ASA Valuation,* March 1991, pp. 34–54.

Books

American Institute of Real Estate Appraisers. *The Dictionary of Real Estate Appraisal.* 2nd ed. Chicago: American Institute of Real Estate Appraisers, 1989.

American Society of Appraisers. *Appraising Machinery and Equipment,* ed. John Alico. New York: McGraw-Hill, 1989.

Appraisal Institute. *The Appraisal of Real Estate.* 10th ed. Chicago: Appraisal Institute, 1992.

Bonbright, James C. *The Valuation of Property.* Charlottesville, Va.: The Miche Company, 1965, Reprint of 1937 ed.

Eck, James R.; William Gary Baker; and David Ensign. *Asset Valuation.* Colorado Springs. Colo.: Shepard's/McGraw-Hill, 1991.

Friedman, Edith J., ed. *Encyclopedia of Real Estate Appraising.* 3rd ed. Englewood Cliffs, N.J.: Prentice Hall, 1978.

Kinnard, William N., Jr., and Byrl N. Boyce. *Appraising Real Property.* Lexington, Mass.: D.C. Heath, 1984.

Smith, Gordon V., and Russell L. Parr. *Valuation of Intellectual Property and Intangible Assets.* New York: John Wiley & Sons, 1989.

Chapter 18

Valuation Synthesis and Conclusion

As presented in previous chapters, there are a variety of alternative small business and professional practice valuation approaches. These approaches include various income capitalization methods, in which the capitalization rate may be derived from security analysis investment criteria, from the capital market activity of "guideline" publicly traded companies, or from merger and acquisition data regarding "guideline" nonpublic companies. These approaches include various discounted future return analyses, including the discounted net cash flow analysis technique. And these approaches include various asset-based methods, including the capitalized excess earnings method (for aggregate asset appraisal) and the asset accumulation method (for discrete asset appraisal).

As we have discussed in previous chapters, each of these approaches has its own strengths and weaknesses. Certainly, in each unique set of circumstances, each approach has its practical application limitations.

This chapter will focus on three fundamental questions:

1. How does the appraiser decide which valuation approach or approaches to use in each individual business valuation?
2. How does the appraiser consider the differing results of alternative valuation approaches in reaching the business valuation synthesis and conclusion?
3. What does the appraiser do when alternative valuation approaches yield materially different valuation conclusions?

Criteria for the Selection of Valuation Approaches

As mentioned above, of the recommended business valuation approaches, there are no clearly right or wrong approaches. This assertion deliberately excludes valuation "approaches" that are not recommended, of course, such as the naive book value "approach." There is also no precise guideline or quantitative formula for selecting which approach or approaches are most applicable in a given business valuation situation. However, the following list presents the most common and most important factors to be considered by the appraiser when selecting among alternative valuation approaches.

1. Quantity and quality of available data.
2. Access to available data.
3. Supply of industry transaction data.
4. Type of business, nature of business assets, and type of industry subject to appraisal.
5. Business interest subject to appraisal.
6. Statutory, judicial, and administrative considerations.
7. Informational needs of appraisal audience.

8. Purpose and objective of appraisal.

9. Professional judgment and expertise of appraiser.

Quantity and Quality of Available Data

Practically, this may be the most important selection criteria. An appraiser simply cannot perform a valuation approach (no matter how conceptually robust it is) if the requisite financial, operational, or market data are not available.

Access to Available Data

In business valuations performed for litigation support and dispute resolution purposes, the appraiser may not have unrestricted access to company data, to company management, to company facilities, and so forth. In these cases, all of the desired historical and prospective data may exist. But the appraiser may not be granted reasonable access to the existing data. Accordingly, in selecting among valuation approaches, the appraiser may have to consider not only what data are available—but what data are available to the appraiser.

Supply of Industry Transaction Data

In some industries, there is a large quantity of publicly available data regarding business sale and purchase transactions. When the supply of reliable industry transaction data is substantial, the appraiser will more likely select and rely upon market-based business valuation approaches.

Type of Business, Nature of Business Assets, and Type of Industry Subject to Appraisal

Certain industries have "rules of thumb" that are used as quick estimates regarding the valuation of businesses in that industry. While these industry rules of thumb, guidelines, or conventions should not be relied upon in a rigorous business valuation, they should not be totally ignored either. And, depending upon the nature of the subject business (e.g., whether it is capital-asset intensive or intangible-asset intensive), different valuation approaches may be more or less applicable.

Business Interest Subject to Appraisal

Obviously, the valuation of a marketable majority interest in a business enterprise is a different assignment than the valuation of a nonmarketable, minority interest in the nonvoting stock of the same business enterprise. In selecting the valuation approach, the appraiser should consider that some valuation approaches are more appropriate for overall business enterprise valuations while other approaches are more appropriate for the analysis of fractional security interests.

Statutory, Judicial, and Administrative Considerations

For those business valuations performed for certain taxation, ESOP, and litigation purposes, the appraiser should be cognizant of which valuation approaches are required—and which valuation approaches are prohibited. Certainly, the IRS has published valuation procedures and guidelines for appraisals performed for gift and estate tax purposes. For example, the specific Chapter 14 guidelines apply for business valuations performed for estate freeze purposes. And certain states require some valuation approaches—and prohibit other approaches—for business valuations performed for appraisal rights pursuant to minority squeeze-out mergers, other shareholder appraisal rights cases, marital dissolution cases, and so forth. The appraiser should be aware of whatever specific statutory requirements, administrative guidance, or judicial precedent affect the subject business valuation.

Informational Needs of Appraisal Audience

The ultimate audience for the appraisal may affect the selection of business valuation approaches. These considerations include the level of sophistication of the appraisal audience and the degree of familiarity of the appraisal audience with the subject company. The ultimate purpose of the appraisal as either notational or transactional may also affect which valuation approach (and how many valuation approaches) will be selected.

Purpose and Objective of Appraisal

Overall, the purpose and objective of the business valuation may influence the selection of the valuation approaches. These appraisal objective factors include the description of the business interest subject to appraisal, the definition (or standard) of value applied, the premise of value applied, and the valuation date. The appraisal purpose factors include the audience for the appraisal and the decision (or decisions) to be influenced by the appraisal.

Professional Judgment and Expertise of Appraiser

When all is said and done, the most important factor affecting the selection of the appropriate business valuation approach or approaches is the professional judgment, technical expertise, and practiced common sense of the appraiser.

Criteria for the Weighting of Valuation Approach Results

As with the selection of which valuation approaches and methods to use, there are no scientific formulae or specific rules to use with regard to the weighting of the results of two or more business valuation approaches. In fact, the same factors or guidelines that affect the selection of the valuation approaches will influence the appraiser with regard to weighting the conclusions of these valuation approaches.

Some appraisers use an implicit weighting scheme in their final valuation synthesis and conclusion. That is, they present the valuation conclusions for each method performed and then jump directly to a valuation conclusion. They do not document or justify the valuation synthesis process.

An example of this implicit weighting scheme follows:

Subject Professional Partnership
Business Valuation Methods and Value Estimates
Valuation Synthesis and Conclusion

Valuation Method	Value Estimate
Capitalization of income	$1,800,000
Discounted future returns	2,000,000
Asset accumulation	2,400,000
Valuation synthesis and conclusion	$2,200,000

This analysis, of course, presents the final valuation conclusion. And that valuation conclusion may be perfectly reasonable. However, the appraiser has not explained the implicit weighting—that is, the intrinsic thought process that led to the $2,200,000 valuation conclusion.

Another procedure is to use an explicit weighting of the several alternative methods. This explicit weighting scheme allows the appraiser to communicate the degree of confidence in the several business valuation methods selected and in the reasonableness of the several business valuation results. In fact, a narrative description of the rationale behind the appraiser's explicit weighting scheme is often included in the narrative valuation opinion report.

An example of this explicit weighting scheme follows:

Subject Professional Partnership
Business Valuation Methods and Value Estimates
Valuation Synthesis and Conclusion

Valuation Method	Value Estimate	Weighting	Weighted Value
Capitalization of income	$1,800,000	25%	$ 450,000
Discounted future returns	2,000,000	25%	500,000
Asset accumulation	2,400,000	50%	1,200,000
Total weighted value			$2,150,000
Valuation synthesis and conclusion (rounded)			$2,200,000

Even if a narrative discussion of the weighting scheme is included in the valuation opinion report, the above explicit weighting provides important information as to the appraiser's thought process regarding—and degree of confidence in—the alternative valuation approaches and the alternative valuation conclusions. This explicit weighting allows the appraisal reader to follow—and reconstruct, if necessary—all of the appraiser's quantitative (if not qualitative) analyses.

It should be noted that there is no objective formula or model that may be used to quantify the weighting factors. The valuation approach weighting will vary for each appraisal. And the weighting assigned to each method in each appraisal is ultimately based upon the experience and judgment of the appraiser.

Discounted Future Returns

The primary criterion for heavy weighting of the discounted future returns method is the existence of a forecast which has reason to be credible. It also becomes important when it is expected that future results will differ significantly enough from past results that reliance on historical results would likely lead to a misleading indication of value. All this, of course, assumes that returns are important to the vaulation, but it would be unusual for this not to be so.

The discounted future returns method is generally more applicable in valuation of a controlling interest than a minority interest. First of all, the control holder has more discretion to take actions to actually realize the forecasted returns. Also, the controlling interest has the discretion to determine the disposition of the returns achieved, usually the amount reinvested.

The method also is more appropriate to the extent that asset values tend to be more of an intangible than a tangible nature.

Capitalization of Earnings

The capitalization of earnings method's validity depends on the ability to estimate some reasonably credible level of normalized earnings (however measured) that can be considered sustainable. As with the discounted future returns method, it assumes that some measure of earning power is important in the valuation. Sometimes it is easier (or more reliable) to develop a "normalized" level of returns than to estimate the timing of returns, as is necessary in the discounted future returns method.

The capitalization of earnings method can also work well if there is a modest and fairly sustainable long-term growth rate expectation.

Excess Earnings Method

The excess earnings method generally is most applicable when there is a high component of intangible asset value, such as often is the case with professional practices. This also assumes, of course, that most of the value derives from earning power. It is also used more often for valuing controlling interests than for valuing minority interests.

Guideline (Comparative) Company Methods

The primary criterion for using guideline (comparative) company methods is the existence of reasonably comparable company data. The general methods can be especially useful for smaller minority interests because of the plethora of public minority interest stock trading data.

It is an almost mandatory method when valuing for tax purposes and ESOPs, given the existing regulatory authority and judicial precedent.

A good analyst can deal with appropriate adjustments for size, marketability, and other differences. If enough good guideline company data are available, it can provide compelling evidence of value.

Gross Revenue Multipliers

Gross revenue multipliers are most useful when one has credible data on the revenues for the subject company and/or comparative company transactions, but does not have credible data for earnings or cash flow figures further down on the income statements. As noted in Chapter 16, the use of gross revenue multipliers for valuation carries an implicit assumption of homogeneity (in terms of return on sales and risk) between the subject company and the companies from which the multipliers are derived. If this is not the case, the valuer must be able to make appropriate adjustments in order for the method to be valid.

Gross revenue multipliers tend to work best for professional practices and service businesses, to some extent for retail/service businesses such as restaurants, and almost not at all for manufacturing companies (most of which are unique). In any case, a company's value ultimately is based on its ability to generate cash flow, and the validity of gross revenue multipliers depends on their ability to indicate potential earning power.

Asset-Based Methods

Asset-based methods are most appropriate for small businesses that are capital intensive or for small businesses or professional practices that are intangible-asset intensive.

They are most appropriate for controlling interests, since minority interests cannot direct the disposition of assets.

They also sometimes are a means of last resort when no meaningful capital market or private transaction data are available.

An Inconsistency of Results among Valuation Approaches and Methods

Ideally, the appraiser will use two or more approaches and methods in the subject business valuation and these will all yield identical valuation conclusions. Practically, this never happens.

Appraisers expect to conclude a range of valuation conclusions when several alternative valuation methods are used. The normal situation occurs when the several valuation methods all conclude a reasonably narrow dispersion of valuation conclusions. These alternative conclusions, then, indicate the reasonable range of values for the subject business. They also provide mutually supportive evidence as to the final valuation synthesis and conclusion.

Occasionally, the situation occurs when two or three valuation methods produce value estimates within a reasonable range—and, then, one valuation method produces a clear and obvious value estimate outlier.

An example of this valuation conclusion outlier phenomenon follows:

Subject Professional Partnership
Business Valuation Methods and Value Estimates
Valuation Synthesis and Conclusion

Valuation Method	Value Estimate
Capitalization of income	$1,800,000
Discounted future returns	2,000,000
Capitalized excess earnings	2,200,000
Asset accumulation (discrete)	1,000,000
Valuation synthesis and conclusion	$2,200,000

In this example, the value estimate of the asset accumulation method (discrete application) is a clear and obvious outlier compared to the three other value estimates. Accordingly, this appraisal requires further analysis and consideration before a valuation conclusion may be reached.

The question is: what is the appraiser to do regarding such an outlier value estimate? There are three alternatives.

First, the appraiser could discard the valuation method that yields the outlier value estimate. This action is based upon the rationale that the outlier valuation method simply does not work given the subject set of facts and circumstances.

Second, the appraiser could keep the outlier valuation method but assign a very low weight to the outlier value estimate. This action is based upon the rationale that if the method is fundamentally sound, even an unreasonable value estimate should be given some weight in the final valuation conclusion.

Third, the appraiser could thoroughly investigate why the outlier method is producing outlier value estimates. The appraiser could attempt to reconcile all of the value estimates. The appraiser could search for an answer, or at least an explanation, to this apparent anomaly. As part of this investigation and reconcilement, the appraiser should recheck all of the quantitative analyses and should rethink all of the qualitative conclusions. The appraiser is most likely to find that an error was made in the analysis and application of the outlier method. (An example may be that one unrecorded intangible asset was inadvertently missed in the asset accumulation method.)

After the analytical or data error is discovered, it can be corrected. Then, the outlier method may produce a more reasonable, and more consistent, value estimate.

Of course, we recommend this third alternative—which involves additional analyses and reconciliation procedures—to handling the phenomenon of an outlier business value estimate. Only with such analysis can such a discrepancy be adequately explained and reconciled with the other indications of value.

Summary

Numerous factors affect the appraiser's decision of which business valuation approaches and methods to select. Of these numerous factors, the professional judgment and expertise of the individual appraiser is the most important factor.

Numerous factors also affect the appraiser's selection of a weighting scheme regarding the value estimates generated by the alternative valuation methods used. The weighting scheme selected indicates the degree of confidence the appraiser has in the selected valuation method and in the derived value estimates. Clearly, the weighting scheme used should be appropriate, given the purpose and objective of the business valuation. Typically, it is preferable that an explicit weighting scheme be presented (and explained) in the final business valuation synthesis and conclusion.

Lastly, alternative valuation methods typically yield value estimates in a reasonably tight range. These value estimates, then, provide mutually supportive evidence regarding the valuation synthesis and conclusion. When a business valuation method derives an outlier value estimate, the appraiser should thoroughly research and reconcile this value estimate, in an attempt to explain—and correct—this apparent anomaly.

Chapter 19

Tradeoff between Cash and Terms

I'll let you name any price you want if you'll let me name the terms.
Deal-Makers' Credo

As noted in previous chapters, most sales of small businesses and professional practices are done on some kind of terms rather than for cash. In most cases, the seller "carries the paper"; that is, the seller accepts an installment payment contract for the balance of the purchase price over and above the down payment.

The main reason for this arrangement is that the typical buyer of a small business or professional practice does not have the personal resources to pay the full purchase price in cash, and most lending institutions would not regard the business or practice being purchased as adequate collateral to support a term loan of the balance of the purchase price. In no other broad category of transactions is it nearly as commonplace for the seller to take an installment contract for a significant portion of the selling price. Larger businesses usually sell to larger corporations, which pay in cash or possibly in stock, if the buyer is a publicly traded company. Buyers of real estate can usually obtain debt financing for a substantial portion of the total purchase price by using the real estate as collateral, thus cashing out the seller.

In a sale of a business or professional practice on terms, the seller is, in effect, making a loan to the buyer to finance the purchase. It is, therefore, of the utmost importance to the seller to have a good contract on the sale, with adequate protective covenants.

The purpose of this chapter is to explain the difference between the face value of a transaction on terms and the equivalent cash value of that transaction. This difference is usually quite significant in the sale of small businesses and professional practices because the rate of interest on contracts carried by the seller is usually far below a market rate of interest for any other comparable contract. We think it fair to say that the typical small business sale at a face value of $100,000 probably has a cash equivalent value somewhere around $80,000, a difference considerably greater than most people realize. Therefore, it is worthwhile for people dealing with small business and professional practice transactions to be able to convert the price of a deal on terms to an equivalent cash value or vice versa. It is also worthwhile to be able to assess the differences in impact (in terms of cash equivalent value) between one set of terms and some alternative set of terms.

Converting a Price on Terms to an Equivalent Cash Value

A Typical Example

Let's start off with an example. John owns a small marina, which he sells on terms for a face amount of $100,000. The terms are as follows:

John's Marina

Sale price	$100,000
Down payment	20%

Balance in equal monthly installments including principal and interest at the rate of 8 percent per annum over a period of 10 years.

Assume that the average yield on 10-year, high-grade corporate bonds is 10 percent. The buyer's installment note, secured by the small marina, is not as high-quality a debt instrument as the high-grade corporate bond, so a reasonable market rate of interest for a note of such characteristics would have to be higher, let's say 13 percent. (We will discuss how to determine an applicable market rate in a subsequent section.)

What is the cash equivalent value of this transaction? The first step is to compute the amount of the monthly payments that John will receive. The buyer will be paying John 120 monthly payments of principal plus interest at 0.67 percent per month (.08 annual rate ÷ 12 months = .0067) on a contract balance of $80,000. This schedule works out to monthly payments of $970.62.

The next step is to convert this stream of 120 monthly payments to a cash equivalent value using a market rate of interest. The question here is: how much cash would a lender pay for this installment contract in order for it to provide him a rate of return of 13 percent per year (1.08 percent per month).

The formula for this is:

$$PV = \sum_{i=1}^{n} \frac{PMT_i}{(1 + r)^i}$$

where:

PV	=	Present value
n	=	Number of payments
PMT	=	Amount of monthly payments in dollars
i	=	The ith payment
r	=	Required rate of return

Substituting values into this formula would give us a calculation as follows:

$$PV = \sum_{i=1}^{120} \frac{\$970.62}{(1 + .0108)^i}$$

$$= \frac{\$970.62}{1.0108} + \frac{\$970.62}{1.0108^2} + ... + \frac{\$970.62}{1.0108^{120}}$$

In this example, John sold his marina for $20,000 cash, plus a note with a present value of $65,007, for a total of $85,007 cash equivalent value.

Some Variations

Extending the Contract. Suppose John has accepted a note under the same terms and conditions but with the payments spread out over 15 years instead of 10. In this case, using the same calculations, he would receive monthly payments of $764.52 for 180 months. Also using the same calculations, the present value of his contract at a 13 percent annual market rate would be $60,424.93, or a total present value of $20,000 + $60,424.93 = $80,425. In this variation, the cash equivalent value is $4,582 less than in the 10-year example.

Accepting a Lower Contract Interest Rate. Let's suppose that John had accepted a contract with an interest rate of 6.0 percent (0.5 percent per month), instead of 8 percent. Using the same calculations, on a 10-year contract, he would receive payments of $888.16 per month for 120 months. At a 13 percent market rate of interest, the present value of his contract balance would be $59,484.27. Adding this amount to his $20,000 down payment would indicate a cash equivalent value for the deal of $79,484, or $5,523 less than the value with an 8 percent interest rate.

Variations in Market Rate of Interest. Suppose that John made the same deal when the market rate of interest on his contract was about 16 percent. He would receive $970.62 per month for 120 months, as in the original example. However, the present value of his contract would have to be figured by discounting his payments back to the present time at 1.3 percent per month (16.00 ÷ 12 = 1.3). Using the same calculations, the present value of his contract would be $57,943. Adding this amount to the down payment of $20,000 would indicate a cash equivalent value for the deal of $77,943, or $7,064 less than if the market rate of interest were 13 percent.

Combining the Variations. For our last variation in this series, we'll assume that John took his $80,000 balance in the form of an installment note with equal monthly payments of principal plus a 7.2 percent annual rate of interest for 15 years (180 months), at a time when a market rate of interest on an installment note such as this would be 16 percent. In this case, he would receive 180 monthly payments of $728.04. The present value of these payments at a 16 percent annual market rate of interest would be $49,570. Adding the $20,000 down payment gives a cash equivalent value for the deal of $69,570, or about 30 percent less than the $100,000 price or face amount of the deal.

Determining the Applicable Market Interest Rate

All of the foregoing is simple mechanical arithmetic, done on an inexpensive pocket calculator in a few seconds. However, determining the applicable market interest rate requires a little bit of data and a little bit of judgment. Exhibit 19–1 offers a quick listing of lending rates current in late 1992.

Data on Market Interest Rates

Bank Lending Rates. Bank prime lending rates (the rates banks charge large borrowers with high credit ratings) are published regularly

Exhibit 19–1

LENDING RATES

		Date	Rate %
a	Prime Lending Rate	Week of 9/28/92	6.00
	Mortgage Lending Rates (Average)		
b	Residential	September 1992	7.95
c	Apartment	2nd Qtr. 1992	9.13
c	Industrial	2nd Qtr. 1992	9.04
c	Office Building	2nd Qtr. 1992	9.50
c	Retail	2nd Qtr. 1992	9.44
	Corporate Bond Rates (Average)		
d	New Issues	3rd Qtr. 1992	7.90
e	Aaa	September 1992	7.92
e	Baa	September 1992	8.62

CURRENT YIELDS f

Certificates of Deposit (3 mos.)	3.15
Money Market Funds	2.91
Prime Lending Rate	6.00
13–Week U.S. Treasury Bills	2.67
5–Year U.S. Treasury Bonds	5.46
20–Year U.S. Treasury Strips	7.99
BBB Corporate Bonds (composite)	8.93

a   *Barron's,* October 5, 1992.

b   *Federal Reserve Bulletin,* December 1992--Average contract rates on new commitments for conventional first mortgages; from Department of Housing and Urban Development.

c   American Council of Life Insurance *Investment Bulletin,* October 7, 1992

d   Standard & Poor's *Trends & Projections,* October 1, 1992--seasonally adjusted annual rate.

e   Moody's *Bond Record,* October 1992.

f   *Barron's,* October 5, 1992; Standard & Poor's *Outlook,* October 7, 1992; and *Federal Reserve Bulletin,* December 1992.

in newspapers and business magazines; or, by a telephone call to any bank, one can learn its current prime lending rate. Banks usually make short-term loans to small businesses at about 2½ to 3 percentage points above their prime lending rates if the business is sound and the loan is well secured, usually by current accounts receivable or inventory. Longer-term loans would normally carry a somewhat higher rate.

Mortgage Rates. General business and real estate publications publish rates for residential mortgages and for various classes of commercial mortgages, such as apartment houses, shopping centers, office buildings, and so forth. These mortgages are usually well secured by good-quality, marketable property, so that the lending institution can foreclose and resell the property fairly readily in case of the borrower's default.

Corporate Bond Rates. Corporate bonds are rated in terms of their quality (degree of certainty that the corporation will be able to pay the bonds' interest and principal on time) by various rating services such as Standard & Poor's and Moody's. Moody's ratings, for example, start with Aaa as the highest and go down through a grade of C, which is very speculative. *Barron's* and other publications show average yields for high-grade corporate bonds down through Baa. For medium-grade and lower-grade corporate bonds, reliable averages are not published, but yields for individual bonds can be found in publications such as the Standard & Poor's *Bond Guide* and Moody's *Bond Record*.

Using an Ounce of Judgment

An installment note receivable, secured by the stock and/or assets of a small business or professional practice, is almost always riskier than any of the foregoing debt instruments and, therefore, must have a higher market interest rate. It is unlikely that an installment contract receivable on a small business sale would have a quality rating any better than grade Caa to C for corporate bonds, if that high.

Furthermore, all the foregoing debt instruments are readily marketable, which an installment contract receivable on a small business is not. Banks sell good-quality loans to other banks. Mortgage lenders sell mortgages to other mortgage lenders. Corporate bonds are traded on the public market (including the New York Stock Exchange, American Stock Exchange, and over-the-counter market). There is no such ready market for installment contracts receivable on small businesses and professional practices.

The number of percentage points that needs to be added to the benchmark rates discussed above, in order to determine an appropriate market rate for a small business installment contract, depends on the degree of risk. If there is a substantial down payment, if the note is relatively short in duration (perhaps three to five years), and it is well secured and well protected by covenants in the purchase agreement, only a few percentage points need to be added. If the down payment is small, the length of the term long, and protective covenants poor or absent, no rate may be high enough.

Converting a Cash Value to a Price on Terms

Let's say that Dusty Trail has concluded that the value of his Paperback Western Bookstore on a cash basis is $150,000, but he expects to sell the business on terms, probably one third ($50,000) down and the balance

Exhibit 19–2

MONTHLY PAYMENT REQUIRED PER $100 OF CONTRACT BALANCE

Contract	Number of Payments												
Int. Rate	12	18	24	30	36	48	60	72	84	96	120	144	180
6%	8.61	5.82	4.43	3.60	3.04	2.35	1.93	1.66	1.46	1.31	1.11	0.98	0.84
7%	8.65	5.87	4.48	3.64	3.09	2.39	1.98	1.70	1.51	1.36	1.16	1.03	0.90
8%	8.70	5.91	4.52	3.69	3.13	2.44	2.03	1.75	1.56	1.41	1.21	1.08	0.96
9%	8.75	5.96	4.57	3.73	3.18	2.49	2.08	1.80	1.61	1.47	1.27	1.14	1.01
10%	8.79	6.01	4.61	3.78	3.23	2.54	2.12	1.85	1.66	1.52	1.32	1.20	1.07
11%	8.84	6.05	4.66	3.83	3.27	2.58	2.17	1.90	1.71	1.57	1.38	1.25	1.14
12%	8.88	6.10	4.71	3.87	3.32	2.63	2.22	1.96	1.77	1.63	1.43	1.31	1.20
13%	8.93	6.14	4.75	3.92	3.37	2.68	2.28	2.01	1.82	1.68	1.49	1.37	1.27
14%	8.98	6.19	4.80	3.97	3.42	2.73	2.33	2.06	1.87	1.74	1.55	1.44	1.33
15%	9.03	6.24	4.85	4.02	3.47	2.78	2.38	2.11	1.93	1.79	1.61	1.50	1.40
16%	9.07	6.29	4.90	4.07	3.52	2.83	2.43	2.17	1.99	1.85	1.68	1.57	1.47
17%	9.12	6.33	4.94	4.11	3.57	2.89	2.49	2.22	2.04	1.91	1.74	1.63	1.54
18%	9.17	6.38	4.99	4.16	3.62	2.94	2.54	2.28	2.10	1.97	1.80	1.70	1.61

($100,000 cash equivalent) on a contract, with interest at something less than a market rate. He now wants to determine the price and terms that would give him his $150,000 cash equivalent value.

The first step is to figure out a market rate of interest for the contract, probably by using one or more of the benchmark rates discussed in the previous section for guidance. Let's say that the high-grade corporate bond yield is 10 percent, and he thinks that the present contract should cost about 2 percent over the high-grade corporate bond rate (or about 12 percent), to obtain the credit on an arm's-length basis in the open market. (That is not a very high premium over the rate for top-quality credit; it implies that he believes there will not be a very high degree of risk associated with the credit.)

The second step is to determine what the monthly payments on the contract will be at a market rate of interest. If he assumes that the contract will run for seven years (84 months), the net level payments of principal and interest on $100,000, at a 12 percent annual rate (1 percent per month), are $1,765.27 per month. The monthly payments per $100 of contract balance for various rates of interest, for various lengths of time, are shown in Exhibit 19–2.

The third and final step is to convert this stream of monthly payments back to a contract face value on the basis of the rate of interest that will be shown on the contract. Let's say that Dusty thinks the rate of interest shown on the contract will be 8 percent per annum, or the equivalent of 0.6667 percent per month. On that basis, the face value of the contract balance should be $113,258.63.

In other words, if the rate of interest on the contract is 8 percent, it takes about $113,000 of face value to have a cash equivalent value of $100,000, if the market rate of interest on such a contract is 12 percent and the term of the contract is seven years. The business could be sold at $163,000, with

$50,000 down and a contract balance of $113,000; the monthly payments would include interest at an 8 percent annual rate for 84 months, and the deal would have a cash equivalent value of about $150,000. Exhibit 19–3 shows the effect of different market rates on various contract terms.

Contingent Payments

Many small businesses and professional practices are sold at a "price" that is actually paid only if certain events occur. Such events may be the achievement of certain levels of revenues and/or profits.

The most common contingency is the retention of existing clients. For example, the "price" may be equal to 100 percent of the latest 12 months' revenues. However, it may be paid over a period of two to five years, and then only to the extent that each existing client produces revenues at or above the level of the last 12 months. To the extent that any client does not, the contingent payments are reduced pro rata with the shortfall in revenue with that client.

To convert a price subject to contingencies to a cash equivalent value, one must use his best judgment to put a probability on the collection of each year's contingent payments, and reduce each year's face value proceeds by the probability of actually realizing those proceeds. Then each year's probability-adjusted revenues from existing clients is discounted to a present value as in the preceding sections.

A simple example will demonstrate the arithmetic. Assume a price of $500,000, with nothing down and $250,000 payable at the end of the first year, and $250,000 payable at the end of the second year, with each payment adjusted pro rata for any existing client revenues not retained. Assume that the $500,000 represents 100 percent of the last 12 months' revenues. Assume 80 percent retention the first year and 60 percent the second year. Assume a discount rate on the payments of 18 percent. The arithmetic is as follows:

Step 1: Probability of realization:

$$\text{Year 1: } \frac{\$400,000}{\$500,000} = .80$$

$$\text{Year 2: } \frac{\$300,000}{\$500,000} = .60$$

Step 2: Multiply probability times amount paid if 100% retained:

	Full Payment		Retention Probability		Expected Payment
Year 1:	$250,000	×	.80	=	$200,000
Year 2:	$250,000	×	.60	=	$150,000

Step 3: Discount expected payment to present value:

$$\frac{\$200,000}{(1 + .18)} + \frac{\$150,000}{(1 + .18)^2}$$

$$= \$169,492 + \$107,728$$

$$= \$277,220$$

In the above case, the estimated cash equivalent value is $272,220, or approximately 55 percent of the "price" of $500,000.

Exhibit 19–3

PRESENT VALUE OF A $1,000 CONTRACT
AT VARIOUS MARKET RATES

"Market Rate" 10%

Contract Int. Rate	Number of Months											
	24	30	36	48	60	72	84	96	120	144	180	240
12%	1,020	1,025	1,029	1,038	1,047	1,055	1,063	1,071	1,086	1,099	1,117	1,141
11%	1,010	1,012	1,015	1,019	1,023	1,027	1,031	1,035	1,042	1,049	1,058	1,070
10%	1,000	1,000	1,000	1,000	1,000	1,000	1,000	1,000	1,000	1,000	1,000	1,000
9%	990	988	986	981	977	973	969	965	959	952	944	932
8%	980	976	971	963	954	946	939	932	918	906	889	867
7%	970	964	957	944	932	920	909	898	879	861	836	803
6%	960	952	943	926	910	895	880	866	840	817	785	742
5%	951	940	929	908	888	869	851	834	803	774	736	684

"Market Rate" 11%

Contract Int. Rate	Number of Months											
	24	30	36	48	60	72	84	96	120	144	180	240
12%	1,010	1,012	1,015	1,019	1,023	1,027	1,031	1,035	1,042	1,048	1,056	1,067
11%	1,000	1,000	1,000	1,000	1,000	1,000	1,000	1,000	1,000	1,000	1,000	1,000
10%	990	988	986	981	977	973	970	966	959	953	945	935
9%	980	976	971	963	955	947	940	933	920	908	892	872
8%	970	964	957	945	933	921	910	900	881	864	841	810
7%	961	952	943	927	911	896	881	868	843	820	791	751
6%	951	940	929	909	889	871	853	837	806	778	742	694
5%	941	928	915	891	868	846	825	806	770	738	696	639

"Market Rate" 12%

Contract Int. Rate	Number of Months											
	24	30	36	48	60	72	84	96	120	144	180	240
12%	1,000	1,000	1,000	1,000	1,000	1,000	1,000	1,000	1,000	1,000	1,000	1,000
11%	990	988	986	981	977	974	970	967	960	954	947	937
10%	980	976	971	963	955	948	940	934	921	910	895	876
9%	970	964	957	945	933	922	911	901	883	866	845	817
8%	961	952	943	927	912	897	883	870	846	824	796	760
7%	951	940	930	909	890	872	855	839	809	783	749	704
6%	942	929	916	892	869	848	828	809	774	743	703	651
5%	932	917	902	875	848	824	801	779	739	704	659	599

Exhibit 19–3 (continued)

PRESENT VALUE OF A $1,000 CONTRACT
AT VARIOUS MARKET RATES

Contract Int. Rate	"Market Rate" 13% Number of Months											
	24	30	36	48	60	72	84	96	120	144	180	240
12%	990	988	986	982	978	974	970	967	961	955	949	940
11%	980	976	972	963	956	948	941	935	923	912	898	881
10%	971	964	958	945	934	923	913	903	885	869	849	824
9%	961	952	944	928	912	898	884	872	848	828	802	768
8%	951	941	930	910	891	873	857	841	813	787	755	714
7%	942	929	916	893	870	849	830	811	778	748	710	662
6%	932	917	903	875	850	826	803	782	744	710	667	612
5%	923	906	890	858	829	802	777	753	710	673	625	563

Contract Int. Rate	"Market Rate" 14% Number of Months											
	24	30	36	48	60	72	84	96	120	144	180	240
12%	980	976	972	964	956	949	942	936	924	914	901	885
11%	971	964	958	946	934	924	914	904	887	872	853	830
10%	961	952	944	928	913	899	886	874	851	832	807	776
9%	952	941	930	911	892	875	859	843	816	792	762	724
8%	942	929	917	893	871	851	832	814	781	753	718	673
7%	933	918	903	876	851	827	805	785	748	716	675	623
6%	923	906	890	859	831	804	780	756	715	679	634	576
5%	914	895	877	843	811	782	754	729	683	644	594	531

Contract Int. Rate	"Market Rate" 15% Number of Months											
	24	30	36	48	60	72	84	96	120	144	180	240
12%	971	964	958	946	935	925	915	906	889	875	858	836
11%	961	953	944	929	914	900	887	875	854	835	812	784
10%	952	941	931	911	893	876	860	846	819	796	768	733
9%	942	930	917	894	873	852	834	816	785	758	725	683
8%	933	918	904	877	852	829	808	788	752	721	683	635
7%	923	907	891	860	832	806	782	760	720	685	642	589
6%	914	895	878	844	813	784	757	732	688	650	603	544
5%	905	884	865	827	793	762	732	705	657	616	565	501

Exhibit 19–3 (concluded)

PRESENT VALUE OF A $1,000 CONTRACT
AT VARIOUS MARKET RATES

"Market Rate" 16%

| Contract Int. Rate | \
Number of Months | | | | | | | | | | |
| --- | --- | --- | --- | --- | --- | --- | --- | --- | --- | --- | --- |
| | 24 | 30 | 36 | 48 | 60 | 72 | 84 | 96 | 120 | 144 | 180 | 240 |
| 12% | 961 | 953 | 945 | 929 | 915 | 901 | 889 | 877 | 856 | 839 | 817 | 791 |
| 11% | 952 | 941 | 931 | 912 | 894 | 877 | 862 | 848 | 822 | 801 | 774 | 742 |
| 10% | 942 | 930 | 918 | 895 | 874 | 854 | 836 | 819 | 789 | 763 | 732 | 694 |
| 9% | 933 | 919 | 905 | 878 | 854 | 831 | 810 | 791 | 756 | 727 | 691 | 647 |
| 8% | 924 | 907 | 891 | 861 | 834 | 808 | 785 | 763 | 724 | 691 | 651 | 601 |
| 7% | 914 | 896 | 878 | 845 | 814 | 786 | 760 | 736 | 693 | 657 | 612 | 557 |
| 6% | 905 | 885 | 865 | 829 | 795 | 764 | 736 | 709 | 663 | 623 | 575 | 515 |
| 5% | 896 | 874 | 852 | 813 | 776 | 742 | 712 | 683 | 633 | 591 | 538 | 474 |

"Market Rate" 17%

Contract Int. Rate	Number of Months											
	24	30	36	48	60	72	84	96	120	144	180	240
12%	952	942	932	913	895	879	864	850	826	805	780	751
11%	943	930	918	896	875	856	838	822	793	768	739	704
10%	933	919	905	879	855	833	812	794	760	732	698	658
9%	924	908	892	862	835	810	787	766	729	697	659	613
8%	915	896	879	846	816	788	763	739	698	663	621	570
7%	906	885	866	830	797	766	739	713	668	630	584	529
6%	896	874	853	814	778	745	715	687	639	598	548	488
5%	887	863	841	798	759	724	692	662	610	567	514	450

"Market Rate" 18%

Contract Int. Rate	Number of Months											
	24	30	36	48	60	72	84	96	120	144	180	240
12%	943	931	919	896	876	857	840	824	796	773	745	713
11%	934	919	906	880	856	835	815	796	764	738	706	669
10%	924	908	893	863	837	812	790	769	733	703	667	625
9%	915	897	880	847	817	790	765	743	703	670	630	583
8%	906	886	867	831	798	769	742	717	673	637	593	542
7%	897	875	854	815	780	748	718	691	644	605	558	502
6%	888	864	841	799	761	727	695	666	616	574	524	464
5%	879	853	829	784	743	706	672	642	589	544	491	428

Summary

A very high percentage of small businesses and professional practices are sold on some terms other than all cash. The terms on the noncash portion of the price most commonly take one or both of two forms: (1) a fixed-price promissory note, usually with interest at a rate below an arm's-length market rate of interest for a promissory note of comparable risk, and/or (2) a variable price based on certain contingencies, most often retention of revenues from existing clients.

Data on such transactions for comparative companies are often used for guidance in negotiating a price for a transaction in a similar company. This is valid if the terms on the subject company transaction are similar to the terms on the guideline company transactions.

However, if transactions on noncash terms are to be used as comparative data for guidance in estimating a cash-equivalent fair market value for a subject company, the price must be adjusted to a cash-equivalent value. This chapter has explained the data to consider and the arithmetic to use to make that adjustment.

Furthermore, if one starts with a cash equivalent value but expects that a transaction is most likely to occur on noncash terms, the chapter has shown how to convert a cash equivalent value to a price on the expected terms.

As the examples have shown, a cash equivalent value can easily be 20 percent to 50 percent less than the face value price under a set of terms favorable to the buyer.

Chapter 20

Making a Sanity Check: Is It Affordable?

As noted in earlier chapters, the large majority of sales of small businesses and professional practices are financed, most often by the seller, sometimes by an outside lender. It is in the interest of both the buyer and the lender (whether the lender is the seller or an outside lender) to make every effort to be sure that the deal is structured so that the debt service (principal and interest payments) can be met. Lack of adequate capital is very high on the list of the most frequent causes of business failure.

One experienced authority discusses the propensity for extended financing terms as follows:

> *Down Payment.* Buyers are worried about how much cash they need to invest. Price resistance goes down as the down payment goes down. Our firm has been able to rapidly sell many businesses with such attractive terms that price becomes a secondary consideration. Of course, a reduced down payment adds risk in the form of other required financing. However, lowering the down payment demand makes the business accessible to more buyers, and many buyers with high aspirations but little cash will pay a premium for the opportunity to get into their own businesses.
>
> Many sellers have reported that they had little trouble selling their businesses for the top price once creative financing and a low down payment requirement were available. I share that experience. Many buyers literally ignore price itself once they're satisfied that they can raise the few dollars to buy the business, and that the business can pay off the loans.[1]

Cash Available for Debt Service

Of course, the key phrase in the quotation above is "satisfied . . . that the business can pay off the loans." In most cases, the source of debt repayment will be cash generated by the business or practice. To measure the ability to cover the debt service, we need a variable not previously defined or discussed in the book, which is referred to as *cash available for debt service.* This phrase is just basic and descriptive, rather than being a term with very specific meaning that is universally accepted in the annals of finance and appraisal, so we can be somewhat creative in how we define it. Determining the amount of cash available for debt service is a matter of using practical common sense, in light of the basic facts of each case.

As a generalized framework to measure affordability, we would suggest defining the cash available for debt service as follows. It is income:

1. Before interest and principal payments (since we are measuring the coverage of those items).
2. Before depreciation and amortization (or other noncash charges).
3. After reasonable compensation for services of owner.
4. After capital expenditures, including both replacements and additions.
5. After federal and state income taxes (based on taxable income per IRS code).

---

[1]Arnold S. Goldstein, *The Complete Guide to Buying and Selling a Business* (New York: New American Library, 1984), p. 102.

The above list assumes that the business or practice itself will be the source of the funds to cover each item on the list. To the extent that funds are available from other sources for one or more of the requirements, the list may be modified.

Amount of Coverage Needed

The amount of coverage of the debt service that should be required depends largely on the degree of risk in the expected cash flow. To the extent that the expected cash flow is highly uncertain or volatile from year to year, the amount of coverage in an average year should be higher.

Paul Baron, a veteran business broker, suggests that debt service should not be more than 35 to 50 percent of after-tax cash flow. (He defines after-tax cash flow in approximately the same way that we have defined cash available for debt service, except that Baron does not deduct from cash flow additions to working capital and capital expenditures for additions.)[2]

Walter Jurek advocates allocating 50 percent of the net cash flow to the servicing of the acquisition debt:

> The entire income stream that is available should not be used for debt service. Any company needs a cushion between its debt service retirement schedule and its net available income for debt service. Normally, only 50 percent of the net available cash flow after taxes and reasonable capital expenditures should be used for debt service or debt retirement.[3]

Possible Adjustments to the Contract

If the terms being considered on the first pass do not seem affordable by a comfortable margin, several adjustments to the contemplated terms may be considered. The length of the contract may be extended; the payments may be varied (perhaps interest only for a time, or an increasing payment schedule, if the cash available is expected to be low at first but increasing); some payments may be contingent on some level of cash flow; or there may be a longer-term amortization with a balloon payment.

Contracts with contingencies in the payment schedule are not unusual for businesses that are known to be cyclical. The principal portion of the payment, or even the entire principal and interest payment, may be suspended for a year if cash flow is negative, extending the length of the contract if that occurs. There may be a range of minimum and maximum payments per year depending on the amount of available cash flow.

A 10-year amortization with a 5-year balloon means that the periodic

---

[2]Paul B. Baron, *When You Buy or Sell a Company,* rev. ed. (Meriden, Conn.: The Center for Business Information, Inc., 1986).

[3]Walter Jurek, *How to Determine the Value of a Business* (Stow, Oh.: Quality Service, Inc., 1977), p. 29.

payments are of a principal and interest amount that would pay off the contract in 10 years, but at the end of the fifth year the remaining contract balance becomes payable all at once. Longer-term amortizations with balloon payments are sometimes used, but we always wonder where the money is going to come from for the balloon payment.

If reasonable alternatives have been considered and do not seem affordable, then, just possibly, in spite of all the valiant valuation exercises done (supposedly in accordance with the previous chapters), the price is simply too high. Back to the drawing board.

Protective Covenants

From the viewpoint of a lender or a seller selling on a contract, it is important to have covenants in the contract that will protect the ability of the business or practice to generate adequate cash flow to cover the debt service. Such covenants usually restrict such items as owner's compensation, capital expenditures, any investments outside of the normal course of the business, and assumption of other indebtedness.

An Example

Exhibit 20–1 uses the Mary's Machinery and Equipment case, as in prior chapters.

Let's begin with an estimated value of $575,000 for Mary's common stock. Mary requires a $200,000 down payment and is willing to extend to the buyer a five-year contract to cover the balance of $375,000 at 12 percent interest. There would be equal annual payments of principal and interest.

The first step in analyzing whether the company can cover this debt service is to calculate the cash available for debt service. The company's pretax income under the new owner, Barney Backhoe, is estimated at $100,000. To calculate the company's taxes, we need to take into consideration that Mary's will receive a tax savings from the increased interest expense if the $375,000 is financed on a contract. The first year's interest expense on the contract will be $45,000 (.12 × $375,000 = $45,000), which will reduce Mary's taxable income to $55,000 ($100,000 − $45,000 = $55,000). Statutory federal taxes on this amount would be $9,750, resulting in a net income of $45,250.

Cash available for debt service equals net income before depreciation and interest related to the contract. That is computed as follows:

Net income	$45,250
Depreciation	33,000
Interest	45,000
Cash available for debt	$123,250

The next step is to determine the debt service requirements that this contract creates. A five-year contract for $375,000 bearing 12

Exhibit 20–1

MARY'S MACHINERY & EQUIPMENT, INC.
ANALYSIS OF DEBT SERVICE

Affordability of debt service related to the purchase of a company increases with either a decreased interest rate or increased term of the loan.

Length of Contract (Years)	5	5	10
Equity Value	$575,000	$575,000	$575,000
Down Payment	200,000	200,000	200,000
Debt	375,000	375,000	375,000
Interest Rate	12.0%	6.0%	12.0%
Projected Pretax Income	100,000	100,000	100,000
Interest Expense Associated with Additional Debt	45,000	22,500	45,000
Adjusted Pretax Income	55,000	77,500	55,000
Statutory Taxes	9,750	13,739	9,750
Net Income	45,250	63,761	45,250
Plus:			
Depreciation	33,000	33,000	33,000
Interest Expense	45,000	22,500	45,000
Cash Available For Debt Service	123,250	119,261	123,250
Debt Service	104,029	89,024	66,369
Debt Service Coverage	1.18 x	1.34 x	1.86 x

percent interest results in annual principal and interest payments of $104,029.

Therefore, the anticipated cash available for debt is less than 1.2 times the projected debt service ($123,250 ÷ $104,029 = 1.18). This level of available cash relative to the requirement for debt service is very low, and a prospective buyer would probably not want to enter into the agreement under these terms. The question about the buyer's ability to pay would make the contract risky from the seller's viewpoint as well.

It is unlikely that Mary will accept less than the $575,000 for her company, since she is not in a real rush to sell. However, if she is going to realize that price, she will probably have to extend more favorable terms. If she extends the length of the contract to 10 years, the annual debt service becomes $66,369. Under this scenario, the cash available to service the debt is almost twice the amount of the debt ($123,250 ÷ $66,369 = 1.86), a much more comfortable level and probably something the buyer could live with. Another alternative, if Mary wanted to keep the contract length to five years, would be to accept a lower interest rate on the debt. Also, since earnings are expected to go up by about 5 percent a year, contract payments could escalate by a similar percentage.

What this example points out is that, while a cash value of $575,000 was indicated for the common stock of Mary's, based on our valuation approaches, the sanity check shows that the company could just barely afford the debt service relating to the purchase of the company if the terms are $200,000 down with the balance payable over 5 years at 12 percent interest. The purchase of the company becomes more affordable if the contract is extended for 10 years or if a lower interest rate is charged. Therefore, the sanity check indicated that a cash equivalent price of $575,000 may be on the high side when affordability is taken into consideration, and the debt service of the company to either the seller or the bank will be a strain unless the terms are spread out over 10 years or a low interest rate is accepted.

The foregoing example was based on normalized earnings, assuming no significant fluctuations from year to year. If cash available for debt service is likely to fluctuate significantly over the years, it would be desirable to make a forecast for several years, perhaps for the full length of the contract.

Summary

One of the last steps in the valuation process should be a "sanity check." By this we mean looking at the suggested price and terms on the basis of "Is it reasonable?" and "Is it affordable?"

"Affordable" in this sense addresses the questions "How long will it take to pay it off?" and "How much cushion is there between expected cash flow and required debt service (principal and interest payments) in case things don't go as well as planned?"

If the review of the proposed deal elicits discomfort on the basis of either reasonableness or affordableness, then the valuation conclusion may be suspect and should be reviewed.

Chapter 21

Common Errors

It is better to know that we do not know than to know not that we know not.

Old Wise Man's Saying

This is a long chapter. It is long because so many different people frequently perpetrate so many common errors in their attempts to determine values of small businesses and professional practices.

We hope that this chapter will assist those who are not professional appraisers to be able to make a reasonably critical review of someone else's appraisal of a business or practice, and to be able to correct, or at least call attention to, some of the errors that seem to recur most frequently. We also hope that the chapter will help the novice appraiser to avoid such pitfalls. Possibly, it will even help one or two veteran but misguided appraisers to mend a few of their wayward ways.

Failure to Clearly Identify and/or Adhere to the Applicable Standard of Value

We cannot count the times that we have seen business appraisals go awry for failure to follow the appropriate standard of value. Be sure that the standard of value is defined at the beginning of the assignment (in the engagement letter) and again at the beginning of the written report. For complete discussion, please refer to Chapter 3.

Half the problems seem to arise from failure to correctly or completely specify the standard of value to begin with. The other half seem to come from not adhering to it in the valuation work product even after it has been defined.

This is especially important in litigation (or potential litigation) situations, where the standard of value is frequently mandated by statute, case precedent, or other binding requirements. Examples include divorce valuation, damage cases, tax cases, dissent or dissolution cases, and valuations pursuant to binding wording found in buy-sell or arbitration agreements. Many times we have seen entire appraisals that were entirely useless because they ignored or misinterpreted the governing legal context.

Rigid Categorization of Business Valuation Methods

Watch out when you hear, "There are currently five accepted methods for valuing a business," or "Three methods exist for valuing a small business," and so on. There is no finite number of commonly accepted methods for valuing small businesses and professional practices. One author references 32 valuation methods.[1]

---

[1]Thomas J. Martin and Mark Gustafson, *Valuing Your Business* (New York: Holt, Rinehart & Winston, 1980), p. 23.

There are three sources from which a business or practice can generate money for its owners: (1) earnings, (2) sales of assets, and (3) sale of the business or practice. All valuation methods attempt to measure one or a combination of these three factors, directly or indirectly, and translate them into a present value. The various methods by which different appraisers approach the problem are not discrete, but rather variations of each other, with considerable overlap.

In our experience, viewing the problem of estimating value in terms of a finite number of specific methods tends to go hand in hand with implementing each of the methods by using some specific formula; more often than not, the formula is applied without the benefit of experienced judgment as to whether or not it conforms to the economic realities of the situation. Estimating the value of a business or professional practice is much more than a mechanical exercise— it requires large doses of informed judgment, distilled out of years of experience and extensive continuing education on developments in the field of business and practice valuation.

Reliance on Real Estate Appraisal Methods

As discussed more extensively in Chapter 6, the traditional world of real estate appraisal has categorized the problem of valuation into three approaches: (1) the cost approach, (2) the market approach, and (3) the income approach. Elements of these approaches are found in generally accepted business appraisal practices. However, some people with a real estate background tend to try to force business appraisal into those three categories as they are applied to real estate, without a full understanding of how the dynamics and personal characteristics of operating businesses and professional practices differentiate such entities from inanimate parcels of real estate.

Chapter 5 deals with differences between valuation of large businesses (some of which may be publicly traded) and valuation of small businesses and professional practices. Chapter 6 deals with differences between appraising real estate and appraising small businesses and professional practices. Between the two, it is our opinion that small businesses and professional practices, with their dynamics of people and operations, have more in common from a valuation viewpoint with their larger brethren than with inanimate real estate. We believe that a person schooled in techniques of security analysis, but without schooling in real estate, can adapt more adequately to the demands of small business and professional practice appraisal than can a real estate appraiser without such schooling in security analysis.

Reliance on Rules of Thumb

The following are a few representative quotes from business and professional practice brokers and appraisers on the subject of rules of thumb:

There seem to be norms for the worth of every imaginable business. My advice: Ignore them. Buying a business is too important for Kentucky windage.[2]

Rules of thumb are dumb . . . greatly oversimplified . . . highly unreliable.[3] They are dangerous and full of pitfalls.[4]

Simplicity is often achieved at the considerable loss of realism.[5]

Over the past five years inflation has affected the pricing of business and thrown traditional "rule of thumb" methods out of whack.[6]

Perhaps the best quote on this topic, especially considering the source, is the following:

> The professional appraiser is always seeking market information as a guide to forming a proper value conclusion. The professional knows not to rely on formulas.[7]

The above quote is from veteran appraiser and writer Glenn Desmond in the *Handbook of Small Business Valuation Formulas.* He goes on to say, "This text should be used only as a guide to rule-of-thumb formulas, which may be considered along with other valuation methods."[8] We can not recount the number of times we've heard formulas from Desmond's *Handbook* quoted as valuation gospel without any reference to these page 1 quotes!

Some of the problems with rules of thumb were discussed in the section on "Problems with Gross Revenue Multipliers," in Chapter 16. Other problems are discussed in the accompanying article (Exhibit 21–1) by Jay Fishman, who, as of this writing, is an active business appraiser and chairman of the American Society of Appraisers Business Valuation Committee.

For industries in which a valuation rule of thumb is widely recognized, the appraiser should consider it, but certainly not accept it at face value.

The "Assets Plus . . ." Method

Some business brokers and others seem to think that every business and practice in existence is worth at least its net tangible asset value (defined as replacement cost new, less depreciation, as discussed in Chapter 7), plus some amount for goodwill and/or whatever other intangible factors may be presumed to exist.

That simply is not always true. Many businesses cannot even generate enough earnings to justify their purchase at net tangible asset value.

---

[2]Thomas P. Murphy, "What Price Independence?" *Forbes,* September 27, 1982, p. 209. Murphy is the head of a venture capital firm.

[3]Glen Cooper, "How Much Is Your Business Worth?" *In Business,* September–October 1984, p. 50.

[4]Alan Johnson, "Figuring the Worth of a Firm," *Computer Systems News,* February 13, 1984, p. 24.

[5]Harry Weber, "An Evaluation of Business Valuation Techniques," *ASA Valuation,* November 1982, p. 104.

[6]*The Business Broker,* February 1985, p. 1.

[7]Glenn Desmond and John Marcello, *Handbook of Small Business Valuation Formulas,* 2nd ed. (Los Angeles: Valuation Press, 1988), p. 1.

[8]Ibid.

Exhibit 21-1

THE PROBLEM WITH RULES OF THUMB
IN THE VALUATION OF CLOSELY-HELD ENTITIES

by Jay E. Fishman, ASA*

Recently we completed the valuation of a pharmacy in a matrimonial matter. Our search for comparable transactions yielded insufficient information to make a direct Market Data Approach useable. Accordingly, we relied on the other traditional methods used in the valuation of closely held businesses, including a Capitalization of Income Approach. Our client reviewed the report and quickly pointed out that we failed to consider the industry rule of thumb for the valuation of pharmacies, as discussed in various pharmacy journals and trade publications. Application of that formula would have produced a negative value for the common stock of the pharmacy and was not used by our client when he purchased the pharmacy three years before. The pharmacist thought that the negative value aspect was perfectly acceptable for matrimonial purposes, but showed great reluctance to use the formula to sell his store.

The pharmacy episode was followed by our involvement in a court case relating to the valuation of a new car dealership. In this matter, the wife's expert determined goodwill grounded on a so-called industry practice which estimated goodwill based on $1,500 for new cars sold on an annual basis. Cross-examination revealed that the so-called industry practice was not derived from actual sales of automobile dealerships, but was based on yet another expert's verbal representation to this witness. Interestingly, the subject new car dealership had an average gross profit margin on the sale of new cars of approximately $500 per car.

The search for a "quick-fix" to the complex problems surrounding the valuation of a closely held enterprise has led many to rely on rules of thumb or industry formulas. The above examples illustrate the enormous potential for abuse in applying these standards to the valuation of a closely held entity.

What are the rules of thumb? Rules of thumb or industry formulas are supposedly market derived units of comparison. The multiple or percentage contained in the formula is an expression of the relationship between gross purchase price and some indicator of the operating results of an enterprise. Accordingly, the sale of a casualty insurance brokerage concern is discussed in terms of cents per retained gallon and the sale of a medical practice is referred to in terms of a multiple or percentage of the gross revenue or of the net disposable income.

The use of a rule of thumb in the valuation of a closely held entity is actually a variation of the Market Comparison Approach. The Market Comparison Approach attempts to establish value via direct comparison with exchanges of similar assets in the marketplace. The use of direct Market Comparison is contingent on the availability of sales involving reasonably comparable businesses in a free and active marketplace. Adjustments for differences between the acquired businesses and the subject entity are then calculated. Examples of adjustments include differences in market share, profitability, capital structure and management depth. These adjustments result in the production of a multiple, usually related to earnings, cash flow or equity which is applied to the subject entity resulting in an expression of value.

Since rules of thumb or industry formulas are a variation of the direct Market Comparison Approach, certain minimum criteria must exist prior to their use in the valuation process. These criteria include the following:
- The single multiple or percentage must be derived from an adequate information base.
- The expert must understand the terms and conditions of each transaction in the information base.
- The transactions should involve reasonably similar businesses.
- Adjustments should be made for differences between the acquired companies and the entity under appraisement.

Problems with industry formulas. We have found that most industry formulas or rules of thumb ar not derived from actual transactions in the marketplace. Industry formulas are commonly derived from textbooks, trade publications, verbal representations or other similar sources of information. Clearly, these sources of information will not provide the expert with sufficient information to render a meaningful opinion of value for the enterprise using these formulas. There are at least three fundamental problems associated with the industry formula "quick fix" approach. All of these fundamental problems are a result of their failure to meet the above minimum criteria.

First, the lack of knowledge concerning the actual transactions that comprise the industry formulas will lead to confusion concerning the property acquired by a buyer during a particular transaction. Buyers will commonly purchase the assets or the equity of an entity. Since the objective of an appraisal for matrimonial purposes is usually

Exhibit 21–1 (concluded)

the common stock or equity portion of an enterprise, reliance on an industry formula that produces a value for the assets of an entity can fundamentally misstate the value of the equity for the subject firm.

Second, the lack of an adequate data base can lead to considerable confusion over the actual purchase price paid for a comparable entity. An opinion of Market Value presumes a 100 percent cash price at the valuation date. Without knowledge of the actual transactions underlying a given group of comparables, the experts would be unable to determine the real purchase price paid for the comparable enterprises.

For example, a gross price of $100,000 could be listed as the purchase price for a comparable entity, but this purchase price could be paid over ten years with no interest. This would further reduce the Market Value paid by the buyer due to the time value of money. If the expert is unaware of the terms of the transaction, he or she would be unable to make such a time value of money adjustment. Therefore, the gross consideration would be confused with a 100 percent cash price at the valuation date and result in a distortion in the opinion of value using the industry formula.

Alternatively, the purchase price could be augmented by a covenant not to compete given to the seller over a period of years. This covenant not to compete could actually be part of the purchase price paid for the business, but was structured in this way for tax purposes. Again, without knowledge of the actual terms of the transaction, a misstatement of value relying on formulas derived from these types of transactions would occur.

Thirdly, most industry formulas in textbooks, trade publications and other sources presume a typical or average entity. Lacking knowledge of actual transactions results in distortions due to differences in profitability, capital structure, management and other important considerations inherent in what a buyer would offer for a business entity. The insufficient information base would result in the expert's inability to make these types of adjustments. The insufficient information base would make it impossible to gauge whether the subject enterprise is typical or atypical, and accordingly, would command a price superior or inferior to the typical multiple displayed in the industry formula.

For example, an accounting firm which could be valued on a one times gross basis would have the same value whether it was profitable or unprofitable. The same would apply as to whether it had a long term lease or short term lease, whether the gross revenue was generated by 100 small clients or 3 large clients. This hypothetical situation indicates the flaws inherent in using industry formulas without sufficient information.

Summary. There are no "quick fixes" to the valuation of closely held entities. It is essential to remember that industry formulas or rules of thumb are commonly not market derived representations of actual transactions. Since most industry formulas or rules of thumb are derived from textbooks, trade publications, verbal representations, or other similar sources of information, they are poor substitutes for the Direct Market Comparison Approach.

* Mr. Fishman is President of Financial Research, Inc. in Ardmore, Pennsylvania.

SOURCE: *FAIR$HARE: The Matrimonial Law Monthly*, Vol. 4, No. 12 (December 1984), p. 13. Reprinted with permission.

If the earning power justifies a price less than the adjusted net tangible asset value but more than the liquidation value, it is rational to expect the value determined by the earning power to predominate. If the value on a capitalized earnings basis is less than liquidation value, it would seem that the rational choice is to liquidate.

Some owners who wish to sell cannot accept the notion that the economic value of the entity could be less than the depreciated replacement cost of its assets. The fact is, however, that there are many such businesses that would never be worth replacing if they did not already exist. They are worth only their economic value based on what they can earn, not what it would cost to replace a business that nobody would choose to replace in its existing form and location.

Most owners who delude themselves into overvaluing their businesses on the basis of an asset value approach without regard to earning power eventually just go quietly out of business, some via bankruptcy.

Indiscriminate Use of Price/Earnings Multiples

Valuation by the good old price/earnings (P/E) multiple has broad appeal. It seems so natural because everyone has heard of it and it is apparently so simple. Just take the earnings, apply a multiplier, and you have a value. P/E multiples for thousands of publicly traded stocks are published daily. By simply picking a P/E multiple and deciding what level of earnings for the subject company to apply it to, you can come up with almost any value you might like. What could be better? It is a valuation method that is simple, widely used, and easily manipulated (albeit more frequently out of ignorance than malice aforethought), and it seems to support almost any desired answer.

One must understand the following characteristics of publicly traded stocks in order to use their P/E multiples for guidance in valuing closely held businesses and professional practices:

1. The publicly traded market prices of the stock represent minority interests, not controlling interests.
2. The stocks are highly liquid—they can almost always be sold in a matter of minutes with cash delivered to the seller within a week.
3. The prices are for stock in a corporation and do not represent a direct purchase of any combination of assets.
4. The P/E multiples apply to earnings after depreciation and amortization, after interest on all short-term and long-term debt, after compensation to all employees in the business, including stockholder/employees, and after all federal and state corporate income taxes.
5. The earnings are from audited statements prepared in accordance with generally accepted accounting principles (GAAP).
6. The price in the P/E multiple usually is the price of the last transaction on the day before the quotation was published.
7. The earnings in the P/E multiple are what are called "latest 12 months' trailing earnings," that is, the earnings for the 12 months ending with the latest quarter for which the company has reported earnings.

Most common errors in the use of P/E multiples stem from failure to recognize one or a combination of the above seven characteristics of public company P/E multiples.

Failure to Identify What One Gets for the Price

For the price that becomes the numerator in the P/E multiple, the buyer receives a share of stock representing a proportionate equity interest in a total corporate enterprise; it is an indirect, residual, proportionate interest in all assets, subject to all liabilities, and with no direct claim on any assets. A common error is to use such a P/E multiple to price an asset purchase of a private business or practice without recognizing the fact that the combination of assets actually being transferred may be quite different from the stock being bought for the price in the P/E multiple.

Applying P/E Multiples to Earnings that Are Not Comparable

Following are a few examples of applying public company P/E multiples to private company earnings that are not comparable:

1. Applying the P/E multiple (based on after-tax earnings) to a private company's pretax earnings.
2. Applying the P/E multiple to a private company's net operating profit (earnings before interest and taxes).
3. Applying the P/E multiple to a private company's operating cash flow (earnings before interest and taxes plus depreciation).
4. Applying the P/E multiple to a private company's seller's discretionary cash (operating cash flow before allowance for compensation to owner).

The potential effects of the four errors above can be illustrated by Exhibit 21–2, which starts with identical income statements and balance sheets for Public Corporation X and Private Corporation Y. Exhibit 21–2 also shows market data for the stock of Public Corporation X and several adjustments to the income statement of Private Corporation Y.

It can readily be seen that the aggregate market value of the outstanding shares of Public Corporation X is $3,600 (300 shares × $12 per share). If one applies the P/E multiple of 6 from Public Company X to the comparable net earnings of Private Company Y, the implied value of Private Company Y's stock is $3,600 (6 × $600 = $3,600). That is a reasonable comparative indication of value before any adjustments for differences in liquidity, for minority or controlling interests, and for any other differences.

However, the following calculations illustrate the potential effects of the four common errors listed above:

1. *P/E applied to pretax earnings:* 6 × $1,000 = $6,000.
2. *P/E applied to net operating profit:* 6 × $1,200 = $7,200.
3. *P/E applied to operating cash flow:* 6 × $1,600 = $9,600.
4. *P/E applied to seller's discretionary cash:* 6 × $2,100 = $12,600.

Nobody could be that far misguided, could he? WAIT! How about combining the above with the "assets plus . . ." syndrome discussed earlier? Suppose the "six times seller's discretionary cash flow" is interpreted to represent only the goodwill or intangible value. As noted on the balance sheets in Exhibit 21–2, the company has a net asset value

Exhibit 21-2

PUBLIC CORPORATION X

Sales	$10,000	
Operating Expenses:		
Salaries	$5,500	
Other Operating Exp.	2,900	
Depreciation	400	
Total Operating Expenses	8,800	
Net Operating Profit (EBIT)	1,200	
Interest Expense	200	
Net Income before Taxes	1,000	
Federal and State Income Taxes	400	
Net Income	600	
Shares Outstanding	300	
Net Income per Share	2	($600 ÷ 300 = $2)
Market Price per Share	12	
Price/Earnings Ratio	6x	($12 ÷ 2 = 6x)
Current Assets	2,000	
Fixed Assets	3,000	
Total Assets	$5,000	
Current Liabilities	$1,000	
Long-Term Liabilities (10%)	2,000	
Stockholders' Equity	2,000	
Total Liabilities & Equity	$5,000	

PRIVATE CORPORATION Y

			"Adjustments"	"Adjusted" Income Statement
Sales		$10,000		$10,000
Operating Expenses:				
Owner's Salary	$500		($500)	
Other Salaries	5,000			
Other Operating Expenses	2,900			
Depreciation	400		(400)	
Total Operating Expenses		8,800		7,900
Net Operating Profit (EBIT)		1,200		
Interest Expense		200	(200)	
Net Income before Taxes		1,000		
Federal and State Income Taxes		400	(400)	
Net Income		600		
"Earnings Available to Owner" or "Seller's Discretionary Cash"				2,100
Current Assets	2,000			
Fixed Assets	3,000			
Total Assets	$5,000			
Current Liabilities	$1,000			
Long-Term Liabilities (10%)	2000			
Owner's Equity	2000			
Total Liabilities & Equity	$5,000			

of $2,000. Adding that to the value derived from number four above would give an indicated value of $14,600!

Applying P/E Multiples When Time Periods Are Not Comparable

We noted that the P/E ratios published in daily newspapers are based on the current stock prices divided by the companies' latest 12 months' actual reported earnings. Using such a P/E multiple, but applying it to any other earnings base for the subject company, can produce significantly misleading results. Following are a few examples of a public company's P/E multiple from one time period being applied to the subject company's earnings for a different time period.

P/E Multiple Applied to a Forecast. Vassar Video, a publicly traded marketer of video cassettes, had 1992 earnings of $4 per share; and early in 1993 the stock traded at $36 per share, for a P/E multiple of 9 ($36 ÷ $4 = 9). Alan Analyst, who has been retained to value the stock of Yale Yuppies, a privately owned company marketing a competitive line of video cassettes, forecasts that Yale will earn $3 per share in 1993. Applying the comparative publicly traded company's P/E of 9 to Alan's forecast of $3 per share for Yale gives Yale stock an indicated value of $27 per share (9 × $3 = $27), on a publicly traded equivalent basis, before adjustments for liquidity and so on.

What Alan overlooked was that analysts following Vassar stock were predicting that Vassar would earn $6 per share in 1993. Therefore, if one divided the current stock price by the forecasted earnings, the P/E multiple so derived would be 6 ($36 ÷ $6 = 6), rather than 9. Applying the P/E multiple of 6 on Vassar's forecasted earnings to Yale's forecasted earnings of $3 would give a publicly traded equivalent indication of value for Yale stock of $18 per share (6 × $3 = $18). Alan erred by applying a P/E multiple based on historical earnings to forecasted earnings in an industry experiencing steep earnings growth at the time.

Failure to Match Historical Time Periods. Alan was called on to value the stock as of December 31, 1992, of Audrey's Automotive Corp., a small subcontractor to the highly cyclical automotive industry. The most comparable publicly traded company was Buddy's, another automotive subcontractor, which earned $5 per share for its latest fiscal year, ended September 30, 1992. Buddy's stock traded at $40 per share on December 31, 1992, so the *Daily Bugle* showed a P/E multiple of 8 ($40 ÷ $5 = 8). Alan applied the P/E multiple of 8 to Audrey's earnings of $4 per share for calendar 1992, resulting in a publicly traded equivalent indicated value of $32 per share for Audrey's stock.

What Alan overlooked was that the fourth quarter of 1992 was a big recovery quarter for the industry, during which Buddy earned $2 per share, compared to a loss of $1 per share in the fourth quarter of 1991 (results not dissimilar to Audrey's). Therefore, for the calendar year 1992, Buddy's stock actually earned $8 per share, and its P/E multiple at December 31, based on 1992 calendar year actual results, was really 5 ($40 ÷ $8 = 5). Applying the P/E multiple of 5, based on Buddy's calendar year 1992 earnings (instead of Buddy's fiscal year earnings), to Audrey's calendar year earnings of $4 would give a publicly traded equivalent indication of value for Audrey's stock of $20 per share (5 × $4 = $20). Alan erred by applying a P/E multiple based on earnings for an earlier time period to actual earnings for a later time period in an industry experiencing a sharp cyclical recovery.

Examples of the application of a P/E multiple derived from earnings of one time period to an earnings base of another time period are endless.

Averaging P/E Multiples over Time. If Alan didn't like the result he got using a current P/E multiple, he had a handy solution: Just use the average of the P/E multiples for the last five years. That way, he applied P/E multiples born out of some set of economic conditions to earnings generated under current economic conditions. About half the time, that variation on the P/E multiple approach helped his case. Alan found that he was only rarely challenged on this anomaly. Alan did a lot of testimony on values of small businesses and professional practices in divorce cases, and he felt that he needed to be flexible in his approaches. Alan was not a member of any professional appraisal association (all of which have codes of ethics).

Using the Reciprocal of the P/E Multiple as the Required Rate of Return

How often we all have heard that the reciprocal of the P/E multiple is the capitalization rate! For example, if a stock is selling at a P/E multiple of 12, the reciprocal would be 8.3 percent (1 ÷ 12 = 0.083). It is not reasonable to expect anyone to buy a stock for an 8.3 percent total rate of return when he could get more on good grade corporate bonds. The reason the P/E is 12 on historical earnings is that the market expects future earnings to be higher.

The capitalization rate applicable to expected earnings is the reciprocal of the public market P/E multiple only in the rare case when the earnings, on which the P/E multiple is based, are expected to be constant over time.[9]

Failure to Make Appropriate Adjustments

Public companies and transactions in publicly traded stocks differ in many ways from exchanges of interests in privately held businesses and professional practices, as discussed in Chapter 5. It is unfortunately common to find uninformed people attempting to practice the art of business appraisal by using P/E multiples to value small businesses and professional practices without taking account of such important factors

---

[9]For a more complete discussion of this relationship, see Chapter 12 in this book and Pratt, *Valuing a Business*, 2nd ed., pp. 94–97.

as size or capital structure of the entity, the degree of liquidity, and the relative proportion of the total company represented by the interest being valued.

Other Errors in Deriving Capitalization Rates

As discussed in Chapters 12 and 14, the capitalization rate must be the one applicable to the earnings base being capitalized, both in terms of definition of the earnings base and the terms of the rate applicable at the particular time. Most errors involve some failure in matching the applicable capitalization rate with the earnings being capitalized.

Using Rates from an Earlier Time Period

The cost of capital varies considerably over time. As the cost of capital goes up, the value of an existing business or practice goes down, and vice versa. Therefore, if capitalization rates used are other than the one actually prevalent at the time of the valuation, the result will be an overstatement or understatement of value.

Incredibly, some people still use the rates given as illustrative at the time in Revenue Ruling 68-609 (Exhibit 15–1) when using the excess earnings method. Since rates have not been that low in many years, the inevitable result of using those rates is overvaluation. This common error is discussed in some detail in the chapter on the excess earnings method.

Applying Rates on "Safe" Investments to Small Business Investments

As discussed in Chapter 12, the biggest variable influencing the capitalization rate is the degree of risk. Many people, however, have never been exposed to this basic economic truth and use some virtually riskless rate, such as the prevailing money market fund or certificate of deposit rate, as a capitalization rate for valuing the expected earnings of small businesses and professional practices. Using too low a capitalization rate results, of course, in an overvaluation.

The rationale for that error is "that is what I can get on my money in an alternative investment." The correct rationale is "what I can get on my money in an alternative investment of equal risk, liquidity, and other characteristics." The lowest rate that is reasonable to use is the rate at which the business or practice can borrow the money. However, the total investment cannot be financed at that low a rate, as discussed in Chapter 12 and the following section.

Failure to Match the Capitalization Rate with the Earnings Base

It is common to find people applying a capitalization rate appropriate to bottom-line net income to other levels of earnings, such as pretax earnings, earnings before depreciation (often called cash flow), earnings before interest, and even earnings before compensation to owners. Most of these errors seem to occur from applying too low a capitalization rate to too high an earnings base, resulting in an overvaluation.

A related common error is applying the company's borrowing rate to the entire equity investment. For example, if the investor thinks he can borrow from the bank for 12 percent, using accounts receivable as collateral, he uses 12 percent as the rate at which to capitalize his entire equity investment. As discussed in Chapter 12, the equity level is where most of the risk is, and an equity investment, therefore, should command a much higher rate of return. The borrowing rate should be used only as a capitalization rate for the percentage of the total investment that actually can be borrowed at that rate.

Mistaking Historical Results for Required Rates of Return

A common fallacy among the uninformed is to use a recent historical average rate of return on equity capital for an industry as a proxy for that industry's cost of equity capital. The following illustrates just how ridiculous that approach really is.

Suppose, for example, a representative group of publicly traded forest products companies earned an average rate of return of 6 percent per year on their equity capital from 1988 through 1992. Does that mean that the appraiser developing an appropriate rate of return by which to discount a projected income stream in 1993 should use 6 percent for the equity portion of the cost of capital? Of course not! To do so would imply that investors in 1993 would be willing to invest in stocks of that industry for a 6 percent expected return, which is far less than the return available on much safer instruments.

All that the 6 percent historical return means is that the forest products industry did not do well in the 1988–1992 period. Adverse factors affected the industry far more than was anticipated

The required rate of return is based on investor expectations. To use historical results as a proxy for expectations can be very misleading, especially when the historical results are for a single industry and for a relatively short time period.

Failure to Estimate a Realistic Normalized Earnings Base

The name of the game is to buy earning power. If that earning power is not correctly assessed, the result will be an overvaluation or undervaluation of the entity.

Reliance on Past Results without Judgment

There is a mind set that can be described as the "mechanistic mentality," for lack of a better expression. It mechanically relies on past data, without considering whether adjustments should be made or whether it is reasonable to expect future results to conform to past results.

Analysis of the earnings patterns of thousands of companies has shown that a pure extrapolation of recent past results more often leads to a poor forecast than to a good forecast. We do not analyze past results for their own sake, but only as a guide to future expectations. The mechanistic mentality may be an excellent tabulator of the past; it fails the test of usefulness for appraisal purposes, however, because it lacks the essential perspective to judge how representative past results are of reasonable future expectations.

Failure to Recognize Any Depreciation

It is common simply to add back all depreciation to get a cash earnings figure, because depreciation is an accounting charge not requiring any cash outlay. Except in the unusual occasion when the property is not wearing out or growing obsolete at all, this practice overstates the true earnings. As discussed in Chapter 8, the correct procedure is to adjust the depreciation charge to an amount that genuinely estimates the degree of wear and tear and/or obsolescence, or else make a separate deduction for the cash outlays that will be required for the average amount of replacements necessary to maintain the income stream. Most business valuation professionals currently favor the latter method, which is one of the steps leading to net free cash flow as the measure of earning power to be discounted or capitalized.

Not Allowing Compensation to Owner/Operator

Another common practice is to add back to the earnings all compensation to the owner(s), which results in a figure often called owner's discretionary cash, or some such appellation. The more correct thinking is that the cash really isn't discretionary until the owner has at least enough to live on, if it is assumed that he will work full-time in the business or practice. As discussed in Chapter 8, the preferred procedure is to consider the value of the owner's services (how much it would cost to hire a comparable worker) as a normal expense of the business in arriving at the earnings base to capitalize.

Any amount that a buyer pays for so-called earnings, which actually includes his own reasonable compensation for his services, can be thought of as an employment fee. There is nothing wrong with a person buying himself a job, as long as he recognizes that that is what he is doing.

Failure to Consider the Full Cost of the Purchase

All too often, a prospective buyer capitalizes the alleged earning power to decide what to offer the seller, only to find that additional investment will be required in order to achieve that earning power. Any additional investment needed to get the earnings should be deducted from the total capitalized earning power value in determining how much should be paid for whatever is being purchased.

Working Capital Requirements

The need for additional investment for working capital frequently is overlooked. Analysis of working capital requirements is covered in Chapter 11.

Deferred Maintenance

Property, leasehold improvements, and equipment should be inspected to determine how well they have been kept up and whether additional investment is needed to bring them up to standards. If so, that amount should be deducted from the purchase price.

Other Investment Needed

It would be an error in valuation to fail to deduct the cost of any investment needed to maintain the earnings stream. Such items could include the cost of relocation, the cost of replacing personnel lost in the transition, the cost of meeting various governmental compliance requirements, and a host of other things. Failure to foresee and adjust the valuation for such expenditures is an extremely common error.

Assuming that the Buyer Will Pay for the Now and the Hereafter

The seller would like to be paid today for what the business could be worth in five years, if a buyer brings in additional capital, manages well, and is very lucky. Some owners seriously entertain that pipe dream.

The buyer, of course, does not see it that way. He wants to pay only for ongoing earnings that the business has already proved it can produce with a high degree of certainty.

With respect to the two positions above, the real world leans much more toward the buyer's perspective than the seller's. So do the divorce courts. Value is based largely on what is there now, as opposed to what might be there sometime. Would-be sellers are misled when they think they should be paid now what the business may be worth after the buyer brings his own magic show to the party.

However, note that in almost every newspaper classified section in the country, the relevant classification does not read "Businesses for Sale," but "Business Opportunities." A genuine opportunity should be worth something—certainly more to one buyer than another, depending on how good the buyer perceives the opportunity to be.

Emphasis of Items Not in Proportion to Their Relative Importance

The most common example of this error is probably the emphasis often accorded to developing the earnings base and the capitalization rates in a capitalization of earnings approach. The two variables are more or less equally critical to a value conclusion using that approach. Yet many reports devote 20 pages to painstakingly developing the earnings base to be capitalized and then cavalierly capitalize that earnings base at a capitalization rate supported only by one or two flimsy sentences. The reader should evaluate the report in light of whether the factors that really matter in reaching the final conclusion are indeed given their due consideration.

Inadequate Documentation

Every number should be justified, not "pulled out of the air." To the extent possible, numbers should be based on the most thorough empirical data practically available. The data should be referenced in a manner such that the reader can look it up and check it should he so desire. It should be laid out in the report so that it is completely clear to the reader what data were used and exactly how the computations based on the data led to each step of the result.

To the extent that the appraiser is forced to rely on judgment in the absence of adequate empirical data, the lack of available market data for the point at hand should be noted. Then the appraiser should describe in reasonable detail the reasons and analysis that led to the judgmental conclusion for which supporting empirical data were not available.

Summary

Most business and professional practice appraisals that miss the mark do so for one or a combination of the following reasons:

- Failure to adequately identify and/or follow the applicable standard of value.
- Using methods and procedures not widely accepted in the professional appraisal community and/or the courts holding jurisdiction.
- Internal inconsistencies.
- Conclusions not supported by clear, rational, and convincing analysis.
- Lack of adequate empirical data.
- Lack of adequate documentation (either in the report or in supporting work papers).

Hopefully, this chapter will be useful to both the appraiser and the user of the appraisal to evaluate the work product and identify and correct common pitfalls.

Chapter 22

A Sample Case: JIT Insurance Company

by Kathryn Daly

JIT Insurance Company (JIT) is a case contrived to illustrate the application of many of the principles and procedures discussed in this book for use in valuing a small business. The hypothetical company is not intended to be patterned after any real-world company, and the reader should not be concerned with whether any of the assumptions bear resemblance to the reader's perception of reality in the insurance agency industry. In this chapter, we describe JIT's business, its operations, and its financial condition. In the next chapter, we illustrate by example the application of a variety of valuation methods used in arriving at the value of the business.

Background of JIT Insurance Company

JIT Insurance Company is an independent general insurance agency in Miami, Florida. The family incorporated the insurance operations in 1925 in the state of Florida. JIT, always owned and operated by family members, has two offices located in Miami and Coral Gables. The company's current owners, Richard and Helen Smythe, inherited the company when their father died in 1968. Both wish to retire, and, neither having children of their own, they have decided to sell the insurance agency. They have asked us to express an opinion as to the fair market value of 100 percent of the common stock of JIT Insurance Company as of December 31, 1991. On a field visit to JIT and through interviews with Mr. and Ms. Smythe, the following information has been gathered.

Economic Data

The Florida economy has traditionally grown more rapidly than the nation as a whole. While the U.S. economy has slowed since 1987 with an employment growth of approximately 1 percent in 1991, the Florida employment growth, at nearly 2 percent, is double the national rate. A diversifying economy, population growth, and the significant tourism industry have driven this strong growth.

Manufacturing

In 1990, Florida moved to the sixth position in the nation in high-tech employment. Between 1980 and 1990, Florida experienced an 18.6 percent increase in manufacturing, while this sector declined 3.3 percent over the same period nationwide. Florida now ranks seventh in the nation in the number of manufacturing plants in a state. During the last two decades, Florida's diversification from an agrarian economy also featured growth in international trade, health care, and financial services.

Population

Since 1980, only Alaska, Arizona, and Nevada had higher population growth rates than Florida. However, Florida's net gain of 2.5 million residents in migration is over twice the population gain of those three states combined. Population is expected to reach 14.2 million by 1993, maintaining Florida's status as the nation's fourth biggest state. The current population of Miami (Florida's largest city) is estimated at 1.85 million.

Tourism

Florida's warm climate, year-round beach life, hundreds of golf courses, and improving highway system attract worldwide tourists as well as retirees. In 1990, 38 million tourists brought $25 billion to Florida's economy. An estimated 11 percent of all jobs in Florida are tourism-related.

Outlook

Florida's deliberate economic diversification may help to avert a state-wide economic slump. The national recession, higher gasoline prices, and a return to costlier airfares will negatively impact Florida's tourism industry. The Miami Convention Bureau projects a flat year for convention attendance in 1992.

The outlook for the Florida economy is for a gradual erosion in the pace of employment growth and slower population growth. No particular factors are to blame, as Florida continues "business as usual" through a nationwide recession.

Operations

JIT is an insurance broker, providing complete insurance coverage to a growing list of commercial clients. Each partner and associate specializes in an insurance area and provides highly technical services to clients. The clients' needs are identified and evaluated on an individual basis through extensive field inspections. Facilities are studied, operations observed, and distribution and use of products are evaluated by one or more skilled staff members.

JIT can provide complete casualty and liability, fire, wet and inland marine, automobile, aviation, bonds, machinery breakdown and boiler, life, employee benefits, group, and personal lines insurance.

The breakdown of JIT's commissions in 1991 and 1990 was as follows:

	1991		1990	
		%		%
Commercial (large & small)	$ 460,000	38.3	$ 430,000	43.0
Employee benefits	300,000	25.0	240,000	24.0
Workers' compensation	200,000	16.7	130,000	13.0
Life	85,000	7.1	70,000	7.0
Personal lines	60,000	5.0	50,000	5.0
Contingent commissions	50,000	4.2	45,000	4.5
Bonds	45,000	3.8	35,000	3.5
Total commissions	$1,200,000		$1,000,000	

The table above indicates that JIT's primary emphasis is on commercial accounts. However, it also reflects the company's strong marketing in the employee benefit and workers' compensation areas. Commercial business improved in total dollars but lost in percentage amounts in 1991 due to the superior growth in workers' compensation commissions. Employee benefits and workers' compensation commissions increased 25 percent and 54 percent, respectively, in 1991 following similar growth in 1990. The company plans to continue to focus on these three lines in 1992.

JIT has two offices, one in downtown Miami, focusing on serving the business or commercial product lines, and another in Coral Gables, with a focus on personal life, automobile, and health policies. The Miami office is the larger, both in terms of revenues and employees, accounting for over 80 percent of 1991 revenues and a staff of 15 employees.

Competition

JIT competes against a wide range of brokers in Miami, both national and large independent brokers. Competition is stiff and company management estimates that roughly 90 percent of the company's new business in 1991 was formerly the business of a different Miami insurance brokerage company. Conversely, JIT loses about 5 percent of its property/casualty business annually to local competition.

Suppliers

JIT has contracts with about 20 insurance companies and uses all 20 for various reasons. However, St. Paul, Royal, Fireman's Fund, Chubb, United Pacific, and Kemper account for the bulk of the company's business.

Premiums have decreased, and are expected to remain flat, for most property/casualty lines. Workers' compensation insurance premiums in Florida have also decreased in 1991. However, premiums are increasing for employee benefits and other insurance lines.

Management and Employees

Chairman of the board and founder John W. Smythe died in late 1968. The position of chairman has remained vacant since Mr. Smythe's death.

President and chief executive officer Richard Smythe has been with JIT since 1962. He assumed his current responsibilities in 1967.

Helen Smythe, CPA, chief financial officer, graduated from Duke University and joined the company in December 1964.

Paul Horst, senior vice president/secretary, joined JIT in 1974 and became senior vice president in 1985. Mr. Horst is an M.B.A. graduate of the University of Florida and was involved in insurance brokerage at Ajax & Ajax prior to joining JIT.

In addition, the company's other senior vice president and three vice presidents have extensive experience in the insurance business, most of it with JIT.

At year-end 1991, JIT's staff totaled approximately 20 people. No major staffing changes are expected in 1992. The average age of the company's producers is down to 40 to 45 years, with an excellent spread of ages, due to the retirement of several people in recent years. Commissions for all of JIT's producers are above their annual salary, which means that the company is not "carrying" any sales personnel. Typically, an insurance agency will pay a new producer a salary that is above what the producer would have made based on his or her production for up to three years. Company management anticipates that the firm may add one or two new producers by the end of 1992.

Customers and Marketing

For the commercial and personal lines offered by JIT, a wide variety of customers exist. Marketing is done by JIT's inside staff of specialized personnel, both through telephone contacts and field visits. Company personnel work hard to maintain a high profile in the community and are active in local organizations. Commercial lines include products for such public bodies as cities and school districts. In fact, JIT is doing an increasing amount of public body business (schools, counties, service organizations) on a fixed-fee basis. Such arrangements increase the stability of the company's revenues, since the fees are not based on premiums, which can vary significantly from year to year. JIT is the broker for many lawyers and for the Florida State Bar Association for both property/casualty lines and employee benefits. In recent years, JIT has placed a major marketing emphasis on workers' compensation and employee benefits. Rates on employee benefits and workers' compensation insurance are expected to rise and management expects this business to grow.

Facilities

JIT's operations are conducted principally through its downtown Miami office, which is leased. The company moved to its new location at Gulf Square in 1991. The new space, which is larger than the old space, has increased rent expense of approximately $20,000 per year. The management expects the new location to be adequate space for the next five years.

Financial Statements

Exhibit 22–1 shows the agency's balance sheet as of December 31, 1991. Mr. and Ms. Smythe intend to withdraw the $450,000 cash account balance before selling their stock.

Exhibit 22–2 illustrates JIT's income statements for the years ended December 31, 1987 through 1991. Helen Smythe's salary is $50,000 per year and has been included in employee compensation. Richard Smythe's salary is $75,000 and is also included in employee compensation. Based on an analysis of comparable industry data, we have determined that these salaries are fair compensation for the services provided.

Richard Smythe expects JIT's net free cash flow (before discretionary bonuses) for the next three years to be $300,000 in 1992, $350,000 in 1993, and $400,000 in 1994, with the $500,000 level sustainable through 1995 and thereafter. The definition of net free cash flow is found in Chapter 12.

Related Financial Data

Exhibits 22–3 through 22–5 provide information that may be used to determine the market value of JIT Insurance Company. Exhibit 22–3 shows financial ratios of insurance agencies as compiled by Robert Morris Associates. Exhibits 22–4 and 22–5 provide balance sheet and income statement data on sales of three similar insurance agencies that were sold recently, along with sale prices and terms.

In the next chapter, we will discuss the analysis of the market value of 100 percent of the common stock of JIT Insurance Company.

Exhibit 22–1

JIT INSURANCE COMPANY
BALANCE SHEETS

| | As of December 31: | | | | | | | | |
| | 1991 | | 1990 | | 1989 | | 1988 | | 1987 | |
	$	%	$	%	$	%	$	%	$	%
ASSETS										
Current Assets:										
Cash	450,000	22.2	400,000	22.3	350,000	20.5	300,000	17.7	300,000	18.0
Accounts Receivable	500,000	24.6	450,000	25.1	450,000	26.3	400,000	23.6	350,000	21.0
Prepaid Expenses	180,000	8.9	180,000	10.1	190,000	11.1	150,000	8.8	130,000	7.8
Total Current Assets	1,130,000	55.7	1,030,000	57.5	990,000	57.9	850,000	50.1	780,000	46.8
Fixed Assets:										
Furniture & Fixtures	1,400,000	69.0	1,200,000	67.0	1,055,000	61.7	1,000,000	59.0	1,000,000	60.1
Less: Accumulated Depreciation	(650,000)	(32.0)	(600,000)	(33.5)	(555,000)	(32.5)	(513,000)	(30.3)	(473,000)	(28.4)
Net Fixed Assets	750,000	36.9	600,000	33.5	500,000	29.2	487,000	28.7	527,000	31.7
Other Assets	150,000	7.4	160,000	8.9	220,000	12.9	358,000	21.1	358,000	21.5
TOTAL ASSETS	2,030,000	100.0	1,790,000	100.0	1,710,000	100.0	1,695,000	100.0	1,665,000	100.0
LIABILITIES & STOCKHOLDERS' EQUITY										
Current Liabilities:										
Notes Payable	20,000	1.0	0	0.0	0	0.0	0	0.0	0	0.0
Accounts Payable	400,000	19.7	250,000	14.0	130,000	7.6	130,000	7.7	110,000	6.6
Other Payables	30,000	1.5	15,000	0.8	10,000	0.6	10,000	0.6	10,000	0.6
Current Portion of LTD	20,000	1.0	20,000	1.1	20,000	1.2	20,000	1.2	20,000	1.2
Total Current Liabilities	470,000	23.2	285,000	15.9	160,000	9.4	160,000	9.4	140,000	8.4
Long-Term Debt, Less Current	200,000	9.9	240,000	13.4	320,000	18.7	340,000	20.1	360,000	21.6
Deferred Income Taxes	50,000	2.5	5,000	0.3	10,000	0.6	0	0.0	0	0.0
Total Liabilities	720,000	35.5	530,000	29.6	490,000	28.7	500,000	29.5	500,000	30.0
Stockholders' Equity:										
Common Equity	10,000	0.5	10,000	0.6	10,000	0.6	10,000	0.6	10,000	0.6
Retained Earnings	1,300,000	64.0	1,250,000	69.8	1,210,000	70.8	1,185,000	69.9	1,155,000	69.4
Total Stockholders' Equity	1,310,000	64.5	1,260,000	70.4	1,220,000	71.3	1,195,000	70.5	1,165,000	70.0
TOTAL LIABILITIES & STOCKHOLDERS' EQUITY	2,030,000	100.0	1,790,000	100.0	1,710,000	100.0	1,695,000	100.0	1,665,000	100.0

SOURCE: Company financial statements.

Exhibit 22–2

JIT INSURANCE COMPANY
INCOME STATEMENTS

	Years Ended December 31:									
	1991		1990		1989		1988		1987	
	$	%	$	%	$	%	$	%	$	%
Total Revenues	1,200,000	100.0	1,000,000	100.0	800,000	100.0	800,000	100.0	650,000	100.0
Cost of Operations:										
Employee Compensation	600,000	50.0	500,000	50.0	370,000	46.3	360,000	45.0	300,000	46.2
General & Administrative	300,000	25.0	250,000	25.0	200,000	25.0	200,000	25.0	160,000	24.6
Depreciation	50,000	4.2	45,000	4.5	42,000	5.3	40,000	5.0	35,000	5.4
Total Operating Expense	950,000	79.2	795,000	79.5	612,000	76.6	600,000	75.0	495,000	76.2
Operating Profit (Loss)	250,000	20.8	205,000	20.5	188,000	23.4	200,000	25.0	155,000	23.8
Other Income (Expenses):										
Interest Expense	(25,000)	(2.1)	(30,000)	(3.0)	(45,000)	(5.6)	(65,000)	(8.1)	(70,000)	(10.8)
Discretionary Employee Bonus	(150,000)	(12.5)	(100,000)	(10.0)	(100,000)	(12.5)	(85,000)	(10.6)	(45,000)	(6.9)
Gain (Loss) on Sale of Assets	5,000	0.4	(10,000)	(0.1)	(3,000)	(0.4)	0	0.0	0	0.0
Total Other Income (Expense)	(170,000)	(14.2)	(140,000)	(13.1)	(148,000)	(18.5)	(150,000)	(18.7)	(115,000)	(17.7)
Pretax Income (Loss)	80,000	6.7	65,000	6.5	40,000	5.0	50,000	6.3	40,000	6.2
Provision for Taxes	(30,000)	(2.5)	(25,000)	(2.5)	(15,000)	(1.9)	(20,000)	(2.5)	(15,000)	(2.3)
NET INCOME (LOSS)	50,000	4.2	40,000	4.0	25,000	3.1	30,000	3.8	25,000	3.9

SOURCE: Company reviewed financial statements.

Exhibit 22–3

SERVICES - INSURANCE AGENTS & BROKERS   SIC# 6411

0-500M	500M-2MM	2-10MM	10-50MM	50-100MM	100-250MM	Type of Statement	6/30/86-3/31/87 ALL	6/30/87-3/31/88 ALL
4	23	35	18	3	4	Unqualified	100	82
2	1	5		1		Qualified	5	5
23	88	44	4		1	Reviewed	158	169
94	92	25	3	1		Compiled	160	179
11	5	1				Tax Returns		
56	51	34	8	2	1	Other	132	128
	217(4/1-9/30/90)		423(10/1/90-3/31/91)					
190	260	144	33	7	6	**NUMBER OF STATEMENTS**	555	563
%	%	%	%	%	%	**ASSETS**	%	%
19.1	21.7	23.9	25.9			Cash & Equivalents	22.6	23.0
23.1	36.8	37.8	19.0			Trade Receivables - (net)	34.4	33.9
.0	.4	.5	3.4			Inventory	1.2	.5
4.0	2.6	6.7	7.6			All Other Current	5.0	4.3
46.2	61.5	68.9	55.9			Total Current	63.1	61.7
21.2	15.1	12.5	15.4			Fixed Assets (net)	13.9	15.1
15.7	11.3	6.8	5.5			Intangibles (net)	7.7	8.1
17.0	12.1	11.8	23.2			All Other Non-Current	15.3	15.1
100.0	100.0	100.0	100.0			Total	100.0	100.0
						LIABILITIES		
13.0	6.5	6.8	9.3			Notes Payable-Short Term	9.4	8.0
6.0	4.6	3.2	4.0			Cur. Mat.-L/T/D	3.8	3.9
26.0	42.8	40.8	15.8			Trade Payables	35.2	35.6
.8	.3	.3	1.1			Income Taxes Payable	1.0	.8
12.5	11.5	14.0	20.2			All Other Current	13.6	13.4
58.2	65.7	65.1	50.4			Total Current	63.0	61.6
21.8	15.0	13.3	13.6			Long Term Debt	12.8	14.0
.1	.2	.2	.3			Deferred Taxes	.7	.6
2.9	1.9	.8	5.9			All Other Non-Current	2.8	2.8
16.9	17.2	20.5	29.7			Net Worth	20.6	21.1
100.0	100.0	100.0	100.0			Total Liabilities & Net Worth	100.0	100.0
						INCOME DATA		
100.0	100.0	100.0	100.0			Net Sales	100.0	100.0
						Gross Profit		
93.8	94.4	95.3	87.1			Operating Expenses	89.9	91.8
6.2	5.6	4.7	12.9			Operating Profit	10.1	8.2
2.0	1.1	.5	1.1			All Other Expenses (net)	1.5	1.0
4.2	4.5	4.2	11.8			Profit Before Taxes	8.6	7.2
						RATIOS		
1.2	1.2	1.2	1.3				1.3	1.3
.8	.9	1.0	1.1			Current	1.0	1.0
.5	.7	.9	1.0				.8	.8
1.1	1.1	1.1	1.3				1.2	1.2
(188) .7	.9	.9	1.0			Quick	1.0	1.0
.4	.7	.8	.6				.7	.7
2 179.8	54 6.8	62 5.9	17 22.1				39 9.3	39 9.3
34 10.6	96 3.8	126 2.9	57 6.4			Sales/Receivables	114 3.2	111 3.3
73 5.0	174 2.1	243 1.5	140 2.6				203 1.8	192 1.9
						Cost of Sales/Inventory		
						Cost of Sales/Payables		
21.6	11.2	7.8	3.2				8.7	9.5
-24.7	-31.3	90.3	11.1			Sales/Working Capital	70.3	384.7
-5.5	-7.1	-9.1	-183.6				-7.6	-9.1
6.3	6.4	6.5	16.4				9.5	8.6
(160) 1.7	(218) 2.7	(116) 2.1	(26) 2.7			EBIT/Interest	(440) 4.0	(445) 3.6
.5	1.1	1.2	1.0				1.7	1.7
3.2	3.7	5.1	3.9				5.8	5.2
(56) .9	(101) 1.8	(69) 2.1	(13) 2.8			Net Profit + Depr., Dep., Amort./Cur. Mat. L/T/D	(244) 2.4	(246) 2.2
.1	.5	.8	1.4				1.3	1.1
.3	.4	.3	.2				.3	.3
2.1	1.7	1.0	.4			Fixed/Worth	.8	1.0
-.7	-1.1	-6.7	2.8				-26.7	-52.3
1.7	2.7	2.3	1.9				2.3	2.2
8.6	12.4	7.0	4.3			Debt/Worth	6.1	6.9
-3.3	-7.5	-33.5	13.1				-126.6	-204.0
90.7	72.8	37.6	57.8				80.3	62.2
(115) 19.1	(167) 22.3	(105) 15.5	(30) 21.0			% Profit Before Taxes/Tangible Net Worth	(413) 31.0	(420) 30.2
-5.1	4.1	3.5	6.1				12.4	11.0
13.3	10.0	6.5	9.8				11.3	10.3
3.8	3.8	2.3	5.7			% Profit Before Taxes/Total Assets	4.9	5.1
-2.5	.2	.4	.6				1.9	1.6
43.8	26.0	22.6	24.9				26.5	23.8
14.5	12.6	12.7	8.0			Sales/Net Fixed Assets	12.5	12.1
7.3	7.2	5.9	5.3				6.6	6.3
3.2	1.6	1.2	1.0				1.5	1.6
1.8	1.2	.9	.7			Sales/Total Assets	1.0	1.0
1.1	.8	.6	.4				.7	.7
1.3	1.8	2.0	2.0				1.9	1.9
(144) 2.8	(203) 2.9	(118) 3.3	(24) 3.8			% Depr., Dep., Amort./Sales	(443) 3.3	(440) 3.4
4.1	4.4	5.1	5.8				5.4	5.3
12.7	12.3	9.5					10.7	12.2
(109) 21.3	(138) 20.2	(72) 17.4				% Officers', Directors' Owners' Comp/Sales	(257) 19.4	(272) 19.4
28.4	28.1	26.2					28.5	28.0
121661M	465371M	657073M	707655M	612781M	1307336M	Net Sales ($)	1951494M	1946448M
49745M	278966M	600703M	776267M	476680M	1017046M	Total Assets ($)	2067178M	1945312M

©Robert Morris Associates 1991

M = $thousand   MM = $million
See Pages 1 through 15 for Explanation of Ratios and Data

Exhibit 22–4

COMPARATIVE MARKET VALUE DATA
SALES OF INSURANCE AGENCIES
BALANCE SHEETS

	Agency One $	Agency Two $	Agency Three $
ASSETS			
Current Assets:			
Cash	800,000	1,250,000	100,000
Accounts Receivable	2,000,000	3,750,000	1,900,000
Prepaid Expenses	200,000	250,000	50,000
Total Current Assets	3,000,000	5,250,000	2,050,000
Fixed Assets:			
Furniture & Fixtures	425,000	750,000	350,000
Less: Accum. Deprec.	(140,000)	(425,000)	(200,000)
Net Fixed Assets	285,000	325,000	150,000
TOTAL ASSETS	3,285,000	5,575,000	2,200,000
LIABILITIES & STOCKHOLDERS' EQUITY			
Current Liabilities:			
Accounts Payable	1,750,000	2,250,000	800,000
Accrued Expenses	225,000	600,000	50,000
Current Portion of LTD	100,000	25,000	0
Notes Payable	75,000	0	175,000
Total Current Liabilities	2,150,000	2,875,000	1,025,000
Long–Term Debt	500,000	100,000	0
Deferred Income Taxes	0	0	50,000
Total Liabilities	2,650,000	2,975,000	1,075,000
Stockholders' Equity	635,000	2,600,000	1,125,000
TOTAL LIABILITIES & STOCKHOLDERS' EQUITY	3,285,000	5,575,000	2,200,000

SOURCE: Willamette Business Sale Data Base. (This data base has now been integrated into the IBA data base. See Chapter 33 for details.)

Exhibit 22–5

COMPARATIVE MARKET VALUE DATA
INSURANCE AGENCIES
INCOME STATEMENTS

	Agency One $	Agency Two $	Agency Three $
Total Revenues	2,375,000	6,750,000	1,750,000
Cost of Operations	1,675,000	5,750,000	1,250,000
Earnings before Interest, Depreciation and Taxes	700,000	1,000,000	500,000
Depreciation	35,000	50,000	20,000
Earnings before Interest and Taxes	665,000	950,000	480,000
Interest Expense	50,000	10,000	0
Pretax Income (Loss)	615,000	940,000	480,000
Transaction Price:			
Face Amount	6,000,000	10,000,000	4,750,000
Terms: Amount of Down Payment	Cash	5,000,000	Cash
Interest Rate on Balance	NA	8%	NA
Payment Terms on Balance	NA	*	NA

* Equal monthly payments of interest and principal over five years.

SOURCE: Willamette Business Sale Data Base. (This data base has now been integrated into the IBA data base. See Chapter 33 for details.)

Chapter 23

Suggested Solution to the Sample Case

by Kathryn Daly

In this chapter, we present an analysis of the market value of 100 percent of the common stock of JIT Insurance Company, as of December 31, 1991. This chapter represents the analysis that the appraiser goes through to arrive at a value, but we have assumed that the Smythes will not require a formal, written appraisal report.[1]

Adjusting the Balance Sheet

The adjusted balance sheet is shown in Exhibit 23–1. Since the Smythes are taking the cash out of the business when they sell it, we need to reduce the current assets by $450,000. Another adjustment is indicated as well—to accounts receivable. Although it is desirable to adjust the balance sheet to reflect the market value of the fixtures and equipment, we have not been provided with information necessary to make that adjustment. However, based on the opinion expressed by Ms. Smythe, such an adjustment would not appear to be significant.

The adjustment to accounts receivable is based on discussions held with Ms. Smythe regarding the aged accounts receivable schedule. Twelve accounts are over 120 days old, and it is unlikely that they will be collected; therefore, accounts receivable need to be reduced by the sum of those twelve accounts: $50,000.

Adjusting the Income Statement

In arriving at the normalized income statement, shown in Exhibit 23–2, two adjustments needed to be made: the removal of the discretionary employee bonus and the removal of nonrecurring items. It should be noted that we have investigated the amount of depreciation expensed by the agency, and in our opinion, it represents the genuine economic depreciation of the fixtures and equipment.

Discretionary Bonus

As can be seen in Exhibit 22–2, actual employee compensation in 1991 was $600,000, or 50 percent of sales. In addition to their salaries, a bonus is paid to Mr. and Ms. Smythe at the end of the calendar year, shown as a separate line item titled "Discretionary Employee Bonus." The amount of that bonus is decided upon by the owners after reviewing draft financial statements. Since their compensation included in the regular Employee Compensation account was considered to be normal, we adjusted the Discretionary Employee Bonus Account to zero.

---

[1]The reader can refer to Chapter 14 in Pratt, *Valuing a Business*, 2nd ed., for an example of a formal written appraisal report.

Exhibit 23–1

JIT INSURANCE COMPANY
ADJUSTED BALANCE SHEETS
AS OF DECEMBER 31, 1991

	Balance Sheet as Reported $	Adjustments $	Balance Sheet as Adjusted $	%
ASSETS				
Current Assets:				
Cash	450,000	(450,000)	0	0.0
Accounts Receivable	500,000	(50,000)	450,000	29.4
Prepaid Expenses	180,000		180,000	11.8
Total Current Assets	1,130,000	(500,000)	630,000	41.2
Fixed Assets:				
Furniture & Fixtures	1,400,000		1,400,000	91.5
Less: Accumulated Depreciation	(650,000)		(650,000)	(42.5)
Net Fixed Assets	750,000		750,000	49.0
Other Assets	150,000		150,000	9.8
TOTAL ASSETS	2,030,000	(500,000)	1,530,000	100.0
LIABILITIES & STOCKHOLDERS' EQUITY				
Current Liabilities:				
Note Payable	20,000		20,000	1.3
Accounts Payable	400,000		400,000	26.1
Other Payables	30,000		30,000	2.0
Current Portion of LTD	20,000		20,000	1.3
Total Current Liabilities	470,000		470,000	30.7
Long-Term Debt, Less Current	200,000		200,000	13.1
Deferred Income Taxes	50,000		50,000	3.3
Total Liabilities	720,000		720,000	47.1
Stockholders' Equity:				
Common Equity	10,000		10,000	0.6
Retained Earnings	1,300,000	(500,000)	800,000	52.3
Total Stockholders' Equity	1,310,000	(500,000)	810,000	52.9
TOTAL LIABILITIES & STOCKHOLDERS' EQUITY	2,030,000	(500,000)	1,530,000	100.0

SOURCE: Company financial statements.

Exhibit 23–2

JIT INSURANCE COMPANY
ADJUSTED INCOME STATEMENTS

	1991 $	1991 %	1990 $	1990 %	1989 $	1989 %	1988 $	1988 %	1987 $	1987 %
					Years Ended December 31:					
Total Revenues	1,200,000	100.0	1,000,000	100.0	800,000	100.0	800,000	100.0	650,000	100.0
Cost of Operations:										
Employee Compensation	600,000	50.0	500,000	50.0	370,000	46.3	360,000	45.0	300,000	46.2
General & Administrative	300,000	25.0	250,000	25.0	200,000	25.0	200,000	25.0	160,000	24.6
Depreciation	50,000	4.2	45,000	4.5	42,000	5.3	40,000	5.0	35,000	5.4
Total Operating Expense	950,000	79.2	795,000	79.5	612,000	76.6	600,000	75.0	495,000	76.2
Operating Profit	250,000	20.8	205,000	20.5	188,000	23.4	200,000	25.0	155,000	23.8
Other Income (Expenses):										
Interest Expense	(25,000)	(2.1)	(30,000)	(3.0)	(45,000)	(5.6)	(65,000)	(8.1)	(70,000)	(10.8)
Discretionary Employee Bonus	0	0.0	0	0.0	0	0.0	0	0.0	0	0.0
Gain (Loss) on Sale of Assets	0	0.0	0	0.0	0	0.0	0	0.0	0	0.0
Total Other Income (Expense)	(25,000)	(2.1)	(30,000)	(3.0)	(45,000)	(5.6)	(65,000)	(8.1)	(70,000)	(10.8)
Pretax Income	225,000	18.7	175,000	17.5	143,000	17.8	135,000	16.9	85,000	13.0

SOURCE: Company reviewed financial statements.

Removal of Nonrecurring Items

The second adjustment we made was to remove the nonrecurring items that appeared under Gain (Loss) on Sale of Assets in the income statement. Since we are interested in the sustainable earning power of the company, and it is unlikely that these events will occur again, their effect needs to be eliminated from the income statement. These items included a loss on sale of nonoperating assets in 1990 and 1989 and gains from the sale of nonoperating assets in 1991.

Analysis of Adjusted Financial Statements

Balance Sheets

Exhibit 23–1 presents the adjusted balance sheet as of December 31, 1991. Current assets totaled $630,000, consisting primarily of accounts receivable. Fixed assets accounted for 49.0 percent of total assets at $750,000.

Current liabilities totaled $470,000 as of December 31, 1991. The largest liability was accounts payable of $400,000, accounting for over 85 percent of total liabilities. Long-term debt was $200,000, or 13.1 percent of total assets. Total liabilities accounted for 47.1 percent of total assets.

Stockholders' equity was $810,000 as of December 31, 1991, or 52.9 percent of total assets.

Income Statements

The adjusted income statements shown in Exhibit 23–2 present an increasing trend of JIT's sales since 1987 from $650,000 to $1.2 million in 1991, for a five-year average annual compound growth rate of 8.6 percent. Operating profit margins have remained stable at around 22 percent, ranging from 20.5 percent to 25.0 percent over the five-year period. Interest expense has been decreased due to the declining debt balance. Pretax profit margins have ranged from 13.1 percent in 1987 to 18.8 percent in the most recent period. Pretax income has averaged around $150,000 the past five years, although the adjusted numbers have shown steady improvement due to reductions in interest expense. Current earnings levels are expected to be a sustainable level of earnings.

Comparison with Industry Averages

Exhibit 23–3 shows a comparison of JIT's ratios with those of Robert Morris Associates (RMA). JIT's operating margin is 15 percentage points higher than RMA.

JIT's operating expenses are lower than RMA, but its other expenses are higher, allowing JIT's pretax profit margin of 18.8 percent to remain above the industry average of 5.8 percent.

JIT has high liquidity ratios, as can be seen by the current ratio

Exhibit 23–3

JIT INSURANCE COMPANY
COMPARISONS WITH INDUSTRY AVERAGES
SIC NO. 6411, INSURANCE AGENTS AND BROKERS

		RMA	JIT
Year:		1991	1991
Asset Size:		$500M–2MM	$1.5MM
Number of Statements:		260	
Gross Sales		100.0%	100.0%
Operating Expenses		94.4	79.2
Operating Profit		5.6	20.8
All Other Expenses (net)		(1.1)	(2.1)
Profit before Taxes		5.0	18.8
RATIOS			
	HI	1.2	
Current	MD	0.9	1.3
	LO	0.7	
	HI	6.8	
Sales/Receivables	MD	3.8	2.7
	LO	2.1	
	HI	11.2	
Sales/Working Capital	MD	(31.3)	7.5
	LO	(7.1)	
	HI	6.4	
EBIT/Interest	MD	2.7	10.0
	LO	1.1	
	HI	2.7	
Debt/Tangible Net Worth	MD	12.4	0.9
	LO	(7.5)	
%Profit Before Taxes/	HI	72.8	
Tangible Net Worth	MD	30.1	27.8
	LO	4.1	
% Profit Before Taxes/	HI	10.0	
Total Assets	MD	3.8	14.7
	LO	0.2	
	HI	1.6	
Sales/Total Assets	MD	1.2	0.8
	LO	0.8	

SOURCES: Robert Morris Associates' *Annual Statement Studies,* 1991 edition; company adjusted financial statements.

and sales/working capital ratios, which were both closest to the upper quartile figures for the industry.

JIT's interest expense coverage ratio (EBIT/interest) is well above the industry average. The company's debt ratio (liabilities/net worth) is higher than the industry average, indicating a relatively stronger equity position. Therefore, on the whole, the company is less leveraged than the industry as a whole and better able to meet interest expense requirements.

JIT's pretax return on tangible net worth was near the industry average while the return on assets was well above the higher quartile. Asset turnover, however, was at the RMA lower quartile.

Overall, JIT has above-average liquidity ratios, asset utilization ratios, and profitability ratios.

Summary of Positive and Negative Factors

Positive Factors

1. The company has a good reputation in Miami and a strong presence in Coral Gables.
2. The company has a solid management organization.
3. The company's financial position is sound, and steps have been taken to further reduce costs.

Negative Factors

1. The outlook for continued high economic growth is not good. Revenues are expected to remain stable with some growth. However, revenues could decline, particularly if the tourism industry remains in a slump and premiums continue to decline in the commercial property/casualty lines.

Deriving Capitalization Rates from Transaction Data

In the previous chapter, information was provided on three agency transactions (Exhibit 22–4). The various price/earnings, price/revenue, and price/book value multiples at which these transactions occurred can provide guidance in valuing JIT. A summary of these multiples and how they were computed appears in Exhibit 23–4.

Adjusting Transaction Data to Cash Equivalent Value

The transaction involving Agency 2 was not a cash transaction, and accordingly we need to convert it to a cash price so that it is comparable to the other two transactions.

Exhibit 23–4

JIT INSURANCE COMPANY
DERIVATION OF COMPARATIVE COMPANY
MARKET VALUE INDICATORS

	Agency One $	Agency Two $	Agency Three $	JIT $		
Cash Price	6,000,000	9,771,580	4,750,000	TBD		
EBT	615,000	940,000	480,000	225,000		
+ Depreciation	35,000	50,000	20,000	50,000		
= EBDT	650,000	990,000	500,000	275,000		
EBT	615,000	940,000	480,000	225,000		
+ Interest Expense	50,000	10,000	0	25,000		
= EBIT	665,000	950,000	480,000	250,000		
EBIT	665,000	950,000	480,000	250,000		
+ Depreciation	35,000	50,000	20,000	50,000		
= EBDIT	700,000	1,000,000	500,000	300,000		
Cash Price	6,000,000	9,771,580	4,750,000	TBD		
+ Long-term Debt (LTD)	500,000	100,000	0	200,000		
+ Current Maturities of LTD	100,000	25,000	0	20,000		
+ Notes Payable	75,000	0	175,000	20,000		
= Price of Invested Capital	6,675,000	9,896,580	4,925,000	240,000		
Total Revenues	2,375,000	6,750,000	1,750,000	1,200,000		
Tangible Book Value	635,000	2,600,000	1,125,000	810,000		

Multiples:					Mean	Median
Cash Price/EBT	9.8	10.4	9.9		10.0	9.9
Cash Price/EBDT	9.2	9.9	9.5		9.5	9.2
Price of Invested Capital/EBIT	10.0	10.4	10.3		10.2	10.3
Price of Invested Capital/EBDIT	9.5	9.9	9.9		9.8	9.9
Cash Price/Revenues	2.53	1.45	2.71		2.23	2.53
EBT Return on Revenues	25.9%	13.9%	27.4%	18.8%		
Cash Price/Book Value	9.45	3.76	4.22		5.81	4.22
EBT Return on Book Value	96.9%	36.2%	42.7%	27.8%		

E = Earnings B = Before D = Depreciation I = Interest T = Taxes
TBD = To Be Determined
SOURCE: Willamette Business Sale Data Base. (This data base has now been integrated into the IBA data base. See
        Chapter 33 for details.)

The terms of the transaction were $5 million down and the balance of $5 million paid in equal monthly installments of principal and interest for five years at 8 percent interest. For purposes of this example, an agency could probably borrow money from the bank at 2½ points above the prime rate of 6½ percent, or about 9 percent. Since a seller's contract may not be secured by specific collateral, as a bank loan is, there is more risk involved. Assuming that the contract is fairly well secured and is protected by covenants in the purchase agreement, a market rate of 10 percent is probably appropriate.

Assuming a market rate of 10 percent, the previously described contract has a cash value of $9,771,580. Refer to Chapter 19 for an explanation of how to make this calculation.

Price/Earnings before Taxes (EBT)

The price/EBT multiples of the three comparative transactions ranged from 9.8 to 10.4 with a mean of 10.0 and a median of 9.9 (see Exhibit 23–4). If we assume that the information provided to us represents what could be considered a sustainable level of earnings, then the reciprocals of the mean and median multiples would indicate what the current capitalization rates are. The reciprocal of the mean and median ratios produce capitalization rates of 10.0 percent and 10.1 percent, respectively.

Price/Earnings before Depreciation and Taxes (EBDT)

The price/EBDT or price/pretax cash flow multiples ranged from 9.2 to 9.9 with a mean and a median of 9.5. We believe, although we do not know for a fact, that the depreciation of the comparative companies is comparable to that of JIT. Again, assuming that the earnings bases are sustainable, the mean and median multiples indicate a capitalization rate of 10.5 percent. This capitalization rate is higher than the rates applicable to EBT because in this calculation we are using cash flow as our earnings base.

Price/Earnings before Interest and Taxes (EBIT)

This method is often referred to as a debt-free method, because in using it we remove the interest expense from the earnings base. When we take out the interest expense from the earnings, however, we also need to add to the transaction price the interest-bearing debt that was assumed. In other words, if no debt was assumed, an investor would have paid a higher price and there would have been no interest expense in the earnings. We have assumed that the amount that the debt is at current market rates. If that was not the case, then it would have to be adjusted to reflect the current market rates. We also assumed that the amount of notes payable throughout the year. The price (including interest-bearing debt)/EBIT ratios for the comparative companies ranged from 10.0 to 10.4, with a mean of 10.2 and a median of 10.3 (Exhibit 23–4). Again, if we assume that the earnings bases of the comparative companies are sustainable, the indicated mean capitalization rate is 9.8 percent and the median capitalization rate is 9.7 percent.

Price/Earnings before Depreciation, Interest, and Taxes (EBDIT)

Price/EBDIT is also a debt-free ratio; it is based on debt-free cash flow. Again, the price used in computing the ratio must include the transaction price plus the amount of the company's interest-bearing debt assumed by the buyer. As computed in Exhibit 23–4, the price/EBDIT ratios ranged from 9.5 to 9.9, with a mean of 9.8 and a median of 9.9, indicating a mean capitalization rate of 10.2 percent and a median capitalization rate of 10.1 percent, based on the previously mentioned assumptions.

Price/Revenue

The price/revenue multiples of the comparative transactions ranged from 145 percent to 271 percent, with a mean of 223 percent and a median of 253 percent (see Exhibit 23–4).

Price/Book Value

The price/book value multiples ranged from 376 percent to 945 percent, with a mean of 581 percent and median of 422 percent.

Capitalization of Normalized Earnings

There are a number of earnings bases that can be capitalized. We chose to look at the following four earnings bases: pretax earnings (EBT), pretax cash flow (EBDT), debt-free pretax earnings (EBIT), and debt-free pretax cash flow (EBDIT). The debt-free methods remove the effect of different debt structures on comparative company data. The pretax cash flow method removes the effect of different depreciation methods, while the debt-free pretax cash flow method removes the effects of *both* different debt structures *and* depreciation methods.

In determining the four earnings bases to capitalize, one can look at current or average earnings. In our opinion, JIT's current earnings reflect its current earning power. Therefore, we chose to look at current earnings in computing the four earnings bases.

In choosing capitalization rates for these various earnings bases, we looked at the comparative company data just discussed. Since the spread between the multipliers of each earnings base was not very wide, in our opinion, they provided a pretty good indication of what current multipliers are in the industry. In choosing which rate to apply to JIT's earnings, we looked at the positive and negative factors relative to JIT, discussed earlier. In our opinion, the positive and negative factors tend to neutralize each other, so a multiple in the middle of the comparative company multiples is appropriate. For each of the following approaches, we chose a multiple near the mean or median multiples.

Price/EBT

As can be seen in Exhibits 23–2 and 23–4, JIT's EBT in 1991 was $225,000. We chose a multiple of 9.9 (the median multiple) to apply to these earnings, resulting in the following indication of value:

EBT		P/E Multiple		Indicated Value
$225,000	×	9.9	=	$2,227,500

Price/EBDT

JIT's EBDT in 1991 was $275,000 (see Exhibit 23–4). We chose a multiple of 9.5 (both the mean and median multiple) to apply to these earnings, resulting in the following indication of value:

EBDT		P/E Multiple		Indicated Value
$275,000	×	9.5	=	$2,612,500

Price/EBIT

JIT's EBIT in 1991 was $250,000 (see Exhibit 23–4). We chose a debt-free earnings multiple of 10.3 (the median multiple) to apply to these debt-free earnings. When we apply this multiple to the EBIT, the resulting value includes the value of the interest-bearing debt. Therefore, to arrive at an indicated value for the equity (stock) of JIT, we need to subtract from that value $240,000, which is the total amount of interest-bearing debt. The following steps summarize the computation described.

EBIT	$250,000
Debt-free multiple	x 10.3
	$2,575,000
Less: Interest-bearing debt	(240,000)
Indicated value	$2,335,000

Price/EBDIT

JIT's EBDIT in 1991 was $300,000 (see Exhibit 23–4). We chose a multiple of 9.9 (which was the median multiple) to apply to these earnings. Again, the amount of interest-bearing debt must be subtracted to arrive at the indicated value, which is derived as follows:

EBDIT	$300,000
Debt-free multiple	x 9.9
	$2,970,000
Less: Interest-bearing debt	(240,000)
Indicated value	$2,730,000

Summary

The four capitalization of normalized earnings methods can be summarized as follows:

	Earnings Base		Capitalization Multiple			Less: Interest-Bearing Debt	Indicated Value
EBT	$225,000	x	9.9	=	$2,227,500	N/A	$2,227,500
EBDT	275,000	x	9.5	=	2,612,500	N/A	2,612,500
EBIT	250,000	x	10.3	=	2,575,000	$240,000	2,335,000
EBDIT	300,000	x	9.9	=	2,970,000	240,000	2,730,000

The mean and median of these four methods is near $2.5 million. In our opinion, since these methods produced a tight range of values, a value of approximately $2.5 million for the stock of JIT is indicated by the capitalization of normalized earnings.

Excess Earnings Method

We considered the possibility of an application of the excess earnings method in our valuation of JIT; however, in our opinion the other methods were more relevant. Therefore, we did not utilize this method. The reader should refer to Chapter 15, "The Excess Earnings Method," for a step-by-step explanation of how the method works and the appropriate situations for this method.

Discounted Future Returns Method

As already discussed in Chapter 13, the discounted future returns method is conceptually the best valuation method in most instances. JIT's net free cash flow before taxes and discretionary bonus for the next three years has been projected as follows:

1992	$300,000
1993	350,000
1994	400,000

Mr. Smythe has informed us that he expects net free cash flow to level off at $500,000 after 1994. Also, his projections are in dollars that include the expected effects of inflation. We assumed that net free cash flow will grow at 4 percent, or the expected inflation rate after 1994.

The next variable that needs to be determined is the appropriate discount rate. Since the future earnings projection is the amount of earnings available to equity, a discount rate applicable to an equity investment should be used. In this case, no discount for lack of marketability was included in our discount rate.

As discussed in Chapter 12, it is necessary to choose a discount rate at which to discount future returns, which reflects returns available on investments without significant risk, plus an adequate premium for the risk and illiquidity of investing in a private company. Because of the long-established nature of JIT Insurance, we will use a discount rate of 20 percent.

The components of our expected rate of return are as follows:

Risk-free rate	8.0%
Equity risk premium	7.4
Small stock premium	5.1
	20.5
	20.0% (rounded)

Discounting these net free cash flows at 20 percent results in an indicated value of $2.3 million for the JIT stock, derived as follows (see Chapter 13 for a detailed explanation):

Present value of earnings from 1992 to 1994:

$$\frac{\$300,000}{(1 + .20)} + \frac{\$350,000}{(1 + .20)^2} + \frac{\$400,000}{(1 + .20)^3} = \$724,537$$

Present value of earnings for 1995 and thereafter:

$$\frac{\$500,000}{.20 - .04} = \$3,125,000$$

$$\frac{\$3,125,000}{(1 + .20)^3} = \$1,808,449$$

Total present value of earnings:

1992 to 1994	$ 724,537
1995 and thereafter	1,808,449
Indicated value	$2,532,986

Gross Revenue Multipler

The capitalization of revenues method is often considered an appropriate method of valuation, especially when it is used in conjunction with several other valuation methods. In a way, it can be considered a shortcut to a capitalization of earnings method, since generally there is an implicit assumption that a certain level of revenues should be able to generate a certain level of earnings in a given type of business. This method is reasonable to use for JIT because there has been a fairly consistent relationship between revenues and profits over the years. Guidance in arriving at the appropriate multiplier of revenues can again be found in the multipliers at which the comparative agency transactions occurred.

The price/revenue (P/R) multipliers for the comparative transactions ranged from 145 percent to 271 percent, with a mean of 223 percent and a median of 253 percent. Before the selection of this revenue multiplier, it is important to note that the pretax profit margins of the three agencies involved in the transactions ranged from 13.9 percent to 27.4 percent and corresponded to the revenue multiples. We selected a price/revenues multiple of 200 percent to apply to JIT's 1991 revenues.

	Price/Revenue Multiple	EBT Return on Revenue
Agency three	2.71	27.4%
Agency one	2.53	25.9
Agency two	1.45	13.9
JIT		18.8

Applying the previously determined multiplier of 200 percent to JIT's 1991 sales results in the following indication of value:

Revenue		P/R Multiple		Indicated Value
$1,200,000	×	2.00	=	$2,400,000

Price/Book Value Method

We considered a book value method, but the value of the book value was nominal in relation to the value found in the revenue and earnings stream, and we did not consider this method appropriate.

Valuation Summary

The three valuation methods we have discussed produced indicated values as summarized below:

Method	Indicated Value
Capitalization of normalized earnings	$2,500,000
Discounted future returns method	2,532,986
Multiple of gross revenues	2,400,000

The three approaches range in value from $2.4 million to $2.53 million, an unusually tight range of indications of value.

Valuation Conclusion

In our opinion, the market value of 100 percent of the common stock of JIT Insurance Company as of December 30, 1991, was $2.5 million.

Part IV

Valuations for Specific Purposes

Chapter 24

S Corporations

by Donna J. Walker, C.F.A., A.S.A.

What Is an S Corporation?

S corporations were enacted in 1958 as part of a tax program to aid small businesses, although they are not limited to small businesses. However, the 1986 Tax Reform Act (TRA 86) propelled S corporations to greater levels of visibility and versatility.

The congressional intent was to lessen tax considerations in the choice of business form by giving certain corporate entities and shareholders the option of being taxed as if they were partnerships. The legislative record indicates that the congressional thinking was that S corporations would be useful for the following:

- To pass corporate net operating losses through to shareholders.
- To eliminate "double" taxation on corporate earnings in the case of a corporation distributing substantial amounts of current earnings.
- To tax corporate earnings at shareholder incremental rates, if lower.

This allowed the S corporation to achieve the coveted corporate characteristics of limited liability combined with the income flow-through attributes of a partnership. However, these advantages did not come without costs.

To qualify for S corporation status, certain requirements must be met:

- The corporation must have no more than 35 shareholders, and all shareholders must be U.S. citizens. (Spouses who hold stock are considered as one shareholder.)
- Shareholders must be individuals (except for estates and certain trusts).
- All shareholders must participate equally in the allocation of profits, losses, and distributions.
- Only common stock can be issued by an S corporation. The corporation may not have more than one class of stock, except that there can be voting and nonvoting shares as long as there are no unequal distribution rights.

As a pass-through tax entity, the earnings of an S corporation are subject to federal taxation only at the shareholder level. Under the pass-through provisions, the income or loss of the S corporation and the resulting tax consequences are allocated on a pro rata ownership basis to the shareholders at each shareholder's personal tax rate. Stockholders are taxed on the earnings of the S corporation whether or not earnings are distributed by the corporation.

The shareholders of the S corporation increase or decrease the basis of their ownership interest in the S corporation to the extent of the income or loss of the corporation recognized by each shareholder. The consequence of such basis adjustment is that income or loss is not taxable to the shareholder again upon distribution or, in the absence of distribution, upon the sale or exchange of the shareholder's interest in the corporation. This allows earnings to be distributed to shareholders free of federal tax, avoiding the double taxation inherent in C corporations, where federal taxes are levied on earnings at the corporate level and on dividends or distributions at the shareholder level.

Why Corporations Elect S Status

Typically, the reasons for electing S corporation status are given as the positive differential between personal and corporate tax rate and the avoidance of double taxation inherent in C corporation distributions. Certainly, the positive differential between corporate and personal tax rates is, at least in part, at the root of the surge of S corporation elections following TRA 86. While the tax advantages are real, as stated previously, the tax implications of S corporations are complex and there are many disadvantages. A qualified tax advisor should be contacted before a C corporation converts to S corporation status. If the goal is strictly to minimize taxes, many private corporations can do so through bonuses or other compensation to employee shareholders. However, for corporations with non-employed shareholders, the S corporation is very useful. It allows nonemployed shareholders to receive distributions that avoid double taxation, thereby allowing for greater return to the shareholder for the same level of payout from the corporation. If 100 percent of earnings are distributed, the net after tax cash available to S corporation shareholders is 51.5 percent greater than that available to C corporation shareholders. This advantage is shown in Exhibit 24–1. It makes sense that these "optimum" S corporations are unlikely to be high-growth companies, because high-growth companies typically plow profits back into the company to fund growth, leaving little or nothing to pay out to shareholders.

Therefore, S corporations that have a handful of shareholders, where employee-shareholders of the corporation are in the minority and/or where the corporation has significant cash flow to distribute, achieve the greatest advantage as measured by tax savings from their S election.

The Pros and Cons of S Status

It is helpful for the appraiser to be aware of the advantages and disadvantages of S corporation status so that these attributes are reflected in the process of determining the value of the subject company.[1]

The major advantage of the S corporation status is avoiding the double taxation on shareholder distributions. Income and loss items pass directly through to shareholders, where income is taxed at the lower effective rate of 31.9 percent (maximum rate in 1992) rather than the corporate tax rate of 34 percent. This means that an S corporation can sell assets (at a purchase price that is often greater than a similar sale of stock) and distribute the proceeds without the corporate level tax (which would apply prior to a C corporation's dividend distribution).

---

[1]Anne Danyluk, "Valuing S Corporations—A Look at Adjustments," presentation at the American Society of Appraisers 1991 International Convention, Philadelphia, Penn., June 18, 1991.

Exhibit 24–1

INCREMENTAL VALUE DIFFERENCE OF
S CORPORATION TAX BENEFITS

100% Earnings Distributed

		C Corporation	S Corporation
Profit before tax	$100	$100	
Corporate tax at 34%		34	0
Net profit		66	100
Retain 0%		0	0
Dividends		66	100
Shareholder tax at 31.9%		21	32
Net after-tax cash		$ 45	$ 68 51.5%

0% Earnings Distributed

		C Corporation	S Corporation
Profit before tax	$100	$100	
Corporate tax at 34%		34	0
Net profit		66	100
Retain 100%		66	66 [a]
Dividends		0	34 [a]
Shareholder tax at 31.9%		0	32
Net after-tax cash		$ 0	$ 2 infinity [b]

[a]   Assumes same dollar amount is retained; thus implies same expected growth.

[b] $\dfrac{(1 - \text{individual tax rate}) - \text{retention rate } (1 - \text{corporate tax rate})^c}{(1 - \text{corporate tax rate}) (1 - \text{retention rate}) (1 - \text{individual tax rate})}$

When 100% earnings distributed:

$\dfrac{(1 - .319) - 0\ (1 - .34)}{(1 - .34)\ (1 - 0)\ (1 - .319)}$ =   1.515 factor or 51.5% increase

When 0% earnings distributed:

$\dfrac{(1 - .319) - 1\ (1 - .34)}{(1 - .34)\ (1 - 1)\ (1 - .319)}$ =   infinity

[c]   Aaron L. Shackelford, "Valuation of S Corporations," *Business Valuation Review* (December 1988), p. 159.

S corporations are not subject to corporate minimum federal taxes. There is no accumulated earnings tax, and there are no personal holding company taxes applicable to S corporations. Non-tax-shelter S corporations are allowed to use the cash method of accounting. At the point of conversion to an S corporation, the C corporation's deferred tax charges are adjusted to retained earnings, improving the appearance of the balance sheet.

Many, but not all, disadvantages of S corporation status apply to C corporations that convert to S corporation status. "Fresh start" S corporations, however, have other distinctions from C corporations, such as:

- S corporation shareholders are liable for taxes on income whether it is distributed or not. Tax-free distributions are allowed only to the extent of the shareholder's basis in the stock. Shareholders typically demand enough cash distributions to pay their taxes, which may limit the amount of earnings available for reinvestment.
- S corporations must generally conform their tax years to their owner's tax years (usually calendar years).
- Each shareholder's deductible share of the S corporation's loss in any year is limited to his adjusted basis in stock and direct shareholder loans, in general. Losses can be carried forward indefinitely at the shareholder level to future S corporation years in which the shareholder creates basis.
- State and local tax compliance can be complicated with multistate S corporations.
- Many fringe benefits for shareholders who own more than 2 percent of the S corporation's stock cannot be deducted by the S corporation.
- The deductibility of pass-through losses for inactive owners is limited.

The major disadvantage of the S corporation which converted from C corporation status is that any gain or income that the corporation recognizes within the 10 post-conversion years is taxed to the extent the asset giving rise to the gain or income was owned at the conversion date. Not only is the corporation subject to the "built-in gains tax" on these items, but the gain or income flows through to the shareholders net of corporate-level tax paid. This creates near double-level tax to the corporation and its shareholders.

Other tax disadvantages of the conversion to S corporation status are that carryover attributes are generally lost (but may be available for built-in gains purposes). There may be a LIFO inventory method recapture tax.

These advantages and disadvantages of S corporation status lead to the following important business concerns:

- Estate planning for S corporation shareholders may require different approaches from those used in C corporations.
- The pool of hypothetical willing buyers cannot include outside corporations, nonresident alien investors, pension plans, or ESOPs.

- S corporations cannot own more than 79 percent of another corporation.
- Buy-sell agreements are important because, while a minority shareholder cannot revoke an S corporation election, he could disqualify the election.

Valuation Issues

In the valuation of the common stock of an S corporation, the central valuation issue is two-fold: First, is there an incremental value attributable to the tax advantages of the S corporation? And, second, if so, how can this incremental value be accounted for in the valuation process?

Business Enterprise Value

If the purpose of the valuation is to determine the fair market value of a controlling interest in the common stock of an S corporation for buying, selling, or merging the company, the company's status as an S corporation will have little or no impact on value. The most likely buyer is a C corporation and, as such, a C corporation will be unwilling to pay for S corporation tax benefits not available to it by definition of its being a C corporation. Generally, in valuations for transaction purposes, valuation methodologies using pretax earnings fundamentals are used, as it is the buyer's tax status that is relevant, not the historical tax status of the selling company.

Valuation of Minority Interests

If the interest being appraised is a minority interest—that is, the appraisal of an ownership interest not having the prerogatives of control—a direct comparison with values of other minority interests is the most appropriate approach to valuation. As discussed earlier in this book, the prices at which the daily transactions in minority interests of publicly traded companies take place offer guidance for the valuation of minority interests.

For the valuation of S corporations, there exists in the public market a comparative subset that can be very useful for the valuation of minority interests. This group is made up of Master Limited Partnerships (MLPs). MLPs are publicly traded partnerships listed on stock exchanges and the NASDAQ over-the-counter quotation service. Traditionally, MLPs were used to finance oil and gas projects, real estate ventures, and natural resource exploration and development. However, the Tax Reform Act of 1986 and the repeal of the General Utilities doctrine triggered a rash of MLPs between 1985 and 1987 in a wide variety of industries.

Because Congress feared a wholesale conversion of corporations into partnerships, the Revenue Act of 1987 decreed that all new publicly traded partnerships would be taxed as corporations. Existing MLPs were given a 10-year tax holiday. This stopped virtually all new MLP issuances beginning in 1988. However, a limited number of MLPs still exist. As partnerships they have similar flow-through tax treatment of income as do S corporations, thus making them useful for comparative valuation purposes in the appraisal of S corporation interests. Unfortunately, the limited number of MLPs results in there being no MLPs existing in many industry categories and only one or two MLPs existing in many industry categories. As stated earlier, the majority of MLPs are still in such industries as natural resources and real estate. For those industries, such as forest products, where MLPs exist, they provide the best comparative valuation guidance for S corporations.

When using MLPs as valuation guidelines, the appraiser should be aware of several caveats. First, many publicly traded partnerships have multitier distribution policies calling for a large percentage of income (often 95 percent) to be paid to the limited partners for a specific length of time followed by a change in the distribution policy in favor of the general partners. It is important to read carefully the partnership agreement and be aware of the distribution policy, especially when applying MLPs' dividend yields to shareholder distributions in the valuation of an S corporation.

Two sources of data on MLPs are *The Stanger Report* and *Realty Stock Review*. Each publication publishes performance summaries for publicly traded master limited partnerships, including listings by industry categories.

If the only appropriate comparative companies are C corporations, the appraiser is faced with deciding how to apply empirical market data derived from C corporations to S corporation fundamentals. There are three alternatives:

1. Apply statutory C corporation tax rates to the S corporation's earnings and apply price/earnings (P/E) multiples derived from C corporation comparative analysis.

   This approach does not recognize the tax advantages accruing to the S corporation shareholder from the positive differential between the highest corporate marginal tax rate and the maximum marginal tax rate for individuals. Some appraisers take this approach and add a premium to the indicated values to capture the advantage of S corporation status.

2. Capitalize S corporation income (before taxes to shareholders) and apply comparative company P/E multiples.

   This approach does not recognize the S corporation shareholders' exposure to taxes on income they don't receive in distributions from the company. It further suffers from a classic apples-to-oranges comparative flaw in its application of an after-tax-derived multiple being applied to a pretax earnings stream.

3. The third approach is to apply the S corporation shareholders' highest personal tax rate to the S corporation's earnings and apply after-tax multiples derived from the comparative (C corporation) companies.

   This approach captures the benefit that accrues to S corporations from the lower personal tax rates. However, such a capitalization of earnings fails to capture the S corporation's ability to distribute earnings on a tax-free basis.

In order to capture this incremental value, one must capitalize shareholders' distributions. Capitalization of dividends or shareholders' distributions is given relatively minor weight in most minority interest valuations involving C corporations. Ultimately, dividends are possible only as a result of earnings. In the valuation of a minority interest, actual dividends rather than dividend-paying capacity are relevant, since the minority stockholder cannot force the payment of dividends, regardless of how much dividend paying capacity the company has. Since many closely held companies either don't pay dividends or pay only minimal dividends because of double taxation on dividends, capitalization of dividends generally receives relatively less weight than other earnings-based approaches. It should be noted, however, that for investors owning a nonmarketable minority interest position in a closely held company, dividends *do* represent the only return the investor is able to realize.

However, the typical S corporation, by virtue of its S election, distributes a significant portion of earnings to shareholders. In addition, it is the S corporation's ability to distribute earnings on a tax-free basis that is at the crux of the S corporation incremental value relative to the C corporation, as shown in Exhibit 24–1. Capitalizing shareholders' distributions captures the incremental value reflected by both the difference in corporate and individual tax rates and elimination of double taxation. If an S corporation distributes all of its earnings, this advantage can result in a 51.5 percent higher after-tax cash flow at the shareholder level (see Exhibit 24–1). Thus, when valuing an S corporation or an interest in it, the capitalization of shareholders' distributions approach should receive a relatively greater proportion of the total weight given to earnings-based methods than is appropriate when valuing a C corporation or an interest in it.

Determination of Appropriate Distribution Rate

If guideline companies are C corporations, dividend yields are inappropriate to apply to S corporation distributions. Once again, MLPs or other publicly traded limited partnerships provide useful comparative data. Ideally, specific MLPs or LPs in the specific industry should be used, if available. If the subject company operates in an industry in which no MLPs or publicly traded LPs exist, a more diverse industry group may have to be used, or the universe of available MLPs and LPs examined and used as an index.

The appraiser may want to compare the payout ratios of the publicly traded LPs or MLPs with the subject company's payout ratio in choosing an appropriate rate at which to capitalize the subject companies' shareholders' distributions. Current as well as average distributions, or both, may be capitalized depending on which best represents the expected future distributions of the subject company.

If the subject S corporation is only distributing earnings sufficient to cover taxes, capitalization of shareholders' distributions is not a meaningful approach to value. Arguably, if an S corporation distributes earnings in addition to those necessary to pay taxes, those earnings only (total distribution less that portion of distributions necessary to pay taxes) should be capitalized. However, publicly traded MLPs or LPs usually report only total distributions without reporting those distributions made to meet shareholders' taxes, making comparative analyses difficult except on a total distribution basis.

Discounted Future Returns Method

Often, a discounted future returns method is used in the appraisal of controlling interests. In such appraisals, the potential or hypothetical buyer will not pay for the S corporation tax advantages if they are not expected to continue in the future. However, if a discounted future returns method is being used in the appraisal of a minority interest, or the S corporation status of the company is expected to continue in the future, an appropriate procedure is to apply the highest applicable personal tax rate to the taxable income and calculate net free cash flow. Select a discount rate as discussed in Chapter 12. To capture avoidance of double taxation on net free cash flow within this valuation framework, one must calculate the future tax savings that would accrue to the S corporation because of its S corporation status. These tax savings should then be present valued at a rate sufficient to reflect the risks that (1) future distributions may be insufficient to cover taxes, (2) the S corporation may lose its election, and (3) the impact of tax legislation relative to personal tax rates may become unfavorable. These risks would seem to imply an equity rate of return as the appropriate discount rate.

In determining the appropriate present value discount rate applicable to the net free cash flows of an S corporation, the appraiser needs to take into consideration whether the S corporation status of the subject corporation increases its cost of capital. The reason that the company's cost of debt capital may be adversely impacted is that some banks are reluctant to loan to S corporations because of their distribution policies. An S corporation's cost of equity capital may be affected by its more circumscribed sources of capital—restricted by both number of investors (shareholders) and type. This increased cost of capital may offset any value increment from the present value of future tax benefits.

Other Valuation Issues

The above methods of determining value have attempted to explicitly deal with the incremental value of S corporations, which stems from the different tax rates paid by an S corporation compared to a C corporation. But the appraiser must take into consideration some of the other characteristics of S corporations and their implications on value. Earlier in this chapter, we listed a number of tax-related advantages and disadvantages of S corporations as well as business concerns for S corporations. These characteristics need to be examined in the valuation of each S corporation to determine whether there are risks specific to the subject company that are not reflected in the comparative valuation methods discussed above. Specific factors to analyze are the outlook for maintenance of the S corporation status; the proportion of earnings paid out both currently and prospectively (examine the historical record, capital needs, and management intentions); shareholder agreements; and the categories of potential buyers (of the entire company or the interest). These specific risks need to be taken into account in appraising an S corporation. These additional risks can be taken into account either in specific discounts or in the multiples or capitalization rates used.

As an example, what would be the impact, presumably negative, of an S corporation paying out distributions insufficient to meet shareholders' tax obligations? Typically, distributions are set to meet the tax obligations of the shareholder with the highest tax rate. S corporations typically have strong cash flows, making this scenario unlikely. If it was anything but a short-term aberration, there would be little advantage to S corporation status, and shareholders would presumably act to disqualify the election. A more likely scenario the appraiser may encounter is that distributions are made and then loaned back to the corporation by the shareholders to meet, for example, a large, one-time capital expenditure requirement. This avoids tax shortfalls for shareholders and increases their basis in the stock.

Lack of Marketability

A lack of marketability discount is still applicable to an S corporation having no ready market for its securities. However, several additional factors need to be considered in determining the appropriate level of such a discount. The discount may be lower because dividends or distributions are more likely to be paid by an S corporation. In fact, the typical S corporation may be distributing a large portion of its earnings. On the other hand, the marketability discount for stock of an S corporation that is not paying out sufficient distributions to cover the tax obligations of its shareholders may be significantly increased.

Because corporations or foreign investors are restricted from ownership interests in S corporations, the universe of potential buyers is more limited, all other things being equal, than is the case for a C corporation.

Converting from C Corporation to S Corporation Status

The argument has been put forth that, given the tax advantage of S corporation election over C corporation status, in valuing a C corporation that could be an S corporation, it should be valued as an S corporation. This fails to take into account that conversion from C corporation to S corporation status is not easily done and, post-TRA 86, has significant tax costs attached to it. In addition, there are less flexibility and greater complexity within the tax code for an S corporation that has past C corporation earnings.

Summary

Intrinsically, the fair market value of a company is unaffected by its choice of corporate form. Over a long period of time, the differences in the taxes paid by S corporations compared to C corporations, taking into consideration all of the relative advantages and disadvantages of each corporate form, may be minimal. This opinion is bolstered by the definition of fair market value that prohibits postulating a specific buyer or seller. As C corporations are the largest and most likely population of hypothetical buyers of the S corporation, the value differential cannot become too great.

However, there is a current cash flow advantage to the S corporation. The valuation methods discussed in this chapter attempt to take into account the explicit tax advantages of S corporation election, giving greater emphasis to the capitalization of shareholder distributions method. However, the appraiser must examine the range of advantages and disadvantages and specific characteristics of the S corporation being appraised on a specific facts and circumstances basis to determine the extent to which the S corporation election of the subject company is ultimately reflected in its fair market value.

The professional business valuation community is still struggling with many issues in the valuation of S corporation stock. As a result, methodologies used by various practitioners in the valuation of S corporation stock are not fully standardized as of this writing.

Selected Bibliography

Articles

"An Improved Tax Status for S Corporations." *Nation's Business*, January 1992, p. 60.

August, Jerald David. "S Corporations." *Journal of Partnership Taxation*, Spring 1988, pp. 67–78.

Bernard, Bruce. "S Status Is Less Advantageous after RRA '90." *Taxation for Accountants*, May 1991, pp. 268–75.

Blackman, Irving L. "Does an S Corporation Make Cents?" *National Petroleum News*, November 1991, p. 62.

Blum, Stephen B. "S-Corporations." *IBBA Journal*, June 1991, pp. 6–8.

Caspar, Frederick J. "S Corporation and Estate Planning: Preserving the S Election including Form Provisions." *S Corporations: The Journal of Tax, Legal and Business Strategies*, Spring 1991, pp. 107–21.

Curtis, Andrew W. "Post-Mortem Planning Tools Available for S Corporations." *Estate Planning*, January–February 1990, pp. 38–41.

———. "Taking Advantage of the Pre-Mortem Planning Options for S Corporations." *Estate Planning*, November–December 1989, pp. 360–65.

Faber, Peter L. "Acquisitions and Liquidations Involving S Corporations after Tax Reform." *Practical Accountant*, September 1987, pp. 99–114.

Gilbert, Gregory. Letter to Editor. *Business Valuation Review,* June 1989, pp. 92–93.

Karlinsky, Stewart S.; John J. Barcal; and Joseph V. Sliskovich. "A New Type of Estate Tax Freeze Vehicle: The S Corporation." *Practical Accountant*, February 1987, pp. 34–36.

Kato, Kelly. "Valuation of 'S' Corporations—Discounted Cash Flow Method." *Business Valuation Review*, December 1990, pp. 117–22.

Lemons, Bruce N.; Richard D. Blau; and Todd A. Fisher. "Consequences of Using S Corporations as Partners." *Journal of Taxation*, June 1990, pp. 324–27.

Lipton, Richard M., and Michael C. Fondo. "The Single-Class-of-Stock Rules, Round Three: The Final Regulations." *Journal of Taxation*, September 1992, pp. 138–41.

Mankoff, Ronald M. "Treasury Issues Replacement Regs. on One Class of Stock." *TAXES*, January 1992, pp. 3–10.

McDowell, Michael T. "S Corporations Provide Shelter for Small Businesses." *Business Credit*, September 1990, pp. 12–13.

Mittelman, Alan J. "S Corporation Buy-Sell Agreements after the Tax Reform Act of 1986." *Journal of American Society of CLU & ChFC*, May 1988, pp. 36–43.

Schlesinger, Michael. "Terminating Part or All of an S Corp.'s Business." *Taxation for Accountants*, November 1991, pp. 288–92.

Shackelford, Aaron L. "Valuation of 'S' Corporations." *Business Valuation Review*, December 1988, pp. 159–62.

Smith, Annette B. "How to Avoid Adverse or Unexpected Tax Consequences in Asset and Stock Acquisitions." Parts 1 and 2. *Tax Adviser*, June 1991 and July 1991, pp. 357–62, 456–60.

Starr, Samuel P., and William J. Dunn. "S Corporations: Knowing When to Say When." *Journal of Accountancy*, July 1989, pp. 46–52.

Zupanic, James D. "S Corporations Deserve Another Look." *Oregon Business*, November 1988, pp. 72–76.

Books

Boucher, Karen J.; Rick J. Taylor; Robert M. Kozub; and William A. Raabe. *Multistate S Corporation Tax Guide*. New York: Panel Publishers, 1990.

Faber, Peter L. *S Corporation Manual*. Englewood Cliffs, N.J.: Maxwell Macmillan, 1989.

Fass, Peter M., and Barbara S. Gerrard. *The S Corporation Handbook*. New York: Clark Boardman Callaghan, 1991.

Foth, Edward C., and Ted D. Engelbrecht. *S Corporations Guide*. Chicago: Commerce Clearing House, 1989.

Goldstein, Arnold S. *Starting Your Subchapter "S" Corporation: How to Build a Business the Right Way*. 2nd ed. New York: John Wiley & Sons, 1992.

Schlesinger, Michael. *The S Corporation Desk Book*. Englewood Cliffs, N.J.: Prentice Hall, 1989.

Starr, Samuel P. *S Corporations* (Tax Management Portfolio). Washington, D.C.: Tax Management Inc., 1986.

Traum, Sydney S., and Judith Rood Traum. *The S Corporation Answer Book*. 3rd ed. New York: Panel Publishers, 1992.

Wood, Robert W. *S Corporations*. Englewood Cliffs, N.J.: Maxwell Macmillan, 1991.

Chapter 25

Employee Stock Ownership Plans (ESOPs)

By Mary B. McCarter, C.F.A., A.S.A., and Kathryn F. Aschwald, C.F.A., A.S.A.

Employee Stock Ownership Plans (ESOPs) have become an increasingly advantageous and popular means of transferring all or any part of a company's ownership to employees. In a single transaction, an owner may sell all his stock to employees through an ESOP, or any proportion of ownership can be sold at any time through one transaction or a series of transactions. An ESOP can be used effectively for financing and can result in significant savings in both income taxes and estate taxes.

In recent years, the use of ESOPs has grown in popularity among smaller companies and professional practices.

What Is an ESOP?

The concept of an ESOP is a plan to allow employees to have an ownership interest in the business. An ESOP is a tax-qualified employee benefit plan designed to invest primarily in the sponsoring company's securities. An ESOP, therefore, is a form of employee benefit plan, subject to the Employee Retirement Income Security Act (ERISA), similar in many respects to a pension or profit-sharing plan. The corporation may contribute cash to the ESOP, and the ESOP may use the cash to buy stock from one or more current stockholders. Alternatively, the corporation may issue additional shares of stock and contribute such shares to the ESOP. The ESOP's ownership interests are allocated among employees on a basis similar to pension and profit-sharing fund ownership allocations.

An ESOP may also borrow money and enter into transactions with related parties to acquire the employer's securities in what would be prohibited transactions under ERISA and the Internal Revenue Code for other types of qualified plans. An ESOP that borrows money to purchase stock is referred to as a *leveraged ESOP*.

Leveraged ESOPs

A leveraged ESOP is one that borrows money, usually from a bank. The money may be used to buy stock from one or more existing owners or to buy stock from the corporation. In either case, the corporation guarantees the loan and makes annual cash contributions to the ESOP, which in turn are used to pay off the loan. Since the contribution is tax-deductible, the loan (both principal and interest) is paid with pretax dollars.

The Leveraged Buyout

If the ESOP borrows money to buy all or part of the company's stock from the current owner or owners, and uses the company's assets as collateral, a perfect example of a leveraged buyout is at work. This avenue is becoming increasingly open to small businesses, partly because of the banks' willingness to make such loans, and partly because of the excellent tax advantages, as detailed in the next section.

The ESOP as a Vehicle for Financing

The ESOP can also borrow money to buy newly issued stock or treasury stock from the corporation. In this situation, the ESOP is used as a vehicle to provide new equity financing to the corporation.

Advantages of ESOPs

Tax-Free Rollover on Sale of Stock to ESOP

A sale of a company's stock to an ESOP will be treated as a tax-free exchange if the ESOP owns at least 30 percent of the total value of the employer's securities outstanding after the transaction and if the selling stockholder invests the proceeds in securities of other domestic corporations. The seller must have held the stock at least one year, and the proceeds must be reinvested within one year in a corporation whose passive investment income is not more than 25 percent of its gross receipts.

Tax-Deductible Dividends

Dividends paid to ESOP participants will be deducted from the employer corporation's taxable income. The corporation may also deduct dividends used to make loan repayments in the case of a leveraged ESOP.

Half of Interest Income Is Tax-Free to Lenders

A commercial lender, such as a bank or insurance company, can exclude from taxable income 50 percent of the interest it receives on the loan an ESOP uses to acquire employee securities, as long as the ESOP owns more than 50 percent of the value in their company's stock after the loan is made.

Estate Tax Liability

An ESOP can assume a stockholder's estate tax liability. Essentially, the government lends the ESOP the money to pay estate taxes, and the company makes contributions to the ESOP, which allows it to pay the estate tax liability. Stock is allocated to the employees' accounts as each payment is made toward the estate tax liability.

Improve Employee Morale and Productivity

There is strong evidence, at least in the United States, that ESOP companies tend to be more efficient than their competitors, particularly if there are meaningful employee participation plans. As part owners, employees may tend to appreciate the need for operating efficiently and are likely to be more aware of the bottom line, particularly where there is an active employee participation plan in place.

Achieve Other Corporate Objectives

An ESOP can also provide a means for achieving other corporate objectives, as follows:

- Facilitate the sale of a division of the company to employees.
- Facilitate the management buyout of the firm.
- Increase the company's capital by selling stock to the ESOP, which uses funds provided by tax-deductible contributions.
- Enhance employee retirement benefits.

Does an ESOP Make Sense for Your Company?[1]

Not every company is a good ESOP candidate. Following are some factors to consider in determining whether or not an ESOP is feasible for your company.

- Value of the company.
- Corporate form.
- Adequacy of payroll.
- Cash flow.
- Owner's departure.
- Corporate culture.

Value of the Company

If an ESOP is being used as a vehicle to buy out an existing owner(s), the first step in this process is to determine how much the owner(s) wants to sell, and over what period of time. From there, a preliminary estimate of the value of the shares to be purchased by the ESOP needs to be determined. With this information, the seller can decide if the price is acceptable and the parties can explore whether the deal is financable.

If the ESOP is not going to be used as a vehicle to buy out a principal owner(s), but is simply to be used as a benefit plan, determination of the feasibility is fairly straightforward. The costs of the ESOP plan should be compared with other potential benefit plans. While ESOPs can be more expensive to administer than other types of plans, the tax deduct-

---

[1]Much of this discussion was drawn from articles appearing in *Employee Ownership Report*, published by The National Center for Employee Ownership, Inc. (NCEO). The NCEO is a private, nonprofit information and research organization headquartered in Oakland, California. They can be contacted by telephone at (510) 272-9461.

ibility of dividends and principal payments and noncash contributions can increase a company's cash flow.

Corporate Form

Currently, ESOPs can only be set up in C corporations. S corporations cannot have trusts (such as an ESOP) as shareholders. As a result, an ESOP would automatically cause the loss of the S corporation tax status. The S corporation could be converted to a C corporation fairly easily, but the costs and benefits associated with doing so should be taken into consideration.

While ESOPs for S corporations are currently not an option, H.R. 2410, which is known as the ESOP Promotion and Improvement Act of 1991, contains provisions that would allow ESOPs in S corporations. As of this writing, H.R. 2410 had not been sent to Congress for a vote.

Adequacy of Payroll

In leveraged ESOPs, companies can contribute up to 25 percent of the covered (or eligible) payroll of plan participants to repay the principal portion of an ESOP loan. In a nonleveraged ESOP, the annual limit is generally 15 percent, although this can be as high as 25 percent under certain limited circumstances. Under some circumstances, dividends can be used to expand these limits. Generally, the amount of the company contribution made to buy the targeted number of shares must fall within these limits, or the ESOP will not work.

Covered payroll is not the same as total payroll. For example, new employees would probably not be participating in the ESOP immediately; some highly compensated employees may have to be excluded under some circumstances; or a union group may not be eligible for participation. These factors reduce the overall level of covered payroll and, thus, allowable contributions.

The above limitations can also be reduced by contributions to other existing defined contribution plans such as profit sharing, 401(k), and defined benefit plans.

If you determine that your company does not have enough payroll, consideration can be given to reducing contributions to existing plans or transferring funds from an existing plan to help fund a portion of the shares to be purchased.

Some experts advise that a company with an annual payroll of less than $500,000 is likely to find that the costs of establishing and operating an ESOP outweigh its short-term benefits.[2]

Cash Flow

An ESOP has two impacts on cash flow. First, cash is needed to make contributions to fund purchases of shares (unless the contributions are

---

[2]Robert W. Smiley, Jr., and Ronald J. Gilbert, *Employee Stock Ownership Plans* (New York: Maxwell MacMillan, 1990), pp. 1-11–1-12.

made in newly issued stock) or to pay off the loan incurred to purchase; and second, to fund the repurchase of shares allocated to participants' accounts when they retire, die, terminate employment, or are disabled. In short, the company needs to analyze the cash available to fund these obligations. If the company's cash flow is shaky to begin with, it is unlikely that it can afford an ESOP without major changes or sacrifices.

Owner's Departure

Some companies are heavily dependent on the existing owner's skills, contacts, and reputation. An abrupt departure of such a key person can have serious implications for a company that is not prepared for such a departure. A management succession plan should be in place, and the new managers/owners must be given the opportunity to develop their own relationship with customers, employees, lenders, and others before the existing owner leaves. Typically if there is such a dependence, the bank will likely require that the selling owner stay on in a consulting capacity or as a corporate officer for a couple of years.

Corporate Culture

Unless employees are treated as owners, an ESOP will not live up to its potential. Management needs to determine if it is really comfortable with employees being owners. Employees as owners are involved with corporate decision making, and typically share in the company's financial information. An ESOP is probably not a good idea in a company where management is not willing to take on the responsibilities of many new shareholders, despite the financial benefits associated with an ESOP. The most important action necessary to ensure that an ESOP realizes all of its benefits, including increased productivity, is to facilitate employee participation and to effectively communicate the ESOP to the employees.

Rules for Valuation of ESOP Shares

Government Regulation

Annual appraisals of ESOP stock by a qualified, independent appraiser became mandatory with the Tax Reform Act of 1986.

Valuation of ESOP shares in privately held companies must meet the requirements of both the IRS and ERISA. The IRS goes by Revenue Ruling 59-60, the general guidelines for gift and estate tax valuations, and, as of this writing, has not issued any supplemental revenue ruling or other guidelines specifically applicable to ESOPs. Section 3(18) of ERISA refers to fair market value determined in good faith "and in accordance with regulations promulgated by the Secretary (of Labor)."

The Department of Labor (DOL) has published a proposed regulation for guidance in valuing ESOP stock. As of this writing, these guidelines have not been finalized.[3] However, the proposed guidelines do embrace Revenue Ruling 59-60 and add provisions specifically applicable to ESOPs.

The appraiser of ESOP shares must know the guidelines set forth in these two documents and must rely on generally accepted appraisal practices and the case law that has developed to date.[4]

When an Appraisal Is Required

An appraisal of the company's ESOP stock is required when:

1. The ESOP makes its first acquisition of stock.
2. Annually thereafter.
3. When there is a transaction with a related (prohibited) party.
4. If the ESOP is selling out.

While typically only an annual appraisal is required, many companies have their ESOP stock valued twice a year, or even on a quarterly basis, to have a more current valuation for transactions several times during the year.

Qualified and Independent Appraiser

The appraiser appointed by the ESOP fiduciaries must meet two basic criteria:

1. The appraiser should be a company or person who regularly engages in the valuation of businesses or business interests.
2. The appraiser must be independent with respect to the issuing company and parties to an ESOP transaction.

Treasury Regulation Section 54.4975-11(d)(5) states: "An independent appraisal will not in itself be a good faith determination of value in the case of a transaction between a plan and a disqualified person. However, in other cases, a determination of fair market value based on at least an annual appraisal independently arrived at by a person who customarily makes such appraisals and who is independent of any party to a transaction under Section 54.4975(b)(9) and (12) will be deemed to be a good faith determination of value."[5]

In order to be considered independent, the appraiser should be a person who does not perform any other services for a party whose interest may be adverse to the ESOP and who would meet an objective standard of impartiality.[6] The regulations make it clear that the appraiser needs to be retained by the ESOP and act as their financial advisor. It is also

---

[3]Proposed Regulation Relating to the Definition of Adequate Consideration, 53 Fed. Reg. 17, 632 (1988) (to be codified at 29 C.F.R. Part 2510).

[4]This is discussed more fully in Pratt, *Valuing a Business*, 2nd edition, Chapter 23.

[5]*Valuing ESOP Shares* (Washington, D.C.: The ESOP Association, 1989), pp. 3–4.

[6]Jared Kaplan and Jack Curtis, "ESOPs," *Tax Management*, 1991, p. A–4.

important for the ESOP to be represented by competent legal advisors with experience in ESOPs. With both competent financial and legal advisors, a leveraged ESOP transaction is much more likely to pass the scrutiny of the various regulatory authorities.

The appraiser should also be experienced in performing ESOP valuations, because the special features of an ESOP, such as the put option, impact the valuation of the shares held by the plan.

ESOP Valuation Problems

Based on our analysis of ESOP court decisions and our own experience, most of the problems with ESOP valuations have occurred in the following situations:

- The appraiser was not independent.
- The appraiser used unconventional procedures not acceptable to the IRS or DOL.
- The appraisal report was not thoroughly documented.
- The appraisal was out of date at the time of the transaction.

Summary

In order to avoid problems with the regulatory authorities with respect to the ESOP valuation, we recommend the following:

- Retain a reputable independent appraisal firm with a good proven track record with regulatory authorities and courts.
- Bring an independent appraisal firm into the professional advisory team at the earliest possible time.
- Allow adequate time and budget to do the job right.
- Do not expect to pressure the independent appraisal firm to reach some predetermined valuation conclusion.

As discussed above, in addition to providing for an employee's retirement, ESOPs, if appropriately considered and implemented, can provide numerous financial advantages, boost employee morale and productivity, and provide a viable means for transferring ownership.

We would encourage any company considering forming an ESOP to contact The ESOP Association, 1726 M Street, N.W., Suite 501, Washington, D.C. 20036, telephone (202) 293-2971. The Association is composed of companies that have ESOPs and can supply names of firms that specialize in installing and administering ESOPs, as well as firms that specialize in appraising ESOP shares. The ESOP Association also offers a variety of informative publications.[7]

---

[7]Note especially, *Valuing ESOP Shares.*

Selected Bibliography

Articles

Ackerman, David. "Innovative Uses of Employee Stock Ownership Plans for Private Companies." *DePaul Business Law Journal*, Spring 1990, pp. 227–54.

Ackerman, David, and Idelle A. Howitt. "Tax-Favored Planning for Ownership Succession via ESOPs." *Estate Planning*, November/December 1992, pp. 331–37.

Blackiston, Henry C., III; Linda E. Rappaport; and Lawrence A. Pasini. "ESOPs: What They Are and How They Work." *Business Lawyer*, November 1989, pp. 85–143.

Block, Stanley B. "The Advantages and Disadvantages of ESOPs: A Long-Range Analysis." *Journal of Small Business Management*, January 1991, pp. 15–21.

Braun, Richard S. "The ESOP Lifecycle." *ESOP Report*, December 1991, pp. 4–5.

————. "ESOP Valuations." In *Financial Valuation: Business and Business Interests*, ed. James H. Zukin and John G. Mavredakis. New York: Maxwell Macmillan, 1990, Ch. 8.

Brockhardt, James, and Robert Reilly. "Employee Stock Ownership Plans after the 1989 Tax Law: Valuation Issues." *Compensation and Benefits Review*, September–October 1990, pp. 29–36.

————. "ESOPs Are Becoming Popular Corporate Financial Tools." *Trusts & Estates*, February 1990, pp. 40–43.

Buxton, Dickson C. "ESOP and Business Perpetuation Plans." *Journal of the American Society of CLU & ChFC*, November 1990, pp. 34–44.

Dema, Robert J., and Duncan Harwood. "Tapping the Financial Benefits of an ESOP." *Journal of Accountancy*, April 1991, pp. 27–28.

Fiore, Nicholas J. "ESOP Fables." *Journal of Accountancy*, February 1990, p. 6.

Gross, Robert J. "ESOP Valuation Issues." *Journal of Employee Ownership Law & Finance*, Winter 1991, pp. 53–62.

Haut, Arthur N., and William P. Lyons. "Issues in the Valuation of Control and Noncontrol Shares in Connection with the Acquisition of Stock by Employee Stock Ownership Plans." *Journal of Pension Planning & Compliance*, Winter 1986, pp. 319–26.

Kaplan, Jared. "Is ESOP a Fable: Fabulous Uses and Benefits or Phenomenal Pitfalls?" *TAXES*, December 1987, pp. 788–95.

Leung, T. S. Tony, and David W. Simpson. "Financing Techniques for Small Business Buy Outs." *Practical Accountant*, February 1990, pp. 66–69.

Lint, Ron J. "ESOP Power." *Management Accounting*, November 1992, pp. 38–41.

McCarter, Mary B., and Shannon P. Pratt. "A Primer to the Appraisal Process." *Employee Ownership Report*, July/August 1987, pp. 1, 6.

Paone, Louis A., and Donna J. Walker. "ESOP Case Law—Valuation." *Journal of Employee Ownership Law and Finance*, Spring 1992, pp. 37–60.

Pratt, Shannon P. "Court Cases Involving ESOP Valuation Issues." *Journal of Pension Planning & Compliance*, Fall 1990, pp. 245–60.

————. "Employee Stock Ownership Plans." Parts 1 and 2. *Journal of Pension Planning & Compliance*, Spring 1989 and Summer 1989, pp. 29–39; pp. 149–58.

————. "ESOPs: Fables, Foibles, and Facts." *Midway*, January 1987, pp. 32–33, 56, 60.

————. "Estate Planning, ESOPs, Buy-Sell Agreements, and Life Insurance for Closely Held Businesses." *Journal of American Society of CLU & ChFC*, September 1986, pp. 74–79.

Reilly, Robert F. "ESOP Formation and Valuation Procedures." *Business Valuation News*, March 1986, pp. 23–35.

————. "ESOPs are Becoming Popular Financial Planning Tools." *Trusts and Estates,* February 1990, pp. 22–24.

————. "Owners of Closely Held Corporations Can Reap Special Benefits from ESOPs." *Taxation for Accountants,* June 1986, pp. 44–46.

————. "Valuing ESOP Shares for Closely Held Businesses." *Small Business Taxation,* July/August 1989, pp. 79–82.

Rosen, Corey. "Sharing Ownership with Employees: ESOPs and Other Options." *Small Business Reporter*, December 1990, pp. 60–69.

————. "Using an ESOP for Business Continuity." *Journal of American Society of CLU & ChFC*, July 1986, pp. 54–58.

Ryterband, Daniel J. "The Decision to Implement an ESOP: Strategies and Economic Considerations." *Employee Benefits Journal*, December 1991, pp. 19–25.

Sayers, William K. "ESOPs Are No Fable." *Small Business Reports*, June 1990, pp. 57–60.

Shaw, Greg. "Employee Ownership in Small Business." *Journal of Employee Ownership Law and Finance*, Summer 1991, pp. 107–28.

Szabo, Joan C. "Using ESOPs to Sell Your Firm." *Nation's Business*, January 1991, pp. 59–60.

Taplin, Polly T. "Employee Stock Ownership Can Sell a Small Business." *Employee Benefit Plan Review*, July 1986, pp. 18, 20.

————. "When an ESOP Is Appropriate in a Small Company." *Employee Benefit Plan Review*, July 1988, pp. 24–25.

Urcinoli, Arthur. "A Piece of the Pie." *Executive Female*, May–June 1991, p. 72.

Van Horn, Bradley. "Consider Establishing an E.S.O.P." *Small Business Forum*, Fall 1991, pp. 20–24.

Welytok, Daniel S. "ESOPs after the Revenue Reconciliation Act of 1989." *TAXES*, April 1990, pp. 330–34.

"What's It Worth?" *Employee Ownership Report*, March/April 1991, p. 9.

Willens, Robert. "ESOPs: A Unique Financing Tool." *Journal of Accountancy*, August 1989, pp. 125–26.

Books

Blasi, Joseph Raphael, and Douglas Lynn Kruse. *The New Owners: The Mass Emergence of Employee Ownership in Public Companies and What It Means to American Business*. New York: HarperCollins, 1991.

Braun, Warren L. *On the Way to Successful Employee Stock Ownership.* Harrisonburg, Va.: Dr. Warren L. Braun, P.E., 1992.

Frisch, Robert A. *The Magic of ESOPs and LBOs.* New York: Farnsworth Publishing Co., 1985.

Kalish, Gerald I., ed. *ESOPs: The Handbook of Employee Stock Ownership Plans.* Chicago: Probus Publishing Co., 1990.

Kaplan, Jared; John E. Curtis, Jr.; and Gregory K. Brown. *ESOPs* (Tax Management Portfolio). Washington, D.C.: Tax Management Inc., 1991.

Quarrey, Michael, and Corey Rosen. *Employee Ownership and Corporate Performance.* Oakland, Calif.: The National Center for Employee Ownership, 1991.

Rosen, Corey; Katherine J. Klein; and Karen M. Young. *Employee Ownership in America: The Equity Solution.* Lexington, Mass.: D.C. Heath and Co., 1986.

Smiley, Robert W., Jr., and Ronald J. Gilbert, eds. *Employee Stock Ownership Plans: Business Planning, Implementation, and Law and Taxation.* Englewood Cliffs, N.J.: Maxwell MacMillan/Rosenfeld Launer, 1991.

Valuing ESOP Shares. Washington, D.C.: The ESOP Association, 1989.

Young, Karen M., ed. *The Expanding Role of ESOPs in Public Companies.* New York: Quorum Books, 1990.

Chapter 26

Estate Planning and Buy-Sell Agreements

By Curtis R. Kimball, C.F.A., A.S.A.

Every business or professional practice has an expected life cycle as surely as the individuals involved in the firm have expected life spans. How a firm copes with the unexpected ownership problems, such as the loss of a key founding owner-manager, or the expected hurdles of the business life cycle, such as transfer of the firm to successor owners, often spells the difference between a successful enterprise and one that founders.

In all such cases, the fair and accurate valuation of the ownership interest is critical. In times of crisis, all parties should be focusing on the successful management of the business rather than being caught up in protracted valuation analysis or disputes. Every owner should have a plan for determining the value of his interest in the firm and for providing any funding that may be required.

This chapter explores these specific purposes for business appraisals. We will follow roughly the order in which these are often faced by a professional or small business owner during his life—from beginning to end. As can be seen, it often pays to devote some time to thinking about the unthinkable in advance to uncover and solve any sticky problems.

Buy-Sell Agreements

When starting out, a professional or small business founder may have partners or coventurers. In addition, the departure of a founder before adequate successors are available or the business reaches some maturity can permanently cripple a firm's growth.

A buy-sell agreement can effectively avoid many of the potential problems regarding disposition of a stock or partnership interest. The buy-sell agreement can be designed to accomplish the following objectives:

1. Identify those situations that will require the buy-sell agreement to be triggered. These include death, mental or physical disability, retirement, departure, divorce, or irreconcilable dissention among the owners.
2. Help all the equity owners by offering a definitive mechanism to obtain liquidity for a departing owner's interest.
3. Provide a definitive and fair provision for determining the price that the departing owner will be paid for the interest.
4. Help the business continue by providing for a fair method to fund the buyout of the departing owner's equity without unduly disrupting the financial stability of the firm.
5. Prevent the ownership interest from being sold or transferred to any party not acceptable to the other owners.
6. Set a price that will be respected by taxing authorities for estate, gift, and income tax purposes, or by courts for divorce or other litigation purposes.
7. Establish coordination with the personal estate planning of the owners.

Types of Agreements

The two basic types of buy-sell agreements relate to the parties who are expected to actually buy the interest under the terms of the agreement.

The first type provides that the firm buy back the interest from the former owner. This is often called an *entity purchase*, a *stock repurchase*, or *redemption agreement*. The second type of buy-sell agreement allows the other owners of the firm to buy the departing owner's interest. This is often identified as a *cross-purchase agreement*. These two concepts can be combined into a hybrid type of *wait-and-see agreement* whereby the firm or the other owners have a right of first refusal to purchase the interest, with the other being mandated to buy if the first refusal option is not exercised. Sometimes key employees or other people who are not currently shareholders are given the opportunity to buy in under the terms of the buy-sell agreement.

The drafting of a buy-sell agreement should be based on the advice of an experienced attorney. In determining the appropriate type of agreement and wording, a good attorney will probe the following areas:

1. What are the desires of the owners regarding who should be allowed to own stock in the firm?
2. Does the buy-sell agreement's proposed language conflict with existing wills or other estate planning objectives of the owners? Conflicts between buy-sell agreements and wills may require expensive litigation to untangle, and may result in the buy-sell agreement restrictions being overturned.[1]
3. What payment terms should be made part of the buyout?
4. What will be the tax effects of such a buyout both on the firm and on the individual owners?
5. What restrictions may exist in state laws on the proposed terms of the buy-sell agreement?
6. What provisions should be made for setting the value?

Provisions for Valuation

The provision for valuation is a critical element of the buy-sell agreement. Under current tax law, the parties have less flexibility than in the past in structuring this provision, particularly when family members are involved, so the language of any agreement must be carefully considered in order to maintain fairness, feasibility, and tax efficiency.

The valuation provision can require the same approach under all circumstances or it can differ for different triggering event purposes, such as voluntary departure from the company as opposed to dismissal or death of the interest's owner. Generally, the vast majority of buy-sell agreements that our firm reviews call for a single value.

If the parties intend to have the buy-sell agreement be binding for purposes other than the transfer itself, such as for estate taxes, then

---

[1] *Globe Slicing Machine* v. *Hasner*, 333 F.2d 413 (2nd Cir. 1964), cert. denied, 379 U.S. 969 (1965).

Beware the "Fair Market Value" Standard In Buy-Sell Agreements

It is important that all parties to a buy-sell agreement and their counsel understand the implications of the valuation provision at the time they enter into the agreement. We at Williamette have seen many horror stories of expensive disputes with resolutions unsatisfactory to one party or another as a result of lack of understanding of the valuation provision. In one case an attorney's insurance company paid over $1 million for not incorporating language into an agreement that reflected his client's understanding and desires regarding implications for value.

The main misconception that we have encountered has been misinterpretation of "fair market value." If you or your client are considering using the phrase "fair market value" in the buy-sell agreement, please read carefully the definition and discussion of this term in Chapter 3 on Defining Value and Chapter 35 on Valuing Minority Interests. Often, a minority owner mistakenly assumes that "fair market value of the shares" means a proportionate share of the value of the equity of the enterprise taken as a whole. The sections referenced make it clear that fair market value of a minority interest is *rarely* equal to a proportionate share of the value of the equity as a controlling interest. In fact, it is not uncommon for the fair market value of a minority interest to be less than half the value of a proportionate share of a controlling interest value! This comes as a devastating shock to many minority owners who were misinformed or uninformed when entering into the agreement.

Such shocks and resulting disputes can be avoided by being sure that all parties to an agreement have a clear understanding of the implications for value arising from the language in the valuation provision.

                                                                                            S.P.P.

---

the standard of value required for the appraisal should be clearly spelled out and should conform with the particular standard. It should be noted that courts tend to put less reliance on a buy-sell agreement that is inconsistent with the purpose for which the court is determining value. For example, gift and estate taxes require the use of "fair market value" as the standard of value. This may not be the appropriate standard of value when, as an example, three equal coventurers actually wish to specify that each other's one-third interest will be repurchased at a price that represents a pro rata one-third portion of the value of the entire firm. In this case, the minority interest discount that is usually appropriate under a fair market value standard is not applicable (see box).

The most common valuation provisions are the following:

1. A price fixed by mutual agreement among shareholders, updated on a periodic basis, typically at least annually.
2. A formula for determining the appraised price. Such a formula may rely on comparative public company price-earnings ratios or other market-related factors, plus premiums and discounts to reflect control and marketability.
3. A requirement for a periodic appraisal by an independent professional appraiser, either annually or upon the occurrence of a triggering event.

Exhibit 26–1

SAMPLE VALUATION ARTICLE FOR BUY-SELL AGREEMENT
(Corporation Stock Redemption Example)

As soon as practical after the end of each fiscal year, the stockholders and the corporation shall agree on the value per share of the stock that is applicable to this agreement. Such value will be set forth in Schedule A, which shall be dated, signed by each stockholder and an officer of the corporation, and attached hereto. Such value shall be binding on both the corporation and the estate of any deceased stockholder whose date of death is within one year of the last dated and signed Schedule A.

If more than a year has elapsed between the date when Schedule A was last signed and the date of death of a deceased stockholder, then the value per share shall be determined, as of the date of death of the stockholder, by mutual agreement between the corporation and the personal representative or administrator of the deceased stockholder's estate.

If the corporation and the personal representative of the deceased stockholder's estate are unable to agree upon such a value within 90 days after such personal representative or administrator has qualified to administer the estate of the deceased stockholder, then such value shall be determined by binding arbitration. Either party may give written notice of such binding arbitration pursuant to this agreement to the other party. Within 30 days of such notice of arbitration, each party shall appoint one arbitrator. Within 30 days of the appointment of the two arbitrators, the arbitrators so appointed will select a third arbitrator. The first two arbitrators will have sole discretion in the selection of the third arbitrator, except that he must be an individual or qualified representative of a firm that regularly engages, as a primary occupation, in the professional appraisal of businesses or business interests. In the event that the first two arbitrators are unable to agree on a third arbitrator within 30 days of their appointment, the Executive Director of the ABC Trade Association shall appoint the third arbitrator.

The standard of value to be used by the arbitrators shall be fair market value of the shares being valued as of the date of death, under the assumption that the stockholder is deceased and the corporation has collected the proceeds, if any, of insurance on the life of the deceased stockholder payable to the corporation.

Each arbitrator shall use his sole discretion in determining the amount of investigation he considers necessary in arriving at a determination of the value of the shares. The corporation shall make available on a timely basis all books and records requested by any arbitrator, and all material made available to any one arbitrator shall be made available to all arbitrators.

Concurrence by at least two of the three arbitrators shall constitute a binding determination of value. The value concluded by the arbitrators shall be reported to the corporation and to the personal representative or administrator of the estate of the deceased in writing, signed by the arbitrators concurring as to the concluded value, within 90 days of the appointment of the third arbitrator unless an extension of time has been agreed upon between the corporation and the personal representative of the estate.

The corporation and the estate shall each be responsible for the fees and expenses of the arbitrators they appoint. The fees and expenses of the third arbitrator shall be divided equally between the corporation and the estate.

A common type of valuation provision calls for the parties to update the value by arm's-length negotiation at least annually, and provides for an independent appraisal if there has been no recent annual appraisal. Exhibit 26–1 is a sample article of a "negotiated price" buy-sell agreement relating to valuation.

Value setting used to be rather arbitrary, with most parties interested in having a reasonably fair price for all involved. Accounting book value was used quite often as a quick, simple, and wholly inadequate proxy for fair market value.

However, in firms controlled by members of the same family, the rules under Section 2703 of Chapter 14 of the Internal Revenue Code—

which applies to all buy-sell agreements created or substantially modified after October 8, 1990—require that three very specific and separate tests be met in order to have such a value determinative for estate and gift tax purposes:[2]

1. It must be a bona fide business arrangement.
2. It must not be a device to transfer such property to members of the family for less than full and adequate consideration.
3. Its terms must be comparable to similar arrangements entered into by persons in an arm's-length transaction.[3]

Thus, family members are treated with particularly close scrutiny, and values must be determined on a truly arm's-length basis, in order to have a buy-sell agreement determine the estate tax value. Adding or removing a party to a "grandfathered" buy-sell agreement in existence prior to October 9, 1990, will generally not be defined as a substantial modification to that agreement, but only if this is required under the terms of the agreement and the added party is not a younger generation family member.[4]

The buy-sell agreement should specify the mechanism or mechanisms not only for pricing the interest but also for terms of payment.

Gift and Estate Taxes

Sometime during life, every successful small business owner or professional should do some serious planning to decide what will happen to his or her business as he or she grows older. Sometimes family firms will be passed on to the next generation; sometimes a professional practice interest is sold, upon death or retirement, to a successor practitioner.

In any case, such transactions may give rise to income taxes or gift and estate taxes. We will discuss below some methods for minimizing gift and estate taxes. References for additional study on each topic are included in the bibliography.

Transfer Tax Rates and Exemptions

Estate and gift taxes are a unified transfer tax system that levies a tax on the fair market value of transfers of assets by gift during life or by will upon death.[5]

Many small businesses and professional practice owners will not have a significant gift or estate tax liability, because the current tax law provides a lifetime unified credit against gift and estate transfer taxes

---

[2]In order for any buy-sell agreement (regardless of who owns the firm) to be determinative for estate tax purposes, the general rules require that (a) the agreement must contain a determinable price; (b) it must be binding on the decedent during life as well as at death; and (c) it must be a bona fide business arrangement.

[3]IRC Section 2703(b). The implication of this requirement is that the agreement must reflect practices that are typical of that specific company's industry.

[4]Final Regulations Section 25.2703-1(c).

[5]If you die without a will, the laws of your state of residence will determine how and to whom your assets will be transferred.

and allows any individual to give away $600,000 in asset values before further transfers are taxed.

In addition, current laws provide effectively for unlimited gifting and estate transfers between spouses. Of course, transferring a growing business interest to your spouse at your death merely postpones the eventual estate tax reckoning and probably increases the amount of taxes eventually owed.

Another useful provision of the law allows an exclusion of a maximum of $10,000 in gifts each year from any single donor to any single donee. Any value over $10,000 per year from any donor to any donee is charged against the $600,000 lifetime gift and estate tax exemption total.

Once the lifetime total of gifts plus the estate exceeds the exemption limit, gift and estate tax rates begin at 37% and rise to 55%, as shown below:

Amount Subject to Tax	Tax Rate (%)
Over $600,000 to $750,000	37
Over 750,000 to 1,000,000	39
Over 1,000,000 to 1,250,000	41
Over 1,250,000 to 1,500,000	43
Over 1,500,000 to 2,000,000	45
Over 2,000,000 to 2,500,000	49
Over 2,500,000 to 3,000,000	53
Over 3,000,000	55

In addition to the federal rates listed above, the benefits of the lower tax rates are recaptured with a special 60 percent rate beginning at $10,000,000. Many states also impose inheritance taxes (with rates generally between 4 percent and 16 percent), which may apply different exemptions than the federal taxes. As can be seen, gift and estate tax rates exceed most of the current levels of income tax rates. Thus, it makes sense to put together a plan to minimize the impact of this largest of taxes.

Penalties for Undervaluation

There are also accuracy-related federal penalties for undervaluation misstatements on gift and estate tax returns. These consist of a 20 percent penalty for understating the value of a business interest at 50 percent or less of the finally determined value with a 40 percent penalty if the undervaluation is 25 percent or less of the finally determined value. Penalties hurt even more because they are ordinarily not deductible expenses for income tax purposes. There are also other penalties for civil fraud that can be levied against the taxpayer and penalties for assisting in the preparation of tax documents in order to knowingly understate tax liabilities that can be levied against tax preparers (including appraisers).

Rules for Valuation

The essential guidelines for valuation of closely held business interests for federal gift and estate tax purposes are contained in Revenue Ruling

59-60,[6] which is included as Appendix B at the end of the book. Most states now follow the same basic guidelines for determining inheritance tax values, but are not bound by any federal-level interpretations for gift and estate tax issues.

In the more than 30 years since Revenue Ruling 59-60 was published, hundreds of gift and estate tax cases have been decided in the courts, giving rise to a body of case law concerning the valuation of small businesses and professional practices. In most situations, the courts will give the most weight to well-documented appraisal reports prepared contemporaneously with the gift or date of death by an appraiser familiar with the existing case law issues. Certainly, having a qualified, well-thought-out appraisal report provides the taxpayer and the tax preparer with a reasonable basis for establishing their position against any subsequent inquiry from the IRS.

Methods Used to Minimize Gift and Estate Taxes

The following types of transactions are methods typically used to minimize the impact of gift and estate taxes for the small business owner and professional practitioner.

Estate Freezing Recapitalizations. Often, the owner of a rapidly growing business wishes his children to receive the value of the business's future appreciation, while retaining an interest that will provide him or her with some income for retirement. One available estate planning method to accomplish this is the estate freezing recapitalization.

In essence, the estate freeze involves dividing the ownership of the firm into two or more classes of senior preferred and junior common interests—either corporate stock or partnership interests. The senior interest will have a nondiscretionary cumulative right to receive cash distributions (e.g., preferred dividends) and other preferences senior to the rights of the junior common interests. The relatively steady return on the distributions will provide a base for the value of the senior preferred interest to be, in effect, frozen, while any appreciation in the value of the entire business is therefore diverted to the junior class(es) of equity. The junior equity interests are then transferred out of the estates of the senior family members to the younger generation of family members.

For all transactions of this nature occurring after October 8, 1990, special valuation rules set forth in the new Chapter 14 of the Internal Revenue Code will apply. The rules are somewhat complex, but basically are designed to force the payment of a market rate of cumulative distributions/dividends to the senior preferred securities and prohibit the use of liquidation, conversion, put rights, or other rights and features to boost the value of the senior securities.

In most of the new estate freezing transactions our firm has seen, the critical issue limiting the amount of value that can be frozen is the

---

[6]Revenue Ruling 59-60 1959-1, CB 237.

available level of the distribution/dividend payout. Because preferred stock dividends are not deductible expenses for corporate income taxes, it would appear that better overall income and estate tax efficiency will be achieved with a partnership freeze. If an estate freezing transaction is contemplated, we recommend retaining at the outset, as part of the estate planning team, a business appraiser who is experienced in recapitalizations. The appraiser can help determine what the feasible freeze limits are for any particular firm under the current market conditions, laws, and regulations.

Revenue Ruling 83-120, included as Exhibit 26–2, provides the IRS view as to guidelines for valuing preferred equity interests.

Minority Block Gifting. Many family-owned businesses can be transferred slowly over a period of time as the next generation of family managers gains experience and demonstrates their ability to succeed the senior generation managers. Succession in management can be accompanied by an increased ownership by having senior family members gift a series of minority blocks of shares to junior family members. The advantage in gifting away control over a period of time by this method is that appraisals of such minority blocks can take full advantage of whatever minority discount and discount for lack of marketability is appropriate for such blocks. These discounts are usually larger for minority blocks than for an interest that represents outright control. We also find that senior generation family owners are often reluctant to part with control of the firm in a single transaction.

The problem with this method arises when the value of the enterprise is growing rapidly. Periodic gifting may not reduce the overall dollar amount of value in the company held by the senior generation even though they own a smaller and smaller percentage of the firm's equity.

Private Annuities and Other Sale Methods. Often, if no clear family successor is available or the owner wishes to completely terminate his direct equity interest in the firm, a sale of the interest back to the firm in exchange for a private annuity, self-canceling installment note, or other type of transaction may be the best method. The remaining shareholders then become the owners of the outstanding common equity of the firm. Sometimes the firm is sold to an employee stock ownership plan (see Chapter 25).

Charitable Contribution. Another method of reducing a senior generation owner's interest in the firm is to make a charitable contribution of at least part of the interest, and thus receive an income tax deduction. Upon the later redemption of this holding (charities rarely wish to continue to own interests in private firms over long periods of time), the remaining junior generation owners will see an increase in their ownership percentage in the firm. The senior owner gets to take a charitable income tax deduction for the full fair market value of the shares contributed, subject to the limits of the current tax law for alternative minimum tax and other rules. Another charitable gifting technique involves the use of a charitable remainder trust to remove closely held business inter-

Exhibit 26–2

Revenue Ruling 83-120

Section 1. Purpose

The purpose of this Revenue Ruling is to amplify Rev. Rul. 59-60, 1959-1 C.B. 237, by specifying additional factors to be considered in valuing common and preferred stock of a closely held corporation for gift tax and other purposes in a recapitalization of closely held businesses. This type of valuation problem frequently arises with respect to estate planning transactions wherein an individual receives preferred stock with a stated par value equal to all or a large portion of the fair market value of the individual's former stock interest in a corporation. The individual also receives common stock which is then transferred, usually as a gift, to a relative.

Sec. 2. Background

.01 One of the frequent objectives of the type of transaction mentioned above is the transfer of the potential appreciation of an individual's stock interest in a corporation to relatives at a nominal or small gift tax cost. Achievement of this objective requires preferred stock having a fair market value equal to a large part of the fair market value of the individual's former stock interest and common stock having a nominal or small fair market value. The approach and factors described in this Revenue Ruling are directed toward ascertaining the true fair market value of the common and preferred stock and will usually result in the determination of a substantial fair market value for the common stock and a fair market value for the preferred stock which is substantially less than its par value.

.02 The type of transaction referred to above can arise in many different contexts. Some examples are:

(a) *A* owns 100% of the common stock (the only outstanding stock) of *Z* Corporation which has a fair market value of 10,500x. In a recapitalization described in section 368 (a) (1)(E), *A* receives preferred stock with a par value of 10,000x and new common stock, which *A* then transfers to *A*'s son *B*.

(b) *A* owns some of the common stock of *Z* Corporation (or the stock of several corporations) the fair market value of which stock is 10,500x. *A* transfers this stock to a new corporation *X* in exchange for preferred stock of *X* corporation with a par value of 10,000x and common stock of corporation, which *A* then transfers to *A*'s son *B*.

(c) *A* owns 80 shares and his son *B* owns 20 shares of the common stock (the only stock outstanding) of *Z* Corporation. In a recapitalization described in section 368(a)(1)(E), *A* exchanges his 80 shares of common stock for 80 shares of new preferred stock of *Z* Corporation with a par value of 10,000x. *A*'s common stock had a fair market value of 10,000x.

Sec. 3. General Approach to Valuation

Under section 25.2512-2(f)(2) of the Gift Tax Regulations, the fair market value of stock in a closely held corporation depends upon numerous factors, including the corporation's net worth, its prospective earning power, and its capacity to pay dividends. In addition, other relevant factors must be taken into account. *See* Rev. Rul. 59-60. The weight to be accorded any evidentiary factor depends on the circumstances of each case. *See* section 25.2512-2(f) of the Gift Tax Regulations.

Sec. 4. Approach to Valuation–Preferred Stock

.01 In general the most important factors to be considered in determining the value of preferred stock are its yield, dividend coverage and protection of its liquidation preference.

.02 Whether the yield of the preferred stock supports a valuation of the stock at par value depends in part on the adequacy of the dividend rate. The adequacy of the dividend rate should be determined by comparing its dividend rate with the dividend rate of high-grade publicly traded preferred stock. A lower yield than that of high-grade preferred stock indicates a preferred stock value of less than par. If the rate of interest charged by independent creditors to the corporation on loans is higher than the rate such independent creditors charge their most credit worthy borrowers, then the yield on the preferred stock should be correspondingly higher than the yield on high quality preferred stock. A yield which is not correspondingly higher reduces the value of the preferred stock. In addition, whether the preferred stock has a fixed dividend rate and is nonparticipating influences the value of the preferred stock. A publicly traded preferred stock for a company having a similar business and similar assets with similar liquidation preferences, voting rights and other similar terms would be the ideal comparable for determining yield required in arms length transactions for closely held stock. Such ideal comparables will frequently not exist. In such circumstances, the most comparable publicly-traded issues should be selected for comparison and appropriate adjustments made for differing factors.

.03 The actual dividend rate on a preferred stock can be assumed to be its stated rate if the issuing corporation will be able to pay its stated dividends in a timely manner and will, in fact, pay such dividends. The risk that the corporation may be unable to timely pay the stated dividends on the preferred stock can be measured by the coverage of such stated dividends by the corporation's earnings. Coverage of the dividend is measured by the ratio of the sum of pre-tax and pre-interest earnings to the sum of the total interest to be paid and the pre-tax

Exhibit 26–2 (concluded)

Revenue Ruling 83-120
(Continued)

earnings needed to pay the after-tax dividends. *Standard & Poor's Ratings Guide, 58* (1979). Inadequate coverage exists where a decline in corporate profits would be likely to jeopardize the corporation's ability to pay dividends on the preferred stock. The ratio for the preferred stock in question should be compared with the ratios for high quality preferred stock to determine whether the preferred stock has adequate coverage. Prior earnings history is important in this determination. Inadequate coverage indicates that the value of preferred stock is lower than its par value. Moreover, the absence of a provision that preferred dividends are cumulative raises substantial questions concerning whether the stated dividend rate will, in fact, be paid. Accordingly, preferred stock with noncumulative dividend features will normally have a value substantially lower than a cumulative preferred stock with the same yield, liquidation preference and dividend coverage.

.04 Whether the issuing corporation will be able to pay the full liquidation preference at liquidation must be taken into account in determining fair market value. This risk can be measured by the protection afforded by the corporation's net assets. Such protection can be measured by the ratio of the excess of the current market value of the corporation's assets over its liabilities to the aggregate liquidation preference. The protection ratio should be compared with the ratios for high quality preferred stock to determine adequacy of coverage. Inadequate asset protection exists where any unforeseen business reverses would be likely to jeopardize the corporation's ability to pay the full liquidation preference to the holders of the preferred stock.

.05 Another factor to be considered in valuing the preferred stock is whether it has voting rights and, if so, whether the preferred stock has voting control. See, however, Section 5.02 below.

.06 Peculiar covenants or provisions of the preferred stock of a type not ordinarily found in publicly traded preferred stock should be carefully evaluated to determine the effects of such covenants on the value of the preferred stock. In general, if covenants would inhibit the marketability of the stock or the power of the holder to enforce dividend or liquidation rights, such provisions will reduce the value of the preferred stock by comparison to the value of preferred stock not containing such covenants or provisions.

.07 Whether the preferred stock contains a redemption privilege is another factor to be considered in determining the value of the preferred stock. The value of a redemption privilege triggered by death of the preferred shareholder will not exceed the present value of the redemption premium payable at the preferred shareholder's death (i.e., the present value of the excess of the redemption price over the fair market value of the preferred stock upon its issuance). The value of the redemption privilege should be reduced to reflect any risk that the corporation may not posses sufficient assets to redeem its preferred stock at the stated redemption price. See .03 above.

Sec. 5. Approach to Valuation–Common Stock

.01 If the preferred stock has a fixed rate of dividend and is nonparticipating, the common stock has the exclusive right to the benefits of future appreciation of the value of the corporation. This right is valuable and usually warrants a determination that the common stock has substantial value. The actual value of this right depends upon the corporation's past growth experience, the economic condition of the industry in which the corporation operates, and general economic conditions. The factor to be used in capitalizing the corporation's prospective earnings must be determined after an analysis of numerous factors concerning the corporation and the economy as a whole. *See* Rev. Rul. 59-60, at page 243. In addition, after-tax earnings of the corporation at the time the preferred stock is issued in excess of the stated dividends on the preferred stock will increase the value of the common stock. Furthermore, a corporate policy of reinvesting earnings will also increase the value of the common stock.

.02 A factor to be considered in determining the value of the common stock is whether the preferred stock also has voting rights. Voting rights of the preferred stock, especially if the preferred stock has voting control, could under certain circumstances increase the value of the preferred stock and reduce the value of the common stock. This factor may be reduced in significance where the rights of common stockholders as a class are protected under state law from actions by another class of shareholders, *see Singer v. Magnavox Co.*, 380 A.2d 969 (Del. 1977), particularly where the common shareholders, as a class, are given the power to disapprove a proposal to allow preferred stock to be converted into common stock. See ABA-ALI Model Bus. Corp. Act, Section 60 (1969).

Sec. 6. Effect on Other Revenue Rulings

Rev. Rul. 59-60, as modified by Rev. Rul. 65-193, 1965-2 C.B. 370 and as amplified by Rev. Rul. 77-287, 1977-2 C.B. 319, and Rev. Rul. 80-213, 1980-2 C.B. 101, is further amplified.

ests from the senior generation's estate, but provide for income during life. (See also the subsequent section on Appraisals for Charitable Contributions.)

Funding with Life Insurance.   A popular method of assuring that the impact of estate taxes on the beneficiaries of the deceased owner and the firm is minimized is to provide for adequate levels of life insurance to:

1. Repurchase the owner's interest from the estate. Often, life insurance funding will be coupled with a buy-sell agreement to provide for a smooth and certain transition and valuation. The previous section above discusses buy-sell agreements in greater detail.
2. Provide liquidity to the estate to pay estate taxes, even if the shares will not be repurchased by the company or by the other owners.
3. Provide liquidity for continuity of the firm if the deceased owner was a key executive whose loss would disrupt operations.

The last decade has seen an explosion of new insurance products designed to address all of these issues and more. It is not within the scope of this book on valuation to try to adequately discuss all of the current policy permutations generated by the creativity of the life insurance industry. We recommend that a good life insurance agent be part of the small business owner's estate planning team.

However, one clear issue should be kept in mind in regard to life insurance funding for small businesses and professional practices. As one practitioner put it: "in each case the right result can only occur if planning determines the product and not vice versa. . . . It is the planning that draws out the client's design specifications and lays the foundation for selection of an appropriate, competitive (insurance) product."[7]

Appraisals for Charitable Contributions

The current tax laws require individuals, closely held corporations (other than S corporations), and personal service corporations (not including S service corporations) to obtain a qualified appraisal for noncash property contributions having a claimed value of more than $5,000. In the case of securities not traded publicly, a qualified appraisal is required if the claimed value of the securities donated to one or more donees is greater than $10,000. The statute stipulates that the appraisal must include a description of the property or security; a statement of its fair market value; the specific basis of the valuation; a statement that the appraisal was prepared for income tax purposes; and qualifications of the appraiser, his signature, and tax identification number. The following are some of the most salient points:

---

[7]Charles Ratner, "Life Insurance Planning: How to Help Clients Get a Perfect Fit," *Probate & Property*, November/December 1991, p. 22.

1. No appraisal will be accepted if all or part of the appraisal fee is based on a percentage of the appraised value of the property.
2. The appraisal must be made by a person qualified to appraise the donated property.
3. The appraisal must be received by the donor before the due date (including extensions) of the return on which the deduction is claimed. The donor must attach to the return on which the deduction is claimed a summary of the written appraisal (IRS Form 8283), also signed by the appraiser.
4. *Appraisers beware.* The requirements include sanctions against appraisers submitting overstated valuations. Appraisers are subject to a civil tax penalty for aiding and abetting an understatement of tax liability (Internal Revenue Code Section 6701). A $1,000 penalty can be imposed against the appraiser, and the appraiser may be barred from presenting evidence in administrative proceedings, causing the appraisal to be disregarded.

Summary

The various owners of a business or professional practice can protect their interests and those of their families by planning for the smooth transfer of their interests during life or at death. Part of the planning process includes an awareness of the value of the business interest and the owner's objectives for the interest. The general objectives are (1) liquidation of the interest, or at least liquidity at death, disability, or departure from the firm; (2) minimization of gift and estate taxes; and (3) continuity of the enterprise.

With adequate legal, accounting, taxation, and valuation advice, these intergenerational wealth transfer objectives can be accomplished on a basis that is fair to all concerned, and that will avoid unnecessary crises. In order to accomplish these intergenerational wealth transfer objectives, small business owners should carefully consider a buy-sell agreement, do gift and estate tax planning, and provide for funds to cover likely eventualities.

Selected Bibliography

Abatemarco, Michael J., and Alfred Cavallaro. "The Importance of Buy-Sell Agreements for Closely Held Corporations." *CPA Journal*, February 1992, pp. 57–59.

Abbin, Byrle M. "IRS Valuation Process Receives a Billion Dollar Setback." *Journal of Taxation*, May 1990, pp. 260–65.

_____. "Taking the Temperature of Asset Value Freeze Approaches: What's Hot, What's Not." *TAXES*, January 1988, pp. 3–32.

Abbin, Byrle M.; David K. Carlson; and Ross W. Nager. "Significant Recent Developments in Estate Planning." Part 3. *Tax Adviser*, December 1990, pp. 773–84.

Adams, Roy M., and David A. Herpe. "Getting Familiar with Proposed Chapter 14 Regs." *Trusts & Estates*, August 1991, pp. 48–49.

Adams, Roy M.; David A. Herpe; and Thomas W. Abendroth. "Highlights of the Chapter 14 Final Regulations." *Trusts & Estates*, April 1992, pp. 35–49.

Beehler, John M. "Corporate Estate Freeze Valuation Rules under the Proposed Section 2701 Regulations." *TAXES*, January 1992, pp. 12–19.

Bell, Lawrence L. "Valuation of Buy-Sell Agreements under Chapter 14 of the Internal Revenue Code." *Journal of the American Society of CLU & ChFC*, September 1992, pp. 48–53.

Blatt, William S. "The Effect of Sec. 2701 on Preferred Interest Freezes." *Trusts & Estates*, March 1991, pp. 8–14.

Blattmachr, Jonathan G. "Don't Be Driven by Tax-Driven Formula Clauses." *Probate & Property*, September/October 1991, pp. 34–38.

Blattmachr, Jonathan G., and Mitchell M. Gans. "An Analysis of the TAMRA Changes to the Valuation Freeze Rules: Parts I and II." *Journal of Taxation*, January and February 1989, pp. 14–19, 74–78.

Blum, Robert. "Common Valuation Errors in Buy-Sell Agreements: How to Avoid Them." *Practical Accountant*, March 1986, pp. 27–37.

Clements, Bruce. "True GRIT: What the Chapter 14 Valuation Rules Mean for Grantor Retained Income Trusts." *Journal of Taxation of Estates and Trusts*, Summer 1991, pp. 13–22.

Cooper, Scott J. "A Guide through the Estate Freeze Maze." *Journal of Taxation of Estates and Trusts*, Winter 1992, pp. 5–10.

Dees, Richard L. "The Slaying of Frankenstein's Monster: The Repeal and Replacement of Section 2036(c)." *TAXES*, March 1991, pp. 151–66.

Doyle, Robert J., Jr., and Stephan R. Leimberg. "New IRS Valuation Rules: Impact on the Tools and Techniques of Estate and Financial Planning." *TAXES*, May 1990, pp. 376–96.

Drake, Dwight J.; Kent Whiteley; and Timothy J. McDevitt. "The Ten Most Common Mistakes of Buy-Sell Agreements." *Journal of Financial Planning*, July 1992, pp. 104–12.

Eastland, S. Stacy, and Margaret W. Brown. "New Attack on Family Business." *Trusts & Estates*, March 1991, pp. 48–56.

Eastland, S. Stacy, and Stephen L. Christian. "Proposed Valuation Regulations Provide Harsh Results under Adjustment and Lapse Rules." *Journal of Taxation*, December 1992, pp. 364–72.

Fiala, David M. "Business Success Planning." *National Public Accountant*, August 1991, pp. 22–27.

Fiore, Owen G. "Chapter 14 Special Valuation Renewed Estate Tax Savings Opportunities via Inter-Vivos Family Wealth Planning." USC Institute on Federal Taxation, January 29, 1992.

Freund, Susan M., and Gregory V. Gadarian. "Buy-Sell Agreements May Have Far-Reaching Tax Consequences." *Journal of Taxation of Estates & Trusts*, Summer 1990, pp. 12–17.

Gamble, E. James. "How Do We Handle Buy-Sell Agreements under Chapter 14?" *Trusts & Estates*, March 1991, pp. 38–46.

Gardner, John H. "Estate Freezes 1990 and Beyond: The Story of the Repeal of Section 2036(c) and the Valuation Rules that Took Its Place." *TAXES*, January 1991, pp. 3–12.

Goodman, Kenneth D. "Keeping It in the Family." *Trusts & Estates*, December 1988, pp. 37–40.

Grassi, Sebastian V., Jr. "Business Problems and Planning—Shareholder Buy-Sell Agreements and the Revenue Reconciliation Act of 1990." *Michigan Bar Journal*, May 1991, pp. 447–49.

_____. "Interim Guidance for Buy-Sell Agreements after the New Law." *Journal of Taxation of Estates and Trusts*, Spring 1991, pp. 4–6.

Harrison, Louis S. "Prop. Regs. Clarify Planning for GRITs, Buy-Sell Agreements." *Estate Planning*, November/December 1991, pp. 323–29.

Harrison, Louis S., and Heather Smith. "Prop. Regs. Address Adjustments and Lapsing Rights." *Estate Planning*, January/February 1992, pp. 3–9.

Hitchner, James R. "Valuation of Closely Held Businesses: Estate and Gift Tax Issues." *Tax Adviser*, July 1992, pp. 471–79.

Hunsberger, Donald A. "Owners and Estates: A Buy-Sell Primer." *Journal of the American Society of CLU & ChFC*, September 1991, pp. 48–52.

Jones, John R., Jr., and Robert W. Fisher. "Income Tax Considerations of Buy-Sell Agreements." *Taxation for Accountants*, January 1991, pp. 34–42.

Jurinski, James John, and W. Ron Singleton. "New Estate Freeze Rules Require Heating Up of Planning Tactics." *Practical Accountant*, May 1991, pp. 21–33.

Kelly, James P., III. "Waiving Rights under Buy-Sell Agreement Affects Stock Value." *Estate Planning*, September/October 1991, pp. 284–291.

Kimball, Curtis R., and Robert F. Reilly. "Kinder, Gentler Gift and Estate Tax Valuation Rules Offer Planning Possibilities." *Journal of Taxation of Estates and Trusts*, Fall 1991, pp. 27–33.

King, Hamlin C. "Final Estate Freeze Rules Simplify Subtraction Method." *TAXES*, July 1992, pp. 460–90.

Kuenster, Richard A. "Estate Planning, Family Businesses, and Divorce." *FAIR$HARE*, October 1991, pp. 7–9.

Lehmert, Robert R. "Surviving the Loss of a Key Person." *Business Age*, March 1989, pp. 20–26.

Leimberg, Stephan R.; Eric Johnson; and Robert J. Doyle, Jr. "The King Is Dead: Long Live the King! A First Glance at the Repeal of IRC 2036(c) and Its Replacement." *Tax Management Financial Planning Journal*, January 15, 1991, pp. 3–16.

Mahon, Joseph C. "Blitzkrieg on Family Business." *Trusts & Estates*, February 1989, pp. 10–20.

Mezzullo, Louis A. "A Guided Tour through Chapter 14." *Probate & Property*, May/June 1991, pp. 28–31.

Mills, Steven R. "Making 'Cents' of the Tax Law." *Business Age*, November–December 1988, pp. 6–11, 64.

Monippallil, Matthew M. "New Estate Freeze Approach Uses Old Valuation Rules." *Taxation for Accountants*, March 1991, pp. 142–49.

Mulligan, Michael D. "Estate Freeze Rules Eased by New Tax Law but Other Restrictions Are Imposed." *Estate Planning*, January/February 1991, pp. 2–7.

Nager, Ross W. "Estate Freeze Rules Repealed, but Uncertainty Remains." *Journal of Taxation of Estates and Trusts*, Winter 1991, pp. 4–7.

Owens, Thomas. "Buy-Sell Agreements." *Small Business Reports*, January 1991, pp. 57–61.

Painter, Andrew D., and Jonathan G. Blattmachr. "How the Final Chapter 14 Anti-Freeze Regulations Affect Estate Planning Strategies." *Journal of Taxation of Estates and Trusts*, Spring 1992, pp. 5–14.

Pennell, Jeffrey N. "2036(c) Is Only a Skirmish: The War Involves Valuation." *Trusts & Estates*, January 1990, pp. 22, 69.

Peterson, James. "Ducking the Cross Fire: Avoiding Disputes in Buy-Sell Agreements." *Journal of Accountancy*, January 1991, pp. 65–69, 71.

Plaine, Lloyd Leva, and Pam H. Schneider. "Prop. Regs. on Valuing Rights and Restrictions Focus on Exceptions." *Journal of Taxation*, October 1991, pp. 204–6.

————. "Proposed Valuation Regulations Provide Workable Exceptions for Transfers in Trust." *Journal of Taxation*, September 1991, pp. 142–49.

Pratt, Shannon P. "Estate Planning, ESOPs, Buy-Sell Agreements, and Life Insurance for Closely Held Businesses." *Journal of the American Society of CLU & ChFC*, September 1986, pp. 74–79.

Reilly, Robert F., and Robert P. Schweihs. "How the Buy/Sell Agreement Smooths a Shift in Control." *Mergers & Acquisitions*, January/February 1991, pp. 52–57.

————. "Stock Valuation for a Buy-Sell Agreement Must Resist Scrutiny." *Small Business Taxation*, July/August 1990, pp. 70–75.

————. "Valuation Aspects of Buy/Sell Agreements Subsequent to the Repeal of Section 2036(c)." *Ohio CPA Journal*, Spring 1991, pp. 38–43.

Rhine, David S. "Final Regs. on Chapter 14 Simplify Valuation Rules." *Taxation for Accountants*, September 1992, pp. 156–67.

Rothberg, Richard S. "Valuation of Interests in Family Businesses after *Newhouse*." *Journal of Taxation of Investments*, Winter 1991, pp. 161–65.

Schindel, Donald M. "Various Methods Exist for Establishing a Sustainable Value for Estate Assets." *Estate Planning*, September/October 1990, pp. 258–64.

Schneider, Pam H., and Lloyd Leva Plaine. "Proposed Valuation Regulations Flesh Out Operation of the Subtraction Method." *Journal of Taxation*, August 1991, pp. 82–90.

Schnur, Robert A. "How to Structure a Shareholder Agreement." *Practical Accountant*, August 1986, pp. 20–32.

Segal, Mark A. "Buy-Sell Agreements—A Valuable Estate Planning Tool." *National Public Accountant*, February 1990, pp. 14–17.

Strauss, Benton C., and James K. Shaw. "Final Chapter 14 Regs. Clarify GRATs, Business Planning." *Estate Planning*, September/October 1992, pp. 259–66.

————. "Final Chapter 14 Regulations Refine Estate Freeze Rules." *Estate Planning*, July/August 1992, pp. 195–202.

Strouse, Jonathan E. "Redemption and Cross-Purchase Buy-Sell Agreements: A Comparison." *Practical Accountant*, October 1991, pp. 44–53.

Ward, Robert E. "An Old Problem, A New Statute." Parts 1 and 2. *Practical Lawyer*, March and April 1991, pp. 13–28, 79–91.

Willens, Robert. "Buy-Sell Agreements: Constructive Dividend Dangers Lurk." *Journal of Accountancy*, February 1992, pp. 49–52.

Part V

Valuing Professional Practices

Chapter 27

Introduction to Professional Practice Valuation

The valuation of professional practices, such as medical, dental, accounting, legal, and architecture/engineering firms, has developed into a profession in its own right. There are many full-time professional practice brokers, appraisers, bankers, lawyers, accountants, and consultants.

This chapter discusses some of the reasons why professional practices are different than small businesses and why they are treated differently when it is necessary to determine the value of a professional practice.

Reasons to Value a Professional Practice

Professional practices often require an appraiser to be retained primarily for two purposes: (1) various buy-sell situations and (2) marital dissolutions.

Appraisals of professional practices for estate tax situations are required less frequently. If the decedent practitioner is a member of a multipractitioner entity, there are usually buy-sell agreements to set a binding value that will be paid to the estate. If the buy-sell agreement is properly drafted, the value set by that agreement may also be used in the estate tax return. If the buy-sell agreement is not as carefully prepared, the Internal Revenue Service may argue that the agreement is self-serving and should be ignored for tax purposes. This type of situation would call for a professional valuation of the decedent's ownership interest.

Dissenting stockholder and corporate or partnership dissolution suits in professional practices are also rare, but they may become necessary when partners or shareholders disagree over how to run the practice. ESOPs, estate planning recapitalizations, and damage suits (involving the value of the practice) are all less common with professional practices than with other businesses.

For these reasons, the focus of this six-chapter unit of the book will be a discussion of valuations for buy-sell and divorce situations. Because the factors involved in the sale of a practice are different from those involved in valuation for a divorce, the elements creating recognizably valuable goodwill may be different. Therefore, the chapter on goodwill (Chapter 29) discusses the elements that are important for each valuation purpose.

A broader list of possible purposes for professional practice valuation is shown as Exhibit 27–1.

Characteristics of a Professional Practice

As the title of this book implies, there are both similarities and differences between a small business and a professional practice. There are several characteristics of a professional practice that, when taken together, distinguish it from other small businesses. These characteristics can be broken down into five categories:

Exhibit 27-1

REASONS FOR A PROFESSIONAL PRACTICE VALUATION

There are numerous reasons--or motivations--why a professional practice may be subject to valuation. However, all of these reasons typically can be grouped into five categories: transaction, taxation, financing, litigation, and management information.

Transaction pricing and structuring motivations
- the purchase or sale of the entire practice
- the purchase or sale of a partnership interest in the practice
- the relative allocation of equity in a two-practice merger
- the relative allocation of equity in the formation of the practice (between individual practitioners)
- the equity or asset allocation during a practice dissolution

Taxation planning and compliance motivations
- estate tax planning
- estate tax compliance
- purchase price allocation
- practice asset basis adjustment

Financing collateralization and securitization motivations
- practice acquisition financing (both asset based and cash flow based financing)
- practice operations financing

Litigation support and dispute resolution motivations
- marital dissolution of the partners
- taxation disputes
- partner squeeze-outs
- claims of fraud or misrepresentation subsequent to a practice purchase or sale

Management information and planning motivations
- long-term estate planning
- formation and operation of partner buy-sell agreements
- partnership formation and dissolution agreements
- evaluation of practice purchase or merger offers
- evaluation of stewardship and effectiveness of practice management
- development and implementation of practice value enhancement techniques

1. The practice is primarily a service business with fewer tangible assets than most small businesses.
2. There is necessarily a relationship of trust and respect between the client and the professional or employee of the practice, because the client must rely on professional expertise that the client himself is not fully capable of understanding or evaluating.
3. The practice or the practitioner often relies upon a referral source or sources.
4. A specific college degree or graduate degree is usually required by regulatory bodies for the professional to practice in his chosen field.
5. The practitioner is licensed by a government or regulatory agency and/or certified by a recognized professional organization.

It is apparent from the list above that the distinction between professional practices and certain kinds of service businesses may be a fine line, at least for some of the characteristics.

Service Business Characteristics

Professional practices provide services of various kinds, from giving tax advice to treating Fido's illnesses. The nature of these services, in light of the professional's specialized training and the client's dependence on the professional's expertise, causes price to be a less important consideration than in the purchase of goods or less-specialized services.

If an individual wants to buy a refrigerator, for example, he will generally shop several appliance stores to find the best price available. However, he is likely to be far less price-conscious in choosing a cardiologist or a defense attorney. Pricing will be important if the particular need is not critical or might be subject to an upper limit of the client's ability to pay, but more important to the selection of a professional than pricing is the expertise that the client or patient needs in his situation. A person with only wage and interest income will probably be completely satisfied with a bookkeeping service preparing his tax return, but a person with complicated investments, capital gains income, and so forth, will want a better qualified certified public accountant (CPA) or attorney to complete his returns. People may purchase refrigerators on the basis of price, but price is usually not the determining factor when choosing a tax preparer.

Client Trust and Respect

The trust and respect that clients hold for the members of the practice are crucial to its success. As long as his trust is maintained, the client will generally return to the practitioner. Personal trust is the chief reason that the goodwill is so strongly related to the practitioner.

Dependence on Referral Sources

New clients choose a professional practice primarily on the basis of referral from another source. They generally do not choose their doctors, lawyers, or accountants from ads in the Yellow Pages, but on the recommendation of someone they know. Some types of practices, however, such as optometrists, dentists, veterinarians, and chiropractors, may get a substantial portion of their new patients by means of their location or by advertisements. At the other extreme, some practices depend totally on new referrals to generate patient visits. An oral surgeon, for example, does not have continuing relationships with his patients, so he must maintain relationships, through professional societies, social clubs, and promotional activities, with the general dentists who can refer patients to him.

Education

The people who make up a professional practice have graduated from institutions offering some kind of specialized education. Although some professions require a bachelor's degree or a certain number of years in a special course of study, others demand a master's or a doctorate degree, plus extensive on-the-job training. This requirement for extensive training affects professional goodwill in two ways: (1) the client's trust and respect are increased or generated by the long years of study involved; (2) the long years of study represent an investment in time and money on the part of the professional, who expects a monetary return on his investment.

Licensing and Certification

Generally, the professional must be licensed by a government or regulatory agency or admitted to a professional organization before he can practice his specialty. This factor has the effect of limiting the number of individuals who can practice, and it creates a barrier to entry to that profession.

Distinctions between Professional Practice and Other Business Valuations

Type of Assets

A greater proportion of professional practice assets tend to be intangible in nature than is the case for other types of enterprises. To this extent, their values tend to be even more dependent on earning capacity than other businesses. If an asset approach to valuation is used, the appraiser should be well versed in the valuation of intangible assets, which themselves derive their values primarily from their contributions to earnings.

Dependence on Professional

Professional practices are more dependent on one or a few individuals than is the case for most businesses. This has two primary implications for valuation:

1. The evaluation of the contribution of the professional(s) is a key factor.
2. In some cases (as discussed in detail in Chapter 29), it is important to distinguish between elements of intangible value that are attached to the practice versus those that are personal to the practitioner.

Licenses

A license to practice usually is a valuable asset. It has intangible value in that it represents an independent third party's endorsement of credibility, usually to the extent of at least acknowledging demonstration of some minimum level of competence. In many cases, it also serves to limit the number of entrants into the field.

A few states (most notably New York) have recognized professional licenses as a valuable marital asset in a dissolution. In most states, the license merely is recognized as one element of the practitioner's goodwill. When a number of licenses are amalgamated within a practice, the collection of licenses held by the practitioners can have intangible value for the practice itself.

Cash Basis Accounting

Since most professional practices use cash basis accounting, it usually is necessary to adjust financial statements to an accrual basis for valuation.

Note, however, that certain comparative data for similar professional practices may be presented on a cash basis. In such a situation, the valuer may need to use cash basis data for comparative purposes and still use accrual-basis data for other aspects of the valuation process.

Limited Life

It can be argued that most professional practices are more constrained to a limited life than most businesses, which often are regarded as having a perpetual life. This constraint arises largely from the limited professional working life of the practitioner(s). Professional practice valuations generally rely heavily on income-based methods, and the limited life characteristic often is reflected in the assumptions underlying the income-based methods employed.

Value Drivers for Professional Practices

For any kind of a business or practice, there usually are a few key factors that are especially important in distinguishing the value of that business or practice from its counterparts in the same industry or profession. These sometimes are referred to as *value drivers*. Exhibit 27–2 provides a succinct checklist of such factors that tend to differentiate the value of one practice from another in the same field of practice. These factors may be reflected in the valuation in a variety of ways, such as influencing multiples, capitalization rates, present value discount rates, and/or a discount for lack of marketability.

Summary

Most professional practice valuations are done either for a transaction or a divorce, although there can be many other reasons for professional

Exhibit 27–2

CHECKLIST OF IMPORTANT FACTORS
AFFECTING VALUES OF PROFESSIONAL PRACTICES

Factor	Most Desirable	Least Desirable
Location and demographics	Urban High growth Affluent Stable population	Rural Mature or declining market Poor Transient population
Client persistence	Very stable	High turnover
Dependence on referrals vs. direct client contact	Large direct client base	One or a few referral sources
Contractual relationships	Strong relationship(s)	Relationship(s) threatened to terminate
Supply/demand relationship (for acquisition of practice)	High demand, low supply	High supply, low demand
Reputation	Stellar, far and wide	Nonexistent or tarnished
Facilities and technology	State of the art	Antiquated
Employees	Adequate and dedicated	Inadequate and/or departing
Practitioner's work habits	Light work load	Workaholic
For medical practices, proportion of "managed care" clients (generally not assignable)	Few or none from health maintenance contracts	High proportion from health maintenance contracts
Vertical potential synergism	High propensity to be source of revenue for prospective acquiree	No synergistic revenue potential for prospective acquiree

practice valuations. Professional practices have certain characteristics that are unique compared to other businesses, requiring the valuer to utilize certain knowledge and analysis that may have little or no applicability in valuing other kinds of businesses. Professional practices also, as a broad generalization, have other distinctions from typical businesses that have a bearing on valuation methods and procedures. Finally, there are certain factors that tend to account for a large part of the differences in value from one practice to another in the same professional field.

This chapter has summarized these characteristics, distinctions, and value drivers in a general sense. Subsequent chapters provide more detail in application of these general considerations in professional practice valuation.

Chapter 28

Adjusting the Professional Practice Balance Sheet

When valuing professional practices, as when valuing small businesses, it is important to analyze and make appropriate adjustments to the entity's tangible and intangible assets and liabilities. The valuation of a professional practice differs from that of the small business, however, because the types of assets possessed by a professional practice are very different from those used by a small business. Perhaps the most important difference is that goodwill plays a much more important part in the professional practice than in the typical small business. The whole process of valuing tangible and intangible assets of the professional practice is further complicated by the cash basis accounting used by most professional practices.

There may be a good deal of value in assets not recorded on the balance sheets of a cash basis entity, such as accounts receivable, work-in-process inventory, and prepaid expenses. Furthermore, fully depreciated equipment still being used by the practice may have been removed from the balance sheet, and leasehold improvements that would be irrelevant to the typical business may form an integral part of the operation of the professional practice. By the same token, such liabilities as accounts payable, accrued vacation time for employees, and accrued taxes may not be recorded on the balance sheet. The appraiser must use judgment to determine whether these assets and liabilities are necessary to the practice operations and how they affect its value.

Assets

Below is a discussion of the most common types of assets that the appraiser can find in professional practices. The list is not all-inclusive, and the appraiser should give specific recognition to the type of practice being appraised in order to develop a list of potential assets the practice may possess.

Cash

The reliability of the cash figure on the balance sheet may depend on whether the statements were audited by an independent accountant or merely compiled by the office manager or a bookkeeping service. If there is reason to believe that the recorded cash balance may be incorrect, the appraiser should request copies of bank statements and statement reconciliations, and should review the deposit activity for a period just following the valuation date. We have found on occasion that checks received in payment were not recorded until they were deposited in the bank the following day. Some practices use a system of tax deferral not authorized by the IRS—for a certain amount of time preceding the fiscal year end: they hold all incoming checks; they then deposit them at the beginning of the next fiscal year, enabling them to include the income on the following year's tax returns. The balance sheet should be adjusted so that these amounts show in either cash or accounts receivable. At the other end of the spectrum of error, petty cash may be shown incorrectly on the books, not to save taxes, but because of poor recordkeeping. The incidence of such anomalies is probably highest among sole proprietorships.

Accounts Receivable

Accounts receivable are not often shown on the balance sheets of professional practices because they generally operate on a cash basis of accounting. It is therefore necessary to determine the value of accounts receivable in order to include them in the value of the professional practice. There are several ways of keeping records of accounts receivable. Gross receivables at any given date are easily determined from the day sheets or accounts receivable journals of most practices.

One system that may cause more difficulty than the normal accounts receivable journal is based on a card file. Under a card system, client charges are recorded on a card that is kept in a file with accounts showing a debit or credit balance. Payments are recorded on the card, and when the account is paid, the card is returned to the client's file. To determine the gross value of outstanding accounts receivable at the current date, the appraiser merely sums the debit and credit amounts on the cards in the "accounts receivable drawer."

If the valuation date precedes the appraiser's field work, however, it can be difficult to reconstruct the accounts receivable due at the valuation date, because accounts with zero balances are simply filed away and there is no record of former balances. The appraiser could extrapolate from current accounts receivable to estimate accounts receivable at the valuation date; or he could analyze the relationship between current and past collection amounts to value the level of receivables at the valuation date. On the other hand, such an estimate can be rendered unusable because the amount of accounts receivable is crucial to the valuation, or because some change in the operation has made a reliable estimate impossible; then the appraiser might request all cards (both in the accounts receivable drawer and in the client files) and use them to recalculate the actual balances that existed at the valuation date. He may also need to request appointment books and collection records for the relevant period of time to verify that all cards have been provided. Obviously, that can be a time-consuming task. Alternatively, he might examine cash deposit records following the valuation date to identify specific payments received.

Another type of receivable often overlooked is accounts that have been turned over to a collection agency, because they are often written off the accounts receivable balance when they are turned over to the agency. Although the value of these accounts is usually small (because the collection agency deducts its fee of as much as 50 percent of amounts collected off the top), the appraiser should be aware of the value and include it in the overall accounts receivable amount.

Having determined the gross value of the accounts receivable, the appraiser must adjust for uncollectible and slow-pay accounts. The two most common methods for estimating uncollectible accounts are:

1. Accounts receivable aging—discounting the accounts on the basis of how long past due they are.

2. Actual payment history—analyzing the payment trends of the specific practice and whether the trend is for more or fewer write-offs.

Both of these methods have positive and negative characteristics, however, and the appraiser should determine which is appropriate for the practice at hand.

Aging of Receivables. The appraiser normally will either acquire or create an accounts receivable aging schedule, such as the one illustrated in Exhibit 7–1. The time periods outstanding generally run in 30-day increments, with the last category including accounts more than 180 days old. After totaling each category, the appraiser applies a discount factor to each, with the further past-due balances receiving higher discounts.

This method of determining uncollectible accounts receivable does not recognize individual payment histories or the payment procedures of the specific practice. For example, to discount by 50 percent all accounts over 180 days past due would cause an underestimation of the value if there were many accounts for which small monthly payments had been arranged and were being paid. In addition, the discount amounts are necessarily subjective, and the result may not reflect the particular payment procedures of the clients of the practice being appraised. If the practice does work for any of various federal agencies, it will be paid for its work eventually, but dependable private clients pay sooner. A 60-day past-due billing for the government should usually not be discounted as much as a 60-day past-due billing for a private client.

Actual Payment History. The second method of estimating the reserve for uncollectible accounts receivable analyzes the practice's individual collection history. It compares the accounts receivable write-offs from one period to the billings generated during the same period. The appraiser requests a payment history for a 36-month to 60-month period. This history would take the form of a schedule showing monthly charges, collections, credit adjustments, debit adjustments, and month-end receivable balances. From these data, the charges, collections, and net adjustments would be totaled for the entire period and for each fiscal year. The appraiser would then calculate the percentage of net adjustments to billings in order to establish an average for the period and for each fiscal year. In this way, the appraiser determines the actual percentage of charges that are never collected and, by analyzing trends for the fiscal years, he can determine if a pattern of higher or lower write-offs is forming.

The problem with computing the percentage of historical net adjustments to the billings is that, if the practice has a significant number of patients who pay immediately and are not billed for services, the total charges would reflect not only accounts receivable, but also cash transactions. Including accounts that were paid when incurred would tend to reduce artificially the percentage of historical write-offs. In that case, the percentage of immediate cash payments on account would need to be considered in the calculation of historical write-offs.

Many practices houseclean their accounts at the end of the fiscal year, writing off the ones they consider uncollectible. The appraiser should be aware if his work follows a housecleaning, so that he does not inadvertently overadjust for uncollectible accounts and so that he can examine the practice's write-off method and adjust for too much or not enough estimation of uncollectible accounts.

As mentioned previously, slow-pay accounts may need to be discounted to allow for the time value of money (see Chapter 7). If the practice collects receivables fairly rapidly, the discount may be very small. However, if collections tend to take a long time, the accounts should be discounted accordingly, netted against any interest the practice charges on past-due amounts.

Work-in-Process Inventory

Many professional practices have unrecorded assets for work they have performed but not yet billed. Typically, work-in-process is an asset found in practices that charge hourly for professional or staff time, such as CPA firms, consulting practices, and law firms, or practices that charge on a percentage of completion basis, such as engineering and appraisal firms. This asset might be called *unbilled accounts receivable.*

Since work-in-process is based on time spent by the professional practice's staff, there are usually (but not always) time records available from which to determine the amount of services that are unbilled. However, it is often the case that most practices can estimate unbilled receivables only at the current date; they cannot reconstruct the work-in-process inventory at any prior date. Therefore, to make a reasonable estimate of the work-in-process inventory at a prior date, the appraiser must understand the billing procedures of the practice—how often the work-in-process is billed and on what day(s) of the month, what procedures are used to compile and bill work-in-process, by what criteria the accounts are determined billable, and what records show work-in-process that has been written off.

It is important to remember that practices using cash basis accounting have probably already recorded all expenses associated with the work-in-process inventory. For that reason, it is unnecessary to calculate the gross or net margins on their work-in-process. The amounts expensed for services that have not been billed to clients, but that are expected to be billed and collected, should be listed as an asset on the practice's financial statements. Then, except for minor adjustments, the appraiser can use the figures shown on the financial statements for the value of the work-in-process. However, under a *modified accrual system*, accounts receivable are included in revenues, but work-in-process is not recognized. In that case, goods and/or margins may become important to the appraiser.

Exhibit 28–1 shows a typical method of calculating the value of work-in-process inventory for a firm using cash basis or modified accrual basis accounting. It is apparent in this exhibit that $32,000 worth of unbilled consulting is not equal to $32,000 of collection. Hours are often written down or written up for a variety of reasons, and the appraiser should calculate an historical percentage to determine how much of the firm's billable time is actually billed. Then the amount is discounted for uncol-

Exhibit 28–1

SMITH & WILSON CONSULTING, INC.
CALCULATION OF VALUE OF WORK–IN–PROCESS INVENTORY
AS OF SEPTEMBER 30, 1992

	J. Smith	K. Wilson	Total
Hours in Unbilled Inventory	130	210	
Hourly Billing Rate	x $125	x $75	
Gross Value of Unbilled Inventory	$16,250	$15,750	
Total Gross Value of Unbilled Inventory			32,000
Less: 3–Year Historical Adjustment to Work–in–Process (Amount Not Billed Is Equal to 7% of Total)			(2,240)
Estimated Work–in–Process Inventory that Will Be Billed			29,760
Less: 3–Year Historical Write–Off on Accounts Receivable (Amount of Charges Not Collected Is Equal to 9% of Total Charges)			(2,678)
Estimated Cash Value of Work–in–Process before Calculation of Discount for Time to Collect			$27,082

lectible receivables, as discussed above, to determine how much is likely finally to be collected. If there are fixed-fee contracts, the appraiser should calculate their value on the basis of the estimated percentage of completion at the valuation date.

One final adjustment may be necessary. The appraiser who finds a significant number of old unbilled hours still in inventory should determine how diligently the firm has housecleaned its inventory. If there has been only haphazard housecleaning, or none at all, the appraiser probably needs to age the work-in-process inventory and significantly discount (or even eliminate) the old unbilled hours.

Some types of professional practices may have contingent work-in-process. For example, a law firm may have work-in-process for which it will collect only if it wins a litigated civil action. The value of such contingent work-in-process may be estimated on the basis of the firm's average historical realizations or on a project-by-project basis. If the practice or an interest in the practice is being sold, this may be resolved by a contingency in the purchase price based on actual realization of the contingent work-in-process.

Inventory of Supplies

The value of the supplies inventory depends on the type of practice. The office supplies of a CPA firm will have a small value compared, for instance, to the inventory of glasses frames in an optometric practice of comparable size. Without a detailed cataloging of inventory items, the appraiser can usually estimate the amount of inventory on hand for practices that do not have substantial value in inventory. Nevertheless, the appraiser normally will tour the practice offices and at least check the level of supplies kept.

A review of the prior year's history of supply purchases can aid the appraiser in estimating the value of supplies on hand. If the practice generally orders supplies once a month, the total supply expense for the prior year could be divided by 12 for an estimate of the value of supplies on hand at any particular time. However, if the practice keeps a 90-day supply on hand, this method would underestimate the value of the supply inventory.

Prepaid Expenses

Two specific expenses are often prepaid—rent and insurance. These two expenses (including insurance policies for errors and omissions and for malpractice) are almost always prepaid, but because they are continuing, their amounts are not necessarily allocated to the periods when they are used. If they do not fluctuate significantly, the IRS will ignore the fact that they are improperly classified in one period, because over several periods, the tax effect will net to zero. The appraiser, on the other hand, is generally concerned with a specific valuation date, and for that reason, prepaid expenses must be classified properly on the balance sheet to recognize the fact that future expenses have already been paid. For example, if the appraiser finds that a physician has paid $5,000 on December 30 for the next year's professional liability insurance, approximately three fourths of the premium is actually prepaid, and therefore an asset, as of the March 30 valuation date.

Equipment

As was true of supplies, the amount and value of equipment necessary to operate any given practice depends very much on the type of practice. A general dentistry practice will require significantly more valuable equipment than a psychiatric practice. The appraiser must judge whether the equipment should be appraised by a professional equipment appraiser; for example, if there is a great deal of equipment, if it is highly specialized, or if there are antiques among the practice's assets. If there is very little equipment, or if it consists primarily of automobiles, the business appraiser could estimate the value himself (for example, using the *Kelly Blue Book*).

An equipment appraiser should be chosen carefully. A qualified equipment appraiser understands *standards of value* and can appraise the equipment using the same standards as the business appraiser, but a used equipment dealer may give as a value only the amount he would pay for it under liquidation conditions.

Several rules-of-thumb valuation methods discussed in Chapter 30 include the value of the equipment. If one of these methods is used to value a professional practice, the appraiser still needs to consider the value of the equipment. It may be old, unnecessary to the practice operation, or extremely specialized; any of these characteristics alter the multiples in the rule-of-thumb method or make them useless for the specific valuation.

Finally, the appraiser may examine the equipment listed on the practice's depreciation schedule. That procedure is wise, but the list should be verified, because assets owned by the practice may have been removed or may never have been listed on the schedule.

Leasehold Improvements

Another important asset is the leasehold improvements of the practice. During the appraiser's tour of the practice office, he should pay attention to the condition of the improvements—in other words, how well the office is packaged. If the leasehold improvements are in good condition and have been fully depreciated on the balance sheet, he may want to adjust their value upward, considering both their life expectancy and the term of the current lease.

Buyers may be reluctant to place much value on leasehold improvements because they will belong to the landlord and cannot be removed if the lessee vacates the premises. However, the fair market value of the leasehold improvements, as part of a going concern, is an allocable amount of the purchase price that the buyer can depreciate for income tax purposes.

In his overall analysis of the practice's assets, the appraiser should continually ask if the asset is necessary to the practice operation. Assets that are unnecessary for the practice's success should be treated as excess to the total practice value, and any income or expenses resulting from these assets should be removed from the income statements.

Intangible Assets

There are many intangible assets that may exist in the professional practice that is the subject of the valuation. Intangible assets that may exist and, therefore, be investigated in the course of the appraiser's analysis are shown in Exhibit 28–2.

As discussed in Chapter 34 on valuing intangible assets, some are amortizable as an expense for income tax purposes and some are not. Because of this differential tax treatment, generally it is worthwhile to specifically identify and value those that are amortizable for tax purposes, rather than lumping all intangibles under "goodwill," which is not amortizable for tax purposes.

For more detail on identifying and valuing intangibles, see Chapter 34, "Valuing Intangible Assets," and Chapter 32, "Illustrative Examples of Professional Practice Valuation Methods."

Liabilities

There may be several categories of liabilities not reflected on the books of a professional practice. On the other hand, from a valuation standpoint

Exhibit 28–2

INTANGIBLE ASSETS FOUND IN
VARIOUS PROFESSIONAL PRACTICES

Computer software	Laboratory notebooks
Computerized data bases	Library
Cooperative agreements	Licenses
Copyrights	Literary works
Customer contracts	Litigation awards & damages
Customer lists	Management contracts
Customer relationships	Marketing and promotional materials
Designs and drawings	Medical charts and records
Employment contracts	Noncompete covenants
Engineering drawings	Patents and patent applications
Favorable leases	Permits
Franchise agreements	Procedural manuals
Going concern	Royalty agreements
Goodwill	Schematics and diagrams
Government contracts	Subscription lists
Historical documents	Supplier contracts
HMO enrollment lists	Technical and specialty libraries
Insurance expirations	Technical documentation
Joint ventures	Trade secrets
Know-how	Trained and assembled workforce

some may appear there (and even be required by GAAP) that are not real debts (such as deferred rent).

Accounts Payable

Cash basis financial statements typically do not show accounts payable. Since most professional practices sell services, their accounts payable usually relate to continuing bills, such as supplies, telephone, utilities, taxes, and so forth, rather than materials for manufacturing or sale. There are two basic methods for estimating accounts payable. Under the first method, the appraiser reviews all unpaid invoices at the valuation date. If field work is done substantially after the appraisal date, the appraiser should request all canceled checks written during a reasonable period of time after the valuation date, along with the corresponding invoices. With this information, the appraiser can determine how much money the practice owed as of the appraisal date.

The second method is less accurate, but it can give a reasonable estimate with less effort. The appraiser begins with the total expenses shown on the practice's income statement. From that amount he subtracts expenses that do not belong with accounts payable—those payable immediately, those that were paid in advance, those not requiring cash,

Exhibit 28–3

SMITH & WILSON CONSULTING, INC.
CALCULATION OF ESTIMATED AMOUNT OF ACCOUNTS PAYABLE
AS OF SEPTEMBER 30, 1992

Total Expenses Shown on Fiscal Year–End		
September 30, 1992, Income Statement		$175,000
Less:		
Those Expenses Paid Immediately When Due:		
Salaries (Officers and Employees)	105,000	
Interest	500	
Those Expenses Paid in Advance:		
Rent	120,000	
Insurance	2,500	
Dues and Subscriptions	200	
Those Expenses Not Requiring Cash:		
Amortization	20	
Depreciation	1,250	
Those Expenses Already Shown as Payables on Financials:		
Pension Plan	20,000	
Payroll Taxes	4,500	
Total of Expenses Not Part of Accounts Payable		(145,970)
Total of Expenses that Can Be Part of Accounts Payable		29,030
Practice Normally Pays Bills after 30 Days, Once per Month		12
Estimated Accounts Payable at September 30, 1992		$2,419

and those shown elsewhere on the balance sheet as payables (e.g., payroll taxes payable). The appraiser considers the practice's regular bill-paying procedures, such as how often all invoices are paid and how long the practice holds them before payment, to calculate the estimated accounts payable at the valuation date. Exhibit 28–3 illustrates this computation.

Accrued Liabilities

Accrued liabilities are expenses, such as payroll, payroll taxes, or interest, which are allocated to a prior period but not yet due. If a note payable calls for interest payments at the end of the year and the appraisal date is at midyear, the appraiser should adjust for accrued interest (unless it is already shown on the financial statements), even though it is not payable for another six months.

Many firms pay employees one to five days after a payroll cycle; if the appraisal takes place at the end of a payroll cycle, there could be a large payable for salaries.

One liability often overlooked is accrued employee vacation time. The appraiser should consider the company's vacation policy and verify the amounts of accrued vacation held by employees. If there is a significant amount of vacation time pending, this liability should be reflected on the balance sheet, or at least disclosed in the appraisal report.

Deferred Liabilities

Deferred liabilities fall into three categories:

1. Deferred revenues.
2. Deferred expenses.
3. Deferred taxes.

Deferred Revenues. Deferred revenues are amounts that have been received for services not yet performed. An obstetrician-gynecologist (OB-GYN) medical practice is likely to have this type of liability, although it may not be shown on the balance sheet. OB-GYN specialists often receive from expectant mothers their entire fees for prenatal care and delivery. If the specialist is on cash basis accounting, he is likely to report this prepayment as current income, although from an accounting viewpoint, there is a liability for services yet to be performed. Deferred revenues may also need to be considered in law firms and consulting firms that receive retainers before beginning work on the case.

Deferred Expenses. Deferred expenses are relatively unusual. One example might be deferred rent. A landlord may offer several months of free rent in return for a tenant's signing of a long-term lease. This situation would warrant a liability account for deferred rent, because the tenant could theoretically have negotiated a lease for the same period of time at a lower monthly rent, had he opted not to accept the free rent, even though the total payments under each option would be equal. Exhibit 28–4 shows entries to account for a deferred rent liability.

As Exhibit 28–4 illustrates, even though the company paid only $1,000 cash toward rent during the first seven months, the financial statements show rental expense of $6,363.63; the difference between the expense and the cash paid was allocated to Deferred Rent. From the appraiser's point of view, this deferral is not a real liability and should be removed; however, when calculating the expected future income, one should adjust the rent expense upward by $90.91 per month.

Deferred Income Taxes. Deferred income tax is the third type of deferred liability. The purpose of deferred income taxes appearing on financial statements is to match income tax expense with the related financial accounting income for the appropriate accounting period.

Exhibit 28–4

SMITH & WILSON CONSULTING, INC.
ACCOUNTING ENTRIES FOR "DEFERRED RENT" ACCOUNT

Assumption: For the signing of a 60–month lease for offices, Smith & Wilson received an additional six months' free rent--the total rent over the term of the lease would total $60,000, or $1,000 per month over 60 months.   Generally accepted accounting principles would require that the rent be charged against income over the 66–month term, or $909.09 per month.

Month 1:	Debit, Rent Expense	909.09	
	Credit, Deferred Rent		909.09
Months 2–6 Totals:	Debit, Rent Expense	4,545.45	
	Credit, Deferred Rent		4,545.45
Month 7:	Debit, Rent Expense	909.09	
	Debit, Deferred Rent	90.91	
	Credit, Cash		1,000.00

Therefore: At the end of seven months, rent expense totaled $6,363.63, cash was decreased by $1,000, and Deferred Rent Expense equaled $5,363.63.

Deferred income taxes usually occur because of the difference in timing between recognition of income or expense for two different accounting systems of the same practice. For example, the practice may use straight-line depreciation on its own financial statements to reflect more accurately economic depreciation, but it might use accelerated depreciation on tax returns. The result of using these two procedures would be to show more income on the financial statements and less on the tax returns. The amount of deferred income taxes on the financial statements is equal to the difference between income taxes actually paid and what they would have been if based on the higher income as shown on the financial statements. When bringing assets onto the balance sheet, the liability for deferred taxes should also be recognized. Adjusting from a cash to an accrual basis for accounts receivable would be an example where recognition of the related deferred tax liability would be appropriate.

For the appraiser, this account may or may not reflect a true liability. If the practice rarely purchases new equipment, the depreciation for tax purposes will ultimately be less than for financial statement purposes, consequently showing more income on the tax returns than on the financial statements. In that case, the taxes actually paid will be higher than taxes shown due on the financial statements, which means that the deferred taxes are an actual liability.

On the other hand, if the practice continually buys new equipment, the financial statements could always show greater profits than the tax returns. In that case, the appraiser could conclude that deferred taxes will never be paid in the foreseeable future and remove them from the balance sheet liabilities.

Long-Term Debt

Long-term debt in professional practices is usually associated with equipment purchases. However, in some instances, it represents amounts due to the former owner of the practice who sold it to the current owner. These situations should alert the appraiser to investigate the past sale. If the appraiser has reason to believe that the amounts listed in long-term debt are incorrect, copies of the debt instrument(s) and payment records should be obtained. Also, the debt instrument will disclose if the practice has an accrued interest liability that is not shown on the balance sheet.

Lease Obligations

The appraiser should always obtain copies of all leases of the practice whether the practice is a lessor or a lessee. The financial statements usually show capital lease obligations, under which the practice will ultimately be obliged to purchase the leased equipment. These future lease payments should be treated as long-term debt, after separating imputed interest payable.

Contingent Liabilities

Contingent obligations, as discussed in Chapter 7, are liabilities (or assets) for which there is insufficient information about the outcome to know how to account for them on the financial statements. The professional may be a defendant or plaintiff in a malpractice suit or there may be disputed billings, and these facts may be disclosed on the financial statement. The appraiser should investigate these types of liabilities (or assets).

Summary

Balance sheet adjustments for professional practices proceed similarly to those for other businesses, as discussed in Chapter 7, which should be used in conjunction with this chapter. In the case of professional practices, there generally is also a need to adjust from a cash to an accrual basis, as discussed in considerable detail in this chapter. This chapter has also discussed other balance sheet adjustments that are particularly unique to professional practices.

Although there has been a great deal of literature written on the subject of professional goodwill and other intangible assets, there has been very little on the valuation of tangible assets of professional practices. These assets may have substantial value, and the appraiser should not overlook them when concentrating on valuing the practice's goodwill. Goodwill usually cannot exist by itself, but is frequently supported by tangible assets of some kind. The reader should refer to Chapter 34 for more direction on identification and valuation of intangible assets.

One caveat: if adjusting the financial statements for comparative purposes (e.g., for comparison to other specific financial statements or some compiled composite data), adjustments should be made only to the extent appropriate to make the data comparable to the comparative data.

Chapter 29

Elements that Create Professional and Practice Goodwill

Goodwill is often defined as the amount of the purchase price for a business or professional practice that is over and above the value of its identifiable tangible and intangible assets and net of the liabilities assumed. It is treated as an asset on the balance sheet of the acquiror, and, because it does not have a determinable life, it generally cannot be amortized against income for income tax purposes. This definition is helpful, however, only to accountants balancing the books. It does not explain goodwill—why it exists, how much of it there is in any given business, or even how it can be built up or dissipated. In professional practices, goodwill is even more difficult to define because it is usually strongly tied to the individual practitioners.

Appraisers often hear professionals say that the practice can't have any goodwill value because "without me, it's worthless." Others believe that there is no way to transfer their professional goodwill because it is so personal. These ideas seem plausible, but they are not necessarily true. With careful planning and cooperation between seller and buyer, at least some portion of the professional goodwill that has been built up can usually be transferred to the new owner.

Distinction between Practice Goodwill and Professional Goodwill

In a professional practice, there are generally two types of goodwill: practice goodwill (sometimes referred to as business goodwill) and professional goodwill (sometimes referred to as personal goodwill). *Practice goodwill* is the goodwill associated primarily with the entity, while *professional goodwill* is the goodwill associated primarily with the individual.

Practice Goodwill

Practice goodwill is specifically an asset of the practice entity and therefore not really different from goodwill that can be held by any other small business. A professional typically cannot sell (as in transfer) his reputation, skills, or knowledge. However, he may use these attributes to establish a successful practice and generate large earnings. In doing so, he has started a business, and through it will acquire many of the elements, such as location, operating systems, staff, and a patient or client base, which are common to both a small business and a professional practice and which make up business (practice) goodwill. These elements and others like them can generate value over and above the entity's net asset value, thus producing goodwill (or going-concern) value.[1] A professional practice that has these elements has a certain amount of practice goodwill, which can be significant in value.

---

[1]Some writers have made a distinction between *goodwill* and *going-concern value*. When this distinction is made, the term *goodwill* generally refers to those factors that generate repeat business, whereas the term *going-concern value* is more of an operations concept: that is, the value of having all the work force and physical elements such as equipment and inventory in place, in balance, and working well together. For the purpose of this chapter, we lump these elements of going-concern value under the general heading of goodwill.

Professional Goodwill

While a professional practice does not possess personal goodwill, the practitioner(s) may have personal goodwill. A certain portion of the practitioner's clients or patients may come to him or her because of the practitioner's personal reputation, thereby causing earnings for the practice. If the practitioner suddenly left the practice, a large majority of the income generated from these personal clients and patients would be likely to leave as well.

A common misconception is that personal goodwill is not marketable because it is never transferable. Although the transfer of personal goodwill is more difficult than the transfer of practice goodwill, there are methods by which the practitioner can facilitate the transfer of his or her goodwill, or at least a portion of his goodwill, to another well-qualified practitioner.

The transfer of client trust and respect from seller to buyer requires the cooperation of both parties. Their efforts would include at least a letter of announcement from the seller to current clients, informing them that the buyer is taking over their cases and that the buyer has the qualifications and expertise to handle their needs. In this way, the selling professional uses his or her reputation to transfer his or her goodwill to the buyer. Another means of ensuring the transfer of personal goodwill would be for the seller to stay with the practice during a transition period so that clients can become familiar and comfortable with the new practitioner. It requires the seller's best efforts to transfer his or her goodwill to the new practitioner. Frequently, the clients will not be made aware that the "buyer" is other than an "associate." This means often proves effective in increasing client retention.

It is more difficult to transfer goodwill if the seller depends upon professional or personal contacts to refer clients. The seller cannot so easily write a letter to his or her friends at the country club and convince them that the person buying the practice should, from now on, get their referrals. Similarly, if an oral surgeon has persuaded general dentists of his expertise through presentations at professional seminars, the oral surgeon buying his practice will not necessarily have an easy time persuading them that his expertise is comparable. On the other hand, the sole cardiac surgeon in a community can relatively easily transfer his referral base to the cardiac surgeon buying the practice. Personal goodwill is hardly ever so personal that none of it can be transferred.

Buying and Selling a Practice—Elements of Goodwill

In order for goodwill to have value transcending a transfer of ownership of the practice, the goodwill must be transferable along with the ownership. Many elements in a professional practice can cause transferable goodwill to exist. The elements that create goodwill in a buy-sell situation are somewhat different from those considered in a divorce valuation. For example, one element that is very important in a buy-sell situation is the marketability of the practice—although that factor is irrelevant under many states' divorce guidelines.

Goodwill is somewhat elusive and hard to define, generated by so many different factors and combinations of factors that it is impossible to list them all. However, several factors are dominant in determining the existence and value of practice and personal goodwill for professional practices:

1. Earnings levels that can be expected in the future.
2. The level of competition.
3. The referral base.
4. The types of patients or clients the practice serves.
5. Work habits of the practitioner.
6. The fees earned (compared to others in the same specialty).
7. Where the practice is located.
8. The practice's employees.
9. The general marketability of the type of practice being sold.

Expected Future Earnings

Like other business enterprises, one of the biggest factors contributing to goodwill value in a professional practice is the level of economic earnings. Although, generally, the higher the earnings, the more goodwill in the enterprise, an abundance of earnings does not inherently indicate an abundance of goodwill, nor does a dearth of earnings inherently indicate its lack. In judging the existence and value of goodwill based on the level of earnings, the appraiser should be sure to know the causes for the economic earnings levels before concluding a value. High economic earnings may result from the professional's skills, reputation, and efficiencies, or from his working longer hours and seeing more clients per day. Like goodwill itself, economic earnings do not occur by themselves, but because of other factors.

The term *economic earnings* does not refer to the practice's net income, because real earnings are usually given out to principals in the form of salaries, perquisites, and benefits; the net income as shown on the books of an incorporated practice is usually close to zero.

To determine the true economic earnings of the practice, the appraiser should analyze five years' worth of financial statements and tax returns, with each account on the income statements and balance sheets compared to the other years and set out in percentages of the relevant figures (on the income statements, all accounts expressed as a percent of revenues; on the balance sheets, all accounts expressed as a percent of total assets). For comparative purposes, economic earnings are usually measured on a cash basis, because professionals generally use that accounting for tax purposes, and because economic earnings surveys are generally on a cash basis.

Trended income statements are also helpful. In our firm, we calculate two types of trended statements—expressing each account as a percentage of the same account in the first year considered, and expressing each account as a percentage of the same account in the year immediately prior. From this information, the appraiser can discover unusual year-to-year activity in specific income accounts (e.g., owner's salaries). The appraiser then requests supporting documents (retirement plan payment allocations, the general ledger, various journals, check registers, invoices, etc.) in order to calculate accurately the practice's available income.

Level of Competition

Approximately 20 to 30 years ago, because of the shortage of physicians in this country, a physician who had met his educational requirements and received his license could hang up his shingle and begin seeing patients during his first week of practice. Because it was so easy to start medical practices, the market for their sale was inactive. Medical schools responded to the shortage by graduating more physicians, and the shortage was eliminated in most parts of the country, followed by an oversupply of physicians in many places.

It is not as easy now to start a successful practice as it was at that time, and, in fact, it is impossible in many areas. For that reason, established medical practices in some areas of the country are selling at prices more attractive to the seller (compared to several years ago), because new physicians are seeking to associate with established practices or to buy them outright. Obviously, as the demand for established practices has increased, so too has their value.

When appraising a professional practice, the appraiser should take into account the number of other practitioners in the same profession in the area, and what proportion they bear to the population at large. The census of supply of professionals has a marked bearing on the value of the professional practice.

Referral Base

Since the sources of referrals are a key characteristic of a professional practice, it is natural that they should also have a profound effect on the value of goodwill. A practice whose referrals come from a large number of current patients and clients will generally have more practice goodwill value than one that relies on referrals from a relatively small client base or from other professionals. Because of the difficulty of transferring the professional goodwill associated with a base of referrals, as discussed earlier in this chapter, the referral base is a more important element of the value of an entire practice than when determining the value of the contribution of a new associate joining the practice or in a valuation for a divorce.

Types of Patients and Clients

Generally, the appraiser should know the types of clients who patronize the practice and why. Typically, he would inquire about how many clients are seen each day, how many new clients seek the practice's services for the first time during a time period and how many cease to do so, and whether the practice depends on any particular client or specific group of clients for a significant portion of its income. Especially in medical and dental practices, the appraiser should inquire about the percentage of patients who have private insurance, who are part of the Medicare program, and who qualify for the government's Medicaid program. The practice with a large percentage of patients who either pay their bills themselves or who have private insurance will have a higher value than one with a preponderance of Medicare and Medicaid patients, because these government insurance programs generally pay less and pay later per procedure than the usual fee charged by the practitioner.

Work Habits of the Practitioner

It's almost a cliché that professionals work long hours. However, some are willing to work longer hours than others. A practice that requires 80 hours a week of a practitioner's time will not be worth as much per dollar of income to a purchaser as one that requires only 50 hours per week. Different work habits may also affect the value of a practice. Some dentists like to spend time with each patient, while others prefer to schedule several patients at a time and delegate more of the procedures to dental assistants or technicians. Obviously, a dentist of the more "personal" type considering purchasing a practice owned by one of the "mass production" type needs to consider how his work habits will alter the earning capacity of that practice. On the other hand, a potential purchaser may find that the selling practitioner liked to spend time on administrative duties that could have been handled by an office manager, and thus that there would be time to generate more revenue or to play more golf.

Fee Schedules

It is important that the appraiser understand the practice's fee schedule. Does it charge by procedure, time spent, or some other measure? How do this practitioner's fees compare with those of others with comparable qualifications? The appraiser should know how often the fees are adjusted and when the last fee adjustment occurred. If fees fall below the community's standard rate, what would happen to the income if the fees were raised, and how many patients or clients would be lost because of a fee increase? All these questions are usually considered in the course of examining the practice's earnings.

The fee schedule also provides an index to the skill and reputation of the practitioner. A practitioner with above-average fees and a large client base could be assumed to have above-average expertise or at least a better reputation.

Practice Location

The location of a practice has a substantial impact on its value. Some areas are perceived to be more desirable than others. Some communities are good "family" towns, while others provide a fast-track lifestyle. Like anyone else, professionals like to practice in the kind of communities in which they like to live. Therefore, areas that provide a comfortable lifestyle for the practitioner and his family, with a growing population or a strong and vibrant economy, will generally have professional practices that are in higher demand and are more expensive than will areas that are personally unattractive and/or economically depressed. The appraiser should investigate local demographics, the economic health of the area, and the overall quality of life in the community.

Employees of the Practice

The employees of a professional practice can be very important to its value. They know the procedures, they know the clients, and the expense of training them has already been incurred. When patients come in for their first visit with the new practitioner (the buyer), the familiar faces of the support personnel will help relieve their anxieties.

The appraiser should inquire about the number of employees and their names, their job titles and job descriptions, their pay scales, and the length of time they have been with the practice. He should inquire whether they plan to stay under the new management.

Particularly important are the nonowner professionals employed by the practice. They may actually hold the goodwill of some clients, and if they chose to leave the practice, their clients might go with them. The appraiser should inquire as to what extent that is the case in the practice at hand. The buyer does not want to pay for professional goodwill value that is ultimately not the seller's to sell, because it is owned by an employee who may or may not stay with the practice. In such a situation, an employment contract and a covenant not to compete might be negotiated with that employee, so that, in effect, the buyer purchases his professional goodwill as well.

Marketability of the Practice

The marketability of the practice depends on a number of factors, some of which have been discussed throughout this chapter. Demand for the practice obviously determines marketability, but often for reasons not directly related to the specific practice itself. If there is a glut of accountants seeking to purchase accounting practices, then the demand for established accounting practices is likely to rise, thus raising their practice goodwill value. If it is relatively easy to enter the specific profession, practice goodwill value will be lower. In many parts of the country, professional practices do not sell at all because the economy is so weak. On the other hand, some professions are inherently unmarketable, such as many psychiatric practices where the trust between patient and doctor is so crucial that it is, for all practical purposes, not transferable. The appraiser should examine these circumstances and use his judgment in determining the market value of professional practices.

Divorce Valuation—Elements of Goodwill

Valuations for divorces are among the most common professional engagements the appraiser of professional practices encounters. Most of the states whose appellate courts have ruled on whether professional goodwill is a marital asset, subject to valuation and division, have held that it is indeed an asset and should be valued and accounted for in the division of property. These states consider the value of the practice in the hands of the professional spouse as part of a going concern. One state (Texas) has consistently held that professional goodwill is not subject to division,[2] but it has held that practice goodwill can be valued.[3]

Even though all the elements that create professional goodwill discussed in the preceding section should be considered in valuing professional goodwill for divorce purposes, some are not necessarily as important in that context as in valuation for a sale of the practice. In a divorce valuation, the marketability of the practice generally does not determine the existence or value of professional goodwill. In a California appellate court ruling, the court was quite specific:

> The value of community goodwill is not necessarily the specified amount of money that a willing buyer would pay for such goodwill. In view of exigencies that are ordinarily attendant on a marriage dissolution, the amount obtainable in the market place may well be less than the true value of the goodwill, and the community goodwill is a portion of the community value of the professional practice as a going concern on the date of dissolution of the marriage.[4]

Other courts in California and other states have taken a similar position.

The difficulty of transferring referral sources is not a consideration for value in divorce cases, primarily because there is no transfer of the professional goodwill occurring. It is more as if the "silent partner" (nonpracticing spouse) is retiring and the practicing spouse is continuing in practice; for that reason, no diminution in professional goodwill will necessarily occur.

The various state courts have been helpful in establishing some fairly uniform guidelines to the factors that must be considered in appraising professional goodwill. The genesis of these factors is the California case, *Lopez* v. *Lopez* (38 Cal. App. 3d 93). The *Lopez* decision is a good treatise on the valuation of professional goodwill for marital dissolutions. It has been widely quoted in many other states in supporting the establishment of value for professional goodwill in divorce cases.

One of the primary sections of the *Lopez* case deals with what elements the appraiser should consider before expressing an opinion of professional goodwill value. The factors it determined to be appropriate included the following:

---

[2]*Nail* v. *Nail*, 486 S.W. 2d 761 (Texas Supreme Court 1972).

[3]*Geesbreght* v. *Geesbreght*, 570 S.W. 2d 427 (Texas Civil Appeals Court 1978).

[4]*In re Marriage of Foster*, 42 Cal. App. 3d 577, 117 Cal. Rptr. 49 (1st Dist. 1974).

1. The age and health of the professional.
2. The professional's demonstrated past earning power.
3. His reputation in the community for judgment, skill, and knowledge.
4. His comparative professional success.
5. The nature and duration of his practice, either as a sole proprietor or as a contributing member of a partnership or professional corporation.[5]

As comprehensive as they seem, these factors have been the source of some confusion among appraisers, attorneys, and the trial courts to determine how they should be measured.

Practitioner's Age and Health

It is far easier to determine the practitioner's age and health than to know how these factors affect professional goodwill value. Naturally, the practitioner's age is important. One close to retirement generally does not have a high professional goodwill value, even though his historical earnings may have been good, because those earnings cannot be expected to continue very far into the future. For example, if the practitioner were going to retire and close his practice two years after the valuation date, any multiple of his earnings (or excess earnings) over two would normally overvalue his professional goodwill. On the other hand, a fairly young practitioner who had only recently started practice would necessarily have a lower earning potential than the "average" practitioner; therefore, adjustments should be made before comparing those earnings to the average practitioner.

Health is another important factor. In one case, the appraiser retained by the nonprofessional spouse reached the opinion that the professional goodwill of the professional spouse—a heart surgeon—was very high because of his past earning power. If that appraiser had inquired as to the doctor's health, he would have learned that the surgeon recently had been diagnosed as having a degenerative disease in his joints, which in a very short period would cause him to curtail his surgical practice. Since the practice was not readily salable and the professional spouse could not expect continued earnings from his practice, the court dismissed the appraiser's determination of value and ruled that only a nominal amount of goodwill existed.

Demonstrated Past Earning Power

As is true in virtually all kinds of business appraisal, future earnings are a very important consideration in determining a value. Because of the peculiar circumstances of property divisions in a divorce, the discounted future earnings approach is not favored by the courts, because they will result from the practitioner's efforts after the marriage is terminated. Future earnings, according to judicial precedent in many jurisdic-

---

[5]*In re Marriage of Lopez*, 38 Cal. App. 3d 93, 113 Cal. Rptr. 58 (3d Dist. 1974).

tions, are not a marital asset. However, the courts have recognized that goodwill value is merely an expression of the value of expected future income, and the best estimate of future income is what has happened in the past. Generally, in practice valuations for divorce purposes, appraisers will consider the past five years of earnings of the practitioner, as of the valuation date.

Reputation for Judgment, Skill, and Knowledge

The practitioner's reputation for judgment, skill, and knowledge is one of the most abstract factors in the measurement of goodwill. After many professional practice valuations, the appraiser begins to get a "feel" for how these elements affect value, but it is difficult to quantify.

The appraiser should request a copy of the practitioner's curriculum vitae and inquire if he has received any special certifications, written any articles, taught classes, received any professional awards, or is a member in any professional societies. Any of these activities might help quantify these elements of a favorable reputation. On the other hand, if the professional has been judged by a court to have committed malpractice (or even been publicly accused of malpractice), that would also have a negative effect on the value of his professional goodwill. An interview form listing the specific questions the appraiser needs to ask can be helpful in discovering information relating to the practitioner's reputation. Experienced appraisers have usually developed proprietary interview forms and valuation worksheets that can be of great assistance to the valuation process.

Comparative Professional Success

Comparative professional success is a crucial factor in establishing professional goodwill. "Success" is usually measured by earnings, but other factors, such as the number of patients seen, hours generally spent working, community standards of living, and so forth, must also be considered.

It is very important to attempt to compare professionals with like professionals. If the appraiser is valuing the professional goodwill of a corporate attorney, it would be best to compare his earnings to other attorneys in corporate law. There are many earnings surveys, and they should be consulted, but to whatever extent possible, the earnings considered should be on a Golden Delicious-to-Golden Delicious basis, not Golden Delicious-to-crab apples.

Nature and Duration of Practice

Goodwill is built up over time, so the length of time the practice has been in existence will have a bearing on goodwill. A long-established law firm will attract more and higher-paying clients than one with wet paint on the shingle. The nature of the practice should also be considered. The following information about it can be relevant in determining goodwill:

- Type of service offered.
- Type of client served.
- Length of time at the current location.
- Length of time remaining on the lease.
- How the fees are billed.
- Source of new clients.
- The individual practitioner's amount of production.
- The number of employees and their length of service.
- Economic and demographic information on the community where the practice is located.
- The number of other professionals in the community offering the same service or specialty.

Summary

Practice goodwill is that which resides with the practice entity rather than any individual practitioner. Professional (personal) goodwill is that which resides with the individual apart from attributes of the practice entity. Even professional goodwill, however, has some degree of transferability with some effort and cooperation by the practitioner.

A divorce valuation is different from a valuation for the sale of a practice or for other purposes, and the appraiser needs to understand the differences. In the discussion of various valuation methods included in the next chapter, methods used primarily in divorce situations are specifically identified. Each state has slightly different case law concerning the valuation of professional goodwill, and any appraisal of goodwill for divorce purposes should recognize that state's particular statutes and case law in arriving at a conclusion. Chapter 39 is devoted to valuations for the purposes of marital property allocation in divorce and should be read in conjunction with any divorce valuation work.

Chapter 30

Determining the Value of the Practice

There is no single correct method of valuing professional practices, any more than there is a single correct method of valuing small businesses. Several methods do predominate, however, depending on the type of practice. This chapter examines several methods of valuing professional practices, along with rules of thumb used by some brokers and appraisers.

Methods of Professional Practice Valuation

Over the years, many methods have been devised to appraise professional practices, most of them ultimately discarded as redundant, invalid, or too complex. Several methods, though, when properly used, have withstood the tests of time and reasonableness and are now the primary methods for valuing professional practices:

1. Discounted cash flow.
2. Capitalization of earnings.
3. Multiple of revenues.
4. Excess earnings.
5. Asset accumulation.
6. Depreciating goodwill.
7. Comparative transactions and buy-ins (market data comparison).
8. Punitive and retirement formulas.

Each method has good and bad points, and not every one will be appropriate to every specific type of practice or valuation assignment.

Discounted Cash Flow

The discounted cash flow method for a professional practice follows the same basic procedures as laid out in Chapter 13, usually focusing on the same definition of net cash flow.

In some instances, the cash flows may be projected on an incremental basis rather than on an absolute basis, i.e., "What is the *difference* between my cash flows from buying this practice and my cash flows if I just hang out my shingle and start practicing?" This incremental version of the discounted cash flow method is shown in the illustrative example of a medical practice valuation in Chapter 31.

Capitalization of Earnings

Chapter 12 presents a long description of capitalization rates and factors that need to be considered in their selection. In professional practices, two types of economic earnings are typically capitalized—pretax earnings after a fair salary to the owner or practitioner, and total earnings (including the owner's or practitioner's salary and benefits). In some cases, aftertax earnings are capitalized. Both definitions of economic earnings assume normalized earnings (having removed nonrecurring income and expenses and adjusting certain expenses to reflect more accurately economic reality).

Choosing a Capitalization Rate. In any given professional practice, the capitalization of each earnings base should produce fairly consistent values, even though the earnings figures (according to the different definitions) are considerably different. When using total earnings (pretax stated earnings plus owner salary and benefits), the capitalization rate should be much higher than when using only pretax earnings after reasonable owner's compensation. It is not unusual to see capitalization rates of 100 percent or more when using total earnings as a base, compared to a 20 to 35 percent capitalization rate for pretax earnings after owner's compensation.

Benefits and Drawbacks of the Capitalization of Earnings Methods. The capitalization of earnings method is both one of the best means of appraising an entity and one of the most abused. Besides the difficulty of selecting an appropriate capitalization rate, proper use of the method requires astute judgments concerning the real earning capacity of the practice and the expected growth in its earnings.

This value generally represents the value of the whole practice—not just the goodwill portion. If a practice has excess assets, or if the assets used in generating income could be replaced by less expensive items with the same function, the appraiser must add the excess asset value back to the calculated value.

Multiple of Revenues

Revenue multiples have been discussed elsewhere in this book, primarily in the context of emphasizing that they should not be used alone. Revenue multiples serve as one of the primary rules of thumb for many industries, particularly professional practices. It is very common to see revenue multiples used in valuations of professional practices for divorces. The multiple of revenues can be a useful valuation approach used in conjunction with others, but it can be misleading if one relies on it solely. Several specific industry revenue multiples are discussed in the "Rule-of-Thumb Methods" section of this chapter.

Revenue multiples are popular in appraising professional practices for several reasons:

1. The method is simple to understand.
2. Revenues are often easier to determine than the economic earnings of the practice.
3. When looking for comparative transactions, sale price-to-revenues is often the only valuation ratio that can be calculated.

Proper Use of the Multiple of Revenues. Revenue multiples are often used in setting prices for sales of professional practices. It is not wise to rely entirely upon them, however, because the specific practice may have certain positive and negative attributes that the multiple would not take into account. For example, if an accounting practice were appraised by the excess earnings method to be $100,000, the appraiser may want to state this value in terms of a multiple of revenue, in order to check it against an industry standard rule-of-thumb revenue multiple. If it seems out of line with the industry, the appraiser knows that he may have erred in calculating value using the excess earnings method (and needs to search for and correct his error), or that the particular practice is so different from the typical accounting practice that it does not fall in the standard revenue multiple range (and the appraiser should analyze such differences).

Benefits and Drawbacks of the Multiple of Revenues Method. The biggest benefit of this appraisal method is that, being relatively easy, it is a good way of making an educated guess at a practice's value. By itself, on the other hand, it does not consider the essence of value, which is the return necessary to justify the risk.

Excess Earnings

The excess earnings method has already been described in detail in Chapter 15, so we do not need to repeat its history or how it is calculated. The excess earnings method is used quite frequently in divorce proceedings—probably more so than in actual transactions. Although most courts have held that there is no single method of valuing professional goodwill, in at least one case, the excess earnings method was the only one discussed as a means of measuring goodwill.[1]

Generally, for a professional practice, *total earnings* are defined as all economic earnings available to the practitioner and are computed as follows:

1. The net income of the practice, including salary and benefits to the practitioner(s) or owner(s).
2. Plus nonrecurring expenses less nonrecurring income.
3. Plus excessive expenses (expenses not related to the generation of practice income).

It was pointed out that a fair salary for the owner/manager should be deducted from earnings in most business valuations. In professional practices, however, earnings are counted before the owner's salary, benefits, and perquisites in most earnings surveys, because, as discussed in Chapter 31, professionals usually pay out most of the practice earnings in salaries, perquisites, and benefits.[2] In comparing the practice earnings

---

[1]*Levy* v. *Levy*, 164 N.J. Super. 542, 397 A.2d 374 (1978).

[2]The two most widely used surveys for medical practice earnings data are *Medical Economics*, a semimonthly periodical that contains an earnings survey each September (along with specific practice specialty surveys throughout the year), and the American Medical Association's *Socioeconomic Characteristics of Medical Practice* (published annually), previously known as *Profile of Medical Practice*.

to the industry level, obviously it is important to be consistent between the practice being appraised and the survey data being used.

Determination of Net Asset Value for Return on Investment Calculation. Chapter 28 discusses methods of valuing net assets for professional practices. The appraiser valuing a practice may wonder how to treat items such as artwork owned by the practice, whether a monetary return should be calculated on this kind of asset. Even though it is arguable that the asset is not essential to the practice operations and that operating earnings should therefore not be charged for a return on nonoperating assets, others would argue that the money for this artwork could have been invested in operating equipment; therefore the total investment in the practice, no matter what type of asset is involved, should realize a return on investment.

Both arguments have merit, and the answer is, as usual, found somewhere between the two extremes. In general, return on net asset value is calculated on operating assets less operating liabilities, but it should give recognition to a certain portion of assets (and/or liabilities) that might not be considered operating, but that are not unusual in the type of practice being appraised. As an example, the value of moderately priced office lithographs would probably be included in net asset value, because the practice's offices need a pleasant atmosphere for its clients. However, if the office contained 50 original M. C. Escher woodcut prints, the fair market value of these prints would most appropriately be removed from the net asset value (along with any associated debt) before calculating a return on capital, because they go far beyond the general requirements of office furnishings.

There are instances when, using the excess earnings method on professional practices, no return on capital is calculated. Sometimes earnings surveys for self-employed professionals include earnings that represent a return on capital to those practitioners. If earnings from such a survey are being used for comparison with earnings of a self-employed professional, it would be improper to remove from that professional's earnings an amount for a return on his capital. On the other hand, if the self-employed professional is being compared against salaries for nonowner professional employees, it is necessary to figure his return on capital because nonowner professionals have no investment at risk.

Earnings Levels. In determining the economic earnings level of the practice, the appraiser should consider at least five years of earnings data, if they are available. A careful analysis of the practice's earning history will provide a basis for estimating the practice's future earning capacity. A five-year average figure may or may not reflect the future earnings potential of the practice, but the five-year history will reveal trends and unusual occurrences that could be buried in an average.

Consider, for example, the partnership of Bean & Bacon, restaurant consultants. If an average earnings figure for the five-year period were routinely accepted by the appraiser as indicative of future earning capacity, then under the following earnings assumptions the appraiser would calculate the average earnings at \$77,400 (\$387,000 ÷ 5 = \$77,400) for Bacon.

	Total Earnings of Bacon	Total Earnings of Bean & Bacon
Latest year	\$100,000	\$200,000
Year 4	120,000	240,000
Year 3	75,000	200,000
Year 2	52,000	175,000
Year 1	40,000	160,000
Total	\$387,000	\$975,000

Even though \$77,400 is the mathematical average of Bacon's five-year earnings, the trend suggests that this average does not represent his future earning capacity. In year 1, Bacon received 25 percent of the practice's total earnings; in year 2, the amount had risen to 30 percent; in year 3 to 37½ percent; and in years 4 and 5, Bacon received 50 percent of total practice earnings.

If the appraiser had investigated, he would have found that partners Bean and Bacon had agreed that Bacon would take a lower percentage of profits in the first three years, but would begin to receive 50 percent in year 4 and continue at that level of earnings from then on. Therefore, Bacon's current earning capacity is 50 percent of the practice's earning capacity; and it should be stated at 50 percent of the five-year average of the partnership's earnings, or \$97,500 (\$975,000 × 50 percent ÷ 5). The appraiser should consider all relevant facts before concluding on current or future earning capacity.

Earnings Surveys. A practitioner's economic earnings should be compared, as much as possible, to those of a like practitioner. The comparative practitioner should be in the same specific field, in the same geographic area, of approximately the same level of experience, and so on, as the professional whose practice is being valued. A psychiatrist, although a medical doctor (MD), should not be compared to a cardiologist, because each specialist has different earnings expectations.

Capitalization Rates. The return expected on the professional practice's net asset value should be neither more nor less than any other small business would expect to receive. Typically, the capitalization rate for the professional's excess economic earnings depends upon the positive and negative influences of the elements of value discussed in Chapter 27. Capitalization rates for the professional's excess economic earnings range from 20 to 100 percent (or multiples of five to one).

Benefits and Drawbacks of the Excess Earnings Method. The primary benefits of the excess earnings method are the following:

1. It is widely used, and therefore recognized and understood by many people.
2. Conceptually, it logically quantifies the value of intangible assets related to excess earnings.

3. It is codified (Rev. Rul. 68-609) and has been approved in many court rulings for valuation of professional practice goodwill.

The primary drawbacks of the excess earnings method are:

1. It is easily misapplied, because it requires so many subjective judgments on the part of the appraiser.
2. It can overstate the value of goodwill because it does not recognize the factor of marketability.
3. It can understate the value of goodwill because it does not always factor in the going-concern elements of a practice already in place, even one that does not have excess earnings.

Asset Accumulation

By the "asset accumulation method" in this context, we really mean adjusted book value (adjusted net worth) including *all* assets, both tangible and intangible, net of the firm's liabilities.

Two examples of the asset accumulation method, including several specific identifiable intangible assets as well as goodwill, are shown in the illustrative valuations of a medical practice and an accounting practice in Chapter 32. In a sense, this method could be viewed as a specific version of the excess earnings method. While the excess earnings method generally lumps all the intangible value into a single pot (often called goodwill), this method specifically identifies and values each individual intangible asset.

Depreciating Goodwill

Goodwill is not constant, but, like most other assets, diminishes in value over time unless something is done to keep or enhance it. Goodwill must be nurtured to maintain its value. That is why the accountant may treat his client to lunch once a year, and the dentist sends out holiday greetings to his patients.

Generally, the depreciating goodwill method uses a modified excess earnings formula.[3] The appraiser establishes a level of excess earnings, but instead of capitalizing those excess earnings at a constant rate, he treats them as a wasting asset, depreciating to zero after a certain period. He then calculates the present value of those depreciating excess earnings using a discount factor that reflects the risk associated with those earnings.

Even though the concept of depreciating goodwill is soundly based and there is no argument with the general procedure of valuing depreciating excess earnings, there is opportunity for some misuse of the method by appraisers.

Common Errors in Depreciating Goodwill. The first common error is that the depreciating excess earnings are generally capitalized at the

---

[3]See, for example, Tony Leung, "Professional Goodwill: A Management Perspective," *Washington State Bar News*, June 1984, pp. 39–41.

same rate used in the capitalization of excess earnings method discussed earlier. Since risk is one of the determining factors in selecting capitalization rates, and since the recognition of the depreciation of goodwill reduces risk, the capitalization rate used in a valuation on the basis of the depreciation of excess earnings should be reduced to reflect the lowered risk, compared to an excess earnings approach that does not factor in depreciation.

The second common error is the assumption that it can be estimated at what date the goodwill will reach zero. A good analogy might be the purchase and nurturing of a houseplant. For the houseplant to live and grow, the weekend horticulturist must water and feed the plant. However, a person with a green thumb will prune the plant, find the most ideal location for it, and probably even mist it regularly, producing a healthy and beautiful plant. Even though both plants will grow, the latter plant will have much more expansive foliage.

The professional practitioner who merely performs services for his clients or patients will see his goodwill diminish, but, like the weekend horticulturist, will probably not see it depreciate to zero. In other words, goodwill, like most other assets, will generally have some salvage value.

Benefits and Drawbacks of the Depreciating Goodwill Method. The concept of depreciating goodwill is appealing because it makes economic sense. However, it is extremely difficult to measure how much depreciation has taken place, or will take place. The type of practice, location, types of clients or patients of the practice, and many other variables affect the rate at which goodwill depreciates. Considering that it is difficult to measure and value by itself, it is almost impossible to determine the life cycle of such an intangible and elusive asset. Perhaps because of the extreme difficulty in developing sound bases for measurement, this method is rarely used in practice.

Comparative Transactions and Buy-Ins (Market Data Comparison)

The use of comparative transactions and buy-ins is not necessarily a set of formulas, such as have been previously discussed, but is a methodology by which various measurements of value can be computed and compared to the practice being appraised.

Comparative Transactions.   For example, assume that a small veterinary practice was being appraised, and the appraiser found 15 comparative sales of similar practices in the same geographic area during the prior 12 months. The price of each practice was probably based on various formulas, several, or all, of which were different from the others. However, if it was found that all sales occurred at a revenue multiple of between 90 and 120 percent of the latest year's net revenue, or at a multiple of the latest year's total earnings of 1.75 to 2.00, these multiples (after adjustments, if appropriate) could be applied to the practice under appraisal. The comparative transactions are not a formula in themselves for establishing value, but can be related to previously discussed methods (excess earnings or revenue multiples, for example), which can then be applied to the practice under appraisal.

Buy-Ins. There is a situation, however, in which the comparative transaction may be based on a formula that the appraiser can rely upon to value the practice. Buy-in formulas may exist in the practice being appraised or in practices similar to it. Typically, they are designed so that a new partner or shareholder of an established practice can buy his interest in the partnership with before-tax dollars, offering only a small down payment, if any.

For example, suppose that Dr. Holladay's practice is expanding so rapidly that he anticipates soon reaching his maximum patient load. He therefore decides to bring in an associate who will be able to increase the number of patients the practice can handle, and ultimately make him a partner. Because of economies of scale, Dr. Holladay would enjoy a higher income with the associate than he would by remaining a sole practitioner. However, Dr. Holladay realizes that he has spent a long time building his practice and thinks that a new associate should be willing to purchase an interest in the practice.

Dr. Holladay could ask a new practitioner to buy a half interest in the practice immediately. However, because such a purchase would require after-tax dollars from the new associate, and would be likely to reduce Dr. Holladay's immediate income as this became shared, he decides to ask for a small down payment and arranges a vesting schedule for the allocation of income between himself and the new associate. According to this schedule, during the early years Dr. Holladay would receive over 50 percent of total practice earnings, even though both doctors spend approximately equal time seeing approximately the same number of patients. The sample appraisal report in the following chapter illustrates this method of valuation.

In other cases, the new doctor comes in as an employee. After a number of years, a buy-in is negotiated, buying the tangible assets and handling the intangible value through a salary differential over time.

Benefits and Drawbacks of the Use of Comparative Transactions and Buy-Ins. When the appraiser has comparative transaction data available, which provide relatively consistent measurements of value, this method is extremely helpful in establishing value. Buy-in transactions, especially in the practice under appraisal, are also very strong evidence of value. Unfortunately, the comparative data can be very sketchy and the prior buy-in may be too remote in time, or may involve unique circumstances, which cause the data to be incomplete or outdated for the current appraisal.

Punitive and Retirement Formulas

Punitive and retirement valuation formulas are established by contract in the practice being appraised. They do not necessarily establish the market value of the practice or the interest in a practice, but they set forth a value for the practitioner's interest when he leaves or retires. Therefore, if the standard of value calls for the appraiser to value good-will on a going-concern basis, these contractual obligations may not necessarily aid in determining that going-concern value.

Purpose of Punitive and Retirement Formulas. A punitive formula is sometimes written into a partnership agreement to discourage partners from leaving the firm. The punitive contract offers the exiting partner a prescribed buyout formula that is lower than the fair market value of his partnership interest. A retirement formula, which is also often included in partnership agreements, may attempt to value the partnership interest at its fair market value, or perhaps even above its fair market value, to reward the partner for many years of valuable service.

Benefits and Drawbacks of the Use of Punitive and Retirement Formulas. Having a prescribed formula for the interest to be valued is helpful if the reason for the appraisal is the event that calls the formula into operation. However, these formulas are generally of little help if the purpose of the appraisal is some reason other than that which would cause the formula to be invoked.

Rule-of-Thumb Methods for Various Types of Practices

A rule of thumb is a homemade recipe for making a guess. It is an easy-to-remember guide that falls somewhere between a mathematical formula and a shot in the dark.[4]

The various methods already discussed can be applied to almost all types of professional practices. However, certain types of practices do have specific formulas (almost all based on revenue multiples) that tend to be commonly used in their respective valuations. Below is a listing of some types of professional practices that have a rule of thumb that can be applied to estimate the practice value.

The appraiser should be cautioned, however, that these are general rules that will be accurate only as averages, given a large number of observations. However, in any specific observation, the rule may need to be adjusted or even discarded if it is not appropriate to the situation at hand. In any case, it is highly recommended that rules of thumb be used only in conjunction with other valuation methods.

Accounting Practices

Small accounting firms tend to sell for their net asset value plus a good-will value, which, when paid over time, is equal to 75 to 150 percent of the latest year's revenues. However, this very simple formula has some complicating adjustments.

---

[4]Tom Parker, *Rules of Thumb* (Boston: Houghton Mifflin, 1983), p. vii.

The goodwill is usually purchased by the buyer's payment to the seller of a certain percentage of fees collected from clients who continue with the practice for a period of time. For example, at the date of sale, a list of past clients may be prepared, and buyer and seller agree that 20 percent of all fees charged to those clients (and paid by them) for the next five years will be transferred to the selling accountant immediately after those fees are paid. This agreement results in a revenue multiple of 1 (20 percent $\times$ 5 = 1). However, at the date of sale, in order to determine a value for the goodwill, the appraiser would need to investigate the attrition rates of clients and also apply a discount to the expected income stream for the time value of money.

Another method of valuing the goodwill of an accounting firm would be to apply a different multiple to each segment of revenue. Generally, an accountant would be willing to pay more for a continuing audit client or a write-up client than for numerous individual tax return clients.

Dental Practices

The old rule was that general dental practices sold for the value of their equipment, furniture, and fixtures plus a value for goodwill of either 25 to 35 percent of revenues, or 50 to 100 percent of total earnings available to the doctor. Others have used factors of all the way from 35 to 75 percent of revenues to value the goodwill and the equipment furniture and fixtures. There may be some upward trend in these percentages due to the large supply of dentists.

Engineering/Architecture Practices

After the first edition of this book was published, a CPA specializing in financial consulting to engineering and architectural practices wrote to say that no rule of thumb exists for engineering and architectural firms. He pointed out that architectural and engineering firms seem to have more characteristics of smaller businesses for valuation purposes than professional practices. Most are regular corporations (not professional corporations) and employ from, say, 50 to 250 people. The adjustments made to the financial statements are more like the ones appropriate for small businesses. Architectural and engineering firms have ESOPs, stock purchase plans, and other transition vehicles that are not usually found in smaller professional practices.

Depending on the type of practice, these firms are valued at their net asset value plus 20 to 40 percent of the latest year's revenues. Practices with continuing clients would tend to sell at the high end of the multiple range. This formula should be used cautiously, because many of these firms possess little, if any, goodwill.

Law Practices

In the past, a general law practice could be sold for its net asset value only, because legal ethics forbade the sale of clients' files or goodwill.

However, some attorneys who wish to retire refer their cases to a new attorney and then split the fee paid by the referred client with the new attorney.

In divorces, many state courts have held that goodwill should be valued, even if it can't be sold. However, no standard rule-of-thumb method exists for this type of appraisal.

In recent years, state laws regarding the sale of legal practices have started to change, in many cases allowing the sale of law practices. So far, not enough data has been developed to provide meaningful generalizations.

Medical Practices

The following comments should be read with the recognition that within the broad spectrum of medical practices there are great differences in valuation depending on the specialty involved.

Ten years ago, medical practices were difficult to sell because the relative ease of entry into the market diminished their value. However, with the oversupply of physicians in many parts of the country, medical practices are selling, and they are commanding goodwill value. Generally, these practices sell in a range of 20 to 60 percent of revenues for the equipment, supplies, and goodwill. Obviously, the type of practice has a large influence on the multiple; referral practices are near the low end, and practices with a continuing patient base are toward the high end of the range.

There is no general rule of thumb for valuing goodwill only. However, the *Goodwill Registry*, a publication produced annually by the Health Care Group in Plymouth Meeting, Pennsylvania, presents a compilation of medical and dental practice valuations. The *Goodwill Registry* has been published since 1981. It reports the sum total of practice intangibles under a term of convenience, *goodwill*. These intangibles can include, for example, beneficial contracts (e.g., "below market" rent), noncompete agreements, and a variety of other intangibles. As reported, for example, in the 1992 *Goodwill Registry*, the 1985–1992 average goodwill value from a total of 101 internal medicine subspecialties showed a mean average of 31 percent and a median of 29 percent of revenue.[5]

While the *Goodwill Registry* is a useful guideline source, it must be used with caution. The authors of the publication recognize that it does not represent a statistically valid sample of any particular population of practices. There are also other limitations. For example, the values shown for goodwill are not necessarily adjusted to cash equivalent value to take into account the time value of money and other factors. Also, the entries do not all represent actual arm's length transactions; some represent appraisals for divorce and other purposes. Recognizing these caveats, the *Goodwill Registry*, used in conjunction with other valuation methods and data, provides some useful insight.

Following a 1992 meeting of the Professional Practice Valuation Study Group at which input was solicited for this book, the following

---

[5]*Goodwill Registry* (Plymouth Meeting, Penn.: The Healthcare Group, 1992), p. 4.

letter was received, which seemed to me to be worth sharing with readers without any editing:[6]

Four new developments will significantly impact on the value and sale of physician, hospital and medical businesses in the 1990s:

1. On July 29, 1991, the Department of Health and Human Services issued long-awaited "Safe Harbor Guidelines" relating to Medicare and State Health Care programs. (Federal Register, Vol. 56, No. 145, 42 CFR Part 1001).

    The regulations address fraud, abuse and kickbacks in federal and state funded health care programs. Two key provisions relate to the sale of medical practices and the percentage of ownership interests that may be held by physicians, hospitals, and others who are in a position to refer downstream business paid for using state or federal funds.

    The impact of these "Safe Harbor Guidelines" on the value of physician, hospital and medical business investments is the most significant in at least a decade. It will require significant restructuring, divestiture, or withdrawal of physician and hospital ownership interests in many businesses formed during the preceding decade.

2. In late 1991 and during 1992, the Internal Revenue Service issued a series of opinions and new "Examination Guidelines" related to (non-profit) hospital joint ventures with physicians and the Service's treatment of unrelated business revenues.

    The effect of these announcements, opinions and private letter rulings has been to add further pressure for the sale or restructuring of many of the physician-joint ventures. The penalty for non-compliance is the loss of a hospital's tax-exemption.

    IRS Announcement 92-70 indicated the Service would, "for a limited time, consider resolution of this tax issue without loss of tax exemption if hospitals terminate the arrangements without further private benefit to the physician investors" and if hospitals enter into a "closing agreement or other arrangement" through a request to the IRS "on or before September 1, 1992."

    The impact of these rulings will further create a national market of forced sales of such businesses.

3. In 1992, the State of Florida (a bellweather health care state) passed legislation requiring physicians to divest themselves of financial interests in businesses to which they refer no later than the end of 1995. Similar proposals are pending in other states and at the federal level.

    The impact of such legislation (or similar regulation) will be to require physicians to divest themselves of ownership interests in such private businesses—creating another "forced sale" market. (Physician investments in publicly held, large capitalization healthcare companies are generally exempt.)

4. On January 1, 1992, the largest single payer of health services instituted a new payment system for physician services. Private insurance carriers are expected to follow suit, increasing the market impact.

    The Resource Based Relative Value Scale (RBRVS) will significantly alter the financial returns to various medical specialties. It is reducing payments to so called "over valued" specialties (specifically thoracic surgery, radiology, ophthalmology, pathology, gastroenterology, neurosurgery, cardiology and orthopedic surgery) while increasing payments

---

[6]Letter to Shannon Pratt from Ronald L. Hammerle, president, Health Resources, Inc., dated May 4, 1992.

to primary care physicians, (especially family practice, internal medicine and pediatrics).

The impact on medical practice values will be to further raise the value of primary care practices, encourage the formation of and acquisition by multi-specialty groups, and anticipate other initiatives by high income physicians to preserve their income.

The best analogy I have been able to share with outsider observers of the U.S. healthcare scene is that "American healthcare in the '90s will look like the American airline industry in the late '80s—unless Congress adopts a single payer system for health insurance.

Optometric Practices

These practices can be more like retail businesses than professional practices, because their location is more important than in other types of professional practices. Generally, the value of an optometric practice's equipment, supplies, patient eye prescriptions, and goodwill can range from 40 percent to 60 percent of the latest year's revenues.

Medical Laboratories

There have been many acquisitions of local laboratories by publicly traded laboratory companies. Acquisition prices as a percent of latest year's revenues have had an extremely wide range, but the vast majority fall in the range of 50 to 80 percent of latest year's revenues for the goodwill and net asset value.

Veterinary Practices

Dog and cat clinics in good locations can command premium prices. Generally, these practices sell for 75 to 125 percent of the latest year's revenues for the goodwill.

Summary

Professional practice valuation follows the basic principles and methods used to value businesses generally, but with certain variations arising from the general nature of professional practices. The choice of actual methods will depend to some extent on the purpose of the valuation, the nature of the practice, and the availability of data. As with other types of businesses, rules of thumb cover such a wide range of potential value for any practice that they cannot be relied on by themselves, but may serve as a check for reasonableness.

Selected Bibliography

Articles

Agiato, Joseph A. "Business Valuations: An Increasingly Important Part of a Professional Practice." *Small Business Taxation*, May/June 1990, pp. 279–85.

Anders, Geoffrey T. "Determining the Market Value of Medical and Dental Practices." In *Valuing Professional Practices and Licenses: A Guide for the Matrimonial Practitioner*. Ronald L. Brown, ed. Clifton, N. J.: Prentice Hall Law & Business, 1987, pp. 179–202.

Arnold, Ralph, and Shannon P. Pratt. "Professional Practices." In *Financial Valuation: Businesses and Business Interests*, James H. Zukin and John G. Mavredakis, eds. New York: Maxwell Macmillan, 1990, pp. 20.1–20.28.

Bentley, Marvin J., and Jay Lieberman. "Goodwill—What Is It Worth in the Market?" *Journal of the American Dental Association*, September 1980, pp. 459–63.

Bern, Brenda, and Arthur Fred Bern. "What Is Your Practice Really Worth?" *Physician's Management*, June 1985, p. 253.

Bernstein, Jack, and John Seigel. "What Is Your Practice Worth?" *Dental Management*, May 1982, pp. 81–83.

Brown, Ronald L. "Valuing Your Practice in a Divorce Case." *National Law Journal*, August 24, 1987, pp. 15–17.

Cheifetz, A. J. "A Practical Guide to Determining the Value of a Professional Practice." *Taxation for Accountants*, February 1982, pp. 102–5.

Cheifetz, Cary B., and Gary N. Skoloff. "Valuation of a Professional Practice." In *Valuation Strategies in Divorce*. 2nd ed. Robert E. Kleeman, ed. New York: John Wiley & Sons, 1992, pp. 75–101."

Christensen, Bobby. "Calculating Your Practice's Worth." *Optometric Management*, March 1989, pp. 45–52.

Cohen, Ray Jeffrey. "It Pays to Appraise Your Practice." *Dental Management*, April 1981, pp. 44–48.

Cosman, Madeleine Peiner; Thomas Russell Lang; and Marin C. Goodheart. "Comparing Medical and Business Goodwill Components." *FAIR$HARE: The Matrimonial Law Monthly*, January 1990, pp. 3–8.

Douglas, Edward P., and Owen E. McCafferty. "Determining Practice Value." *Veterinary Economics*, July 1977, pp. 21–51.

Florescue, Leonard G. "Business Value of Law License." *New York Law Journal*, August 21, 1990, p. 3.

Gellman, Stuart A. "Valuing Law and Medical Practices: The Accounting Approach." *FAIR$HARE: The Matrimonial Law Monthly*, May 1986, pp. 16–20.

Gerhardt, Charles D. "Putting a Value on a Medical Practice." *Family Advocate*, Summer 1984, pp. 10–13.

Getz, Lowell V. "How Much Is Your Firm Really Worth?" *Consulting Engineer*, March 1985, pp. 51–56.

Giangrego, Elizabeth. "Determining the Value of Your Practice: A Realistic Approach." *Journal of the American Dental Association*, September 1984, pp. 402–12.

Goodman, Stanely L. "Valuing Dr. O'Brien's Medical Degree: A View from Inside." *FAIR$HARE: The Matrimonial Law Monthly*, May 1986, pp. 10–13.

Harrison, Doane. "Pump Up and Preserve Your Practice Goodwill." *Medical Economics*, April 15, 1985, pp. 107–12.

Hempstead, John E. "Putting a Value on a Law Practice." *Family Advocate*, Summer 1984, pp. 15–19.

Holdren, Richard C. "How Much Is My Practice Worth?" *Nebraska Medical Journal*, August 1985, p. 306.

Horvath, James L. "Valuing Professional Degrees and Licenses." *Canadian Family Law Quarterly*, April 1988, pp. 1–22.

Hubler, Richard S. "A New Approach to Evaluating the Worth of a Practice." *Optometric Management*, March 1987, pp. 40, 42, 44.

Irving, Raymond N. "How a Broker Values a Practice." *Optometric Management*, May 1982, pp. 33, 37, 39.

————. "How Much Is Your Practice Worth?" *Dental Management*, October 1981, pp. 16–20.

Jackson, James B. "Determining the Value of Your Practice: A Realistic Approach." *Journal of the American Dental Association*, September 1984, pp. 402–12.

Keyes, James. "Measuring Practice Value." *Dental Economics*, May 1986, p. 38.

Klein, Ronald. "Techniques for Valuing Law Practices." In *Valuing Professional Practices and Licenses: A Guide for the Matrimonial Practitioner*. Ronald L. Brown, ed. Clifton, N. J.: Prentice Hall Law and Business, 1987, pp. 127–43.

Kline, Michael E. "Law Practice Goodwill: An Evolving Concept." *FAIR$HARE: The Matrimonial Law Monthly*, April 1991, pp. 6–8.

Leimberg, Stephan R. "Putting a Price on the Practice." *Best's Review (Life/Health Insurance Edition)*, July 1987, p. 62.

Leung, T. S. Tony. "Valuation of Professional Goodwill." *Business Valuation News*, June 1983, pp. 11–18.

Lonergan, Wayne. "What Is a Professional Practice Really Worth? *Australian Accountant*, April 1992, pp. 26–32.

Lurvey, Ira. "How to Value a Lawyer's Practice." *TRIAL*, June 1986, pp. 36–40.

Martin, J. Thomas. "Don't Overlook These Crucial Points in a Practice Sale: Whether You're Selling or Buying, This Checklist Will Help Protect You Against Financial and Tax Risks." *Medical Economics*, January 6, 1992, pp. 95–97.

Mastracchio, Nicholas J. "How to Value a Professional Practice." *Practical Accountant*, December 1985, pp. 22–26.

McCafferty, Owen E. "How to Price Your Practice." Parts 1, 2, and 3. *Veterinary Economics*, August, September, and October 1987, pp. 38–55; 62–71; and 62.

McGovern, Margaret F. "Licenses v. Degrees: Is There a Difference?" *Family Advocate*, Fall 1986, pp. 14–17.

Monath, Donald. "Differentiating Commercial Professional Goodwill from Personal Professional Goodwill." Parts I and II. *FAIR$HARE: The Matrimonial Law Monthly*, October and November 1990, pp. 13–15; 6–8.

_____. "Professional Goodwill: Is It Marital Property." *Family Advocate*, Fall 1991, pp. 52–53.

_____. "Valuation Part I: How to Value a Medical Clinic—A Case Study." *Family Advocate*, Winter 1989, pp. 48–52.

_____. "Valuation Part II: Valuing Specialized Private Medical Practice." *Family Advocate*, Spring 1989, pp. 55–57.

Nielsen, Gordon L., and Dennis H. Hudson. "How to Value an Accounting Practice." *Practical Accountant*, April 1987, pp. 44–50.

Paone, Louis A., and Kathryn F. Aschwald. "Determining the Value of A/E Firms." *ASCENT*, September/October 1991, pp. 6–7.

Park, William R. "Fair Market Value of an Ongoing Business." *Consulting Engineer*, March 1985, pp. 72–76.

Parkman, Allen. "The Treatment of Professional Goodwill in Divorce Proceedings." *Family Law Quarterly*, Summer 1984, pp. 213–23.

Petrie, Kurt J. "Evaluating the Worth of a Practice." *Optometric Management*, November 1986, pp. 18–19.

Pratt, Shannon P. "Valuing a Practice: Choosing the Right Capitalization Rates." *CA Magazine*, April 1987, pp. 49–52.

Pratt, Shannon P., and Ralph Arnold. "Placing a Value on Your Professional Practice." *Lawyer/Manager*, May/June 1989, pp. 42–48.

_____. "Specific Methods for Determining the Value of Your Law Practice." *Lawyer/Manager*, July/August 1989, pp. 41–49.

Reilly, Robert F. "How Much Is Your Practice Worth." *Today's CPA*, May/June 1991, pp. 27–37.

_____. "The Valuation of a Medical Practice." *Health Care Management Review*, Summer 1990, pp. 25–34.

_____. "The Valuation of Chiropractic and Similar Professional Practices." Parts 1 and 2. *Digest of Chiropractic Economics*, January/February 1991; March/April 1991, pp. 17–21; 24–28.

_____. "The Valuation of Medical, Dental, and Similar Professional Practices." *Business Valuation Review*, March 1989, pp. 7–27.

_____. "Valuation of the Professional Medical Practice." Parts 1 and 2. *Small Business Taxation*, November/December 1988, January/February 1989, pp. 107–10, 173–78.

Reilly, Robert F., and Robert P. Schweihs. "Valuation of Accounting Practices." *Ohio CPA Journal*, Autumn 1990, pp. 19–26.

_____. "Valuation of Accounting Practices—What's It Worth?" *National Public Accountant*, February 1991, pp. 20–29.

Rosen, Harvey S., and John Burke, Jr. "Putting a Value on a Professional License." *Family Advocate*, Summer 1984, pp. 23–27.

Samuelson, Elliot D. "Putting a Value on a Professional Practice." *Family Advocate*, Summer 1984, pp. 5–7, 40.

Shayne, Mark. "Valuing Your Law Practice." *New York State Bar Journal*, July-August 1992, pp. 54–56.

Shultz, Clayton G. "What's a Professional Practice Really Worth?" *CA Magazine*, June 1983, pp. 36–40.

Steiner, Erwin H., and Ronald J. Kudla. "Valuation of Professional Practices." *Law Office Economics and Management* 31, no. 2 (1990), pp. 197–206.

Strogen, Edward M., Jr., and Leif C. Beck. "The Market Approach to Valuing Medical and Dental Practices." *FAIR$HARE: The Matrimonial Law Monthly*, May 1986, pp. 14–16.

Thal, Lawrence S. "The Practice Sale: Getting to the Bottom Line." *Optometric Management*, June 1986, pp. 66–67.

Thompson, Gary W. "Is That Practice Worth the Price?" *Medical Economics*, June 8, 1987, pp. 151+.

Tibergien, Mark C., and Leung, T. S. Tony. "Pricing a Practice." *Financial Planning*, October 1984, pp. 203–4.

Vinso, Joseph D. "Valuing Professional Goodwill: The *Slivka* Case Revisited." *Business Valuation Review*, December 1987, pp. 156–63.

Zaumeyer, David J. "Are Professional Licenses and Practices Inseparable Assets?" *FAIR$HARE: The Matrimonial Law Monthly*, May 1986, pp. 13–14.

Books

Brown, Ronald L., ed. *Valuing Professional Practices and Licenses: A Guide for the Matrimonial Practitioner*. Clifton, N.J.: Prentice Hall Law and Business, 1987.

Desmond, Glen M. *How to Value Professional Practices*. Marina Del Rey, Calif.: Valuation Press, 1980.

General Guidelines for Establishing the Worth of an Optometric Practice. St. Louis, Mo.: American Optometric Association, 1988.

Horvath, James L. *Valuing Professional Practices*. Ontario, Canada: CCH Canadian Limited, 1990.

Jackson, James B., and Roger K. Hill. *New Trends in Dental Practice Valuation and Associateship Arrangements*. Chicago: Quintessence Publishing, 1987.

Shangold, Jules, and Frank Greenberg. *How to Buy, Sell, and Share a Practice of Podiatric Medicine*. Mount Kisco, N.Y.: Future Publishing Co., 1977.

Skoloff, Gary N., and Theodore P. Orenstein. *When A Lawyer Divorces: How to Value a Professional Practice*. Chicago: American Bar Association Press, 1986.

Unland, James J. *Valuation of Hospitals and Medical Centers*. Chicago: Health Management Research Institute, 1989.

Valuation of a Dental Practice: A Brief Overview for Buyers and Sellers. Chicago: American Dental Association, 1984.

Valuing a Medical Practice: A Short Guide for Buyers and Sellers. Chicago: American Medical Association, 1987.

Zweig, Mark, & Associates. *Valuation Survey of A/E/P & Environmental Service Firms*, 2nd ed. Natick, Mass.: Mark Zweig & Associates, 1992.

Additional Sources of Information

Sources of Value Data

Comparative Performance of U.S. Hospitals: The Sourcebook. Baltimore: Health Care Investment Analysts. Annual.

Financial Studies of the Small Business. Orlando, Fla.: Financial Research Associates. Annual.

Goodwill Registry. Plymouth Meeting, Penn.: The Health Care Group. Annual.

Reasonable Compensation Resources for Accounting Firms

Management of an Accounting Practice Handbook. Fort Worth, Tex.: American Institute of Certified Public Accountants and Practitioners Publishing Company (includes operating statistics gathered at the annual AICPA practice management and small firm conferences). Annual.

Practice Management Survey, National Results for 1991. Dallas, Tex.: Texas Society of Certified Public Accountants. Annual.

Reasonable Compensation Resources for Dental Practices

The Survey of Dental Practice. Chicago: American Dental Association, Bureau of Economic and Behavioral Research. Annual.

Dental Economics magazine. Tulsa: Pennwell Publishing Company. Salary survey published annually.

Reasonable Compensation Resources for Law Firms

Small Law Firm Economic Survey. Newtown Square, Penn.: Altman Weil Pansa. Annual.

The Survey of Law Firm Economics. Newtown Square, Penn.: Altman Weil Pensa. Annual.

Reasonable Compensation Resources for Medical Practices

Physician Compensation Survey. Englewood, Colo.: Center for Research in Ambulatory Health Care Administration, Medical Group Management Association. Annual.

Physician Marketplace Statistics. Chicago: American Medical Association. Annual.

Medical Economics Magazine. Montvale, N.J.: Medical Economics Publishing. Salary survey published annually.

Note: The reader may wish to consult the chapter-end bibliographies of Chapters 36 and 39 for references relating to professional practice valuation issues.

Chapter 31

Sample Professional Practice Valuation Report

Introduction

Dr. Stanley McNee's practice is a case contrived to illustrate the application of some of the practice valuation methods and procedures discussed in previous chapters. It is not patterned after any specific real-world practice. The point of the chapter is simply to illustrate one possible way of valuing a practice and organizing and presenting the valuation in the form of a written appraisal report.

Description of the Assignment

Willamette Management Associates has been requested by Robert A. Attorney to appraise Dr. Stanley McNee's interest in the medical practice known as Internal Medicine Associates, Inc., located in Sacramento, California, and to appraise his professional goodwill. The valuations are as of February 1992, using information available at that time. The appraisal is being conducted for the marital dissolution of Dr. and Mrs. McNee.

In completing this appraisal, we have followed the standards and guidelines established by the California courts in regard to professional practice valuation.

Summary Description of the Practice

Internal Medicine Associates, Inc., is a medical corporation located in Sacramento, California, with two shareholders, Dr. McNee and Dr. Leon Chandler. Each individual has a 50-percent ownership in the medical practice.

Sources of Information

In preparing this appraisal report, we have reviewed the following documents:

1. Annual compiled financial statements prepared by the corporation's independent certified public accounting firm for the fiscal years ending January 31, 1988, through January 31, 1992.
2. U.S. corporate income tax return for the corporation for the fiscal years ending January 31, 1988, through January 31, 1992.
3. U.S. individual income tax returns for Stanley and Kathleen McNee for the years 1987 through 1991.
4. A copy of the lease agreement between the corporation and Professional Medical Building, Inc., for the building that houses the practice.
5. The fee schedule in effect in February 1992 for the practice.
6. Depreciation schedules for furniture, fixtures, and equipment owned by the practice.
7. The articles of incorporation, by-laws, and minutes of shareholders' and board of directors' meetings for the years 1990 through 1992.
8. Schedules of gross fees charged, gross fees charged that were attributable to Dr. McNee, gross fees charged that were attributable to Dr.

Chandler, and adjustments to accounts receivable for the fiscal years 1988 through 1992.
9. The past three years' appointment books for Drs. McNee and Chandler.

Anita Analyst toured the offices of the practice and interviewed Dr. McNee and Dr. Chandler, as well as the independent accountant for the practice.

For economic data, we considered *Employment Data Research*, produced by the state of California; Sacramento area Council of Government's *1992 Sacramento Business Handbook*; and information from the Sacramento Metropolitan Chamber of Commerce, the California State Board of Quality Assurance, and the California Medical Association.

For industry data, we considered the American Medical Association's *Socioeconomic Characteristics of Medical Practice, 1991*, as well as various articles appearing in the periodical *Medical Economics*.

Summary and Conclusion

Based upon the analysis completed and discussed in this report, it is our opinion that the current value of Dr. McNee's equity interest in the practice is equal to $70,500. It is also our opinion that the value of Dr. McNee's professional goodwill as of February 1992 was equal to $86,000. The total values of these two items are $156,500.

Sacramento Economic Profile

Overview

The four-county Sacramento region, one of California's interior economies, is slated for continued growth and prosperity. According to the Center for Continuing Study of the California Economy (CCSCE) and the Bank of America, inland regions will outpace coastal areas, traditionally California's major growth centers.

The CCSCE predicts that the Sacramento region will see a 24.0 percent growth in population and a 33.7 percent increase in households by the year 2000. Personal income will rise from 53.0 percent to 73.1 percent in the same period, according to the same source. These figures compare to a statewide average of 3.9 percent to 51.5 percent growth in personal income.

The per capita income of the four-county region—Sacramento, Yolo, Placer, and El Dorado—was $11,248 in 1989 and was estimated to be $13,336 to $15,089 in constant dollars by 2000. Average household income was expected to grow from $29,893 to between $33,026 and $37,365. Taxable sales were expected at least to double in constant dollars, from $6.75 billion in 1990 to a predicted $13.43 billion in 2000.

The short-range economy was also promising. James H. Pattersen, a private consultant and former economist for the state legislature, predicted employment to rise by 3.5 percent by 1993 with similar increases through 2006. Pattersen expected a growth rate of 6 percent in the manufacturing sector. His projections for other employment sectors were optimistic as well.

Government was the largest employment sector, with 149,200 workers, or 33.5 percent of nonagricultural workers. Not surprising for a state capital, more than 81 percent of those workers were involved with state or local government. Total nonagricultural employment in the Sacramento four-county metro area during 1991 was 445,000. The service sector accounted for 20.4 percent of the work force, retail trade 19.7 percent, wholesale trade 5.0 percent, and manufacturing 6.7 percent. Unemployment in the Sacramento metro area at the close of 1991 was 10.7 percent.

The population of Sacramento County was predicted by the Population Research Unit of the state Department of Finance to top 1 million by the year 2000. A population of 1.5 million was predicted by 2030. Those projections, based on the 1990 census data, represented major increases over projections based on the prior census. The population for the metro area was projected to exceed 1.4 million by 2003 and reach 1.7 million by 2010. The 1993 population for Sacramento County was projected to reach 889,800, a 4.9 percent increase from the 1991 population of 848,400. The metro area population was estimated to be at one-third million by 1993.

Health Care

As one of the fastest-growing areas in the state, medical services and health care were expanding in the Sacramento area. Current services and care were considered excellent. The area had 18 hospitals and an in-patient capacity of 2,663 licensed beds.

There are 2,799 licensed physicians in the four-county area, including approximately 160 internists, according to the state Board of Medical Quality Assurance and the area county medical societies. The ratio of 314.5 physicians per 100,000 civilian population was above the state average of 232.1 physicians per 100,000 civilian population.

Four health maintenance organizations (HMOs) offered services in the Sacramento area: Foundation Health Plan, Healthcare, Kaiser Foundation Health, and TakeCare.

Foundation offered medical and hospital services on a direct service basis. It had 111,000 members in February 1992 and was predicted to be at 150,000 by January 1994. It had 1,500 private practice physicians under contract. Foundation served a five-county area, including Sacramento, Yolo, El Dorado, Nevada, and Placer Counties.

Healthcare served 15,266 people and was a federally qualified HMO. It operated three primary care facilities and offered complete medical and hospital services through approximately 170 private-practice physicians.

Kaiser Foundation Health was a direct services plan providing medical and hospital services through its exclusive physicians and facilities.

Kaiser currently served three clinics in the Sacramento area, with 348 full-time and 40 part-time physicians under contract.

TakeCare was affiliated with Blue Cross of California. The HMO emphasized preventive care, as well as treatment for illness. The plan provided complete health care services to its members for a prepaid monthly fee. It served 11,000 members through six clinics and had 32 on-site and 100 off-site physicians under contract.

Survey of the Medical Practice Field

The private medical practice field is in a period of relatively rapid change. Largely unaffected by the 1981–82 economic recession, which had profound effects on most segments of the United States industrial business service sectors, private medical practice instead has been affected by a series of socioeconomic changes in the way the public approaches and receives medical services.

Among the forces cited as bringing about change in the medical practice environment are an increased surplus of doctors, relaxation of restrictions on physicians' advertising, the introduction of contract, prepaid health care delivery systems, a general crackdown on the high cost of health care, and provider arrogance in dealing with patients.

Competition

Physicians are facing an increasingly competitive environment. Several factors have contributed to this trend. Patients and purchasers of health services are increasingly more cost-conscious due to the rise in health care costs. Medical costs are rising at a brisk 7 percent to 8 percent per year. That rate is projected to increase the nation's present health bill to $750 billion by the year 2000. For the average individual, health care costs per year will rise from $1,500 to $3,000 by 2000.

Secondly, the number of physicians has greatly increased in the last decade. Since 1980, the number of physicians has increased at a rate four times faster than the general population. During the same period, the cost of practicing medicine rose sharply, according to the American Medical Association.

These pressures have made it more difficult for some physicians to attract and retain patients. Physicians' concern over the cost-effectiveness of their practices is on the rise as a result of the more competitive environment within the medical profession.

Additionally, changes in practice services and the adoption of new marketing strategies by physicians have come about as a result of these competitive pressures.

Changes in Practice Services

The most evident impact of competition on medical practice services is the increased use of nonphysician employees. Nonphysician personnel employed by physicians increased 22 percent in the two-year 1989–90 period. This trend in hiring nonphysician staff is stronger in younger physicians, whose less-developed practices are more vulnerable to competitive pressure. Physicians in practice for 10 years or less increased their nonphysician staff 34 percent in the same two-year period, compared to 18 percent for physicians in practice longer than 10 years. Physicians, in response to competition, have not significantly increased their house calls or weekend and evening office hours, according to 1990 data compiled by the American Medical Association. However, physicians have begun to use marketing strategies to identify patient needs and attract new patients. According to *Socioeconomic Characteristics of Medical Practice, 1991*, 40 percent of physicians surveyed have used at least one marketing strategy in the last five years. The most common strategy was a study of community demographics; 27 percent of physicians surveyed said they had employed such a marketing strategy.

The extent to which physicians adopt marketing strategies is affected by physician characteristics. Younger physicians and those in group practices were more likely to use marketing techniques than their older colleagues in solo practice (46 percent of those in practice 10 years or less compared to 38 percent with more than 10 years of practice; 53 percent of group practices in contrast to 32 percent of solo practices). Similar delineations are found by geographic region and specialty group. In the West, where competition is higher due to greater physician population ratios, 48 percent of physicians used marketing techniques, compared to 40 percent of physicians throughout the country. By specialty, 51 percent of medical specialists have used marketing strategies as compared to 38 percent of surgical and other specialists and 33 percent of general family practitioners.

Prepaid Health Care

The delivery of health care services in the United States is changing. The evolution is easy from a physician-dominated health care system to one geared toward consumer needs and preferences, operating as a business with full exposure to the competitive forces of the free marketplace.

Beginning in the 1970s, prepaid, contracted systems of health care emerged in contrast to the fee-for-service approach typified in the traditional private medical practice. Health maintenance organizations (HMOs) have led the prepaid care movement. With the dramatic increase in the 1970s and 1980s in health care costs, HMOs and other prepaid services offered a method of containing price increases.

Health care analysts predict the trend toward prepaid health care to increase in the 1990s. In 1988, there were 235 HMOs in the country, serving 4 percent of the population, or 9 million patients. HMOs now serve 12 million patients, and that number is predicted to increase to 25 to 30 million patients by 2000.

Industry analysts also predict a trend toward fewer solo practices, with group practices growing (there were 88,000 group practices in the country in 1988) because of the complexity and cost of technology, the increasing necessity of expensive marketing programs, and stringent reimbursement systems, which make solo practices less practical. More physicians are also expected to be employees by the end of the decade, working for contract health-delivery systems instead of as solo or group practitioners.

Personal Background

Dr. McNee is 54 years old and describes his health as good. In 1959, he received his bachelor of science degree from Holy Cross College in Worcester, Massachusetts. His medical school training was at the College of Medicine, University of Cincinnati, and was completed in 1962. He served his internship at St. Luke's Hospital in San Francisco and served his residency at the University of California Medical Center, San Francisco. In June 1968, he opened his medical practice in Sacramento, California. He was board-certified by the American Board of Internal Medicine in June 1973. He is also a member of the American Medical Association, American College of Physicians, and American Heart Association (Fellow).

Dr. McNee sees 10 to 15 patients per day in his office, in addition to patients he sees on daily hospital visits. His patients fall in all age ranges and he generally spends 10 to 15 minutes per patient, although at times as much as one hour.

Approximately 10 percent of the patients he sees are either on medicare or medicaid, with the balance generally having private medical insurance. Dr. McNee works from 8 A.M. to 6 P.M., Monday through Friday (except Wednesdays, when he finishes at 2 P.M.). He is on call every other weekend to the hospitals where his patients are staying. Dr. McNee estimates that he spends a total of 10 to 12 hours per day, four days a week, on practice-related activities and approximately 6 hours per day on Wednesdays. He works approximately three to four hours on the weekends when he is on call to the hospitals.

Practice History

Dr. McNee owns a 50-percent interest in a professional corporation named Internal Medicine Associates, Inc., with one other doctor, in Sacramento, California. The practice is located at 1501 A Street, across from one of Sacramento's main hospitals, Sacramento Memorial Hospital. The general area in which the practice is located has many other professional offices (medical, legal, accounting, and so on) in downtown Sacramento. The office was opened in 1968 by Dr. McNee.

In 1988, Dr. McNee was working nearly 60 to 70 hours per week because of a large increase in the number of patients he was seeing. Because he felt overworked, he decided to bring in an associate internist,

Dr. Leon Chandler, who would purchase a 50-percent interest in his practice.

Dr. Chandler paid $100,000 for the net asset value and intangible value for the 50-percent interest in the practice. Based upon the sales agreement, $75,000 was attributable to the net assets of the practice and $25,000 attributable to the practice's goodwill.

Generally, the purchase price allocation between assets purchased and goodwill purchased is strongly influenced by income tax considerations rather than the actual fair market value of the various assets purchased. However, in this particular sale, our investigation revealed that the allocations were based on informed negotiations between Drs. McNee and Chandler and that the $75,000 allocated to 50 percent of the net tangible assets of the practice reasonably approximated the fair market value of those assets at that time.

Dr. Chandler signed an employment agreement in which it was agreed that during the fiscal years ended January 31, 1989, through January 31, 1991, he would take a lower salary than Dr. McNee. Of the total officers' salaries to be paid, Dr. Chandler would receive the following percentages for each of the fiscal years:

1989	32%
1990	40%
1991	45%

Thereafter, the officers' salaries would be equally divided between Dr. McNee and Dr. Chandler.

The suite in which the practice is located is in a medical building in downtown Sacramento. It has approximately 2,500 square feet, including four examination rooms, a reception and office area, two doctor's offices, an employee lounge, and a storage area.

The practice has two full-time and one part-time nonowner employees. Edna Smith has been with Dr. McNee for 12 years as a receptionist/assistant. Janet Dollar has been with Dr. McNee for 10 years as the office bookkeeper. Donna Fisher works 16 hours per week as Dr. McNee's assistant.

Financial Statement Analysis

Internal Medicine Associates, Inc., has a fiscal year ending January 31. The financial statements are compiled by the accounting firm of Martin & Mastroleo, certified public accountants.

Balance Sheets

Table I (Exhibit 31–1) is a schedule of cash basis balance sheets for the fiscal years ended January 31, 1988, through January 31, 1992. This schedule shows both dollar amounts and the amounts expressed as a percent of total assets.

Exhibit 31–1

CASH BASIS BALANCE SHEETS

TABLE I
INTERNAL MEDICINE ASSOCIATES, INC.
STATEMENT OF ASSETS, LIABILITIES, AND STOCKHOLDERS' EQUITY (CASH BASIS)
As of January 31

	1992 $	1992 %	1991 $	1991 %	1990 $	1990 %	1989 $	1989 %	1988 $	1988 %
ASSETS										
Cash & Equiv.	908	6.8	3,324	17.0	1,677	21.1	(424)	(7.3)	18,750	42.7
Marketable Securities (Cost)	0	0.0	0	0.0	0	0.0	0	0.0	19,950	45.5
	908	6.8	3,324	17.0	1,677	21.1	(424)	(7.3)	38,700	88.2
Furniture, Fixtures, and Equip. (Cost)	44,390	330.1	44,390	226.7	31,168	391.8	27,560	476.3	21,168	48.3
Accum. Deprec.	(31,850)	(236.9)	(28,135)	(143.7)	(24,890)	(312.9)	(21,350)	(369.0)	(16,002)	(36.5)
Net Fixed Assets	12,540	93.2	16,255	83.0	6,278	78.9	6,210	107.3	5,166	11.8
TOTAL ASSETS	13,448	100.0	19,579	100.0	7,955	100.0	5,786	100.0	43,866	100.0
LIABILITIES & EQUITY										
Payroll Taxes Pay.	445	3.3	211	1.1	295	3.7	350	6.1	413	0.9
Note Payable	0	0.0	7,500	38.3	0	0.0	0	0.0	0	0.0
Pension Cont. Pay.	0	0.0	5,000	25.5	0	0.0	15,600	269.6	59,000	134.5
Shareholder Payable (Demand)	0	0.0	0	0.0	5,789	72.8	12,354	213.5	0	0.0
Total Liabilities	445	3.3	12,711	64.9	6,084	76.5	28,304	489.2	59,413	135.4
Shareholders' Equity	13,003	96.7	6,868	35.1	1,871	23.5	(22,518)	(389.2)	(15,547)	(35.4)
TOTAL LIABILITIES & EQUITY	13,448	100.0	19,579	100.0	7,955	100.0	5,786	100.0	43,866	100.0

SOURCE: U.S. corporation income tax returns.

In 1989, the amount of total assets of the practice decreased significantly from the fiscal year end January 1988. However, since that date, assets have continually increased. The primary reason for the decrease in 1989 was expenses associated with the expansion of the offices and additional leasehold improvements and new equipment (some of which was not capitalized), which became necessary when Dr. Chandler joined the practice.

During the entire period considered, liabilities have continually decreased from a total of $59,413 in January 1988 to $445 in January 1992. The primary reason for the decrease has been a change in philosophy on the payment of bills. Dr. McNee stated that one of the agreements that he made with Dr. Chandler was to carry less debt on the books and to pay all bills on a timely basis. This philosophy is reflected primarily in the pension contributions, which are generally paid currently over the 12-month period instead of in one lump sum at the end or after the end of a fiscal year.

The cash basis financial statements show that shareholders' equity was in negative amounts during 1988 and 1989 fiscal years end; however, it has increased each year since.

The cash and equivalents and marketable securities shown in 1988 were equal to almost 90 percent of total assets. However, the company has held a much lower value in current assets in the last four years. Conversely, the company also has a much lower value in current liabilities (total liabilities) than in 1988.

It should be noted that the balance sheet is on a cash basis and does not reflect such assets as accounts receivable or prepaid expenses, which in this particular case are quite meaningful. Also, the balance sheets as presented do not show accrued and unpaid bills.

Income Statements

Table II (Exhibit 31–2) presents cash basis income statements for the practice for the fiscal years ended January 31, 1988, through January 31, 1992.

Total fees received have been increasing each year during the period considered. Also, there has been a continual increase in officers' salaries, although in 1992 officers' salaries dropped somewhat as a percent of total fees received.

Total operating expenses have generally averaged approximately 95 percent to 100 percent of total fees received; however, operating expenses include such items as officers' salaries, directors' fees, and other discretionary expenses.

In 1989, Dr. McNee sold marketable securities held by the corporation and realized a $32,500 gain on their sale. These securities were sold because of the large loss taken by the practice in that fiscal year and because of the expenditures for additional equipment and new leasehold improvements when Dr. Chandler joined the practice. Net income during the period fluctuated greatly, from the high in 1988 of $18,146 to a loss in 1989 of $6,971. During the past two years, the company has made nominal net income. This low or nonexistent net income is not unusual

Exhibit 31–2

CASH BASIS INCOME STATEMENTS

TABLE II
INTERNAL MEDICINE ASSOCIATES, INC.
STATEMENT OF CASH RECEIVED AND EXPENSES PAID
Years Ended January 31

	1992 $	1992 %	1991 $	1991 %	1990 $	1990 %	1989 $	1989 %	1988 $	1988 %
Fees Received	483,818	100.0	442,069	100.0	422,789	100.0	375,447	100.0	298,894	100.0
Operating Expenses:										
Officers' Salaries	310,500	64.2	292,500	66.2	258,000	61.0	230,000	61.3	126,679	42.4
Other Salaries	51,978	10.7	44,448	10.0	43,475	10.3	43,551	11.6	34,150	11.4
Automobile	2,258	0.5	4,565	1.0	2,898	0.7	1,778	0.5	1,324	0.4
Travel	610	0.1	1,131	0.3	0	0.0	0	0.0	0	0.0
Promotion	3,204	0.7	3,189	0.7	2,590	0.6	0	0.0	0	0.0
Directors' Fees	7,895	1.6	410	0.1	0	0.0	0	0.0	0	0.0
Education	1,439	0.3	0	0.0	0	0.0	0	0.0	0	0.0
Accounting & Legal	14,120	2.9	3,892	0.9	3,611	0.9	3,425	0.9	3,516	1.2
Retire. Plan Contrib.	38,209	7.9	46,009	10.4	46,912	11.1	96,289	25.7	78,921	26.4
Other Expenses	48,783	10.1	42,384	9.6	40,907	9.7	42,139	11.1	35,796	12.0
Total Oper. Expenses	478,996	99.0	438,528	99.2	398,393	94.3	417,182	111.1	280,386	93.8
Operating Income	4,822	1.0	3,541	0.8	24,396	5.7	(41,735)	(11.1)	18,508	6.2
Other Income (Expense):										
Interest Income	2,361	0.5	2,192	0.5	2,113	0.5	1,875	0.5	768	0.3
Interest Expense	(98)	(Nil)	0	0.0	0	0.0	0	0.0	0	0.0
Gain on Sale of Assets	0	0.0	0	0.0	0	0.0	32,500	8.7	0	0.0
Total Other Income	2,263	0.5	2,192	0.5	2,113	0.5	34,375	9.2	768	0.3
Pretax Income (Loss) (Cash Basis)	7,085	1.5	5,733	1.3	26,509	6.2	(7,360)	(1.9)	19,276	6.5
Income Tax Paid	(950)	(0.2)	(736)	(0.2)	(2,120)	(0.5)	389	0.1	(1,130)	(0.4)
Net Income	6,135	1.3	4,997	1.1	24,389	5.7	(6,971)	(1.8)	18,146	6.1

Nil = Inconsequential amount, greater (or less) than zero.

SOURCE: U.S. corporation income tax returns.

for a professional practice because generally, officers' salaries, perquisites, and benefits are calculated to an amount that will eliminate income from the corporation.

When considering the sum of officers' salaries, retirement plan contributions, and pretax income, this practice's total earnings have fallen in a range of 73.6 percent to 85 percent of yearly revenues—an extremely high percentage compared to various medical surveys that show internists generally have total earnings of 50 percent to 60 percent of yearly revenues.

Since this practice has such a high percentage of total earnings to revenues, it may be at a greater risk of a loss of a portion of those earnings because of increased competition by others that want to participate in this large net profit margin. In fact, the practice has seen its total earnings, as a percent of revenues, drop during the past three years (in fiscal 1990 total earnings equaled 78.4 percent while in fiscal 1992 they fell to 73.6 percent).

Table III (Exhibit 31–3) is a statement of income as a percent of 1988. As can be seen, fees received in 1992 were 61.87 percent greater than in 1988. Generally, expenses have also increased over this period.

Operating income has decreased as a percent of the 1988 operating income, while other income has increased. On a net income basis, 1992 income was approximately one third of the 1988 income.

Before one can conclude that this practice is making less money, the total economic earnings of the practice should be examined.

Table IV (Exhibit 31–4) calculates total compensation (earnings) of Internal Medicine Associates, Inc. This schedule, in calculating total earnings, considers not only the corporation's net income, but also salaries paid to officers, officers' retirement benefits, and other extraordinary expenses and income that are not normal to the practice. As can be seen from this schedule, the extraordinary expenses included directors' fees of $7,895 paid in 1992. In essence, these fees, which were paid to the officers, are more accurately classified as officers' salary.

Our investigation also showed that there were excess legal and accounting expenses for the fiscal year ended January 31, 1992, for tax planning done for the personal benefit of each of the doctors.

In 1991, excess automobile expenses occurred. We learned that these expenses were accrued from prior years and did not necessarily represent the normal annual automobile expense for the practice.

Lastly, we removed the gain on the sale of securities that occurred in 1989, because that is not normal operating earnings of a medical practice. By means of these adjustments, we determined the total practice earnings. These earnings are discretionary and are the earnings a buyer of the practice would consider. Since we are valuing only a 50-percent interest in Internal Medicine Associates, Inc., we have removed the earnings and benefits received by the other shareholder, Dr. Chandler. As this schedule shows, we have removed the salary, fees, benefits, and income (including excess expenses and income) that Dr. Chandler received or that are attributable to his portion of the corporation. This computation gives us Dr. McNee's total compensation. However, Dr. McNee's total compensation includes excess payments made to him in

Exhibit 31–3

STATEMENTS OF INCOME AS A PERCENT OF A BASE YEAR

TABLE III
INTERNAL MEDICINE ASSOCIATES, INC.
STATEMENT OF CASH RECEIVED AND EXPENSES PAID
AS PERCENT OF 1988 AMOUNTS

	Fiscal Years Ended January 31				
	1992 %	1991 %	1990 %	1989 %	1988 %
Fees Received	161.87	147.90	141.45	125.61	100.00
Expenses of Operation:					
Officers' Salaries	245.11	230.90	203.66	181.56	100.00
Other Salaries	152.20	130.16	127.31	127.53	100.00
Automobile	170.54	344.79	218.88	134.29	100.00
Travel	NM	NM	NM	NM	NM
Promotion	NM	NM	NM	NM	NM
Directors' Fees	NM	NM	NM	NM	NM
Education	NM	NM	NM	NM	NM
Legal & Accounting	401.59	110.69	102.70	97.41	100.00
Retirement Plan Contrib.	48.41	58.30	59.44	122.01	100.00
Other Expenses	136.28	118.40	114.28	117.72	100.00
Total Oper. Expenses	170.83	156.40	142.09	148.79	100.00
Operating Income	26.05	19.13	131.81	(255.50)	100.00
Other Income (Expense):					
Interest Income	307.42	285.42	275.13	244.14	100.00
Interest Expense	NM	NM	NM	NM	NM
Gain on Sale of Assets	NM	NM	NM	NM	NM
Total Other Income	294.66	285.42	275.13	4,475.91	100.00
Pretax Income (Loss) (Cash Basis)	36.76	29.74	137.52	(38.18)	100.00
Income Tax Paid	84.07	65.13	187.61	(34.42)	100.00
Net Income (Loss)	33.81	27.54	134.40	(38.42)	100.00

NM = Not Meaningful.
SOURCE: Table II.

accordance with the buy-in agreement with Dr. Chandler. We have calculated these payments and have deducted them from Dr. McNee's total compensation to make a determination of Dr. McNee's normal compensation over the past five years. In this way, we can gauge more accurately what Dr. McNee can expect to receive in the future.

Exhibit 31–4

TABLE IV
INTERNAL MEDICINE ASSOCIATES, INC.
SCHEDULE OF OWNERS' TOTAL COMPENSATION

	Fiscal Years Ended January 31				
	1992	1991	1990	1989	1988
	$	$	$	$	$
Corporation's Net Income	6,135	4,997	24,389	(6,971)	18,146
Salaries to Officer(s)	310,500	292,500	258,000	230,000	126,679
Retirement Benefits for					
Officers' Benefit	34,500	42,000	44,500	91,000	76,500
Extraordinary Expenses (Income)					
Directors' Fees	7,895				
Excess Legal & Accounting	10,000				
Excess Automobile		3,500			
Gain on Sale of Securities				(32,500)	
Total Practice Earnings	369,030	342,997	326,889	281,529	221,325
Less: Dr. Chandler's Portion of:					
Officers' Salary	(155,250)	(131,625)	(103,200)	(73,500)	0
Directors' Fees	(3,948)	0	0	0	0
Retirement Benefits	(20,000)	(17,500)	(15,000)	(10,000)	0
Corporate Income	(3,068)	(2,499)	(12,195)	3,486	0
Excess (Expenses) & Income	(5,000)	(1,750)	0	16,250	0
Dr. McNee's Total Compensation	181,764	189,623	196,494	217,765	221,325
Less: Portion paid to Dr.					
McNee per Buy-In Agmt.	0	(14,625)	(25,800)	(41,500)	0
Dr. McNee's Normal Compensation	181,764	174,998	170,694	176,265	221,325

SOURCE: U.S. corporation income tax return; practice's books and records, retirement plan documents, and
Dr. Chandler's Employment Agreement.

As can be seen from this schedule, Dr. McNee's normal compensation dropped during fiscal years ended January 31, 1988, through 1990; it has increased from that time through January 31, 1992. Because of the changes in ownership and the compensation levels, which occurred in accordance with the employment agreement with Dr. Chandler, we decided that the last three years (fiscal years ended January 31, 1990, through January 31, 1992) are more representative of Dr. McNee's future compensation than the years that came before.

Valuation of a Medical Practice and Professional Goodwill

In the following sections, we calculate the value of Dr. McNee's equity in Internal Medicine Associates, Inc., and his professional goodwill.

Medical Practice

Table V (Exhibit 31–5) is a statement of assets, liabilities, and shareholders' equity on both a cash basis and an adjusted accrual basis.

In calculating the net asset value of the company, it is inappropriate to use cash basis balance sheets, because they do not reflect various assets and liabilities that do, in fact, exist. Therefore, it is important that cash basis balance sheets be adjusted to an accrual basis and that assets not recorded at estimated market value be increased (or decreased) to reflect their current market value. Table V shows these calculations.

We adjusted the cash basis financial statements as of January 31, 1992, for the following purposes:

1. Our review indicated that there were checks worth $4,395 received by the practice on January 31, 1992, which were not deposited into the bank, although they had been adjusted out of accounts receivable. On the following day (February 1, 1992), these checks were deposited in the bank. Since the cash was in hand and in the doctors' office, we have reflected this sum as if it were cash already received.
2. We recorded accounts receivable for services performed but for which fees have not yet been collected, and we also estimated the reserve for uncollectible accounts receivable. This reserve for uncollectible accounts was based upon a review of the past three years' accounts receivable activity to determine the percentage of the accounts that have been written off compared to total charges made.
3. Based on discussions with Dr. McNee, we determined that approximately $1,250 worth of medical and office supplies was in inventory at January 31, 1992.
4. Based upon a review of the malpractice and other liability insurance policies carried by the practice, $3,650 of previous expense was actually a prepaid asset of the practice as of the valuation date.
5. After reviewing an appraisal completed by ABC Equipment Appraisers, we have adjusted the furniture, fixtures, equipment, and leasehold improvements to $31,000 from a stated net book value of $12,540 to reflect more accurately the depreciated replacement value of those assets.
6. The last asset adjustment was to reflect a nominal ($500) value for the professional library maintained by the practice.
7. Various liabilities were recognized that had not been recorded on the books, including unpaid bills (accounts payable), additional payroll taxes, and payroll payable, which represents payroll due to the three non-owner employees for the period January 16 through January 31, 1992. According to Dr. McNee, this payroll will be paid on February 5, 1992.

As can be seen in Table V, the total value of the shareholders' equity in the clinic is equal to $140,821. Dr. McNee's 50-percent interest in this equity is equal to $70,400 (rounded).

Professional Goodwill

We have also calculated the value of Dr. McNee's professional goodwill as of January 31, 1992.

Exhibit 31–5

TABLE V
INTERNAL MEDICINE ASSOCIATES, INC.
ADJUSTED ACCRUAL BASIS BALANCE SHEET
AS OF JANUARY 31, 1992

| | As Shown (Cash Basis) | Adjustments | | Adjusted Balance Sheet (Accrual Basis) |
		Debit	Credit	
ASSETS				
Current Assets:				
Cash & Equivalents	908	4,395 a		5,303
Accounts Receivable	0	119,954 b	10,196 c	109,758
Supplies	0	1,250 d		1,250
Prepaid Insurance	0	3,650 e		3,650
Total Current Assets	908	129,249	10,196	119,961
Furniture, Fixtures & Equipment	12,540	31,000 f	12,540 f	31,000
Library	0	500 g		500
TOTAL ASSETS	13,448	160,749	22,736	151,461
LIABILITIES & SHAREHOLDERS' EQUITY				
Liabilities:				
Accounts Payable	0		4,695 h	4,695
Payroll Taxes Payable	445		500 i	945
Payroll Payable	0		5,000 j	5,000
Total Liabilities	445		10,195	10,640
Shareholders' Equity	13,003	32,931 k	160,749 k	140,821
TOTAL LIABILITIES & SHAREHOLDERS' EQUITY	13,448		170,944	151,461

a   To add to assets and cash in transit, not shown in either bank balance or accounts receivable.
b   To add to assets the face value of accounts receivable, per accounts receivable journal.
c   To reduce accounts receivable for estimated uncollectible accounts (based on 8.5% historical write-off of receivables by practice).
d   To add to assets the estimated value of supply inventory (medical and office) on hand.
e   To add to assets six-month prepaid malpractice insurance for Drs. McNee and Chandler.
f   To increase the value of fixed assets to "depreciated replacement cost," per equipment appraisal completed by ABC Equipment Appraisers.
g   To add to assets the value of the professional library (estimated).
h   To add unrecorded unpaid bills to liabilities.
i   To increase payroll taxes payable for taxes due for pay period from 1/16/92 to 1/31/92.
j   To add to liabilities the payroll due on 2/5/92 for pay period from 1/16/92 to 1/31/92.
k   Reversing entries.

SOURCE: U.S. corporation income tax returns, practice's books and records, equipment appraisal report, and interview with Dr. McNee.

We have used two primary methods for calculating this goodwill. The first method is commonly known as the *excess earnings* method; the second method considers the value received by Dr. McNee in the sale of the 50-percent interest in this practice to Dr. Chandler in February 1988.

Excess Earnings. Table VI (Exhibit 31–6) is a schedule of various earnings (compensation) surveys conducted by the publication *Medical Economics* and by the American Medical Association. These earnings represent not only salaries paid to self-employed physicians, but the net income of the practice and benefits received by each physician.

As can be seen from this schedule, we have considered all the categories that could possibly include Dr. McNee. In 1990, the comparative earnings of physicians such as Dr. McNee ranged from $75,000 (all internists, median) to $113,550 (all incorporated multiphysician practices, median). In choosing an appropriate comparative earnings figure, it is our opinion that the earnings of incorporated multiphysician practices are the best comparative earnings amount to use. Our investigation has revealed that the primary reason for Dr. McNee's high earnings (giving consideration to the hours he spends on practice-related activities) is generally a result of the economies of scale achieved by associating with Dr. Chandler. Also, various earnings surveys indicate that multiphysician practices usually have much higher income per practitioner, compared to a solo practitioner. For these reasons, we believe the most comparative earnings figure to use is the figure for incorporated multiphysician practices.

Table VII (Exhibit 31–7) is a calculation of the value of goodwill using the excess earnings method. Of the past three years of Dr. McNee's income, we have weighted fiscal year January 31, 1992 (identified as 1991), one half of the total; 1990, one third; and 1989, one sixth. Based on these calculations, Dr. McNee's three-year weighted average compensation was equal to $177,665.

As previously mentioned, in our opinion, the median compensation of all incorporated multiphysician practices (for each practicing physician) is the best indicator of comparative earnings in comparison to Dr. McNee. As shown in Table VI, the compound average annual increase in compensation for this group of doctors from 1987 through 1990 has been 8.76 percent. As of this date, no data are available for 1991, so we have estimated 1991's total compensation in this category to be equal to an 8.76 percent increase over the 1990 level. That would indicate a comparative compensation for 1991 of $123,497. By weighting these earnings in the same way as we weighted Dr. McNee's, we have derived a comparative three-year weighted average compensation level of $117,698 for a comparable physician. That indicates that Dr. McNee's excess earnings are equal to $59,966.

In choosing an appropriate rate at which to capitalize these excess earnings, we have given specific recognition to the following factors:

1. Excess earnings are generally considered to have a higher risk of being maintained compared to earnings that are primarily generated by a return on a passive investment.

Exhibit 31–6

TABLE VI
INTERNAL MEDICINE ASSOCIATES, INC.
SCHEDULE OF COMPARATIVE COMPENSATION

	Compounded Average Annual Increase %	1990 $	1989 $	1988 $	1987 $
Median Compensation, All Physicians (1)	6.73%	93,270	86,210	83,700	76,720
Median Compensation, All Internists (1)	4.52%	85,910	79,710	74,310	75,230
Median Compensation, Far Western State Physicians (1)	5.49%	87,220	80,630	81,610	74,290
Median Compensation, Incorporated Internists (1)	5.69%	NA	89,120	80,630	79,790
Median Compensation, All Incorporated Multi–Physician Practices (1)	8.76%	113,550	108,600	100,210	88,270
Median Compensation, All Physicians (2)	6.69%	85,000	78,000	NA	70,000
Median Compensation, All Internists (2)	2.33%	75,000	74,500	NA	70,000
Median Compensation, Far Pacific State Physicians (2)	4.55%	80,000	80,000	NA	70,000
Median Compensation, Non–Solo Practice Physicians (2)	8.74%	90,000	81,000	NA	70,000
Median Compensation, All Physicians in Metro Areas of 1,000,000 or Greater (2)	4.55%	80,000	75,000	NA	70,000
Median Compensation, All Physicians between the Ages of 46 Years to 55 Years (2)	7.72%	100,000	95,000	NA	80,000

NA = Not available.

SOURCE: (1) Annual earnings surveys, *Medical Economics;* (2) *Socioeconomic Characteristics of Medical Practice, 1991,* American Medical Association.

Exhibit 31–7

TABLE VII
INTERNAL MEDICINE ASSOCIATES, INC.
CALCULATION OF GOODWILL
USING EXCESS EARNINGS METHOD

	Year	Normal Compensation		Weighting Factor	Weighted Compensation
Calculation of Dr. McNee's Weighted					
Average Normal Compensation	1991	181,764	x	3	545,292
(See Table IV)	1990	174,998	x	2	349,996
	1989	170,694	x	1	170,694
	Total			6	1,065,982
	Divided by Sum of Weighting Factors				6

Dr. McNee's 3–year Weighted Average Compensation   177,664

	Year	Comparative Compensation		Weighting Factor	Weighted Compensation
Calculation of Comparative Weighted					
Average Compensation	1991	123,497	x	3	370,491
	1990	113,550	x	2	227,100
	1989	108,600	x	1	108,600
	Total			6	706,191
	Divided by Sum of Weighting Factors				6

Comparative 3–year Weighted Average Compensation   117,699

Dr. McNee's Excess Earnings   59,965
Capitalized at 50% (Equal to a Multiple of 2)   50%

Indicated Value of Dr. McNee's Goodwill (Rounded)   120,000

SOURCE: Tables IV and VI.

2. Dr. McNee is at the end of what is generally regarded as the high income-producing years of a physician (generally, high-income years fall between the ages of 45 to 55 years).
3. Major changes are now occurring in the health care industry that are being mandated by government, health insurance underwriters, and private industry to control the growth in costs of providing health care.

Generally, excess earnings are capitalized at rates from 20 percent (equal to a multiple of 5) to 100 percent (equal to a multiple of 1). The median multiple, 3, is equal to a capitalization rate of 33⅓ percent.

Because of the factors listed above, we believe that Dr. McNee's excess earnings should be capitalized at an amount greater than the median rate, and therefore it is our opinion that a capitalization rate of 50 percent (equal to a multiple of 2) is appropriate. These computations produce an indicated value of $120,000 (rounded) for Dr. McNee's goodwill.

Prior Transactions

One of the most reliable methods of valuing a practice, if the information is available, is a prior transaction in the practice being appraised. Fortunately, such a transaction is available for guidance in this valuation. As discussed earlier in this report, in 1989, Dr. Chandler purchased a 50 percent interest in the practice for $100,000. Of this amount, $25,000 was allocated to goodwill (in accordance with the buy-in agreement). As previously mentioned, our investigation revealed that this transaction was an arm's-length sale of 50 percent of this practice and that the allocation of net tangible asset value and goodwill value appeared to be reasonable.

However, that $100,000 was not the only value received by Dr. McNee. A review of the appointment books revealed that Dr. McNee and Dr. Chandler have both worked an equal amount of time in the practice and have seen approximately the same number of patients per day. However, the employment agreement signed at the same time as the sale of the 50 percent interest indicated that Dr. McNee would receive a larger portion of the earnings of the practice for three years than would Dr. Chandler. The percentages were discussed earlier in this report. Therefore, Dr. McNee was receiving additional compensation, even though he was not seeing more patients or spending more time with the practice than was Dr. Chandler. Therefore, the difference between half of the officers' salaries and the amount received by Dr. McNee is an additional payment received by Dr. McNee for each of the three years that the employment agreement was in existence. Table VIII (Exhibit 31–8) shows the calculations of these excess payments. As this table discloses, Dr. McNee received the following excess payments:

1989	$41,500
1990	25,800
1991	14,625

We have discounted the value of these payments to recognize that, as of the sale date, they were not worth their full face value. Because many uncertainties exist at the sale date for any enterprise, we believe that relatively high yield rates should be realized on these types of future payments and therefore have used a yield rate of 20 percent. Discounting these payments (as of the sale date) to give an annual yield of 20 percent produces the following present values for each of the future payments:

1989	$34,583
1990	17,917
1991	8,463

Adding these amounts to the original $25,000 received for goodwill value produces a total value for goodwill of $85,963.

Exhibit 31–8

TABLE VIII
INTERNAL MEDICINE ASSOCIATES, INC.
CALCULATION OF GOODWILL
USING PRIOR TRANSACTION

Cash Payment Made by Dr. Chandler for 50% of Corporate Stock		100,000	
Less: Portion Attributable to Net Tangible Assets		(75,000)	
Cash Payment Received for Goodwill Value			25,000
Calculation of Present Value (at Sale Date) of Deferred Payments (Agreed–Upon Reduction in Dr. Chandler's Salary and Increase in Dr. McNee's Salary):			
Dr. McNee's 1989 Officer Salary		156,500	
1989 Total Officer Salaries	230,000		
50% of 1989 Officer Salaries	x 50%	115,000	
Excess Payments Received by Dr. McNee		41,500	
Present Value Factor––Payable at the End of 12 Months to Yield 20%		0.83333	
Present Value of 1989 Deferred Payments			34,583
Dr. McNee's 1990 Officer Salary		154,800	
1990 Total Officer Salaries	258,000		
50% of 1990 Officer Salaries	x 50%	129,000	
Excess Payments Received by Dr. McNee		25,800	
Present Value Factor––Payable at the End of 24 Months to Yield 20%		0.69444	
Present Value of 1990 Deferred Payments			17,917
Dr. McNee's 1991 Officer Salary		160,875	
1991 Total Officer Salaries	292,500		
50% of 1991 Officer Salaries	x 50%	146,250	
Excess Payments Received by Dr. McNee		14,625	
Present Value Factor––Payable at the End of 36 Months to Yield 20%		0.57870	
Present Value of 1991 Deferred Payments			8,463
Present Value of Payments Received by Dr. McNee for Goodwill Value as of Sale Date			85,963

SOURCE: Sale agreements and employment agreements between Drs. McNee and Chandler.

Goodwill Valuation Conclusion. Based upon the two methods for calculating the value of professional goodwill considered in this report, we have a valuation range of $86,000 to $120,000. In testing these values, we have considered the results of a survey conducted by The Health Care Group (Plymouth Meeting, Pennsylvania), which compares the goodwill value paid in sales of 100 percent of practices against that practice's latest year's fees. That survey showed that in 1991 practices were generally selling with a goodwill value equal to 25 percent to 38 percent of the prior year's fees received.

Another rule of thumb for the valuation of a medical practice (besides goodwill plus equipment and supplies) is that the practice should sell for 20 percent to 60 percent of the latest year's revenues. Although Dr. McNee's practice has been established for over 24 years, the current economic and medical industry conditions would tend to dilute its value. For that reason, in our opinion, the appropriate percentage would be 33. Applying that percentage rate to the practice's last year's fees would produce a value of $160,000 (rounded). Dr. McNee's interest in that goodwill figure would equal $80,000.

Considering the excess earnings and actual transaction methods, it is our opinion that the actual transaction is a more appropriate method for this particular case, because we have an arm's length sale between Dr. McNee and Dr. Chandler for a 50 percent interest in the practice we are appraising. Also, the value is relatively close to the range of goodwill values according to The Health Care Group survey. Therefore, in our opinion, the value of Dr. McNee's professional goodwill is equal to $86,000.

Valuation Conclusion

Based upon the analysis completed in this report and the conclusions reached, it is our opinion that the value for Dr. McNee's professional goodwill and his 50 percent interest in the corporation known as Internal Medicine Associates, Inc., as of February 1992, is equal to:

One-half equity in practice (rounded)	$ 70,500
Professional goodwill	86,000
Total value	$156,500

Chapter 32

Illustrative Examples of Professional Practice Valuation Methods

This chapter provides two illustrative professional practice valuation exercises: a medical practice valuation and an accounting practice valuation. To facilitate the brevity of the illustration, almost all of the background material and analysis are omitted, and only the application of the chosen valuation methods is presented.

Illustrative Example of a Medical Practice Valuation

Three Practice Valuation Approaches

This appraisal uses one method within each of the following three general approaches to value a medical practice:

1. The discounted net cash flow (or earnings capacity) method.
2. The market data comparable (or analysis of transactional data) method.
3. The asset accumulation (or adjusted net worth) method.

Unlike the traditional business and stock appraisal, the appraisal of a medical practice is typically conducted on an incremental basis. The basic appraisal premise regarding a manufacturer, wholesaler, retailer, and so forth, is: What is the income-generating capacity of the firm's assets? However, the basic appraisal premise regarding a medical practice is: What is the incremental income-generating capacity of the subject practice—when compared to the income-generating potential of a hypothetical start-up practice?

The relative ease of creation of a medical practice is the principal reason for this incremental appraisal analysis. The physician contemplating the purchase of a practice would have to consider the following with respect to the transaction valuation: How much would I pay for the going-concern value of the subject practice—as opposed to starting my own practice?

Two recent trends reinforce this theoretical practice valuation construct. First, many hospitals are financing the start-up practices of primary care physicians, and even subspecialty practice physicians. The reason hospitals finance these start-up practices, of course, is to ensure a steady stream of patient referrals and admissions into their institution. Therefore, a start-up practice is a viable alternative to many physicians, particularly younger doctors, who would be the primary buyers in practice transactions in any event. Second, the recent popularity of corporate-owned, free-standing primary care clinics has greatly augmented employment opportunities for physicians. Clearly, the rational physician would have to consider this: How much am I willing to pay (incrementally) for a practice that nets $120,000 per year when I can earn $100,000 per year as a primary-care center salaried physician (and not be required to finance any investment at all)?

Illustrative Example Fact Set

Young Dr. John Kilpatient has just completed a residency in internal medicine and a fellowship in infectious disease medicine. Dr. Kilpatient is contemplating the purchase of the established practice of old Ben Crazy, M.D. Ben Crazy is also an internist who wishes to sell his practice and retire after a distinguished 30-year medical career.

Quantitatively, Ben Crazy's practice is fairly lucrative. The practice grosses (on a cash receipts basis) $300,000 per year. Kilpatient estimates that the practice will continue to increase at the compound rate of 10 percent per year. As a practical matter, the maximum revenues that a sole practitioner general internist can generate is $400,000 per year.

The total expenses of operating Dr. Crazy's office equal 50 percent of net revenues. This includes support staff, rent, utilities, office supplies, insurance, and so forth—all expenses except Crazy's compensation. Included in these expenses is $10,000 per year of depreciation expense.

Dr. Kilpatient has inspected Ben Crazy's office and has concluded that he would have to spend $50,000 in the first year for new office furniture and fixtures and new medical equipment. After the first year, Dr. Kilpatient estimates that annual capital expenditures would approximate $10,000. These capital expenditures will increase depreciation expense to $20,000 per year, for the next five years. However, even with the increased depreciation, Kilpatient believes he can maintain the practice's 50-percent profit margin.

Most importantly, Dr. Kilpatient has evaluated two career options as alternatives to buying Ben Crazy's practice. First, Kilpatient has carefully analyzed the local competitive environment for general internists. Although it would be an arduous task, Kilpatient is convinced that he could develop a reasonably successful competitive practice to the Ben Crazy practice—from a start-up position—in five years. Second, Kilpatient could obtain employment from a local primary care clinic, at an annual salary of $100,000 per year.

Lastly, it is important to note that the Ben Crazy practice is very highly regarded in the local medical community. Ben Crazy, a highly published and learned internist, is well liked by his patients and well respected by his colleagues. He admits to the most prestigious hospitals in town. In fact, he has had several prestigious committee appointments at these hospitals in recent years. Due to his infectious disease orientation, Ben Crazy receives frequent referrals from family practitioners and other internists. And he refers his patients only to the most prominent subspecialists in town. The only significant detriment to the Ben Crazy practice is that Dr. Crazy has been somewhat "winding down" over the last few years, in anticipation of retirement.

Dr. Kilpatient is considering acquiring the Ben Crazy practice on or about December 31, 1991. Additional data regarding the Ben Crazy practice are presented in the several exhibits that are essential components of this valuation.

Discounted Net Cash Flow Method

Exhibit 32–1 presents the results of our discounted net cash flow practice valuation analysis. It is important to reiterate that five years is considered to be the reasonable period to start up a reasonably successful internal medicine practice. Of course, under the incremental valuation premise, there is no residual value to the subject value—after the discrete forecast period. The discounted net cash flow value of the Ben Crazy practice is: $270,000.

Market Data Comparable Method

Exhibit 32–2 presents the results of a systematic analysis of actual medical practice sale and purchase transactions during the periods 1990 and 1991. This exhibit presents the reasonable range of medical practice transaction values by medical practice subspecialty. Exhibit 32–3 presents the results of our practice valuation analysis of the Ben Crazy practice using the market data comparable method. The market data comparable value of the Ben Crazy practice is: $270,000.

Asset Accumulation Method

This section will briefly describe the mechanics of the asset accumulation method. All medical practice assets are typically grouped into three categories: financial assets, tangible real and personal property, and intangible assets.

Financial assets normally include cash, accounts receivable, prepaid expenses, and inventory and supplies. Since the objective of the appraisal is to state the property in terms of its current cash value, the value of the cash account is already stated at fair market value. The fair market value of accounts receivable is the present value of anticipated collections. Prepaid expenses would include, for example, prepaid rent, prepaid insurance, prepaid utilities, and so on. The historical cost of these assets is typically indicative of their fair market value. Medical practice inventory includes both office materials and supplies and medical materials and supplies. Materials and supplies that are used in current operations should be valued at current replacement cost.

The tangible real and personal property will typically include office furniture and fixtures, medical equipment, leasehold improvements, and leasehold interests. To appraise the owned real and personal property, estimates are made of the cost to replace all owned office furniture and medical equipment. An allowance is made to recognize the physical deterioration, functional obsolescence, technological obsolescence, and economic obsolescence associated with each piece of office or medical equipment.

The typical medical practice has the following intangible assets: patient charts and records, a favorable office lease or office location, a trained and assembled work force, physician/employee employment contracts, a currently hospitalized patient population, patient referrals from general practitioners, going-concern value, and goodwill. Each of these intangible assets is subject to appraisal. And any of these intangible assets can represent the most significant portion of the overall value of the medical practice.

Several of the most common medical practice intangible assets— that is, patient charts and records, a trained and assembled work force, going-concern value, and goodwill—will be illustrated in our example.

Exhibit 32–1

MEDICAL PRACTICE OF BEN CRAZY, M.D.
FAIR MARKET VALUE
DISCOUNTED NET CASH FLOW ANALYSIS
AS OF DECEMBER 31, 1991
(in $000s)

	Account Projection	Year 1	Year 2	Year 3	Year 4	Year 5
	Practice cash revenues	330	363	399	400	400
Less:	Start–up practice revenues	120	144	173	207	249
Equals:	Incremental practice revenues	210	219	226	193	151
Less:	Incremental operating expenses	105	109	113	97	75
Equals:	Incremental before–tax profit	105	110	113	96	76
Times:	Effective tax rate, 40%	42	44	45	38	30
Equals:	Incremental after–tax profit	63	66	68	58	46
Plus:	Depreciation expense	20	20	20	20	20
Less:	Capital expenditures	50	10	10	10	10
Plus:	Start–up capital expenditures	100	0	0	0	0
Equals:	Incremental net cash flow	133	76	78	68	56
Times:	Present value factor, at 20%	0.833	0.694	0.579	0.482	0.402
Equals:	Net present value	111	53	45	33	22
Equals:	Total net present value	264				
Rounded:	Practice fair market value	270				

Notes:

(1) Practice revenues represent last year Crazy revenues, compounded at 10% per year, to a maximum of $400,000.

(2) Start–up practice revenues represent our estimate of the net revenues generated by Kilpatient's hypothetical start–up ("opportunity cost") practice.

(3) Start–up capital expenditures represent our estimate of the leasehold improvements, office furniture and fixtures, and medical equipment required to create the hypothetical start–up practice; these expenditures will not be incurred if Kilpatient buys the Crazy practice.

(4) This example assumes that there is no acquired practice long–term debt.

(5) This example assumes a 20% present value discount rate––i.e., an alternative cost of equity capital rate, risk adjusted.

Exhibit 32–2

THE VALUATION OF MEDICAL PRACTICES
MARKET DATA COMPARABLE METHOD
RANGE OF TRANSACTIONAL ANALYSIS DATA
BASED UPON MEDICAL PRACTICE SALES AND PURCHASES
FOR THE YEARS 1990 AND 1991

Medical Practice Specialty	Fair Market Value Transaction Price (Expressed as a % of Annual Net Revenues)		
	Low Value	High Value	Median Value
General/Family Practice	55%	95%	75%
Internal Medicine	70%	100%	85%
Surgery	80%	100%	90%
Pediatrics	55%	75%	65%
Obstetrics/Gynecology	80%	100%	90%
Radiology	80%	100%	90%
Psychiatry	65%	85%	75%
Anesthesiology	90%	110%	100%

Notes:
  (1) All fair market value range observations have been rounded to the nearest 5%, for
      simplicity of presentation.
  (2) In order to present relevant reasonable ranges, outlier data points were eliminated from
      the reasonable range determination; that is, any data point observations in excess of plus
      or minus two standard deviations around the initial mean were eliminated from the
      population.
  (3) No attempt was made to--and the quantity and quality of data would not permit--further
      disaggregation of medical sub-specialties (e.g., different surgical sub-specialities).
  (4) No attempt was made to disaggregate the total data base by geographical region,
      although this would be statistically feasible.
  (5) The data included in this analysis are from transaction prices represented to us and
      deemed to be accurate; however, no attempt was made to independently verify these
      transaction prices.

Virtually all medical practices have patient charts and records. These patient charts include the medical histories (and billing histories) of the current population of practice patients. These patient charts and records are typically appraised using an income approach. That is, the value of the charts and records is the present value of the anticipated prospective income to be earned from the current patient population.

The first step in this intangible asset appraisal is to quantify the expected remaining life of the current patient population. This step requires a physical inspection and quantitative analysis of both the current patient charts and the inactive patient charts. Inactive charts represent patients who no longer use the subject medical practice, for whatever

Exhibit 32–3

MEDICAL PRACTICE OF BEN CRAZY, M.D.
FAIR MARKET VALUE
MARKET DATA COMPARABLE METHOD
AS OF DECEMBER 31, 1991
(in $000s)

Annual revenues of Ben Crazy, M.D. practice, year ended 12/31/91	$300
Range of fair market value transaction prices for general interest sub–specialty	70% – 100%
Point estimate fair market value selected for Crazy practice, based upon quantitative and qualitative analysis	90%
Estimate of fair market value of the internal medicine practice of Ben Crazy, M.D. ($300,000 x 90%)	$270

Notes:

(1) The point estimate of the subject practice within the reasonable range of practice values is admittedly subjective. Therefore, this estimation should be made by an appraiser with significant experience in the valuation of medical, dental, and similar professional practices.

(2) In the instant case, the point estimate was based upon the reputation, size, and profitability of the subject practice––modified by the fact that Crazy has been "winding down" his practice in recent years.

reason. This remaining useful life analysis can encompass a simple turnover rate analysis or a more comprehensive actuarial or mortality statistical curve-fitting analysis. First, the expected average life of the entire patient population must be determined. Second, the expected remaining life of the current patient population must be quantified.

The second step in the intangible asset appraisal process is to quantify the expected net economic income (i.e., net cash flow) per patient—for each year over the expected life of the patient population.

The last step in the appraisal of patient charts and records is to determine the present value of the net economic income to be derived from the current patient population over its expected useful life. Exhibit 32–4 presents an example of this analysis.

A trained and assembled work force is a very valuable intangible asset for many medical practices. This work force includes the salaried employee/physicians and clerical and medical support staff on the permanent payroll of the practice. A common method of valuing an assembled work force is the cost to recruit, hire, and train a replacement work force of comparable quality and experience. The rationale to this method is that if the medical practice did not have a trained and assembled work

Exhibit 32–4

MEDICAL PRACTICE OF BEN CRAZY, M.D.
FAIR MARKET VALUE
VALUATION OF INTANGIBLE ASSETS
AS OF DECEMBER 31, 1991
(in $000s)

Patient Charts and Records

Total number of active patient charts in the practice	5,000
Average revenue per patient per year	
(includes both office revenue and hospital revenue)	$60
Average before-tax profit margin	50%
Average before-tax profit margin per patient per year	$30
Effective tax rate	40%
Average after-tax profit per patient per year	18
Fair return on other practice assets (assume 15% of revenues)	9
Practice return attributable to patient population	9
Total practice return attributable to patient population (5,000 patients x $9)	$45,000
Average expected life of patient relationship--4 years	
Average expected remaining life of patient relationship--2 years	
Present value discount rate--20%	
Present value of annuity factor, at 20% for 2 years	1.527
Present value of patient charts and records ($60,000 x 1.527)	$91,620

Trained and Assembled Work Force

Dr. Crazy has three loyal and competent staff members, all of whom have worked for the practice for several years. The appraisal of this workforce follows:

Staff Member	Annual Salary	Cost to Recruit, Hire & Train	Fair Market Value of Work Force
Rhonda Receptionist	$12,000	10%	$1,200
Nancy Nurse	$20,000	10%	$2,000
Mary Medtech	$24,000	15%	$3,600
Total (rounded)			$7,000

Going-Concern Value

We estimate that it would take 3 months to create our nascient medical practice (i.e., to lease an office, hire employees, order and install office and medical equipment, etc.). During that 3-month period, the Ben Crazy practice will generate $20,000 of positive net cash flow--compared to zero cash flow for the start-up practice. Accordingly, the Crazy practice going-concern value is $20,000.

Exhibit 32–4 (concluded)

MEDICAL PRACTICE OF BEN CRAZY, M.D.
FAIR MARKET VALUE
VALUATION OF INTANGIBLE ASSETS
AS OF DECEMBER 31, 1991
(in $000s)

Goodwill

The following is a projection of practice net cash associated with goodwill (in $100s).

		Year 1	Year 2	Year 3	Year 4	Year 5
	Aggregate practice before–tax profit	165	182	200	200	200
Less:	Alternative employment income	100	120	140	140	140
Equals:	Incremental practice profit	65	62	60	60	60
Times:	Effective tax rate, 40%	26	25	24	24	24
Equals:	Incremental after–tax profit	39	37	36	36	36
Less:	Fair return on all other practice assets	30	30	30	30	30
Equals:	Incremental economic return on practice ownership	9	7	6	6	6
Times:	Present value factor, at 20%	0.833	0.694	0.579	0.482	0.402
Equals:	Present value of economic return	7	5	3	3	2
Rounded:	Practice fair market value	21				

Notes:
(1) The remaining life calculation for patient charts is based upon an analysis of historical patient turnover rates.
(2) The cost to recruit, hire, and train a replacement work force is based upon our estimate.
(3) The start–up period used to calculate going-concern value is based upon our analysis of the subject practice.
(4) The alternative employment income is based upon our projection of prospective salaried internist wage rates.

force in place, the practice would immediately have to develop such a work force—at a substantial replacement cost.

This method requires a schedule of each salaried employee's name, position, and annual salary. Next, for each employee, an estimate is made of the cost (in terms of a percent of annual salary) to recruit, hire, and train an experienced replacement. These costs would include, among others, newspaper help-wanted ads, employment agency fees, the cost of the physician/owner's time for interviews and reference checks, and so on. For certain employee physician and office management employees, the costs could include executive search firm fees, employee signing bonuses, and employee relocation expenses.

For all replacement employees, even those with substantial experience, there will be a training and orientation period as the new employee learns the administrative ways of the practice. These costs, in total, could easily sum to between 10 and 50 percent of the employee's annual salary. As described, the replacement cost for each employee is calculated. The fair market value of the collective trained and assembled work force is the sum of the replacement costs for each salaried employee.

Going-concern value represents the fact that the subject medical practice is an up-and-running, fully operational, revenue-producing business. Going-concern value represents the difference in the value of a practice "on paper" (e.g., a business plan associated with the creation of a new practice) and the value of a practice that is already a "going concern" (e.g., a practice with all assets in place and currently generating revenues, profits, and cash flow). Clearly, to any medical practice that is generating positive cash flow, going-concern value is an important intangible asset.

As with all intangible assets, there are several methods for quantifying going-concern value. A common method quantifies the difference in cash flow associated with the going-concern practice (i.e., the subject practice) versus the cash flow associated with a hypothetical start-up practice.

This method requires the appraiser to predict a start-up period—associated with the recreation (from scratch) of a competitive medical practice. This start-up period is the amount of time required to plan and design all of the practice asset requirements, construct the practice physical facilities, and assemble all of the assets. It is important to note that the going-concern value does not typically include the time and costs to produce any promotional materials (otherwise appraised separately), to develop patient relationships (otherwise captured in the patient charts and records appraisal), and to reproduce the practice employee base (otherwise captured in the assembled work force appraisal).

The value of the going concern is the difference between the cash flow associated with the hypothetical start-up and the cash flow associated with the established practice during the start-up period. For the start-up practice, the cash flow will likely be all negative, including start-up expenses and interest on equipment purchases and facilities construction. For the established practice, the cash flow during this period should be positive—the incremental cash flow after providing for all operating expenses and for normal working capital, capital expenditure, and debt service requirements. The difference between these two cash flow projections (start-up practice versus established practice) over the projected start-up period represents the going-concern value of the subject medical practice.

Goodwill is frequently considered a "catch all" intangible asset designed to encompass all other value not specifically captured in the identified tangible and intangible assets. Basically, then, goodwill is the value of everything else that does not otherwise show up on the fair market value balance sheet. Many analysts (and courts) use the term *goodwill* in the classic sense of the factors that cause clients to return to the stand—reputation, location, and so forth. While there are many formulas to quantify goodwill, the most common method is the capitalization of excess earnings method. Under this method, goodwill will be the most significant asset for many highly profitable practitioners. However, for medical practices that have made substantial investments in other assets, there may be no goodwill at all.

The excess earnings method first requires the valuation of all of the practice's other assets, both tangible and intangible. For this reason, goodwill is usually the last asset to be appraised in a practice valuation. The second step is to determine fair return on the practice's asset. There are several variations of this method. These variations involve alternative definitions of fair return. For example, fair return can involve return on net tangible assets, on net total assets, or on total assets. However, if these alternative definitions are appropriately applied (i.e., consistently with the appraisal of all other tangible and intangible assets), then the resulting practice valuation conclusion should remain the same. For purposes of this chapter, fair return will be defined as return on total assets.

Since a medical practice is appraised on an incremental economic benefit basis, the excess return associated with goodwill is also calculated on an incremental basis. The excess return is calculated after an estimate of the physician's opportunity cost—that is, foregone wages as a salaried physician.

The return on the practice's total assets is quantified for either a single-year or multiple-year period. The industry average return on total assets is quantified by reference to published industry statistical data. The difference between the subject practice's return on total assets and the industry return on total assets is determined. If the difference is positive, then goodwill exists. If the difference is negative, then no goodwill exists. If the difference is positive, then this excess rate of return on total assets is multiplied by the fair market value of total assets. This product represents the "excess earnings" of the subject medical practice.

This excess earnings amount is capitalized—as an annuity in perpetuity—by an appropriate discount rate. This discount rate represents the practice's risk-adjusted cost of equity capital. Since the asset accumulation method values the practice by calculating the value of all identified assets, it is important that the excess earnings method reference return on total assets and not just on tangible assets. This will avoid the double counting of the value of identified intangible assets. Obviously, it is also important that the industry average return on assets be calculated in the same way as the subject practice return on assets. This capitalized excess earnings represents the medical practice goodwill.

Exhibit 32–4 presents an illustrative example of the valuation of the intangible assets associated with the hypothetical practice of Ben Crazy, M.D.

The value of the medical practice's total assets, then, is the summation of the fair market values of the practice's financial assets, real property, tangible personal property, and identified intangible assets, including goodwill. This total represents the collective value of the practice's assets as a going-concern business, but not the fair market value of the practice's equity. In order to determine the value of the equity, the current value of the practice's liabilities must be subtracted from the fair market value of the practice's assets.

Medical practice liabilities may be grouped into two categories: current liabilities and long-term liabilities. The first step in the appraisal of liabilities is to remove from the balance sheet all accounts that are not bona fide liabilities of the practice. This adjustment typically involves the reclassification of liability accounts, which are, in fact, truly equity accounts. Examples of liabilities that may be reclassified as equities include notes payable to physician/owners or immediate family members of major physician/shareholders. If these liabilities are really considered to be equity positions by the creditors—and if the practice does not have a plan for the repayment of these obligations—then they may be reclassified as equity.

The typical current liabilities include accounts payable, wages payable, taxes payable, and accrued expenses. The appraiser should determine the current value of each of these liability accounts. Typically, the current value of these accounts is represented by the historical carrying amount. If these liabilities are not interest-bearing and payable in less than one year, then it is reasonable to value these liabilities at historical amounts.

The long-term liabilities of a medical practice typically include mortgages and notes payable. Each of these debts should be restated to current value. The current value of a long-term debt instrument is a function of term-to-maturity, remaining principal payments, periodicity of principal payments, imbedded interest rates, and current market interest rates for instruments of similar risk and maturity.

When the imbedded interest rate is greater than the current market rate, the current value of the instrument will exceed the principal outstanding. In other words, if interest rates have decreased since the debt was created, it would be valued at a premium over par. For debt instruments with an imbedded interest rate less than current market rates, the fair market value of that debt is less than the principal outstanding. In other words, if interest rates have increased since the debt was issued, its current value will be below par. The objective of these current value analyses is to determine what a current payoff amount would be to extinguish the liability between the debtmaker and the debtholder.

The fair market value of all long-term liabilities is the summation of the current values of each long-term debt outstanding. The fair market value of the medical practice's total liabilities is the sum of the current value of all current liabilities plus the current value of all long-term liabilities.

The fair market value of the medical practice's equity interest is, quite simply, the difference between the fair market value of the assets and the current value of the liabilities. Algebraically, this relationship is expressed: FMV business enterprise equals FMV total assets minus FMV total liabilities. If the asset accumulation method has been properly applied, the fair market value of the business enterprise represents what a willing buyer would pay for a 100 percent equity interest in the practice.

Exhibit 32–5 presents an illustrative example of the application of

Exhibit 32–5

MEDICAL PRACTICE OF BEN CRAZY, M.D.
FAIR MARKET VALUE
ASSET ACCUMULATION METHOD
AS OF DECEMBER 31, 1991
(in $000s)

	At Historical Cost	At Fair Market Value
ASSETS		
Current Assets:		
Cash	10	10
Accounts receivable	40	40
Prepaid expenses	10	10
Medical and office supplies	10	20
Total Current Assets	70	80
Plant, Property, and Equipment:		
Office furniture and fixtures	100	60
Medical equipment	100	60
Gross Plant, Property and Equipment	200	120
Less: Accumulated depreciation	100	0
Net Plant, Property, and Equipment	100	120
Intangible Assets:		
Patient charts and records	0	69
Trained and assembled workforce	0	7
Going–concern value	0	20
Goodwill	0	21
Total Intangible Assets	0	117
TOTAL ASSETS	170	317
LIABILITIES AND OWNER'S EQUITY		
Liabilities:		
Accounts payable	10	10
Wages payable	10	10
Taxes payable	20	20
Total Liabilities	40	40
Owner's Equity	130	277
TOTAL LIABILITIES AND OWNER'S EQUITY	170	317
CONCLUSION		
Fair Market Value of Practice Equity ($277 rounded)		280

Notes:

(1) The fair market value of current assets and of property, plant, and equipment is based upon depreciated replacement cost appraisals.

(2) The fair market value calculation regarding intangible assets is presented in Exhibit 32–4.

the asset accumulation method to the medical practice valuation of Ben Crazy, M.D. This example illustrates both the revaluation of on-balance sheet assets and liabilities and the revaluation (creation through appraisal) of off-balance sheet intangible assets.

Based upon the asset accumulation method, the fair market value of the Ben Crazy medical practice is: $280,000.

Fair Market Value of the Medical Practice

Exhibit 32–6 presents our valuation synthesis and conclusion with respect to the Ben Crazy, M.D., practice. Based upon a synthesis of the three valuation approaches, we would estimate the fair market value of this hypothetical practice to be: $270,000.

This chapter presented an analysis designed to quantify the value of a 100 percent equity interest. This chapter has assumed a simple capital structure: only one class of stock outstanding—voting common stock. The asset accumulation method can be adjusted to accommodate the valuation of less than a 100 percent interest and the valuation of a practice with a complex capital structure. However, these adjustments are significant.

In the instance when less than a 100 percent equity interest is being valued, appropriate discounts and premiums should be quantified for minority ownership interests, majority (but less than 100 percent) ownership control, lack of marketability, illiquidity, and blockage. In the instance of a practice with several classes of stock outstanding, each class of stock should be valued separately: common and preferred stock—voting versus nonvoting, cumulative versus noncumulative, participative versus nonparticipative, and primary versus secondary liquidation preference. An analysis of the appropriate adjustments to the asset accumulation method—to accommodate either less than 100 percent equity interest or complex capital structures—is beyond the scope of this chapter.

Summary and Conclusion

There are numerous reasons to value medical, dental, and similar health care professional practices. These reasons fall into the following categories: taxation (compliance and planning), transaction (pricing), financing (cash flow based and asset based), litigation (and dispute resolution), and management (i.e., ownership) information purposes.

There are various methods that may be applicable to the valuation of medical practices. For example, the appraiser could value the subject practice by reference to the pricing data derived from the actual sales of guideline or comparative medical practices. This is often called the *market data transaction method*. The appraiser could value the subject practice by reference to the incremental economic income (often defined as net cash flow) that the subject practice will generate prospectively—when compared to a hypothetical start-up practice. This is often called the *discounted future returns method*. Or the appraiser could value the

Exhibit 32–6

MEDICAL PRACTICE OF BEN CRAZY, M.D.
FAIR MARKET VALUE
VALUATION SYNTHESIS AND CONCLUSION
AS OF DECEMBER 31, 1991
(in $000s)

Discounted net cash flow method	270
Market data comparable method	270
Asset accumulation method	280
Total valuation synthesis and conclusion	270

Notes:

(1) The valuation synthesis and conclusion is based upon the weighted average of the results of the various valuation methods employed.

(2) The weighted average averaging scheme is based upon the quantity and quality of available data, the experience and judgment of the professional appraiser, and the degree of confidence placed upon each valuation method by the professional appraiser.

subject practice by reference to the sum of the discrete values (on a going-concern basis) of the individual component tangible and intangible assets that comprise the practice. This is often called the *asset accumulation method.*

In this section, an illustrative example of the asset accumulation method to medical practice valuation was presented. This method has particular application in a number of practice valuation instances, including litigation between a practice owner and another party (e.g., marital dissolution cases), litigation between practice owners (e.g., partner or shareholder disputes), the allocation of equity in a merger of medical practices, the allocation of assets in a separation or split-up of medical practices, and the actual pricing and structuring of the sale of a medical practice.

The utility of the asset accumulation valuation method is based on several factors. First, most medical practice sales are asset sales. Accordingly, the buyer wants to know exactly what assets (tangible and intangible) he or she is buying. This practice valuation method provides a ready-made purchase price allocation of the purchased practice, for both general accounting and tax reporting purposes. This method allows the buyer, and other parties, to estimate the amount of financing (both cash flow based and asset based) that may be available to finance the practice acquisition. And this method allows the practice owners, and other parties, to quantify what assets are available for distribution after professional or personal litigation. This valuation method can satisfy these diverse objectives because it quantifies the income-generating capacity of the overall professional practice, since it componentizes the value of each contributory tangible and intangible asset of the practice.

Illustrative Example of an Accounting Practice Valuation

Applying the Asset Accumulation Method

To illustrate the asset accumulation method to accounting practice valuation, we will analyze the hypothetical firm of Precise and Accurate, CPAs. Although hypothetical, the firm of Precise and Accurate, CPAs, is representative of many small, two-partner accounting firms. The objective of this hypothetical appraisal is to determine the fair market value of 100 percent of the partners' equity capital as of December 31, 1991. We will appraise Precise and Accurate, CPAs, under the premise of value in continued use as a going-concern business enterprise.

Exhibit 32–7 presents a summary of the asset accumulation method used to value Precise and Accurate, CPAs. Exhibit 32–7 also presents the historical cost basis balance sheet and the fair market value basis balance sheet of the firm as of December 31, 1991. The value of the practice equity is based upon this fair market value basis balance sheet.

In Exhibit 32–7, the financial assets were appraised to net realizable value. This appraisal resulted in a slight devaluation in the client receivables and the client work in process. Also in Exhibit 32–7, each item of the firm's tangible real and personal property was appraised to fair market value in continued use. The appraisal of these assets was the result of a depreciated replacement cost analysis.

The next section of the hypothetical example illustrates the identification, valuation, and remaining useful life analysis of the accounting practice intangible assets.

Exhibit 32–8 presents the valuation of the leasehold interest. This asset represents the favorable economic element of the Precise and Accurate, CPAs, leased office space.

Exhibit 32–9 presents the valuation of the practice's trained and assembled work force. This asset represents the cost to recruit, hire, and train a replacement work force of comparable experience and expertise to the Precise and Accurate, CPAs' work force.

Exhibit 32–10 presents the valuation of the practice client workpaper files. This asset represents the cost to recreate the workpaper files related to recurring audit, accounting, and taxation clients. Since clients normally return to the accounting firm that maintains their historical and permanent accounting and tax files, these files represent an important intangible asset for Precise and Accurate, CPAs.

Exhibit 32–11 presents the valuation of the practice client relationships. The first step in this valuation is the determination of the average remaining life of the client relationships in place as of the valuation date. Various procedures commonly used to determine the average remaining life of client relationships include the turnover rate procedure, the original group procedure, the select and ultimate

Exhibit 32–7

PRECISE AND ACCURATE, CPAs
ASSET ACCUMULATION METHOD
FAIR MARKET VALUE AS OF DECEMBER 31, 1991

	At Historical Cost	At Fair Market Value
ASSETS		
Financial Assets:		
Cash	$10,000	$10,000
Client accounts receivable	240,000	200,000
Work in process	120000	100000
Prepaid expenses	40,000	40,000
Total Financial Assets	410,000	350,000
Tangible Real & Personal Property:		
Office furniture and fixtures	120,000	100,000
Computer equipment	60,000	40,000
Leasehold improvements	40,000	30000
Gross Real & Personal Property	220,000	170,000
Less: Accumulated depreciation	100,000	0
Total Tangible Real & Personal Property	120,000	170,000
Intangible Real & Personal Property:		
Leasehold interests	0	110,000
Trained and assembled work force	0	150,000
Client workpaper files	0	30,000
Client relationships	0	400,000
Goodwill	0	200,000
Total Intangible Real & Personal Property	0	890,000
TOTAL ASSETS	**$530,000**	**$1,410,000**
LIABILITIES AND OWNERS' EQUITY		
Current Liabilities:		
Accounts payable	$100,000	$100,000
Accrued expenses	100,000	100,000
Total Current Liabilities	200,000	200,000
Total Liabilities	200,000	200,000
Owners' Equity:		
Partners' Capital	330,000	1,210,000
Total Partners' Capital	330,000	1,210,000
TOTAL LIABILITIES AND OWNERS' EQUITY	**$530,000**	**$1,410,000**
FAIR MARKET VALUE OF PARTNERS' CAPITAL (ROUNDED)		**$1,200,000**

Exhibit 32–8

PRECISE AND ACCURATE, CPAs
LEASEHOLD INTEREST
FAIR MARKET VALUE AS OF DECEMBER 31, 1991

1	Net size of leased office space	6,000 square feet
2	Current market rent for comparable space	$22 per foot
3	Current rental rate per lease	$16 per foot
4	Favorable leasehold advantage--per foot (3 - 2)	$6 per foot
5	Total annual favorable leasehold advantage (4 x 1)	$36,000
6	Number of years remaining in lease term	5 years
7	Appropriate before-tax present value discount rate	20%
8	Present value of annuity factor, 20% for 5 years	2.99
9	Present value of favorable leasehold advantage (8 x 5)	$107,640
10	Fair market value of leasehold interest (rounded)	$110,000

Exhibit 32–9

PRECISE AND ACCURATE, CPAs
TRAINED AND ASSEMBLED WORK FORCE
FAIR MARKET VALUE AS OF DECEMBER 31, 1991

Category of Employee	Total Annual Compensation	Percent of Annual Compensation to				Replacement Cost
		Recruit	Hire	Train	Total	
Professional staff	$250,000	10%	10%	30%	50%	$125,000
Paraprofessional staff	40,000	10%	0%	20%	30%	12,000
Support staff	40,000	10%	0%	10%	20%	8,000
Total cost to recruit, hire, and train replacement work force						$145,000
Fair market value of assembled work force (rounded)						$150,000

procedure, and the retirement rate procedure. For the Precise and Accurate, CPAs' client relationships, we have determined that the average remaining life is five years.

The second step in this valuation is a projection of the net fee revenues from the current client relationships. This projection requires consideration of expected changes in the levels of service provided, of the practice billing rates, and of the practice allowance (or charge off) rate.

The third step in this valuation is a projection of the contribution

Exhibit 32–10

PRECISE AND ACCURATE, CPAs
CLIENT WORKPAPER FILES
FAIR MARKET VALUE AS OF DECEMBER 31, 1991

Type of Client	Number of Clients	Hours to Recreate Permanent File	Cost Per Hour	Cost to Recreate Each Client File	Cost to Recreate All Client Files
Recurring audit	30	10	$40	$400	$12,000
Recurring bookkeeping	60	5	30	150	9000
Recurring tax--corporate	100	2	30	60	6000
Recurring tax--individual	200	1	20	20	4000
Total cost to recreate client workpaper files					$31,000
Fair market value client workpaper files (rounded)					$30,000

Exhibit 32–11

PRECISE AND ACCURATE, CPAs
CLIENT RELATIONSHIPS
FAIR MARKET VALUE AS OF DECEMBER 31, 1991
(in $000s)

	Year 1	Year 2	Year 3	Year 4	Year 5
Net client fees	1,260	1,323	1,389	1,459	1,532
Contribution margin	20%	20%	20%	20%	20%
Contribution	252	265	278	292	306
Increase in net financial assets	10	11	11	12	12
Return on assets employed	142	142	142	142	142
Economic income	100	112	125	138	152
Present value factor *	0.909	0.758	0.631	0.526	0.438
Present value of economic income	91	85	79	72	67
Fair market value of client relationship (rounded)					400

* 20% present value discount rate, mid–year convention

margin (or profit margin) associated with the current clients. This contribution margin is calculated after an allowance for basic partner compensation, but before consideration of any partner profit distributions. In other words, in order to calculate the contribution margin, partners are treated as highly compensated employees, and not as owners of the firm.

The fourth step is to convert the projection of net earnings into a projection of economic income. This is accomplished by subtracting any increments in net financial assets due to the projected increase in net client fees. Net financial assets are typically defined as accounts receivable plus work-in-process less accounts payable. Also, the net earnings from the client relationships should be reduced by a fair return on the assets employed in the service of those clients. The fair return is often calculated as the practice-specific discount rate times the fair market value of the assets employed on the valuation date. The discount rate typically represents the firm's weighted-average cost of capital. And the assets employed include both the tangible (e.g., office furniture and fixtures) and intangible (e.g., client workpaper files) of the practice. The final step of this valuation is the determination of the present value of the economic income over the average remaining life of the client relationships. Of course, this procedure requires the quantification of the appropriate present value discount rate. Typically, this discount rate is the weighted-average cost of capital for the firm. The present value of the projected economic income represents the value of the recurring client relationships to Precise and Accurate, CPAs.

Exhibit 32–12 presents the statement of results of operations of Precise and Accurate, CPAs, for the year ended December 31, 1991. This statement of operating results is used in the determination of the value of the goodwill of the accounting practice. It should be noted that partners are treated as employees in the preparation of this statement. In other words, the partners' basic compensation is treated as an operating expense; and the statement presents the amount of firm profits available for periodic distribution to the firm partners.

Exhibit 32-13 presents the determination of the value of the Precise and Accurate, CPAs' practice goodwill. For practice valuation purposes, goodwill is often calculated by a capitalized excess earnings method.

The first step in the goodwill valuation is the determination of the fair market value of all of the identified assets of the practice. These assets include financial assets, tangible real and personal property assets, and specifically identified intangible assets. The sum of these values is the total fair market value of all identified assets. The second step is the determination of the current value of all identified liabilities of the practice. The third step is the determination of the fair market value of net assets of the practice (i.e., total identified tangible and intangible assets less liabilities).

The fourth step is the determination of a fair return on the practice net assets. There are several procedures for quantifying a fair return on net assets. One common procedure is to use the firm-specific, present value discount rate. Since this discount rate is based upon a weighted-average return on capital, it should provide for a weighted-average fair return on net assets. This is the procedure illustrated in Exhibit 32–13.

Exhibit 32–12

PRECISE AND ACCURATE, CPAs
STATEMENT OF RESULTS OF OPERATIONS
FOR THE FISCAL YEAR ENDED DECEMBER 31, 1991
(in $000s)

Net Client Revenues	1,200
Less Operating Expenses:	
Partner basic compensation	200
Staff salaries	330
Employment taxes and benefits	70
Rent expense	96
Telephone and utilities	54
Postage and stationery	50
Professional liability and other insurance	50
Data processing expenses	50
Depreciation	40
Interest expense	20
Total Operating Expenses	960
Net Income	240

It is important to note that the fair return is typically calculated based upon the appraised value of all of the practice assets—both tangible and intangible.

The fifth step is a comparison of the actual net income of the practice to the calculated fair return on net assets. If the actual return exceeds the "fair" return, then excess earnings exist. The capitalization of this fair return represents the value of the practice goodwill. If the actual return is less than the "fair" return, economic obsolescence occurs. In that case, the value of the identified tangible and intangible assets may have to be reduced—to equal the amount of economic support for those assets.

If excess earnings exist, the final step is to capitalize those earnings as an annuity in perpetuity. Again, the firm-specific discount rate is often used as the annuity capitalization factor. These capitalized excess earnings represent the fair market value of the Precise and Accurate, CPAs, goodwill.

Using the asset accumulation method, the value of the practice equity is the fair market value of the firm assets less the current value of the firm liabilities. Exhibit 32–7 presents the fair market value of the firm assets (i.e., $1,410,000) and the current value of the firm liabilities (i.e.,

Exhibit 32–13

PRECISE AND ACCURATE, CPAs
GOODWILL
FAIR MARKET VALUE AS OF DECEMBER 31, 1991

Fair Market Value of Identified Assets:	
Financial assets	$350,000
Tangible real and personal property	160,000
Intangible assets (including goodwill)	690,000
Total fair market value	1,200,000
Current Value of Short–Term Liabilities	
Accounts payable	100,000
Accrued expenses	100,000
Total current value	200,000
Net Fair Market Value of Identified Assets	1,000,000
Times: Present Value Discount Rate	x 20%
Equals: Fair Return on Net Assets	200,000
Net Income of Precise and Accurate, CPAs	240,000
Excess Earnings (i.e., Actual Net Income Less Fair Return)	40,000
Capitalized as an Annuity in Perpetuity	x 5.00
Equals: Fair Market Value of Goodwill	$200,000

$200,000). Accordingly, the fair market value of the partners' equity in Precise and Accurate, CPAs, is $1,200,000 (rounded).

Caveats Regarding Professional Practice Valuations

Due to space constraints, our illustrative example did not consider all of the discounts and premiums associated with professional practice valuation issues. For example, appropriate discounts should be applied for a minority interest (e.g., individual partner's interest), key partner dependence, key client dependence, and so forth. In addition, appropriate premiums should be applied for majority control of a practice, for significant practice diversification, and so forth. While the asset accumulation method can be modified to accommodate many of the issues, the consideration of minority discounts, control premiums, and so on, are beyond the scope of this analysis.

Summary and Conclusion

Various reasons to perform a valuation of an accounting practice include transaction, financing, taxation, litigation, and management information motivations. There are several approaches commonly used in the valuation of accounting practices, including the market data comparison, discounted net cash flow, and asset accumulation methods. Of these methods, the asset accumulation method is the most structured, most rigorous, and best substantiated method. A comprehensive illustrative example of this method was provided. The asset accumulation method not only concludes an overall practice valuation, it componentizes the elements of that valuation into the individual tangible and intangible assets of the accounting practice.

While actual transaction data should not be ignored in any professional practice valuation, the asset accumulation method is often particularly applicable to the appraisal of an accounting practice. First, accountants are familiar with the traditional balance sheet format in which the results of this method are presented. Second, accountants recognize that the asset accumulation method results in a ready-made purchase price allocation (assuming an actual practice sale) that may be used for financial accounting and tax reporting purposes. Third, accountants appreciate that this method quantifies not only an overall practice value, but also the contributory value of each of the component tangible and intangible assets of the practice. Therefore, accountants can use this method to explain and justify the overall practice value to current partners, potential partners, merger candidates, bankers, and so forth.

Lastly, the asset accumulation method has specific application when the subject practice may, in fact, be involved in a transaction. This method is relevant to the allocation of equity values when two practices merge, based upon the relative asset contributions of each practice. This method is relevant when a practice splits in two and assets have to be allocated to partners based upon their capital accounts. This method is also applicable when the practice faces financing, refinancing, bankruptcy, partner or marital dissolution, or in many other instances when the total value of the practice's tangible and intangible assets are directly relevant to the business value of the subject accounting practice.

Part VI

Topics Related to Valuation

Chapter 33

Transaction Data Bases

One frustration that constantly plagues appraisers of small businesses and professional practices is lack of comparative transaction data. Unlike transactions in either real estate or publicly traded securities, there is no legal requirement that transfers of ownership of most closely held businesses be reported anywhere.

To date, only a smattering of work has been done on the collection of closely held business and professional practice transaction data. The work reported here is a little more than was reported in the first edition, but does not represent a great deal of progress for a period of seven years. This chapter presents descriptions and samples of those data bases that we currently know to exist.

In the first edition, we reported the results of the Willamette Business Sale Data Base. Since then, we have provided those data to the Institute of Business Appraisers data base, which is described in this chapter.

If readers know of any additional data bases, please contact Shannon Pratt at Willamette Management Associates, 111 S.W. Fifth Avenue, Suite 2150, Portland, Oregon 97204, (503) 222-0577. We hope to update this synopsis with more information in future editions of both this book and other publications.

The IBA Market Data Base

The Institute of Business Appraisers (IBA) maintains a data base of information on actual sales of closely held businesses. Exhibit 33–1 is a printout of the data included for SIC Code 2752, commercial printing, lithographic. The data are available to IBA members at no charge.

Description of the IBA Data Base

According to Ray Miles, executive director of IBA, in a presentation at the IBA 1992 national convention, the IBA data base contains the following information for those companies for which it was made available to IBA (although not every item is included in the standard printout, as shown in Exhibit 33–1):

- SIC number.
- Business type.
- Annual gross revenue.
- Annual earnings.
- Owner's compensation.
- Year and month of sale.
- Selling price of business.
- Value of real estate, if any.
- Whether asset or stock sale.
- Net worth (book value).
- Down payment.
- Terms.
- Geographical location.

Exhibit 33-1

THE INSTITUTE OF BUSINESS APPRAISERS, INC.
P. O. Box 1447, Boynton Beach, FL 33425   Phone: 407-732-3202

The information below is supplied in response to your request for data to be used in applying the "market data approach" to business appraisal. Because of the nature of the sources from which the information is obtained, we are not able to guarantee its
accuracy. Neither do we make any representation as to applicability of the information to any specific appraisal situation.

Following is an explanation of the entries in the data table:

"Business Type"	= Principal line of business.
"SIC No."	= Principal Standard Industrial Classification number applicable to business sold.
"Ann. Gr."	= Reported annual sales volume of business sold.
"Ann. Earn."	= Reported annual earnings before owner's compensation, interest and taxes.
"Own. Comp."	= Reported owner's compensation.
"Sale Price"	= Total reported consideration i.e. cash, notes, liabilities assumed, etc. excluding real estate.
	A = Asset Sale; S = Stock Sale
"Sales Price/Gross"	= Ratio of total consideration to reported annual gross.
"Price/Ann. Earn.	= Ratio of total consideration to reported annual earnings.
"Yr/Mo of Sale"	= Month and year during which transaction was consummated.

DATA FOR MARKET COMPARISON   10/15/92

Business type	SIC	Ann.Gr. $000's	Ann Earn. $000's	Own Comp. $000's	Sale Price $000's	Sale Pr./ Gross	Price/ Ann Earn.	Geographical Location	Yr/Mo of Sale
Printer, specialized	2752	1228	95		529 S	0.43	5.57	Canada	90/02
Printing, quick		259	87	41	200 A	0.77	2.30	AZ	90/02
Commercial printing		530	45		221 A	0.42	4.91	Mid-west	90/02
Printing Shop		80	25		50	0.63	2.00	TX	90/03
Printing/copying		760	100	45	510 A	0.67	5.10	CA	90/04
Printing, quick		1091			1000 A	0.92		FL	90/04
Printing shop		723	55		530 A	0.73	9.64	West coast	90/05
Printing Shop		500	72		214	0.43	2.97	OH	90/05
Printer, commerc.		190	50	26	80 A	0.42	1.60	CO	90/05
Printing Shop		230	48		105	0.46	2.19	MN	90/10
Printer, commercial		178	56	56	105 A	0.59	1.88	FL	90/11
Printing Shop		250	45		155	0.62	3.44	OH	91/01
Printing Shop		1283	283		761	0.59	2.69	TN	91/07
Printing Shop		3800	725		2900	0.76	4.00	OH	92/01
Printing		280	65	54	108 A	0.39	1.66	NY	92/02
Printing		102	12		55 A	0.54	4.58	FL	92/03

SOURCE: Provided courtesy of The Institute of Business Appraisers, Inc., Boynton Beach, Florida.

Information for the IBA Market Data Base is obtained from IBA members and other sources having actual knowledge of sales. The amount of information about each sale is limited by practical considerations as to the amount of information that IBA's sources have about the sale of a closely held business, and are willing to take the time to record and submit to IBA.

As of the IBA 1992 national convention, the IBA data base contained one or more entries on each of 366 SIC categories. Of these, 84 SIC categories had six or more entries and 26 SIC categories had 20 or more entries. Business types with the largest numbers of entries were the following:

- Restaurants (435).
- Drinking places (173).
- Fast food (172).
- Retail groceries (168).
- Accounting (117).
- Retail liquor (106).
- Miscellaneous services (106).
- Pizzerias (105).

Limitations of the IBA Data Base

Miles notes the following limitations, among others, of the IBA data base:

- Data on individual sales may be flawed as a result of circumstances such as misinterpretation of some data items, inaccurate reporting by source, data entry errors, and so forth.
- Location of business is given only in terms of general geographic area.
- Data are useful primarily for statistical purposes (averages, ranges, correlations, etc.) rather than for direct comparison of individual sales.

In addition to the above limitations, the IBA transactions are spread over a time period in excess of 10 years. The extent of this limitation is discussed in the following section.

How Does Business Value Vary with Time?

The IBA addressed the significance of the time of the sale by correlating value ratios with the date of sale. Specifically, they performed a linear regression of the price/earnings ratio ("earnings" as defined in Exhibit 33–1) on date of sale for the years 1982 through 1991. They also regressed the price/gross sales ratio on the date of sale for the same years. The results of this exercise show that "price to net and price to gross ratios of closely held businesses sold during the period 1982 through 1991 show essentially zero correlation with date of sale."[1]

---

[1]Raymond C. Miles, "Business Appraising in the Real World: Evidence from the IBA Market Data Base," presentation to The Institute of Business Appraisers 1992 National Conference, February 6–7, 1992 in Orlando, Florida.

From the results of the above exercise, the following conclusion is stated:

> The variation of business value with time does not appear to be significant in comparison with other influences affecting business value. Consequently, there is no need to restrict choice of "comparables" to sales within the very recent past.[2]

However, the above conclusion may be misleading. Often, important information contained in subsets of data is masked by analyzing the data only on a mass basis. This phenomenon is particularly true of linear regression statistics. In this case, two of the significant data subsets that are masked are (1) time periods that are characterized by significantly different economic circumstances, such as interest rates and the availability of capital and (2) differing patterns of pricing of the businesses over time among different industry groups.

The above suggests further study. For example, if one compared the average value ratios during the period of highest capital costs with the ratios during the periods of lowest capital costs, or made comparisons between different phases of the economic cycle (recession versus expansion), one would be surprised if there were not differences. (One would need to be careful, however, in analyzing terms of sale, because sellers tend to counter high interest rates with "creative financing," a euphemism for a discount in the form of a contract for a larger balance, for a longer time, and further below general market interest rate levels.)

It is also reasonable to believe that value ratios for industry groups tend to rise and fall with the relative popularity of investing in different industry groups at different times.

One leading restaurant broker once told us that average value ratios (such as price to gross sales) dropped fully a third within a six-month period in his market due to a combination of tight and expensive financing and some detrimental publicity regarding restaurant investments.

We are not suggesting that if recent transactions are not available, older transactions are useless. We believe that there is some stability to ranges of value ratios that persist over time. However, we believe that value ratios from transactions from periods of different conditions need to be adjusted to reflect differences between those conditions and current conditions as one factor in estimating where within the long-term range the value ratio for the subject transaction should fall.

The data are useful in that they seem to contain one fairly important implication: over the decade 1982 through 1991, they do not show any long-term secular trend either upward or downward in the overall levels of value ratios.

How Is Price Affected by Terms?

The IBA addressed the significance of terms by correlating value ratios with the percentage down payment. They regressed the value ratios on the down payment expressed as a percentage of the price. The results of

---

[2]Ibid.

this exercise show that "the correlation between price to net ratio and down payment is negligible, and the correlation between price to gross ratio and down payment is very low."[3]

From the results of this exercise, the following conclusion is stated:

Terms of payment can usually be neglected as a consideration when appraising closely held businesses.[4]

It is also noteworthy that the above conclusion may be misleading if taken as a stand-alone statement without reference to the very limited study to which it actually applies. There are at least a half dozen significant elements in the "terms of payment" that influence the price of a small business or professional practice sale:

1. Down payment percentage.
2. Length of contract payout.
3. Extent to which contract payout is fixed or dependent on contingencies.
4. Interest rate (especially relative to market rates at the time of the transaction).
5. Strength of contract, collateral, covenants, and remedies in case of default.
6. Other consideration (employment contracts, covenants not to compete, and so on).

Again, further study is warranted. It would be surprising if a multiple regression (or some other statistical approach) that reflected all the above factors would not reveal differences in price reflecting differences between cash versus various types of terms. (See Chapter 19, "Tradeoff between Cash and Terms.")

Bizcomps™

A potentially promising recent development is a data base published in a series of books called *Bizcomps*™.[5] There are three geographical editions: Western, Central, and Eastern. The present plan is to update each geographical edition annually. Between editions, updated transaction information is available by SIC code from the publisher, Jack R. Sanders, (619) 457-0366, for a fee.

A sample page from the Bizcomps™ 1992 Central Edition is shown as Exhibit 33–2. A summary of the averages of certain parameters from that edition is shown as Exhibit 33–3.

In addition to a listing of all sales in the data base, the book provides the following breakdowns:

---

[3]Ibid.

[4]Ibid.

[5]*Bizcomps*™, by Jack R. Sanders (San Diego: Asset Business Appraisal, 1992).

Exhibit 33–2

ALL BUSINESSES IN DATA BASE

File: SALE.BASE.CENTR
Report: CENTRAL STATES

SBIC BUS TYPE	ASK PR	ANN GR	ADJ NET	SALE DATE	SALE PR	% DOWN	TERMS	SALE/GR	SALE/NET	RENT/SALES	FF&E	AREA
0782 Office Plant Leasing	310	1,200	200	Oct 90	250	100%	N/A	.21	1.2	2%	100	Central Texas
0782 Landscape Nursery	165	507	98	Aug 87	165	76%	N/A @ 8%	.33	1.7	N/A	N/A	Brentwood, TN
1711 Contr-Htg & AC	59	452	79	Jun 90	59	73%	7 yrs @ 10%	.13	.7	1%	30	New Glarus, Wisconsin
1711 Contr-Plumb Htg & AC	66	135	48	Apr 90	36	80%	6 Mos @ 10%	.34	.8	3.0%	19	NW Arkansas
1742 Contr-Asbestos Removal	1,186	1,863	534	Apr 91	1,186	33%	5 Yrs-Earno	.64	2.2	1%	95	Southern Wisconsin
1751 Mfg-Cabinets	35	94	47	Dec 91	28	64%	6 Yrs @ 10%	.30	.6	5.7%	15	Dallas/Fort Worth
2022 Food Processor-Cheese	1,144	5,068	167	Nov 91	1,144	100%	N/A	.23	6.9	.4%	560	Southern Wisconsin
2097 Mfg-Ice	450	435	150	Oct 90	425	100%	N/A	.98	2.8	N/A	88	Central Missouri
2396 Silk Screen Printing	430	1,841	82	Mar 92	338	100%	N/A	.18	4.1	1.2%	159	Des Moines, IA
2431 Mfg-Millwork	234	240	95	Mar 91	165	49%	5 Yrs @ 9%	.69	1.7	N/A	65	Des Moines, IA
2515 Mfg-Mattresses	172	635	(38)	May 91	152	26%	N/A	.24	0.0	9.1%	10	Madison, Wisconsin
2741 Publication	25	91	12	Feb 91	25	100%	N/A	.27	2.1	3%	N/A	Minneapolis, MN
2741 Publication	67	55	(33)	Sep 88	61	41%	3 Yrs @ 11%	1.11	1.8	N/A	N/A	Brentwood, TN
2751 Printing Shop	85	94	32	Jul 90	85	12%	4 Yrs @ 11%	.90	2.7	10.5%	45	Madison, Wisconsin
2752 Printing Shop	2,900	3,800	725	Jan 92	2,900	50%	10 Yrs @ 10	.76	4.0	2.5%	N/A	Cincinnati, OH
2752 Printing Shop	850	1,283	283	Jul 91	761	71%	10 Yrs @ 9	.59	2.7	N/A	443	Brentwood, TN
2752 Printing Shop	165	250	45	Jan 91	155	65%	5 Yrs @ 10%	.62	3.4	N/A	25	Cincinnati, OH
2752 Printing Shop	125	230	48	Oct 90	105	25%	7 Yrs @ 10%	.46	2.2	3%	75	St. Paul, MN
2752 Printing Shop	226	500	72	May 90	214	71%	N/A	.43	3.0	N/A	50	Cincinnati, OH
2752 Printing Shop	50	80	25	Mar 90	50	40%	5 Yrs @ 10%	.62	2.0	4.5%	35	Dallas/Fort Worth
2752 Printing Shop	150	200	65	Sep 89	129	100%	N/A	.64	2.0	N/A	35	Brentwood, TN
2752 Printing Shop	125	276	52	Sep 88	125	32%	N/A	.45	2.4	N/A	25	Nolensville, TN
2752 Printing Shop	50	70	18	Oct 86	36	42%	3 Yrs @ 10%	.51	2.0	N/A	8	Nashville, TN
2791 Graphics & Art Work	120	150	20	Jan 87	50	100%	N/A	.33	2.5	N/A	22	Nashville, TN
3082 Mfg-Plastic Extruder	385	500	108	Mar 91	325	44%	5 Yrs @ 10%	.65	3.0	4%	200	Minneapolis, MN
3441 Mfg-Structural Steel	975	1,700	600	Aug 90	1,125	54%	N/A	.66	1.9	N/A	200	Cincinnati, OH
3443 Mfg-Pressure Vessels	1,410	4,955	478	Oct 90	810	50%	5 Yrs @ 10%	.16	1.7	1%	553	Houston, TX
3444 Mfg-Drain Gutters	194	500	85	May 90	149	42%	7 Yrs @ 10%	.30	1.8	1.3%	95	Dallas/Fort Worth
3499 Mfg-Trailer Parts	10,358	27,218	4,443	Jun 89	10,358	67%	N/A	.38	2.3	.3%	2,28	Dallas/Fort Worth
3569 Mfg-Service Equipment	248	820	130	Feb 91	225	40%	10 Yrs @ 10	.27	1.7	4%	100	Minneapolis, MN
3589 Mfg-Office Signs	398	820	130	Feb 91	375	40%	10 Yrs @ 10	.46	2.9	N/A	100	Nashville, TN
3599 Mfg-Machine Shop	375	648	112	Jul 90	375	30%	5 Yrs @ 10%	.62	3.3	4%	150	Minneapolis, MN
3600 Mfg-Small Parts	600	5,000	525	Jan 92	495	100%	N/A	.10	.9	N/A	150	La Vergne, TN
3711 Mfg-Auto Body Parts	1,640	2,400	560	Jul 91	1,463	82%	5 Yrs @ 8%	.61	2.6	N/A	150	Cincinnati, OH
3724 Aircraft Parts Repair	90	130	53	Oct 89	74	100%	N/A	.57	1.4	N/A	20	Antioch, TN
3724 Aircraft Engine Repair	58	126	31	Sep 87	58	35%	3 Yrs @ 10%	.46	1.9	N/A	8	Nashville, TN
3993 Sign Manufacturer	155	197	61	Mar 91	155	25%	5 Yrs @ 10%	.79	2.5	3%	71	Minneapolis, MN
3993 Sign Manufacturer	265	950	90	Jan 91	200	20%	N/A	.21	2.2	5%	225	Minneapolis, MN
3993 Sign Manufacturer	194	500	70	Mar 90	184	59%	5 Yrs @ 10%	.37	2.6	N/A	30	Cincinnati, OH
3995 Mfg-Burial Vaults	111	130	N/A	Jul 91	73	100%	N/A	.56	0.0	N/A	60	Des Moines, IA
3999 Mfg-Silk Flowers	160	159	91	Jan 92	135	33%	5 Yrs @ 0%	.85	1.5	5.4%	37	Dallas/Fort Worth
4119 Ambulance Service	375	834	140	Sep 91	325	77%	7 Yrs @ 10%	.40	2.3	N/A	200	Brentwood, TN
4119 Limousine Service	300	307	55	Mar 90	270	100%	N/A	.88	4.9	N/A	10	Brentwood, TN
4121 Taxi Cab Fleet	252	466	139	Mar 92	229	50%	1 Yr @ 0%	.49	1.6	1%	229	Dallas/Fort Worth
4121 Taxi Cab Fleet	112	355	112	Jan 92	108	52%	1 Yr @ 0%	.30	1.0	1%	108	Dallas/Fort Worth
4121 Taxi Cab Fleet	224	519	198	Dec 91	180	27%	1 Yr @ 0%	.35	.9	1%	180	Dallas/Fort Worth
4121 Taxi Cab Fleet	210	497	162	Feb 91	150	25%	1 Yr @ 0%	.30	.9	1%	150	Dallas/Fort Worth
4339 Record Destruction Servi	155	147	60	Jan 90	158	47%	5 Yrs @ 10%	1.07	2.6	N/A	30	Cincinnati, OH
4424 Freight Forwarding	480	1,374	100	Dec 91	130	5%	Assume Debt	.09	1.2	1.6%	44	Dallas/Fort Worth
4724 Travel Agency	43	360	15	Aug 91	21	100%	N/A	.06	1.4	10.6%	20	Dallas/Fort Worth

SOURCE: *Bizcomps*tm, 1992 Central Edition, p. 13. Used with permission.

- Businesses sold with terms.
- Businesses sold for cash.
- Businesses sold for under $100K.
- Businesses sold for over $500K.
- Businesses sold for over 2 times "profit."
- Fifteen industry groupings.

The 1992 Central edition contained 299 transactions contributed by 16 business brokers. Jack advised me that he expected to have over 1,300 transactions in the three editions combined for 1993.

The 1992 Central edition of Bizcomps™ contains some interesting analysis, portions of which are abstracted in Exhibit 33–4.

Exhibit 33–3

CENTRAL STATES
SUMMARY OF SALE DATA

Item	Actual Sale /Ask Price	Actual Sale /Gross Sales	ActualSale /True Net	Average Dn Pay	Average Percent Rent
All Businesses	82.1%	.41	1.9	59%	7.2%
All Businesses Net Prof Over 2.0	87.7%	.54	2.7	58%	8.1%
Businesses Sold For Terms	85.7%	.42	1.9	43%	7.0%
Businesses Sold For Cash	69.9%	.36	1.8	100.0%	7.9%
Businesses Sold For Under $100K	72.0%	.36	1.6	60%	8.3%
Businesses Sold For Over $500K	89.6%	.52	2.9	58%	3.2%
Food Services	71%	.32	1.7	60%	9.0%
All Retail Bus.	67%	.23	1.6	62%	12.0%
Service Business	83%	.58	2.1	59%	8.0%
Service Business Net Prof Over 2.0	89%	.69	2.8	57%	10.0%
Manufacturing	94%	.45	2.5	58%	3.4%
Whsle/Distr	74%	.37	2.0	51%	3.4%
Printing	95%	.59	2.5	58%	4.7%
Transportation	86%	.56	1.9	55%	1.0%
Restr & Fast Food	72%	.32	1.8	51%	9.3%
Deli's	75%	.36	1.4	68%	9.6%
Cocktail Lounges	71%	.36	1.6	70%	12.3%
Mini-Marts	75%	.14	1.3	91%	2.8%
Food Markets	78%	.16	1.7	74%	N/A
Coin Laundries	76%	.91	2.2	64%	21.0%
Dry Cleaners	87%	.74	2.8	61%	9.0%
Video Tape Rental	83%	.70	1.9	72%	16.0%

SOURCE: *Bizcomps*™, 1992 Central Edition, p. 11. Used with permission.

Exhibit 33–4

ANALYSIS OF SELECTED BUSINESS SALE DATA

The business sales surveyed here have been grouped first in total by Small Business Industry Code (SIC) and then sorted into a number of more meaningful groups.

The first sub-group is by type of sale. Those businesses that sold for all cash were separated from those sold with terms. 26% percent of the businesses surveyed actually sold for cash. It is not known how many of those businesses were marketed as "cash only" sales, or were converted to a cash sale at some point during the transaction. In general, business brokers will do everything possible to avoid marketing a business as an all cash sale. It has a very negative effect on the buyer's perception of the business.

The significant statistic here is that businesses sold with terms sold for an average of 86% of listed sale price while those that sold for cash sold for 70% of listed sale price. On the average, businesses that sold for all cash appear to have been discounted 16% more than those business sold on a terms basis. This discount is appropriate when you consider the general lack of strong collateral for seller provided financing and that the buyer always has the alternative of purchasing a larger, more leveraged business.

The second sub-group is by profitability. All businesses in the data base are compared with only the businesses that sold for more than 2.0 times True Net Profit. This group of businesses had a Price to Gross Sales ratio that was 13% higher than of all businesses in the data base. The same comparison was made of all Service Businesses in the data base to those Service Businesses that sold for more than 2.0 times True Net Profit. The Service Businesses Sale Price to Gross Sales ratio was 11% higher than that of all Service Businesses in the data base.

This comparison confirms that gross sales multipliers are generally poor indicators of business value. Methods that use some form of profits are much more reliable. Future studies will have more comparisons of this nature as the data base increases.

The third sub-group is by the size of the sale. Businesses that sold for under $100,000 (179) and businesses that sold for over $500,000 (15) have been separated from the rest of the data base and their characteristics compared.

Substantial differences appear. Sale Price to Gross Sales Ratios are 44% greater for the businesses that sold for over $500,000. The Average Sale Price to True Net Profit are nearly twice as large for the larger businesses as well. They also sold for almost 18% more of their asking prices and they had Rent to Gross Sales Percentages about one third of the percentages for smaller businesses.

In general, these ratios confirm what one might suspect--that larger businesses are more profitable, pay less rent and sell for much higher (by ratio) prices than do smaller businesses.

The fourth sub-group is by the type of business. The larger categories are Food Service, Retail, Service, Manufacturing, and Wholesale/Distribution. Significant differences appear in the Sale Price/Gross Sales ratios although the Sale Price/True Net Profit ratios remain relatively constant. The Sale Price/Gross Sales ratios are Food Service (.32), Retail (.23), Service (.58), Manufacturing (.45), and Wholesale/Distribution (.37), while the Sale Price/True Net Profit ratios are (1.7), (1.6), (2.1), (2.5), and (2.0) respectively.

Their averages are as follows:

Item	Actual Sale /Ask Price	Actual Sale /Gross Sales	Actual Sale /True Net	Average Down Pmt.	Average Percent Rent
Food Service	71%	.32	1.7	60%	9.0%
Retail Businesses	67%	.23	1.6	62%	12.0%
Service Businesses	83%	.58	2.1	59%	8.0%
Manufacturing	94%	.45	2.5	58%	3.4%
Whsle/Distr.	74%	.37	2.0	51%	3.4%

SOURCE: *Bizcomps*tm, 1992 Central Edition, pp. 7-9. Used with permission.

Geneva Business Sale Data Base

Geneva acts as an intermediary in the sale of businesses primarily in the range of $500,000 to $20 million in value, most in the lower half of that range. As an example of the data that they collect and preserve, they provided us with transaction information on 14 sales of manufacturing companies, shown as Exhibit 33–5.

It is interesting to note that, even though the average size of the companies is considerably larger than the typical small business discussed in this book, only 5 of the 14 sales were structured as stock sales, the rest being asset sales. It is also interesting that not a single one of the 14 sold for all cash, and that slightly over half (8 of 14) included in the "price" a contingency in the form of an earnout. It is also interesting to note the wide discrepancies (both ways) between the total sale price and the estimated fair market value based on information prior to the sale.

The UBI Business Sale Data Base

With over 25 years in the field of business brokerage, United Business Investments (UBI) has long been aware of the need to arrive at a method of valuing companies on a basis other than standard methods relative to stated earnings. As a result of the discretionary variations reflected in small companies' income statements, a method tied to a more closely structured financial basis, gross revenue, was found to much better serve as a point of comparison for businesses in similar industries.

The UBI business sale data base, known as "Analyx," is compiled from all the sales of businesses consummated by the brokerage offices that are members of the UBI franchise business brokerage system. The material in the data base is available only to UBI franchisees.

Description of the UBI Data Base

The following data are entered for each transaction:

1. Listing price.
2. Sale price.
3. Down payment.
4. Volume (gross revenue).

The listing and sale price in "Analyx" do not reflect either inventory or real property. From the above data, the following ratios are calculated for each category:

1. The historical ratio of sale price to gross revenue.
2. The current ratio of sale price to gross revenue.
3. An indication of the trend of sale price from the historical value to the current value.

Exhibit 33–5

THE GENEVA COMPANIES
Extract from Database of Companies Sold

Information from Valuation Prior to Sale

Co.	Est FMV	Sales	EBIT	Pretax	Equity
		-----	Recast	-----	
A	300	750	66	100	145
B	800	1,300	207	207	507
C	500	2,000	108	107	422
D	1,300	3,200	317	317	1,180
E	500	1,400	283	283	1,141
F	1,000	2,100	227	221	701
G	3,600	6,867	567	567	1,179
H	1,300	5,000	308	157	474
I	3,500	2,400	603	603	994
J	5,000	3,250	883	883	502
K	2,700	6,200	689	689	1,960
L	3,000	6,900	546	546	1,788
M	6,000	7,000	1,279	1,279	1,693
N	5,000	5,800	1,315	1,314	2,835

Information from Sale of Company

Co.	Type	Cash at Closing	Notes, Agrmnts	Earnout	Total Price	Sales	Pretax	Equity	Sales	Pretax	Equity
						-- Recast --			-- Per Books --		
A	Asset	175	200	125	500	750	75	150	750	50	150
B	Stock	275	62	225	562	1,096	100	314	1,096	65	304
C	Asset	518	359		877	1,683	74	361	1,686	43	462
D	Stock	813	500		1,313	2,900	210	1,000	2,900	160	1,000
E	Stock	375	551	500	1,426	2,395	130	76	2,395	193	98
F	Asset	400	1,160		1,560	2,500	287	615	2,500	287	615
G	Asset	2,138	1,004		3,142	5,867	870	2,345	5,867	482	1,578
H	Asset	1,420	1,365	500	3,285	5,853	400	1,370	5,853	253	673
I	Asset	1,185	1,590	750	3,525	2,780	520	1,406	2,780	520	1,406
J	Asset	2,900	800		3,700	2,600	650	900	2,600	290	920
K	Stock	2,700		1,000	3,700	7,200	893	1,900	7,500	389	1,400
L	Asset	400	3,120	250	3,770	7,000	450	1,544	7,000	200	2,044
M	Asset	3,100	1,400	3,000	7,500	6,700	1,300	1,300	6,700	1,200	1,300
N	Stock	7,650	230		7,880	5,700	1,500	2,500	5,700	1,300	2,200

NOTE: Sample derived from smaller manufacturing companies sold by Geneva between early 1989 and late 1991.

SOURCE: Provided courtesy of Geneva Business Research Corporation, Irvine, California.

Results of the UBI Data Base by Industry Category

UBI divides the transactions in its data base into 30 separate groupings. Among the latest 1,000 transactions as of January 1992, UBI president David Scribner considered 28 of the 30 groupings contained enough transactions among companies that were homogeneous enough to produce meaningful averages.

Exhibit 33–6 is a sample page from UBI's Analyx Data Base.

Professional Practice Valuation Study Group

The Professional Practice Valuation Study Group consists primarily of brokers of medical and dental practices.

In 1990, the staff of Willamette Management Associates compiled data on transactions of professional practices from 1987 through 1989. The transactions are from members of the Professional Practice Valuation Study Group, who broker such practices. A summary of the transaction results is shown as Exhibit 33–7, and excerpts from the underlying data are shown in Exhibit 33–8. It should be noted that about 90% of the reported transactions are of dental practices. Willamette Management Associates plans to do an update study in the future.

The Professional Practice Valuation Study Group meets every six to nine months. Information on the group can be obtained from Mike Carroll or John Cahill at Carroll/Cahill Associates, 250 Executive Park Boulevard, Suite 4300, San Francisco, California 94134, (415) 468-3880.

Carroll/Cahill Associates Data Base

Carroll/Cahill Associates (CCA) is a firm that has been assisting dentists for over 22 years in the greater San Francisco Bay Area. They are in the practice brokerage business assisting both buyers and sellers in all aspects of practice sales and buy-in transactions, as well as practice appraisals to establish the fair market value.

The CCA data base was started as a way to track the sales made by the firm. It has developed into a tool that allows them to track trends in the professional practice sales field, such as the average selling price for a specific area, or the average percentage that a selling price is to the gross receipts of a practice. Information such as this reinforces the values used in the evaluation and sales process.

The following are the fields that are tracked in the data base:

- Type of practice.
- Seller.
- Professional corporation/solo/group/partnership.
- Buyer.

Exhibit 33–6

UBI AnalyX

UBI BUSINESS BROKERS, INC. - UPDATE - JANUARY, 1992

CATEGORY	BAKRY	CON MKT	LIQUOR STORE	DRY CLEANG	COIN(3) LAUNDRY
LIST PRICE	80,000	160,800	156,667	164,333	146,576
SALE PRICE	56,667	141,000	150,000	150,000	124,950
DOWN PMNT	36,667	109,000	146,667	43,667	56,364
VOLUME	152,000	398,400	366,000	175,000	99,600
SALE PRICE/ VOL (HIST)	52.1%	37.4%	47.0%	87.5%	125.0%
SALE PRICE/ VOL (CURR)	37.3%	35.4%	41.0%	85.7%	125.0%
PRICE TREND	–	FLAT	–	FLAT	N/A

CATEGORY	COIN VEND	RTL CL ACCSRS	FLORST	GIFT CARD	GEN RTL
LIST PRICE	93,333	71,510	48,333	70,667	63,857
SALE PRICE	64,500	57,974	45,000	61,083	33,857
DOWN PMNT	58,667	29,661	21,333	36,917	29,071
VOLUME	100,000	287,000	126,667	150,667	221,429
SALE PRICE/ VOL (HIST)	76.1%	21.4%	31.0%	41.0%	16.2%
SALE PRICE/ VOL (CURR)	64.5%	20.2%	35.5%	40.5%	15.3%
PRICE TREND	–	FLAT	+	FLAT	FLAT

SOURCE: Provided courtesy of UBI Business Brokers, Inc., Tarzana, California.

- Practice location.
- Valuation or listing price.
- Selling price.
- Terms of purchase.
- Closing date of sale.
- Gross receipts for past two full years.
- Adjusted net income for past two full years.
- Asset value (equipment, furniture, fixtures, etc.).

Exhibit 33–7

PROFESSIONAL PRACTICE VALUATION STUDY GROUP
TRANSACTION DATA BASE AVERAGES

	Count	High Value	Low Value	Median Value	Mean Value	Standard Deviation	Coeff. of Variation
Last Year Cash Flows	98	$414,627	$4,702	$56,692	$76,370	$61,843	80.98%
Last Year Revenues	102	$873,169	$37,420	$161,812	$204,077	$146,245	71.66%
Second Year Revenues	89	$728,689	$33,107	$156,000	$204,166	$135,672	66.45%
Third Year Revenues	72	$607,294	$33,000	$186,631	$213,671	$132,853	62.18%
Fourth Year Revenues	33	$669,562	$72,614	$207,819	$216,677	$121,946	56.28%
Fifth Year Revenues	10	$592,211	$129,172	$244,700	$275,638	$150,502	54.60%
Value of Tangible Assets	84	$164,271	$3,000	$33,500	$40,542	$32,197	79.42%
Debt Assumed	8	$50,000	$3,053	$20,000	$23,717	$17,836	75.21%
Total Purchase Price	107	$750,000	$15,000	$92,500	$117,930	$110,879	94.02%
Value of Intangible Assets	84	$612,746	($14,000)	$47,986	$73,858	$90,618	122.69%
% of Price Paid Down	102	100.00%	–	100.00%	35.54%	39.90%	112.28%
% of Price Financed, 3rd Party	102	100.00%	–	–	29.23%	39.47%	135.05%
% of Price from Buyer	102	100.00%	–	75.00%	64.76%	35.63%	55.02%
% of Price Financed by Seller	102	100.00%	–	27.00%	35.23%	35.63%	101.15%
Seller's Interest Rate	51	13.50%	50.00%	10.25%	10.28%	1.25%	12.12%
Seller's Time Period on Note	57	10.00	1.00	5.00	5.12	1.51	29.49%

Note: There were a total of 107 transaction forms input into the data base. The sales all took place in the years 1987–1989. Data was supplied by members of the Professional Practice Valuation Study Group and was compiled by the staff of Willamette Management Associates, Portland, Oregon.

- Supplies and consumables.
- Goodwill.
- Covenant not to compete (radius + number of years).
- Number of active patients (within past 18 to 24 months).
- New patients per month.
- Number of operations.
- Hygiene days per week.

Exhibit 33-8

PROFESSIONAL PRACTICE VALUATION STUDY GROUP
TRANSACTION DATA BASE
SAMPLE PAGE OF UNDERLYING DATA

Number	Price/ Cash Flow	Price/ Revs.	Price/3-yr. Avg. Revs.	Intang. Price/ Cash Flow	Intang. Price/ Revs.	Intang. Price/3-yr. Avg. Revs.	Type	Specialty	Population	Sale Date
1	2.06	0.67		2.06	0.46		1 a	1	2 c	01/27/88
2	3.49	0.60		3.49	0.43		1	1	2	06/30/87
3	1.35	0.69	0.68	1.35	0.37	0.82	1	2	5	07/01/88
4	1.96	0.68	0.66	1.96	0.35	0.84	1	1	5	06/30/87
5							1	1	4	07/17/87
6	0.45	0.30	0.29	0.45	(0.10)	1.16	1	1	5	07/25/87
7	0.70	0.34	0.37	0.70	0.23	0.17	1	5	5	08/04/87
8	0.55	0.20		0.55	0.00		1	1	5	08/27/87
9	0.77	0.30		0.77	0.07		1	4	5	08/28/87
10	1.67	0.23		1.67	0.03		1	1	5	09/01/87
11	1.62	0.67	0.73	1.62	0.48	0.52	1	1	5	10/09/87
12	2.26	0.68		2.26	0.49		1	1	5	10/23/87
13	1.78	0.92		1.78	0.46		1	1	5	12/18/87
14							1	5	5	02/18/88
15	2.34	0.54	0.50	2.34	0.41	0.22	1	1	5	04/28/88
16	1.20	0.66		1.20	0.45		1	1	5	05/05/88
17	1.34	0.71	0.70	1.34	0.61	0.04	1	1	5	10/10/86
18	1.89	0.73	0.72	1.89	0.53	0.29	1	1	5	11/07/86
19	1.44	0.79		1.44	0.38		1	1	5	09/16/87
20	1.09	1.28		1.09	0.88		1	1	3	01/29/88
21	0.71	0.55	0.47	0.71	0.18	0.56	1	1	5	04/08/88
22	1.36	0.42		1.36	0.00		1	1	1	03/28/88
23	1.50	0.39	0.40	1.50	0.24	0.27	1	1	1	06/14/88
24	1.06	0.48	0.51	1.06	0.29	0.39	1	1	5	05/15/88
25	1.47	0.60	0.51	1.47	0.48	0.15	1	1	1	06/09/88
26	1.11	0.42	0.38	1.11	0.24	0.31	1	1	1	08/11/88
27	8.73	0.67	0.64	8.73	0.27	1.09	1	1	5	12/31/87
28	1.79	0.69	0.71	1.79	0.35	1.04	1	1	5	01/31/87
29	1.21	0.47	0.45	1.21	0.21	0.68	1	1	5	10/10/86
30	2.49	0.81		2.49	0.39		1	1	3	06/01/88
31	1.80	0.86	0.70	1.80	0.66	0.41	1	1	5	07/07/87
32	0.63	0.38	0.40	0.63	0.24	0.33	1	3	4	05/31/88
33	0.99	0.41	0.42	0.99	0.14	0.80	1	1	5	01/31/87
34	0.60	0.45	0.40	0.60	0.04	1.04	1	1	5	04/29/88
35	3.19	0.36		3.19	(0.36)		1	1	3	07/01/87
36	1.28	0.70	0.87	1.28	0.54	0.28	1	1	5	07/15/88
37	2.01	0.61	0.64	2.01	0.54	0.14	1	1	5	08/01/88
38	2.38	0.64	0.69	2.38	0.54	0.20	1	1	5	12/15/88
39	3.25	0.57	0.83	3.25	0.51	(0.19)	1	1	5	08/08/88
40	2.89	0.69	0.69	2.89	0.57	0.26	1	1	3	09/01/88
41	3.47	0.73	0.75	3.47	0.61	0.19	1	1	4	03/31/88
42	1.92	0.67	0.67	1.92	0.55	0.14	1	1	3	04/29/88
43	1.23	0.55		1.23	0.46		1	1	5	09/30/87
44	1.50	0.56	0.56	1.50	0.48	0.06	1	1	5	04/01/88
45	2.95	0.59		2.95	0.43		1	1	5	12/31/87
46	1.50	0.63	0.62	1.50	0.51	0.25	1	1	4	01/02/89
47	1.60	0.50	1.50	1.60	0.31	0.32	1	1	5	01/02/89
48	1.28	0.67	0.96	1.28	0.53	0.42	1	1	3	07/01/88
49	1.76	0.75	1.03	1.76	0.52	0.62	1	1	1	03/01/87
50	0.91	0.42	0.44	0.91	0.17	0.68	1	1	1	07/01/87
51	0.74			0.74			2	2	1	12/01/87
52	0.81	0.46	0.52	0.81	0.22	0.65	1	1	1	09/01/88
53		0.71	0.73		0.49	0.60	1	1	5	01/01/88
54		0.77	0.42		0.52	0.23	1	1	5	03/01/88
55	0.32	0.18		0.32	(0.04)		1	1	5	12/16/86

a Type represents type of practice, e.g., 1 is General Dentistry.

b Specialty is subspecialty of type, e.g., cardiology is a subspecialty of medical practice.

c Population relates to size of city in which transaction occurred.

Exhibit 33-9

SELLING PRICE TO GROSS PRODUCTION
PRACTICES SOLD IN THE SAN FRANCISCO/SAN MATEO AREA

LOCATION	GROSS RECIEPTS	SELLING PRICE	SELLING %
SAN FRANCISCO	$200,000.00	$26,000.00	0.13
SAN FRANCISCO	$172,795.00	$55,000.00	0.32
SAN FRANCISCO	$216,727.00	$75,000.00	0.35
SAN FRANCISCO	$184,915.00	$66,250.00	0.36
SAN MATEO	$935,597.00	$350,000.00	0.37
SAN FRANCISCO	$172,845.00	$65,000.00	0.38
SAN MATEO	$285,397.00	$110,000.00	0.39
MILLBRAE	$125,779.00	$50,000.00	0.40
HALF MOON BAY	$181,909.00	$75,000.00	0.41
LOS GATOS	$105,932.00	$45,000.00	0.42
SAN FRANCISCO	$342,891.00	$175,000.00	0.51
SAN BRUNO	$86,675.00	$45,000.00	0.52
SAN MATEO	$138,820.00	$73,475.00	0.53
SAN FRANCISCO	$260,507.00	$142,500.00	0.55
SAN MATEO	$154,666.00	$85,000.00	0.55
Mountain View	$574,053.00	$340,000.00	0.59
MILLBRAE	$47,179.00	$30,000.00	0.64
MILLBRAE	$254,545.00	$165,000.00	0.65
APTOS	$83,529.00	$55,000.00	0.66
BELMONT	$33,787.00	$22,500.00	0.67
SAN MATEO	$186,065.00	$129,000.00	0.69
LOS ALTOS	$229,479.00	$160,000.00	0.70
SAN CARLOS	$249,150.00	$175,000.00	0.70
SAN FRANCISCO	$155,000.00	$110,000.00	0.71
MENLO PARK	$188,341.00	$135,000.00	0.72
BELMONT	$286,993.00	$210,000.00	0.73
SAN FRANCISCO	$84,000.00	$62,500.00	0.74
SAN MATEO	$200,158.00	$155,000.00	0.77
FOSTER CITY	$234,060.00	$200,000.00	0.85
MILLBRAE	$38,679.00	$35,000.00	0.90
SAN FRANCISCO	$73,128.00	$75,000.00	1.03

Average: $209,148.42 $112,813.71   0.58
Count: 31

SOURCE: Provided courtesy of Carroll/Cahill Associates, San Francisco, California.

The data base's strongest feature is its reporting capabilities. Any of the items that are tracked can be reported. The reports can be as simple as the average selling price, or as complex as the percentage of equipment and goodwill to the selling price, or average gross receipts of a practice. There are a number of ways that the report can be sorted (alphabetical, ascending percentages, etc.) and a variety of ways to retrieve the practice information.

Exhibit 33–9 is a sample report of practices sold in the San Francisco/Peninsula area of California. The report shows the most recent gross receipts for the practice, the selling price, and the percentage the selling price was to the gross receipts. There is a count at the bottom of the report to show the number of practices for this report. Additionally, there is an average line for the remaining columns: gross receipts, selling price, and selling percentage.

This report has not taken into account any anomalies that might occur in a sample of practices, such as the sale of a practice in a death situation or other abnormal situations. Although a "true" report considers all sales, a report can be generated omitting the special situation sales.

IBBA Merger and Acquisition Data

As we go to press, the International Business Brokers Association (IBBA) is planning to launch an effort to collect data on business sales aimed at those above a half million dollars in value. The data base will be known as The M&A Source Sold Company Data Base. It will be compiled by members of The M&A Source, a division of the IBBA, and will be available to members of the division. Information on this can be obtained through Frank Beane, Jr. at The International Business Brokers Association, P.O. Box 786, Wilton, Connecticut 06897, telephone (203) 834-0070.

Summary

This chapter has described and shown excerpts from the data bases we currently know to be available on sales of small privately held businesses and professional practices. The data are far less complete than what are generally available for publicly held companies. Also, since the data are for private companies, it rarely is possible to fully verify the information. Therefore, the data can seldom provide the sole basis for a small company or professional practice appraisal. Nevertheless, there are some expansions and improvements in the available data from a few years ago, and the data often can help to identify some reasonable range of value.

Chapter 34

Valuing Intangible Assets

Introduction

This chapter will present the fundamental concepts and methodologies with regard to the identification and valuation of intangible assets and intellectual properties. These concepts will be developed from two perspectives. The first perspective is the valuation of an assemblage of intangible assets as part of the appraisal of a small business or professional practice. The second perspective is the valuation of a single intangible asset (or of a portfolio of intangible assets) appraised separately and independently of the equity of a going-concern business.

It is important to emphasize that concepts will be developed within our overall framework of small businesses and professional practices. As we will see, there are numerous reasons why the intangible assets of a small business may be subject to appraisal. And, certainly, the existence and value of the intangible assets of the business should be important considerations with regard to the appraisal of any small business. And, just as certainly, the identification and valuation of individual intangible assets is an integral and essential part of the adjusted net worth approach to the appraisal of small businesses and professional practices.

As a result of our overall framework of small business valuation, we will not present a comprehensive treatise on intangible asset valuation. Certainly, the basics of intangible asset valuation will be developed adequately to allow for the appraisal of the typical small business. However, the technical development of some of the more esoteric issues regarding intangible asset valuation (e.g., the quantification of the remaining useful life of specific intangibles) will have to be reserved for other books.

In terms of the outline of this chapter, we will first discuss the fundamentals of any appraisal of the intangible assets related to a small business or a professional practice. Second, we will discuss the legal and economic attributes associated with the identification of the existence of intangible assets. Third, we will discuss the three generally accepted categories of approaches with regard to the valuation of all intangible assets and intellectual properties. Last, we will discuss general concepts regarding the remaining useful life analysis of intangible assets; and we will explain the impact of the remaining useful life analysis on the determination of value of the subject intangible asset.

Fundamentals of the Appraisal

Before conducting an appraisal of intangible assets, the appraiser should document certain fundamental issues regarding the appraisal assignment. This documentation should be in writing and should be clear and complete with regard to each fundamental issue. And this documentation should be agreed upon by the appraiser and the client before the appraiser begins any quantitative or qualitative valuation analyses.

Exhibit 34-1

VALUATION OF INTANGIBLE ASSETS
ALTERNATIVE PREMISES OF VALUE

There are several premises of value that may apply in the valuation of intangible assets. A premise of value states an assumption as to the overall conceptual framework within which the appraiser applies quantitative analysis and qualitative judgment to ultimately reach a conclusion of the definition of value sought. An intangible asset appraisal may result in materially different valuation conclusions for the same asset--using the same definition of value-- depending on which premise of value is applied.

The four most common alternative premises of value for an intangible asset appraisal are as follows:

♦ **Value in use, as part of a going concern.** This premise contemplates the contributory value of the intangible asset as part of a mass assemblage of tangible and intangible assets, to an income-producing business enterprise.

♦ **Value in place, as part of an assemblage of assets.** This premise contemplates that the intangible asset is fully functional, is part of an assemblage of assets that is ready for use, but is not currently engaged in the production of income.

♦ **Value in exchange, in an orderly disposition.** This premise contemplates that the intangible asset will be sold, in its current condition, with normal exposure to its appropriate secondary market, but without the contributory value of any associated tangible or intangible assets.

♦ **Value in exchange, in a forced liquidation.** This premise contemplates that the intangible asset is sold piecemeal, in an auction environment, with an artificially abbreviated exposure to its secondary market.

The definition of an intangible asset appraisal assignment includes the following:

1. A detailed description of the intangible assets subject to appraisal.
2. A description of the specific bundle of legal rights of ownership subject to appraisal.
3. A specification of the valuation "as of" date.
4. A description of the definition of value—or standard of value—that is being sought.
5. A description of the premise of value under which the subject assets are being appraised.
6. The use to which the appraisal is to be put.

Exhibit 34-1 presents a listing and description of the most common alternative premises of value with respect to the appraisal of intangible assets.

The statement of the objective of an intangible asset appraisal, therefore, answers the following questions:

1. What—what particular intangible assets are the subject of the appraisal?

2. With—what particular legal and ownership rights are associated with the subject intangible assets?
3. When—when is the valuation date effective?
4. Who—we are seeking a value of the assets by reference to whom?
5. How—how, or under what conditions, will the transfer of ownership of the assets take place?
6. Why—for what utilization will the appraisal be valid?

While there are numerous individual reasons for conducting an intangible asset appraisal, all of these individual reasons can be grouped into a few categories of motivations to conduct such an appraisal:

1. Transaction pricing and structuring, for either the sale or license (i.e., transfer pricing) of intangible assets.
2. Financing securitization and collateralization, for both cash flow-based financing and asset-based financing.
3. Taxation planning and compliance, with regard to amortization, abandonment, charitable contribution, gifting, intercompany transfer pricing, and other federal taxation matters and with regard to state and local ad valorem taxation matters.
4. Management information and planning, including business value enhancement purposes, estate planning, and other long-range strategic issues.
5. Bankruptcy and reorganization analysis, including the value of the estate in bankruptcy, debtor in possession financing, traditional refinancing, restructuring, and assessment of the impact of proposed reorganization plans.
6. Litigation support and dispute resolution, including infringement, fraud, lender liability, and a wide range of deprivation-related reasons.

Clearly, there are many reasons to conduct an intangible asset appraisal. Of these six categories of reasons, many of the most common reasons that practicing appraisers value intangible assets relate to the litigation support and dispute resolution purposes. Within this category of appraisal purposes, a common subcategory relates to deprivation appraisals. And within this subcategory, there are the following general five types of litigation-related deprivation appraisals:

1. Eminent domain—including municipal condemnations, nationalization of properties and industry, and expropriation.
2. Property damages—including slander, libel, and other forms of damage to a party's name, reputation, or goodwill.
3. Infringement—including the unauthorized use of (and resulting damage to) patents, trademarks, copyrights, and other intellectual properties.
4. Squeeze-out transactions—including any involuntary deprivation of the minority ownership party in an asset, property, or business interest by the majority ownership party (and the associated loss of economic satisfaction by the minority owners).

5. Breach of contract—including the loss of economic satisfaction realized by a party suffering from the breach of a contract to buy or sell assets or to consume or provide services.

In all of these cases, an intangible asset appraisal is usually called for. That intangible asset appraisal will be performed more effectively and efficiently if the appraiser begins the assignment with a clear and complete statement of the purpose and objective of the appraisal.

Identification of Intangible Assets

Appraisers familiar with the intangible asset valuation discipline could easily create a list of over 100 intangible assets commonly found in the industrial and commercial environment. For an intangible asset to exist from a valuation, accounting, and legal perspective, it must possess certain attributes. Some of the common attributes for an intangible asset to be subject to valuation include the following:[1]

- It must be subject to specific identification and recognizable description.
- It must be subject to legal existence and protection.
- It must be subject to the right of private ownership, and this private ownership must be legally transferable.
- There must be some tangible evidence or manifestation of the existence of the intangible asset (e.g., a contract or a license or a registration document).
- It must have been created or have come into existence at an identifiable time or as the result of an identifiable event.
- It must be subject to being destroyed or to a termination of existence at an identifiable time or as the result of an identifiable event.

In other words, there must be a specific bundle of legal rights (and/or other natural properties) associated with the existence of any intangible asset.

For an intangible asset to have a quantifiable value from an economic perspective, it must possess certain additional attributes. Some of these additional requisite attributes include the following:

- It must generate some measurable amount of economic benefit to its owner. This economic benefit could be in the form of an income increment or of a cost decrement. This economic benefit may be measured in any of several ways, including present value of net income, net operating income, net cash flow, and so on.
- It must enhance the value of other assets with which it is associated; the other assets may include tangible personal property and tangible real estate.

---

[1]Professional goodwill as an asset in a marital dissolution property distribution may not possess all the attributes here listed. See "Elements that Create Professional and Practice Goodwill," Chapter 29.

Clearly, there may be a substantial distinction between the legal existence of an intangible asset and the economic value of that asset. An example of this phenomenon would be the new registration of a legally binding and enforceable patent that, upon creation, is immediately and permanently locked in the corporate vault. If the patent is never used in the production of, or the protection of, income, then it has no economic value—even though it has legal existence.

Categorization of Intangible Assets

Generally, professional appraisers will categorize the aforementioned 100 plus individual intangible assets into several distinct categories. This categorization of intangible assets is used for general asset identification and classification purposes and, therefore, it is relevant for purposes of implementing an intangible asset transfer program.

Intangible assets in each category are generally similar in nature and function. Also, intangible assets are grouped in the same category when similar valuation and transfer pricing methodologies apply to that group of assets.

The most common categorization of intangible assets follows:

- Technology-related (e.g., engineering drawings).
- Customer-related (e.g., customer lists).
- Contract-related (e.g., favorable supplier contracts).
- Data processing-related (e.g., computer software).
- Human capital-related (e.g., a trained and assembled work force).
- Marketing-related (e.g., trademarks and trade names).
- Location-related (e.g., leasehold interests).
- Goodwill-related (e.g., going-concern value).

There is a specialized classification of intangible assets called intellectual properties. Intellectual properties manifest all of the legal existence and economic value attributes of other intangible assets. However, because of their special status, intellectual properties enjoy special legal recognition and protection.

Unlike other intangible assets that may be created in the normal course of business operations, intellectual properties are created by human intellectual and/or inspirational activity. Such activity (although not always planned) is specific and conscious. Such creativity can be attributed to the activity of identified, specific individuals. Because of this unique creation process, intellectual properties are generally registered under, and protected by, specific federal and state statutes.

Like other intangible assets, intellectual properties are generally grouped into like categories. The intellectual properties in each category are generally similar in nature, feature, method of creation, and legal protection. Likewise, similar valuation, transfer pricing, and other methods of economic analysis would apply to the intellectual properties in each category.

The most common categorization of intellectual properties follows:

- Creative (e.g., copyrights).
- Innovative (e.g., patents).

Listing of Intangible Assets

There is no such thing as a complete or comprehensive listing of all intangible assets that may be subject to appraisal. As industries and business evolve, new intangible assets are periodically created in the normal course of business operations. Also, as valuation technology improves over time, appraisers become better equipped to identify and appraise previously ignored intangible assets.

Exhibit 34-2 presents a listing of over 100 industrial and commercial intangible assets commonly subject to appraisal. This listing is presented to illustrate the diversity and variety of the types of intangible assets subject to appraisal. It is not intended to present a comprehensive listing or checklist of all intangible assets that may be appraised.

Valuation of Intangible Assets

As was described in Chapter 17, "Asset-Based Methods," there are three fundamental categories of approaches with regard to the valuation of assets. These three approaches to value apply equally to tangible assets and to intangible assets. Of course, within each fundamental category of valuation approaches, numerous different methods or techniques may be used to appraise individual intangible assets.

The three traditional approaches to intangible asset valuation include the following:

- The market approach.
- The income approach.
- The cost approach.

All individual appraisal methods and techniques used with regard to intangible asset valuation are derived from these three traditional approaches to value. For each intangible asset appraisal, one or more of these traditional approaches will prove more or less relevant. Therefore, the appraiser should consider and (if possible) use all three generally accepted approaches during the appraisal of individual intangible assets. Each technique results in a preliminary and (ultimately) a final indication of the value of the subject intangible asset. In the valuation synthesis step of the appraisal process, the appraiser integrates the results of applying the various analytical techniques. This integration considers all of the appraisal approaches and methods utilized, and results in a synthesis of value that indicates the appraiser's final conclusion about the value of the intangible asset subject to appraisal.

Exhibit 34–2

ILLUSTRATIVE LISTING OF INTANGIBLE ASSETS
AND INTELLECTUAL PROPERTIES
COMMONLY SUBJECT TO APPRAISAL

- Advertising campaigns and programs
- Agreements
- Airport gates and slots
- Appraisal plants
- Awards and judgments
- Bank customers--deposit, loan, trust, and credit card
- Blueprints
- Book libraries
- Brand names
- Broadcast licenses
- Buy-sell agreements
- Certificates of need
- Chemical formulations
- Claims
- Computer software
- Computerized databases
- Contracts
- Cooperative agreements
- Copyrights
- Credit information files
- Customer contracts
- Customer lists
- Customer relationships
- Designs
- Development rights
- Distribution networks
- Distribution rights
- Drilling rights
- Easements
- Employment contracts
- Engineering drawings
- Environmental rights
- FCC licenses
- Favorable financing
- Favorable leases
- Film libraries
- Food flavorings and recipes
- Franchise agreements
- Franchise ordinances

- Going concern
- Goodwill
- Government contracts
- Government programs
- Governmental registrations
- Historical documents
- HMO enrollment lists
- Insurance expirations
- Insurance in force
- Joint ventures
- Know-how
- Laboratory notebooks
- Landing rights
- Leasehold estates
- Leasehold interests
- Literary works
- Litigation awards and damages
- Loan portfolios
- Location value
- Management contracts
- Manual databases
- Manuscripts
- Marketing and promotional materials
- Masks and masters
- Medical charts and records
- Mineral rights
- Musical compositions
- Natural resources
- Newspaper morgue files
- Noncompete covenants
- Nondiversion agreements
- Open orders
- Options, warrants, grants, rights
- Ore deposits
- Patent applications
- Patents--both product and process
- Patterns
- Permits
- Personality contracts

- Possessory interest
- Prescription drug files
- Prizes and awards
- Procedural manuals
- Production backlogs
- Product designs
- Property use rights
- Proposals outstanding
- Proprietary computer software
- Proprietary processes
- Proprietary products
- Proprietary technology
- Publications
- Purchase orders
- Regulatory approvals
- Reputation
- Retail shelf space
- Royalty agreements
- Schematics and diagrams
- Securities portfolios
- Security interests
- Shareholder agreements
- Solicitation rights
- Stock and bond instruments
- Subscription lists
- Supplier contracts
- Technical and specialty libraries
- Technical documentation
- Technology
- Technology sharing agreements
- Title plants
- Trade secrets
- Trained and assembled workforce
- Trademarks and trade names
- Training manuals
- Unpatented technology
- Use rights--air, water, land
- Work in process

We will first describe the three basic approaches to intangible asset valuation. Then we will discuss several specific methodologies within each approach. Last, we will present several caveats that appraisers should be mindful of when reaching a valuation synthesis and conclusion with regard to intangible assets.

Market Approach

The market approach provides a systematic framework for estimating the value of an intangible asset based on an analysis of actual sale or transfer transactions of intangible assets that are reasonable guideline comparatives to the subject asset.

This approach requires comparing the intangible asset being studied with guideline intangible assets that have been listed for sale or have been sold in their appropriate primary or secondary markets. Correlations between actual sale transaction prices are also examined.

Factors that are considered include:

- The income-generating capacity of the guideline intangible assets.
- The markets served by the guideline asset.
- The historical and expected prospective return on investment earned by the guideline asset.
- The historical age and the expected remaining useful life of the guideline asset.
- The time of the sale.
- The degree of—and the future risk of—obsolescence of the guideline intangible asset (including physical, functional, technological, and economic).
- Special terms and conditions of the sale (such as special seller financing, an earn-out agreement, noncompete agreement, and so on).

These factors are analyzed discretely for each comparable intangible asset transaction and the data are adjusted as appropriate.

Generally speaking, it is difficult for appraisers to practically use the market approach to value most intangible assets. This is true for several reasons. First, intangible assets often are not sold separately from other business assets. In other words, they are sold as part of a mass assemblage of income-producing (tangible and intangible) business assets. Therefore, the appraiser faces the problem of allocating a lump-sum market transaction price among all of the assets transferred—including the specific guideline intangible asset. Second, much more than in the case of transactions involving the sale of real estate or tangible personal property, buyers and sellers of intangible assets tend to keep actual transactional data very proprietary. So, appraisers face difficulty in obtaining, verifying, and confirming data on the actual terms of arm's-length sales of intangible assets. Last, the appraiser also faces the challenge of data purification and cash equivalency analysis. That is, even if the guideline intangible asset was sold without any accompanying fixed assets, there are often short-term servicing agreements and long-term noncompete agreements that accompany the transfer of intangible assets. And if there is an earn-out or other payment terms (as is often the case with the transfer of intangible assets), the appraiser has to perform a cash equivalency analysis to estimate the actual guideline transaction price to be used for further analysis.

Nonetheless, most appraisers would agree that—when it can be used—the market approach is the best method to use to estimate the value of an intangible asset. It is equally true for intangible assets as for tangible assets that an actual and active secondary market provides the best indicator of value for any asset, property, or business interest. Of course, this assertion assumes that a secondary transfer market exists, that it is sufficiently active, and that the appraiser can obtain verifiable pricing data regarding the actual asset transfers.

Some intangible assets do lend themselves very well to an application of the market approach. These would include situations where there are often "naked sales" of intangibles within an industry. A naked sale occurs when the subject intangible asset is sold "naked"—or separately and independently from any other tangible assets or intangible assets. For example, in the financial institutions industry, bank "core deposit" accounts, loan portfolios, credit card portfolios, mortgage servicing rights, and trust customer accounts are often sold separately and independently—in negotiated arm's-length transactions—from the rest of the assets of the bank or savings and loan institution.

In the real estate industry, leasehold interests, possessory interests, air rights, water rights, mineral rights, other development rights, easements, and other real estate-related intangible assets are often bought and sold—in an active secondary marketplace—separately from the actual underlying real estate (and separately from any other intangible assets).

In the aviation industry, airport landing rights (sometimes called "slots" at controlled airports), airline routes, airline reservation systems, FAA licenses, aircraft parking or "tiedown" rights, and airport gate positions are frequently bought and sold—in negotiated arm's-length transactions—independently from the rest of the assets of the going-concern airline business.

In fact, many licenses and permits are sold separately from other business assets. This may include Federal Communication Commission (FCC) licenses, liquor licenses, franchise agreements, territory development agreements, and so on.

Obviously, in industries where intangible assets are sold "naked" from other business assets, in an active secondary market, and where "pure" and verifiable transactional data are available, the appraiser should seriously consider the application of the market approach as one method in the appraisal of the subject intangible asset.

Income Approach

The income approach provides a systematic framework for estimating the value of an intangible asset based on income capitalization or on the present value of future "economic income" to be derived from the use, forbearance, license, or rental of that intangible asset.

Under the income approach to intangible asset appraisal, *economic income* can be defined several ways, including:

- Net income before tax.
- Net income after tax.
- Net operating income.
- Gross or net rental income.
- Gross or net royalty or license income.
- Gross (or operating) cash flow.
- Net (or net free) cash flow.

The income capitalization procedure can also be accomplished in several ways, including:

- Capitalizing current year's income.
- Capitalizing an average of several years' income.
- Capitalizing a normalized or stabilized period's income.
- Projecting future income over a discrete time period and determining a present value.

Quantifying the appropriate capitalization or present value discount rate is an essential element of the income approach.

The appropriate capitalization or present value discount rate should reflect a fair return on the stakeholders' investment in the subject intangible asset and should consider:

- The opportunity cost of capital.
- The time value of money (including consideration of a real rate of return and expected inflation over the investment horizon).
- The term of the investment (including consideration of the expected remaining life of the subject intangible asset).
- The risk of the investment.

The most important factor to remember with regard to deriving the appropriate capitalization or discount rate is that the selected rate must be consistent with the measurement of economic income used. In other words, a before-tax capitalization rate should be applied to a before-tax measurement of economic income. An after-tax capitalization rate should be applied to an after-tax measurement of economic income. An economic income stream representing a return to stockholders only should be capitalized by a rate based upon a cost of equity capital only. An economic income stream representing a return to stakeholders (i.e., both debtholders and equityholders) should be capitalized by a rate based upon a blended—or weighted average—cost of debt and equity capital.

There are many ways to assign an economic income stream to a particular intangible asset. With regard to the appraisal of intangible assets, economic income can be derived from two categorical sources: (1) increments to revenue or (2) decrements to cost. From an appraisal perspective, either categorical source of economic income is an equally valid contributor to the value of the subject intangible asset.

With regard to incremental revenue, certain intangible assets may allow the asset owner (typically an operating business) to sell more products than otherwise, sell products at a higher average selling price (than otherwise), gain a larger market share, enjoy a monopolistic market position, ensure a relatively sure source of recurring customers, ensure a relatively sure source of future business, generate add-on or renewal business, develop new markets, introduce new products, and so on.

With regard to decremental costs, certain intangible assets may allow the asset owner (typically an operating business) to incur lower labor costs, incur lower material costs, incur lower scrap (or other waste) costs, enjoy lower rent expense, enjoy low utilities expense, enjoy lower advertising or promotional expenses, defer the costs to recruit and train employees, avoid start-up costs, avoid construction period interest, avoid interest in an otherwise greater level of receivables or inventory, avoid or defer design or development costs, supply a low-cost and dependable source of financing, avoid or defer software development or ongoing data processing costs, and so on.

Some intangible assets lend themselves very well to the application of the income approach. Such contract-related or customer-related assets as favorable leases, favorable supply contracts, favorable labor agreements, customer lists, and customer contracts would seem to be likely candidates for an application of the income approach. Other technology-related intangible assets and certain intellectual properties are also likely candidates for an application of the income approach. These intangible assets may include patents, proprietary technology or processes, trademarks and trade names, copyrights, and so forth.

Obviously, for intangible assets that generate a measurable and predictable stream of economic income—whether that represents an increment to revenues or a decrement to costs—the appraiser should seriously consider the application of the income approach as one method in the appraisal of the subject intangible asset.

When using an income approach valuation technique, the appraiser must be particularly mindful of the expected remaining life of the subject intangible asset. Clearly, the economic income projection associated with the subject intangible asset should not extend beyond the term of the expected remaining useful life for that intangible asset.

Also, the appraiser should be careful not to double-count the economic income associated with the subject intangible asset during the valuation process. That is, the appraiser must ensure that the same stream of economic income (whether it represents a revenue increment or a cost decrement) is not assigned to more than one asset. For example, the same stream of excess earnings for a particular business should not be assigned both to the firm's patent and to the firm's trademark. Clearly, only one of these assets deserves to be associated with that specific stream of economic income. (The other intangible asset in this example, though it has legal existence, may have little or no economic value.) And the appraiser should be careful to consider only that stream of economic income that associates with the particular intangible asset in the valuation process. To be mindful of this caveat, the appraiser should be careful to assign a fair return on the tangible assets used in the production of income related to the subject intangible asset. This fair return on associated fixed assets should be subtracted from the economic income stream assigned to the subject intangible asset in order to avoid the double counting of asset values during the valuation process.

Cost Approach

The cost approach provides a systematic framework for estimating the value of an intangible asset based on the principle of substitution. In other words, a prudent investor would pay no more for an intangible asset than the cost that would be incurred to replace that intangible with a comparable substitute.

Replacement Cost New

Replacement cost new establishes the maximum amount that a prudent investor would pay for an intangible asset. To the extent that an intangible asset is less useful than an ideal replacement asset, the value of the subject intangible asset must be adjusted accordingly.

The subject intangible asset's replacement cost new is adjusted for losses in economic value due to:

- Physical deterioration.
- Functional obsolescence.
- Technological obsolescence (a specific form of functional obsolescence).
- Economic obsolescence (which is often called external obsolescence).

Physical deterioration is the reduction in the value of an intangible asset due to physical wear and tear resulting from continued use.

Functional obsolescence is the reduction in the value of an intangible asset due to its inability to perform the function (or yield the periodic utility) for which it was originally designed.

Technological obsolescence is a decrease in the value of an intangible asset due to improvements in technology that make an asset less than the ideal replacement for itself. Technological obsolescence occurs when, due to improvements in design or engineering technology, a new replacement intangible asset produces a greater standardized measure of utility production than the intangible asset being appraised.

Economic obsolescence is a reduction in the value of the subject intangible asset due to the effects, events, or conditions that are external to—and not controlled by—the current use or condition of the intangible asset. The impact of economic obsolescence is typically beyond the control of the intangible asset's owner. For that reason, economic obsolescence is typically considered incurable.

In determining the amounts (if any) of physical deterioration, functional obsolescence, technological obsolescence, and economic obsolescence related to the subject intangible asset, the consideration of the subject asset's actual age—and its expected remaining useful life—is essential to the proper application of the cost approach.

Under the cost approach, the typical formula for quantifying an intangible asset's replacement cost is: Reproduction cost new − Incurable functional and technological obsolescence = Replacement cost new.

To estimate the intangible asset value, the following formula is used: Replacement cost new − Physical deterioration − Economic obsolescence − Curable functional and technological obsolescence = Value.

Curable versus Incurable Obsolescence

An intangible asset's deficiencies are considered curable when the prospective economic benefit of enhancing or modifying it exceeds the current cost (in terms of material, labor, and time) to change it.

An intangible asset's deficiencies are considered incurable when the current costs of enhancing or modifying it (in terms of material, labor, and time) exceed the expected future economic benefits of improving it.

Reproduction Cost

Reproduction cost is the cost (at current price) to construct an exact duplicate or replica of the subject intangible asset. This duplicate would be created using the same materials, standards, design, layout, and quality of workmanship used to create the original intangible asset.

Therefore, an intangible asset's reproduction cost encompasses all the deficiencies, "superadequacies," and obsolescence that exist in the subject intangible asset. Many of these conditions or characteristics are inherent in the subject intangible asset and are thus incurable.

Replacement Cost

The replacement cost of an intangible asset is the cost to create, at current prices, an asset having equal utility to the intangible asset subject to appraisal. However, the replacement asset would be created with modern methods and constructed according to current standards, state-of-the-art design and layout, and the highest available quality of workmanship.

The difference between an intangible asset's reproduction cost and its replacement cost is typically the quantification of incurable functional and technological obsolescence. That is, in an ideal replacement intangible asset, all elements of incurable functional and technological obsolescence are removed or "re-engineered" from the subject asset.

An intangible asset's replacement cost is sometimes quantified using a *green-field* approach. That is, the replacement cost of an intangible asset is the cost to redesign and reengineer an ideal replacement intangible asset on the drawing board from scratch—i.e., on a virgin "green field."

Some intangible assets lend themselves very well to the application of the cost approach. These intangible assets are typically used—or used up—in the generation of income for the firm. Examples of intangible assets that may be likely candidates for the cost approach include computer software and automated data bases, technical drawings and documentation, blueprints and engineering drawings, laboratory notebooks, technical libraries, chemical formulations, food and other product recipes, and so on.

Obviously, for intangible assets that are used or used up in the production of income for the firm—and for which accurate replacement cost estimates are available—the appraiser should seriously consider the application of the cost approach as one method in the appraisal of the subject intangible asset.

Remaining Useful Life Analysis of Intangible Assets

One factor that has been mentioned in our discussion of all three valuation approaches is the estimation of the remaining useful life of the subject intangible asset. This estimation (sometimes called "*lifing*" the assets) is obviously important in the market approach because the appraiser will want to select guideline sale transactions where the sold intangible asset has a similar remaining useful life to the subject intangible asset. This estimation is obviously important in the income approach because the appraiser will need to estimate the time period or duration over which to project (and capitalize) the economic income associated with the subject intangible asset. And this estimation is obviously important in the cost approach because the appraiser will need an assessment of the remaining functionality of the subject intangible asset in order to identify and quantify the elements of physical depreciation, functional obsolescence, technological obsolescence, and economic obsolescence.

There are several methods for analyzing and estimating the remaining useful life for intangible assets. The most common methods for assessing the remaining life of an intangible asset are listed below:

1. Remaining legal (or legal protection) life (e.g., remaining term of trademark protection).
2. Remaining contractual term of period (e.g., remaining term on a lease).
3. Statutory or judicial life (e.g., some courts have allowed a "standardized" life of five years for computer software).
4. Remaining physical life (e.g., some intangible assets just wear out from continued use, like blueprints).
5. Remaining functional life (e.g., some intangible assets just become dysfunctional with the passage of time, like chemical formulations that need to be continuously updated).
6. Remaining technological life (e.g., period until the current technology becomes obsolete, for patents, proprietary processes, etc.).

7. Remaining economic life (e.g., period after which the intangible asset will no longer generate income, such as a legally valid copyright on a book that's out of print).
8. Actuarial mortality life analysis (e.g., estimating the remaining life of group assets—such as customer accounts—by reference to the historical turnover [or mortality] of such accounts).

Generally, an appraiser should consider all of these measures of remaining useful life in the analysis of an intangible asset. Also, generally, the shortest resulting measurement of remaining useful life will be used in the appraisal of each intangible asset. For example, it is not as relevant that the remaining legal life on a particular patent is 15 years if the expected remaining technological life on the patented technology is only 5 years.

In any event, regardless of the valuation approach used, an assessment of the remaining useful life of the subject intangible is an important step in any valuation of intangible assets.

Summary

Clearly, there are numerous small business and professional practice intangible assets that may be subject to apraisal. And there are numerous reasons to conduct an appraisal of the intangible assets related to small businesses and professional practices.

Appraisers should have a clear understanding of the purpose and objective of the appraisal before they begin the valuation of an intangible asset. The purpose and objective of the appraisal should clearly specify the intangible asset subject to appraisal and the bundle of legal rights subject to appraisal. The purpose and objective of the appraisal will, in good measure, dictate the appropriate definition (or standard) of value to be used and the appropriate premise of value to be used.

Depending upon the definition of value sought and the premise of value used, appraisers may use a market approach, income approach, and/ or cost approach to value the subject intangible asset. The appraiser will also consider the quantity and quality of available data, and the nature and unique characteristics of the subject intangible asset, when selecting which valuation approach or approaches to use. Clearly, some intangible assets lend themselves more to one valuation approach than to another.

Regardless of which valuation approach is used, the appraiser should consider not only the legal and physical existence of the subject intangible asset but the economic validity of the intangible asset as well. Also, regardless of which valuation approach is used, an assessment of the remaining useful life is an important step in any intangible asset appraisal.

Ideally, the appraiser will be able to form a valuation synthesis and conclusion based upon the results of two or more valuation approaches. In the valuation synthesis and conclusion, the appraiser will weigh the results of the various valuation approaches based upon his degree of confidence in the applicability and validity of each approach with regard to the subject intangible asset.

Selected Bibliography

Cosman, Madeleine Pelner; Thomas Russell Lang; and Marin C. Goodheart. "Comparing Medical and Business Goodwill Components." *FAIR$HARE: The Matrimonial Law Monthly*, January 1990, pp. 3–7.

Dal Santo, Jacquelyn. "Valuation Concerns in the Appraisal of Covenents Not to Compete." *Appraisal Journal*, January 1991, pp. 111–14.

Dezart, James H. "New Turns in the Slugfest on Amortizable Intangibles." *Mergers & Acquisitions*, March/April 1991, pp. 41–46.

Fenton, Edmund D.; Lucinda VanAlst; and Patricia Isaacs. "The Determination and Valuation of Goodwill: Using a Proven, Acceptable Method to Withstand IRS Challenge." *Tax Adviser*, September 1991, pp. 602–12.

Fiore, Nicholas J. "Valuing Intangibles." *Journal of Accountancy*, September 1986, p. 12.

Gehan, Raymond F. "How to Establish a Limited Useful Life in Order to Amortize Purchased Intangibles." *Taxation for Accountants*, June 1986, pp. 356–59.

Henszey, Benjamin N. "Going Concern Value after *Concord Control, Inc.*" *TAXES*, November 1983, pp. 699–705.

Hollingsworth, Danny P., and Walter T. Harrison, Jr. "Deducting the Cost of Intangibles." *Journal of Accountancy*, July 1992, pp. 85–90.

King, Jerry G., and Paul D. Torres. "The Purchase of a Going Concern: Planning for Intangibles." *National Public Accountant*, March 1991, pp. 32–35.

McMullin, Scott G. "The Valuation of Patents." *Business Valuation News*, September 1983, pp. 5–13.

Millon, Tom. "Computer Software Valuation: Don't Be Led Astray by a Quick Approach." *National Public Accountant*, September 1992, pp. 14–17.

Osborne, Philip H. "Amortization of Intangibles." *Business Valuation Review*, September 1991, pp. 127–28.

Paulsen, Jon. "Measuring Rods for Intangible Assets." *Mergers & Acquisitions*, Spring 1984, pp. 45–49.

Reilly, Robert F. "Appraising and Amortizing Noncomplete Covenants." *CPA Journal*, July 1990, pp. 28–38.

———. "How to Determine the Value and Useful Life of Core Deposit Intangibles." *Journal of Bank Taxation*, Winter 1991, pp. 10–18.

———. "The Valuation and Amortization of Noncompete Covenants." *Appraisal Journal*, April 1990, pp. 211–20.

———. "The Valuation of Computer Software." *ASA Valuation*, March 1991, pp. 34–54.

Reilly, Robert F., and Daniel Lynn. "The Valuation of Leasehold Interests." *Real Estate Accounting & Taxation*, Winter 1992, pp. 24–33.

Reilly, Robert F., and Robert P. Schweihs. "The Valuation of Intangible Assets." *ASA Valuation*, June 1988, pp. 16–25.

Russell, Lee C. "How to Value Covenants Not to Compete." *Journal of Accountancy*, September 1990, pp. 85–92.

Schweihs, Robert P., and Robert F. Reilly. "The Valuation of Intellectual Properties." *Licensing Law and Business Report*, May–June 1988, pp. 1–12.

Chapter 35

Valuing Minority Interests

The value of a partial interest in a business or practice may be equal to, more than, or less than a proportionate share of the value of a 100 percent interest in the business or practice.

This revelation comes as a shock to many people, who may have always assumed that a partial interest would be worth a pro rata portion of the value of the total enterprise. To compound the frustration of the uninitiated, it is also true that the sum of the values of the individual parts does not necessarily equal the value of the whole.

How can this be? As the King mused, " 'Tis a puzzlement."[1]

Elements of Control

The following is a list of some of the more common prerogatives of control:

1. Appoint management.
2. Determine management compensation and perquisites.
3. Set policy and change the course of business.
4. Acquire or liquidate assets.
5. Select people with whom to do business and award contracts.
6. Make acquisitions.
7. Liquidate, dissolve, sell out, or recapitalize the company.
8. Sell or acquire treasury shares.
9. Register the company's stock for a public offering.
10. Declare and pay dividends.
11. Change the articles of incorporation or bylaws.

From the above list, it is apparent that the owner of a controlling interest in an enterprise enjoys some very valuable rights that an owner not in a controlling position does not.

Degree of Control

The matter of a control position versus a minority position is not an either/or proposition. Relevant state statutes, a company's articles of incorporation and bylaws, and the way the overall ownership of the entity is distributed have a bearing on the relative rights of minority and controlling stockholders.

Effect of State Statutes

Statutes affecting the relative rights of controlling versus minority stockholders vary from state to state.

---

[1]Oscar Hammerstein II, *The King and I* (New York: Random House, 1951).

Supermajority Vote Requirements. In some states, a simple majority can approve major actions such as a merger, sale, or liquidation of the company. Other states require a two-thirds or even greater majority to approve such actions, which means that a minority of just over one third (in a few states even less) has the power to block such actions.

State Dissolution Statutes. Under the statutes of California, New York, Delaware, Rhode Island, and some other states, minority stockholders enjoy certain rights under some circumstances that minority stockholders in other states do not. Specifically, under certain circumstances, minority stockholders can bring suit to dissolve a corporation. If the suit is successful and the control stockholders wish to avoid dissolution, the remedy is to pay the minority stockholders the "fair value" for their stock. The variations in state law concerning what rights are given to what proportion of ownership can have an important bearing on the valuation of certain percentage interests in some cases.

Effect of Articles of Incorporation and Bylaws

As with state statutes, a company's articles of incorporation or bylaws may require supermajorities for certain actions and/or may confer special rights to minority stockholders under certain conditions. The variety of possibilities is almost without limit. The analyst should be sure to read the articles of incorporation and bylaws (and all amendments thereto) to be sure to understand any factors affecting the minority stockholders' degree of control.

Effect of Distribution of Ownership

If one person owns 49 percent of the stock and another owns 51 percent, the 49 percent holder has little or no control of any kind; however, if two stockholders own 49 percent each and a third owns 2 percent, the 49 percent stockholders may be on a par with each other, depending on who owns the other 2 percent. The 2 percent stockholder may be able to command a considerable premium over the pro rata value for that particular block of stock because of its swing vote power.

If each of three stockholders or partners owns a one-third interest, no one has complete control, but no one is in a relatively inferior position, unless two of the three have close ties with each other, which are not shared by the third. Normally, equal individual interests are each worth less than a pro rata portion of what the total enterprise would be worth, so that the sum of the values of the individual interests is normally less than what the total enterprise could be sold for to a single buyer. However, the percentage discount from pro rata value for each of such equal interests would not normally be as great as for a minority interest that had no control whatsoever.

Each situation has to be analyzed individually with respect to the degree of control, or lack of it, and the implications for the value of the minority interest.

Distinction between Discount for Minority Interest and Discount for Lack of Marketability

Much confusion exists because some writers and appraisers fail to distinguish between a minority interest discount and a discount for lack of marketability. These are two separate concepts, although there is some interrelationship between them.

The concept of *minority interest* deals with the relationship between the interest being valued and the total enterprise, based on the factors discussed in the first two sections of this chapter. The primary factor bearing on the value of the minority interest in relation to the value of the total entity is how much control the minority interest does have over the particular entity.

The concept of *marketability* deals with the liquidity of the interest—how quickly and certainly it can be converted to cash at the owner's discretion.

People sometimes overlook the fact that discounts are meaningless until the base from which the discount is to be taken has been defined. Since a minority interest discount reflects lack of control, the base from which the minority interest discount is subtracted is its proportionate share in the total entity value, including all rights of control. Since a discount for lack of marketability reflects lack of liquidity, the base from which the discount is subtracted is the value of an entity or interest that is otherwise comparable but enjoys higher liquidity.

Even controlling interests suffer to some extent from lack of marketability. It usually takes a few months to sell a company. The relationship between the discount for lack of marketability and the discount for minority interest lies in the fact that, even after discounting a minority interest for its lack of control, it still is usually much harder to sell a minority interest than to sell a controlling interest in a closely held business.

If one is valuing a minority interest in a closely held company by comparing it with values of publicly held stocks, one must discount only for lack of marketability, because a minority interest discount is already reflected in the public stock's trading price.

Exhibit 35–1 graphically illustrates the relationship between controlling interest value, minority interest value if readily marketable, and minority interest value if not readily marketable.

How the Applicable Standard of Value Affects Minority Interests

As discussed in Chapter 3, the applicable standard of value for the vast majority of valuation situations falls into one of four categories: (1) fair market value, (2) investment value, (3) intrinsic value, or (4) fair value. The applicable standard of value is determined primarily by the purpose and circumstances of the valuation. In some situations, the applicable

Exhibit 35–1

**EXAMPLE OF RELATIONSHIPS BETWEEN
CONTROL PREMIUMS, MINORITY INTEREST DISCOUNTS,
AND DISCOUNTS FOR LACK OF MARKETABILITY**

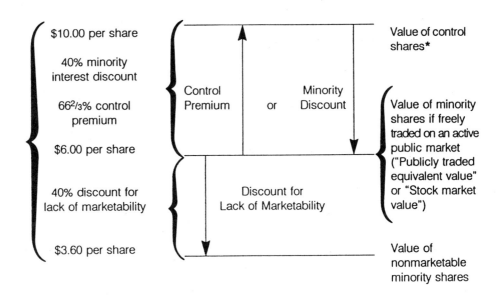

A combined 40% minority interest discount and a 40% discount for lack of marketability equals a total of 64% discount from value of control shares*

$10.00 per share

40% minority interest discount

66²/₃% control premium

$6.00 per share

40% discount for lack of marketability

$3.60 per share

Control Premium or Minority Discount

Discount for Lack of Marketability

Value of control shares*

Value of minority shares if freely traded on an active public market ("Publicly traded equivalent value" or "Stock market value")

Value of nonmarketable minority shares

* **Note:** Control shares in a privately held company may also be subject to some discount for lack of marketability, but usually not nearly as much as minority shares.

SOURCE: Reprinted with permission of Practitioners Publishing Company, Fort Worth, Texas, from *Guide to Business Valuations*, Second Edition, July 1992.

standard of value is mandated by law. In other situations, the choice of the standard of value lies within the discretion of the parties involved.

Fair Market Value

Recall from Chapter 3 that the fair market value standard implies a price at which an arm's-length transaction would be expected to take place between normally motivated investors under open market conditions, without considering any special benefits that might be related to the transaction for any particular buyer or seller. Considering the unattractiveness of minority interests in closely held companies to investors at large, the discount from a proportionate share of enterprise value under the fair market value standard would normally be quite large.

Investment Value

In Chapter 3, we indicated that *investment value* takes into consideration the value to a *particular* buyer or seller. We noted that consideration could be given to the investor's cost of capital, perception of risk, and other characteristics unique to that investor.

When valuing minority interests, one characteristic unique to a particular investor that may be important is the investor's relationship with other owners. Such a relationship might give the minority owner some elements or benefits that otherwise might be available only to a control owner.

Intrinsic Value

Intrinsic value, as noted in Chapter 3, arises from analysis of the characteristics of the investment, such as value of the firm's assets, likely future earnings, likely future dividends, and likely future dividend rates.

The relative importance of these factors, however, may be different for minority valuations than for control valuations. Dividends may take on increased importance for a minority investor because dividends are something the minority investor gets. Assets, on the other hand, may have little or no importance to a minority investor unless the minority investor perceives that the assets will somehow translate into a benefit to the investor. The same thing can be said of future earnings and growth.

Fair Value

As noted in Chapter 3, the fair value standard suffers from lack of consistent definition from one context to another. It crops up most often as the statutory standard of value applicable to appraisals under dissenting stockholders' rights. Such valuations, by their nature, are valuations of minority interests. The need to interpret the meaning of this standard of value from a study of the legal precedents in dissenting stockholder actions in each of the 50 states and Canada poses a continuing challenge to the appraisal profession. Certain precedents have suggested that fair value be interpreted to mean fair market value without a minority interest discount (a proportionate share of enterprise value). However, I cannot emphasize enough that research of the specifically applicable legal precedents is very important in each context to which the fair value standard is determined to apply.

Approaches to Valuation of Minority Interests

There are three basic ways of approaching the valuation of minority interests: (1) a proportionate share of the total enterprise value, or a discount from this value; (2) a direct comparison with values of other minority interests; and (3) a "bottom up" approach of estimating the benefits the minority interest holder will realize over the life of the investment.

Proportion of the Enterprise Value less a Discount

One way to approach the valuation of a minority interest is the following three-step process:

1. Determine the value of the total enterprise.
2. Compute the minority owner's pro rata interest in the total.
3. Determine the amount of discount, if any, applicable to the pro rata value of the total enterprise to reflect properly the value of the minority interest.

The value of the total enterprise should be determined as discussed in the earlier part of this book, with certain possible variations noted in a later section. The proportionate value is normally a straightforward computation, although occasionally there may be complications due to special rights of different classes of partners or stockholders.

The amount of discount to reflect the minority interest can be a matter of great controversy. The degree of control or lack of it, as discussed in an earlier section, definitely has a bearing on the applicable discount, but there is no magic formula for quantifying this factor. Also, the discount is generally lower for stocks that pay cash dividends, or partnerships that distribute considerable cash flow, than for those that do not, but there is no formula to quantify that factor, either. Some guidance to typical discounts and ranges of discounts found in actual transactions is included in later sections of this chapter.

Valuation by Comparison with Other Minority Interests

If the appraiser can find data on actual sales of other comparable minority interests, he might be able to reach a conclusion of value by direct comparison to such transactions, without ever going through the step of estimating a value for the total enterprise. The appraiser can value the subject minority interest using parameters similar to those used for valuing a total company. Such parameters would include, for example, capitalization of earnings, capitalization of cash flow, capitalization of dividends or partnership withdrawals, a ratio of price to book value or adjusted net asset value, and so on. Guidance for the quantification of the market value parameters would be taken from the comparative minority interest transaction data.

Sources of Comparative Data. One source of comparative data could be prior arm's-length transactions involving minority interests in the same company.

There is no generally available source of data on any broad group of minority interest transactions in closely held companies, but there is, of course, a readily available data base on daily transactions in minority interests in thousands of publicly traded companies. Subject to several limitations discussed earlier in the book, guidance for parameters for the valuation of minority interests might be drawn from the prices of publicly traded stocks.

Adjustments for Risk and Marketability. As discussed earlier in this book, if the comparison with public stock prices approach is taken, adjustments need to be made for differences in risk and other factors. The most important of these factors is the lack of liquidity (lack of marketability) of the minority interest in the closely held company, compared with the virtually instant marketability of a publicly traded stock.

This difference in marketability is a more important factor with respect to value than most people who have not had experience in dealing with it realize. The fair market values of minority interests in closely held companies average about 35 to 50 percent less than prices of comparable minority interests in very liquid, publicly traded companies, all other things being equal.[2]

"Bottom Up" Approach

In the two previous sections, we started with something and, in some cases, took a discount or two to arrive at the value of a minority interest. In the "bottom up" approach, we start with nothing and try to estimate what the minority interest owner might sometime realize.

In most cases, the benefits the minority interest holder may realize fall into two simple categories:

1. Dividends or partnership withdrawals.
2. Proceeds realized on sale of the interest.

What this really boils down to is an application of the discounted future returns method of valuation, as discussed in Chapter 13. The steps are as follows:

1. Forecast the expected distributions (dividends or partnership withdrawals).
2. Forecast a time and an amount at which the interest can be expected to be sold.
3. Determine an appropriate discount rate, using the methods and information discussed in Chapter 12.
4. Discount the forecasted distributions and sale price to a present value, using the formula in Chapter 13.

Errors to Avoid

The following points should help the reader avoid certain common errors in the valuation of minority interests and to identify such errors when they appear in someone else's minority interest valuation analysis.

[2]For a detailed discussion of the impact of marketability or lack of it, see Pratt, Chapter 10, "Data on Discounts for Lack of Marketability," in *Valuing a Business*, 2nd ed., pp. 238–62.

The Public Offering Myth

Incredibly, we have frequently seen authors and analysts use the estimated cost of a public offering as a method for quantifying the discount for lack of marketability for a minority interest in a closely held company. The rationale for such an approach is that if the difference in value compared to a publicly traded minority interest is lack of marketability, the discount should be no more than the cost of overcoming that deficiency. The fallacy in that approach is the basic fact that a minority stockholder does not have the legal right to register the company's stock for a public offering. Since registration for public offering is not an alternative available to a minority stockholder, the matter of what it would cost him to do so is not pertinent.

Irrelevant Financial Statement Adjustments

In Part II, "Analyzing the Company," we suggested that in developing the company's earnings capacity, the appraiser might want to remove from expenses such items as Uncle Rusty's consulting fees and the cost of Grandpa's chauffeured Cadillac. At that time, we were contemplating valuation of the entire company, and we were assuming that it was within the controlling owner's discretion to remove such expenses with no significant impairment to revenues. The minority stockholder, however, has no such power, so these adjustments may not be relevant in estimating an earnings base for the valuation of minority interests, unless there is reason to believe that the changes are actually going to be made.

The same general concept applies to adjustments to the balance sheet to reflect the values of excess assets. Unless the controlling person or group is expected to take action to liquidate such assets, their value to the minority stockholders is remote.

Comparison with Real Estate Minority Discounts

Discounts for minority interests in direct investment in real estate, when taken at all, are usually only about 10 to 20 percent below a pro rata proportion of the value of the total parcel. Sometimes people more familiar with direct investments in real estate than with investments in businesses impute similarly low minority interest discounts to investments in business interests.

There are at least two reasons for this disparity in discounts for minority interest between businesses and direct real estate investments. The first is that direct fractional owners of real property normally have the right to partition. That means that if they are dissatisfied with the investment, they can institute action to divide the property and ultimately own 100 percent of a fractional proportion of it. Another reason for the disparity in minority interest discounts is the greater diversity of options available to the control owner of most operating businesses compared to the generally narrower range of options available to the control owners of most parcels of real estate.

Data on Sales of Minority Interests

Very few reliable data exist on sales of minority interests in closely held businesses. The market for publicly traded stocks, on the other hand, provides thousands of reported transactions every day.

Trust and Estate Sales

Some of the most convincing data we have found on actual sales prices of minority interests in closely held businesses were compiled by a bank trust officer responsible for administering estates that owned all or portions of closely held businesses. For openers, he offers the following generalities:

> A number of years of experience has demonstrated that it is extremely difficult to find any market for minority interests . . . despite efforts to do so. . . . On the relatively rare occasions when an offer is made to buy a minority interest, it is almost always for an amount far less than the fiduciary and the beneficiary expect to get.[3]

The trust officer compiled data on 30 actual sales of minority interests. He found that the average transaction price was 36 percent below book value, and he concludes with the following observations:

> Only 20 percent of the sales were made at discounts less than 20 percent. A little more than half the sales (53⅓ percent) were made at discounts that ranged from 22 percent to 48 percent, and 23⅓ percent of the sales were made at discounts of from 54.4 percent to 78 percent.
> It would be dangerous to draw too many generalizations from the survey, but those sales where the discounts were below 20 percent involved, with one exception, purchases from close relatives where friendly relations existed. The exception was the sale by a holder of swing shares who used his leverage well, but still took a 4.3 percent discount. At the other end of the spectrum was the settlement of a three year bitter dispute between two families; the majority family raised its token offer only after threat of a lawsuit, but the price the minority interest took nonetheless represented a 78 percent discount.[4]

Note that the discounts in the foregoing surveys were from book value, not from the value of the enterprise as a whole. Book value, of course, recognizes no appreciation in assets above depreciated net asset value, although, in a very few cases in the survey referenced above, the discounts were computed from an adjusted book value reflecting appreciation in real estate values. We would expect that the total enterprise value would be above the book value in most cases. If that was true in the survey, then the discounts from the owners' proportionate shares of the total enterprise values were even greater than the discounts as shown in the survey, which were from book value.

---

[3]H. Calvin Coolidge, "Fixing Value of Minority Interest in a Business: Actual Sales Suggest Discount as High as 70 Percent," *Estate Planning*, Spring 1975, p. 141.
[4]Ibid.

An update published in 1983 indicates a trend toward even higher discounts when disposing of minority interests in closely held corporations. In the update, a much higher concentration of discounts from book value was at the high end of the range, and the average discount for the two studies combined was approximately 40 percent. The updated study concludes as follows:

> Each of the sales used in the survey involved a combination of factors that made it somewhat unique. To use any of the data, or any classification of the data, as definitive proof of the discount to be applied in a prospective valuation would be dangerous. This should not, however, obscure the true significance of the data, which is that in the actual marketplace, the typical discount is not of token size, but of substantial magnitude.[5]

To the best of our knowledge at press time, no comparable studies have been published since the above.

Public Stock Market Data

The thousands of daily stock transactions on stock exchanges and in the over-the-counter market are, of course, minority interest transactions. The prices per share at which these transactions take place are usually significantly below the prices stockholders receive when an entire company or a controlling interest is purchased.

The following are some examples involving companies that have names familiar to many readers.

Name of Company Acquired	Date of Buyout	Premium Paid over Market[a]	Implied Minority Interest Discount[b]
Golden Valley Microwave Foods Inc.	7/12/91	57.0%	36.3%
BizMart Inc.	7/15/91	39.0	28.1
Bohemia, Inc.	8/15/91	18.5	15.6
Square D Co.	8/22/91	75.0	42.9
Ashton-Tate Corp.	10/14/91	64.6	39.2
WestAir Holdings Inc.	11/08/91	64.4	39.2
Petroleum Equipment Tools Co.	12/04/91	29.6	22.8

[a]The premium paid over market is a percentage based on the buyout price over the market price of the seller's stock five business days prior to the announcement date.
[b]Formula: $1 - [1 \div (1 + \text{Premium paid})]$; for example, $1 - (1 \div 1.570) = 1 - .637 = .363$.

SOURCE: W.T. Grimm's *Mergerstat Review 1991* (Chicago: W.T. Grimm & Co., 1992) and Willamette Management Associates' calculations.

The average percentage discount from the buyout price at which stocks were selling immediately prior to announcements of acquisitions for the years 1980 through 1991 were as follows:

1980	33.3%
1981	32.4%
1982	32.2%
1983	27.4%
1984	27.5%

---

[5]H. Calvin Coolidge, "Survey Shows Trend towards Larger Minority Discounts," *Estate Planning*, September 1983, p. 282.

1985	27.1%
1986	27.6%
1987	27.7%
1988	29.5%
1989	29.1%
1990	29.6%
1991	26.0%

SOURCE: *Mergerstat Review 1991*. Discount calculated by Willamette Management Associates.

A Few Personal Experiences

The following anecdotes from firsthand experiences should cast some light on the realities of the values of minority interests.

Split-Up of the Brothers-in-Law

Two brothers-in-law owned a small service business, which was incorporated. One brother-in-law owned two thirds of the stock and the other one third. There was no buy-sell agreement. The brother-in-law who owned one third left the company and requested that the two-thirds owner buy his stock at book value, either personally or through the corporation. The two-thirds owner declined, but offered to buy at a lower price. The one-third owner, believing that he should receive book value, declined the counteroffer. Ten years went by, during which time the business prospered and grew greatly. The two-thirds owner kept increasing his salary, and the retained earnings built up mountainously. No dividends were ever paid on the stock. At the end of the 10 years, the two-thirds owner offered to buy the stock at what the book value had been 10 years earlier (the price the one-third stockholder had originally asked), and the one-third stockholder accepted.

The Lost Sheep Out in the Cold

One stockholder in a family-controlled corporation has wanted to sell his stock for years. The business is successful, but the stock pays no dividends, and the family member who wants to sell receives no benefit from owning the stock. He lives hundreds of miles from the location of the business operation, and there is little or no social or other communication among the family members. He would accept 10 percent of book value. In spite of repeated efforts, he has been unable to get an offer from anyone to buy his stock at any price.

When the Controlling Interest Is Sold

One corporation had two stockholders, one owning 70 percent of the stock and the other owning 30 percent. The 70 percent stockholder sold his stock for $50 per share. The buyer had no obligation to purchase the minority owner's stock at $50 per share or at any price. The minority owner agreed to accept an offer of $20 per share from the new controlling owner for the remaining 30 percent of the stock.

The foregoing example is representative of several that I know. Many people assume that minority stockholders will automatically receive the same treatment as a controlling stockholder, if a controlling interest is sold. However, unless minority stockholders are protected either by statute or agreement, they do not necessarily receive equal treatment when a controlling interest is sold. This startling revelation has been the genesis of many lawsuits.

When the Buy-Sell Agreement Is Triggered

Many are the times that minority stockholders have cried "foul!" when a buy-sell agreement was triggered. The reason is that the typical closely held company minority stockholder who is party to a buy-sell agreement expects the stock to be valued as a pro rata proportion of the total enterprise value, not at some discount from that amount.

The fair market value of a minority interest is usually less than a pro rata proportion of the value of the enterprise. If fair market value is to be the standard of value for the buy-sell agreement, all parties to the agreement (preferably including spouses of owners as well as directly named owners) should understand the implications of that standard of value.

Summary

Minority interests are not necessarily (or even usually) worth a pro rata proportion of the value of the total business. They are usually worth less because there are many decisions over which the majority interest has control and the minority interest holder does not. The many factors that affect the rights and powers of the minority interest holder must be analyzed and evaluated in each case.

The concepts of minority interest versus control and ready marketability, or lack of it, are two different notions. Minority interest deals with lack of control. Marketability deals with the degree of ready liquidity to sell the interest or lack of it. These two factors should be recognized and analyzed separately.

The applicable standard of value (e.g., fair market value, investment value) may have different implications for the appropriate methodology and relative importance of factors when valuing minority interests than when valuing controlling interests.

There are three broad ways to approach the value of minority interests:

1. Enterprise value less appropriate discounts.
2. Comparison with value of other minority interests.
3. Discounted value of expected distributions and eventual sale proceeds.

The chapter discussed some errors frequently encountered in minority interest valuations. It also discussed some sources of empirical data on minority interest valuations. Finally, the chapter concluded with a few relevant anecdotes from firsthand experiences with minority interest valuations.

Selected Bibliography

Arneson, George S. "Minority Discounts beyond Fifty Percent Can Be Supported." *TAXES*, February 1981, pp. 97–107.

Bolten, Steven E. "Discounts for Stocks of Closely Held Corporations." *Trusts & Estates*, December 1990, pp. 47–48.

Coolidge, H. Calvin. "Fixing Value of Minority Interest in Business: Actual Sales Suggest Discounts as High as 70%." *Estate Planning*, Spring 1975, pp. 138–41.

Curtis, Andrew M. "Discounting Minority Stock Interests in Closely Held Corporations: When and How Much?" *Journal of Taxation of Estates and Trusts*, Spring 1991, pp. 26–30.

Dant, Thomas W., Jr. "Courts Increasing Amount of Discount for a Minority Interest in a Business." *Journal of Taxation*, August 1975, pp. 104–9.

Fiore, Nicholas J. "All in the Family: Determining the Value of a Minority Interest in Stock in a Closely Held Corporation." *Journal of Accountancy*, September 1991, p. 14.

Fishman, Jay E.; Shannon P. Pratt; J. Clifford Griffith; and D. Keith Wilson. "Premiums and Discounts in Business Valuations." Parts I and II. *FAIR$HARE: The Matrimonial Law Monthly*, May and June 1992, pp. 11–17, 14–16.

Harper, John S., Jr. "Minority Shareholders: It's the Cash You Get that Counts: Discounting Expected Future Cash Distributions to Determine the Fair Market Value of a Minority Ownership Interest in a Partnership or Corporation." *Tax Management Estates, Gifts, and Trusts Journal*, November–December 1990, pp. 215–21.

Harris, James Edward. "Minority and Marketability Discounts: Are You Taking Enough?" *Probate and Property*, January/February 1990, pp. 6–11.

Herpe, David A., and Carter Howard. "Minority Discounts Revisited: The Estate of Murphy." *Trusts & Estates*, December 1990, pp. 35–38.

Hitchner, James R., and Kevin J. Rudd. "The Use of Discounts in Estate and Gift Tax Valuations." *Trusts & Estates*, August 1992, pp. 49–56, 60.

Horsman, Steven E. "Minority Interest Discounts on Gifts among Family Members." *Trusts & Estates*, July 1987, pp. 54–55.

Janiga, John M., and Louis S. Harrison. "Valuation of Closely Held Stock for Transfer Tax Purposes: The Current Status of Minority Discounts for Intrafamily Transfers in Family-Controlled Corporations." *TAXES*, May 1991, pp. 309–17.

Lauer, Eliot, and Benard V. Preziosi, Jr. "A Fair Share for Minority Shareholders." *New York Law Journal*, June 1, 1992, p. 7.

Maher, J. Michael. "An Objective Measure for a Discount for a Minority Interest and a Premium for a Controlling Interest." *TAXES*, July 1979, pp. 449–54.

Nath, Eric W. "Control Premiums and Minority Interest Discounts in Private Companies." *Business Valuation Review*, June 1990, pp. 39–46.

Trieschmann, James S.; E. J. Leverett; and Peter J. Shedd. "Valuing Common Stock for Minority Stock and ESOPs in Closely Held Corporations." *Business Horizons*, March–April 1988, pp. 63–69.

Chapter 36

Buying or Selling a Business or Practice

The ultimate objective of the buyer's and seller's valuation deliberations is to arrive at a *price* and a set of *terms* acceptable to both of them. Consequently, this chapter attempts to give equal consideration to the perspectives of both the buyer and the seller. Besides the entity's fair market value (as defined in Chapter 3), these factors bear on the price determined to be mutually acceptable:

1. Special circumstances of the particular buyer and seller.
2. Tradeoff between cash and terms (as discussed in Chapter 19).
3. Relative tax consequences for the buyer and seller, which depend on how the transaction is structured.

All too often, however, price negotiations become an exercise in futility because the prospective buyers and sellers should never have gotten that far in the first place. For that reason, we will step back from the price negotiations and briefly consider the decision to sell or buy that must precede the determination of the specific price.

To Sell or Not to Sell

Ideally, the nonfinancial reasons for selling would become manifest at the same time that buyers would be willing to pay the seller an attractive price for the business. Unfortunately, it is usually true that the desire to sell does not coincide with the timing for the best price attainable. A prospective seller who considers in advance factors that affect the sell decision and factors that affect the price can synchronize his sell decision with conditions that bring a good price.

Reasons to Sell

Common reasons to sell a business include the following:

1. Death of an owner.
2. Ill health.
3. Retirement (or "exit strategy sale"—senior slows down and younger associate takes over).
4. Desire to start a new business or alternate career.
5. Boredom (or burnout).
6. Frustration and/or disillusionment.
7. Disputes among owners.
8. Need for a parent company with the capital and resources necessary to perpetuate the business and realize its growth potential.
9. Poor financial condition and/or losing money.

Several of the reasons are so strong that they may be defined as *compulsion*; they are discussed under "Differing Perceptions and Circumstances of Sellers and Buyers," later in this chapter.

Factors Affecting Price

Some of the most important factors affecting price are the following:

1. Recent profit history.
2. General condition of the company (such as condition of facilities, completeness and accuracy of books and records, morale, and so on).
3. Market demand for the particular type of business.
4. Economic conditions (especially cost and availability of capital and any economic factors that directly affect the business).
5. Ability to transfer goodwill or other intangible values to a new owner.
6. Future profit potential.

(For more detail on factors affecting prices of professional practices, see Chapter 30, "Determining the Value of the Practice.").

Timing of the Sell Decision

When comparing these lists of reasons to sell and factors affecting price, it becomes obvious that the reasons to sell are not necessarily likely to surface at the same time that the business is most ripe for sale in terms of the factors affecting price. Owners who wish to sell their business at the best possible price should consider the following suggestions:

1. Anticipate the possibility of a sale, whether or not one is imminent, and prepare accordingly.
2. Make the sale when the timing is good from a financial standpoint, rather than holding back and risking a forced sale under less advantageous circumstances.
3. Hold off on selling when the seller is convinced that significantly higher profitability is on the immediate horizon, especially if the full potential of the increased profitability would not be immediately apparent to an outsider (which is almost always the case). If this realization does not materialize, however, especially if there is a downturn, it could be a significant loss to the seller.

In some respects, there is an inherent conflict between running the business the way an owner likes on an ongoing basis and preparing the business for sale. An owner typically makes a variety of discretionary expenditures that result in reduced reported profits. It may or may not be possible to convince a prospective buyer to adjust fully for these items when assessing profitability. An owner may do many things his own way when he is operating the business, but this may not make the business most attractive to the typical potential buyer. Ideally, the efforts to sell should be aimed at a time when the business can put its best foot forward.

Some owners find the decision to sell emotionally difficult to reach. Victor Niederhoffer, operating as a broker who finds small companies available to be purchased by larger companies, puts it this way:

It's very threatening to sell your company, perhaps harder than getting married. Some sellers get neurotic and kind of flip out. They let emotion get in the way of facts and analysis.

We're working with one guy who probably ruined his chances of selling his company. Two years ago, he was approached by a company that wanted to pick up his company at book value. Out of a fear of getting taken, he picked out a price out of the air, three times the company's worth. He's left for Germany. I don't think he'll ever sell his company.[1]

Sellers often procrastinate when the timing for the sale is financially opportune, and then they decide to sell later, after the economy, or other factors, have made it inopportune and it is impossible to find buyers willing to pay as much as they would have when conditions were better. If an active owner dies, value almost always diminishes because the owner is no longer available to facilitate the transfer of goodwill to a new owner.

If the owner is confident of a sharp rise in profits, it will almost always be financially beneficial to keep the business until the increased profitability can be demonstrated to a buyer rather than just projected. Concerning the decision to keep or sell a small business, Stephen Einhorn, an acquisition specialist, has this to say:

> **Step I. Determine future profits: If I don't sell the business, what will be the most probable result? . . .**
>
> Step I is the key step in discussions with the potential seller. If his expectations and justifications for his future estimated results differ dramatically from most purchasers' perception of his potential, he probably is not truly prepared to sell his business. An owner who knows that his business is about to improve quickly and substantially would not normally want to sell his temporarily undervalued business.[2]

Niederhoffer cites a case in point: "One company projected $800,000 in earnings for the year ahead, when it had three years of $100,000 earnings. A prospective buyer asked them why they didn't just wait a year to show the $800,000, and then sell. It was a reasonable question."[3]

An article in the *Harvard Business Review* makes the following points regarding picking the right time to sell:

> Timing is everything in selling a company. Here are a few suggestions regarding timing:
>
> Sell when business profits show a strong upward trend.
> Sell when the management team is complete and experienced.
> Sell when the business cycle is on the upswing, with potential buyers in the right mood and holding excess capital or credit for acquisitions.
> Sell when you are convinced that your company's future will be bright.
> Don't sell when the opposite of any of the previous suggestions holds.[4]

---

[1]"Getting Top Dollar for Your Company," *Inc.*, April 1980, p. 84.

[2]Stephen Einhorn, "Notes on the Decision to Keep or Sell a Small Business," *Mergers & Acquisitions*, Summer 1977, pp. 29–30.

[3]"Getting Top Dollar," p. 84.

[4]Charles W. O'Connor, "Packaging Your Business for Sale," *Harvard Business Review*, March–April 1985, p. 56.

Preparing the Business for Sale

One broker offers the following explanation of the need for long-term preparation for the sale of a business:

> In many cases, for reasons of age or health, the owner will find it necessary to sell his business.
>
> When he attempts to sell, his past use of accounting and financial management techniques for the primary purpose of tax avoidance produces the predictable result that he is either unable to sell the business or must sell it at a grossly understated value.
>
> Reconstruction of records: It is possible to reconstruct the financial statements of a small business to show the true net operating income and therefore give an accurate indication of the value of that business. However, such reconstruction aggravates the problem of selling the business at its true value because reconstruction may result in claims for back income taxes and penalties for the owner.
>
> Thus a small business owner must either sell at an understated value or plan a five- to seven-year preparation period for selling, based on accurate financial statements. This lead time is required so that accounting methods can be altered gradually over a three- to four-year period, thus avoiding IRS investigation and so that several years of accurate financial statements will be available to a prospective purchaser.[5]

The previously referenced *Harvard Business Review* article makes the following observation: "More often than not, the successful sale of smaller companies is the result of a carefully orchestrated long-term strategy. Making the strategy work are effective financial planning, internal organization, timing, and valuation analysis."[6]

The following are six suggestions for preparing the business for sale:

1. Have excellent records.
2. Clean up the balance sheet.
3. Have a good profit record.
4. Have the business in good general condition.
5. Have adequate personnel.
6. Get a valuation analysis.

Have Excellent Records

In most cases, excellent records will help a seller to obtain the best possible price for his business. The most credible statements are five or more years of financial statements audited by a CPA firm. The next best are financial statements reviewed by a CPA firm. The next best after that are statements compiled by an independent CPA, including the footnote disclosures that normally would be included in audited or reviewed statements. Internally prepared statements should be done as meticulously as possible and accord as closely as possible with procedures

---

[5]Robert F. Everett, "What Is the Business Worth?" *Real Estate Today*, October 1978, p. 46.

[6]O'Connor, "Packaging Your Business," p. 52.

that would be used if an independent CPA were preparing them. If the company has only income tax returns, good supporting documents should be readily available.

Good supporting schedules of the details contained within line items found on the statements are very helpful. Detailed schedules of expenses are especially useful if items are categorized so that they are comparable with industry averages. The list of property and equipment, and the related depreciation schedule, should be complete and up-to-date.

In general, the material listed in Exhibit 37–2, "Documents and Information Checklist," should be as complete and accurate as possible.

Clean Up the Balance Sheet

By "cleaning up the balance sheet," We mean removing items that a purchaser would consider undesirable. Such items would likely include any nonoperating assets. If the business owns real estate, the seller may be wise to place the real estate in a separate corporation or partnership, charging rent at a market rate to the business or practice that is to be sold. In some cases, the same course might be advantageous for machinery and equipment. Depending on the nature of the business and the potential buyer, the seller may be able to get more for the business itself by keeping the hard assets and leasing them to a new owner than by selling them in a package with the business. (If there is any question about how to handle the fixed assets, the prudent owner will seek guidance from a business broker familiar with the particulars of selling his type of business.)

Many companies keep negative balances in their cash accounts, operating on the "float" provided by checks outstanding but not yet drawn from the account. This practice appears on the balance sheet either as a negative balance in the cash account on the asset side or as an overdraft on the liability side, neither of which looks very sound to readers of balance sheets. The seller should try to have a positive balance in the cash account as of the balance sheet date, even if it means delaying a few payables. Receivables from and/or payables to owners or related parties should generally be removed from the balance sheet.

Have a Good Profit Record

A good profit record is probably the single most important factor in preparing the business to sell for the best possible price. The best record is one of profits increasing steadily each year, with the profitability for the period immediately prior to the offer to sell at, or above, industry averages according to such measures as return on equity, return on assets, and return on sales. Establishing a good profit record may require careful management and relinquishing some hidden perks for a time, but it should be worthwhile to be able to produce a well-documented record of profitability at the time of the sale.

Have the Business in Good General Condition

Like a house, car, or almost anything else, a business should fetch a better price if everything is clean, neat, and in good working order.

Inventory should be current and well balanced. Promotional material should be attractive and up-to-date. Everything should work together efficiently and harmoniously.

Have Adequate Personnel

A buyer is likely to look more favorably on a business if the personnel needed to perform the various tasks are in place, well trained, and working together with esprit. A buyer is likely to discount the price if he faces the chore of recruiting and training new personnel.

Get a Valuation Analysis

A valuation analysis will help the seller determine a range of reasonable prices before exposing the business to the marketplace. He should find out at what prices similar businesses are currently selling. These prices should be compared to their respective revenues, earnings, assets, and other fundamental factors. A complete written appraisal is not necessary for determining a range of acceptable prices. Many business appraisal firms offer consulting services on an hourly or daily basis and provide worthwhile guidance without a full formal written report. The seller should have in mind at least an objectively determined negotiating range before his first serious conversation with a potential buyer or broker about listing the business. In the case of a professional practice, it is prudent to have this completed prior to any potential buy-in by an associate in order to avoid future conflict.

A written appraisal report, however, may be useful by providing more detailed information for the buyer, as well as for some potential sources of buyer financing, if the seller chooses to carry a contract. The expense of a credible written appraisal report may be recovered many times over if the selling price increases over what might be achieved without such a report. (In some cases, a hospital will pay appraisal fees to assist a loyal medical practitioner to exit his practice.)

In any case, whether the valuation work is informal consulting or a formal report, good independent business appraisal work will help the owner to understand the factors that add or detract value, and can help the business to achieve a better price. A recent article recommends regular appraisals:

> Even if a small-business owner is not planning to sell the business, experts believe it is a good idea to have the firm appraised every year or two to learn more about its operation. A professional valuation involves examining the company's entire operation, from scrutinizing financial records to interviewing key managers. The company facets that appraisers consider include management's background and experience, uniqueness of product, diversity of customers, market size, capital reserves, competition, and past and potential earnings.[7]

Even if a lower price is indicated by the independent appraisal, it may make the seller more realistic about the selling price and therefore help facilitate the transaction.

---

[7]Doreen Mangan, "What Is Your Company Worth?" *Executive Female*, November–December 1990, p. 74.

Deciding What to Buy

Some successful entrepreneurs will buy almost anything that comes along if they find it interesting and think the price is right—but not very many of them. Most who will buy almost anything eventually go broke because, sooner or later, they overextend themselves on what turns out to be a bad deal. This may happen several times. (Entrepreneurs are very resilient.) Successful potpourri buyers succeed "on balance": that is, they succeed because some good winners offset the losses from many mistakes.

We do not advocate that most potential buyers take a shotgun approach to potential acquisition targets. We suggest that a potential buyer carefully think out and write down his criteria for a business that he would consider buying, that he diligently pursue businesses worthy of consideration, and that he make an offer only for a business that meets the predetermined criteria. At a minimum, the list of criteria for a potential purchase should cover the following points:

1. The type of business or practice.
2. Acceptable geographic locations.
3. The minimum and maximum size the buyer considers worthwhile and that he is realistically capable of managing.
4. The amount of cash available for purchase. (If outside sources are to be used, the buyer should at least explore the availability of funds from such sources before he goes shopping for a business.)
5. Whether, and for how long, the buyer will need assistance from existing management, and/or the duration and structure of a management transition period.
6. Whether the buyer wants a smooth-running and profitable operation, or a "fixer-upper," an operation currently not doing so well.

With these and any other relevant criteria firmly in mind, the buyer should be ready to screen brokers' listings and companies advertised in newspapers and trade publications in order to develop a list of possibilities for purchase.

Preparing to Make an Offer

Once the buyer has screened potential acquisitions and identified one or a few that meet his criteria, it is time for his own valuation analysis. He may do one on his own or consult with a business appraiser, or he may have the appraiser prepare the whole analysis. His analysis should cover the elements discussed in this book, but will not usually require a formal written report.

In preparing to make an offer, the buyer and/or his appraiser should have available all the documents listed in Exhibit 37–2, "Documents and Information Checklist." Moreover, they should have access to whatever records are necessary to verify any items that may be unclear or in question. If the seller is unwilling to supply enough documentation for the buyer to be totally comfortable with his offer, the buyer should walk away and consider something else. The financial and nonfinancial investment in a business is too high to buy a pig in a poke. Naturally, however, the buyer should be willing to sign a confidentiality agreement with respect to the seller's information.

A special problem arises when the seller and prospective buyer are competitors: should the deal fall through, the seller would be at a competitive disadvantage if the buyer had access to his financial information. We have seen the buyer handling this situation by engaging an independent appraiser to analyze the information, with the independent appraiser keeping most of the details confidential from the buyer until the negotiations appeared very likely to result in a completed transaction.

Buyers almost always expect to improve the profitability of the business they are considering buying. They should prepare, or have someone prepare, pro forma statements, as discussed in Chapter 11, that reflect their expectations for the business under their ownership. The further into the future the buyer can prepare meaningful pro forma statements, the better; but no benefit is derived from extending them to the point where they are completely speculative.

Arnold Goldstein, a veteran small business dealmaker, has this to say:

> When I counsel prospective buyers, I use a *pro forma* profit and loss statement. Before I even allow a buyer to think price, I put him through the exercise of planning his profit profile. Not only does this quantify earnings expectation, it forces the buyer to think through virtually every phase of the business as he would operate it.
>
> To get to that bottom line, the buyer starts at the top with sales and works his way down, through anticipated cost of goods and every last expense. Once he defines, justifies, and verifies each item on his projected P&L, he can measure forecasted earnings with some degree of confidence.[8]

The buyer's appraisal of the business as it stands (which may be somewhat less than the seller's appraisal of the business as it stands) probably represents the floor of a negotiating range, provided that the seller is under no compulsion to sell. A capitalization of earnings or discounted cash flow analysis, based on the buyer's pro forma statements (assuming that they are soundly conceived), should provide the absolute top of a negotiating range.

Conditions in the market for the particular kind of business or practice will determine where in the range an offer is likely to be successful without being too high. The buyer should investigate recent sales of comparative companies or practices and the supply and demand for the particular type of company in order to assess how much, if any, premium should be offered over the value of the company as its stands, before considering any improvement to profits caused by the buyer's efforts. Comparative transactions are very difficult to find. A business broker

---

[8]Arnold S. Goldstein, *The Complete Guide to Buying and Selling a Business* (New York: New American Library, 1983), p. 105.

or a business appraiser may be helpful in this regard, perhaps using transaction data such as described in Chapter 33, "Transaction Data Bases."

Differing Perceptions and Circumstances of Sellers and Buyers

> Value is nothing more than perception, and we each bring to the valuation process our own ideas on what that "right" perception is. . . .
>
> That's what makes the process of placing a value on a business so interesting. So few buyers and sellers share that same perspective.[9]

Frequently, buyers and sellers use different criteria to reach conclusions about a particular business's value to them; each has his own reasons, which are valid under their respective circumstances. Obviously, both must be satisfied, whether or not for different reasons, in order for a transaction to be consummated. Goldstein's experience has led him to be somewhat caustic about the extent to which rationality influences many buyers' and sellers' assessments of their own situations.

> For every knowledgeable buyer or seller, there are five others whose value system is on the blink. They invariably end up wondering about the deal that never was or worse—buying or selling at precisely the wrong price.[10]
>
> Having handled over 1,500 transactions, I can assure you from firsthand experience that the rationality of the numbers seldom sells the buyer, but rather it's what the business does to the buyer's mind. For the small business buyer it's probably 80 percent psychological and 20 percent arithmetic. It may be an ego trip or a certain lifestyle. For the unemployed, the business may represent a tonic for anxiety and insecurity. A seller may simply be too tired or aggravated to continue, or perhaps his energies are directed to a new career.[11]

Assessment of Future Profits and Risk

The overexuberance typical of sellers is exemplified by one more quote from Niederhoffer:

> A buyer is looking for a company that's going to keep growing, but I've never met a seller who doesn't think his business won't be three times bigger five years down the road. And they'll tell you that with unlimited capital their businesses would be tenfold larger. . . . Sellers always believe their companies will grow, but only half of them will. . . . All sellers believe their geese are swans.[12]

There is evidence, however, that buyers also tend to be overoptimistic:

---

[9]Ibid., p. 95.

[10]Ibid., pp. 95–96.

[11]Ibid., p. 103

[12]"Getting Top Dollar," p. 84.

A study by Northeastern University shows that 80 percent of the buyers surveyed responded that they thought they could *improve* profits by 50 percent or more. The results showed a different picture:

55 percent earned less money than their predecessors.

25 percent normally increased profits or continued to operate at the same level of profitability.

15 percent increased profits by as much as 49 percent.

Only 5 percent of the respondents actually increased profits by 50 percent or more within the target date.

> This same lack of objectivity can filter throughout the earnings forecast. The buyer may foresee considerably improved operating margins or reduced expenses. Under this faulty forecasting, any business can show a considerable improvement in profitability.
>
> The accountant will ordinarily have to defer to the client in forecasting such items as sales and margins on the assumption the client should have a better idea of how the business will, or can be operated than will the accountant. The accounting projection is only a projection of the business, but the accountant must be able to assess the competency of the client in planning the forecast. For the first-time buyer, the most conservative approach possible should be adhered to. It is only when the client is well experienced and has a proven track record in the type business under investigation that the accountant can view the projections with more confidence.[13]

Obviously, different expectations of future profits would logically lead buyers and sellers to reach different conclusions of value. The foregoing quotes, however, suggest that both buyers and sellers tend to overestimate future profits. This condition can lead to transactions that are consummated at prices higher than the values that the parties would have estimated if their expectations of future profits had been accurate. The foregoing quotations characterize the reality of the small business market and that more businesses sell above, than sell below, the values indicated if the prices were based on accurate projections of future profits.

The bias toward overpricing is further exacerbated by buyers, sellers, and small-business brokers who tend to underestimate the risk, thus leading to unjustifiably low capitalization rates (that is, multiples that are too high).

Opportunity

As mentioned elsewhere in this book, it's interesting that the classified ads in most newspapers don't list businesses for sale, but rather business opportunities. We know business brokers who adhere to the philosophy that a buyer should never pay more than the value of the business as it stands (which may be less than the tangible asset value). The value of any opportunity would be part of the buyer's profits that result from a judicious entrepreneurial exploitation of the opportunity. We know other

---

[13]Arnold S. Goldstein, *Business Transfers: An Accountant's and Attorney's Guide* (New York: John Wiley & Sons, 1986), pp. 115–16.

brokers who believe that a buyer should always pay more than the tangible asset value for the opportunity that comes with the business.

The value of opportunity per se is a matter for each individual to decide, not a matter that can be financially analyzed. We do not buy state lottery tickets because we are unwilling to accept a 40 cent average expected return for our dollar, in order to have the opportunity for the big win. However, we appreciate the fact that our taxes are lower than they otherwise might be because many other people do choose to buy them, thus contributing large sums of money to state treasuries. In other words, lottery tickets sell at a fair market value of $1 even though that price is about two and a half times their intrinsic or fundamental value of $.40. Prices at which some businesses sell bear a similar relationship. We're not sure how much of such premiums over intrinsic or fundamental value represent willingness to pay for opportunity and how much really represent failure to analyze intrinsic or fundamental value adequately.

Personal Rewards

A buyer may be willing to pay more than the value indicated by financial analysis because of personal rewards. He may fall in love with the physical location of an operation. The business may conduct an activity the buyer enjoys as a hobby. The buyer may desire the prestige associated with ownership of a certain business, or he may find the location and operating hours especially convenient. It can certainly be advantageous to a seller to find a buyer who perceives extra value in the business because of intangible personal benefits, whatever they may be.

Synergism

One of the most important factors that may add to the transaction price in a sale, over and above its value on a stand-alone basis, is *synergism*, the concept that the value of the combined operations is greater than the sum of the values of the individual operations. An example would be two pickle packers, one with substantial excess production capacity and the other without nearly enough capacity to serve the demand created by its very successful marketing.

If there really is synergism, as there often may be between potential merger mates, how much of the value of the synergism will the seller be able to add into the selling price, and how much will be left to be reflected in the buyer's future returns? The answer, of course, is a matter of negotiation, but the respective parties' negotiating posture depends to a great extent on supply of, and demand for, the particular type of company. If many such companies are available for sale and there is only one buyer, or a few potential buyers, very little synergism is likely to be reflected in the transaction price. On the other hand, if there is only one or a few similar companies available for sale, and several active potential buyers, the seller is likely to be able to receive a premium for a significant portion of the synergism.

Obviously, it is in the seller's interest to seek out buyers who would have synergism with the selling company, because such buyers might well be able to afford to pay more than anybody else for the particular company.

Compulsion

The definition of fair market value assumes that neither buyer nor seller is under any compulsion to buy or to sell. In many cases in the real world, however, that assumption is not met, and compulsion leads to the transfer of businesses at prices that are different from what reasonably might be considered to be fair market value.

The most common source of compulsion that drives owners to sell is foreclosure of credit, usually by banks. Other common sources of compulsion are illness, death of an owner or family member, and irreconcilable differences among present owners; these make it virtually impossible to operate the business effectively under current ownership.

Compulsion affecting buyers arises most often because of synergistic effects that might be lost if the deal falls through. For example, a buyer might feel compelled to buy the business of a key customer from the estate of a deceased owner in order to keep it from failing or falling into the hands of a competitor.

Working with a Business Broker

The intermediaries who put together the large mergers and acquisitions in Corporate America are known as "investment bankers," while those that perform a similar service for small businesses and professional practices are known by the less elegant but much more descriptive designation of "business brokers." Those who broker medium-size transactions are often known as "merger and acquisition specialists."

Services Offered by Business Brokers

The basic service of a business broker, of course, is bringing together a buyer and a seller and negotiating the transaction. Some business brokers also offer appraisal services, and some serve to find financing for the buyer.

Most business brokers have typically represented the seller of a business through an agency relationship as the seller's sole and exclusive agent. More recently, however, some brokers are being asked to represent buyers. This gives the buyer the advantage of the broker's expertise and can save the buyer considerable time and money that might otherwise be wasted.

Among other services offered by business brokers is fee consulting with buyer or seller clients who may have located a business on their own and need assistance in valuing or structuring the transaction.

A professional broker should provide sellers or buyers practical advice on many of the following issues:

- Probability of business being sold.
- Necessary steps, legal and otherwise, to prepare the business for sale.
- Estimate of costs involved to buyer/seller.
- Responsibility of the parties in the sale process: broker, buyer, seller, attorney, accountant, lender.
- Estimate of total transaction time from engagement to closing.
- Confidentiality requirement.
- Timing on offers, counteroffers, escrow, closing.
- Purchaser cash requirements.
- Skills required to operate the business.
- Other listings in this range and alternate investment options.
- Suggested selling price and deal structure.
- Pre-closing and post-closing responsibility of the parties.
- Estimated net proceeds at closing.

Should You Use a Business Broker or Not?

The utilization of brokerage services has increased dramatically in the last 25 years. We have seen significantly increased professionalism and capabilities of participants in the business brokerage industry.

Part of this increase in broker utilization is due in part, according to Don R. McIver of American Business Group, Inc., in Dallas, to the fact that more buyers than ever before are looking for alternative careers and are opting for their own business. In the 1970s and 80s, the number of active business brokers expanded thanks to heavy agent recruiting by growing brokerage franchise companies. Additionally, the professional brokerage associations (statewide and internationally) began to offer educational programs leading to certification (such as CBC, BCB, CBI, and others). As more agents joined the field, advertising solicitation (both direct and by mail) was increased, leading to greater recognition of the business brokerage profession.

The primary function of the business broker is to find buyers for sellers, and vice versa. If the seller needs to locate potential buyers or the buyer needs to locate potential acquisition candidates, then a business broker can be useful. If the seller is already personally acquainted with all the potential buyers (or the buyer with the potential sellers), which is highly unlikely, a broker still may be very helpful. The broker not only acts as an intermediary and buffer between buyer and seller but also serves other important functions, such as the negotiation of price and terms and the handling of transaction and escrow documents. A broker can be invaluable to either seller or buyer in navigating through the uncharted mine field, which includes all the details of getting the contingent elements agreed to in the contract fulfilled, and completing the myriad of details to close the transaction and transfer the ownership from one party to the next. Also, the broker can provide anonymity to the buyer and/or seller, at least up to the point of serious negotiation.

Criteria for Selecting a Broker

A seller should select a broker whose direct sales efforts, or whose particular listing network, will be likely to reach the potential buyers for that seller's business. A buyer would be wise to make his interests known to several different brokers who may have access to listings that would be of interest.

The following criteria deserve more or less weight in selecting a broker with whom to work, depending on the situation:

1. Types of businesses commonly brokered.
2. Size of businesses commonly brokered.
3. Geographical scope.
4. Overall competence of the broker.
5. Success ratio (percentage of listings actually sold).
6. Willingness of broker to spend money advertising the business for sale.

Types of Businesses. Certain brokers specialize in specific types of businesses and practices, such as radio and TV stations, magazines, beer distributorships, auto dealerships, funeral homes, hotels and motels, accounting practices, or medical practices. Others specialize in more general categories, such as wholesalers, retailers, or manufacturers. Many others do not necessarily specialize as a matter of policy, but they simply have considerable experience in transactions in one or a few industries. A broker experienced in an industry would usually have an advantage over a broker without such experience in finding buyers and sellers in that industry and in negotiating a mutually satisfactory transaction.

Size of Businesses. Most brokers tend to concentrate their efforts within a certain price range. Some brokers may do very well with businesses priced under $100,000, while others find their level of comfort and success in the $100,000-to-$500,000 range, and still others do most of their business in the $500,000-and-up category. Buyers and sellers should seek brokers who generally handle transactions in the appropriate size category.

Geographical Scope. Regional and national connections are not important to a seller whose business would appeal only to a local buyer, such as small retailers, taverns, and so on. However, if a buyer could conceivably come from elsewhere in the region or nation, the seller would want to contact a broker whose connections extend outside the local area. A seller should inquire whether the brokers' networks would facilitate the exposure of his listing in the various markets where buyers might be located. Much more networking is available among brokers nationally now than was the case a few years ago.

A buyer seeking to locate in a particular city logically would talk to brokers in that city. If he thinks he might be interested in one of several cities, however, he should talk to brokers belonging to the multiple-listing networks, or to one who has connections with brokers in other cities.

General Competence. Naturally, a broker's competence is an important consideration, but that is not easy to judge. A seller or buyer can inquire about the broker's educational and professional credentials (such as CBC or CBI), how long he has been in the business, and what his experience has been with the type of company in mind. Beyond that, sellers or buyers should ask for and contact the broker's references. Some brokers may be reluctant to give out names and addresses of previous clients as references due to the confidentiality request of both buyers and sellers. Most brokers, however, can and freely will give out names of their banker, accountant, attorney, and other professional references that will satisfy the purchaser's or seller's need for some comfort level with references.

Success Ratio.   Naturally, a buyer or seller will want to select a broker whose track record looks good. Find out the ratio of sales per listings.

Willingness of a Broker to Spend Money on Advertising a Business for Sale.   Unless a brokerage firm is willing to spend some money on advertising, the chances for optimum exposure to the market diminish, possibly decreasing the likelihood of a timely sale.

Locating the Broker

The *Yellow Pages* in every city offer many listings under the classification "Business Broker," but they give little or no information to assist a prospective buyer or seller in deciding which brokers would be most suitable for any particular situation. A better locally published source in most cases is the Sunday "Business Opportunities" classified ads. They indicate which brokers are advertising businesses in which particular industries.

It may be ideal to locate a business broker by referral from someone who knows the person or firm first hand. In some cases, an attorney, accountant, banker, business appraiser, or insurance agent may be familiar with some of the local brokers either directly or through their clients.

The headquarters offices of various organizations of business brokers listed in Exhibit 36–1 can give names of member firms in the area, and in some cases can suggest which ones might be best suited to the buyer's or seller's particular needs. For example, Wally Stabbert, executive director of the Institute of Certified Business Counselors, is personally acquainted with most of the several hundred members of that group and their respective areas of specialization and strengths. Tom West, the executive director of the International Business Brokers Association, has similar familiarity with many members of his organization. Any of the organizations listed will be glad to send a list of members and/or to speak personally with anyone seeking the services of a broker.

Exhibit 36–2 lists networks and franchisors in business brokerage. Franchisors typically offer a training program, standardized forms for all aspects of the business, varying programs of ongoing management consulting, and a computerized network through which to access business listings of all offices throughout the franchise group.

Exhibit 36–1

BUSINESS BROKERAGE ORGANIZATIONS

NATIONAL

The International Business Brokers Association (IBBA)
Thomas L. West, Executive Director
P.O. Box 704
Concord, MA 01742
(508) 369-2490

The Institute of Certified Business Counselors (CBC)
Wally Stabbert, President
P.O. Box 70326
Eugene, OR 97401
(503) 345-8064

STATE AND LOCAL [a]

Arizona Association of Business Brokers
Carl A. Barton, Chairman
Business Centre
5620 N. Kolb, Suite 164
Tucson, AZ 85715

Association of Midwest Business Brokers (AMBB)
John Torrence, CBI, President
Torrence Enterprises
483 N. Mulford
Rockford, IL 61107
(815) 399-4410

Business Brokers Association of Southern California
Terry Hogan, President
625 W. Broadway
Glendale, CA 91204
(818) 243-4271

Business Opportunity Council of California (BOCC)
Ron Schuster, Membership
Century 21/Hunter
1240 E. Wardlow
Long Beach, CA 90807
(310) 426-6577

California Association of Business Brokers (CABB)
Mel Weisblatt, President
Probus, Inc.
307 Orchard City Drive, Suite 100
Campbell, CA 95008
(408) 370-9500

Florida Business Brokers Association (FBBA)
Ken Stebbins, President
Stebbins Commercial Brokers
2001 N.W. 62nd Street, Suite 101
Ft. Lauderdale, FL 33309
(303) 493-7861

Georgia Business Brokers Association
Nick Nicholson, President
Nicholson & Associates
402 E. Wesley Road
Atlanta, GA 30305
(404) 261-6276

Heartland Association of Business Intermediaries (HABI)
John C. Johnson
1427-B East 41st Street
Tulsa, OK 74105
(918) 627-6500

Michigan Association of Business Brokers
c/o Jim Hines, CBI
Inexco Business Brokerage & Development Co.
6200 28th Street, S.E.
Grand Rapids, MI 49546
(616) 949-4374

New England Business Brokers Association (NEBBA)
c/o Ted Burbank, CBI
The Burbank Group Business Investments
135 Boston Turnpike
Shrewsbury, MA 01545
(508) 791-5600

Ohio Business Brokers Association
Whitten S. Humphreys, CBI
2130 Arlington Avenue
Columbus, OH 43221
(614) 488-2245

Ontario Business Brokers Association
A.L. (Roy) Brown, CBI
ROI Corporation
2624 Dunwin Drive, Suite 1
Missisauga, Ontario, Canada L5L 3TS
(416) 820-4145

Exhibit 36–1 (*concluded*)

BUSINESS BROKERAGE ORGANIZATIONS

Texas Association of Business Brokers
    Carl Monnin, CBI
    Corporate Investment International
    7320 N. Mopac Expressway, Suite 305
    Austin, TX 78731
    (512) 346-4444

Texas Association of Business Brokers/Austin Chapter
    James J. McNeal, President
    7320 N. Mopac Expressway, Suite 305
    Austin, TX 78731
    (512) 346-4444

Texas Association of Business Brokers/Dallas-Fort Worth Chapter
    Bud Moore, BCB, President
    15851 Dallas Parkway, Suite 500
    Dallas, TX 75248
    (214) 450-5975

Texas Association of Business Brokers, Inc./Houston Chapter
    William Bumstead, BCB
    5433 Westheimer, Suite 1110
    Houston, Texas 77056
    (713) 621-5474

Texas Association of Business Brokers, Inc./San Antonio Chapter
    Rich Tomlinson, President
    7911 Broadway
    San Antonio, Texas 78209
    (512) 824-6395

Washington DC Area
    Lauri Katz
    K.F. Business Brokers
    15200 Shady Grove Road, Suite 350
    Rockville, MD 20850
    (301) 670-2823

[a]   State and local organizations elect officers each year, so the contact people may change, but the people listed should be able to provide information.

Pricing and Listing a Business or Practice for Sale

The essential elements of the listing agreement are:

1. The property being offered for sale.
2. The offering price and terms.
3. The commission.
4. The duration of the listing agreement.

The matter of defining what is being offered for sale was discussed in Chapter 2. Commissions are discussed later in this chapter. The duration of the agreement with most brokers is usually between six months and one year on an exclusive basis, so that the broker has adequate opportunity to work the listing, because it usually takes several months to sell a business. Most brokers will not even accept nonexclusive listings.

How the seller and the broker will set the price and terms of the listing varies a great deal from one type of business to another and, especially, from one broker to another. At the one extreme, some brokers insist on doing their own appraisal and accept the listing only if the price

Exhibit 36–2

BUSINESS BROKERAGE NETWORKS AND FRANCHISORS

Business Brokers Network
Contact: Gerald Nance, President
9330 LBJ, Suite 900
Dallas, TX 75243
(214) 680-9969

Business Exchange Network
Contact: Jorge Couto or Frank DeSantis
P.O. Box 43
Broomail, PA 19008
(215) 353-8244

Corporate Finance Associates (CFA)
Contact: James L. Baker
1801 Broadway, Suite 1200
Denver, CO 80202
(303) 296-6300

Country Business, Inc. (CBI)
Contact: Brian Knight
Box 1071
Manchester Center, VT 05255
(802) 362-4710

Franchise Brokers Network
Contact: N. Norman Schutzman, President
3617A Silverside Road
Wilmington, DE 19810
(302) 472-0200

Nation-List
Contact: Chip Fuller
1660 South Albion Street, Suite 407
Denver, CO 80222
(800) 525-9559

UBI Business Brokers, Inc.
Contact: David Scribner, President
18663 Ventura Boulevard, Suite 223
Tarzana, CA 91356
(818) 343-8263

VR Business Brokers, Inc.
Contact: Don Taylor, Chairman
1151 Dove Street, Suite 100
Newport Beach, CA 92660
(800) 377-8722

approximates their appraisal. At the other extreme, some brokers have nothing to do with the pricing and simply list a property at whatever price the seller designates. Most brokers will fall somewhere in between. They will offer some practical guidance if the seller wants it, but normally will not do a complete appraisal.

In any case, a seller should have a pretty good idea of a reasonable price before contacting the broker. It is part of the purpose of this book to provide the seller the guidance to develop a reasonable range of possible values. If the seller wants objective guidance, he may seek a professional appraisal from an independent fee appraiser rather than from a broker before offering the business for sale. It is a waste of both the seller's and the broker's time to start out by offering the business at a price inflated beyond a realistic range. On the other hand, a seller should naturally expect to get all he reasonably can, and not leave money on the table by underpricing the business.

Since most small businesses and professional practices are sold on terms rather than for cash, the listing price should be set to reflect just about the most generous terms the seller would be willing to accept. Chapter 19 shows how to convert a cash equivalent value to a higher price that appropriately reflects extended terms of sale. Then, if a deal looks possible on terms more favorable to the seller (or even better, if a cash deal looks possible), the seller can negotiate to a lower price that reflects the terms more favorable to the seller. It does not work psychologically to list the business priced on the basis of a cash deal, and then to raise the face amount to reflect the discount in value received as a result of extending terms to a buyer.

Statistics suggest that the average business sold closes at a price around 80 percent of its original listing price, but this average varies greatly from one brokerage office to another. The more sophisticated the seller and the broker are about realistic pricing, the higher the odds that the business will actually be sold, and the more likely that the price will be at or near the listing price.

Typical Fees

Brokers typically receive commissions of 10 to 15 percent of the stated sales price on sales up to about $500,000 (sometimes even up to $1,000,000) and somewhat lower percentages on higher amounts. Most brokers also have some minimum commission, the amount of which varies considerably from one brokerage firm to another. The broker receives his commission in cash at closing. Thus, if the down payment is 30 percent of the face amount and the commission is 10 percent, the commission amounts to one third of the down payment.

Fees for finding financing are usually about 2.5 to 5 percent of the amount of money raised.

Business brokerage has traditionally been a strictly commission business. However, there has been a trend recently for some brokers to charge sellers nonrefundable retainers that are usually deducted from the commission if the business is sold. The services covered by such retainers vary considerably. In some cases, the retainer may entitle the seller to receive the broker's opinion as to an appropriate price for the business. However, brokers do not often provide appraisal services of the scope discussed in this book. The retainer may cover the development of a presentation package that highlights relevant information about the business or practice.

Some brokers' retainers run several thousand dollars. However, it is more typical for a retainer for a small business to be $1,000 to $2,000. The retainer helps to cover some of the broker's out-of-pocket expenses and to weed out sellers who are not serious and would merely waste the broker's time. From the seller's viewpoint, the retainer should help to get the broker's full attention and at least enhance his moral obligation to pursue rigorously the sale of the business.

Working with the Broker

The more the seller or buyer understands the functions of brokers in general and the broker he is working with in particular, the smoother the relationship will be, and the more likely that it will be successful. Both sellers and buyers should respect the broker's time, and should try to accomplish maximum results with a minimum amount of the broker's time.

The Seller's Role. The seller's main job is to provide the broker with business information that is as complete as possible, as discussed in Chapter 37, and updating it as necessary. The seller should encourage as many of the brokerage's representatives as possible to tour the place of business so that they will be familiar with it.

The seller should give the broker and other representatives of his firm a narrative account of the nature of the business and why it should be attractive to a buyer. He should make himself readily available to answer the broker's questions and to provide potential purchasers an opportunity to tour the premises and ask questions about the business. The information he provides should be complete, honest, and not exaggerated.

The Buyer's Role. The buyer's first step is to make clear to the broker exactly what he is looking for—the type of business, acceptable price and size range, acceptable geographical area, the cash he has available for the down payment, and any other appropriate description of what is or is not acceptable. It is not fair for a buyer to waste a broker's time on "fishing expeditions" until he has thought these things through and answered these questions in his own mind. If he has not, he should be up-front and tell the broker so, seeking the broker's guidance, if appropriate.

A buyer who is serious about a business should be entitled to full disclosure of pertinent information. He should have access to all of the information necessary to complete all the steps in the valuation process discussed in this book. Obviously, such information is confidential, and the buyer should treat it that way. It is totally appropriate for the seller to require the buyer to sign a confidentiality agreement before releasing information.

Because of the lack of multiple-listing cooperation among business brokers within virtually all cities, a buyer may need to review the listings of several brokers in order to find the business or practice most suitable for him.

Closing the Deal

A problem constantly facing brokers is buyers and sellers trying to make a deal excluding the broker, so that the broker loses his commission. If a broker has introduced a buyer to a property, it is both unethical and illegal to avoid paying his commission if the deal is consummated. He is entitled to be paid for his services, and this obligation should be respected by both buyers and sellers.

The broker probably has offer-to-purchase and/or purchase agreement forms available. The comprehensiveness of these forms varies considerably from one brokerage firm to another, and the need for comprehensive forms varies considerably from one transaction to another.

Even if the parties choose to use the standard forms provided by the broker or obtained elsewhere, it is appropriate that both buyer and seller have their attorneys review the documents before finalizing the deal. However, both parties should expect their attorneys to be both expeditious and reasonable in the language they suggest in the purchase agreement. Too many deals have been killed unnecessarily by attorneys either failing to act on a timely basis or unreasonably demanding language that is unacceptable to the other party.

A significant proportion of the transactions put into escrow through some brokerage firms never close, and many that do close take an excruciatingly long time. We have heard of brokerage firms which, on the average, close less than half the transactions put into escrow. Firms that close over 90 percent of the transactions put into escrow tend to be very proud of that record. High closing records come with firms that have qualified buyers with cash available and sellers that provide full and timely disclosure of all information that a buyer needs and can verify. If these conditions are met, a transaction should clear escrow on a timely basis, to the satisfaction of both buyer and seller.

Structuring a Deal

Tax and other consequences of the structure of a transaction can have a significant impact on the transaction price. The following points are broadly generalized simplifications, and we recommend that both seller and buyer consult a tax attorney and/or an accountant regarding tax and legal implications of the terms of the transaction.

Stock versus Asset Sale

As noted elsewhere, the smaller the business the more likely the transaction will involve a transfer of assets rather than of corporate stock, even if the selling company is a corporation.

Generally speaking, from an income tax viewpoint, an asset transaction is more favorable to the buyer and a stock transaction more favorable to the seller. In a stock transaction, the seller receives capital gains treatment on the difference between his cost basis and the amount received, and the buyer's cost basis for the assets remains the same as the seller's cost basis. In an asset transaction, the buyer gets a new cost basis, equal to the amount paid to the seller, for the assets purchased, but the seller is subject to ordinary income tax for any depreciation recapture and/or gain on inventory.

Selling on an Installment Contract

Most sellers would prefer to sell for cash. Usually, however, they ultimately sell for some combination of cash and a contract on the balance carried by the seller. This happens because most buyers of small businesses do not have the resources to pay the full purchase price in cash. See Chapter 19, "Tradeoff between Cash and Terms," for a discussion of how to price a sale on an installment contract to achieve the desired cash equivalent value.

A contract sale is automatically treated as an installment sale for tax purposes (regardless of amount of the down payment or even if there is no down payment); this means that the seller pays taxes on the proceeds in the year he receives them. The seller, however, has the option of electing to include all the profit in the year of sale by reporting the transaction on IRS Form 4797.

When a seller accepts an installment contract, he is putting himself in the position of a lender; and the contract should contain the same kind of protective covenants that a bank or other lender would require. Such covenants usually cover such items as limiting salaries and withdrawals of the new owners, preventing pledging the assets as collateral for other debt, and maintaining certain financial ratios and levels of working capital and net worth. There are a variety of horror stories involving contract sales without such covenants, in which the buyer soon got the company in such a position that he was unable to make the contract payments.

Rexford Umbenhaur of Rexford Business Consultants in San Diego offers the following commentary on the prevalence of seller financing of small business transactions:

> For the small business sale, the majority of financing is arranged with the seller. I feel the largest contributing factors to the preponderance of this is found in the following:
> 1. Most small businesses and closely held corporations report their income to reflect little or no profit.
> 2. Many have poor records of income and expenses.
> 3. The recasting of the statements can subject the business owner to an IRS audit so they do not want a recast done.
> 4. The income/expense statements look lousy to bankers and other third party financiers (not bankable).
> 5. If the financial statements are recast, the recast line items look like the owner didn't buy anything personally last year but paid for his "life" through the business. (which is true . . . but the lenders don't like it).
> 6. The small business buyer in most all cases has never been in the business or industry in which he is attempting to buy into and his lack of direct experience and provable success is too risky for third party lenders to get involved with.[14]

Most of the above problems can be avoided by following the suggestions in the section on "Preparing the Business for Sale" earlier in this chapter.

Selling for Stock of the Buying Company

If a selling corporation receives the stock of the purchasing company, the transaction may be treated as a tax-free exchange, meaning that the seller does not pay taxes on the gain until he eventually sells the stock of the buying corporation. Of course, receiving stock in another company

---

[14]Letter from Rexford Umbenhaur to the author dated October 5, 1992.

creates the whole problem of appraising the stock of the buying company, lest the seller finds himself in the position of the little boy who sold his dog for $10,000, receiving two $5,000 cats as the consideration.

Also, stock of a publicly traded corporation received in exchange for another company is normally restricted from resale on the open market for a period of two years. Restricted stock is usually valued at a discount from freely tradeable stock.[15]

Leveraged Buyouts

The willingness of banks and other institutions to make loans for leveraged buyouts, including leveraged buyouts of small businesses, has made this form of transaction increasingly popular the past several years. The basic concept of the leveraged buyout is to use the assets of the selling company as collateral for a loan to buy the business.

Small businesses that do not have enough assets to secure a completely leveraged deal might be able to sell on the basis of a partly leveraged buyout. The buyer could raise part of the purchase price by means of a bank loan secured by the company's assets and give the seller a contract for the balance secured by the company's stock. Naturally, it is in the interest of both the buyer and the seller to analyze carefully the company's ability to pay off both the bank loan and the seller's contract.

Employee stock ownership plans (ESOPs) have been used more frequently in recent years in buyouts of smaller companies, and bank financing has been available. Consequently, in this edition, we have added a new chapter (Chapter 25) on ESOPs.

Earn-Outs

If the buyer and seller would like to make a deal but can't get together on a fixed price because of differing earnings expectations or different degrees of confidence in the projections, the answer sometimes is to structure the transaction with some amount of cash and a specified participation in earnings for a certain period of time, often three to five years. There is no limit to the variety of earn-out arrangements. For example, if earnings before interest and taxes exceed 25 percent on the buyer's investment, the sellers might receive 40 percent of the excess for a specified period of time. In some cases, a minimum and/or maximum amount for the earn-out may be indicated.

Our advice to sellers contemplating an earn-out arrangement is to be sure that they retain control of the operation for the full period of the earn-out, in order to protect themselves from changes in personnel and policies that might diminish or eliminate the value of the earn-out.

Contingencies

Occasionally, an unresolved contingency remains at the time a transaction is contemplated. The most common contingencies are the outcome of

---

[15]For data on discounts for restricted stock, see "Data on Discounts for Lack of Marketability," Chapter 10 in Pratt, *Valuing a Business,* 2nd edition.

lawsuits, settlements of tax liabilities or refunds from past periods, and costs of compliance with regulatory requirements. In such cases, the problem of the uncertain effect of the contingency's outcome on the value of the entity can be solved by creating an escrow account. Any proceeds from collection of contingent amounts, or money left over after payment of contingent liabilities, can be distributed from the escrow account to the seller.

Covenants Not to Compete

We would estimate that in well over half of the sales of small businesses and professional practices, the seller provides the buyer with a covenant not to compete. The covenant usually covers certain activities within a specific geographical area for a specific period of time. It may be incorporated into the purchase agreement, or it may be a separate document. Payments over the life of a covenant not to compete are ordinary income to the seller and tax-deductible expenses to the buyer. The tax deductibility of the covenant can make this feature very desirable to the buyer. It is important to have the covenant professionally valued at the time of the transaction. (See Chapter 34 on "Valuing Intangible Assets.")

Employment Contracts

The value of a business can also be enhanced by having employment contracts with one or more key employees. The value attributable to such contracts is usually amortizable for tax purposes over the life of the contracts. Such contracts should also be valued at the time of the transaction.

Allocating the Purchase Price

From the buyer's viewpoint, the most desirable objective is to allocate as much of the purchase price as possible to assets that can be expensed, depreciated, or amortized most quickly. The seller would normally have an opposite viewpoint, since the kind of allocations that create the most write-offs for the buyer tend to create the most ordinary income, as opposed to capital gains, for the seller.

The buyer normally wants to see as much of the purchase price as possible allocated to such items as amortizable intangibles, inventory, and quickly depreciable fixed assets. The buyer prefers to have little or none of the purchase price allocated to goodwill because goodwill cannot be amortized for income tax purposes.

If the purchase price significantly exceeds the value of the tangible assets, many buyers examine the possibility of allocating some or all of the excess to specifically identifiable intangible assets that can be amortized. Chapter 34 deals with the subject of identifying and valuing specific intangible assets. The justification for the allocation to various depreciable and amortizable assets should be through documents in writing. If there is to be no allocation to the covenant not to compete, that should be specified in the purchase contract.

The relative income tax circumstances of the buyer and seller usually have a major bearing on the eventual agreement about allocating the purchase price, and the agreement may have a measurable impact on the price finally agreed upon.

In the sale of the assets of a business, the Internal Revenue Service (IRS) requires that Form 8594 be completed and filed by both buyer and seller when filing their next income tax return. It requires, among other things, information on how the sale price was allocated, especially the amounts for goodwill or going concern value, employment agreements, and covenants not to compete. Form 8594 requires that both the buyer and seller disclose the allocated amount for each asset and that they agree on these amounts.

The following are some of the items that make up the purchase price of a business and therefore are part of the allocation:

Furniture, fixtures, equipment, and machinery.

Leasehold improvements.

Licenses (liquor).

Vehicles.

Land.

Buildings and improvements.

Franchise cost.

Covenant not to compete.

Employment or consulting agreements.

Patents, copyrights, mailing lists.

Training and transition period.

Use of trade name, telephone number, etc.

Goodwill or going concern value.

Form 8594 and its instructions are shown in Exhibit 36–3.

Summary

This chapter has dealt with the entire gamut from deciding to buy or sell to closing the deal and allocating the purchase price. Good advance planning can help to smooth the way and raise the chances of making a sound deal.

Often, the terms and structure of a deal are more important than the price. Chapter 19 discussed the trade-off between cash and various sets of terms, and this chapter discussed various sale structures.

In many cases, a business broker can be instrumental in finding buyers or sellers and negotiating a deal. Business brokers' abilities to network among cities across the country have increased significantly in recent years. Business brokers can also be helpful in preparing purchase documents.

Exhibit 36–3

Form **8594**	**Asset Acquisition Statement**	OMB No. 1545-1021

Form **8594**
(Rev. July 1990)
Department of the Treasury
Internal Revenue Service

Asset Acquisition Statement
Under Section 1060
▶ **Attach to your Federal income tax return.**

OMB No. 1545-1021
Expires: 4-30-93

Attachment
Sequence No. **61**

Name as shown on return	Identification number as shown on return

Check the box that identifies you: ☐ Buyer   ☐ Seller

Part I   General Information—To be completed by all filers

1 Name of other party to the transaction	Other party's identification number

Address (number and street)

City, state, and ZIP code

2 Date of sale	**3** Total sales price

Part II   Assets Transferred—To be completed by all filers of an original statement

1 Assets	Aggregate Fair Market Value (Actual Amount for Class I)	Allocation of Sales Price
Class I	$	$
Class II	$	$
Class III	$	$
Class IV		$
Total		$

2 Did the buyer and seller provide for an allocation of the sales price in the sales contract or in another written document signed by both parties? . . . . Yes ☐ No ☐

If "Yes," are the aggregate fair market values listed for each of asset Classes I, II, and III the amounts agreed upon in your sales contract or in a separate written document? . . . . Yes ☐ No ☐

3 **To be completed by buyer only:** In connection with the purchase of the group of assets, did you also purchase a license or a covenant not to compete, or enter into a lease agreement, employment contract, management contract, or similar arrangement with the seller (or managers, directors, owners, or employees of the seller)? . . . . Yes ☐ No ☐
If "Yes," specify (a) the type of agreement, and (b) the maximum amount of consideration (not including interest) paid or to be paid under the agreement. *(Attach additional sheets if more space is needed.)*

_____

_____

_____

_____

_____

_____

_____

For Paperwork Reduction Act Notice, see instructions.   Form **8594** (Rev. 7-90)

Exhibit 36–3 *(continued)*

Form 8594 (Rev. 7-90)　　　　　　　　　　　　　　　　　　　　　　　　　　　　　　　Page **2**

Part III **Class III, Intangible Amortizable Assets Only— Complete if applicable. The amounts shown below also must be included under Class III assets in Part II.** *(Attach additional sheets if more space is needed.)*

Assets	Fair Market Value	Useful Life	Allocation of Sales Price
	$		$
	$		$
	$		$
	$		$
	$		$
	$		$
	$		$
	$		$
	$		$

Part IV **Supplemental Statement— To be completed only if amending an original statement or previously filed supplemental statement because of an increase or decrease in consideration.**

1　Assets	Allocation of Sales Price as Previously Reported	Increase or (Decrease)	Redetermined Allocation of Sales Price
Class I	$	$	$
Class II	$	$	$
Class III	$	$	$
Class IV	$	$	$
Total	$	////////	$

2　Reason(s) for increase or decrease *(Attach additional sheets if more space is needed.)*

_____

_____

_____

_____

_____

_____

_____

_____

_____

_____

3　Tax year and tax return form number with which the original Form 8594 and any supplemental statements were filed

Exhibit 36–3 (continued)

Form 8594 (Rev. 7-90)   Page **3**

Instructions

(Section references are to the Internal Revenue Code, unless otherwise noted.)

Paperwork Reduction Act Notice.—We ask for the information on this form to carry out the Internal Revenue laws of the United States. You are required to give us this information. We need it to ensure that taxpayers are complying with these laws and to allow us to figure and collect the right amount of tax.

The time needed to complete and file this form will vary depending on individual circumstances. The estimated average time is:

Recordkeeping	.10 hrs., 46 mins.
Learning about the law or the form	30 mins.
Preparing and sending the form to IRS	42 mins.

If you have comments concerning the accuracy of these time estimates or suggestions for making this form more simple, we would be happy to hear from you. You can write to both IRS and the Office of Management and Budget at the addresses listed in the instructions of the tax return with which this form is filed.

Purpose of Form.—The seller and buyer of a group of assets constituting a trade or business must report to IRS on Form 8594 if goodwill or a going concern value attaches, or could attach, to such assets and if the buyer's basis in the assets is determined only by the amount paid for the assets ("applicable asset acquisition," defined below).

Who Must File.—Both the buyer and the seller of the assets must prepare and attach Form 8594 to their Federal income tax returns (Forms 1040, 1041, 1065, 1120, 1120S, etc.).

Exceptions.—You are not required to file Form 8594 if any of the following apply:
(1) The acquisition is not an applicable asset acquisition.

(2) The asset acquisition occurs under a binding contract in effect on May 6, 1986, and at all times thereafter.

(3) A group of assets that constitutes a trade or business is exchanged for like-kind property in a transaction to which section 1031 applies. However, if section 1031 does not apply to all the assets transferred, Form 8594 is required for the part of the group of assets to which section 1031 does not apply. For information about such a transaction, see Regulations section 1.1060-1T(b)(4).

(4) A partnership interest is transferred. See Regulations section 1.755-2T for special reporting requirements.

When To File.—Generally, attach Form 8594 to your Federal income tax return for the year in which the sale date occurred. If the amount allocated to any asset is increased or decreased after Form 8594 is filed, the seller and/or buyer (whoever is affected) must complete Part I and the supplemental statement in Part IV of a new Form 8594 and attach the form to the Federal tax return for the year in which the increase or decrease is taken into account.

Penalty.—If you fail to file a correct Form 8594 by the due date of your return and you cannot show reasonable cause, you may be subject to a penalty. See sections 6721 through 6724.

Definitions

Applicable asset acquisition means a transfer of a group of assets that constitutes a trade or business in which the buyer's basis in such assets is determined wholly by the amount paid for the assets. An applicable asset acquisition includes both a direct and indirect transfer of a group of assets, such as a sale of a business.

A group of assets constitutes a **trade or business** if goodwill or going concern value could under any circumstances attach to such assets. A group of assets could qualify as a trade or business whether or not they qualify as an active trade or business under section 355 (relating to controlled corporations). Factors to consider in making this determination include (a) any excess of the total paid for the assets over the aggregate book value of the assets (other than goodwill and going concern value) as shown in the buyer's financial accounting books and records, or (b) a license, a lease agreement, a covenant not to compete, a management contract, an employment contract, or other similar agreements between buyer and seller (or managers, directors, owners, or employees of the seller).

The buyer's **consideration** is the cost of the assets. The seller's **consideration** is the amount realized.

Fair market value is the gross fair market value unreduced by mortgages, liens, pledges, or other liabilities. However, for determining the seller's gain or loss, generally, the fair market value of any property is not less than any nonrecourse debt to which the property is subject.

Class I assets are cash, demand deposits, and similar accounts in banks, savings and loan associations and other depository institutions, and other similar items that may be designated in the Internal Revenue Bulletin.

Class II assets are certificates of deposit, U.S. Government securities, readily marketable stock or securities, foreign currency, and other items that may be designated in the Internal Revenue Bulletin.

Class III assets are all tangible and intangible assets that are not Class I, II, or IV assets. Examples of Class III assets are furniture and fixtures, land, buildings, equipment, a covenant not to compete, and accounts receivable.

Class IV assets are intangible assets in the nature of goodwill and going concern value.

Allocation of Consideration

An allocation of the purchase price must be made to determine the buyer's basis in each acquired asset and the seller's gain or loss on the transfer of each asset. Use the residual method for the allocation of the sales price among the goodwill and other assets transferred. See Regulations section 1.1060-1T(d). The amount allocated to an asset, other than a Class IV asset, cannot exceed its fair market value on the purchase date. The amount you can allocate to an asset also is subject to any applicable limits under the Internal Revenue Code or general principles of tax law. For example, see section 1056 for the basis limitation for player contracts transferred in connection with the sale of a franchise.

First, reduce the consideration by the amount of Class I assets transferred. Next, allocate the remaining consideration to Class II assets in proportion to their fair market values on the purchase date, then to Class III assets in proportion to their fair market values on the purchase date, and finally to Class IV assets.

Reallocation After an Increase or Decrease in Consideration

If an increase or decrease in consideration that must be taken into account to redetermine the seller's amount realized on the sale or the buyer's cost basis in the assets occurs after the purchase date, the seller and/or the buyer must allocate the increase or decrease among the assets. If the increase or decrease occurs in the same tax year as the purchase date, consider the increase or decrease to have occurred on the purchase date. If the increase or decrease occurs after the tax year of the purchase date, consider it in the tax year in which it occurs.

For an increase or decrease related to a patent, copyright, etc., follow the rules under *Specific allocation,* described on page 4.

Allocation of Increase.—Allocate an increase in consideration as described above under *Allocation of Consideration.* If an asset has been disposed of, depreciated, amortized, or depleted by the buyer before the increase occurs, any amount allocated to such asset by the buyer must be properly taken into account under principles of tax law applicable when part of the cost of an asset (not previously reflected in its basis) is paid after the asset has been disposed of, depreciated, amortized, or depleted.

Exhibit 36–3 (*concluded*)

Allocation of Decrease.—Allocate a decrease in the following order: (1) reduce the amount previously allocated to Class IV assets, (2) reduce the amount previously allocated to Class III assets in proportion to their fair market values on the purchase date, and (3) reduce the amount previously allocated to Class II assets in proportion to their fair market values on the purchase date.

You cannot decrease the amount allocated to an asset below zero. If an asset has a basis of zero at the time the decrease is taken into account because it has been disposed of, depreciated, amortized, or depleted by the buyer, the decrease in consideration allocable to such asset must be properly taken into account under principles of tax law applicable when the cost of an asset (previously reflected in basis) is reduced after the asset has been disposed of, depreciated, amortized, or depleted. An asset is considered to have been disposed of to the extent the decrease allocated to it would reduce its basis below zero.

Patents, Copyrights, and Similar Property.—You must make a *specific allocation* if an increase or decrease is the result of a contingency that directly relates to income produced by a particular intangible asset, such as a patent, a secret process, or a copyright, and the increase or decrease is related only to such asset and not to other assets. If the specific allocation rule does not apply, make an allocation of any increase or decrease as you would for any other assets as described above under *Allocation of Increase* and *Allocation of Decrease.*

Specific allocation.—Limited to the fair market value of the asset, any increase or decrease is allocated first specifically to the patent, copyright, or similar property to which the increase or decrease relates, and then to the other assets in the order described above under *Allocation of Increase* and *Allocation of Decrease.* For purposes of applying the fair market value limit to the patent, copyright, or similar property, the fair market value of such asset is redetermined when the increase or decrease is taken into account by considering only the reasons for the increase or decrease. However, the fair market values of the other assets are not redetermined.

Specific Instructions

For an original statement, complete Parts I, II, and, if applicable, III. For a Supplemental Statement, complete Parts I and IV.

Enter your name and taxpayer identification number (TIN) at the top of the form. Then identify yourself as the buyer or seller by checking the proper box.

Part I, Item 1.—Enter the name, address, and TIN of the other party to the transaction (buyer or seller). You are required to enter the TIN of the other party. If the other party is an individual or sole proprietor, enter the social security number. If the other party is a corporation, partnership, or other entity, enter the employer identification number.

Part I, Item 2.—Enter the date on which the sale of the assets occurred.

Part I, Item 3.—Enter the total consideration transferred for the assets.

Part II.—For a particular class of assets, enter the total fair market value of all the assets in the class and the total allocation of the sales price. For item 3, to determine the maximum consideration to be paid, assume that any contingencies specified in the agreement are met and that the consideration paid is the highest amount possible. If you cannot determine the maximum consideration, state how the consideration will be computed and the payment period.

Part III.—Enter in Part III only those Class III assets that are intangible and amortizable. Be sure to enter the total Class III assets in Part II.

Part IV.—Complete Part IV and file a new Form 8594 for each year that an increase or decrease in consideration occurred. Give the reason(s) for the increase or decrease in allocation. Also, enter the tax year and form number with which the original and any supplemental statements were filed. For example, enter "1988 Form 1040." If an original or supplemental Form 8594 was not required to be filed, so state.

The buyer and seller should agree on the allocation of purchase price if the sale is structured as an asset (rather than stock) sale, and IRS form 8594, Asset Acquisition Statement, should be filed.

Selected Bibliography

Articles

Berkowitz, Richard K., and Joseph A. Blanco. "Putting a Price Tag on Your Company." *Nation's Business*, January 1992, pp. 29–31.

Bernstein, Jack. "The Purchase and Sale of a Practice. What Are Your Assets? When Should You Sell?" *Oral Health*, January 1984, pp. 53–57.

Cohen, Ira D. "Ten Tips When Selling Your Firm." *Small Business Reports*, August 1990, pp. 42–45.

Cohrs, Denis A. "Guidelines for Purchasing an Accounting Practice." *Practical Accountant*, August 1989, pp. 17–24.

Cole, Stephen R. "No Agreement, No Sale." *CA Magazine*, April 1992, pp. 51–55.

Cook, J. J. "Buying and Selling a Property Management Business." *Journal of Property Management*, July/August 1985, pp. 6–12.

Cosman, Madeleine Pelner. "How to Price and Sell a Practice." *Opthalmology Management*, June 1987, pp. 22–26.

Finegan, Jay. "The Insider's Guide: Fifteen Steps to Owning the Company That's Right for You." *Inc.*, October 1991, pp. 26–28+.

Fox, Bruce A. "Let the Buyer Beware." *Small Business Reports*, September 1991, pp. 12–16.

Fox, James, and Steven Elek. "Selling Your Company." *Small Business Reports*, May 1992, pp. 49–58.

Fraser, William M. "To Buy or Not to Buy?" *Management Accounting*, December 1989, pp. 34–37.

Gallagher, James K. "The Trustee's Role in Selling a Closely Held Business." *Trusts and Estates*, September 1990, pp. 45–50.

Ginsberg, Linda Gartner. "Phase-Out Agreement Provides the Best Way to Sell a Practice." *Dental Economics*, January 1983, pp. 81–89.

Haas, G.C. "The Price Is Right." *Beverage World*, February 1985, pp. 51–52.

Hartman, John W. "A Dozen Mistakes You Can Make Selling Your Company." *Advertising Age*, February 19, 1990, p. 31.

Hitchings, Bradley. "Selling Your Small Company." *Business Week*, February 4, 1985, p. 101.

Holdren, Richard C. "Timing Is Everything When Selling Your Practice." *Ocular Surgery News*, October 1, 1988, pp. 46–49.

Hubler, Richard S. "How to Buy (or Maybe Sell) an Optometric Practice." *Optometric Management*, May 1982, pp. 27–32.

Kuhn, Robert Lawrence, and David H. Troob. "When It's Time to Sell the Firm." *Nation's Business*, July 1992, pp. 47–49.

Lang, Stuart S. "Buying, Merging, or Selling an Accounting Practice." *Practical Accountant*, November 1983, pp. 87–95.

Levy, Jerome T. "Don't $ell Your Practice Short." *Optometric Management*, January 1986, pp. 49–52.

Mangan, Doreen. "What Is Your Company Worth?" *Executive Female*, November–December 1990, p. 74.

Martin, J. Thomas. "Don't Overlook These Crucial Points in a Practice Sale." *Medical Economics*, January 6, 1992, pp. 95–101.

McCord, Sam, and Tom Tole. "Partnerships: If There's a Beginning, There's an End." *National Public Accountant*, April 1992, pp. 18–22.

Richards, Fred F., Jr. "Preparing a Small Company for the Best Sale Price." *Mergers & Acquisitions*, September/October 1986, pp. 62–65.

Riggs, Carol D. "When You Want to Sell Your Business." *D&B Reports*, March–April 1991, pp. 20–23.

Scharfstein, Alan J. "The Right Price for a Business." *CPA Journal*, January 1991, pp. 42–47.

Singletary, Michelle L., and Kevin D. Thompson. "So, You Want to Buy a Business." *Black Enterprise*, April 1991, pp. 47–48.

Stollings, George D. "Selling a Dental Practice." *Dental Economics*, April 1992, pp. 31–36.

Thal, Lawrence S. "The Practice Sale: Getting to the Bottom Line." *Optometric Management*, June 1986, pp. 66–67.

Tibergien, Mark C., and T. S. Tony Leung. "Pricing a Practice." *Financial Planning*, October 1984, pp. 203–4.

Ward, John L., and Craig E. Aronoff. "To Sell or Not to Sell." *Nation's Business*, January 1990, pp. 63–64.

Wooley, Suzanne. "Rule No. 1 for Selling Your Company: Don't Rush." *Business Week*, April 3, 1989, pp. 114–15.

Books

Buying & Selling Medical Practices: A Valuation Guide. Chicago: American Medical Association, 1990.

Cosman, Madeleine, and Thomas Russell Lang. *Selling the Medical Practice: The Physicians' and Surgeons' Guide*. Tenafly, N.J.: Bard Hall Press, 1988.

Goldstein, Arnold S. *Business Transfers*. New York: John Wiley & Sons, 1986.

————. *The Complete Guide to Buying and Selling a Business*. New York: John Wiley & Sons, 1984.

Hagendorf, Stanley. *Tax Guide for Buying and Selling a Business*. Englewood Cliffs, N.J.: Prentice Hall, 1989.

Hansen, James M. *Guide to Buying or Selling a Business*. Mercer Island, Wash.: Grenadier Press, 1979.

Horwich, Willard D. *Lawyer's and Accountants' Guide to Purchase and Sale of a Small Business*. New York: Rosenfeld Launer, 1991.

Klueger, Robert F. *Buying and Selling a Business—A Step by Step Guide*. New York: John Wiley & Sons, 1988.

Lane, Marc J. *Purchase and Sale of Small Businesses*. 2nd ed. New York: John Wiley & Sons, 1991.

Ness, Theodore, and William F. Indoe. *Tax Planning for Dispositions of Business Interests*. 2nd ed. Boston: Warren, Gorham & Lamont, 1990.

Nunes, Morris A. *The Right Price for Your Business*. New York: John Wiley & Sons, 1988.

Schaub, Gary R. *Selling or Buying a Medical Practice*. Oradell, N.J.: Medical Economics Books, 1988.

Shangold, Jules, and Frank Greenberg. *How to Buy, Sell, and Share a Practice of Podiatric Medicine*. Mount Kisco, N.Y.: Future Publishing Co., 1977.

Silton, Lawrence C. *How to Buy or Sell the Closely Held Corporation*. Englewood Cliffs, N.J.: Prentice Hall, 1987.

Smith, Brian R., and Thomas L. West. *Buying Your Own Small Business*. Lexington, Mass.: The Stephen Greene Press, 1985.

Stefanelli, John. *The Sale and Purchase of Restaurants*. 2nd ed. New York: John Wiley & Sons, 1990.

West, Thomas L. *1992 Business Brokers Reference Guide*. Concord, Mass.: Business Brokerage Press, 1992.

Chapter 37

Working with a Business Appraiser

In any transaction where "value" is the most important issue, a competent, experienced, and professional appraiser should be consulted on behalf of the client to determine the true value of an enterprise.[1]

Situations that may call for a professional appraisal can include any of those listed in Chapter 4, as well as a few others. In addition to the basic service of appraising the business or practice, the professional appraiser may be able to provide related services.

Services Typically Offered by Business Appraisers

Although not all business appraisers necessarily offer all services, the following are some services typically offered by business appraisers.

- Preliminary appraisal opinions.
- Complete appraisals, with oral reports only, brief letter reports, relatively short written reports, or comprehensive, fully documented appraisal reports.
- Expert testimony.
- Service as arbitrator in valuation disputes.
- Assistance with purchase or sale negotiations.
- Assistance in structuring purchase or sale terms.
- Fairness opinion on a proposed transaction.
- Solvency opinion on a proposed transaction.
- Assistance in designing classes of business interests in corporate or partnership reorganizations.
- Litigation support research.
- Allocation of purchase price among classes of assets.

Finding and Engaging an Appraiser

The task of locating the right expert appraiser for the job at hand is sometimes undertaken by the owner(s) of the business or professional practice in question. More often, however, assistance in finding an appraiser is provided by the owner's attorney, CPA, insurance agent, or other professional advisor.

These individuals are usually familiar with the qualifications of one or several business appraisers, some of whom they may have worked with on past occasions. If a referral is not available, a list of Senior Members of the American Society of Appraisers accredited in business valuation is available from the national headquarters of that organization, P.O. Box 17265, Washington, D.C. 20041, (703) 478-2228. A list of those certified by the Institute of Business Appraisers is also available

---

[1]John E. Moye, *Buying and Selling Businesses* (Minneapolis: National Practice Institute, 1983), p. 25.

from that organization, Box 1447, Boynton Beach, FL 33425, (407) 732-3202.

Selecting the Appraiser

The more the client or his advisors know about the qualifications of any business appraisal firm or individual being considered, the greater the likelihood of selecting the appraiser who is best suited for the particular assignment. An appraiser being considered will usually have available a brochure describing his firm and a resume of his own qualifications, and will provide references on request. It is appropriate to interview a prospective appraiser, either on the telephone or in person. At that time, it is proper to inquire about his and/or his firm's specific experience relating directly to the assignment at hand. Alternatively, the appraisal firm or appraiser may be contacted in writing, with the assignment described and an inquiry made about the appraiser's qualifications to perform it.

The exact qualifications desired depend to some degree on the specific situation. Certainly, if there is litigation or potential litigation involved, experience with court testimony is an important factor. In any case, it is desirable that the appraiser be familiar with the law as it relates to the particular valuation situation. An article in *Inc.* magazine offered the following "Five Tips on Choosing a Valuation Expert":

1. Select someone with documented valuation experience, including a minimum of two years in the field and the references to prove it.
2. Choose an individual who is familiar with your industry.
3. Hire a professional who is willing to quote his rates in advance.
4. Pick a person who knows valuation law.
5. Find an expert with experience defending his valuations in court and before Internal Revenue Service agents.[2]

The article also adds:

Seeking a valuator who is a member of the American Society of Appraisers (A.S.A.) is also a good idea. To become a member an individual must pass written and oral tests, have a minimum of two years' full-time experience as a professional appraiser, and abide by the organization's code of ethics. Distinctions are made by discipline and level of experience: Regular members have worked two to four years as professional appraisers, while senior members have five or more years of experience.[3]

When contacting a prospective appraiser, it is desirable to be as up-front and complete as possible about such matters as the identity, nature, and size of the company; the purpose and scope of the appraisal assignment; and the desired schedule. Disclosure of confidential client information to unauthorized parties is prohibited, of course, by the codes of ethics of the American Society of Appraisers and the Institute of Busi-

---

[2]Donna Sammons, "Evaluating the Valuators," *Inc.*, May 1983, p. 186.
[3]Ibid.

ness Appraisers. Confidentiality of client information should not be a problem when dealing with a reputable appraisal firm.

If there are any possible conflicts of interest, this matter should be explored at the outset of the contract with the prospective appraiser. If the prospective appraiser contacted has any conflict of interest with respect to either the client or the assignment, he would be expected to disclose such conflict immediately.

Fees and Scheduling

Besides determining that the prospective appraiser is properly qualified, the client should reach a mutual understanding with the appraiser about fees and schedule. Most appraisal firms base their fees on the amount of time that the engagement will require for one or several members of the appraisal staff, plus out-of-pocket expenses. Most appraisers have an hourly or daily billing rate, much as in a law practice. Some assignments, especially ones where the required time is difficult or impossible to estimate accurately, may be undertaken strictly on an hourly basis, usually with some estimated range of cost. If the appraiser has been furnished with sufficient information, and if the assignment can be well defined, most appraisers are willing to commit to a fixed fee for their services, plus out-of-pocket expenses. If court testimony or arbitration may be involved, the appraiser may quote a fixed fee for the basic appraisal, with the trial preparation, depositions, and court time charged on an hourly or daily basis, since the amount of such time required is usually out of the appraiser's control.

The following information about a prospective appraisal assignment would be helpful to an appraiser for quoting a fixed or estimated fee for an assignment, as well as for discussing scheduling:

1. Line(s) of business.
2. Location(s) of operations.
3. Form of organization (corporation, S corporation, general or limited partnership, sole proprietorship).
4. Purpose of the appraisal.
5. Interest to be valued (100 percent or some partial interest).
6. Applicable valuation date or dates.
7. Status of financial statements (audited, reviewed, externally compiled, internally compiled, tax returns only, records in shoe boxes, and whether on cash or accrual basis).
8. Any subsidiaries or financial interest in other companies.
9. Annual revenues.
10. Annual profits.
11. Approximate book value.
12. Form and extent of appraisal report desired.
13. Desired schedule.

Some clients or their attorneys wait until the last minute to contact an appraiser, failing to allow a comfortable lead time to do the job thoroughly. In some cases, the client has received an unexpected offer for the purchase of his company, and he needs the opinion of the expert appraiser in only a few days in order to formulate his response. Most appraisal firms have enough flexibility in their staff scheduling to accommodate such urgent needs when necessary. Hopefully, however, those who have read this book have gained some appreciation of the complexities of business appraisal, and will give their appraisers as much lead time as possible to do the job properly. In most cases, that means a matter of weeks rather than days. If litigation is involved, lead time for adequate preparation—60 to 90 days in most cases—becomes even more important.

Professional Services Agreement

Once the appraiser has been selected and the assignment and fee arrangements agreed upon, the engagement should be committed to writing, usually through the appraisal firm's professional services agreement or engagement letter, supplemented as necessary to provide complete details of the assignment. Basically, the professional services agreement should cover the definition of the valuation assignment, as discussed in some detail in Chapter 1. To summarize, the professional services agreement, engagement letter, or whatever form is used to formalize the engagement in writing should cover the following points:

1. The property to be valued.
2. The purpose or purposes of the valuation.
3. The valuation date or dates.
4. The applicable standard of value.
5. The form and extent of the appraisal report.
6. The expected schedule.
7. Fee arrangements.
8. Whatever limiting conditions may be applicable.

The engagement document should be signed by the appraiser and the client. It should be supplemented by written addenda if any of the factors are changed during the course of the engagement.

Contingent and Limiting Conditions

Exhibit 37–1 is a sample statement of contingent and limiting conditions applicable to an appraisal engagement. One of the most important is that the appraisal is valid only for the appraisal date and for the specific use stated in the professional services agreement. We have seen that the appraisal date and the use to which the appraisal will be put are critical to the appraisal. There have been many misuses of appraisals—using them for some date and/or some use for which they were not prepared. The most certain way to prevent such misuse is to include the above limitation in the written professional services agreement, as well as in the final written report. The 1993 update of the Uniform Standards of Professional Appraisal Practice also suggests including such language in the engagement document.

Exhibit 37–1

CONTINGENT AND LIMITING CONDITIONS

This appraisal is subject to the following contingent and limiting conditions:

1. Information, estimates, and opinions contained in this report are obtained from sources considered reliable; however, no liability for such sources is assumed by the appraiser.

2. Client company and its representatives warranted to appraiser that the information supplied to appraiser was complete and accurate to the best of client's knowledge. Information supplied by management has been accepted without further verification as correctly reflecting the company's past results and current condition in accordance with generally accepted accounting principles, unless otherwise noted.

3. Possession of this report, or a copy thereof, does not carry with it the right of publication of all or part of it, nor may it be used for any purpose by anyone but the client without the previous written consent of the appraiser or the client and, in any event, only with proper attribution.

4. Appraiser is not required to give testimony in court, or be in attendance during any hearings or depositions, with reference to the company being appraised, unless previous arrangements have been made.

5. The various estimates of value presented in this report apply to this appraisal only and may not be used out of the context presented herein. This appraisal is valid only for the appraisal date or dates specified herein and only for the appraisal purpose or purposes specified herein.

SOURCE: Willamette Management Associates.

Information to Provide the Appraiser

Exhibit 37–2 provides a generalized checklist of documents and other information that may be necessary or helpful for the appraisal. Naturally, not all of the listed items are applicable for every appraisal, and, for some situations, relevant, specialized information will not be included on the list. The list should be helpful to the client, however, in anticipating and preparing for the information requirements of the appraisal. The types of analysis to be done on the various data have already been discussed throughout the book, of course, so they will not be repeated in this chapter.

Financial Statements

The key phrase about the length of time for which financial statements should be provided is the "relevant period." If operations have changed significantly, financial statements may be relevant only for the period since operations have been as they are now. On the other hand, for a very cyclical business, the appraiser may require statements for a long period of time to make an assessment of normalized earning power.

For many small businesses, financial statements may be somewhat incomplete or even nonexistent. If the appraiser has to try to create the necessary financial information from original source documents (invoices, check records, and so on), the process can be time-consuming and expensive. In any case, the appraiser has to do the best work he can with what is available, and his appraisal report will contain appropriate disclaimers regarding any information that is unavailable or unverifiable.

Other Financial Data

The list in Exhibit 37–2 is pretty much self-explanatory and covers a wide spectrum of data. The relative importance of the items varies from case to case, of course, and common sense should suggest which ones are most important in any given situation. Documents that can be easily copied or prepared can be provided to the appraiser prior to his visit to the premises and interview(s) with owners and/or management. Those that are somewhat voluminous can generally be reviewed on-site by the appraiser during his visit to the company.

Company Documents

Unless the company is a sole proprietorship, the appraiser will usually want to review the basic corporate or partership documents and any special agreements among the parties. These documents contain information about the various rights and restrictions related to the interests, and thus can have an important bearing on value. These documents can be either provided to the appraiser separately from his field visit or inspected on the premises or at the offices of the client's legal adviser.

Other Information

The "other information" category covers a universe of possibilities, and it is difficult to offer useful generalizations about it. The suggested list in Exhibit 37–2 should provide enough guidance to trigger the necessary thinking about the most important categories of relevant information. Again, the extent to which various materials are provided to the appraiser, prior to his on-site visit, is largely a matter of convenience and scheduling.

If the totality of Exhibit 37–2 and other aspects of client involvement in the appraisal process seem overwhelming, talk to the appraiser about what he really needs in light of the scope and purpose of the assignment. An experienced appraiser will get out his Occam's razor to whittle away at multiplicity of data and effort, and get to what is specifically relevant to the appraisal issue at hand. Most appraisers will cooperate to the utmost to avoid making the process any more time-consuming or disrup-

Exhibit 37–2

DOCUMENTS AND INFORMATION CHECKLIST

Financial Statements

Balance sheets, income statements, statements of changes in financial position, and statements of stockholders' equity or partners' capital accounts for up to the last five fiscal years, if available

Income tax returns for the same years

Latest interim statements if valuation date is 90 days or more beyond end of last fiscal year and interim statements for the comparable period the year before

List of subsidiaries and/or financial interests in other companies, with relevant financial statements

Other Financial Data

Equipment list and depreciation schedule

Aged accounts receivable list

Aged accounts payable list

List of prepaid expenses

Inventory list, with any necessary information on inventory accounting policies (including work in progress, if applicable)

Lease or leases (if lease does not exist or is not transferable, determine what new lease or rental terms will be)

Any other existing contracts (employment agreements, covenants not to compete, supplier and franchise agreements, customer agreements, royalty agreements, equipment lease or rental contracts, loan agreements, labor contracts, employee benefit plans, and so on)

List of stockholders, or partners, with number of shares owned by each or percentage of each partners' interest in earnings and capital

Compensation schedule for owners, including all benefits and personal expenses

Schedule of insurance in force (key-man life, property and casualty, liability)

Budgets or projections, if available

Latest business plan or operating forecast

Company Documents

If a corporation, articles of incorporation, by-laws, and any amendments to either, and corporate minutes

If a partnership, articles of partnership, with any amendments

Any existing buy-sell agreements, options to purchase stock or partnership interest, or rights of first refusal

Other Information

Brief history, including how long in business and details of any changes in ownership and/or bona-fide offers received

Brief description of business, including position relative to competition and any factors that make the business unique

Marketing literature (catalogs, brochures, advertisements, and so on)

List of locations where company operates, with size, and whether owned or leased

List of states in which licensed to do business

If customer or supplier base concentrated, list of major accounts, with annual dollar volume for each

List of competitors, with location, relative size, any other relevant factors

Resumes of key personnel, with age, position, compensation, length of service, education, and prior experience

Trade associations to which company belongs or would be eligible for membership

Relevant trade or government publications

Any existing indicators of asset values, including latest property tax assessments and any appraisals that have been done

List of patents, copyrights, trademarks, and other intangible assets

Any contingent or off-balance-sheet assets or liabilities (pending lawsuits, compliance requirements, warranty or other product liability, and so on)

Any filings or correspondence with regulatory agencies

Information on prior transactions in the stock

SOURCE: Willamette Management Associates.

tive for the client than is absolutely necessary to get the job done properly.

Field Visit

In the vast majority of appraisal assignments, it is desirable to have the appraiser visit the operating location(s). This first-hand visit to the operating premises can usually help the appraiser to gain an understanding of the operation beyond what is possible in an "armchair" appraisal (done entirely on the basis of interviews and a study of the documents without a visit to the facilities). If testimony may be required, courts tend to place more credibility on testimony of an appraiser that has visited the premises of the company than on testimony of one who has not.

Preparation

To the extent possible, the appraiser usually wants to review and analyze financial statements and as many documents as conveniently possible before the field trip. This way, he can have an understanding of the business before arriving there and can be prepared with a list of general and specific questions that otherwise would have to be covered at some other time, or might even be overlooked.

Mission

The kinds of information the appraiser will want to glean through his field visit have been discussed throughout the previous chapters. As discussed in the immediately previous section, the field trip can be a convenient time to review some of the documents that would be cumbersome or inconvenient to supply to the appraiser away from the premises.

The field trip is usually an excellent time to interview owners and/ or managers. The appraiser's physical presence on the premises might help to trigger relevant questions that might not occur to him in the surroundings of the appraiser's own conference room or office. If interviews with several people are appropriate, it is usually more convenient to conduct them on the premises. Also, information usually is at hand for any questions management is unable to answer completely from memory.

Generally speaking, the mission of the field trip consists of gaining a good overview of operations, getting whatever specific information is needed that has not been obtained by other means, and assessing all the qualitative factors discussed in Chapter 10. As noted elsewhere, one of the main objectives is to assess factors that might cause the future to differ from what the past record might indicate.

Confidentiality

Confidentiality is one problem with which the appraiser has to deal carefully on field trips. If a business is being put up for sale, the owners frequently do not want the employees or other people to know about it; and there can be many other good reasons for confidentiality. Experienced appraisers have learned to work around this problem. They can dress and act unobtrusively. If they have to be introduced or identified to someone who is not a confidant in the situation, they are "consultants," which is an accurate and adequately abstruse label.

As a last resort, the appraiser might visit the premises after working hours, when employees are not present. However, that will not give the appraiser as good a picture as he gets if he sees the facility in operation.

Adversary Proceedings

Another problem that the appraiser sometimes faces is opposition to an adequate facilities visit (or sometimes any facilities visit at all), in the case of an adversary proceeding. Undoubtedly, this problem most commonly occurs in appraisals being made for the purpose of property settlements in divorces.

If that is a problem, it is the responsibility of the client's attorney to make the necessary arrangements for the appraiser to visit the facilities and interview the necessary people. The parties should understand that the field visit is a standard part of the appraiser's work. They should understand that the appraiser himself is not an adversary party and is not an advocate for either party, but has been retained to render an independent opinion about value, as discussed in the final section of this chapter. When using a reputable, professional appraiser, the parties should not have to be concerned with confidentiality, as discussed elsewhere in this chapter. Furthermore, the party who is in the adversary position to the appraiser's client should welcome the opportunity to tell his side of the story to the appraiser.

If all discovery has to proceed through interrogatories and court orders, the process will be much more time-consuming, costly, and disruptive to the business operation. It is usually a good business decision for parties on both sides of a dispute to cooperate with independent appraisers. More discussion on adversary proceedings is included in Part VII on "Litigation and Dispute Resolution."

The Appraisal Report

As noted earlier, the scope of the appraisal report should be addressed when the appraiser is engaged. The form, length, and content are dictated primarily by the purpose of the appraisal and the audience for the report. In some cases, the report format is mandated or heavily influenced by law or convention. In such cases, an experienced appraiser can give the client guidance as to the appropriate form and scope of the report. In other cases, the scope of the written report is largely or totally a matter of client preference.

In some cases, only an oral report is necessary. In such an instance, it is usually best if it can be done in a meeting, so that the appraiser can go over work papers and other materials to the extent necessary for the client to understand how the appraiser arrived at his opinion about the value. Sometimes, however, logistics dictate that a telephone conversation will have to suffice for the oral report.

In some cases, only a brief letter report is required; sometimes a single sentence. More commonly, a letter report is one or two pages, outlining concisely the assignment, the steps taken, the approaches used, and the conclusion.

The next level would be a slightly longer letter report, which would fill in more detail on steps taken and information sources utilized. It would usually give specific numbers, such as earnings, capitalization rates, and asset values used in the various approaches. The report might also include one or a few supporting tables.

A complete formal appraisal report could run from 15 pages to well over 100 pages, depending on the purpose of the report, how complex the appraisal was, and how great the need for a comprehensive and documented written report.

One example of a formal report is included as Chapter 31, "Sample Professional Practice Valuation Report." Since this book is primarily about small business and professional practice valuations, I have not included a sample of a longer, more comprehensive report, which normally would be used in conjunction with larger businesses. An entire chapter on written reports, plus an example of a longer, comprehensive written report, are included in my other book.[4]

The purpose and the intended (or possible) audience of the report are all-important. Reports strictly for a client's internal use usually do not need to include nearly so much detail as those intended for outside use. An appraisal report for a possible sale of a business or practice, for example, might be fairly brief if it is just for the guidance of the owner. If prospective purchasers will, or might, see it, however, considerably more detail is usually warranted.

Similarly, appraisal reports strictly for buy-sell agreements and to determine life insurance needs may be fairly brief. However, if the same report will also be used for gift or estate taxes, a longer report is necessary in order to encompass all the factors contained in Revenue Ruling 59-60.

If so desired by the client or his attorney or other representative, the appraiser can be quite helpful in making suggestions as to the appropriate format, content, and length of the report, once he has a good idea of the purpose of the appraisal assignment.

Independence of Appraiser

In most situations, the appraiser is independent of the client who has retained him for the appraisal. That means the appraiser has no financial interest in the property being appraised, is not an employee or agent of the client, and neither has nor has had any financial or other dealing with the

---

[4]Pratt, *Valuing a Business*, 2nd ed., pp. 317–84.

client that would prejudice his ability to render a fair and impartial opinion about the value of the subject property. Professional ethics require that disclosure be made to the extent that these conditions are not met.

Unless otherwise made clear, when a professional appraiser expresses his independent opinion about value, whether in a written report, court testimony, or some other context, he is acting neither as an agent nor as an advocate of the client, but he is an advocate of his own opinion. That does not mean that someone who has made an appraisal cannot assume a role that is not independent, such as that of a negotiator or agent for the client in effecting a transaction; but that role is different from the role of an independent appraiser, and the relationship must be made clear to the parties involved. When an appraiser accepts an assignment as an "arbitrator," he maintains his role as an independent appraiser and is not an agent of any principal, as discussed more fully in the last chapter of this book.

Summary

Business appraisers not only value businesses or business interests, but also offer many related services. These include arbitration, negotiation, litigation support (consultation and/or expert testimony), deal structuring, tax planning, fairness opinions, solvency opinions, assistance drafting buy-sell and/or arbitration agreements, purchase price allocation among categories of assets, and many other services.

Qualified appraisers may be located by referrals or through professional appraisal associations. Qualifications to consider include academic and professional credentials, relevant experience, and knowledge of applicable valuation law.

The chapter has covered the information that should be provided to the appraiser so that the appraiser can make a reasonable engagement proposal, including a realistic fee and schedule. The chapter has also given a summary of the general information the appraiser will ultimately need to complete the assignment. The chapter has also discussed the mission and importance of the field visit.

Generally speaking, it should be expected that the appraiser will be independent and will provide a best estimate of value according to the applicable standard of value, without bias. There may be exceptions to this when the appraiser is retained in the role of a consultant or negotiator. The role of the appraiser should be made clear at the time of the engagement. Should this role change, such change should be documented in writing.

Far too many attorneys and business executives underestimate the time and cost required to do a proper business appraisal. It is important to allow an adequate budget and enough lead time for the appraiser to perform all the appraisal steps adequately. Without adequate time and resources, the appraisal is almost certain to suffer from inadequacies, often with severe consequences.

Part VII

Litigation and Dispute Resolution

Chapter 38

Litigation

Frequently, litigation follows a dispute over the value of a business or professional practice (or an interest in one). The following are the most common reasons that owners of small businesses and professional practices become involved in litigation concerning the value of holdings:

- Divorce.
- Damage cases.
- Corporate and partnership dissolutions.
- Dissenting stockholder actions.
- Estate, gift, and income taxes.
- Bankruptcy/insolvency/reorganization situations.
- State and local property taxes.
- Intellectual property rights infringement.

Imminent or potential litigation requires that the appraiser understand the legal context within which the appraisal is being made. The appraiser must tailor his valuation methods and criteria to relevant statutory and case law, which often varies considerably from one valuation purpose to another, and from one jurisdiction to another. The first major section of this chapter discusses assessing the legal context, a step that is essential in all litigation and dispute resolution.

The following sections of this chapter discuss valuations in various contexts, including:

- Corporate and partnership dissolutions.
- Dissenting stockholder actions.
- Estate, gift, and income taxes.
- Bankruptcy/insolvency/reorganization situations.
- State and local property taxes.
- Intellectual property rights infringement.

The next two chapters discuss valuations for divorces and damage cases, respectively. The final chapter discusses arbitration.

The Legal Context

Whenever a valuation involves litigation or potential litigation, a thorough understanding of the legal context is essential. The appraiser and the attorney must work very closely together so they are both fully cognizant of how the legal context may influence certain aspects of the valuation procedures and conclusion.

The primary aspects of the legal context are the following:

1. Statutes.
2. Regulations and administrative rulings.

3. Case law.
4. Court directives and preferences.

Statutes

Federal law governs valuation issues in some types of cases, such as gift and estate tax matters and damages in antitrust actions. State statutes apply to many other valuation issues, such as divorces, damages resulting from condemnation, dissenting stockholder actions, and values for ad valorem taxation. Statutes governing these issues vary considerably from state to state, and states change their statutes from time to time. If there is a chance that litigation involving a valuation issue will arise, the appraiser should look into the legal jurisdiction and the relevant statutes.

Regulations and Administrative Rulings

Statutes may be supplemented by regulations and administrative rulings, some of which have the force of law, and some that do not. For example, to implement the federal tax laws, the U.S. Treasury Department issues regulations which have the force of law. However, the Internal Revenue Service (IRS) issues Revenue Rulings, representing the opinion of the IRS on various issues, which do not have the force of law. The appraiser should know what regulations and rulings exist, and also what is their force and impact on the matter at hand.

Case Law

Case law is defined as past judicial cases to which courts may look for established precedent on a particular issue. Since most courts follow precedents established by other cases within their jurisdictions, it behooves the appraiser to be familiar with the relevant case law. Courts may also consider precedents established in the decisions of courts in other jurisdictions, but they would not accept those decisions as binding.

Because courts rely heavily on case law, it plays an important part in valuations involving litigation. Some appraisers have studied case law in depth and maintain extensive files of court cases involving the valuation of businesses and professional practices. Others rely on the attorney involved in the case to research the case law and provide them with the relevant cases for their study. Either way, gaining the necessary understanding of relevant case law is an important area of cooperation between the appraiser and the attorney in any valuation situation involving litigation or potential litigation.

Court Directives and Preferences

Most courts prefer not to hear valuation cases at all, and will try to encourage a settlement if possible. Some courts exercise considerable discretion in the handling of valuation cases, determining such matters as when or whether the retention of experts must be disclosed to the opposing side, rules for discovery, and whether or not written appraisal reports must be prepared and exchanged.

Some of the foregoing items are standing matters of law or policy in certain jurisdictions, and others are left to the discretion of the judge in the particular case. When litigation is involved, the appraiser should find out from the attorney at the outset what are the known ground rules and what are the court's preferences about the procedures of the case, so that the appraiser may plan accordingly.

Corporate and Partnership Dissolutions

Corporate or partnership dissolutions have many characteristics in common with divorces. People are terminating a relationship, frequently under antagonistic circumstances. Generally speaking, there is little or no statutory or case law to provide any guidance for the issue of valuation.

In many instances, a buy-sell agreement exists that may specify a standard of value. (See Chapter 26 entitled "Estate Planning and Buy-Sell Agreements" for a discussion of buy-sell agreements.) In other cases, the parties may draw up a document specifically for the purpose of providing guidance on the valuation of the interest and other aspects of the dissolution. Arbitration can be a useful way to resolve valuation differences in conjunction with a corporate or partnership dissolution (see Chapter 41, "Arbitrating Disputed Valuations").

A few states (e.g., California, New York, Rhode Island) have "dissolution statutes" that allow minority stockholders to demand a dissolution of a corporation under certain circumstances. In these states, the company can avoid the dissolution by paying the stockholders the "fair value" of their stock. See Chapter 35 on "Valuing Minority Interests" for further discussion.

Dissenting Stockholder Actions

In all states, stockholders controlling some percentage of the stock (ranging from 50 percent plus one share up to 90 percent, depending on the state) can force out minority stockholders by effecting a "statutory merger," often referred to colloquially as a "squeeze-out merger." The merger can be effected either with an already existing company or with a new company created by the controlling stockholders for the purpose of the merger. This and other corporate actions can give rise to dissenting stockholder actions requiring appraisal of, and cash payment for, shares held.

Reasons for Squeeze-Out Mergers

Some common reasons for squeeze-out mergers include the cost or nuisance of having minority stockholders, disagreements with minority stockholders, and needs for additional capital infusion into a company which minority stockholders are not willing or able to share on a pro rata basis.

Dissenting Stockholder Appraisal Rights

In all states except West Virginia, stockholders who dissent to certain corporate actions have the right to have their stock appraised and to be paid the value of the stock in cash. The corporate actions giving rise to the dissenting stockholders' appraisal rights vary from state to state. In general, though, events triggering dissenters' appraisal rights include a merger, the sale of the company, a sale of major corporate assets, or some other fundamental organizational change.

Standard of Value

Statutes governing the value of stock pursuant to dissenting stockholders' appraisal rights in most states designate fair value as the standard of value.

None of the statutes defines fair value, so the appraiser must look to case law for interpretation of the concept in the context of dissenting stockholders' appraisal rights. Since so many companies are incorporated in Delaware, that state provides a significant portion of the case law regarding dissenting stockholders' appraisal rights. Traditionally, appraisals under the Delaware dissenting stockholder statutes have followed what some call the Delaware Block Rule, which holds that various weightings should be given to each of four relevant factors: (1) earnings, (2) assets values, (3) dividends, and (4) market value. However, a landmark case in 1983 said that the traditional factors alone were not necessarily sufficient; all relevant factors must be taken into consideration. In the particular case, the court specifically made the point that projections of future earnings were available and should be considered. The court also made the point that not only did the conclusion as to value need to be fair, but the appraisal procedures needed to be fair as well.[1]

In some cases, the concept of fair value under dissenting stockholders' appraisal rights has been interpreted to mean a proportionate share of the value of the total enterprise, with no discount for the marketability nor the fact that the shares at issue represent a minority interest. This is opposed to the standard of fair market value, under which minority shares would normally be valued at something less than a proportionate share of the total enterprise value. However, two Canadian decisions have interpreted fair value to mean a proportionate share of enterprise value plus a premium for the taking![2]

The only way to really understand the standard of value for dissenting stockholder actions is to study the case law relevant to the particular state. New case law results in continuous changes to the standard of value in this kaleidoscopic arena of litigation.

---

[1] *Weinberger* v. *U.O.P. Inc.*, 457 A2d 701 (Del. Supr. 1983), rev. and remanding 426 A2d 1333.

[2] *Domglas Inc.* v. *Jarislowsky, Fraser & Co.*, (1980) C.S. 925, 13 BLR 135, affirmed (1982) C.A. 377, 22 BLR 121, 138 DLR (3d) 521 (C.A.); *Les Investissements Mont Soleil Inc.* v. *National Drug*, (1982) C.S. 716, 22 BLR 139 at 176. Both cases added a 20 percent premium for the taking.

Estate, Gift, and Income Taxes

The standard of value for estate, gift, and income tax transactions is fair market value. There is an extensive body of business valuation precedent through court cases that interprets fair market value for estate, gift, and income taxes.[3] See Chapter 3 for a discussion of the fair market value standard, and Chapter 26 for a discussion of estate planning, using the fair market value standard.

Bankruptcy/Insolvency/Reorganization Situations

Creditors, debtors, consultants, lawyers, and others involved in the bankruptcy and reorganization process often rely upon appraisers. Appraisers are relied upon for a number of traditional asset and equity valuation purposes. One factor that distinguishes the bankruptcy appraisal process is the broad array of potential uses of the appraisal work product.

Appraisals of assets, properties, and business interests are a routine part of the bankruptcy and reorganization process. Appraisals are relied upon to conclude various definitions and premises of value (e.g., going-concern value versus liquidation value) for such uses as debtor-in-possession financing, restructurings, reorganization financing, recapitalizations, out-of-court reorganizations, and turnarounds.

If properly understood, traditional business valuations can well serve the management information and decision-making needs of debtors, creditors, and other parties in interest to the bankruptcy. Appraisal clients and third-party users should understand the foundation elements of the appraisal upon which they are relying. And appraisal clients and third-party users should recognize the inherent limitations of all appraisals and consider their degree of reliance accordingly.

The appraisal work product in the bankruptcy/reorganization environment may be used for either notational purposes or for transactional purposes.

In addition to the traditional appraisal uses listed above, professional appraisers have experience and expertise that may serve debtors, creditors, and others with a wide range of insolvency and troubled debt analyses. The skills and judgment of professional appraisers serve the needs of property owners and other parties in areas such as:

- Restructuring strategies for recovery of property value.
- Creation of troubled property workout plans.
- Assessment of troubled property workout plan feasibility.
- Identification of asset or business spinoff opportunities.
- Valuation of asset or business spinoff opportunities.
- Valuation of adequate protection plans.

---

[3]For analysis of important precedent-setting court cases regarding federal taxes, see Chapters 21 and 22 in Pratt, *Valuing a Business*, 2nd ed.

- Valuation of claims for purchase or sale.
- Fraudulent conveyance analyses.
- Reorganization, recapitalization, and restructuring analyses.

Professional appraisers can often assist property owners both before and after they reach reorganization status. Appropriately experienced appraisers can serve the informational, analytical, and assessment needs of debtors in possession, of secured and unsecured creditors, and even of the bankruptcy court. These analyses are designed to identify—and maximize—all elements of tangible and intangible property value, to the benefit of all parties in interest to the reorganization.

All appraisals are quantitative analyses based upon qualitative judgments. Notational appraisals are prepared for accounting or management information purposes only. A purchase or sale transaction will not be consummated based upon the appraisal analysis or conclusion. An example of a notational appraisal may be the periodic valuation of a portfolio of real estate. The valuation may be performed to measure the appreciation or depreciation in the portfolio (compared to a general real estate market index). However, no actual purchase or sale of a property is planned.

On the other hand, transactional appraisals are performed in anticipation of an actual purchase or sale transaction. These appraisals may be used to establish a transaction price, to negotiate a transaction price, to obtain transactional financing, and so on. In any event, a real transaction will be consummated based, in part, upon the appraisal. Due to their transactional nature, these appraisals usually involve greater documentation and substantiation than do notational appraisals. Client users, and appraisers should understand the difference between transactional and notational appraisal when considering the bankruptcy valuation process.

State and Local Property Taxes

Special-purpose properties and income-producing properties subject to state and local property taxes may, in certain cases, be valued using business valuation techniques. Such properties include, for example, mining operations, timberland and forestry operations, farm land and agricultural properties, chemical processing plants, utilities and cogeneration plants, data processing and telecommunications facilities, high-technology properties, hotels, motels, strip and enclosed shopping malls, and mixed-use properties.

The first step in the valuation process is to quickly develop a thorough understanding of the definitions of value, the valuation elements and methodology, and the assessment process—all as allowed or required by the statutory authority of the relevant jurisdiction. The valuation work program, procedures and methodologies, and valuation opinion report should be tailored to be consistent with the value definitions and approaches in the local jurisdiction.

Additionally, location-specific, intangible real estate interests may become part of the valuation process to ensure that only the real property interests that are taxable are appraised. Depending on local ordinances, such location-specific real estate interests may include franchise agreements, FCC licenses, certificates of need, licenses and permits, possessory interests, leasehold interests, and so on. When these intangible assets would otherwise be grouped with the real estate and taxed as a bundle of rights, it may be appropriate to separately identify, value, and determine the remaining useful life of these assets. That way, in jurisdictions where intangible assets are not subject to state or local property taxation, their value can be appropriately separated from the balance of the real estate value.

Intellectual Property Rights Infringement

Once the infringement has been proven, the question of the amount of damages caused by the infringement becomes an important issue. There are several methods available with which to quantify the damages caused by the infringement. Two of the more common methods are (1) incremental market value of property during infringement period, and (2) present value of lost income during the infringement period.

The first method requires a comparative valuation (i.e., a valuation of the intangible asset or intellectual property on two different "as of" valuation dates). That is, analysts value the intellectual property before the inception of the infringement act and, then, value the intellectual property again at the termination of the infringement act.

The second method requires that the analyst determine the present value of the economic income (as defined) that was foregone by the owner of the intellectual property during the infringement period. This lost economic income could represent either actual lost earnings or cash flow or the loss of hypothetical rents, royalties, or payments that would normally accrue to the ownership of such an intellectual property.

The most common categorization of intangible assets follows:

- Technology-related (e.g., engineering drawings).
- Customer-related (e.g., customer lists).
- Contract-related (e.g., favorable supplier contracts).
- Data processing-related (e.g., computer software).
- Human capital-related (e.g., a trained and assembled work force).
- Marketing-related (e.g., trademarks and trade names).
- Location-related (e.g., leasehold interests).
- Goodwill-related (e.g., going-concern value).

Many of the typical business valuation theories and techniques can be applied in order to quantify the impact of an infringement upon such intellectual properties as trademarks, trade names, copyrights, patents, proprietary technology, computer software, and so forth.

Those intellectual property valuation techniques are often applied by business appraisers when multistate corporations transfer legal title to various corporate intangible assets and intellectual properties to their Delaware subsidiary. This intangible asset-transfer program is often implemented for strategic planning, asset management, and tax reduction purposes.

Multinational corporations often recognize another application of these intellectual property valuation techniques when their intercompany pricing decisions regarding these assets may be scrutinized by interested third parties, such as the Internal Revenue Service or joint venture partners.

Summary

Any valuation done for litigation, or where potential litigation may be involved, must be done in conformance with the applicable legal context. This context includes statutes, regulations, court case precedents, and directives or preferences of the court of jurisdiction.

Standards of value and acceptable valuation methodologies are defined differently from one legal context to another. A study of the valuation law in the relevant valuation context is essential to any valuation involving known or potential litigation.

Chapter 39

Divorce

By Ralph Arnold, CFA, ASA

One of the most common reasons an appraiser is retained to value a small business or professional practice is to establish value for a marital dissolution. In fact, the adoption of the *no-fault* divorce and the application of the equitable distribution of marital property statutes in the 1970s by the various state legislatures significantly influenced the development of the business valuation profession.

Unlike valuations for other purposes, the valuation standards, appraisal methods, and valuation dates are as diverse as the geography of the 50 states.

Divorce Valuation Survey

In preparation for this chapter, we prepared a survey form on business valuations for divorce purposes, which was sent to all *Accredited Senior Appraisers* certified in business valuation by the American Society of Appraisers. The survey questions dealt with the appraiser's experience during the past three years involving business valuations for marital dissolutions. Information requested included the number of divorce cases handled, the growth trend of divorce valuations experienced, and the standards and methods of valuation most commonly used.

Of the 300 forms sent out, 117 responses were received. Of those appraisers responding, 54 percent had been involved in at least one divorce valuation during the past three years. The most common reason why the other 46 percent had not been involved in divorce valuations was that of the low fees generated. Most likely, the low fees are not because of the valuation purpose, but because most businesses being valued for divorces are small businesses and professional practices.

Those that had been involved in divorce valuations in the past three years averaged 32 divorce valuations during that time period. However, certain appraisers had specialized in divorce valuations. The top 20 percent of appraisers (based on number of divorce appraisals completed) averaged 91 cases during the past three years, while the remaining 80 percent averaged 15 cases.

The survey results suggest that the demand for business and professional practice valuations related to marital dissolutions is increasing— 41 percent of the respondents indicated that the divorce cases were growing in number, while only 11 percent saw a decline (another 7 percent decided not to handle divorce valuations in the future).

The survey respondents, who are generally full-time appraisers, indicated that on average, 41 percent of the other professionals completing divorce valuations were also full-time business appraisers, 20 percent were forensic accountants, 17 percent were general accountants, 8 percent were business brokers and the subject company's accountant (each), and 6 percent were other professionals. Also, professional practice valuation represented 22 percent of all divorce valuations for all appraisers, while 24 percent of the valuations were of professional practices by those appraisers (the top 20 percent) handling the most divorce valuations.

Divorce and Litigation

Obviously, any appraiser considering divorce valuation is considering litigation valuation. The emotions of the parties in many divorces can have an impact upon their ability to compromise valuation differences. We were involved in a case where the total valuation difference between the appraisers was $25,000, less than 5 percent of the value opined by either appraiser. Both attorneys and appraisers recommended to their clients that the difference in value be split as a compromise—a recommendation that was rejected by both parties, even though the cost of litigating the difference was more than the difference in value. While this may seem to be a totally illogical choice by the divorcing couple, the emotions involved as a result of the breakup of the marriage were greater than the logic suggested by all the professionals representing the parties.[1]

Those surveyed appraisers involved in divorce valuations indicated that 24 percent of all divorce cases ended in litigation where the value of the business or professional practice was at issue. Those appraisers specializing in divorce valuations experienced a slightly lower litigation percentage of 19 percent.[2]

Because of the high incidence of divorce valuations ending up contested in the courtroom, the appraiser considering valuations for divorce purposes needs to be well versed in effective testimony methods and courtroom procedure. Also, as is discussed in the following sections of this chapter, each state's courts are the primary body that determines the proper standards of value that are to be used in that state's divorce cases, so the appraiser in the divorce situation needs to be apprised of relevant state court precedents.

The valuation of small businesses for divorce purposes requires the appraiser to be more of an investigative appraiser compared to other situations that call for valuation. Small businesses tend to have less reliable, compiled financial statements. Also, many times the parties have expensed many personal expenses through the business. Therefore, the appraiser may need to assume a more active role in restating the financial statements in order to better reflect the economic operations of the business or reconstruct the revenues and/or expenses of the business before any valuation of the business is completed. The appraiser who diligently calculates the correct capitalization rate to apply, but does not take the time to evaluate the accuracy of the prior financial statements from an economic point of view, may find that his valuation report is totally meaningless. Many times, it is advisable for the appraiser to retain an accountant (or to recommend that the client retain an accountant) to restate the prior income statements and balance sheets if the appraiser does not have the time or knowledge to produce more reliable financial statements based on the company's supporting records.

---

[1]Ultimately, the judge adopted one of the appraiser's values and did not split the difference.
[2]This percentage is far higher than for disputed valuations in most other contexts.

Date of Valuation

A question that should always be asked of the divorce attorney by the appraiser is: What valuation date or dates should be used? Three primary dates can be used in a divorce proceeding: the date closest to trial, the date of separation, and the date of marriage. As a general rule, a business primarily dependent on the efforts of one of the parties getting the divorce will be valued at the date of separation. Businesses whose success is more dependent on many individuals, location, underlying asset values, and so forth, will be valued at a date closest to trial. A date of marriage valuation is generally necessary where it is claimed that one of the spouses is only allowed to receive one half (or some percentage) of the increase in value of the business during the period of marriage.

Many states have rules as to what valuation dates are appropriate,[3] while many states do not provide any statute or case law that clarifies the date. The appropriate date of valuation may be further confused because the divorcing couple cannot even agree on what date they separated or because the trial date is continually postponed. In one case in which we were involved, valuations were required for four different dates: date of marriage, date of separation claimed by the wife, date of separation claimed by the husband, and the date of trial.

In those situations where the increase in the business's value is the portion to be divided equitably, the increase in value from the date of marriage to either the date of separation or date of trial will need to be calculated by appraising the business as of both dates. Various allocation formulas can then be applied in order to determine the marital portion of the business to be divided. There are two primary methods for allocating this increase.

The *Periera* method treats the value at date of marriage as an investment that should generate an appropriate rate of return during marriage. Therefore, the value of the marital property would be equal to the assets' date of separation (or trial) value, less the value at date of marriage and the expected normal yearly returns during marriage based on the value at date of marriage.

The *Van Camp* method considers the value of services of the employee/spouse during the term of the marriage and compares that value to the compensation received. If the employee/spouse is underpaid, the underpayment is allocated as marital property (including a return on the underpayment to the date of trial).

Generally, the Periera method is preferred by the nonoperating spouse, while the Van Camp method is preferred by the employee/spouse. While each method can give similar values for the marital property, it is more likely that the two methods will give extremely different allocations between marital and separate property values. One method of resolving a large conflict between the two allocation methods is a third method, called the *Todd* method and sometimes referred to as the

---

[3]For example, California professional practices are generally valued at the date of separation, while commercial businesses not totally dependent on the owner's efforts are valued as of trial date.

combination method. An example of this method, along with examples of the Periera and Van Camp methods, are shown in Exhibit 39–1.

Standard of Value

Most state divorce statutes require the equal or equitable division of the marital property between the spouses. Many of the state statutes require that the assets be "valued." However, the statutes themselves are generally silent as to what standard of value should be used in setting the value. As a result, the states' appellate courts have been responsible for addressing this issue. This means that there is no universal standard of value among the various states and, in fact, there is not necessarily a single standard for all divorce valuations in any single state.

While many divorce courts will use the fair market value standard, there are many situations where this standard is not necessarily used. As examples, the required valuation of nonmarketable professional goodwill or the valuation of licenses or educational degrees cannot be based on the fair market value standard because these assets cannot be sold in any marketplace. Therefore, the intrinsic value standard may be more appropriate.

Many state courts tend to ignore the value set in a company's buy-sell agreement, even when that agreement may limit the fair market value of the stock interest to the agreement's stated value. The intrinsic value of holding onto the company's stock may exceed the buy-sell value. In fact, only 2 percent of the surveyed appraisers indicated that the court *always* follows the buy-sell agreement in setting value, and 11 percent indicated that the court gives *substantial* weight to an agreement. On the other hand, 79 percent of the appraisers indicated that the courts give *some* weight to the agreement and another 8 percent indicated *little if any* weight is given to buy-sell agreements by the divorce courts.

The appraiser needs to be knowledgeable about the statutory and case law as related to divorce for each state in which that appraiser practices so that the applicable standard of value is considered (as well as the valuation date).

The standard of value used most by the appraisers responding to the divorce valuation survey was fair market value—84 percent of all respondents indicated that they had used this standard of value in at least one divorce valuation during the past three years. However, when valuing professional practices, only 66 percent of the appraisers indicated that they used the fair market value standard.

Discovery

The reliability of any valuation of a company is primarily contingent on the accuracy of the information used in the appraisal. Because of the animosity often attendant in divorce proceedings, the appraiser may find

Exhibit 39–1

MARITAL PROPERTY ALLOCATION METHODS

Periera Method

Value of Business, Date of Separation		$750,000
Value of Business, Date of Marriage	100,000	
Return on Investment, 10% per annum (simple)		
Year 1	10,000	
Year 2	10,000	
Year 3	10,000	
Year 4	10,000	
Year 5	10,000	
Value of Separate Property		(150,000)
Value of Marital Property		$600,000

Van Camp Method

Value of Business, Date of Separation $750,000

	Market Compensation	Compensation Paid	Difference	Return on Investment	Total	
Year 1	60,000	40,000	20,000	0	20,000	
Year 2	65,000	55,000	10,000	2,000	12,000	
Year 3	71,000	55,000	16,000	3,000	19,000	
Year 4	77,000	65,000	12,000	4,600	16,600	
Year 5	80,000	65,000	15,000	5,800	20,800	
Value of Marital Property						(88,400)
Value of Separate Property						$661,600

Todd Method (Combination Method)

Return on Separate Property (Periera Method)	50,000	36.1%
Value of Unpaid Services	88,400	63.9%
Total	138,400	100.0%

Value of Separate Property	
Value of Business, Date of Separation	$750,000
Value of Business, Date of Marriage	100,000
Increase in Business Value	650,000
Separate Property Portion of Increase	x 36.1%
Separate Property Increase in Value	234,650
Value of Business, Date of Marriage	100,000
Value of Separate Property	$334,650

Value of Marital Property	
Increase in Business Value	650,000
Marital Property Portion of Increase	x 63.9%
Value of Marital Property	$415,350

that one or both of the parties will not be willing to provide the company information necessary for the valuation of the company. This is frequently a problem for the appraiser who is retained by the nonoperating spouse. The attorney for the nonoperating spouse will need to rely upon the appraiser for guidance as to the types of information necessary to be subpoenaed from the other party and/or the subject company. Therefore, the appraiser should provide a detailed and specific list of documents that are necessary. Because the process of subpoenaing documents is cumbersome, lengthy, and has specific cut-off dates, the appraiser should ask for all documents that may reasonably exist that may have any impact on the company value. Many times it is difficult, if not impossible, to go back for a second (or third) request of documents.

Also, the appraiser may need to interview the company's management by providing the attorney with a list of all questions to be asked by interrogatory or by deposition. Also, it may be necessary for the appraiser to have the attorney go to the court in order to get permission for a site visit to the business, or to review records at the business.

Obviously, because the appraisal will only be as good as the information used to reach a value opinion, the ability of the appraiser and attorney, working together, to procure the necessary and complete information is of critical importance to the appraiser.

It should be remembered that the company is not the only source of documents regarding company information. The company's accountants, bankers, insurance agents, and attorneys also maintain information on the company. These sources of information may also need to be investigated by the appraiser.

Methods of Valuation

There are no *standard* methods of valuation for divorce purposes. However, certain methods tend to be used more than others. Valuation methods using publicly traded company data (price/earnings multiples, etc.) are typically not used when valuing small businesses or professional practices. Also, many state courts have held a business's value resulting from the efforts of the operating spouse after separation are not marital property. As a result, divorce courts tend not to use financial projections that are necessary to complete the discounted future returns method of valuation.

The appraisers responding to the divorce valuation survey indicated a preference for the capitalization of earnings method of valuation—94 percent of all respondents indicated that they had used the method in divorce valuations of business interests and 61 percent for professional practices. Other methods used for business valuation, and the percent of appraisers that have used them, were as follows:

	Commercial Businesses	Professional Practices
Prior sales of company	77%	52%
Capitalization of cash flow	73	47
Publicly traded companies	73	26

	Commercial Businesses	Professional Practices
Adjusted book value	71	52
Excess earnings method	66	62
Revenue multiples	58	55
Discounted future returns	58	32
Book value multiples	57	32
Buy-sell agreement formula	55	53
Nonpublic sales, other companies	53	42
Merger and acquisition data	53	24
Adjusted tangible assets and goodwill	44	50
Rules of thumb	42	44
Book value (unadjusted)	40	37
Liquidation value	39	24
Capitalization of dividends	36	18
Original investment	24	23
Cost to recreate	24	21

Clearly, the facts of each situation will determine the method of valuation to be used. For example, a company that is highly profitable and not intending to liquidate would not be valued using a liquidation method.

Valuation Discounts

Discounts for taxes, minority interest, and lack of marketability are not necessarily universal when valuing businesses and professional practices for divorce purposes. In the state of Oregon, for example, the appellate court has held that in a family-owned company, no discounts for minority interest or marketability are appropriate when valuing an individual family member's interest for divorce purposes.

When using the adjusted book value method, many state courts have held that no corporate capital gains tax should be considered unless the tax is *immediate and specific*. Based on the survey, 51 percent of the appraisers polled indicated that the courts rarely or never allowed this discount, while the remainder indicated that the courts usually allowed the taxes to be computed.

Based on the survey, the application of minority and marketability discounts was influenced by the factors that might influence the discount. Given a situation where the interest being appraised (for divorce purposes) represented a minority interest in a company controlled by the spouse's family, 37 percent of the appraisers would apply a discount, 37 percent sometimes applied a discount, and 26 percent never applied a discount. On the other hand, given the same situation, 52 percent would always apply a marketability discount, while 34 percent sometimes applied a discount, and 14 percent would never consider a marketability discount.

Only 15 percent of the appraisers would usually apply a minority interest discount for a 50 percent interest in the company, while 58 percent would never apply this discount. If the interest being appraised represented control, only 21 percent would usually apply a marketability discount, while 32 percent would never apply such a discount.

Clearly, the facts in each situation will have a direct impact upon the application of, and amount of, minority interest and marketability discounts in divorce valuations.

Summary

Valuations for divorce purposes represent a significant portion of all professional valuations of small businesses and professional practices. Our practitioner survey indicated that the demand for professional valuations in connection with divorces is continuing to grow.

A significant proportion (about 20 to 25 percent, according to the practitioner survey) of all valuations for divorces culminate in litigation. Divorce valuations are complicated by inconsistencies in standards and methods of value, and also applicable valuation dates from one jurisdiction to another (and sometimes within the same jurisdiction). The appraiser needs to work closely with the attorney to understand the applicable standards and dates as well as accepted valuation methods in each case.

Discovery is often more difficult in valuations for divorces than for other purposes. The appraiser should work closely with the attorney to ensure adequate discovery.

The appraiser involved in valuations for divorces must be alert and willing to understand the legal requirements in each case and adopt procedures and appraisal methodology to meet the respective requirements.

Selected Bibliography

Articles

Arnold, Ralph. "Putting a Value on Future Interests." *Family Advocate*, Summer 1984, pp. 32–36, 42.

Broecker, H.W. "Cross-Examination of a Business Valuation Expert Witness." *American Journal of Family Law*, Fall 1989, pp. 213–21.

Cenker, William J., and Carl J. Monastra. "The Basics of Business Valuation in Divorce Settlements." *Practical Accountant*, January 1991, pp. 18–26.

Cohen, Harriet N., and Patricia Hennessey. "Valuation of Property in Marital Dissolutions." *Family Law Quarterly*, September 1989, pp. 339–81.

DuCanto, Joseph N., and David H. Hopkins. "Tax Aspects of Dissolution and Separation." *Illinois Family Law*, 1988, Chapter 17.

Fishman, Jay E. "The 'Key Man' Concept in Business Valuation Upon Divorce." *FAIR$HARE: The Matrimonial Law Monthly*, June 1982, pp. 3–4.

Gallinger, George W. "Valuation of Community Goodwill in Divorce Proceedings Involving Closely Held Businesses." *ASA Valuation*, January 1992, pp. 34–41.

Henszey, Benjamin N., and Arnold F. Shapiro. "Distribution of Pension Benefits on Divorce: Some Unresolved Analytical Issues." *Journal of Risk and Insurance*, September 1991, pp. 480–96.

Kalcheim, M. W. "Problems in Valuing Professional Goodwill in Divorce Proceedings." *Illinois Bar Journal*, February 1990, pp. 80–87.

Kelsey, David. "The Real Bottom Line in Divorce." *National Public Accountant*, November 1991, pp. 28–30.

Klein, Ronald. "The Role of the Expert in Divorce Valuation." *FAIR$HARE: The Matrimonial Law Monthly*, May 1986, pp. 3–6.

Kuenster, Richard A. "Estate Planning, Family Businesses, and Divorce." Parts I and II. *FAIR$HARE: The Matrimonial Law Monthly*, October 1991 and November 1991, pp. 7–9, 11–14.

"Legal Briefs: When Company Owners D-I-V-O-R-C-E." *Inc.*, October 1991, p. 161.

Maccarrone, Eugene T., and Martha S. Weisel. "The CPA License at Divorce." *CPA Journal*, March 1992, pp. 22–27.

Marmer, Jack. "Divvying up Matrimonial Assets." *CA Magazine*, April 1988, pp. 54–56.

McGovern, Margaret F. "Licenses v. Degrees: Is There a Difference?" *Family Advocate*, Fall 1986, pp. 14–17.

Monath, Donald. "Professional Goodwill: Is It Marital Property?" *Family Advocate*, Fall 1991, pp. 52–53.

Morse, Ed. "The Appraisal of Community Property." *Appraisal Journal*, October 1988, pp. 477–81.

Murphy, John W. "Using an Appraiser to Value the Closely Held Business." *FAIR$HARE: The Matrimonial Law Monthly*, March 1992, pp. 6–7.

Parkman, Allen. "The Treatment of Professional Goodwill in Divorce Proceedings." *Family Law Quarterly*, Summer 1984, pp. 213–23.

Riebesell, H. F., Jr. "Divorce of a Closely Held Business Owner." *FAIR$HARE: The Matrimonial Law Monthly*, May 1992, pp. 3–8.

Rosen, Howard S., and J. Burke. "Putting a Value on a Professional License." *Family Advocate*, Summer 1984, pp. 23–27.

Trugman, Gary R. "An Appraiser's Approach to Business Valuation." Parts I and II. *FAIR$HARE: The Matrimonial Law Monthly*, July 1991 and August 1991, pp. 3–8, 8–13.

Zipp, Alan S. "Business Valuation for Divorce." *Journal of Accountancy*, April 1992, pp. 43–48.

————. "Divorce Valuation of Business Interests: A Capitalization of Earnings Approach." *Family Law Quarterly*, Spring 1989, pp. 89–129.

Books

Brown, Ronald, ed. *Encyclopedia of Matrimonial Practice.* Englewood Cliffs, N.J.: Prentice Hall Law & Business, 1991.

————. *Valuing Professional Practices and Licenses: A Guide for the Matrimonial Practitioner.* Clifton, N.J.: Prentice Hall Law Business, 1987.

Foster, Henry H., Jr., and Ronald L. Brown, eds. *Contemporary Matrimonial Law Issues: A Guide to Divorce Economics & Practice.* New York: Law & Business, Inc., 1985.

Goldberg, Barth H. *Valuation of Divorce Assets*. St. Paul, Minn.: West Publishing Co., 1984; Supplemented 1989.

Kleeman, Robert E., ed. *Valuation Strategies in Divorce*. 2nd ed. New York: John Wiley & Sons, 1992.

McCahey, John P., ed. *Valuation and Distribution of Marital Property*. New York: Matthew Bender & Co., 1992.

Oldham, J. T. *Divorce, Separation and the Distribution of Property*. New York: Law Journal Seminars Press, 1987.

Shank, Steven J., and Richard K. Olson. *Practical Divorce Valuation and Financial Analysis*. Eau Claire, Wis.: Professional Education Systems, 1986.

Skoloff, Gary N., and Theodore P. Orenstein. *When a Lawyer Divorces: How to Value a Professional Practice; How to Get Extraordinary Remedies*. Chicago: American Bar Association, 1986.

Trugman, Gary R. *Equitable Distribution Value of Small Closely Held Businesses and Professional Practices*. (Thesis for Degree of Master of Valuation Sciences, Lindenwood College.) Morristown, N.J.: Gary R. Trugman, 1990.

Zipp, Alan S. *Handbook of Tax and Financial Planning for Divorce and Separation*. Englewood Cliffs, N.J.: Prentice Hall, 1985.

Chapter 40

Damages

By Charles A. Wilhoite, CPA, CMA

In an economic sense, the term *damages* relates to the notion of one party experiencing a loss in value, however measured, as a result of another party's actions. In a business sense, this loss usually represents out-of-pocket costs and any other reasonably foreseeable amounts relating to increased costs, lost profits, or decreases in overall business value resulting from the wrongful actions of another. Although wrongful terminations, wrongful death, and permanent or total disability might immediately come to mind, as these circumstances often require damage calculations for wage and salary losses, our concern is that of damage cases involving the valuation of a business or professional practice, or lost profits thereof. The most common types of damage cases involving valuation of a business or practice are the following:

1. Breach of contract.
2. Condemnation.
3. Lost business opportunity.
4. Antitrust actions.
5. Personal injury.
6. Insurance claims.
7. Infringement of intellectual property.
8. Business torts.
9. Violation of securities laws.

Regardless of the specific type of damage involved, the common thread of a legitimate damage case is the fact that, because of the actions of another party, the affected business did not operate as it would have if the charged party had not undertaken the event(s) causing the damage. This leads to the consequential "but-for" claims of the damaged party, alleging that "but for" the actions of Company Z, "my business would have realized X profits or cash flows during this time period," or, in the most extreme circumstance, "my business would have continued to operate as a going concern," implying the total loss of the business. Another type of damage claim is the loss of a partial interest in a business or an entire business or business opportunity. "Had it not been for this wrongful deprivation, I would own X percentage of Z company." The job of the appraiser is to determine what that interest would be worth as of some particular date, usually (but not always) the date that the damage event occurred.

A noteworthy factor that often differentiates damage cases from other litigation involving business valuations is that damage cases are usually tried before a jury, but most other valuation-related litigation, such as divorce cases, dissenting stockholder suits, and tax cases, are usually tried before a judge without a jury. Preparation for a jury trial requires every possible effort to simplify the presentation of the complex subject of business or professional practice valuation, along with graphic exhibits to illustrate major points.

The Fact of Damages versus the Amount of Damages

From a legal standpoint, different proofs are required to establish whether or not damages occurred as opposed to establishing the amount of damages. William Cerillo, a California civil litigation and antitrust attorney, explains as follows:

> The fact of damage relates to whether plaintiff has been injured as a result of defendant's conduct. The amount of damage involves an estimate of plaintiff's loss. These are separate proofs. The burden as to the former is more stringent than the burden as to the latter. There must be evidence of the fact of injury before a jury is allowed to estimate the amount of damage.[1]

The business valuation expert may be called on in conjunction with either or both of these two essential elements of any damage case.

Establishing the Fact of Damages

Three legal principles govern the establishment of the fact of damages:

1. Proximate cause.
2. Reasonable certainty.
3. Foreseeability.

Proximate Cause

The plaintiff's "but-for" charge raised against the defendant addresses the requirement that the defendant's wrongful actions were the proximate, or approximate, cause of the losses. As suggested by the term approximate, this does not imply that the defendant's actions were the sole cause of the plaintiff's actions, but rather, that they were at least the major cause. Thus, necessary emphasis should be placed by experts on both sides to understand both the plaintiff's position within its industry and the direction of the industry, as well as the actual and projected impact that external factors were expected to have on the performance of participants within the industry during the alleged damage period in order to sufficiently support or refute the plaintiff's charge of proximate cause.

Reasonable Certainty

Reasonable certainty alludes to the notion that damages were actually experienced by the plaintiff. If the plaintiff achieves growth and profitability that greatly exceeded both industry norms and its own previous operating history *after* the alleged wrongful conduct of the defendant, a plaintiff might experience some difficulty recovering damages because of the inability to prove that actual damages were incurred. However, a plaintiff who has actually incurred damages and suffers significant losses after a defendant's wrongful actions, but who has failed to maintain adequate financial records and consequently provides an expert with little evidential support, may encounter similar, if not more, difficulty in proving actual damages. Thus, significant uncertainty as to the fact, or actual occurrence, of damages is potentially fatal to any damage claim.

---

[1]William A. Cerillo, *Proving Business Damages*, 2nd ed. (New York: John Wiley & Sons, 1991), p. 7.

Foreseeability

Foreseeability relates to the idea that resultant damages alleged by the plaintiff were a foreseeable natural result of a breach of contract at the time the contract was made or the time that the wrongful acts were committed. The concept of foreseeability is relevant only in the law of contracts. With tort claims, the foreseeability of injury is not a legal requirement, that is, a tortfeasor will be held liable regardless of whether damage was foreseeable or not. This point should be made clearer. It is what separates contract from tort law.

In contract situations, the immediate effect of breaches, either by the buyer or seller, are foreseeable in the sense that the buyer often has to find replacement goods or services at a higher cost, or the seller loses a sale and the related profits. One step further, even related effects are conceivably foreseeable, as a buyer who is the victim of a seller's breach may not only have to acquire replacement goods at a higher cost, but may also suffer the effects of lost sales that were dependent on the timely receipt of the contracted material that happened to be an integral component of the buyer's ultimate product. On the other hand, many sellers who operate as wholesalers may be deemed to have a virtually unlimited capacity to conduct business, and though a breach of contract by one buyer may have been easily fulfilled by a replacement buyer, courts have often ruled that based on the seller's capacity, both sales were conceivable and foreseeable, thereby accepting the seller's damage claim for both the difference in lost profits between the first contracted sale and the replacement sale, as well as the total lost profits on the first sale.

In order to support or refute a plaintiff's claim of damages, expertise in several areas is often required in order to establish the significant factors affecting the plaintiff's success in his particular industry and to ascertain whether the defendant's actions were indeed the principal cause for the demise of the plaintiff's operations. Only those knowledgeable in the plaintiff's industry and the impact that external forces and actions would exert on the plaintiff's performance within that industry are able to determine with any degree of certainty the foreseeable result of certain actions. For this very reason, damage cases of significant dollar amounts often result in numerous experts—industry, accounting, finance, economics— being retained by both the plaintiff and the defendant in order to adequately address specific questions relating to their areas of expertise and the impact that certain actions would have on the plaintiff's operation.

Calculating the Amount of Damages

Although the burden of proof regarding damages rests with the plaintiff, and at times may appear to represent a near monumental task, defendants assume significant risk when they bank on a plaintiff's inability to calculate exact damages, as the courts merely require that the plaintiff's presentation be reasonable. It is essential that defendants provide excellent expert evidence as to the actual amount of damages (or lack of damages). Otherwise, a defendant may end up facing a significant liability at the conclusion of the trial, regardless of how weak the plaintiff's presentation may have been, for the simple reason that it was the best, or only, proof provided.

Though the circumstances surrounding different damage claims will determine the specific type of claim filed (i.e., breach of contract, antitrust, lost business opportunity, etc.), the methods used to calculate claims are fairly standard. With the exception of a breach of contract, which is often covered by liquidated damages and other provisions within the contract itself, current literature suggests that most damage claims can be calculated by administering one or more of the following methods:

1. Before-and-after.
2. Yardstick (comparable).
3. Sales projection ("but-for").

Simple in theory only, these methods have the underlying theme of requiring an estimated performance level for the damaged party, absent the effects of the defendant's actions, and comparing these projected results to actual results that were experienced by the plaintiff.

The Before-and-After Method

Using the before-and-after method, which is probably most suited to antitrust and other similar business interruption situations, operations for the plaintiff are estimated during the damage period based on results (1) attained prior to the alleged damaging acts, and/or (2) after the effects of the alleged acts have subsided, and either or both of these is compared to results during the period of the effect of the alleged acts. The success of this method depends, of course, on the ability of the plaintiff's expert to establish and support a proven historical financial record for the plaintiff's business so that operations preceding and succeeding the alleged damage are able to serve as "damage bookends," clearly illustrating the effects of the interruption or antitrust violation period. Ideally, operations before and after the damage period will show similar trends, thereby enabling the expert to estimate the company's performance during the damage period using either pre- or postdamage operations as a performance standard with comparable damage amounts resulting. In many cases only the "before" period or the "after" period is available to use to predict the "but-for" performance during the damage period.

The Yardstick (Comparable) Method

The yardstick, or comparable, method requires the expert to identify companies or industries that are comparable to the plaintiff's company and plot the performance of the plaintiff's company along the lines of the comparable companies' or industries' performances. This method, of course, requires that the expert not only satisfy the often difficult task of identifying similar companies or industries, but also that the companies or industries selected by the expert be themselves unaffected by the alleged damaging acts of the defendant. Applying as a proxy the performance of another company or a particular industry to project the performance of the plaintiff's company, absent the alleged damaging actions of the defendant, is a straightforward, understandable approach in estimating losses. Once again, the key lies in carefully identifying the most appropriate comparable companies or industry. In some instances, a comparable but unaffected branch or division of the plaintiff's own company may provide the yardstick needed.

Sales Projections ("But-For") Method

The sales projections, or "but-for," method entails the creation of a performance model for the plaintiff's company, complete with growth and return assumptions. Using the model, operations for the plaintiff's company are projected during the damage period absent (i.e., "but-for") the alleged effects of the defendant's actions. The returns suggested by the model are then compared with the actual results realized by the defendant during the damage period.

Of the three methods mentioned above, probably the most recurring method applied in practice is some variation of the sales projection method. Typically, most business operators are in a position to provide sales projections for their businesses, and fit within one of a countless number of industries subject to annual, semiannual, or even quarterly forecasts by a variety of both public and private data sources. Such circumstances lend themselves quite nicely to the development of simulation models designed specifically for the plaintiff's business. However, a key factor to keep in mind when developing a sales projection and the resulting profits is that courts tend to prefer projections based on historical track records, even in light of numerous concurring industry forecasts and other published financial data regarding "normal" growth and returns for participants within the relevant industry.

Regardless of the method undertaken, the extent that projected results exceed actual results represents the plaintiff's loss. This loss often not only represents profits lost during the damage period, but also can and often does represent a decrease in overall business value separate from lost profits. Whatever is represented by the total damage claim, all concerned parties should bear in mind that the sum total of combined lost profits and any decrease in overall business value is limited to the present value of total future profits anticipated by the business prior to the alleged damaging acts. The reason is that the value of any business is the present (discounted) value of all expected future profits. Intuitively, this should serve as a recurring reasonableness check throughout the calculation process.

Some Comments on Projections

A review of the plaintiff's operations for a reasonable period prior to the damaging acts—preferably 5 to 10 years, if available—should provide the expert with a reasonable basis for making some general estimations regarding growth patterns and returns for the plaintiff's business, absent the effects of the defendant's alleged damaging acts. At this point, the expert would be wise to research the plaintiff's industry, comparing the plaintiff's historical record with the historical record of the industry for the relevant time period in order to determine whether the plaintiff's operations were below, at, or above industry averages.

Many times, a plaintiff will be unable to provide much historical information, either because operations are in the development stages, or for other reasons, and industry information will be all that the expert will have to go on in projecting operating results for the plaintiff during the damage period. In circumstances such as these, it is critical that the expert thoroughly investigates and understands the industry and develops a sound argument supporting why the plaintiff's operations should be expected to parallel, or exceed, industry averages before applying industry return and growth rates to the plaintiff's operations.

Armed with return and growth assumptions, the plaintiff's expert is in a position to project the plaintiff's operations over the damage period. A simple presentation of the projected, but-for operating results parallel to the actual results, with a column indicating the differences—that is, losses—will illustrate clearly the alleged damages experienced by the plaintiff.

A word of warning, however, regarding projections. Though the analysis may be quite simple and the final numbers may appear to speak for themselves, analysis of the projected results is required in order to determine their reasonableness. Implied revenue and profit growth rates should be analyzed to determine if they are reasonable over the damage period. Further, projected profits should be compared with initial investments and revenues in order to determine if returns are reasonable for businesses within the relevant industry. Unreasonable results suggest that your model may have one or more unreasonable assumptions.

Particular attention should be paid to the implications of revenue growth and the resulting profits. Projections often fail to consider the limitations placed on revenue and profit growth by a particular business's given capacity at the time of the projections. Revenues projected several years down the road would often be unattainable without significant capital investments and costs being incurred by the related business. Required investments may include expanded operating space or new facilities and additional equipment. Additional costs might include an increased employee base, with related benefit expenses. Each of these, of course, imply reductions in profits and should be incorporated into projected results. The only way for such information to be appropriately reflected in projected results is for the expert to have gained a thorough understanding of the plaintiff's industry.

Having incorporated all relevant costs and the effects of any capital demands into the projections, the resulting summed losses represent the total loss for the plaintiff, which has not taken into consideration any prejudgment interest earnings that may be accruable to the plaintiff. If losses have been projected past the date of adjudication, the principle of discounting, or bringing the loss to a present value, must also be considered.

Prejudgment Interest and Discounting Anticipated Returns

Assume a court determines that damages commenced two years prior to the judgment date and were projected for seven years after the judgment date, for a total damage period of nine years. In order to make the plaintiff whole—that is, award the plaintiff with a fund that, if invested, would provide payments that would put him in the same financial position that he would have been in prior to the damaging acts—losses prior to the judgment date would have to be compounded upward, and losses projected subsequent to the judgment date would have to be discounted. Though the compounding of past year amounts, known as prejudgment interest, and the discounting of future losses make sound economic sense, many court jurisdictions do not allow prejudgment interest calculations, and occasionally have refused to recognize that future losses should be discounted. However, this has usually occurred when the arguments have not been made.

The question, now, is what rate to use for compounding or discounting losses. In general, most theorists will agree that future profits should be discounted at an appropriate rate; however, most are reluctant to state what the appropriate rate is, and whether the same rate should be applied in calculating prejudgment interest. In personal injury situations, discussed below, courts have accepted both prejudgment and discount real (i.e., inflation-adjusted) rates based on U.S. government securities. In strict business applications, the courts have taken a less firm stance. Therefore, determining an acceptable discount rate requires that the expert first establish the degree of risk relating to the expected returns from investing in the relevant business, and then proceed as analysts would in the market by developing a rate implicit with inflation and other premiums that would properly reflect the risk associated with the anticipated returns.

Intuitively, most would argue that investing in any business is riskier than investing in U.S. securities; the extent that risk premiums are added to the "riskless" government security rate in determining the particular business's appropriate discount rate depends on the size of the business and potential for its failure (i.e., financial or default risk), as well as the variability of returns experienced by the business and others in its industry. The key factor in determining discount rates is the need to equate the expected returns from investing in a particular concern with risk of achieving those returns.

The damage calculation is complete after the effects of any prejudgment interest and discounting have been incorporated, unless, of course, the calculation relates to an antitrust or situation allowing for trebled damages. Statutes and case law for the particular jurisdiction should always be reviewed in order to determine the courts' views on prejudgment interest and discounting.

Common Damage Cases

As mentioned earlier, some of the most common types of damage cases involving valuation of a business or practice include breach of contract, condemnation, lost business opportunity, antitrust actions, personal injury, and insurance claims. Each of these six types of damage cases is discussed briefly below.

Breach of Contract

A variety of breach-of-contract actions can give rise to a lawsuit requiring a valuation of a business or a fractional interest in a business as a measure of damages. As mentioned earlier, substantiating or refuting the assumptions regarding proximate cause, reasonable certainty, and foreseeability are vitally important in contract disputes resulting in damage claims. A stockholder or partner's claim of a contract breach resulting in his ousting from a company, business venture, or the denial of a stock or partnership interest, or a breach from either side between a buyer and seller—each of these circumstances presents a situation with readily available facts to address the issues of proximate cause, reasonable certainty, and foreseeability.

The denial of a right to a business interest is usually a normal, straightforward valuation problem involving the value of whatever interest in an entity was denied as a result of the breach of contract. However, if the breach of contract damages the business itself, this creates the need to determine the value of lost profits, and often, the diminution in the total value of the business resulting from the damaging acts. In general, damage claims resulting from contract breaches should contemplate foreseeable and reasonably estimable losses reflecting a type of opportunity cost incurred by the damaged party. In other words, as a result of the breach, the damaged party was not able to enjoy benefits that it was contractually entitled to, and further, the damaged party may even experience additional costs in the form of both increased actual costs and lost profits.

Condemnation

A frequent cause of damages is the taking of business premises through eminent domain proceedings. Condemnation may result in the total loss of the business, if relocation is not feasible, or in a temporary loss of profits plus relocation costs. These temporary costs may also be combined with some permanent loss of locational goodwill, since it is unlikely that all patrons would follow a business or practice to a new location. Ideally, one would like to be able to document the loss of locational goodwill by the use of customer lists before and after the condemnation, but few businesses are likely to have such records.

Lost Business Opportunity

The most common scenario leading to a damage claim for lost business opportunity is an employee coming upon an opportunity through contacts made through the employer company, and then exploiting the opportunity on his own, or through another company, without offering it to the initial employer. In this case, the measure of damages is usually the value lost to the initial employer as a result of not being offered the business opportunity.

Antitrust Actions

Perhaps the most complicated of all categories of business damage cases is the antitrust area, or those situations where certain business activities are deemed by the courts to result in the restraint of normal competition. The hard-line stance adopted by the courts in dealing with violators of antitrust laws is based primarily on the premise that most monopolistic circumstances result in consumers being forced to accept higher prices for goods and services. A victorious plaintiff under the federal antitrust laws has the right to recover treble damages in many circumstances.

In the realm of antitrust litigation, the law is the greatest ally of the party pressing suit because allegations arising from clearly illegal acts of a defendant require that the plaintiff prove only that the act has occurred. The defendant's liability to the plaintiff is created by his violation of the relevant antitrust law, and the plaintiff is thereby relieved of the need to prove specific damage to competition. Examples, and brief explanations of some such violations include the following:

> *Price fixing*: Horizontal price fixing results when collusive behavior among competitors within a particular market results in price stabilization. An example is situations in which larger companies, or companies with significant market share, are able to sustain a period of pricing below average unit costs long enough to drive both existing and potential competitors from the market. At such times, prices are usually raised to reap the benefits of monopolistic profits due to the absence of competitors. The difficulty in proving such behavior, known as predatory pricing, lies in establishing an appropriate cost structure for the relevant industry in order to verify that the charged party is pricing below cost.

> *Horizontal market division*: As the name suggests, horizontal market division results in participants within the same industry dividing up a particular market with the end result that each participant has a virtual monopoly in his particular segment of the market. Such divisions can occur on a variety of bases, including citywide, regional, and end-user classifications. The simple act of two competitors simultaneously withdrawing from a particular market area often suggests some degree of horizontal market division activity. Another example of horizontal arrangements is the group boycott, during which competitors agree to refrain from dealing with specific suppliers or customers.

> *Resale price maintenance*: A form of vertical price fixing, resale price maintenance occurs when a manufacturer establishes a contract with a retailer, establishing either a maximum or minimum price at which the retailer can ultimately sell the product to the consumer. Under a maximum price arrangement, the manufacturer attempts to en-

hance competitiveness for its own product relative to other products. Under a minimum price-fixing arrangement, the manufacturer attempts to ensure that its product receives exposure comparable to that of its competitors' products by way of demonstration and store location. Such exposure is normally disproportionately allocated to the higher margin products, and a minimum price arrangement is established to produce a margin floor for the manufacturer's product.

As in all damage situations, antitrust violations require that the expert calculate a reasonable and supportable amount of profits that the damaged party would have realized were it not for the antitrust violations, and compare this amount with profits that were actually generated. This may use the "before-and-after," "yardstick," or "projections" approaches described earlier in the chapter.

Antitrust actions typically are tried in federal court for violation of either the Sherman or Clayton Acts. Each circuit of the federal court system develops its own case law. Courts usually consider case law developed in other circuits, but they are not bound by precedents from other circuits, some of which may conflict with the local circuit. Therefore, the expert should be aware of the local circuit case law as it affects the determination of damages in antitrust matters.

Some antitrust actions are tried in state courts under state antitrust statutes. Many states' antitrust laws are patterned after the federal statutes but may have some differences.

Personal Injury

Sometimes a personal injury impairs a person's ability to carry on his business or practice. In such cases, the amount of the economic loss is normally the measure of damages, usually estimated by the discounted future returns method. The process entails identifying the amount of returns lost, the duration of the loss period, and the appropriate discount factor. The discounting of future returns is required because the purpose of the award of damages is to provide a fund that, amortized over time, will yield the damaged party an amount equivalent to his loss. Though courts have not reached a consensus regarding the absolute need to discount future returns, the principle has often been approved. Discount rates accepted by the courts in personal injury situations have tended to suggest that the courts continue to view individuals as being risk-averse, as the rates normally reflect returns that could reasonably be expected by investing funds in riskless securities.

The measure of returns to be discounted would normally be net cash flows that would have been expected to be available to the damaged party. If the cash flows are in the form of taxable earnings, the taxes would not be deducted because the damage award itself would normally be subject to tax.[2]

---

[2]The circumstances under which a person suffering personal injury may recover damages equivalent to business loss are limited. Personal injury damages are generally limited to lost income, and lost business profits are recoverable only when the court can be persuaded that they are equivalent to lost income or lost earnings, typically of a sole proprietor. For a discussion of this point, see Robert L. Dunn, *Recovery of Damages for Lost Profits*, 4th ed. (Westport, Conn.: Lawpress Corporation, 1992).

Insurance Casualty Claims

Frequently, businesses are interrupted or destroyed by casualty losses, such as fires or storms. The discounted future returns method commonly comes into play to estimate the loss, offset by whatever value is salvaged. In dealing with insurance claims, careful attention should be paid to the wording in the policies before a damage estimate is submitted. Inappropriate attention to coverage provisions can often result in the forfeiture of potential recoveries or calculations of losses that were not insured.

Mitigation

An often crucial aspect regarding damage claims of all types, particularly contract breaches, is the principle of mitigation. This principle suggests that even victims of contract breaches have a duty to mitigate damages—that is, keep them as low as possible—and that damages are not recoverable for losses that the injured party could have avoided without undue risk, burden, or humiliation. Even in fraud situations, courts have long held that once a plaintiff learns of the fraud, alleged damages that accrue thereafter are not caused by the fraud, but rather by the plaintiff's decision to continue its relationship with the defendant irrespective of his knowledge of the fraud.

With regard to buyers and sellers of goods or services, the buyer is required by the principle of mitigation to "cover" by making reasonable efforts to find replacement goods or services to purchase, while a breached seller is obligated to make reasonable efforts to find an alternative purchaser for the breached goods or services. Excess costs incurred by the buyer in acquiring replacement goods, differences between the contracted price and the resale price incurred by the seller, and incidental damages such as expenses incurred in stopping the manufacture of goods, inspecting, transporting, receiving, or storing goods that resulted from the breach are normally recoverable.

Summary

In general, damage cases require a creative, but realistic, approach to calculating "hypothetical" values absent the alleged effects of the damaging party's actions. A thorough understanding of the damaged party's industry is a must in any damage calculation, and, if available, a historical record of the damaged party's operations should prove very beneficial. Knowledge of case law will provide the expert important guidance regarding approaches and methods that the courts will and will not accept in the calculation of damages in the specific legal context in question.

Selected Bibliography

Articles

Ackerman, Alan T. "Just Compensation for Condemnation of Going-Concern Value." *ASA Valuation*, June 1986, pp. 42–55.

Bagby, J. W., et al. "The Determination of Compensatory Damages: A Valuation Framework." *American Business Law Journal*, Spring 1984, pp. 1–39.

Bjorklund, Paul R. "Calculating Lost Earnings for Damage Awards." *Practical Accountant*, June 1991, pp. 62–70.

Blair, Roger D. "Measuring Damages for Lost Profits in Franchise Termination Cases." *Franchise Law Journal*, Fall 1988, pp. 3–12.

Budge, Bruce. "Damage Control." *Washington Law*, December 1990, pp. 26–27.

Lansche, James M. "Business Damages: What Are They Worth?" *Washington State Bar Association Business Law Newsletter*, October 1990, pp. 1–3.

Lanzillotti, R. F., and A. K. Esquibel. "Measuring Damages in Commercial Litigation: Present Value of Lost Opportunities." *Journal of Accounting, Auditing & Finance*, Winter 1990, pp. 125–44.

Liddle, Jeffrey L., and William F. Gray, Jr. "Proof of Damages for Breach of a Restricted Covenant or Noncompetition Agreement." *Employee Relations Law Journal*, Winter 1983–84, pp. 455–73.

Love, Vincent J., and Steven Alan Reiss. "Guidelines for Calculating Damages." *CPA Journal*, October 1990, p. 36.

O'Brien, Vincent E., and Joan K. Meyer. "A Guide to Calculating Lost Profits." *National Law Journal*, January 29, 1990, pp. 17–19.

Wagner, Michael J. "How Do You Measure Damages? Lost Income or Lost Cash Flow?" *Journal of Accountancy*, February 1990, pp. 28–31.

———. "The Accountant's Role in the Process of Damage Measurement." *Practical Accountant*, July 1990, pp. 52–60.

Zerter, William B. "Statistical Approaches to Loss of Profits Valuations." *Business Valuation News*, September 1985, pp. 25–28.

Books

Cerillo, William A. *Proving Business Damages.* 2nd ed. New York: John Wiley & Sons, 1991.

Dunn, Robert L. *Recovery of Damages for Lost Profits.* 4th ed. Westport, Conn.: Lawpress Corporation, 1992.

Frank, Peter B.; Michael J. Wagner; and Roman L. Weil. *Litigation Services Handbook: The Role of the Accountant as Expert Witness.* New York: John Wiley & Sons, 1990.

Link, Albert N. *Evaluating Economic Damages: A Handbook for Attorneys.* Westport, Conn.: Greenwood Press, 1992.

McCarthy, John C. *Recovery of Damages for Bad Faith.* 5th ed. Kentfield, Calif.: Law Press Corporation, 1990.

_____ Chapter 41

_____ Arbitrating Disputed Valuations

Disputes over the values of businesses and professional practices arise from a variety of circumstances, such as divorces, corporate or partnership dissolutions, dissenting stockholder actions, and assorted damage cases. There has been a growing trend in recent years to resolve such disputes through arbitration rather than taking them through a court trial. We have been involved in many such arbitrations in the last few years, and have frequently found this to be a preferable alternative to a court trial.[1]

There can be much potential grief, however, for both the principals and the arbitrators, if all the essential elements of the arbitration process are not anticipated, understood, and agreed upon by all the parties involved. We hope that the following pages, which are based heavily on our experiences as arbitrators and as consultants in arbitration situations, will assist principals, their attorneys and other advisors, and those who may act as arbitrators to use the arbitration process efficiently and with results that are fair to all. Not all situations are suitable for arbitration, and a decision to arbitrate should be cleared by the principal's attorney in each case.

Advantages of Arbitration versus Court Trial

The primary advantages of arbitration over a court trial are the following:

1. Usually takes less elapsed time from start to finish.
2. Usually costs less. Attorneys' time is reduced considerably, and experts' fees are usually less than for a court trial. The appraisal process itself may not be less expensive, but the time required to prepare for cross-examination and to prepare to rebut an opposing expert in court can be very expensive.
3. Scheduling can usually be made more convenient for all parties involved.
4. Usually less formal and less taxing on all participants, especially the principals in the disputed issue.
5. Less likelihood of an outlandish result in favor of one side over the other, if the arbitrators are qualified, professional business appraisers.
6. The award of the arbitrators in most situations is final and binding and can be confirmed in court on motion.

Independent Role of Arbitrators

The most important point to understand about the arbitration process is that at least from the arbitrators' viewpoint, it is not an adversary proceed-

---

[1]For discussions of preparation and presentation of expert testimony in court on disputed business valuations, see Chapter 28, "Expert Testimony," in Shannon P. Pratt, *Valuing a Business*, 2nd ed., pp. 657–73; and Brian P. Brinig, "The Art of Testifying," Chapter 5, in Frank, Wagner, Weil, *Litigation Services Handbook*, pp. 87–95.

ing, but a cooperative effort to reach a fair and equitable conclusion. All the parties should realize that each arbitrator, regardless of who appointed him, is not an agent of any principal (as might be the case in a negotiation for a sale); he is acting independently in using his expertise and judgment to reach a conclusion that is fair to all parties. The neutrality of party-appointed arbitrators should be established at the outset.

This attitude of cooperation is especially significant in the way expert appraisers appointed as arbitrators normally interact during the arbitration process, as opposed to their interaction when presenting expert testimony in a court proceeding. In a court proceeding, there is normally no direct communication whatsoever between experts. Expert testimony is limited to answering the questions posed by attorneys on direct or cross-examination, or to questions posed by the court. In an arbitration proceeding, on the other hand, maximum communication among arbitrators is expected from the outset; discussion is expected to cover all points thoroughly and impartially, and not be limited to answering questions posed by opposing attorneys, each acting from the perspective of advocacy.

Situations Giving Rise to Arbitration

Almost any dispute over the value of a business or professional practice or a partial interest in one can lend itself to resolution by arbitration instead of trial. The following have been the major categories in our experiences.

In divorces and corporate or partnership dissolutions, a decision ahead of time to determine any matters of valuation by arbitration may prevent their ever reaching the point of dispute.

Divorces

Of all situations involving disputed valuations of businesses or professional practices, we believe that those arising from divorces are the most difficult for the parties to resolve by amicable negotiation. Although divorces are only a small part of our staff's valuation practice, they account for a large proportion of the times that we prepare for, and appear on, the witness stand in court presenting expert testimony.

Disputed valuation issues can become a major element in the already intense emotional strain accompanying divorce proceedings. Frequently, the valuation for the property settlement is the major, if not the only, disputed issue. Besides the time and cost advantages, arbitration spares the parties the tension and added antagonism associated with fighting it out in court.

Corporate and Partnership Dissolutions

Akin to a divorce situation is a corporate or partnership dissolution. We would also include in this general category the buyout of a minority stockholder or partner pursuant to a buy-sell agreement. By arbitrating the valuation issue, the principals can part on as friendly a basis as possible, whatever the circumstances of the dissolution may be.

Dissenting Stockholder Actions

A merger, sale, or other major corporate action can give rise to dissenting stockholders' appraisal rights under the statutes of all states except West Virginia. The expediency and lower cost make the arbitration process an attractive alternative to a trial in such cases, especially smaller ones for which prolonged and expensive court proceedings can result in a no-win situation for everyone.

Damage Cases

Damage cases, in which the valuation of a business or practice is often the central issue in determining the amount of relief, include the following:

1. Breach of contract.
2. Condemnation.
3. Antitrust.
4. Lost profits.
5. Lost business opportunity.
6. Amount of casualty insurance proceeds or allocation of proceeds among parties at interest.
7. Infringement of intellectual property.
8. Business torts.
9. Violation of securities laws.

The risk of an outlandish determination of value by a court is generally greater in damage cases, especially breach of contract and antitrust cases, than in any other major category of disputed valuation cases. This inclination toward an extreme decision one way or the other may result from a tendency of some juries or courts to allow the damage event to affect their objective view of the valuation issue; or perhaps some sentiment about the parties involved can affect them. This risk can be reduced significantly through the use of an arbitration process using qualified appraisers as arbitrators.

Selection of Arbitrators

Two factors need to be delineated regarding the selection of arbitrators: the criteria and the procedure for selection.

Criteria for Selection

The arbitration process produces the most equitable results for all parties if all the arbitrators (or the arbitrator) are experienced, qualified, professional appraisers of businesses and/or professional practices. If there are three arbitrators, it is most desirable that all three should be full-time professional appraisers, but two out of three are better than only one or none at all.

In some cases, if the business or profession is highly specialized, it may be desirable to seek as arbitrators one or more appraisers who have experience in appraising the specific line of business or professional practice. It is generally not desirable to gain the desired industry expertise by utilizing as an arbitrator someone who is an active or retired participant in the industry or profession involved, or who has done ancillary functions such as accounting or economic analysis work in the industry or profession, but who is not experienced in matters related directly to valuation. Many of these people lack the requisite training to deal professionally with the specific issue of valuation, and there is also the risk that such people's biases toward the industry or profession could prevent objective valuation. The expertise of industry experts can be gained through informal discussion with the arbitrator(s) or by formal testimony presented to the arbitrator(s). This is preferable to having them act as arbitrators themselves.

We have observed sound valuation conclusions reached by arbitration panels composed of industry people knowledgeable in finance, along with attorneys knowledgeable in both the industry and valuation matters. However, in these instances, costs were incurred not only for the three arbitrators, but also for expert testimony to be presented to the arbitration panel by at least two appraisers in each case. We have also seen nonprofessional panels reach conclusions that we do not believe a consensus of responsible professional appraisers would consider to be supportable within a reasonable range of value.

Obviously, one criterion for selection is the availability of the desired arbitrator(s) so that the arbitration can take place reasonably promptly.

Procedure for Selection

The most typical procedure is that each party selects one arbitrator and the two arbitrators select the third. It is preferable for the two arbitrators appointed by the parties to have complete authority to select the third, rather than having the selection of the third arbitrator subject to the approval of the principals. This avoids delays and dealing with pressures arising from the principals' biases, which are almost sure to be injected.

It is important that there be an alternative procedure for the selection of a third arbitrator in case of a deadlock. Plan this contingency procedure in advance or in conjunction with entering into the arbitration agreement. There should be a deadline, at which time the alternate selection process takes effect if the first two arbitrators have failed to reach agreement on a third arbitrator. In case of a deadlock, the procedure should call for the appointment of the third arbitrator who is a qualified appraiser by some predetermined entity, such as the American Arbitration Association, a court, or some designated official in the industry or profession. This procedure will almost assure that at least two of the three arbitrators will be professional appraisers, if your side has already chosen one. If your side insists that the third arbitrator be a qualified professional appraiser, and presents a list of appraisers who are independent of the principals involved, it is not likely that anyone charged with making such an appointment would select someone not so qualified over someone who was.[2]

Another possibility is to establish the procedure so that the two arbitrators attempt to reach agreement, bringing in the third arbitrator only if they are unable to do so. In that case, it is recommended that the prospective third arbitrator be agreed upon between the first two at the outset, before they get involved in other aspects of interaction with each other in the arbitration process. This procedure could be established as part of the language in a buy-sell agreement.

If a court appoints an arbitrator, he may be an equal part of a three-member arbitration panel, or he may be a "special master," where the conclusion reached does not require the concurrence of any other arbitrator, although he would normally be expected to take their respective positions into consideration.

American Arbitration Association Procedure

The American Arbitration Association (AAA) procedure for appointing arbitrators is different than that described in the foregoing section. When parties agree to submit a disputed matter to arbitration through the AAA, the association sends the parties a list of suggested arbitrators from the association's panel of arbitrators. Each party may veto nominees and indicate its preferences, but the final decision is made by the AAA.

In a letter discussing an early draft of this chapter in the first edition of this book, Robert Coulson, president of the American Arbitration Association, makes the following observation:

> Although you encourage parties to use the party-appointed system, many arbitration experts have come to believe that using neutral arbitrators is more reliable and less subject to a concern that one of the party-appointed arbitrators might be prejudiced in favor of the party that appointed him.

Mr. Coulson also says, "I, too, believe that qualified appraisers are often the best arbitrators for such valuation questions." However, there is no assurance that a panel appointed by the AAA will be composed of appraisers unless the arbitration clause so provides, or the parties so agree. Of three recent arbitration panels where we were not in the role of arbitrators but presented testimony on valuation issues to the panel, two panels included no valuation experts and one was composed of two attorneys and one business appraiser.

In many AAA arbitrations, each party will retain its own expert appraiser who will present testimony before the arbitration panel, rather than having the expert actually participate as an arbitrator. In this sense, the preparation and presentation of expert testimony is similar to a court trial, although it is slightly less formal. For additional informa-

---

[2]A list of accredited senior appraisers of the American Society of Appraisers who are certified in business valuation may be obtained from the American Society of Appraisers, P.O. Box 17265, Washington, D.C. 20041.

tion, the address of the American Arbitration Association is: 140 West 51st Street, New York, New York 10020.

The balance of this chapter discusses the type of situation where the appraiser is acting in the role of a member of the arbitration panel rather than a presenter of expert testimony.

Engagement and Compensation of Arbitrators

Once the arbitrators have been appointed, the engagement should be committed to writing. The description of the engagement may take the form of a standard professional services agreement initiated by an appraiser serving as arbitrator, an engagement letter drafted by one of the attorneys or parties, or both. All aspects of the engagement should be adequately covered. Sometimes, addenda to the initial engagement document(s) may be necessary, since decisions on some items, such as schedules and some expenses, may be made or changed as the engagement progresses.

The engagement document(s) should include by reference the document(s) giving rise to the arbitration (e.g., a buy-sell agreement) and should cover compensation of the arbitrator and all necessary instructions not addressed or not made clear in the arbitration document(s).

All documents relating to the engagement of an arbitrator should be signed by the arbitrator and whoever is responsible for compensating him for his services. The most common compensation arrangement is that each party assumes responsibility for the compensation and expenses of the arbitrator it has nominated or appointed, with the parties equally sharing the compensation and expenses of the third arbitrator. Such arrangements vary, however, from case to case.

The amount of compensation is usually based on each arbitrator's normal professional hourly or daily billing rate (or some mutually agreed-upon rate) plus out-of-pocket expenses. It is much less common for an arbitrator's compensation to be based on a fixed fee, because it is very difficult to determine in advance just how much time the total appraisal and arbitration process will require. However, it is reasonable to expect to discuss some estimate of probable fees and the daily rate or other basis for the fees. Under the procedures of the American Arbitration Association, these arrangements are carried out by a representative of that organization. If they are to be directed to appoint qualified business appraisers, they should also be directed to expect to pay the fees normally charged by such qualified appraisers.

Establishing the Ground Rules for Arbitration

The ground rules by which the arbitration will proceed are of critical importance. They start with a document mandating certain elements of the arbitrators' assignment. This document may be, for example, a buy-sell agreement, a prenuptial agreement, or an agreement drawn up specifically for the purpose of the arbitration. Sometimes, an agreement such as a buy-sell agreement will be supplemented by written instructions agreed upon by the attorneys involved. It is important that the written agreement directing the arbitration specify what factors are mandated by the agreement and what factors are left to the discretion of the arbitrators.

Factors Specified in the Arbitration Agreement

Factors that should be mandated by the agreement include the following:

1. Procedure for selection of arbitrators.
2. Definition of the property to be valued.
3. The date as of which the property is to be valued.
4. The standard of value to be used (as discussed in Chapter 3 and elsewhere in the book).
5. What constitutes a conclusion by the arbitrators, such as:
   a. Agreement by at least two out of three.
   b. Average of the two closest to each other.
   c. The conclusion of the third (neutral) arbitrator, such as in a "special master" situation.
6. The format and procedure for the arbitrators to render their conclusion.
7. The terms of payment of the amount determined by the arbitrators, including interest, if any.
8. The time schedule for the various steps in the arbitration process, at least the selection of arbitrators and some outside time limit for the total process.

Failure to specify any of the matters above may leave the door open for costly and extensive legal battles. Most state statutes specify that the standard of value for dissenting stockholders' appraisal rights is fair value, although a minority of states specify fair market value. In other cases, the arbitrators must look to the arbitration document to establish the standard of value.

Some buy-sell agreements specify fair market value as the standard of value. In cases of minority interests, this standard of value, of course, implies a discount from a proportionate share of the fair market value of the total entity, a fact that many owners (and even some attorneys) may overlook when drafting the agreement. Some buy-sell agreements specify that the valuation is to be a proportionate share of the fair market value of the total enterprise, with no minority interest discount. We recommend that the drafter of the agreement discuss this with the parties to the agreement (see the chapter on "Estate Planning" for sample wording).

A reporting deadline may be specified in the agreement or a reporting schedule may be worked out in conjunction with the process of engaging the arbitrators.

Because of the many ramifications inherent in the wording of the arbitration agreement, we recommend that an appraiser experienced in arbitration be consulted when drafting the agreement. This consultation will help to avoid both important omissions and unintentional implications of the wording discussing the valuation (such as the standard of value to be used).

Factors Left to the Arbitrators' Discretion

Factors that can, and in most cases should, be left to the discretion of the arbitrators include the following:

1. Whether or not each arbitrator is expected or required to make a complete, independent appraisal, or the extent to which each arbitrator considers it necessary to do independent work, as opposed to relying on certain data or analyses furnished by other arbitrators and/ or appraisers.
2. The obligation of the arbitrators to communicate with each other (writing, telephone calls, personal meetings), and the rules for sharing information.
3. Scheduling of the arbitrators' work and meetings, within the constraint of the agreed-upon reporting schedule.
4. The valuation approaches and criteria to be taken into consideration, within the constraints of any legally mandated criteria.
5. The facts, documents, and other data on which to rely (although the principals may agree to stipulate certain facts or assumptions, which could make the arbitrators' job easier with respect to some matters of possible uncertainty).

The Arbitration Process

One of the major variables in the arbitration process is the extent to which each arbitrator is expected or required to carry out independent appraisal work. Some arbitration documents specify that each expert on the arbitration panel do a complete, independent appraisal. More commonly, however (and we think preferably in most cases), the extent of independent appraisal work to be done is left to the judgment of each individual arbitrator, or to the arbitration panel as a group. This subject should be discussed with the parties or their representatives before the arbitration commences. It would be useful to have this addressed in the arbitrators' engagement letter, preferably allowing them considerable discretion.

Review of Arbitration Document

Each arbitrator should begin with a careful review of the document(s) giving rise to the arbitration. If there is any confusion or disagreement about any details of the assignment, such as the exact definition of the property, the effective date of the valuation, or the applicable standard of value, the arbitrators should seek clarification immediately. This should be done in writing to avoid any possible disputes later.

Initial Communication among Arbitrators

We recommend that the arbitrators establish communication among themselves at the earliest possible time after their appointment. A face-to-face meeting is ideal if geographic proximity to each other makes that feasible, but a conference call or a series of conference calls is usually sufficient, perhaps supplemented by correspondence. While each case is unique, the following is a generalized list of points to try to establish early:

1. Status of work already accomplished, if any (who has done what work up to that point).
2. An agreement as to sharing of information. (Our preference is to agree that all information gathered or developed by one arbitrator will be shared with the other arbitrators as quickly as possible.)
3. An agreement, if possible, as to the relevant valuation approaches to consider. (Where this becomes an issue, it seems fair to allow the parties' representatives to be heard as to their preferences. However, in our experience, this often results in highly biased supplications by parties' representatives who have no technical knowledge of relevant valuation approaches.)
4. A list of documents and data needed, and assignment of responsibility for obtaining each and seeing that the necessary distribution to other arbitrators is made. (It should be agreed up front that any such documents in the possession of the parties will be provided as evidence to the arbitrators promptly and completely.)
5. Any other possible division of the research effort, such as searches for comparable transactions, development of economic and/or industry data, and routine financial statement analysis (spread sheets, ratio analysis, comparison with industry averages, and so on). Division of research effort, of course, must depend on each arbitrator's willingness to accept certain efforts of another, which must be based on a judgment of professional ability and unbiased presentation of data and analysis.
6. Scheduling.

Field Visit

In most cases, arbitrators will want to visit the operating premises and interview relevant principals and/or management. It works out best if the arbitrators can conduct this field trip together, if possible, rather than separately. Together, the arbitrators will see the same things at the same time, and all can benefit from hearing each other's questions and answers first-hand. A joint field trip also gives the arbitrators an opportunity to address any items not fully covered in their previous communications. Also, this gives arbitrators who did not know each other previously an opportunity to get to know each other and form a basis for working together.

Hearings

The arbitrators should offer each party the opportunity to present oral and written information and opinions if they so desire. It is frequently convenient to hold a meeting to accommodate such input in conjunction with the field trip.

The Valuation Meeting

Usually, the arbitrators will meet in person to reach the valuation conclusion. In some instances, this meeting may be replaced by a conference call. In either case, all should be as prepared as possible, having exchanged and assimilated as much information as possible prior to the meeting.

In the meeting, it is usually most productive to come to agreements issue by issue, identifying and keeping track of each point of agreement and disagreement. Good notes should be kept so that it is clear exactly what points have been agreed upon, and what the respective positions are on points that have been addressed but on which agreement has not been reached. Each arbitrator should be receptive to the others' information and viewpoints and attempt to reach compromises on points where reasonable judgments may differ.

It is most desirable to come to a conclusion that can be endorsed as fair by all members of the arbitration panel. This agreement can usually be achieved if all of the arbitrators are qualified professional business appraisers. If unanimous agreement cannot be reached, the arbitrator in the minority position may render a dissenting opinion for the record, if he so desires.

Reporting the Results of the Arbitration

The formal report of the valuation conclusion reached by the arbitrators is usually contained in a very brief letter that does no more than reference the arbitration agreement, state that the arbitrators have completed their assignment in accordance with the agreement, and state the conclusion reached. The letter is signed by the arbitrators concurring in the conclusion. In the parlance of arbitration, this is called an *award*. In some cases, the letter must be notarized as well as signed.

In a significant proportion of cases, the principals on both sides would like to have a brief report explaining how the valuation conclusion was reached. In arbitration parlance, this is called an *opinion*. In such situations, we suggest that such an advisory report be the sole responsibility of the third appraiser. To make such a report a joint task of two or more arbitrators, each of whom probably judged various factors a little bit differently—though they were able to agree on a conclusion—would usually be an unnecessarily complicated and costly exercise.

If the valuation conclusion is reached unilaterally by a special master, normally he would be the only one to sign the report. An explanation of the procedures and criteria used is usually included.

Summary: The Most Critical Elements

The two most critical elements for an expeditious and successful arbitration are (1) a definitive arbitration agreement that provides the arbitrators with unambiguous instructions on the key matters listed above and (2) the appointment of independent arbitrators who will be both fair and competent in reaching a conclusion about the value of the subject property. If these two elements are properly addressed, the arbitration process can be a very efficient and fair way of resolving business or professional practice valuation matters.

Selected Bibliography

Arneson, George S. "Effects of Proposed Changes in Federal Rules of Civil Procedure and Evidence on Appraisers as Experts in Litigation." *ASA Valuation*, June 1992, pp. 2–8.

Carper, Donald L. "Remedies in Business Arbitration." *Arbitration Journal*, September 1991, pp. 49–58.

Kaufman, Steve. "See You Out of Court: Mediation Used in Resolving Business Disputes." *Nation's Business*, June 1992, pp. 58–60.

Koritzinsky, Allan R.; Robert M. Welch, Jr.; and Stephen W. Schlissel. "The Benefits of Arbitration." *Family Advocate*, Spring 1992, pp. 45–52.

Nicolaisen, Donald T., and Albert A. Vondra. "How Arbitration Can Reduce the Cost of Disputes." *CPA Journal*, September 1991, p. 10.

Pearson, Claude M. "Using Streamlined Arbitration to Resolve Valuation Disputes for an Accounting Partnership." *Practical Accountant*, September 1987, pp. 116–17.

Popell, S. D. "Mediating the Value of Small Businesses and Professional Firms." *Community Property Journal*, Winter 1983, pp. 17–27.

Appendix A

American Society of Appraisers Business Valuation Standards*

---

*Permission to reprint granted, American Society of Appraisers, November 1992.

American Society of Appraisers

Business Valuation Standards©

This release of the approved Business Valuation Standards of the American Society of Appraisers contains all standards approved through September 30, 1992, and are to be used in conjunction with the Uniform Standards of Professional Appraisal Practice (USPAP) of The Appraisal Foundation and the Principles of Appraisal Practice and Code of Ethics of the American Society of Appraisers.

It contains the following sections, with the effective approval date of each:

AMERICAN SOCIETY OF APPRAISERS
Business Valuation Standards

Preamble©

Approved by the ASA Board of Governors, September 1992

I. To enhance and maintain the quality of business valuations for the benefit of the business valuation profession and users of business valuations, the American Society of Appraisers, through its Business Valuation Committee, has adopted these standards.

II. The American Society of Appraisers (in its Principles of Appraisal Practice and Code of Ethics) and The Appraisal Foundation (in its Uniform Standards of Professional Appraisal Practice) have established authoritative principles and a code of professional ethics. These standards include these requirements, either explicitly or by reference, and are designed to clarify and provide additional requirements specifically applicable to the valuation of businesses, business ownership interests or securities.

III. These standards incorporate, where appropriate, all relevant business valuation standards adopted by the American Society of Appraisers through its Business Valuation Committee.

IV. These standards provide minimum criteria to be followed by business appraisers in the valuation of businesses, business ownership interests or securities.

V. If, in the opinion of the appraiser, circumstances of a specific business valuation assignment dictate a departure from any provisions of any Standard, such departure must be disclosed and will apply only to the specific departure.

VI. These Standards are designed to provide guidance to ASA Appraisers conducting business valuations and to provide a structure for regulating conduct of members of the ASA through Uniform Practices and Procedures. Deviations from the Standards are not designed or intended to be the basis of any civil liability; and should not create any presumption or evidence that a legal duty has been breached; or create any special relationship between the appraiser and any other person.

AMERICAN SOCIETY OF APPRAISERS
Business Valuation Standard

BVS-I   Terminology©

Adopted by the ASA Business Valuation Committee, June 1988
Approved by the ASA Board of Governors, January 1989
Revisions Approved, September 1992

ADJUSTED BOOK VALUE	— The book value which results after one or more asset or liability amounts are added, deleted or changed from the respective book amounts.
APPRAISAL	— The act or process of determining value. It is synonymous with valuation.
APPRAISAL APPROACH	— A general way of determining value using one or more specific appraisal methods. (See Asset Based Approach, Market Approach and Income Approach definitions.)
APPRAISAL DATE	— The date as of which the appraiser's opinion of value applies.
APPRAISAL METHOD	— Within approaches, a specific way to determine value.
APPRAISAL PROCEDURE	— The act, manner and technique of performing the steps of an appraisal method.
APPRAISED VALUE	— The appraiser's opinion or determination of value.
ASSET BASED APPROACH	— A general way of determining a value indication of a business's assets and/or equity interest using one or more methods based directly on the value of the assets of the business less liabilities.
BOOK VALUE	— 1. With respect to assets, the capitalized cost of an asset less accumulated depreciation, depletion or amortization as it appears on the books of account of the enterprise.
	2. With respect to a business enterprise, the difference between total assets (net of depreciation, depletion and amortization) and total liabilities of an enterprise as they appear on the balance sheet. It is synonymous with net book value, net worth and shareholders' equity.
BUSINESS APPRAISER	— A person who by education, training and experience is qualified to make an appraisal of a business enterprise and or its intangible assets.
BUSINESS ENTERPRISE	— A commercial, industrial or service organization pursuing an economic activity.
BUSINESS VALUATION	— The act or process of arriving at an opinion or deter-

mination of the value of a business enterprise or an interest therein.

CAPITALIZATION	— 1. The conversion of income into value 2. The capital structure of a business enterprise. 3. The recognition of an expenditure as a capital asset rather than a period expense.
CAPITALIZATION FACTOR	— Any multiple or divisor used to convert income into value.
CAPITALIZATION RATE	— Any divisor (usually expressed as a percentage) that is used to convert income into value.
CAPITAL STRUCTURE	— The composition of the invested capital.
CASH FLOW	— Net income plus depreciation and other non-cash charges.
CONTROL	— The power to direct the management and policies of an enterprise.
CONTROL PREMIUM	— The additional value inherent in the control interest, as contrasted to a minority interest, that reflects it's power of control.
DISCOUNT RATE	— A rate of return used to convert a monetary sum, payable or receivable in the future, into present value.
ECONOMIC LIFE	— The period over which property may be profitably used.
ENTERPRISE	— See BUSINESS ENTERPRISE.
EQUITY	— The owner's interest in property after deduction of all liabilities.
FAIR MARKET VALUE	— The amount at which property would change hands between a willing seller and a willing buyer when neither is acting under compulsion and when both have reasonable knowledge of the relevant facts.
GOING CONCERN	— An operating business enterprise.
GOING CONCERN VALUE	— 1. The value of an enterprise, or an interest therein, as a going concern. 2. Intangible elements of value in a business enterprise resulting from factors such as having a trained workforce, an operational plant, and the necessary licenses systems and procedures in place.
GOODWILL	— That intangible asset which arises as a result of name, reputation, customer patronage, location, products and similar factors that have not bee separately identified and/or valued but which generate economic benefits.
INCOME APPROACH	— A general way of determining a value indication of a business, business ownership interest or security using one or more methods wherein a value is determined by converting anticipated benefits.

INVESTED CAPITAL — The sum of the debt and equity in an enterprise on a long term basis.

MAJORITY — Ownership position greater than 50% of the voting interst in an enterprise

MAJORITY CONTROL — The degree of control provided by a majority position.

MARKET APPROACH — The market approach is a general way of determining a value indication of a business, business ownership interest or security using one or more methods that compare the subject to similar businesses, business ownership interests or securities that have been sold.

MARKETABILITY DISCOUNT — An amount or percentage deducted from an equity interest to reflect lack of marketability.

MINORITY INTEREST — Ownership position less than 50% of the voting interest in an enterprise.

MINORITY DISCOUNT — The reduction, from the pro rata share of the value of the entire business, which reflects the absence of the power of control.

NET ASSETS — Total assets less total liablities.

NET INCOME — Revenue less expenses, including taxes.

RATE OF RETURN — An amount of income realized or expected on an investment, expressed as a percentage of that investment.

REPLACEMENT COST NEW — The current cost of a similar new item having the nearest equivalent utility as the item being appraised.

REPORT DATE — The date of the report. May be the same or different than the APPRAISAL DATE.

REPRODUCTION COST NEW — The current cost of an identical new item.

RULE OF THUMB — A mathematical relationship between or among a number of variables based on experience, observation, hearsay or a combination of these, usually applicable to a specific industry.

VALUATION — See APPRAISAL.

VALUATION RATIO — A factor wherein a value or price serves as the numerator and financial, operating or physical data serve as the denominator.

WORKING CAPITAL — The amount by which current assets exceed current liabilities.

AMERICAN SOCIETY OF APPRAISERS
Business Valuation Standards

BVS-II   Full Written Business Valuation Report©

Adopted by the ASA Business Valuation Committee, June 1990
Approved by the ASA Board of Governors, June 1991

I. Preamble

A. To enhance and maintain the quality of business valuation reports, for the benefit of the business valuation profession and users of business valuation reports, the American Society of Appraisers, through its Business Valuation Committee, has adopted this standard. This standard is required to be followed in the preparation of full, written business valuation reports by all members of the American Society of Appraisers, be they candidate, accredited or senior members.

B. The purpose of this standard is to define and describe the requirements for the written communication of the results of a business valuation, analysis or opinion, but not the conduct thereof.

C. The American Society of Appraisers, in Section 7.4 and 8 of its <u>Principles of Appraisal Practice and Code of Ethics</u>, includes requirements with respect to written appraisal reports, as does The Appraisal Foundation, in Section 10 of its <u>Uniform Standards of Professional Appraisal Practice</u>. The present standard includes these requirements, either explicitly or by reference, and is designed to provide additional requirements specifically applicable in full, written business valuation reports.

D. The American Society of Appraisers, through its Business Valuation Committee, has adopted, in Business Valuation Standard BVS-I (1/88), a set of defined terms used in business valuation. In the preparation of reports in accordance with the present standard, BVS-I (1/88) should be followed.

E. The present standard provides minimum criteria to be followed by business appraisers in the preparation of full, written reports.

F. Written reports must meet the requirements of the present standard unless, in the opinion of the appraiser, circumstances dictate a departure from the standard; if so, such a departure must be disclosed in the report.

G. For the purpose of this standard, the appraiser is the individual or entity undertaking the appraisal assignment under a contract with the client.

II. Signature and Certification

A. An appraiser assumes responsibility for the statements made in the full, written report and indicates the acceptance of that responsibility by signing the report. To comply with this standard, a full, written report must be signed by the appraiser.

B. Clearly, at least one individual is responsible for the valuation conclusion(s) expressed in the report. A report must contain a certification, as required by Standard 10 of the

<u>Uniform Standards of Professional Appraisal Practice</u> of The Appraisal Foundation, in which the individuals responsible for the valuation conclusion(s) must be identified.

III. Assumptions and Limiting Conditions

The following assumptions and/or limiting conditions must be stated:

1. Pertaining to bias—a report must contain a statement that the appraiser has no interest in the asset appraised, or other conflict, which could cause a question as to the appraiser's independence or objectivity or if such an interest or conflict exists, it must be disclosed.

2. Pertaining to data used—where appropriate, a report must indicate that an appraiser relied on data supplied by others, without further verification by the appraiser, as well as the sources which were relied on.

3. Pertaining to validity of the valuation—a report must contain a statement that a valuation is valid only for the valuation date indicated and for the purpose stated.

IV. Definition of the Valuation Assignment

The precise definition of the valuation assignment is a key aspect of communication with users of the report. The following are key components of such a definition and must be included in the report:

1. The business interest valued must be clearly defined, such as 100 shares of the Class A common stock of the XYZ Corporation or a 20% limited partnership interest in the ABC Limited Partnership. The existence, rights and/or restrictions of other classes of ownership in the business appraised must also be adequately described if they are relevant to the conclusion of value.

2. The purpose and use of the valuation must be clearly stated, such as the determination of fair market value for ESOP purposes or a determination of fair value for dissenters' rights purposes. If a valuation is being done pursuant to a particular statute, the particular statute must be referenced.

3. The standard of value used in the valuation must be stated and defined. The premise of value, such as a valuation on a minority interest basis or an enterprise basis, must be stated.

4. The appraisal date must be clearly identified. The date of the preparation of the report must be indicated.

V. Business Description

As evidence of the appraiser's due diligence in obtaining the pertinent facts about the business appraised, and to aid the user's comprehension of the valuation conclusion, a full, written business valuation report must include a business description which covers all relevant factual areas, such as:

1. Form of organization (corporation, partnership, etc.)
2. History
3. Products and/or services and markets and customers
4. Management
5. Major assets, both tangible and intangible

---

6. Outlook for the economy, industry and company
7. Past transactional evidence of value
8. Sensitivity to seasonal or cyclical factors
9. Competition
10. Sources of information used.

VI. Financial Analysis

A. An analysis and discussion of a firm's financial statements is an integral part of a business valuation and must be included. Exhibits summarizing balance sheets and income statements for a period of years sufficient to the purpose of the valuation and the nature of the subject company must be included in the valuation report.

B. Any adjustments made to the reported financial data must be fully explained.

C. If projections of balance sheets or income statements were utilized in the valuation, key assumptions underlying the projections must be included and discussed.

D. If appropriate, the company's financial results relative to those of its industry must be discussed.

VII. Valuation Methodology

A. The valuation method or methods selected, and the reasons for their selection, must be discussed. The steps followed in the application of the method or methods selected must be described and must lead to the valuation conclusion.

B. The report must include an explanation of how any variables such as discount rates, capitalization rates or valuation multiplies were determined and used. The rationale and/or supporting data for any premiums or discounts must be clearly presented.

VIII. Full, Written Report Format

The full, written report format must provide a logical progression for clear communication of pertinent information, valuation methods and conclusions and must incorporate the other specific requirements of this standard, including the signature and certification provisions.

IX. Confidentiality of Report

No copies of the report will be furnished to persons other than the client without the client's specific permission of direction unless ordered by a court or competent jurisdiction.

X. Address

Copies of this standard and BVS-I (1/88) may be obtained from the American Society of Appraisers, P.O. Box 17265, Washington, DC 20041.

AMERICAN SOCIETY OF APPRAISERS
Business Valuation Standard

BVS-III   General Performance Requirements For Business Valuation©

As Adopted by the Business Valuation Committee, June 1991
Approved by the ASA Board of Governors, January 1992

I.   Preamble

A. To enhance and maintain the quality of business valuations for the benefit of the business valuation profession and users of business valuations, the American Society of Appraisers, through its Business Valuation Committee, has adopted this standard. This standard is required to be followed in all valuations of businesses, business ownership interests, and securities by all members of the American Society of Appraisers, be they Candidates, Accredited Members (AM), or Accredited Senior Appraisers (ASA), or Fellows (FASA).

B. The purpose of this standard is to define and describe the requirements for performance of valuations of businesses, business ownership interests, and securities but not the reporting therefor.

C. The American Society of Appraisers, in its <u>Principles of Appraisal Practice and Code of Ethics,</u> and The Appraisal Foundation in its <u>Uniform Standards of Professional Appraisal Practice,</u> establish authoritative principles and a code of professional ethics. This present standard includes these requirements, either explicitly or by reference, and is designed to clarify and provide additional requirements specifically applicable to the valuation of businesses, business ownership interests and securities.

D. This standard incorporates, where appropriate, all relevant business valuation standards adopted by the American Society of Appraisers through its Business Valuation Committee.

E. The present standard provides minimum criteria to be followed by business appraisers in the valuation of businesses, business ownership interests and securities.

F. If in the opinion of the appraiser circumstances of a specific business valuation assignment dictate a departure from any provisions of this standard, such departure must be disclosed and will apply only to the specific departure.

II.   The Valuation Assignment shall be Appropriately Defined

A. The valuation assignment to be performed must be defined determining

1. The business, business ownership interest, or security to be valued.

2. The appraisal date.

3. The standard of value.

4. The purpose and the intended use of the valuation.

B. The scope of the assignment must be adequately defined. Acceptable scopes of work

---

would generally be of three types as delineated below. Other scopes of work should be explained and described in appropriate detail in related reporting.

1. Appraisal
   a. The objective of an appraisal is to express an unambiguous opinion as to the value of the business, business ownership interest, or security, which is supported by all procedures that the appraiser deems to be relevant to the valuation.
   b. An appraisal has the following qualities:
      (1) It is expressed as a single dollar amount or as a range.
      (2) It considers all relevant information as of the appraisal date available to the appraiser at the time of performance of the valuation.
      (3) The appraiser conducts appropriate procedures to collect and analyze all information expected to be relevant to the valuation.
      (4) The valuation is based upon consideration of all conceptual approaches deemed to be relevant by the appraiser.

2. Limited Appraisal
   a. The objective of a limited appraisal is to express an estimate as to the value of a business, business ownership interest, or security, which lacks the performance of additional procedures that are required in an appraisal.
   b. Limited appraisal has the following qualities:
      (1) It is expressed as a single dollar amount or as a range.
      (2) It is based upon consideration of limited relevant information.
      (3) The appraiser conducts only limited procedures to collect and analyze the information which such appraiser considers necessary to support the conclusion presented.
      (4) The valuation is based upon the conceptual approach(es) deemed by the appraiser to be most appropriate.

3. Calculations
   a. The objective of calculations is to provide an approximate indication of value based upon the performance of limited procedures agreed upon by the appraiser and the client.
   b. Calculations have the following qualities:
      (1) They may be expressed as a single dollar amount or as a range.
      (2) They may be based upon consideration of only limited relevant information.
      (3) The appraiser performs limited information collection and analysis procedures.
      (4) The calculations may be based upon conceptual approaches as agreed upon with the client.

III. Information Collection and Analysis

The appraiser shall gather, analyze, and adjust relevant information to perform the valuation as appropriate to the scope of work. Such information shall include the following:

A. Characteristics of the business, business ownership interest or security to be valued including rights, privileges and conditions, quantity, factors affecting control and agreements restricting sale or transfer.

B. Nature, history and outlook of the business.

C. Historical financial information for the business.

D. Assets and liabilities of the business.

E. Nature and conditions of the relevant industries which have an impact on the business.

F. Economic factors affecting the business.

G. Capital markets providing relevant information, e.g. available rate of return on alternative investments, relevant public stock transactions, and relevant mergers and acquisitions.

H. Prior transactions involving the subject business, interest in the subject business, or its securities.

I. Other information deemed by the appraiser to be relevant.

IV. Approaches, Methods, and Procedures

A. The appraiser shall select and apply appropriate valuation approaches, methods, and procedures.

B. The appraiser shall develop a conclusion of value pursuant to the valuation assignment as defined, considering the relevant valuation approaches, methods, and procedures, and appropriate premiums and discounts, if any.

V. Documentation and Retention.

The appraiser shall appropriately document and retain all information and work product that were relied on in reaching the conclusion.

VI. Reporting

The appraiser shall report to the client the conclusion of value in an appropriate written or oral format.

VII. Address

Copies of this standard may be obtained from the American Society of Appraisers, P.O. Box 17265, Washington, D.C. 20041.

AMERICAN SOCIETY OF APPRAISERS
Business Valuation Standard

BVS-IV   Asset Based Approach to Business Valuation©

As Adopted by the Business Valuation Committee, June 1991
Approved by the ASA Board of Governors, January 1992

I.   Preamble

A. To enhance and maintain the quality of business valuations, for the benefit of the business valuation profession and users of business valuations, the American Society of Appraisers, through its Business Valuation Committee, has adopted this standard. This standard is required to be followed in all business valuation assignments where the Asset Based Approach is used by members of the American Society of Appraisers, be they Candidates, Accredited Members (AM), Accredited Senior Appraisers (ASA), or Fellows (FASA).

B. The purpose of this standard is to define and describe the requirements for the use of the Asset Based Approach to business valuation and the circumstances in which it is appropriate.

C. The American Society of Appraisers, in its Principles of Appraisal Practice and Code of Ethics, and The Appraisal Foundation, in its Uniform Standards of Professional Appraisal Practice, establish authoritative principles and a code of professional ethics. The present standard includes these requirements, either explicitly or by reference, and is designed to provide additional requirements specifically applicable to business valuation through the Asset Based Approach.

D. This standard incorporates, where appropriate, all relevant business valuation standards adopted by the American Society of Appraisers through its Business Valuation Committee.

E. The present standard provides minimum criteria to be followed by business appraisers in their use of the Asset Based Approach to business valuation.

F. If in the opinion of the appraiser circumstances of a specific business valuation assignment dictate a departure from any provisions of this standard, such departure must be disclosed and will apply only to the specific departure.

II.   The Asset Based Approach

A. In business valuation the Asset Based Approach may be analogous of the Cost Approach of other disciplines.

B. Assets, liabilities and equity relate to a business that is an operating company, a holding company, or a combination thereof (mixed business).

　　1. An operating company is a business which conducts an economic activity by generating and selling, or trading, in a product or service.

　　2. A holding company is a business which derives its revenues by receiving returns on its assets which may include operating companies and/or other businesses.

C. The Asset Based Approach should be considered in valuations conducted at the <u>total entity level</u> and involving the following:

1. An investment or real estate holding company

2. A business appraised on a basis other than as a going concern.

   Valuations of <u>particular ownership interests</u> in an entity may or may not require the use of the Asset Based Approach.

D. The Asset Based Approach should not be the sole appraisal approach used in assignments relating to operating companies appraised as going concerns. Unless it is customarily used by sellers and buyers. In such cases, the appraiser must support the selection of this approach.

III. Address

Copies of this standard may be obtained from the American Society of Appraisers, Post Office Box 17265, Washington, D.C. 20041.

Copyright, © American Society of Appraisers — 1992

AMERICAN SOCIETY OF APPRAISERS
Business Valuation Standard

BVS-V   The Guideline Company Valuation Method©

As Adopted by the Business Valuation Committee, June 1991
Approved by the ASA Board of Governors, January 1992

I. Preamble

A. To enhance and maintain the quality of business valuations for the benefit of the business valuation profession and users of business valuations, the American Society of Appraisers, through its Business Valuation Committee, has adopted this standard. This standard is required to be followed in the use of the guideline company valuation method for the valuation of businesses, business ownership interests or securities by all members of the American Society of Appraisers, be they Candidates, Accredited Members (AM), Accredited Senior Appraisers (ASA), or Fellows (FASA).

B. The purpose of this standard is to define and describe the requirements for the use of guideline companies in the valuation of businesses, business ownership interests or securities.

C. The American Society of Appraisers, in its <u>Principles of Appraisal Practice and Code of Ethics</u>, and The Appraisal Foundation, in its <u>Uniform Standards of Professional Appraisal Practice</u> establish authoritative principles and a code of professional ethics. The present standard includes these requirements either explicitly or by reference, and is designed to provide minimum requirements specifically applicable to the use of guideline companies in the valuation of businesses, business ownership interests or securities.

D. This standard incorporates, where appropriate, all relevant business valuation standards adopted by the American Society of Appraisers through its Business Valuation Committee.

E. The present standard provides minimum criteria to be followed by business appraisers for the use of guideline companies in the valuation of businesses, business ownership interests or securities.

F. If in the opinion of the appraiser circumstances of a specific business valuation assignment dictate a departure from any provisions of this standard, such departure must be disclosed and will apply only to the specific departure.

II. Conceptual Framework

A. Market transactions in businesses, business ownership interests or securities can provide objective, empirical data for developing value measures to apply in business valuation.

B. The development of value measures from guideline companies should be considered for use in the valuation of businesses, business ownership interests or securities, to the extent that adequate information is available.

C. Guideline companies are companies that come as close as possible to the investment characteristics of the company being valued. Ideal guideline companies are in the same industry as the company being valued; but if there is insufficient transaction evidence available in the same industry it is necessary to select companies with an underlying similarity of relevant investment characteristics such as markets, products, growth, cyclical variability and other salient factors.

III. Search for and Selection of Guideline Companies

A. A thorough, objective search for guideline companies is required to establish the credibility of the valuation analysis. The procedure must include criteria for screening and selecting guideline companies.

B. Empirical data from guideline companies can be found in transactions involving either minority or controlling interests in either publicly traded or closely held companies.

IV. Financial Data of the Guideline Companies

A. It is necessary to obtain and analyze financial and operating data on the guideline companies, as available.

B. Consideration should be given to adjustments to the financial data of the subject company and the guideline companies to minimize differences in accounting treatments when such differences are significant. Unusual or nonrecurring items should be analyzed and adjusted as appropriate.

V. Comparative Analysis of Qualitative and Quantitative Factors

A comparative analysis of qualitative and quantitative similarities and differences between guideline companies and the subject company must be made to assess the investment attributes of the guideline companies relative to the subject company.

VI. Valuation Ratios Derived From Guideline Companies

A. Price information of the guideline companies must be related to the appropriate underlying financial data of each guideline company in order to compute appropriate valuation ratios.

B. The valuation ratios for the guideline companies and comparative analysis of qualitative and quantitative factors should be used together to determine appropriate valuation ratios for application to the subject company.

C. Several valuation ratios may be selected for application to the subject company and several value indications may be obtained. The appraiser should consider the relative importance accorded to each of the value indications utilized in arriving at the valuation conclusion.

D. To the extent that adjustments for dissimilarities with respect to minority and control, or marketability, have not been made earlier, appropriate adjustments for these factors must be made, if applicable.

VII. Address

Copies of this standard may be obtained from the American Society of Appraisers, P.O. Box 17265, Washington, D.C. 20041.

AMERICAN SOCIETY OF APPRAISERS
Business Valuation Standards

BVS-VI   Market Approach to Business Valuation©

As Adopted by the Business Valuation Committee, June 1992
Approved by the ASA Board of Govenors, September 1992

I.   Preamble

A. This standard is required to be followed in all valuations of businesses, business ownership interests, and securities by all members of the American Society of Appraisers, be they Candidates, Accredited Members (AM), Accredited Senior Appraisers (ASA), or Fellows (FASA).

B. The purpose of this standard is to define and describe the requirements for use of the market approach in valuation of businesses, business ownership interests, and securities, but not the reporting therefor.

C. This present standard is applicable to appraisals and may not necessarily be applicable to limited appraisals and calculations as defined in BVS-III, Section III.B.

D. This standard incorporates the general preamble to the Business Valuation Standards of the American Society of Appraisers.

II. The Market Approach

A. The market approach is a general way of determining a value indication of a business, business ownership interest or security using one or more methods that compare the subject to similar businesses, business ownership interests and securities that have been sold.

B. Examples of market approach methods include the Guideline Company method and analysis of prior transactions in the ownership of the subject company.

III. Reasonable Basis for Comparison

A. The investment used for comparison must provide a reasonable basis for the comparison.

B. Factors to be considered in judging whether a reasonable basis for comparison exists include:

1. Sufficient similarity of qualitative and quantitative investment characteristics.

2. Amount and verifiability of data known about the similar investment.

3. Whether or not the price of the similar investment was obtained in an arms length transaction, or a forced or distress sale.

IV. Manner of Comparison

A. The comparison must be made in a meaningful manner and must not be misleading. Such comparisons are normally made through the use of valuation ratios. The computation and use of such ratios should provide meaningful insight about the pricing of the subject considering all relevant factors. Accordingly, care should be exercised in the following:

1. Selection of underlying data used for the ratio.

2. Selection of the time period and/or averaging method used for the underlying data.

3. Manner of computing and comparing the subject's underlying data.

4. The timing of the price data used in the ratio.

B. In general, comparisons should be made using comparable definitions of the components of the valuation ratios. However, where appropriate, valuation ratios based on components which are reasonably representative of continuing results may be used.

V. Rules of Thumb

A. Rules of thumb may provide insight on the value of a business, business ownership interest or security. However, value indications derived from the use of rules of thumb should not be given substantial weight unless supported by other valuation methods and it can be established that knowledgeable buyers and sellers place substantial reliance on them.

AMERICAN SOCIETY OF APPRAISERS
Business Valuation Standards

BVS-VII	Income Approach to Business Valuation©

As Adopted by the Business Valuation Committee, June 1992
Approved by the ASA Board of Govenors, September 1992

I. Preamble

A. This standard is required to be followed in all valuations of businesses, business ownership interests, and securities by all members of the American Society of Appraisers, be they Candidates, Accredited Members (AM), Accredited Senior Appraisers (ASA), or Fellows (FASA).

B. The purpose of this standard is to define and describe the requirements for use of the income approach in valuation of businesses, business ownership interests, and securities, but not the reporting therefor.

C. This present standard is applicable to appraisals and may not necessarily be applicable to limited appraisals and calculations as defined in BVS-III, Section III.B.

D. This standard incorporates the general preamble to the Business Valuation Standards of the American Society of Appraisers.

II. The Income Approach

A. The income approach is a general way of determining a value indication of a business, business ownership interest or security using one or more methods wherein a value is determined by converting anticipated benefits.

B. Both capitalization of benefits methods and discounted future benefits methods are acceptable. In capitalization of benefits methods, a representative benefit level is divided or multiplied by a capitalization factor to convert the benefit to value. In discounted future benefits methods, benefits are estimated for each of several future periods. These benefits are converted to value by the application of a discount rate using present value techniques.

III. Anticipated Benefits

A. Anticipated benefits, as used in the income approach, are expressed in monetary terms. Depending on the nature of the business, business ownership interest or security being appraised and other relevant factors, anticipated benefits may be reasonably represented by such items as net cash flow, dividends, and various forms of earnings.

B. Anticipated benefits should be estimated considering such items as the nature, capital structure, and historical performance of the related business entity, expected future outlook for the business entity and relevant industries, and relevant economic factors.

IV. Conversion of Anticipated Benefits

A. Anticipated benefits are converted to value using procedures which consider the expected growth and timing of the benefits, the risk profile of the benefits stream and the time value of money.

B. The conversion of anticipated benefits to value normally requires the determination of a capitalization rate or discount rate. In determining the appropriate rate, the appraiser should consider such factors as the level of interest rates, rates of return expected by investors on relevant investments, and the risk characteristics of the anticipated benefits.

C. In discounted future benefits methods, expected growth is considered in estimating the future stream of benefits. In capitalization of benefits methods, expected growth is incorporated in the capitalization rate.

D. The rate of return or discount rate used should be consistent with the type of anticipated benefits used. For example, pre-tax rates of return should be used with pre-tax benefits; common equity rates of return should be used with common equity benefits; and net cash flow rates of return should be used with net cash flow benefits.

AMERICAN SOCIETY OF APPRAISERS
Business Valuation Standards

BVS-VIII   Reaching a Conclusion of Value©

As Adopted by the Business Valuation Committee, June 1992
Approved by the ASA Board of Govenors, September 1992

I.   Preamble

A. This standard is required to be followed in all valuations of businesses, business ownership interests, and securities by all members of the American Society of Appraisers, be they Candidates, Accredited Members (AM), Accredited Senior Appraisers (ASA), or Fellows (FASA).

B. The purpose of this standard is to define and describe the requirements for reaching a final conclusion of value in valuation of businesses, business ownership interests, and securities.

C. This present standard is applicable to appraisals and may not necessarily be applicable to limited appraisals and calculations as defined in BVS-III, Section III.B.

D. This standard incorporates the general preamble to the Business Valuation Standards of the American Society of Appraisers.

II.   General

A. The conclusion of value reached by the appraiser shall be based upon the applicable standard of value, the purpose and intended use of the valuation, and all relevant information obtained as of the appraisal date in carrying out the scope of the assignment.

B. The conclusion of value reached by the appraiser will be based on value indications resulting from one or more methods performed under one or more appraisal approaches.

III. Selection and Weighing of Methods

A. The selection of and reliance on the appropriate method and procedures depends on the judgment of the appraiser and not on the basis of any prescribed formula. One or more approaches may not be relevant to the particular situation. More than one method under an approach may be relevant to a particular situation.

B. The appraiser must use informed judgment when determining the relative weight to be accorded to indications of value reached on the basis of various methods or whether an indication of value from a single method should dominate. The appraiser's judgment may be presented either in general terms or in terms of mathematical weightings of the indicated values reflected in the conclusion. In any case, the appraiser should provide the rationale for the selection or weightings of the method or methods relied on in reaching the conclusion.

C. In formulating a judgment about the relative weights to be accorded to indications of value determined under each method or whether an indication of value from a single method should dominate, the appraiser should consider factors such as:

1. The applicable standard of value;

2. The purpose and intended use of the valuation;

3. Whether the subject is an operating company, a real estate or investment holding company, or a company with substantial non-operating or excess assets;

4. Quality and reliability of data underlying the indication of value;

5. Such other factors which, in the opinion of the appraiser, are appropriate for consideration.

III. Additional Factors to Consider.

As appropriate for the valuation assignment as defined, and if not considered in the process of determining and weighting the indications of value provided by various procedures, the appraiser should separately consider the following factors in reaching a final conclusion of value:

A. Marketability, or lack thereof, considering the nature of the business, business ownership interest or security, the effect of relevant contractual and legal restrictions, and the condition of the markets.

B. Ability of the appraised interest to control the operation, sale, or liquidation of the relevant business.

C. Such other factors which, in the opinion of the appraiser, are appropriate for consideration.

AMERICAN SOCIETY OF APPRAISERS
Business Valuation Standards

BVS-IX   Financial Statement Adjustments©

As Adopted by the Business Valuation Committee, June 1992
Approved by the ASA Board of Govenors, September 1992

I. Preamble

A. This standard is required to be followed in all valuations of businesses, business ownership interests, and securities by all members of the American Society of Appraisers, be they Candidates, Accredited Members (AM), Accredited Senior Appraisers (ASA), or Fellows (FASA).

B. The purpose of this standard is to define and describe the requirements for making financial statement adjustments in valuation of businesses, business ownership interests, and securities.

C. This present standard is applicable to appraisals and may not necessarily be applicable to limited appraisals and calculations as defined in BVS-III, Section III.B.

D. This standard incorporates the general preamble to the Business Valuation Standards of the American Society of Appraisers.

II. Conceptual Framework

A. Financial statements should be analyzed and, if appropriate, adjusted as a procedure in the valuation process. Financial statements to be analyzed include those of the subject entity and any entities used as guideline companies.

B. Financial statement adjustments are modifications to reported financial information that are relevant and significant to the appraisal process. Adjustments may be necessary in order to make the financial statements more meaningful for the appraisal process. Adjustments may be appropriate for the following reasons, among others: (1) To present financial data of the subject and guideline companies on a consistent basis; (2) To adjust from reported values to current values; (3) To adjust revenues and expenses to levels which are reasonably representative of continuing results; and (4) To adjust for non-operating assets and liabilities and the related revenue and expenses.

C. Financial statement adjustments are made for the purpose of assisting the appraiser in reaching a valuation conclusion and for no other purpose.

III. Documentation of adjustments

Adjustments made should be fully described and supported.

Appendix B

Revenue Ruling 59–60

REVENUE RULING 59-60

In valuing the stock of closely-held corporations, or the stock of corporations where market quotations are not available, all other available financial data, as well as all relevant factors affecting the fair market value must be considered for estate tax and gift tax purposes. No general formula may be given that is applicable to the many different valuation situations arising in the valuation of such stock. However, the general approach, methods and factors which must be considered in valuing such securities are outlined.

SECTION 1. PURPOSE.

The purpose of this Revenue Ruling is to outline and review in general the approach, methods and factors to be considered in valuing shares of the capital stock of closely-held corporations for estate tax and gift tax purposes. The methods discussed herein will apply likewise to the valuation of corporate stocks on which market quotations are either unavailable or are of such scarcity that they do not reflect the fair market value.

SECTION 2. BACKGROUND AND DEFINITIONS.

.01 All valuations must be made in accordance with the applicable provisions of the Internal Revenue Code of 1954 and the Federal Estate Tax and Gift Tax Regulations. Sections 2031(a), 2032 and 2512(a) of the 1954 Code (sections 811 and 1005 of the 1939 Code) require that the property to be included in the gross estate, or made the subject of a gift, shall be taxed on the basis of the value of the property at the time of death of the decedent, the alternate date if so elected, or the date of gift.

.02 Section 20.2031-1(b) of the Estate Tax Regulations (section 81.10 of the Estate Tax Regulations 105) and section 25.2512-1 of the Gift Tax Regulations (section 86.19 of Gift Tax Regulations 108) define fair market value, in effect, as the price at which the property would change hands between a willing buyer and a willing seller when the former is not under any compulsion to buy and the latter is not under any compulsion to sell, both parties having reasonable knowledge of relevant facts. Court decisions frequently state in addition that the hypothetical buyer and seller are assumed to be able, as well as willing, to trade and to be well informed about the property and concerning the market for such property.

.03 Closely-held corporations are those corporations the shares of which are owned by a relatively limited number of stockholders. Often the entire stock issue is held by one family. The result of this situation is that little, if any, trading in the shares takes place. There is, therefore, no established market for the stock and such sales as occur at irregular intervals seldom reflect all of the elements of a representative transaction as defined by the term "fair market value."

SECTION 3. APPROACH TO VALUATION.

.01 A determination of fair market value, being a question of fact, will depend upon the circumstances in each case. No formula can be devised that will be generally applicable to the multitude of different valuation issues arising in estate and gift tax cases. Often, an appraiser will find wide differences of opinion as to the fair market value of a particular stock. In resolving such differences, he should maintain a reasonable attitude in recognition of the fact that valuation is not an exact science. A sound valuation will be based upon all the relevant facts, but the elements of common sense, informed judgment and reasonableness must enter into the process of weighing those facts and determining their aggregate significance.

.02 The fair market value of specific shares of stock will vary as general economic conditions change from "normal" to "boom" or "depression," that is, according to the degree of optimism or pessimism with which the investing public regards the future at the required date of appraisal. Uncertainty as to the stability or continuity of the future income from a property decreases its value by increasing the risk of loss of earnings and value in the future. The value of shares of stock of a company with very uncertain future prospects is highly speculative. The appraiser must exercise his judgment as to the degree of risk attaching to the business of the corporation which issued the stock, but that judgment must be related to all of the other factors affecting value.

.03 Valuation of securities is, in essence, a prophesy as to the future and must be based on facts available at the required date of appraisal. As a generalization, the prices of stocks which are traded in volume in a free and active market by informed persons best reflect the consensus of the investing public as to what the future holds for the corporations and industries represented. When a stock is closely held, is traded infrequently, or is traded in an erratic market, some other measure of value must be used. In many instances, the next best measure may be found in the prices at which the stocks of companies engaged in the same or similar line of business are selling in a free and open market.

SECTION 4. FACTORS TO CONSIDER.

.01 It is advisable to emphasize that in the valuation of the stock of closely-held corporations or the stock of corporations where market quotations are either lacking or too scarce to be recognized, all available financial data, as well as all relevant factors affecting the fair market value, should be considered. The following factors, although not all-inclusive are fundamental and require careful analysis in each case:

(a) The nature of the business and the history of the enterprise from its inception.

(b) The economic outlook in general and the condition and outlook of the specific industry in particular.

(c) The book value of the stock and the financial condition of the business.

(d) The earning capacity of the company.

(e) The dividend-paying capacity.

(f) Whether or not the enterprise has goodwill or other intangible value.

(g) Sales of the stock and the size of the block of stock to be valued.

(h) The market price of stocks of corporations engaged in the same or a similar line of business having their stocks actively traded in a free and open market, either on an exchange or over-the-counter.

.02 The following is a brief discussion of each of the foregoing factors:

(a) The history of a corporate enterprise will show its past stability or instability, its growth or lack of growth, the diversity or lack of diversity of its operations, and other facts needed to form an opinion of the degree of risk involved in the business. For an enterprise which changed its form of organization but carried on the same or closely similar operations of its predecessor, the history of the former enterprise should be considered. The detail to be considered should increase with approach to the required date of appraisal, since recent events are of greatest help in predicting the future; but a study of gross and net income, and of dividends covering a long prior period, is highly desirable. The history to be studied should include, but need not be limited to, the nature of the business, its products or services, its operating and investment assets, capital structure, plant facilities, sales records and management, all of which should be considered as of the date of the appraisal, with due regard for recent significant changes. Events of the past that are unlikely to recur in the future should be discounted, since value has a close relation to future expectancy.

(b) A sound appraisal of a closely-held stock must consider current and prospective economic conditions as of the date of appraisal, both in the national economy and in the industry or industries with which the corporation is allied. It is important to know that the company is more or less successful than its competitors in the same industry, or that it is maintaining a stable position with respect to competitors. Equal or even greater significance may attach to the ability of the industry with which the company is allied to compete with other industries. Prospective competition which has not been a factor in prior years should be given careful attention. For example, high profits due to the novelty of its product and the lack of competition often lead to increasing competition. The public's appraisal of the future prospects of competitive industries or of competitors within an industry may be indicated by price trends in the markets for commodities and for securities. The loss of the manager of a so-called "one-man" business may have a depressing effect upon the value of the stock of such business, particularly if there is a lack of trained personnel capable of succeeding to the management of the enterprise. In valuing the stock of this type of business, therefore, the effect of the loss of the manager on the future expectancy of the business, and the absence of management-succession potentialities are pertinent factors to be taken into consideration. On the other hand, there may be factors which offset, in whole or in part, the loss of the manager's services. For instance, the nature of the business and of its assets may be such that they will not be impaired by the loss of the manager. Furthermore, the loss may be adequately covered by life insurance, or competent management might be employed on the basis of the consideration paid for the former manager's services. These, or other offsetting factors, if found to exist, should be carefully weighed against the loss of the manager's services in valuing the stock of the enterprise.

(c) Balance sheets should be obtained, preferably in the form of comparative annual statments for two or more years immediately preceding the date of appraisal, together with a balance sheet at the end of the month preceding that date, if corporate accounting will permit. Any balance sheet descriptions that are not self-explanatory, and balance sheet items comprehending diverse assets or liabilities, should be clarified in essential detail by supporting supplemental schedules. These statements usually will disclose to the appraiser (1) liquid position (ratio of current assets to current liabilities); (2) gross and net book value of principal classes of fixed assets; (3) working capital; (4) long-term indebtedness; (5) capital structure; and (6) net worth. Consideration also should be given to any assets not essential to the operation of the business, such as investments in securities, real estate, etc. In general, such nonoperating assets will command a lower rate of return than do the operating assets, although in exceptional cases the reverse may be true. In computing the book value per share of stock, assets of the investment type should be revalued on the basis of their market price and the book value adjusted accordingly. Comparison of the company's balance sheets over several years may reveal, among other facts, such developments as the acquisition of additional production facilities or subsidiary companies, improvement in financial position, and details as to recapitalizations and other changes in the capital structure of the corporation. If the corporation has more than one class of stock outstanding, the charter or certificate of incorporation should be examined to ascertain the explicit rights and privileges of the various stock issues including: (1) voting powers, (2) preference as to dividends, and (3) preference as to assets in the event of liquidation.

(d)   Detailed profit-and-loss statements should be obtained and considered for a representative period immediately prior to the required date of appraisal, preferably five or more years. Such statements should show (1) gross income by principal items; (2) principal deductions from gross income including major prior items of operating expenses, interest and other expense on each item of long-term debt, depreciation and depletion if such deductions are made, officers' salaries, in total if they appear to be reasonable or in detail if they seem to be excessive, contributions (whether or not deductible for tax purposes) that the nature of its business and its community position require the corporation to make, and taxes by principal items, including income and excess profits taxes; (3) net income available for dividends; (4) rates and amounts of dividends paid on each class of stock; (5) remaining amount carried to surplus; and (6) adjustments to, and reconciliation with, surplus as stated on the balance sheet. With profit and loss statements of this character available, the appraiser should be able to separate recurrent from nonrecurrent items of income and expense, to distinguish between operating income and investment income, and to ascertain whether or not any line of business in which the company is engaged is operated consistently at a loss and might be abandoned with benefit to the company. The percentage of earnings retained for business expansion should be noted when dividend-paying capacity is considered. Potential future income is a major factor in many valuations of closely-held stocks, and all information concerning past income which will be helpful in predicting the future should be secured. Prior earnings records usually are the most reliable guide as to the future expectancy, but resort to arbitrary five-or-ten-year averages without regard to current trends or future prospects will not produce a realistic valuation. If, for instance, a record of progressively increasing or decreasing net income is found, then greater weight may be accorded the most recent years' profits in estimating earning power. It will be helpful, in judging risk and the extent to which a business is a marginal operator, to consider deductions from income and net income in terms of percentage of sales. Major categories of cost and expense to be so analyzed include the consumption of raw materials and supplies in the case of manufacturers, processors and fabricators; the cost of purchased merchandise in the case of merchants; utility services; insurance; taxes; depletion or depreciation; and interest.

(e)   Primary consideration should be given to the dividend-paying capacity of the company rather than to dividends actually paid in the past. Recognition must be given to the necessity of retaining a reasonable portion of profits in a company to meet competition. Dividend-paying capacity is a factor that must be considered in an appraisal, but dividends actually paid in the past may not have any relation to dividend-paying capacity. Specifically, the dividends paid by a closely-held family company may be measured by the income needs of the stockholders or by their desire to avoid taxes on dividend receipts, instead of by the ability of the company to pay dividends. Where an actual or effective controlling interest in a corporation is to be valued, the dividend factor is not a material element, since the payment of such dividends is discretionary with the controlling stockholders. The individual or group in control can substitute salaries and bonuses for dividends, thus reducing net income and understating the dividend-paying capacity of the company. It follows, therefore, that dividends are less reliable criteria of fair market value than other applicable factors.

(f)   In the final analysis, goodwill is based upon earning capacity. The presence of goodwill and its value, therefore, rests upon the excess of net earnings over and above a fair return on the net tangible assets. While the element of goodwill may be based primarily on earnings, such factors as the prestige and renown of the business, the ownership of a trade or brand name, and a record of successful operation over a prolonged period in a particular locality, also may furnish support for the inclusion of intangible value. In some instances it may not be possible to make a separate appraisal of the tangible and intangible assets of the business. The enterprise has a value as an entity. Whatever intangible value there is, which is supportable by the facts, may be measured by the amount by which the appraised value of the tangible assets exceeds the net book value of such assets.

(g)   Sales of stock of a closely-held corporation should be carefully investigated to determine whether they represent transactions at arm's length. Forced or distress sales do not ordinarily reflect fair market value nor do isolated sales in small amounts necessarily control as the measure of value. This is especially true in the valuation of a controlling interest in a corporation. Since, in the case of closely-held stocks, no prevailing market prices are available, there is no basis for making an adjustment for blockage. It follows, therefore, that such stocks should be valued upon a consideration of all the evidence affecting the fair market value. The size of the block of stock itself is a relevant factor to be considered. Although it is true that a minority interest in an unlisted corporation's stock is more difficult to sell than a similar block of listed stock, it is equally true that control of a corporation, either actual or in effect, representing as it does an added element of value, may justify a higher value for a specific block of stock.

(h)   Section 2031(b) of the Code states, in effect, that in valuing unlisted securities the value of stock or securities of corporations engaged in the same or a similar line of business which are listed on an exchange should be taken into consideration along with all other factors. An important consideration is that the corporations to be used for comparisons have capital stocks which are actively traded by the public. In accordance with section 2031(b) of the Code, stocks listed on an exchange are to be considered first. However, if sufficient comparable companies whose stocks are listed on an exchange cannot be found, other comparable companies which have stocks actively traded on the over-the-counter market also may be used. The essential factor is that whether the stocks are sold on an exchange or over-the-counter there is evidence of an active, free public market for the stock as of the valuation date. In selecting corporations for comparative purposes, care should be taken to use only comparable companies. Although the only restrictive requirement as to comparable corporations specified in the statute is that their lines of business be the same or similar, yet it is obvious that consideration must be given to other relevant factors in order that the most valid comparison possible will be obtained. For illustration, a corporation having one or more issues of preferred stock, bonds or debentures in addition to its common stock should not be considered to be directly comparable to one having only common stock outstanding. In like manner, a company with a declining business and decreasing markets is not comparable to one with a record of current progress and market expansion.

SECTION 5. WEIGHT TO BE ACCORDED VARIOUS FACTORS.

The valuation of closely-held corporate stock entails the consideration of all relevant factors as stated in section 4. Depending upon the circumstances in each case, certain factors may carry more weight than others because of the nature of the company's business. To illustrate:

(a)   Earnings may be the most important criterion of value in some cases whereas asset value will receive primary consideration in others. In general, the appraiser will accord primary consideration to earnings when valuing stocks of companies which sell products or services to the public; conversely, in the investment or holding type of company, the appraiser may accord the greatest weight to the assets underlying the security to be valued.

(b)   The value of the stock of a closely-held investment or real estate holding company, whether or not family owned, is closely related to the value of the assets underlying the stock. For companies of this type the appraiser should determine the fair market values of the assets of the company. Operating expenses of such a company and the cost of liquidating it, if any, merit consideration when appraising the relative values of the stock and the underlying assets. The market values of the underlying assets give due weight to potential earnings and dividends of the particular items of property underlying the stock, capitalized at rates deemed proper by the investing public at the date of appraisal. A current appraisal by the investing public should be superior to the retrospective opinion of an individual. For these reasons, adjusted net worth should be accorded greater weight in valuing the stock of a closely-held investment or real estate holding company, whether or not family owned, than any of the other customary yardsticks of appraisal, such as earnings and dividend-paying capacity.

SECTION 6. CAPITALIZATION RATES.

In the application of certain fundamental valuation factors, such as earnings and dividends, it is necessary to capitalize the average or current results at some appropriate rate. A determination of the proper capitalization rate presents one of the most difficult problems in valuation. That there is no ready or simple solution will become apparent by a cursory check of the rates of return and dividend yields in terms of the selling prices of the corporate shares listed on the major exchanges of the country. Wide variations will be found even for companies in the same industry. Moreover, the ratio will fluctuate from year to year depending upon economic conditions. Thus, no standard tables of capitalization rates applicable to closely-held corporations can be formulated. Among the more important factors to be taken into consideration in deciding upon a capitalization rate in a particular case are: (1) the nature of the business; (2) the risk involved; and (3) the stability or irregularity of earnings.

SECTION 7. AVERAGE OF FACTORS.

Because valuations cannot be made on the basis of a prescribed formula, there is no means whereby the various applicable factors in a particular case can be assigned mathematical weights in deriving the fair market value. For this reason, no useful purpose is served by taking an average of several factors (for example, book value, capitalized earnings and capitalized dividends) and basing the valuation on the result. Such a process excludes active consideration of other pertinent factors, and the end result cannot be supported by a realistic application of the significant facts in the case except by mere chance.

SECTION 8. RESTRICTIVE AGREEMENTS.

Frequently, in the valuation of closely-held stock for estate and gift tax purposes, it will be found that the stock is subject to an agreement restricting its sale or transfer. Where shares of stock were acquired by a decedent subject to an option reserved by the issuing corporation to repurchase at a certain price, the option price is usually accepted as the fair market value for estate tax purposes. See Rev. Rul. 54-76, C.B. 1954-1, 194. However, in such case the option price is not determinative of fair market value for gift tax purposes. Where the option, or buy and sell agreement, is the result of voluntary action by the stockholders and is binding during the life as well as at the death of the stockholders, such agreement may or may not, depending upon the circumstances of each case, fix the value for estate tax purposes. However, such agreement is a factor to be considered, with other relevant factors, in determining fair market value. Where the stockholder is free to dispose of his shares during life and the option is to become effective only upon his death, the fair market value is not limited to the option price. It is always necessary to consider the relationship of the parties, the relative number of shares held by the decedent, and other material facts, to determine whether the agreement represents a bonafide business arrangement or is a device to pass the decedent's shares to the natural objects of his bounty for less than an adequate and full consideration in money or money's worth. In this connection see Rev. Rul. 157 C.B. 1953-2,255, and Rev. Rul. 189, C.B. 1953-2,294.

SECTION 9. EFFECT ON OTHER DOCUMENTS.

Revenue Ruling 54-77, C.B. 1954-1,187, is hereby superseded.

Appendix C

Present Value Tables

Present Value of One Dollar Due at the End of *n* Periods

$$PV = \frac{\$1}{r} - \frac{\$1}{r(1+r)^n}$$

PV = present value; r = discount rate; n = number of periods payment is made.

n	1%	2%	3%	4%	5%	6%	7%	8%	9%	10%
1	.99010	.98039	.97007	.96154	.95238	.94340	.93458	.92593	.91743	.90909
2	.98030	.96117	.94260	.92456	.90703	.89000	.87344	.85734	.84168	.82645
3	.97059	.94232	.91514	.88900	.86384	.83962	.81630	.79383	.77218	.75131
4	.96098	.92385	.88849	.85480	.82270	.79209	.76290	.73503	.70843	.68301
5	.95147	.90573	.86261	.82193	.78353	.74726	.71299	.68058	.64993	.62092
6	.94204	.88797	.83748	.79031	.74622	.70496	.66634	.63017	.59627	.56447
7	.93272	.87056	.81309	.75992	.71068	.66506	.62275	.58349	.54703	.51316
8	.92348	.85349	.78941	.73069	.67684	.62741	.58201	.54027	.50187	.46651
9	.91434	.83675	.76642	.70259	.64461	.59190	.54393	.50025	.46043	.42410
10	.90529	.82035	.74409	.67556	.61391	.55839	.50835	.46319	.42241	.38554
11	.89632	.80426	.72242	.64958	.58468	.52679	.47509	.42888	.38753	.35049
12	.88745	.78849	.70138	.62460	.55684	.49697	.44401	.39711	.35553	.31863
13	.87866	.77303	.68095	.60057	.53032	.46884	.41496	.36770	.32618	.28966
14	.86996	.75787	.66112	.57747	.50507	.44230	.38782	.34046	.29925	.26333
15	.86135	.74301	.64186	.55526	.48102	.41726	.36245	.31524	.27454	.23939
16	.85282	.72845	.62317	.53391	.45811	.39365	.33873	.29189	.25187	.21763
17	.84438	.71416	.60502	.51337	.43630	.37136	.31657	.27027	.23107	.19784
18	.83602	.70016	.58739	.49363	.41552	.35034	.29586	.25025	.21199	.17986
19	.82774	.68643	.57029	.47464	.39573	.33051	.27651	.23171	.19449	.16351
20	.81954	.67297	.55367	.45639	.37689	.31180	.25842	.21455	.17843	.14864
21	.81143	.65978	.53755	.43883	.35894	.29415	.24151	.19866	.16370	.13513
22	.80340	.64684	.52189	.42195	.34185	.27750	.22571	.18394	.15018	.12285
23	.79544	.63414	.50669	.40573	.32557	.26180	.21095	.17031	.13778	.11168
24	.78757	.62172	.49193	.39012	.31007	.24698	.19715	.15770	.12640	.10153
25	.77977	.60953	.47760	.37512	.29530	.23300	.18425	.14602	.11597	.09230

Present Value of One Dollar Due at the End of n Periods

n	11%	12%	13%	14%	15%	16%	17%	18%	19%	20%	n
1	.90090	.89286	.88496	.87719	.86957	.86207	.85470	.84746	.84034	.83333	1
2	.81162	.79719	.78315	.76947	.75614	.74316	.73051	.71818	.70616	.69444	2
3	.73119	.71178	.69305	.67497	.65752	.64066	.62437	.60863	.59342	.57870	3
4	.65873	.63552	.61332	.59208	.57175	.55229	.53365	.51579	.49867	.48225	4
5	.59345	.56743	.54276	.51937	.49718	.47611	.45611	.43711	.41905	.40188	5
6	.53464	.50663	.48032	.45559	.43233	.41044	.38984	.37043	.35214	.33490	6
7	.48166	.45235	.42506	.39964	.37594	.35383	.33320	.31392	.29592	.27908	7
8	.43393	.40388	.37616	.35056	.32690	.30503	.28478	.26604	.24867	.23257	8
9	.39092	.36061	.33288	.30751	.28426	.26295	.24340	.22546	.20897	.19381	9
10	.35218	.32197	.29459	.26974	.24718	.22668	.20804	.19106	.17560	.16151	10
11	.31728	.28748	.26070	.23662	.21494	.19542	.17781	.16192	.14756	.13459	11
12	.28584	.25667	.23071	.20756	.18691	.16846	.15197	.13722	.12400	.11216	12
13	.25751	.22917	.20416	.18207	.16253	.14523	.12989	.11629	.10420	.09346	13
14	.23199	.20462	.18068	.15971	.14133	.12520	.11102	.09855	.08757	.07789	14
15	.20900	.18270	.15989	.14010	.12289	.10793	.09489	.08352	.07359	.06491	15
16	.18829	.16312	.14150	.12289	.10686	.09304	.08110	.07078	.06184	.05409	16
17	.16963	.14564	.12522	.10780	.09293	.08021	.06932	.05998	.05196	.04507	17
18	.15282	.13004	.11081	.09456	.08080	.06914	.05925	.05083	.04367	.03756	18
19	.13768	.11611	.09806	.08295	.07026	.05961	.05064	.04308	.03669	.03130	19
20	.12403	.10367	.08678	.07276	.06110	.05139	.04328	.03651	.03084	.02608	20
21	.11174	.09256	.07680	.06383	.05313	.04430	.03699	.03094	.02591	.02174	21
22	.10067	.08264	.06796	.05599	.04620	.03819	.03162	.02622	.02178	.01811	22
23	.09069	.07379	.06014	.04911	.04017	.03292	.02702	.02222	.01830	.01509	23
24	.08170	.06588	.05322	.04308	.03493	.02838	.02310	.01883	.01538	.01258	24
25	.07361	.05882	.04710	.03779	.03038	.02447	.01974	.01596	.01292	.01048	25

Present Value of One Dollar Due at the End of *n* Periods

n	21%	22%	23%	24%	25%	26%	27%	28%	29%	30%	n
1	.82645	.81967	.81301	.80645	.80000	.79365	.78740	.78125	.77519	.76923	1
2	.68301	.67186	.66098	.65036	.64000	.62988	.62000	.61035	.60093	.59172	2
3	.56447	.55071	.53738	.52449	.51200	.49991	.48819	.47684	.46583	.45517	3
4	.46651	.45140	.43690	.42297	.40960	.39675	.38440	.37253	.36111	.35013	4
5	.38554	.37000	.35520	.34111	.32768	.31488	.30268	.29104	.27993	.26933	5
6	.31863	.30328	.28878	.27509	.26214	.24991	.23833	.22737	.21700	.20718	6
7	.26333	.24859	.23478	.22184	.20972	.19834	.18766	.17764	.16822	.15937	7
8	.21763	.20376	.19088	.17891	.16777	.15741	.14776	.13878	.13040	.12259	8
9	.17986	.16702	.15519	.14428	.13422	.12493	.11635	.10842	.10109	.09430	9
10	.14864	.13690	.12617	.11635	.10737	.09915	.09161	.08470	.07836	.07254	10
11	.12285	.11221	.10258	.09383	.08590	.07869	.07214	.06617	.06075	.05580	11
12	.10153	.09198	.08339	.07567	.06872	.06245	.05680	.05170	.04709	.04292	12
13	.08391	.07539	.06780	.06103	.05498	.04957	.04472	.04039	.03650	.03302	13
14	.06934	.06180	.05512	.04921	.04398	.03934	.03522	.03155	.02830	.02540	14
15	.05731	.05065	.04481	.03969	.03518	.03122	.02773	.02465	.02194	.01954	15
16	.04736	.04152	.03643	.03201	.02815	.02478	.02183	.01926	.01700	.01503	16
17	.03914	.03403	.02962	.02581	.02252	.01967	.01719	.01505	.01318	.01156	17
18	.03235	.02789	.02408	.02082	.01801	.01561	.01354	.01175	.01022	.00889	18
19	.02673	.02286	.01958	.01679	.01441	.01239	.01066	.00918	.00792	.00684	19
20	.02209	.01874	.01592	.01354	.01153	.00983	.00839	.00717	.00614	.00526	20
21	.01826	.01536	.01294	.01092	.00922	.00780	.00661	.00561	.00476	.00405	21
22	.01509	.01259	.01052	.00880	.00738	.00619	.00520	.00438	.00369	.00311	22
23	.01247	.01032	.00855	.00710	.00590	.00491	.00410	.00342	.00286	.00239	23
24	.01031	.00846	.00695	.00573	.00472	.00390	.00323	.00267	.00222	.00184	24
25	.00852	.00693	.00565	.00462	.00378	.00310	.00254	.00209	.00172	.00142	25

Present Value of an Annuity of One Dollar for n Periods

$PV = \dfrac{\$1}{(1+r)^n}$

PV = present value; r = discount rate; n = number of periods until payment.

n	1%	2%	3%	4%	5%	6%	7%	8%	9%	10%	n
1	.9901	.9804	.9709	.9615	.9524	.9434	.9346	.9259	.9174	.9091	1
2	1.9704	1.9416	1.9135	1.8861	1.8594	1.8334	1.8080	1.7833	1.7591	1.7355	2
3	2.9410	2.8839	2.8286	2.7751	2.7232	2.6730	2.6243	2.5771	2.5313	2.4868	3
4	3.9020	3.8077	3.7171	3.6299	3.5459	3.4651	3.3872	3.3121	3.2397	3.1699	4
5	4.8535	4.7134	4.5797	4.4518	4.3295	4.2123	4.1002	3.9927	3.8896	3.7908	5
6	5.7955	5.6014	5.4172	5.2421	5.0757	4.9173	4.7665	4.6229	4.4859	4.3553	6
7	6.7282	6.4720	6.2302	6.0020	5.7863	5.5824	5.3893	5.2064	5.0329	4.8684	7
8	7.6517	7.3254	7.0196	6.7327	6.4632	6.2098	5.9713	5.7466	5.5348	5.3349	8
9	8.5661	8.1622	7.7861	7.4353	7.1078	6.8017	6.5152	6.2469	5.9852	5.7590	9
10	9.4714	8.9825	8.5302	8.1109	7.7217	7.3601	7.0236	6.7101	6.4176	6.1446	10
11	10.3677	9.7868	9.2526	8.7604	8.3064	7.8868	7.4987	7.1389	6.8052	6.4951	11
12	11.2552	10.5753	9.9539	9.3850	8.8632	8.3838	7.9427	7.5361	7.1607	6.8137	12
13	12.1338	11.3483	10.6349	9.9856	9.3935	8.8527	8.3576	7.9038	7.4869	7.1034	13
14	13.0038	12.1062	11.2960	10.5631	9.8986	9.2950	8.7454	8.2442	7.7861	7.3667	14
15	13.8651	12.8492	11.9379	11.1183	10.3796	9.7122	9.1079	8.5595	8.0607	7.6061	15
16	14.7180	13.5777	12.5610	11.6522	10.8377	10.1059	9.4466	8.8514	8.3125	7.8237	16
17	15.5624	14.2918	13.1660	12.1656	11.2740	10.4772	9.7632	9.1216	8.5436	8.0215	17
18	16.3984	14.9920	13.7534	12.6592	11.6895	10.8276	10.0591	9.3719	8.7556	8.2014	18
19	17.2261	15.6784	14.3237	13.1339	12.0853	11.1581	10.3356	9.6036	8.9501	8.3649	19
20	18.0457	16.3514	14.8774	13.5903	12.4622	11.4699	10.5940	9.8181	9.1285	8.5136	20
21	18.8571	17.0111	15.4149	14.0291	12.8211	11.7640	10.8355	10.0168	9.2922	8.6487	21
22	19.6605	17.6580	15.9368	14.4511	13.1630	12.0416	11.0612	10.2007	9.4424	8.7715	22
23	20.4559	18.2921	16.4435	14.8568	13.4885	12.3033	11.2722	10.3710	9.5802	8.8832	23
24	21.2435	18.9139	16.9355	15.2469	13.7986	12.5503	11.4693	10.5287	9.7066	8.9847	24
25	22.0233	19.5234	17.4131	15.6220	14.0939	12.7833	11.6536	10.6748	9.8226	9.0770	25

Present Value of an Annuity of One Dollar for *n* Periods

n	11%	12%	13%	14%	15%	16%	17%	18%	19%	20%	n
1	.9009	.8929	.8850	.3772	.8696	.8621	.8547	.8475	.8403	.8333	1
2	1.7125	1.6901	1.6681	1.6467	1.6257	1.6052	1.5852	1.5656	1.5465	1.5278	2
3	2.4437	2.4018	2.3612	2.3216	2.2832	2.2459	2.2096	2.1743	2.1399	2.1065	3
4	3.1024	3.0373	2.9745	2.9137	2.8550	2.7982	2.7432	2.6901	2.6386	2.5887	4
5	3.6959	3.6048	3.5172	3.4331	3.3522	3.2743	3.1993	3.1272	3.0576	2.9906	5
6	4.2305	4.1114	3.9976	3.8887	3.7845	3.6847	3.5892	3.4976	3.4098	3.3255	6
7	4.7122	4.5638	4.4226	4.2883	4.1604	4.0386	3.9224	3.8115	3.7057	3.6046	7
8	5.1461	4.9676	4.7988	4.6389	4.4873	4.3436	4.2072	4.0776	3.9544	3.8372	8
9	5.5370	5.3282	5.1317	4.9464	4.7716	4.6065	4.4506	4.3030	4.1633	4.0310	9
10	5.8892	5.6502	5.4262	5.2161	5.0188	4.8332	4.6586	4.4941	4.3389	4.1925	10
11	6.2065	5.9377	5.6869	5.4527	5.2337	5.0286	4.8364	4.6560	4.4865	4.3271	11
12	6.4924	6.1944	5.9176	5.6603	5.4206	5.1971	4.9884	4.7932	4.6105	4.4392	12
13	6.7499	6.4235	6.1218	5.8424	5.5831	5.3423	5.1183	4.9095	4.7147	4.5327	13
14	6.9819	6.6282	6.3025	6.0021	5.7245	5.4675	5.2293	5.0081	4.8023	4.6106	14
15	7.1909	6.8109	6.4624	6.1422	5.8474	5.5755	5.3242	5.0916	4.8759	4.6755	15
16	7.3792	6.9740	6.6039	6.2651	5.9542	5.6685	5.4053	5.1624	4.9377	4.7296	16
17	7.5488	7.1196	6.7291	6.3729	6.0472	5.7487	5.4746	5.2223	4.9897	4.7746	17
18	7.7016	7.2497	6.8399	6.4674	6.1280	5.8178	5.5339	5.2732	5.0333	4.8122	18
19	7.8393	7.3658	6.9380	6.5504	6.1982	5.8775	5.5845	5.3162	5.0700	4.8435	19
20	7.9633	7.4694	7.0248	6.6231	6.2593	5.9288	5.6278	5.3527	5.1009	4.8696	20
21	8.0751	7.5620	7.1016	6.6870	6.3125	5.9731	5.6648	5.3837	5.1268	4.8913	21
22	8.1757	7.6446	7.1695	6.7429	6.3587	6.0113	5.6964	5.4099	5.1486	4.9094	22
23	8.2664	7.7184	7.2297	6.7921	6.3988	6.0442	5.7234	5.4321	5.1668	4.9245	23
24	8.3481	7.7843	7.2829	6.8351	6.4338	6.0726	5.7465	5.4509	5.1822	4.9371	24
25	8.4217	7.8431	7.3300	6.8729	6.4641	6.0971	5.7662	5.4669	5.1951	4.9476	25

Present Value of an Annuity of One Dollar for *n* Periods

n	21%	22%	23%	24%	25%	26%	27%	28%	29%	30%	n
1	.8264	.8197	.8130	.8065	.8000	.7937	.7874	.7813	.7752	.7692	1
2	1.5095	1.4915	1.4740	1.4568	1.4400	1.4235	1.4074	1.3916	1.3761	1.3609	2
3	2.0739	2.0422	2.0114	1.9813	1.9520	1.9234	1.8956	1.8684	1.8420	1.8161	3
4	2.5404	2.4936	2.4483	2.4043	2.3616	2.3202	2.2800	2.2410	2.2031	2.1662	4
5	2.9260	2.8636	2.8035	2.7454	2.6893	2.6351	2.5827	2.5320	2.4830	2.4356	5
6	3.2446	3.1669	3.0923	3.0205	2.9514	2.8850	2.8210	2.7594	2.7000	2.6427	6
7	3.5079	3.4155	3.3270	3.2423	3.1611	3.0833	3.0087	2.9370	2.8682	2.8021	7
8	3.7256	3.6193	3.5179	3.4212	3.3289	3.2407	3.1564	3.0758	2.9986	2.9247	8
9	3.9054	3.7863	3.6731	3.5655	3.4631	3.3657	3.2728	3.1842	3.0997	3.0190	9
10	4.0541	3.9232	3.7993	3.6819	3.5705	3.4648	3.3644	3.2689	3.1781	3.0915	10
11	4.1769	4.0354	3.9018	3.7757	3.6564	3.5435	3.4365	3.3351	3.2388	3.1473	11
12	4.2785	4.1274	3.9852	3.8514	3.7251	3.6060	3.4933	3.3868	3.2859	3.1903	12
13	4.3624	4.2028	4.0530	3.9124	3.7801	3.6555	3.5381	3.4272	3.3224	3.2233	13
14	4.4317	4.2646	4.1082	3.9616	3.8241	3.6949	3.5733	3.4587	3.3507	3.2487	14
15	4.4890	4.3152	4.1530	4.0013	3.8593	3.7261	3.6010	3.4834	3.3726	3.2682	15
16	4.5364	4.3567	4.1894	4.0333	3.8874	3.7509	3.6228	3.5026	3.3896	3.2832	16
17	4.5755	4.3908	4.2190	4.0591	3.9099	3.7705	3.6400	3.5177	3.4028	3.2948	17
18	4.6079	4.4187	4.2431	4.0799	3.9279	3.7861	3.6536	3.5294	3.4130	3.3037	18
19	4.6346	4.4415	4.2627	4.0967	3.9424	3.7985	3.6642	3.5386	3.4210	3.3105	19
20	4.6567	4.4603	4.2786	4.1103	3.9539	3.8083	3.6726	3.5458	3.4271	3.3158	20
21	4.6750	4.4756	4.2916	4.1212	3.9631	3.8161	3.6792	3.5514	3.4319	3.3198	21
22	4.6900	4.4882	4.3021	4.1300	3.9705	3.8223	3.6844	3.5558	3.4356	3.3230	22
23	4.7025	4.4985	4.3106	4.1371	3.9764	3.8273	3.6885	3.5592	3.4384	3.3254	23
24	4.7128	4.5070	4.3176	4.1428	3.9811	3.8312	3.6918	3.5619	3.4406	3.3272	24
25	4.7213	4.5139	4.3232	4.1474	3.9849	3.8342	3.6943	3.5640	3.4423	3.3286	25

Appendix D

Bibliography

General Valuation Issues

Articles

Alerding, R. James, Jr. "IRS Valuation Methods Lag Behind Business Practice." *Taxation for Accountants*, July 1992, pp. 4–9.

Angelini, James P., and Spencer J. Martin. "Judicial Trends in Closely Held Business Valuation." *National Public Accountant*, July 1989, pp. 28–32.

Berkowitz, Richard K., and Joseph A. Blanco. "Putting a Price Tag on Your Company." *Nation's Business*, January 1992, pp. 29–31.

Bielinski, Daniel W. "The Comparable-Company Approach: Measuring the True Value of Privately Held Firms." *Corporate Cashflow Magazine*, October 1990, pp. 64–66.

Blue, Ian; Pamela Meneguzzi; and Stephen R. Cole. "Business Valuation: Creature from the Green Lagoon." *CA Magazine*, July 1992, pp. 42–44, 47.

Cole, Stephen R. "Business Valuation: No Agreement, No Sale." *CA Magazine*, April 1992, pp. 51–55.

Cooper, Glen. "How Much Is Your Business Worth? *In Business*, September–October 1984, pp. 50–54.

DeThomas, Arthur R. "Valuing the Ownership Interest in the Privately Held Small Firm." *American Journal of Small Business*, Winter 1985, pp. 50–59.

Dukes, William P., and Oswald D. Bowlin. "Valuation of Closely Held Firms." *Business Valuation Review*, December 1990, pp. 127–37.

Eber, Victor I. "The Valuation of Closely Held Corporations." *Journal of Accountancy*, June 1984, pp. 103–4.

Emory, John D. "Why Business Valuation and Real Estate Appraisal Are Different." *Business Valuation News*, June 1990, pp. 5–8.

Faris, John; Walter R. Holman; and Patrick A. Martinelli. "Valuing the Closely Held Business." *Mergers & Acquisitions*, Fall 1983, pp. 53–59.

Feinberg, Andrew. "What's It Worth?" *Venture*, January 1988, pp. 27–31.

Field, Irving M. "A Review of the Principles of Valuation." *ASA Valuation*, June 1986, pp. 2–10.

Fiore, Nicholas J. "Valuing Closely Held Businesses." *Journal of Accountancy*, April 1990, p. 10.

Fishman, Jay E. "The Alternate Market Comparison Approach in Valuing Closely Held Enterprises." *FAIR$HARE: The Matrimonial Law Monthly*, October 1988, pp. 7–8.

————. "The Problem with Rules of Thumb in the Valuation of Closely Held Entities." *FAIR$HARE: The Matrimonial Law Monthly*, December 1984, pp. 13–15.

Forbes, Wallace F. "Putting a Value on a Closely Held Company." *Family Advocate*, Summer 1984, pp. 28–30.

Graham, Michael D. "Selection of Market Multiples in Business Valuation." *Business Valuation Review*, March 1990, pp. 8–12.

Gray, Gerald. "When Is Fair Market Value Unfair?" *ASA Valuation*, June 1984, pp. 2–7.

Haas, R. Victor, Jr. "What's Your Business Worth?" *Small Business Reports*, February 1992, pp. 20–24.

Hitchner, James R. "Valuation of a Closely Held Business." *Tax Adviser*, July 1992, pp. 471–79.

Hoeppner, James B. "Closely Held Business Interests—Valuation Strategies." *Tax Adviser*, April 1990, pp. 218–20.

Jones, Jeffrey D. "Rule of Thumb Formulas for Small Businesses." *Business Valuation News*, December 1982, pp. 7–18.

Kaplan, Steven P., and Egon Fromm. "The Impact of Taxes on the Value of Close Corporations." *Estate Planning*, May/June 1992, pp. 137–42.

Kissin, Warren, and Ronald Zulli. "Valuation of a Closely Held Business." *Journal of Accountancy*, June 1988, pp. 38–40.

Klaris, Raynor J. "Valuing the Family Business." *Trusts & Estates*, February 1990, pp. 18–29.

Kleeman, Robert E., Jr. "Valuing the Closely Held Business Entity: A Lawyer's Guide to Business Valuation." *American Journal of Family Law*, Winter 1990, pp. 385–96.

Kurzman, Stephen A. "How to Value a Closely Held Business." *Practical Accountant*, May 1988, pp. 64–74.

Kuttner, Monroe S. "Business Valuation: An Important Management Advisory Service." *Journal of Accountancy*, November 1989, pp. 143–46.

Lammers, Teri. "Business Valuations: Know Your Worth." *Inc.*, August 1991, pp. 90–91.

LeClair, Mark S. "Valuing the Closely-Held Corporation: The Validity and Performance of Established Valuation Procedures." *Accounting Horizons*, September 1990, pp. 31–42.

Ledereich, Leonard, and Joel G. Siegel. "What's a Business Worth? Valuation Methods for Accountants." *National Public Accountant*, February 1990, pp. 18–22.

Leung, T. S. Tony. "Tax Reform Act of 1986: Considerations for Business Valuations." *Business Valuation Review*, June 1987, pp. 60–63.

Lewis, Lawrence D. "How to Value a Small Business." *Business* (Atlanta, Ga., monthly magazine), July–August 1988, pp. 46–49.

Longenecker, Ruth R. "A Practical Guide to Valuation of Closely Held Stock." *Trusts & Estates*, January 1983, pp. 32–41.

Mangan, Doreen. "What Is Your Company Worth?" *Executive Female*, November–December 1990, p. 74.

Mard, Michael J. "The Business Valuation Process." *FAIR$HARE: The Matrimonial Law Monthly*, November 1991, pp. 25–26.

Margolis, Nell. "Something of Value." *Inc.*, January 1986, pp. 103–4.

Meyers, William. "Determining a Value." *Venture*, January 1985, pp. 35–36.

Moskowitz, Jerald I. "What's Your Business Worth?" *Management Accounting*, March 1988, pp. 30–34.

Murphy, John W. "Using an Appraiser to Value the Closely Held Business." *FAIR$HARE: The Matrimonial Law Monthly*, March 1992, pp. 6–7.

"The Opinion of the College on Defining Standards of Value." *ASA Valuation*, June 1989, pp. 65–72.

Peterson, Renno L. "A Guide to Valuing the Closely Held Business." *Practical Accountant*, April 1989, pp. 34–39.

Pratt, Shannon P. "Business Buyer's Valuation Guide." *In Business*, March/April 1987, pp. 58–59.

Randisi, Martin P. "Comparable Company Method of Valuing a Closely Held Business." *FAIR$HARE: The Matrimonial Law Monthly*, January 1991, pp. 3–5.

Reilly, Robert F. "What Financial Advisors Need to Know about Business Valuation and Security Analysis Services." *Corporate Growth Report*, January 1992, pp. 11–14, 18.

Sammons, Donna. "Evaluating the Valuators." *Inc.*, May 1983, pp. 186–88.

Scharfstein, Alan J. "The Right Price for a Business." *CPA Journal*, January 1991, pp. 42–47.

Schilt, James H. "Challenging Standard Business Appraisal Methods." *Business Valuation News*, December 1984, pp. 4–14.

Siciliano, Peter J., and Mark Jones. "Business Valuation for the Nonspecialist: Finding the Best Value." *Practical Accountant*, September 1991, pp. 70+.

Singleton, Margaret. "What's It Worth to You?" *Inc.*, September 1986, pp. 113–14.

Sliwoski, Leonard J. "The Value Cannot Be Determined by One Precise Mathematical Formula." *Small Business Forum*, Fall 1991, pp. 15–20.

Stevens, Mark. "Valuations as a Business Report Card." *D&B Reports*, November–December 1991, pp. 50–51.

Taub, Maxwell J. "Can Market Comparables Be Used in Valuing Small Businesses?" *IBBA Journal*, October 1991, pp. 10–14.

Thornton, Roy C. "What's a Business Worth? A Practical Guide to Valuation." *Practical Accountant*, November 1984, pp. 54–58.

Trugman, Gary R. "What Is Fair Market Value? Back to Basics." *FAIR$HARE: The Matrimonial Law Monthly*, June 1990, pp. 11–13.

Walker, Donna J., and Curtis R. Kimball. "Business Valuations: What Are They Worth to You?" *Business Age*, November/December 1988, pp. 54–58.

Weiss, Gary. "How to Take the Guesswork out of Valuing a Business." *Canadian Business*, May 1986, pp. 130–31.

West, Thomas L. "Pricing Businesses: The Use of Comparables." *Business Broker*, June 1992, pp. 1–4.

Worley, Joel K., and Fess B. Green. "Determinants of Risk Adjustment for Small Business Valuation in a Growth Industry." *Journal of Small Business Management*, October 1989, pp. 26–33.

Books

Babcock, Henry A. *Appraisal Principles and Procedures*. Washington, D.C.: American Society of Appraisers, 1980.

Blackman, Irving L. *The Valuation of Privately Held Businesses*. Chicago: Probus Publishing Co., 1986.

Blum, Robert R. *A Practical Guide to Business Valuation*. New York: McGraw-Hill, 1986.

Bonbright, James C. *The Valuation of Property*. Charlottesville, Va.: The Miche Company, 1965. Reprint of 1937 ed.

Burke, Frank M. *Valuation and Valuation Planning for Closely Held Businesses*. Englewood Cliffs, N.J.: Prentice Hall Law & Business, 1981.

Copeland, Thomas; Tim Koller; and Jack Murrin. *Valuation: Measuring and Managing the Value of Companies.* New York: John Wiley & Sons, 1989.

Desmond, Glenn M., and Richard E. Kelley. *Business Valuation Handbook.* 2nd ed. Marina del Rey, Calif.: Valuation Press, 1985.

Desmond, Glenn M., and Sandra Storm, ed. *Handbook of Small Business Formulas.* 3rd ed. Culver City, Calif.: Valuation Press, forthcoming in 1993.

Fishman, Jay E.; Shannon P. Pratt; J. Clifford Griffith; and D. Keith Wilson. *Guide to Business Valuations.* 2nd ed. Fort Worth, Tex.: Practitioners Publishing Co., 1992.

Horn, Thomas. *Business Valuation Manual.* Lancaster, Pa.: Charter Oak Press, 1985.

Kramer, Yale. *Valuing a Closely Held Business* (Accountant's Workbook Series). New York: Matthew Bender & Company, 1987.

McCarthy, George D., and Robert E. Healy. *Valuing a Company: Practices and Procedures.* New York: Ronald Press Company, 1971.

Miles, Raymond C. *Basic Business Appraisal.* New York: John Wiley & Sons, 1984.

————. *How to Price a Business.* Englewood Cliffs, N. J.: Prentice Hall, 1987.

Pratt, Shannon P., ed. *Readings in Business Valuation.* Washington, D.C.: American Society of Appraisers, 1986.

————. *Valuing a Business: The Analysis and Appraisal of Closely Held Companies.* 2nd ed. Homewood, Ill.: Dow Jones-Irwin, 1989.

Schnepper, Jeff A. *The Professional Handbook of Business Valuation.* Reading, Mass.: Addison-Wesley Publishing, 1982.

Smith, Gordon V. *Corporate Valuation—A Business and Professional Guide.* New York: John Wiley & Sons, 1988.

Smith, Gordon V., and Russell L. Parr. *Valuation of Intellectual Property and Intangible Assets.* New York: John Wiley & Sons, 1989.

West, Thomas L. *1992 Business Brokers Reference Guide.* Concord, Mass.: Business Brokerage Press, 1992.

West, Thomas L., and Jeffrey D. Jones, eds. *Handbook of Business Valuation.* New York: John Wiley & Sons, 1992.

Woolery, Arlo, ed. *The Art of Valuation.* Lexington, Mass.: Lexington Books, 1978.

Wright, Jeffrey P. *What Is a Business Worth?: For Buyers, Sellers, and Brokers.* Scottsdale, Ariz.: E.V.S. Publications, 1990.

Zukin, James H., and John G. Mavredakis, eds. *Financial Valuation: Businesses and Business Interests.* New York: Maxwell Macmillan, 1990.

Valuation of Specific Industries

Articles

Adams, P. E. "It's Not Difficult to Put a Price Tag on a Pharmacy." *American Druggist,* March 1982, pp. 77–78.

Anikeeff, Michael A. "Car Care Centers." *Real Estate Appraiser & Analyst,* Summer 1990, pp. 73–77.

Battersby, M.E. "Putting a Value on Your Beverage Business." *Beverage World*, November 1984, pp. 126+.

Blatt, Julius M. "Appraising the Multiplex Movie Theater." *Appraisal Journal*, October 1988, pp. 508–21.

Buono, Thomas J. "Valuations in Broadcasting." *Appraisal Journal*, July 1984, pp. 382–88.

Burke, Brian H. "Appraising Independent Insurance Agencies." *Business Valuation Review*, September 1989, pp. 114–19.

Clatanoff, Robert M. *The Valuation of Resort and Recreational Property: A Classified Annotated Bibliography*. Chicago: International Association of Assessing Officers, 1984.

de Vries, Ted. "What Is Your Business Really Worth?" *Rental Age*, October 1982, p. 40.

Duryee, David A. "Valuation of an Insurance Agency." *Broker World*, October 1988, pp. 40–48.

Fairchild, Bruce H., and Keith W. Fairchild. "How to Value Personal Service Practices." *Practical Accountant*, August 1989, pp. 27–30, 32–40.

Fisher, Douglas P. "Restaurant Valuation: A Financial Approach." *Cornell Hotel and Restaurant Administration Quarterly*, February 1991, pp. 88–92.

Gimmy, Arthur E., and Mary G. Gates. "Health Care Facilities: Valuation Issues for the 1990s." *Real Estate Finance Journal*, Summer 1992, pp. 63–67.

Grabowski, Roger J. "How Much Is Your Foundry Worth?" *Modern Casting*, October 1990, pp. 30–31.

Hall, Jeremy G. "Valuation of a Fully Automatic Carwash." *Appraisal Journal*, October 1990, pp. 445–50.

Halloran, Jim. "How Much Does Your Shop Pay You?" *Motor Service*, June 1991, pp. 24–27.

————. "Just How Much Is Your Shop Worth?" *Motor Service*, June 1990, pp. 20–22.

Hirsh, Lawrence A. "Golf Courses—Valuation and Evaluation." *Appraisal Journal*, January 1991, pp. 38–47.

Johnson, Alan W. "How Much Is Your Company Worth?" *Apparel Industry Magazine*, November 1982, pp. 34–38.

Keesey, Robert L. "The Campground Resort—A Valuation Model." *Real Estate Appraiser and Analyst*, Spring 1984, pp. 8–13.

Kerr, Stephen J. "Formulas for Informed Printing Company Buyers." *Printing Journal*, June 1989, pp. 12–13.

King, Clive A., and Frics Mai. "Appraising Wines and Vines." (Part 2, The Valuation of Vineyards and Wineries). *Wines & Vines*, July 1991, pp. 42–43.

Kudla, Ronald J. "Valuation of an Independent Insurance Agency." *American Journal of Family Law*, Summer 1989, pp. 149–55.

McKay, Cecil R., Jr. "Golf Course Appraisals." *ASA Valuation*, November 1981, pp. 100–107.

Monath, Donald. "Appraising Fair Value of a Dealership." *Automotive News*, July 15, 1985, pp. 25–26.

Moore, Sharon K., and Robert F. Reilly. "Pricing Your Brokerage Business: What to Consider." *Commercial Investment Real Estate Journal*, Summer 1990, pp. 34–41.

Moyse, John S. "The Valuation of Existing Business in a Life Insurance Practice." *Journal of the American Society of CLU & ChFC*, July 1990, pp. 66–71.

Ninker, Robert W. "Your Funeral Home's Worth: Do Your Job Now." *The Director*, May/June 1984, pp. 5, 12–13, 47–48.

Pettit, Laurence C.; Michael D. Atchison; and Robert S. Kemp. "The Valuation of Small or Closely Held Banks." *Journal of Bank Accounting & Auditing*, Spring 1991, pp. 23–31.

Pratt, Shannon P. "Valuing a Property Management Company." (A research study) Chicago: Institute of Real Estate Management Foundation, 1988.

Reilly, Robert F. "The Business Valuation of a Typical Construction Company." *Cost Engineering*, January 1990, pp. 13–22.

———. "The Valuation of Construction Companies." *Buyouts & Acquisitions*, March/April 1988, pp. 41–56.

———. "The Valuation of Real Estate Brokerage Firms." *Real Estate Accounting & Taxation*, Spring 1991, pp. 52–60.

———. "Valuing the Commercial Brokerage Firm." *Small Business Taxation*, May/June 1990, pp. 297–303.

Roberts, Joe R., and Eric Roberts. "Reviewing a Nursing Home Appraisal Report." *Appraisal Review & Mortgage Underwriting Journal*, Spring 1992, pp. 60–73.

Roddewig, Richard J.; Steven P. Schiltz; and Gary Papke. "Appraising Theme Parks." *Appraisal Journal*, January 1986, pp. 85–108.

Rosen, Bob. "Valuing Your Company." *Graphic Arts Monthly*, December 1988, pp. 72–76.

Shepard, Richard C. "Valuation of a Property Management Company for Acquisition." *Real Estate Issues*, Spring/Summer 1992, pp. 13–16.

Shulman, William. "Bagel Bakeries: Plugging the Valuation Holes." *FAIR-$HARE: The Matrimonial Law Monthly*, August 1989, pp. 26–27.

Stefanelli, John M. "Valuation of Restaurants." *Business Valuation Review*, December 1986, pp. 16–24.

Townsley, William J. "Valuation of Golf Courses." *Property Tax Journal*, September 1985, pp. 161–95.

Wise, Richard M. "The Valuation of Insurance Agencies." *CA Magazine*, December 1985, pp. 80–83.

Selected Sources of Composite Financial Data

Manufacturing

Annual Key Ratio Survey of the Folding Carton and Rigid Box Industry
National Paperbox and Packaging Association
1201 East Abingdon Drive
Suite 203
Alexandria, Virginia 22314
Telephone: (703) 684-2212
Annual. Price $75 per copy.

Industry Norms and Key Business Ratios
Dun & Bradstreet Credit Services
Dun's Analytical Services
One Diamond Hill Road
Murray Hill, New Jersey 07974-0027
Telephone: (800) 223-0141
Annual. Price varies with content.

Metal Treating Institute Operational Cost Survey
Metal Treating Institute
302 Third Street, Suite 1
Neptune Beach, Florida 32266-5138
Telephone: (904) 249-0449
Annual. Price: Free to participants; $100 prepaid to nonparticipating members;
$150 prepaid to nonmembers.

Printing Industries of America, Inc. Annual Financial Ratio Studies
Printing Industries of America, Inc.
Financial Services Department
100 Dangerfield Road
Alexandria, Virginia 22314-2888
Telephone: (703) 519-8138
Annual. Price: $85 per book, $625 for a complete set for members; $100 per book,
$900 for a complete set for nonmembers.

*Special Statistical Report on Profit, Sales and Production Trends of the Men's
and Boys' Clothing Industry*
Clothing Manufacturers Association of the U.S.A.
1290 Avenue of the Americas
New York, New York 10104
Telephone: (212) 757-6664
Annual. Price: $25 per single copy.

Statistics of Paper, Paperboard & Wood Pulp
American Paper Institute
260 Madison Avenue
New York, New York 10016
Telephone: (212) 340-0600
Annual. Price: $345.

Retailing

Annual Financial Review
Food Marketing Institute
1750 K Street, N.W.
Washington, D.C. 20006
Telephone: (202) 452-8444
Annual. Price: $30 per copy for nonmembers.

Cost of Doing Business Survey
National Association of Retail Dealers of America
10 East 22nd Street, Suite 310
Lombard, Illinois 60148
Telephone: (708) 953-8950
Annual. Price: $50 to members; $75 to nonmembers.

Cost of Doing Business Survey for Retail Sporting Goods Stores
National Sporting Goods Association
1699 Wall Street
Mt. Prospect, Illinois 60056
Telephone: (708) 439-4000
Biennial. Price: $95 per copy

Dealer Compensation Survey Report
National Office Products Association
301 N. Fairfax Street
Alexandria, Virginia 22314-2696
Telephone: (703) 549-9040
Triennial. Price: $50 to members; $100 to nonmembers.

Distributors Profit Survey Report
National Truck Equipment Association
38705 Seven Mile Road, Suite 345
Livonia, Michigan 48152
Telephone: (313) 462-2190
Annual. Price: $75 to nonparticipants.

Financial and Operating Results of Department and Specialty Stores
National Retail Federation
100 W. 31st Street
New York, New York 10001
Telephone: (212) 244-8780
Annual. Price: $37 to members; $69 to nonmembers.

FTD Retail Florists' Operating Survey
Florists' Transworld Delivery Association
29200 Northwestern Highway
Southfield, Michigan, 48034
Telephone: (313) 355-6385
Price: $50 to members; $100 to nonmembers.

Industry Norms and Key Business Ratios
Dun & Bradstreet Credit Services
Dun's Analytical Services
One Diamond Hill Road
Murray Hill, New Jersey 07974-0027
Telephone: (800) 223-0141
Annual. Price varies with content.

NHFA Operating Expenses
National Home Furnishings Association
Post Office Box 2396
High Point, North Carolina 27261
Telephone: (919) 883-1650
Annual. Price: $50 to members; $300 to nonmembers.

NOPA Dealer Operating Results
National Office Products Association
301 N. Fairfax Street
Alexandria, Virginia 22314-2696
Telephone: (703) 549-9040
Annual. Price: $50 per copy to members; $100 to nonmembers.

Operations Review
Food Marketing Institute
1750 K Street, N.W.
Washington, D.C. 20006
Telephone: (202) 452-8444
Quarterly. Price: $25 to members; $50 to nonmembers.

Petroleum Marketing Databook
Petroleum Marketing Education Foundation
5600 Roswell Road
Prado North, #318
Atlanta, Georgia 30342
Telephone: (404) 255-7600
Biennial. Price: $53.50 to members; $78.50 to nonmembers.

Restaurant Industry Operations Report
National Restaurant Association
1200 17th Street, N.W.
Washington, D.C. 20036
Telephone: (202) 331-5900
Annual. $39 per copy to members; $78 to nonmembers.

Supermarket Financial Performance Study
Food Marketing Institute
1750 K Street, N.W.
Washington, D.C. 20006
Telephone: (202) 452-8444
Annual. Price: $25 to members; $50 to nonmembers.

Service and Construction

Construction Industry Annual Financial Survey
Construction Financial Management Association
Princeton Gateway Corporate Campus
707 State Road, Suite 223
Princeton, New Jersey 08540-1413
Telephone: (609) 683-5000
Annual. Price: $100 to members; $195 to nonmembers.

Cost of Doing Business Survey
American Rental Association
1900 19th Street
Moline, Illinois 61265
Telephone: (309) 764-2475
Annual. Price: One free copy to all members; $30 to nonmembers.

Dollars & Cents of Convenience Centers: A Special Report
The Urban Land Institute
625 Indiana Avenue, N.W.
Washington, D.C. 20004-2930
Telephone: (800) 321-5011
Price: $42 prepaid to members; $54 prepaid to nonmembers.

Dollars & Cents of Shopping Centers: 1990
The Urban Land Institute
625 Indiana Avenue, N.W.
Washington, D.C. 20004-2930
Telephone: (800) 321-5011
Triennial (next edition 2/93). Price: $180 prepaid to members; $225 to nonmembers.

Financial Performance Report
National Electrical Contractors Association
7315 Wisconsin Avenue
Bethesda, Maryland 20814
Telephone: (301) 657-3110
Biennial. Price: Free to members; $50 prepaid to nonmembers.

Financial Report of the Hospital Industry
Healthcare Financial Management Association
Two Westbrook Corporate Center, Suite 700
Westchester, Illinois 60154
Telephone: (800) 252-4362, ext. 309
Annual. Price: $260.

Gas Facts
American Gas Association
1515 Wilson Boulevard
Arlington, Virginia 22209
Telephone: (703) 841-8559
Annual. Price: $25 to members; $50 to nonmembers.

Industry Norms and Key Business Ratios
Dun & Bradstreet Credit Services
Dun's Analytical Services
One Diamond Hill Road
Murray Hill, New Jersey 07974-0027
Telephone: (800) 223-0141
Annual. Price varies with content.

MGMA Annual Cost and Production Survey Report
Medical Group Management Association
104 Inverness Terrace East
Englewood, Colorado 80112
Telephone: (303) 799-1111
Annual. Price: $60 to members; $185 prepaid to nonmembers.

Mortgage Banking: Financial Statements and Operating Ratios
Mortgage Banking Association of America
1125 15th Street, N.W.
Washington, D.C. 20005
Telephone: (202) 861-6574
Annual. Price: $35 to members; $55 prepaid to nonmembers.

Radio Financial Report
National Association of Broadcasters
1771 N Street, N.W.
Washington, D.C. 20036-2891
Telephone: (800) 368-5644
Annual. Price: $125 to members; $225 to nonmembers.

Railroad Revenues, Expenses, and Income
Association of American Railroads
50 F Street, N.W.
Room 5401
Washington, D.C. 20001
Telephone: (202) 639-2302
Quarterly. Price: $50 prepaid for annual subscription.

Television Financial Report
National Association of Broadcasters
1771 N Street, N.W.
Washington, D.C. 20036-2891
Telephone: (800) 368-5644
Annual. Price: $125 to members; $225 to nonmembers.

Trends in the Hotel Industry—U.S. Edition
Pannell Kerr Forster
262 North Belt East, Suite 200
Houston, Texas 77060
Telephone: (713) 999-5134
Annual. Price: $100 prepaid.

Wholesaling

Industry Norms and Key Business Ratios
Dun & Bradstreet Credit Services
Dun's Analytical Services
One Diamond Hill Road
Murray Hill, New Jersey 07974-0027
Telephone: (800) 223-0141
Annual. Price varies with content.

Operating Performance Report
American Supply Association
222 Merchandise Mart Plaza
Suite 1360
Chicago, Illinois 60654
Telephone: (312) 464-0090
Annual. Price: $35 to members; $150 per copy prepaid to nonmembers.

Paper Merchant Performance
The National Paper Trade Association, Inc.
111 Great Neck Road
Great Neck, New York 11021
Telephone: (516) 829-3070
Annual. Price: $300 per copy.

Profitability Analysis Report
The Industrial Distribution Association
Three Corporate Square, Suite 201
Atlanta, Georgia 30329
Telephone: (404) 325-2776
Annual. Price: Free to members; $250 to nonmembers.

Selected Sources of Officer Compensation

Almanac of Business and Industrial Financial Ratios (Leo Troy, Ph.D., Englewood Cliffs, N.J.: Prentice Hall) presents financial ratios of companies by SIC code, asset size, and profitability. Compensation of officers includes salary and wages, bonuses or bonds, and other identified benefits paid to officers for personal services rendered. Pensions, profit sharing, stock bonuses, annuity, and other deferred compensation is specifically excluded from officer compensation and is reported elsewhere.

Annual Statement Studies (Philadelphia, Pa.: Robert Morris Associates) contains composite financial data on companies in manufacturing, wholesaling, retailing, service, and contracting. The information is collected by member banking institutions from their borrowing customers and is presented by SIC code. The officer compensation to sales ratio measures the total amount of monetary remuneration paid to the company officers (exclusive of pension contributions).

Executive Compensation: Survey Results (New York, N.Y.: National Association of Business Management, Inc.) presents the results of surveys conducted by BDO/Seidman and the Research Institute of America, Inc. The results are separated into officer position (CEO, Marketing, Sales, Manufacturing, Finance, EDP, and Human Resources), regional (New England, Middle Atlantic, South Atlantic, West North Central, West South Central, East North Central, East South Central, Mountain, and Pacific), base salary, extra compensation, and industry type.

Financial Studies of the Small Business (Orlando, Fla.: Financial Research Associates) shows data from financial statements of more than 30,000 financial statements submitted by over 1,500 independent certified public accountant firms. The information is broken down by asset size, sales volume, industry, and profitability.

The Hay Report (Wellesley, Mass.: Hay Group) provides benchmarks for measuring against other companies within an industry. Drawn from research encompassing thousands of companies, hundreds of individual compensation plans, and more than 1 million U.S. workers, this comprehensive annual update of pay and benefits practices in American businesses and industry offers detailed data with findings enumerated by specific industry for industrial, financial, and insurance organizations, and by specific job function and level, including executives.

Officer Compensation Report (Greenvale, N.Y.: Panel Publishers, Inc.) is a comprehensive study of officer compensation for more than 1,000 companies with annual revenues less than $60 million, based on a survey of 50,000 companies. The study examines the ownership structure, profitability, and economic profile and is further broken down by officer position and industry. Compensation is defined as salary plus all other direct remuneration received.

Source Book Statistics of Income (Washington, D.C.: Internal Revenue Service) is a collection of balance sheet, income statement, tax, and selected other financial information by industry type and asset size. The information is collected by the Internal Revenue Service from a sampling of corporate tax returns filed.

Online Information Retrieval

Online information retrieval is computer-assisted access to several hundred data bases covering information on many topics, including business. Some data bases provide references to magazines and newspaper articles; others cover conference papers, statistical data, and technical reports. Many of the data bases are also available as printed indexes in libraries and can often be efficiently searched manually.

Online searches produce varying results depending on the nature of the data bases:

- References to articles (bibliographic citations).
- Abstracts or full texts of articles.
- Statistics, charts, lists, or customized reports.

Why are online searches valuable?

- Speed.
- Currency.
- Access to information not available in print.
- Access to topics combining multiple ideas.
- Ability to sift quickly through vast amounts of information.

If your company does not have a library or information center, large public libraries and university libraries will search for you. Vendors like Dialog, Dow Jones News/Retrieval, and LEXIS/NEXIS are among the most widely used. You may contact these vendors directly for more information about their services:

Dialog Information Services, Inc.
3460 Hillview Avenue
Palo Alto, California 94304
(800) 3-DIALOG

Dow Jones News/Retrieval
Post Office Box 300
Princeton, New Jersey 08543-0300
(609) 452-1511

LEXIS/NEXIS
Mead Data Central, Inc.
9393 Springboro Pike-DM
Post Office Box 933
Dayton, Ohio 45401
(800) 227-4908

Online systems remain the most heavily used electronic sources for business searching, but they are by no means the only medium at the researcher's disposal. Important business data bases can be found with increasing frequency on CD-ROMs. Data base searching on Compact Disk-Read Only Memory (CD-ROM) has become an extremely popular alternative to online information retrieval in recent years. Using laser technology, information producers are able to store an incredible amount of data on a single compact disk. Because a single CD can hold up to 1,500 times the data on a floppy diskette, large databases can be installed on a microcomputer for local use. Many libraries subscribe to CD-ROM services and allow their patrons to search for themselves.

Index